One World, Many Cultures

One World, Many Cultures

Third Edition

———————◆———————

STUART HIRSCHBERG

Rutgers: The State University of New Jersey, Newark

TERRY HIRSCHBERG

Allyn and Bacon

Boston ✦ *London* ✦ *Toronto* ✦ *Sydney* ✦ *Tokyo* ✦ *Singapore*

Executive Editor: Eben W. Ludlow
Editorial Assistant: Linda M. D'Angelo
Marketing Manager: Lisa Kimball
Editorial Production Service: Lachina Publishing Services
Manufacturing Buyer: Suzanne Lareau
Cover Administrator: Linda Knowles

Library of Congress Cataloging-in-Publication Data

One world, many cultures / [compiled by] Stuart Hirschberg, Terry
  Hirschberg. — 3rd ed.
    p.   cm.
  Includes indexes.
  ISBN 0-205-26777-7 (pbk.)
    1. College readers.   2. Pluralism (Social sciences)—Problems,
  exercises, etc.   3. Ethnic groups—Problems, exercises, etc.
  4. English language—Rhetoric.   5. Readers—Social sciences.
  I. Hirschberg, Stuart.   II. Hirschberg, Terry.
  PE1417.O57   1997
  808'.0427—dc21   97-21967
                                                              CIP

Printed in the United States of America
10 9 8 7 6 5 4 3 2   02 01 00 99 98

In memory of
Henry A. Christian, III
and
Peter Christian

Contents

5   *Class Conflicts*   284

9　*The Unseen World*

Preface

◆

This third edition of *One World, Many Cultures* is a global, contemporary reader whose international and multicultural selections offer a new direction for freshman composition courses.

In nine thematic chapters, seventy-one readings (thirty-four of which are new to this edition) by internationally recognized writers from thirty-five countries, we explore cultural differences and displacement in relation to race, class, gender, region, and nation. *One World, Many Cultures* also reflects the new emphasis on cultural studies that has become an integral part of many college programs since the second edition. The selections challenge readers to see similarities between their own experiences and the experiences of others in radically different cultural circumstances. Compelling and provocative writings by authors from the Caribbean, Africa, Asia, Europe, South America, and Central America reflect the cultural and ethnic heritage of many students.

The fifty-one nonfiction selections include diaries, essays, journalists' reports, interviews, autobiographies, scholarly articles, prison memoirs, and speeches. These and the twenty short stories (over half of which are fact-based) encourage readers to perceive the relationship between a wide range of experiences in different cultures and corresponding experiences of writers within the United States. The third edition of *One World, Many Cultures* continues to provide a rich sampling of accounts by writers who are native to the cultures they describe, allowing the reader to hear authentic voices rather than filtered journalistic reports.

New to This Edition

- A fifteen-page introduction covers important aspects of critical reading, keeping a journal and responding to the text, and includes a sample selection by Edward T. Hall ("Hidden Culture") for students to annotate.
- Nearly twenty percent of the text consists of selections that represent the different kinds of work being done in the field of cultural studies. These include:

"The Flesh and the Devil" (Kim Chernin) Ch. 3
"Talk in the Intimate Relationship" (Deborah Tannen) Ch. 3

"Visualizing the Disabled Body" (Lennard J. Davis) Ch. 3
"What Are Homosexuals For?" (Andrew Sullivan) Ch. 3
"Ornamental Cookery" (Roland Barthes) Ch. 5
"A Small Place" (Jamaica Kincaid) Ch. 5
"The Odour of the Other" (Constance Classen) Ch. 5
"Decolonising the Mind" (Ngũgĩ wa Thiong'o) Ch. 6
"Reflections on Exile" (Edward Said) Ch. 6
"Individualism as an American Cultural Value" (Poranee
Natadecha-Sponsel) Ch. 7
"The Power of Meat" (Nick Fiddes) Ch. 7
"Home" (Raymonde Carroll) Ch. 8
"The Language of Clothes" (Alison Lurie) Ch. 8

- Thirty-four new selections reflect current worldwide concerns.
- More readings by Native-American authors are offered.
- More short works of fiction are included.
- More selections by writers from different ethnic backgrounds within the United States are included.

Chapter Descriptions

The nine chapters move from the most personal sphere of family life through adolescent turning points, male and female relationships, the responsibilities of working, and the conflicts of class and race to more encompassing social and spiritual dimensions.

Chapter 1, "The Family in Different Cultures," introduces families in Russia, Guatemala, Japan, India, Lebanon, and the Congo, and, within the United States, an African-American family and a Mexican-American family. These selections illustrate that the "family," however defined (as a single-parent household, a nuclear family, or the extended family of an entire community), passes on the mores and values of a particular culture to the next generation.

Chapter 2, "Turning Points," provides insights into both formal and informal rites of passage and initiation ceremonies in the lives of a Chinese-American girl, a Kiowa Native-American, and young people in Ireland, Tanzania, Egypt, Lebanon, Italy, and Finland and illustrates how these turning points are celebrated across a broad spectrum of cultures.

Chapter 3, "How Culture Shapes Gender Roles," explores the role of culture in shaping sexual identity. Readers can gain insight into how gender roles are culturally conditioned rather than biologically determined. The extent to which sex role expectations, both heterosexual and homosexual, differ from culture to culture can be seen in societies as diverse as those of Puerto Rico, Mali, Finland, and the United States.

Chapter 4, "How Work Creates Identity," explores work as a universal human experience through which we define ourselves and others. The role of culture in shaping attitudes toward work can be seen in the different values of a female auto mechanic in Vermont and a village goldsmith in Guinea. We can share the work experiences of a radiation expert following the Chernobyl disaster in Russia, a Chinese martial-arts master exchanging instruction for English lessons, a sex show performer in Bangkok, a Mexican-American worker in Chicago, an Indian novelist turned filmmaker, and an auto mechanic in a former communist country.

Chapter 5, "Class Conflicts," takes up the crucial and often unrecognized relationships between race, identity, and class through readings that explore positions of power and powerlessness. Selections include Roland Barthes's analysis of advertisements for food in French magazines, Jo Goodwin Parker's poignant revelation of what it means to be poor in the southern United States, and Mahdokht Kashkuli's story of a family in modern-day Iran who must place one of their children in an orphanage. The voices heard are those of men and women of many races and several nations, including Antonio, a teenage contract killer in Colombia's drug capital, Medellín. Unusual perspectives on class issues are provided by Jamaica Kincaid's thought-provoking analysis of tourism in Antigua, Mary Crow Dog's account of her experiences in a government-run school for Native-Americans, Constance Classen's analysis of olfactory symbolism across cultures, and Catherine Lim's bittersweet fable of a couple who speculate in the Singapore Stock Exchange, drawn by the lure of becoming wealthy overnight.

Chapter 6, "Politics and Power," looks at the resilience and courage of ordinary citizens pitted against civil war in Croatia and state tyranny in the China of Mao Tse-tung during the Cultural Revolution and in Vietnam after the war. We gain insight into the formation of the state of Israel. We hear the voices of writers of conscience and survivors of oppressive regimes in Algeria under the French, Kenya during British colonial rule, and in Cyprus during the liberation struggle against the British.

Chapter 7, "Strangers in a Strange Land," explores the condition of exiles—whether refugees, immigrants, or travelers—who are caught between two cultures but are at home in neither. The need of those who have left "home" to make sense of their lives in a new place is a theme explored by Edward Said, William M. Kephart, Joan Didion, Le Ly Hayslip, Luis Alberto Urrea, Poranee Natadecha-Sponsel, and Gloria Anzaldúa.

Chapter 8, "The Role Customs Play in Different Cultures," focuses on the role that ritual, religion, and belief play in shaping social behavior. The decisive influence of cultural values is explored through an analysis of how the symbolism of meat eating varies from culture to culture, the role of aggression among the Yąnomamö Indians in Brazil, and the reasons for French and American cultural misunderstandings of the idea of privacy. We gain insight into the role customs play in accounts of a Kiowa Indian Sun Dance in Wyoming, the symbolism of clothes and body decorations across cultures, reciprocal gift giving in New Guinea, fiestas in Mexico, and the place of revenge in Bedouin culture.

Chapter 9, "The Unseen World," shows how people in many different cultures throughout the world look at themselves in relationship to the absolute, eternal, cosmic, or supernatural. Gino Del Guercio investigates the role of voodoo in Haitian society. Leslie Marmon Silko explores the relationship between the natural and spiritual worlds of the Laguna Pueblo Indians; Bessie Head tells how a family resorted to an outlawed tribal ritual to produce rain in Botswana; and Aung San Suu Kyi describes the influence of Buddhism on Burmese culture. We read Abioseh Nicol's bittersweet ghost story from Sierra Leone, Naguib Mahfouz's provocative metaphysical parable, Carol Spindel's account of the function of blessings in Côte d'Ivoire, and conclude with Premchand's classic depiction of the Brahman priest in Indian society.

Editorial Apparatus

Chapter introductions discuss the theme of each chapter as related to the individual selections. Biographical sketches preceding each selection give background information on the writer's life and identify the cultural, historical, and personal context in which the selection was written. Background information on countries represented by multiple selections (e.g., Brazil, China, Egypt, Finland, France, India, Lebanon, Mexico, Russia, and Thailand) is keyed to the subject of each reading.

The questions that follow each selection are designed to encourage readers to discover relationships between personal experiences and ideas in the text, to explore points of agreement and areas of conflict sparked by the viewpoints of the authors, and to provide ideas for further research and inquiry.

The first set of questions, "Evaluating the Text," asks readers to think critically about the content, meaning, and purpose of the selections and to evaluate the author's rhetorical strategy, voice projected in relationship to his or her audience, evidence cited, and underlying assumptions.

The questions in "Exploring Different Perspectives" focus on relationships between readings within each chapter that illuminate differences and similarities between cultures. These questions encourage readers to make connections between diverse cultures, to understand the writer's values and beliefs, to enter into the viewpoints of others, and to understand how culture shapes perception and a sense of self.

The questions in "Extending Viewpoints Through Writing" invite readers to extend their thinking by seeing wider relationships between themselves and others through writing of many different kinds, including personal or expressive as well as expository and persuasive writing and more formal research papers.

Following each chapter, "Connecting Cultures" challenges readers to make connections and comparisons between selections within the chapter and throughout the book. These questions provide opportunities to consider additional cross-cultural perspectives on a single issue or explore a particular topic in depth.

A geographical index, a rhetorical index, a pronunciation key to names and places, and a map of the world identifying countries mentioned in the selections are included to allow the text to accommodate a variety of teaching approaches.

Instructor's Manual

An *Instructor's Manual* provides guidelines for using the text, supplemental bibliographies of books and periodicals, suggested answers to discussion questions in the text, and a filmography for instructors who wish to use films and videos connected to particular selections.

Acknowledgments

Once again, we want to acknowledge our appreciation for the encouragement, sound advice, and patience of our editor, Eben W. Ludlow, and our gratitude to all those teachers of composition who offered their thoughtful comments and gave this third edition the benefit of their scholarship and teaching experience. We would very much like to thank the following reviewers who commented on changes they wanted to see from the second edition:

Joan G. Brand
Cincinnati State Technical
and Community College

Dana J. Ringuette
Eastern Illinois University

Annabel Servat
Southeastern Louisiana University

Denis Sivack
Kingsborough Community
College, CUNY

Michele Geslin Small
Northland College

For their dedication and skill, we owe much to Allyn and Bacon's able staff, especially Marjorie Payne, production supervisor. We are most grateful to Fred W. Courtright and Amanda Sumner for their outstanding work as permissions editors.

Introduction

◆

Critical Reading for Ideas and Organization

One of the most important skills to have in your repertoire is the ability to survey unfamiliar articles, essays, or excerpts and come away with an accurate understanding of what the author wanted to communicate and how the material is organized. On the first and in subsequent readings of any of the selections in this text, especially the longer ones, pay particular attention to the title, look for introductory and concluding paragraphs (with special emphasis on the author's statement or restatement of central ideas), identify the headings and subheadings (and determine the relationship between these and the title), and identify any unusual terms necessary to fully understand the author's concepts.

As you work your way through an essay, you might look for cues to enable you to recognize the main parts of the argument or help you perceive the overall organization of the article. Once you find the main thesis, underline it. Then work your way through fairly rapidly, identifying the main ideas and the sequence in which they are presented. As you identify an important idea, ask yourself how this idea relates to the thesis statement you underlined or to the idea expressed in the title.

Finding a Thesis

Finding a thesis involves discovering the idea that serves as the focus of the essay. The thesis is often stated in the form of a single sentence that asserts the author's response to an issue that others might respond to in different ways. For example, the opening paragraph of "Reflections on Exile" presents Edward Said's assessment of an important aspect of contemporary society:

> **Exile is strangely compelling to think about but terrible to experience.** It is the unhealable rift forced between a human being and a native place, between the self and its true home: its essential sadness can never be surmounted. And while it is true that literature and history contain heroic, romantic, glorious, even triumphant episodes in an exile's life, these are no more than efforts meant to overcome the crippling sorrow of estrangement. The achievements of exile are permanently undermined by the loss of something left behind for ever.

1

The thesis (in bold type) represents the writer's view of a subject or topic from a certain perspective. Here, Said states a view of exile that will serve as a focus for his essay. Writers often place the thesis in the first paragraph or group of paragraphs so that the readers will be able to perceive the relationship between the supporting evidence and this main idea.

As you read, you might wish to underline the topic sentence or main idea of each paragraph or section (since key ideas are often developed over the course of several paragraphs). Jot it down in your own words in the margins, identify supporting statements and evidence (such as examples, statistics, and the testimony of authorities), and try to discover how the author organizes the material to support the development of important ideas. To identify supporting material, look for any ideas more specific than the main idea that is used to support it. Also look for instances where the author uses examples, descriptions, statistics, quotations from authorities, comparisons, or graphs to make the main idea clearer or prove it to be true.

Pay particular attention to important transitional words, phrases, or paragraphs to better see the relationships among major sections of the selection. Noticing how certain words or phrases act as transitions to link paragraphs or sections together will dramatically improve your reading comprehension. Also look for section summaries, where the author draws together several preceding ideas.

Writers use certain words to signal the starting point of an argument. If you detect any of the following terms, look for the main idea they introduce:

> since, because, for, as, follows from, as shown by, inasmuch as, otherwise, as indicated by, the reason is that, for the reason that, may be inferred from, may be derived from, may be deduced from, in view of the fact that

An especially important category of words is that which includes signals that the author will be stating a conclusion. Words to look for are these:

> therefore, hence, thus, so, accordingly, in consequence, it follows that, we may infer, I conclude that, in conclusion, in summary, which shows that, which means that, and which entails, consequently, proves that, as a result, which implies that, which allows us to infer, points to the conclusion that

You may find it helpful to create a running dialogue with the author in the margins, posing and then trying to answer the basic questions *who, what, where, when,* and *why,* and to note observations on how the main idea of the article is related to the title. These notes can later be used to evaluate how effectively any specific section contributes to the overall line of thought.

Responding to What You Read

When reading an essay that seems to embody a certain value system, try to examine any assumptions or beliefs the writer expects the audience to share. How is this assumption related to the author's purpose? If you do not agree with these assumptions, has the writer provided sound reasons and evidence to persuade you to change your mind?

You might describe the author's tone or voice and try to assess how much it contributed to the essay. How effectively does the writer use authorities, statistics, or examples to support the claim? Does the author identify the assumptions or values on which his or her views are based? Are they ones with which you would agree or disagree? To what extent does the author use the emotional connotations of language to try to persuade his or her reader? Do you see anything unworkable or disadvantageous about the solutions offered as an answer to the problem the essay addresses? All these and many other ways of analyzing someone else's essay can be used to create your own. Here are some specific guidelines to help you.

When evaluating an essay, consider what the author's purpose is in writing it. Was it to inform, explain, solve a problem, make a recommendation, amuse, enlighten, or achieve some combination of these goals? How is the tone or voice the author projects toward the reader related to his or her purpose in writing the essay?

You may find it helpful to write short summaries after each major section to determine whether you understand what the writer is trying to communicate. These summaries can then serve as a basis for an analysis of how successfully the author employs reasons, examples, statistics, and expert testimony to support and develop his or her main points.

For example, if the essay you are analyzing cites authorities to support a claim, assess whether the authorities bring the most timely opinions to bear on the subject or display any obvious biases, and determine whether they are experts in that particular field. Watch for experts described as "often quoted" or "highly placed reliable sources" without accompanying names, credentials, or appropriate documentation. If the experts cited offer what purports to be a reliable interpretation of facts, consider whether the writer also quotes equally trustworthy experts who hold opposing views.

If statistics are cited to support a point, judge whether they derive from verifiable and trustworthy sources. Also, evaluate whether the author has interpreted them in ways that are beneficial to his or her case, whereas someone who held an opposing view could interpret them quite differently. If real-life examples are presented to support the author's opinions, determine whether they are representative or whether they are too atypical to be used as evidence. If the author relies on hypothetical examples or analogies to dramatize ideas that otherwise would be hard to grasp, judge whether these examples are too far-fetched to back up the claims being made. If the essay depends on the stipulated definition of a term that might be defined in different ways, check whether the author provides clear reasons to indicate why one definition rather than another is preferable.

As you list observations about the various elements of the article you are analyzing, take a closer look at the underlying assumptions and see whether you can locate and distinguish between those assumptions that are explicitly stated and those that are implicit. Once the author's assumptions are identified, you can compare them with your own beliefs about the subject, determine whether these assumptions are commonly held, and make a judgment as to their validity. Would you readily agree with these assumptions? If not, has the author provided sound reasons and supporting evidence to persuade you to change your mind?

Marking as You Read

The most effective way to think about what you read is to make notes as you read. Making notes as you read forces you to go slowly and think carefully about each sentence. This process is sometimes called annotating the text, and all you need is a pen or a pencil. There are as many styles of annotating as there are readers, and you will discover your own favorite technique once you have done it a few times. Some readers prefer to underline major points or statements and jot down their reactions to them in the margin. Others prefer to summarize each paragraph or section to help them follow the author's line of thinking. Other readers circle key words or phrases necessary to understand the main ideas. Feel free to use your notes as a kind of conversation with the text. Ask questions. Express doubts. Mark unfamiliar words or phrases to look up later. If the paragraphs are not already numbered, you might wish to number them as you go to help you keep track of your responses. Try to distinguish the main ideas from supporting points and examples. Most importantly, go slowly and think about what you are reading. Try to discover whether the author makes a credible case for the conclusions he or she reaches. One last point: take a close look at the idea expressed in the title before and after you read the essay to see how it relates to the main idea.

Distinguishing between Fact and Opinion

As you read, distinguish between statements of fact and statements of opinion. Statements of fact relate information that is widely accepted and objectively verifiable; facts are used as evidence to support the claim made by the thesis. By contrast, an opinion is a personal interpretation of data or a belief or feeling that however strongly presented should not be mistaken by the reader for objective evidence. For example, consider the following claim by Edward T. Hall in "Hidden Culture":

> Each culture and each country has its own language of space, which is just as unique as the spoken language, frequently more so. In England, for example, there are no offices for the members of Parliament. In the United States, our congressmen and senators proliferate their offices and their office buildings and simply would not tolerate a no-office situation.

The only statement that could be verified or refuted on the basis of objective data is "In England . . . there are no offices for the members of Parliament." All the the other statements, *however persuasive they may seem,* are Hall's interpretations of a situation (multiple offices and office buildings for U.S. government officials) that might be interpreted quite differently by another observer. These statements should not be mistaken for statements of fact.

A reader who could not distinguish between facts and interpretations would be at a severe disadvantage in understanding Hall's essay. Part of the difficulty in separating fact from opinion stems from the difficulty of remaining objective about statements that match our own personal beliefs.

Take a few minutes to read and annotate the following essay. Feel free to "talk back" to the author. You can underline or circle key passages or key terms. You can make observations, raise questions, and express your reactions to what you read.

A SAMPLE ESSAY FOR STUDENT ANNOTATION

Edward T. Hall

Hidden Culture

———————◆———————

1   A few years ago, I became involved in a sequence of events in Japan that completely mystified me, and only later did I learn how an overt act seen from the vantage point of one's own culture can have an entirely different meaning when looked at in the context of the foreign culture. I had been staying at a hotel in downtown Tokyo that had European as well as Japanese-type rooms. The clientele included a few Europeans but was predominantly Japanese. I had been a guest for about ten days and was returning to my room in the middle of an afternoon. Asking for my key at the desk, I took the elevator to my floor. Entering the room, I immediately sensed that something was wrong. Out of place. Different. I was in the wrong room! Someone else's things were distributed around the head of the bed and the table. Somebody else's toilet articles (those of a Japanese male) were in the bathroom. My first thoughts were, "What if I am discovered here? How do I explain my presence to a Japanese who may not even speak English?"

2   I was close to panic as I realized how incredibly territorial we in the West are. I checked my key again. Yes, it really was mine. Clearly they had moved somebody else into my room. But where was my room now? And where were my belongings? Baffled and mystified, I took the elevator to the lobby. Why hadn't they told me at the desk, instead of letting me risk embarrassment and loss of face by being caught in somebody else's room? Why had they moved me in the first place? It was a nice room and, being sensitive to spaces and how they work, I was loath to give it up. After all, I had told them I would be in the hotel for almost a month. Why this business of moving me around like someone who has been squeezed in without a reservation? Nothing made sense.

3   At the desk I was told by the clerk, as he sucked in his breath in deference (and embarrassment?) that indeed they had moved me. My particular room had been reserved in advance by somebody else. I was given the key to my new room and discovered that all my personal ef-

6

fects were distributed around the new room almost as though I had done it myself. This produced a fleeting and strange feeling that maybe I wasn't myself. How could somebody else do all those hundred and one little things just the way I did?

Three days later, I was moved again, but this time I was prepared. There was no shock, just the simple realization that I had been moved and that it would now be doubly difficult for friends who had my old room number to reach me. *Tant pis,* I was in Japan. One thing did puzzle me. Earlier, when I had stayed at Frank Lloyd Wright's Imperial Hotel for several weeks, nothing like this had ever happened. What was different? What had changed? Eventually I got used to being moved and would even ask on my return each day whether I was still in the same room.

Later, at Hakone, a seaside resort where I was visiting with friends, the first thing that happened was that we were asked to disrobe. We were given *okatas,* and our clothes were taken from us by the maid. (For those who have not visited Japan, the okata is a cotton print kimono.) We later learned, when we ventured out in the streets, that it was possible to recognize other guests from our hotel because we had all been equipped with identical okatas. (Each hotel had its own characteristic, clearly recognizable pattern.) Also, I noted that it was polite to wave or nod to these strangers from the same hotel.

Following Hakone, we visited Kyoto, site of many famous temples and palaces, and the ancient capital of Japan.

There we were fortunate enough to stay in a wonderful little country inn on the side of a hill overlooking the town. Kyoto is much more traditional and less industrialized than Tokyo. After we had been there about a week and had thoroughly settled into our new Japanese surroundings, we returned one night to be met at the door by an apologetic manager who was stammering something. I knew immediately that we had been moved, so I said, "You had to move us. Please don't let this bother you, because we understand. Just show us to our new rooms and it will be all right." Our interpreter explained as we started to go through the door that we weren't in that hotel any longer but had been moved to *another* hotel. What a blow! Again, without warning. We wondered what the new hotel would be like, and with our descent into the town our hearts sank further. Finally, when we could descend no more, the taxi took off into a part of the city we hadn't seen before. No Europeans here! The streets got narrower and narrower until we turned into a side street that could barely accommodate the tiny Japanese taxi into which we were squeezed. Clearly this was a hotel of another class. I found that, by then, I was getting a little paranoid, which is easy enough to do in a foreign land, and said to myself, "They must think we are very low-status people indeed to treat us this way."

8   As it turned out, the neighborhood, in fact the whole district, showed us an entirely different side of life from what we had seen before, much more interesting and authentic. True, we did have some communication problems, because no one was used to dealing with foreigners, but few of them were serious.

9   Yet, the whole matter of being moved like a piece of derelict luggage puzzled me. In the United States, the person who gets moved is often the lowest-ranking individual. This principle applies to all organizations, including the Army. Whether you can be moved or not is a function of your status, your performance, and your value to the organization. To move someone without telling him is almost worse than an insult, because it means he is below the point at which feelings matter. In these circumstances, moves can be unsettling and damaging to the ego. In addition, moves themselves are often accompanied by great anxiety, whether an entire organization or a small part of an organization moves. What makes people anxious is that the move usually presages organizational changes that have been coordinated with the move. Naturally, everyone wants to see how he comes out vis-à-vis everyone else. I have seen important men refuse to move into an office that was six inches smaller than someone else's of the same rank. While I have heard some American executives say they wouldn't employ such a person, the fact is that in actual practice, unless there is some compensating feature, the significance of space as a communication is so powerful that no employee in his right mind would allow his boss to give him a spatial demotion—unless of course he had already reached his crest and was on the way down.

10   These spatial messages are not simply conventions in the United States—unless you consider the size of your salary check a mere convention, or where your name appears on the masthead of a journal. Ranking is seldom a matter that people take lightly, particularly in a highly mobile society like that in the United States. Each culture and each country has its own language of space, which is just as unique as the spoken language, frequently more so. In England, for example, there are no offices for the members of Parliament. In the United States, our congressmen and senators proliferate their offices and their office buildings and simply would not tolerate a no-office situation. Constituents, associates, colleagues, and lobbyists would not respond properly. In England, status is internalized; it has its manifestations and markers—the upper-class received English accent, for example. We in the United States, a relatively new country, externalize status. The American in England has some trouble placing people in the social system, while the English can place each other quite accurately by reading ranking cues, but in general tend to look down on the importance that Americans attach to space. It is very easy and very natural to look at

things from one's own point of view and to read an event as though it were the same all over the world.

I knew that my emotions on being moved out of my room in Tokyo were of the gut type and quite strong. There was nothing intellectual about my initial response. Although I am a professional observer of cultural patterns, I had no notion of the meaning attached to being moved from hotel to hotel in Kyoto. I was well aware of the strong significance of moving in my own culture, going back to the time when the new baby displaces older children, right up to the world of business, where a complex dance is performed every time the organization moves to new quarters. 11

What was happening to me in Japan as I rode up and down elevators with various keys gripped in my hand was that I was reacting with the cultural part of my brain—the old, mammalian brain. Although my new brain, my symbolic brain—the neocortex—was saying something else, my mammalian brain kept repeating, "You are being treated shabbily." My neocortex was trying to fathom what was happening. Needless to say, neither part of the brain had been programmed to provide me with the answer in Japanese culture. I did have to put up a strong fight with myself to keep from interpreting what was going on as though the Japanese were the same as I. This is the conventional and most common response and one that is often found even among anthropologists. Any time you hear someone say, "Why *they* are no different than the folks back home—they are just like I am," even though you may understand the reasons behind these remarks you also know that the speaker is living in a single-context world (his own) and is incapable of describing either his world or the foreign one. 12

The "they are just like the folks back home" syndrome is one of the most persistent and widely held misconceptions of the Western world, if not the whole world. There is very little any outsider can do about this, because it expresses views that are very close to the core of the personality. Simply talking about "cultural differences" and how we must respect them is a hollow cliché. And in fact, intellectualizing isn't much more helpful either, at least at first. The logic of the man who won't move into an office that is six inches smaller than his rival's is *cultural* logic; it works at a lower, more basic level in the brain, a part of the brain that synthesizes but does not verbalize. The response is a total response that is difficult to explain to someone who doesn't already understand, because it is so dependent on context for correct interpretation. To do so, one must explain the entire system; otherwise, the man's behavior makes little sense. He may even appear to be acting childishly—which he most definitely is not. 13

It was my preoccupation with my own cultural mold that explained why I was puzzled for years about the significance of being 14 moved around in Japanese hotels. The answer finally came after further experiences in Japan and many discussions with Japanese friends. In Japan, one has to "belong" or he has no identity. When a man joins a company, he does just that—joins himself to the corporate body—and there is even a ceremony marking the occasion. Normally, he is hired for life, and the company plays a much more paternalistic role than in the United States. There are company songs, and the whole company meets frequently (usually at least once a week) for purposes of maintaining corporate identity and morale.

15   As a tourist (either European or Japanese) when you go on a tour, you *join* that tour and follow your guide everywhere as a group. She leads you with a little flag that she holds up for all to see. Such behavior strikes Americans as sheeplike; not so the Japanese. The reader may say that this pattern holds in Europe, because there people join Cook's tours and the American Express tours, which is true. Yet there is a big difference. I remember a very attractive young American woman who was traveling with the same group I was with in Japan. At first she was charmed and captivated, until she had spent several days visiting shrines and monuments. At this point, she observed that she could not take the regimentation of Japanese life. Clearly, she was picking up clues, such as the fact that our Japanese group, when it moved, marched in a phalanx rather than moving as a motley mob with stragglers. There was much more discipline in these sightseeing groups than the average Westerner is either used to or willing to accept.

16   It was my lack of understanding of the full impact of what it means to belong to a high-context culture that caused me to misread hotel behavior at Hakone. I should have known that I was in the grip of a pattern difference and that the significance of all guests being garbed in the same okata meant more than that an opportunistic management used the guests to advertise the hotel. The answer to my puzzle was revealed when a Japanese friend explained what it means to be a guest in a hotel. As soon as you register at the desk, you are no longer an outsider; instead, for the duration of your stay you are a member of a large, mobile family. *You belong.* The fact that I was moved was tangible evidence that I was being treated as a family member—a relationship in which one can afford to be "relaxed and informal and not stand on ceremony." This is very highly prized state in Japan, which offsets the official properness that is so common in public. Instead of putting me down, they were treating me as a member of the family. Needless to say, the large, luxury hotels that cater to Americans, like Wright's Imperial Hotel, have discovered that Americans do tenaciously stand on ceremony and want to be treated as they are at home in the States. Americans don't like to be moved around; it makes them anxious. Therefore, the Japanese in these establishments have learned not to treat them as family members.

Keeping a Reading Journal

The most effective way to keep track of your thoughts and impressions and to review what you have learned is to start a reading journal. The comments you record in your journal may express your reflections, observations, questions, and reactions to the essays you read. Normally, your journal would not contain lecture notes from class. A reading journal will allow you to keep a record of your progress during the term and can also reflect insights you gain during class discussions and questions you may want to ask, as well as unfamiliar words you intend to look up. Keeping a reading journal becomes a necessity if your composition course will require you to write a research paper that will be due at the end of the semester. Keep in mind that your journal is not something that will be corrected or graded, although some instructors may wish you to share your entries with the class.

TURNING ANNOTATIONS INTO JOURNAL ENTRIES

Although there is no set form for what a journal should look like, reading journals are most useful for converting your brief annotations into more complete entries that explore in depth your reactions to what you have read. Interestingly, the process of turning your annotations into journal entries will often produce surprising insights that will give you a new perspective. For example, a student who annotated Edward T. Hall's "Hidden Culture" converted them into the following journal entries:

- Hall's personal experiences in Japan made him realize that interpreting an action depends on what culture you're from.
- Hall assumes hotels should treat long-term guests with more respect than overnight guests. "Like someone who had been squeezed in without a reservation" shows Hall's feelings.
- What does having your clothes replaced with an okata—cotton robe—have to do with being moved from room to room in a hotel? The plot thickens!
- The hotel in Hakone encourages guests—all wearing the same robes—to greet each other outside the hotel in a friendly, not formal, manner.
- Hall says that in America, size of office = personal value and salary. Hall compared how space works in the U.S. in order to understand Japanese attitudes towards space.
- Thesis—"culturally defined attitudes toward space are different for each culture." Proves this by showing how unimportant space is to members of Parliament in England when compared

with the great importance office size is to U.S. congresspersons and senators.

- Hall is an anthropologist. He realizes his reactions are instinctual. Hall wants to refute idea that people are the same all over the world. Says what culture you are from determines your attitudes and behavior.
- He learns from Japanese friends that workers are hired for life and view their companies as family. Would this be for me? In Japan, group identity is all-important.
- Hall describes two tour groups, one Japanese and one American, as an example of Japanese acceptance of regimentation, whereas Americans go off on their own.
- The answer to the mystery of why he was being moved: moving him meant he was accepted as a member of the hotel family. They were treating him informally, as if he were Japanese: a compliment not an insult. Informality is highly valued because the entire culture is based on the opposite—regimentation and conformity.

SUMMARIZING

Reading journals may also be used to record summaries of the essays you read. The value of summarizing is that it requires you to pay close attention to the reading in order to distinguish the main points from the supporting details. Summarizing tests your understanding of the material by requiring you to restate, concisely, the author's main ideas in your own words. First, create a list composed of sentences that express in your own words the essential idea of each paragraph, or each group of related paragraphs. Your previous underlining of topic sentences, main ideas, and key terms (as part of the process of critical reading) will help you follow the author's line of thought. Next, whittle down this list still further by eliminating repetitive ideas. Then formulate a thesis statement that expresses the main idea behind the article. Start your summary with this thesis statement, and combine your notes so that the summary flows together and reads easily.

Remember that summaries should be much shorter than the original text (whether the original is one page or twenty pages long) and should accurately reflect the central ideas of the article in as few words as possible. Try not to intrude your own opinions or critical evaluations into the summary. Besides requiring you to read the original piece more closely, summaries are necessary first steps in developing papers that synthesize materials from different sources. The test for a good summary, of course, is whether a person reading it without having read the original article would get an accurate, balanced, and complete account of the original material.

Writing an effective summary is easier if you first compose a rough summary, using no more than two complete sentences to summarize each of the paragraphs or group of paragraphs in the original article. A student's rough summary of Hall's essay might appear as follows. Numbers show which paragraphs are summarized from the article.

1–3 Hall describes how a seemingly inexplicable event that occurred while he was staying in a Tokyo hotel, frequented mostly by Japanese, led him to understand that the same action can have a completely different significance from another culture's perspective. Without telling him, the hotel management had moved his personal belongings to a new room and had given his room to another guest.

4 Three days later when Hall is again moved without warning, he is less startled but begins to wonder why this had never happened during his stay at Frank Lloyd Wright's Imperial Hotel in Tokyo.

5 At another hotel in Hakone, Hall is given an *okata*, a kind of cotton robe, to wear instead of his clothes and is encouraged to greet other guests wearing the same *okata* when he sees them outside the hotel.

6–7 At a third hotel, a country inn near Kyoto, Hall discovers that he has been moved again, this time to an entirely different hotel in what he initially perceives to be a less desirable section of town. Hall interprets this as an insult and becomes angry that the Japanese see him as someone who can be moved around without asking his permission.

8 The neighborhood he had initially seen as less desirable turns out to be much more interesting and authentic than the environs of hotels where tourists usually stay.

9 Hall relates his feelings of being treated shabbily ("like a piece of derelict luggage") to the principle that in the United States, the degree of one's power and status is shown by how much control one has over personal space, whether in the Army or in corporations, where being moved to a smaller office means one is considered less valuable to the company.

10–11 Hall speculates that the equation of control over space with power may pertain only to the United States, since in England, members of Parliament have no formal offices, while their counterparts in the United States—congressmen and senators—attach great importance to the size of their offices. Hall begins to realize that he has been unconsciously applying an American cultural perspective to actions that can be explained only in the context of Japanese culture.

12 Hall postulates the existence of an instinctive "cultural logic" that varies from culture to culture, and he concludes that it is necessary to understand the cultural context in which an action takes place in order to interpret it as people would in that culture.

13–14 Once Hall suspends his own culturally based assumption that one's self-esteem depends on control over personal space, he learns from conversations with Japanese friends that in Japan one has an identity only as part of a group. Japanese workers are considered as family by the companies that hire them for life.

15 The emphasis Japanese society places on conforming to a group is evident in the behavior of Japanese tourists, who move as a coordinated group and closely follow their guide, while American tourists refuse to accept such discipline.

16 Hall realizes that wearing an *okata* and being moved to different rooms and to another, more authentic, hotel means that he is being treated in an informal manner reserved for family members. What Hall had misperceived as an insult—being moved without notice—was really intended as an honor signifying he had been accepted and was not being treated as a stranger.

Based on this list, a student's formulation of a thesis statement expressing the essential idea of Hall's essay appears this way:

> Every society has a hidden culture that governs behavior that might seem inexplicable to an outsider.

The final summary should contain both this thesis and your restatement of the author's main ideas without adding any comments that express personal feelings or responses to the ideas presented. Keep in mind that the purpose of a summary or concise restatement of the author's ideas in your own words is to test your understanding of the material. The summary would normally be introduced by mentioning the author as well as the title of the article:

> Edward T. Hall, writing in "Hidden Culture," believes every society has a hidden culture that governs behavior that might seem inexplicable to an outsider. In Japan, Hall's initial reactions of anger to being moved to another room in a hotel in Tokyo, having his clothes replaced by a cotton kimono or *okata* in Hakone, and being relocated to a different hotel in Kyoto led him to search for the reasons behind such seemingly bizarre events. Although control over space in America is related to status, Hall realizes that in other cultures, like England, where members of Parliament have no offices, this is not the case. Hall discovers that rather than being an insult, being treated informally meant he was considered to be a member of the hotel "family."

Although some features of the original essay might have been mentioned, such as the significance of office size in corporations in the United States, the student's summary of Hall's essay is still an effective one. The summary accurately and fairly expresses the main ideas in the original.

USING YOUR READING JOURNAL
TO GENERATE IDEAS FOR WRITING

You can use all the material in your reading journal (annotations converted to journal entries, reflections, observations, questions, rough
and final summaries) to relate your own ideas to the ideas of the person
who wrote the essay you are reading. Here are several different kinds
of strategies you can use as you analyze an essay in order to generate
material for your own:

1. What is missing in the essay? Information that is not mentioned
is often just as significant as information the writer chose to include.
First, you must have already summarized the main points in the article.
Then, make up another list of points that are not discussed, that is,
missing information that you would have expected an article of this
kind to have covered or touched on. Write down the possible reasons
why this missing material has been omitted, censored, or downplayed.
What possible purpose could the author have had? Look for vested interests or biases that could explain why information of a certain kind is
missing.

2. You might analyze an essay in terms of what you already know
and what you didn't know about the issue. To do this, simply make a
list of what concepts were already familiar to you and a second list of
information or concepts that were new to you. Then write down three
to five questions you would like answered about this new information
and make a list of possible sources you might consult.

3. You might consider whether the author presents a solution to a
problem. List the short-term and long-term effects or consequences of
the action the writer recommends. You might wish to evaluate the solution to see whether positive short-term benefits are offset by possible
negative long-term consequences not mentioned by the author. This
might provide you with a starting point for your own essay.

4. After clearly stating what the author's position on an issue is,
try to imagine other people in that society or culture who would view
the same issue from a different perspective. How would the concerns
of these people be different from those of the writer? Try to think of as
many different people, representing as many different perspectives, as
you can. Now, try to think of a solution that would satisfy both the author and at least one other person who holds a different viewpoint. Try
to imagine that you are an arbitrator negotiating an agreement. How
would your recommendation require both parties to compromise and
reach an agreement?

1

The Family in Different Cultures

◆————————

The family has been the most enduring basis of culture throughout the world and has provided a stabilizing force in all societies. The complex network of dependencies, relationships, and obligations may extend outward from parents and children to include grandparents, cousins, aunts and uncles, and more distantly related relatives. In other cultures the entire community or tribe is seen as an extended family. The unique relationships developed among members of a family provide a universal basis for common experiences, emotions, perceptions, and expectations. At the same time, each family is different, with its own unique characteristic relationships and bonds. Family relationships continue to exert a profound influence on one's life long after childhood. In the context of the family we first learn what it means to experience the emotions of love, hope, fear, anger, and contentment. The works in this chapter focus on parent-child relationships, explore the connections between grandparents and grandchildren, and depict the impact of the cultural values on these relationships.

The structure of the family is subject to a wide range of economic and social influences in different cultures. For example, child-rearing in Russia is a vastly different enterprise from what it is in American society because of the enormous differences in economic circumstances and political systems. Yet, the family in different cultures still serves its age-old role of nurturing, protecting, and instilling values and social mores. The variety of family structures depicted by writers of many different nationalities offers insight into how the concept of the family is modified according to the constraints, beliefs, and needs of particular societies.

For many families, the family history is inseparable from the stories told about a particular member of the family, which define the character of the family and its relationship to the surrounding society. These stories can be told for entertainment or education and often explain old loyalties and antagonisms. Some are written and some are part of an oral history related by one generation to the next. The complex portraits of family life offered in this chapter allow us to share, sympathize, and identify with writers from diverse cultures and more completely understand our own family experiences in the light of theirs.

The African-American writer Gayle Pemberton, in "Antidisestablishmentarianism," describes how her no-nonsense grandmother taught her to think for herself. A fascinating glimpse into communal life in Russia's heartland is offered by Boris Yeltsin in "Childhood in Russia." Rigoberta Menchú, in "Birth Ceremonies," offers a unique perspective on the significance of rituals and ceremonies performed to usher a newborn baby into the Guatemalan Indian community. Nicholas Bornoff, in "The Marriage Go-Round," analyzes how social and familial expectations control courtship and marriage in modern-day Japan. Serena Nanda, in "Arranging a Marriage in India," describes her participation in the lengthy process of getting her friend's son married. The Lebanese writer Shirley Saad, in "Amina," tells the story of a woman who has given birth to only girls and fears that her husband will take another wife in order to have a son. Pat Mora, in "Remembering Lobo," recalls the integral part her aunt played in her Mexican-American family's life. Based on his fieldwork in the Congo, Colin Turnbull, in "The Mbuti Pygmies," describes the importance of rituals in shaping the behavior of children in Mbuti society. A father's boorish insensitivity undermines what was to have been a happy reunion between a son and his father in John Cheever's story "Reunion."

Gayle Pemberton

Antidisestablishmentarianism

———————◆———————

Gayle Pemberton is currently the social director of Afro-American Stud-ies at Princeton University. Born in 1948, she spent her childhood in Chi-cago and Ohio. She received a Ph.D. in English and American Literature at Harvard University and has taught at Smith, Reed, and Bowdoin Col-leges. The Hottest Water in Chicago: On Family, Race, Time, and American Culture *(1992) is part memoir, part social analysis, and part literary criticism. Pemberton focuses on her experiences growing up as an Afro-American female in mid-twentieth-century America. The title de-rives from her father's experience in 1954 as an organizer with the Urban League who had the dubious honor of integrating a Chicago hotel. As Pemberton recounts, it was a desperately dirty establishment for tran-sients whose owner had shamelessly boasted of offering "the hottest water in Chicago." The chapter from this book, "Antidisestablishmentarian-ism," describes the influential role played by Pemberton's grandmother in shaping her outlook.*

1   Okay, so where's Gloria Lockerman? I want to know. Gloria Lock-erman was partially responsible for ruining my life. I might never have ended up teaching literature if it had not been for her. I don't want to "call her out." I just want to know how things are, what she's doing. Have things gone well, Gloria? How's the family? What's up?

2   Gloria Lockerman, in case you don't recall, won scads of money on "The $64,000 Question." Gloria Lockerman was a young black child, like me, but she could spell anything. Gloria Lockerman became my nemesis with her ability, her a-n-t-i-d-i-s-e-s-t-a-b-l-i-s-h-m-e-n-t-a-r-i-a-n-i-s-m.

3   My parents, my sister, and I shared a house in Dayton, Ohio, with my father's mother and her husband, my stepgrandfather, during the middle fifties. Sharing is an overstatement. It was my grandmother's house. Our nuclear group ate in a makeshift kitchen in the basement; my sister and I shared a dormer bedroom, and my parents actually had a room on the main floor of the house—several parts of which were off-limits. These were the entire living room, anywhere within three feet of Grandma's African violets, the windows and venetian blinds, anything with a doily on it, the refrigerator, and the irises in the backyard.

4   It was an arrangement out of necessity, given the unimpressive state of our combined fortunes, and it did not meet with anyone's satis-

faction. To make matters worse, we had blockbusted a neighborhood. So, for the first year, I integrated the local elementary school—a thankless and relatively inhuman experience. I remember one day taking the Sunday paper route for a boy up the block who was sick. It was a beautiful spring day, dewy, warm. I walked up the three steps to a particular house and placed the paper on the stoop. Suddenly, a full-grown man, perhaps sixty or so, appeared with a shotgun aimed at me and said that if he ever saw my nigger ass on his porch again he'd blow my head off. I know—typical American grandfather.

Grandma liked spirituals, preferably those sung by Mahalia Jackson. She was not a fan of gospel and I can only imagine what she'd say if she were around to hear what's passing for inspirational music these days. She also was fond of country singers, and any of the members of "The Lawrence Welk Show." ("That Jimmy. Oh, I love the way he sings. He's from Iowa.") She was from Iowa, Jimmy was from Iowa, my father was from Iowa. She was crazy about Jimmy Dean too, and Tennessee Ernie Ford, and "Gunsmoke." She could cook with the finest of them and I wish I could somehow recreate her Parkerhouse rolls, but I lack bread karma. Grandma liked flowers (she could make anything bloom) and she loved her son.

She disliked white people, black people in the aggregate and pretty much individually too, children—particularly female children—her daughter, her husband, my mother, Episcopalianism, Catholicism, Judaism, and Dinah Shore. She had a hot temper and a mean streak. She also suffered from several nagging ailments: high blood pressure, ulcers, an enlarged heart, ill-fitting dentures, arteriosclerosis, and arthritis—enough to make anyone hot tempered and mean, I'm sure. But to a third grader, such justifications and their subtleties were ultimately beyond me and insufficient, even though I believe I understood in part the relationship between pain and personality. Grandma scared the daylights out of me. I learned to control my nervous stomach enough to keep from getting sick daily. So Grandma plus school plus other family woes and my sister still predicting the end of the world every time the sirens went off—Grandma threatened to send her to a convent—made the experience as a whole something I'd rather forget, but because of the mythic proportions of family, can't.

I often think that it might have been better had I been older, perhaps twenty years older, when I knew Grandma. But I realize that she would have found much more wrong with me nearing thirty than she did when I was eight or nine. When I was a child, she could blame most of my faults on my mother. Grown, she would have had no recourse but to damn me to hell.

Ah, but she is on the gene. Grandma did everything fast. She cooked, washed, cleaned, moved—everything was at lightning speed. She passed this handicap on to me, and I have numerous bruises, cuts, and burns to show for it. Watching me throw pots and pans around in the creation of a meal, my mother occasionally calls me by my grandmother's first name. I smile back, click my teeth to imitate a slipping upper, and say something unpleasant about someone.

9   Tuesday nights were "The $64,000 Question" nights, just as Sundays we watched Ed Sullivan and Saturdays were reserved for Lawrence Welk and "Gunsmoke." We would all gather around the television in what was a small, informal family section between the verboten real living room and the mahogany dining table and chairs, used only three or four times a year. I don't remember where I sat, but it wasn't on the floor since that wasn't allowed either.

10   As we watched these television programs, once or twice I sat briefly on Grandma's lap. She was the world's toughest critic. No one was considered worthy, apart from the above-mentioned. To her, So-and-So or Whosits could not sing, dance, tell a joke, read a line—nothing. In her hands "Ted Mack's Amateur Hour" would have lasted three minutes. She was willing to forgive only very rarely—usually when someone she liked gave a mediocre performance on one of her favorite shows.

11   I must admit that Grandma's style of teaching critical thinking worked as well as some others I've encountered. My father had a different approach. Throughout my youth he would play the music of the thirties and forties. His passion was for Billie Holiday, with Ella Fitzgerald, Peggy Lee, Sarah Vaughan, and a few others thrown in for a touch of variety. He enjoyed music, and when he wanted to get some musical point across, he would talk about some nuance of style that revealed the distinction between what he called "really singing" and a failure. He would say, "Now, listen to that there. Did you catch it? Hear what she did with that note?" With Grandma it was more likely to be:

12   "Did you hear that?"

13   "What?" I might ask.

14   "That. What she just sang."

15   "Yes."

16   "Well, what do you think of it?"

17   "It's okay, I guess."

18   "Well, that was garbage. She can't sing a note. That stinks. She's a fool."

19   Message across. We all choose our own pedagogical techniques.

20   Game shows are, well, game shows. I turned on my television the other day, and as I clicked through channels looking for something to watch I stopped long enough to hear an announcer say that the guest contestant was going to do something or other in 1981. Reruns of game shows? Well, why not? What difference does it make if the whole point is to watch people squirm, twist, sweat, blare, weep, convulse to get their hands on money and gifts, even if they end up being just "parting

gifts?" (I won some of them myself once: a bottle of liquid Johnson's Wax, a box of Chunkies, a beach towel with the name of a diet soda on it, plus a coupon for a case of the stuff, and several boxes of Sugar Blobs—honey-coated peanut butter, marshmallow, and chocolate flavored crispies, dipped in strawberry flavoring for that special morning taste treat!)

Game shows in the fifties were different, more exciting. I thought   21
the studio sets primitive even when I was watching them then. The clock on "Beat the Clock," the coat and crown on "Queen for a Day"— nothing like that mink on "The Big Payoff" that Bess Meyerson modeled—and that wire card flipper on "What's My Line" that John Charles Daly used—my, was it flimsy looking. The finest set of all, though, was on "The $64,000 Question." Hal March would stand outside the isolation booth, the door closing on the likes of Joyce Brothers, Catherine Kreitzer, and Gloria Lockerman, the music would play, and the clock would begin ticking down, like all game show clocks: *TOOT-toot-TOOT-toot-TOOT-toot-BUZZZZZZ.*

There were few opportunities to see black people on television in   22
those days. I had watched "Amos 'n' Andy" when we lived in Chicago. But that show was a variation on a theme. Natives running around or jumping up and down or looking menacing in African adventure movies; shuffling, subservient, and clowning servants in local color movies (or any other sort); and "Amos 'n' Andy" were all the same thing: the perpetuation of a compelling, deadly, darkly humorous, and occasionally laughable idea. Nonfictional blacks on television were limited to Sammy Davis, Jr., as part of the Will Mastin Trio and afterward, or Peg Leg Bates on "The Ed Sullivan Show" on Sunday, or the entertainers who might show up on other variety shows, or Nat King Cole during his fifteen-minute program. Naturally, the appearance of Gloria Lockerman caused a mild sensation as we watched "The $64,000 Question," all assembled.

"Look at her," Grandma said.   23

I braced myself for the torrent of abuse that was about to be leveled   24
at the poor girl.

"You ought to try to be like that," Grandma said.   25

"Huh?" I said.   26

"What did you say?"   27

"Yes, ma'am."   28

I was shocked, thrown into despair. I had done well in school, as   29
well as could be hoped. I was modestly proud of my accomplishments, and given the price I was paying every day—and paying in silence, for I never brought my agonies at school home with me—I didn't need Gloria Lockerman thrown in my face. Gloria Lockerman, like me, on television, spelling. I was perennially an early-round knockout in spelling bees.

30   My sister understands all of this. Her own story is slightly different and she says she'll tell it all one day herself. She is a very good
singer and has a superb ear; with our critical training, what more
would she need? Given other circumstances, she might have become a
performer herself. When she was about eleven Leslie Uggams was on
Arthur Godfrey's "Talent Scouts" and was soon to be tearing down the
"Name That Tune" runway, ringing the bell and becoming moderately
famous. No one ever held Leslie Uggams up to my sister for image
consciousness-raising. But my sister suffered nevertheless. She could
out-sing Leslie Uggams and probably run as fast; she knew the songs
and didn't have nearly so strange a last name. But, there she was, going nowhere in the Middle West, and there was Leslie Uggams on her
way to "Sing Along With Mitch." To this day, my sister mumbles if she
happens to see Leslie Uggams on television—before she can get up to
change the channel—or hears someone mention her name. I told her I
saw Leslie Uggams in the flesh at a club in New York. She was sitting
at a table, just like the rest of us, listening with pleasure to Barbara
Cook. My sister swore at me.

31   Grandma called her husband "Half-Wit." He was a thin, small-
boned man who looked to me far more like an Indian chief than like a
black man. He was from Iowa too, but that obviously did not account
for enough in Grandma's eyes. He had a cracking tenor voice, a head
full of dead straight black hair, reddish, dull brown skin, and large sad,
dark brown eyes. His craggy face also reminded me of pictures I'd seen
of Abraham Lincoln—but, like all political figures and American forefathers, Lincoln, to my family, was fair game for wisecracks, so that re-
semblance did Grandpa no good either. And for reasons that have gone
to the grave with both of them, he was the most thoroughly henpecked
man I have ever heard of, not to mention seen.

32   Hence, domestic scenes had a quality of pathos and high humor as
far as I was concerned. My sister and I called Grandpa "Half-Wit"
when we were alone together, but that seemed to have only a slight effect on our relations with him and our willingness to obey him—
though I cannot recall any occasions calling for his authority. Grandma
was Grandma, Half-Wit was Half-Wit—and we lived with the two of
them. I have one particularly vivid memory of Grandma, an aficionada
of the iron skillet, chasing him through the house waving it in the air,
her narrow, arthritis-swollen wrist and twisted knuckles turning the
heavy pan as if it were a lariat. He didn't get hurt; he was fleet of foot
and made it out the back door before she caught him. My father's real
father had been dead since the thirties and divorced from Grandma
since the teens—so Half-Wit had been in place for quite some years and
was still around to tell the story, if he had the nerve.

33   Grandma had a glass menagerie, the only one I've seen apart from
performances of the Williams play. I don't think she had a unicorn, but

she did have quite a few pieces. From a distance of no less than five feet I used to squint at the glass forms, wondering what they meant to Grandma, who was herself delicate of form but a powerhouse of strength, speed, and temper. I also wondered how long it would take me to die if the glass met with some unintended accident caused by me. Real or imagined unpleasantries, both in the home and outside of it, helped develop in me a somewhat melancholic nature. And even before we had moved to Ohio I found myself laughing and crying at the same time.

In the earlier fifties, in Chicago, I was allowed to watch such programs as "The Ernie Kovacs Show," "Your Show of Shows," "The Jackie Gleason Show," "The Red Skelton Show," and, naturally, "I Love Lucy." I was continually dazzled by the skits and broad humor, but I was particularly taken with the silent sketches, my favorite comedians as mime artists: Skelton as Freddy the Freeloader, Caesar and Coca in a number of roles, thoroughly outrageous Kovacs acts backed by Gershwin's "Rialto Ripples." My father was a very funny man and a skillful mime. I could tell when he watched Gleason's Poor Soul that he identified mightily with what was on the screen. It had nothing to do with self-pity. My father had far less of it than other men I've met with high intelligence, financial and professional stress, and black faces in a white world. No, my father would even say that we were all poor souls; it was the human condition. His mimicking of the Gleason character—head down, shoulders tucked, stomach sagging, feet splayed—served as some kind of release. I would laugh and cry watching either of them.

But my absolute favorite was Martha Raye, who had a way of milking the fine line between tragedy and comedy better than most. I thought her eyes showed a combination of riotous humor and terror. Her large mouth contorted in ways that seemed to express the same two emotions. Her face was a mask of profound sadness. She did for me what Sylvia Sidney did for James Baldwin. In *The Devil Finds Work,* Baldwin says, "Sylvia Sidney was the only American film actress who reminded me of a colored girl, or woman—which is to say that she was the only American film actress who reminded me of reality." The reality Raye conveyed to me was of how dreams could turn sour in split-seconds, and how underdogs, even when winning, often had to pay abominable prices. She also could sing a jazz song well, with her husky scat phrasing, in ways that were slightly different from those of my favorite singers, and almost as enjoyable.

There were no comedic or dramatic images of black women on the screen—that is, apart from Sapphire and her mother on "Amos 'n' Andy." And knowing Grandma and Grandpa taught me, if nothing else suggested it, that what I saw of black life on television was a gross burlesque—played to the hilt with skill by black actors, but still lacking reality.

37   Black female singers who appeared on television were, like their music, sacrosanct, and I learned from their styles, lyrics, and improvisations, lessons about life that mime routines did not reveal. Still, it was Martha Raye, and occasionally Lucille Ball and Imogene Coca at their most absurd, that aligned me with my father and his Poor Soul, and primed me to both love and despise Grandma and to see that in life most expressions, thoughts, acts, and intentions reveal their opposite polarities simultaneously.

38   Grandma died in 1965. I was away, out of the country, and I missed her funeral—which was probably a good idea since I might have been tempted to strangle some close family friend who probably would have launched into a "tsk, tsk, tsk" monologue about long-suffering grandmothers and impudent children. But, in another way, I'm sorry I didn't make it. Her funeral might have provided some proper closure for me, might have prompted me to organize her effect on my life sooner than I did, reconciling the grandmother who so hoped I would be a boy that she was willing to catch a Constellation or a DC-3 to witness my first few hours, but instead opted to take the bus when she heard the sad news, with the grandmother who called me "Sally Slapcabbage" and wrote to me and my sister regularly, sending us the odd dollar or two, until her death.

39   I remember coming home from school, getting my jelly sandwich and wolfing it down, and watching "The Mickey Mouse Club," my favorite afternoon show, since there was no afternoon movie. I had noticed and had been offended by the lack of black children in the "Club," but the cartoons, particularly those with Donald Duck, were worth watching. On this particular episode—one of the regular guest act days—a group of young black children, perhaps nine or ten of them, came on and sang, with a touch of dancing, "Old MacDonald Had a Farm," in an up-tempo, jazzy version. In spite of the fact that usually these guest days produced some interesting child acts, I became angry with what I saw. I felt patronized, for myself and for them. Clearly a couple of them could out-sing and out-dance any Mouseketeer—something that wasn't worth giving a thought to—but this performance was gratuitous, asymmetrical, a nonsequitur, like Harpo Marx marching through the Negro section in *A Day at the Races*, blowing an imaginary horn and exciting the locals to much singing, swinging, and dancing to a charming ditty called "Who Dat Man?"

40   I must have mumbled something as I watched the group singing "Old MacDonald." Grandma, passing through, took a look at what was on the screen, and at me, turned off the television, took my hand, led me to her kitchen, and sat me down at the table where she and Half-Wit ate, poured me some milk, and without so much as a blink of her eye, said, "Pay no attention to that shit."

✦ *Evaluating the Text*

1. What impression do you get of the circumstances surrounding Pemberton's early life? How do they help explain why her grandmother was so influential in shaping her outlook on life?

2. How would you characterize the voice that you hear in Pemberton's essay? What personality traits does she possess as a writer?

3. How is the grandmother's response to Gloria Lockerman so unexpected in light of her customary reactions to television performers?

4. In what ways was the media's presentation of African-Americans in the 1950s a stereotyped one? How does this help explain Pemberton's grandmother's reaction to Gloria Lockerman?

5. Why is it important to know that the narrator's family was the only black family in that neighborhood and what inferences can you form about her experiences at school?

✦ *Exploring Different Perspectives*

1. Compare the influence of Boris Yeltsin's grandfather in "Childhood in Russia" in shaping his outlook with the effect of Pemberton's grandmother on her. In what way are they comparable?

2. To what extent do the observations on the importance of the extended family in Pemberton's account also pertain to Rigoberta Menchú's "Birth Ceremonies"?

✦ *Extending Viewpoints Through Writing*

1. To what extent did one of your grandparents or relatives exert a shaping influence on your outlook, personality, and expectations? Describe one or two key incidents that illustrate this.

2. In your view, what television shows either reflect or fail to reflect African-American life in the United States today?

Boris Yeltsin

Childhood in Russia

◆

Born in the Russian heartland, near the Ural Mountains, and raised in a communal hut with twenty other families, Boris Yeltsin experienced the hardships of the Soviet system firsthand. His success as an engineer attracted the local Communist Party, and he was appointed district representative. In this post, he was instrumental in alleviating chronic food shortages throughout the region. Mikhail Gorbachev then brought Yeltsin to Moscow as a member of the party elite. Yeltsin's initial support of Gorbachev's perestroika *program gave way to criticism so severe that he was expelled from the politburo and the party. Yeltsin's comeback began when he won a seat in the National Legislature. The following year, Yeltsin was elected president of the Russian Republic, the largest of the fifteen Soviet republics. Yeltsin has proposed a "500-day" plan designed to turn the economy of the Russian Republic into a free-market system. "Childhood in Russia" is taken from Yeltsin's 1990* Against the Grain: An Autobiography, *translated by Michael Glenny.*

 Russia is the largest of the fifteen former Soviet republics and the largest country in the world. It is nearly twice the size of the United States. Russia is bounded by the Arctic Ocean in the north, by the Pacific Ocean in the east, and in the south and west by many countries in Europe and Asia. The first Russian ruler, Ivan the Terrible (1533–1584), expanded Russia's territory, as did Peter the Great (1682–1724) and Catherine the Great (1762–1796). In 1812 Russian troops defeated France's Napoleon. In 1917 Vladimir Lenin, head of the Bolshevik party, led a revolt that put the communists in power. Their rule was consolidated under the authoritarian regimes of Joseph Stalin, Nikita Khruschev, and Leonid Brezhnev. After emerging as a new leader of the Soviet Union, Mikhail Gorbachev attempted to reform the system with the policy of perestroika *in 1986. The failure of these reforms led to an unsuccessful coup in August 1991 and the unraveling of the Soviet Union. Russia became an independent country and Russia's first elected president, Boris Yeltsin, has found it difficult to introduce free-market reforms because of opposition from hardliners in the parliament. A new constitution was adopted by referendum in December 1993. In 1996 Boris Yeltsin faced a serious health crisis after having been reelected for another five-year term as president.*

1 I was born on February 1, 1931, in the village of Butko in the Talitsky district of Sverdlovsk province, where all my forebears had lived.

They had plowed the land, sown wheat, and passed their lives like all other country people. Among the people in our village there were the Yeltsins, my father's family, and the Starygins, my mother's family. My father married my mother there, and soon I made my appearance in the world—their first child.

My mother used to tell me the story of what happened at my baptism. The little church, with its priest, was the only one for the whole district, which consisted of several villages. The birth rate for the area was quite high, but even so the baptismal service was held only once a month. Consequently, that day was a busy one for the priest, and the church was filled to bursting with parents, babies, relatives, and friends. The baptism was conducted in the most primitive fashion: There was a tub full of holy liquid, water seasoned with something or other, in which each baby was completely immersed. The squalling infant was then christened and given a name, which was entered in the parish register. And of course, as was the custom in villages all over Russia, the parents offered the priest a glass of home-brewed beer, moonshine, or vodka—whatever they could afford.

Since my turn did not come until the afternoon, the priest, having drunk many toasts, could barely stand. When my mother, Klavdia Vasilievna, and my father, Nikolai Ignatievich, handed me to him, the priest dropped me into the tub and, being drawn into an argument with a member of the congregation, forgot to take me out. At first, my parents, who were standing at some distance from the baptismal font, didn't know what had happened. When they finally realized what was going on, my mother screamed, leapt forward, and fished me out from somewhere at the bottom of the tub.

They then shook the water out of me. The priest was not particularly worried. He said, "Well, if he can survive such an ordeal, it means he's a good, tough lad—and I name him Boris."

Thus I became Boris Nikolayevich. I won't say that after that I developed any special affinity for religion; of course not.

My childhood was passed during hard times: very bad harvests and no food. We were all forced to join a collective farm—and all of us were treated like peasants. To make matters worse, gangs of outlaws roamed at large, and almost every day we saw shootouts, murders, and robbery.

We lived in near poverty, in a small house with one cow. We did have a horse, but when it died, we were left without an animal to pull the plow. In 1935, the situation became more unbearable—even our cow died—and my grandfather, who was over sixty, was forced to go from house to house, building stoves. Besides being a plowman, he was also a carpenter and cabinetmaker—a complete jack-of-all-trades.

In order to save the family, my father decided to leave the farm to find work on a construction site. It was then Stalin's so-called period of industrialization. He knew that construction workers would be needed for the building of a potash plant at Berezniki in the neighboring province of Perm, so he moved the family there. We all harnessed ourselves to the cart, loaded it with our few possessions, and set off for the railway station—itself a distance of twenty miles.

9   After we arrived at Berezniki and my father signed on at the construction site as a laborer, we were housed in one of the communal huts typical of that time—which, to this day, are still to be found in a few places—built of clapboard, through which drafts whistled relentlessly. The hut had a central corridor and twenty small rooms, naturally without any modern conveniences; there was only an outdoor toilet and water drawn from a well. We were given a few sticks of furniture, and we bought a goat to supply us with milk. My brother and my sister, the youngest, had already been born by then. The six of us, including the goat, slept on the floor, huddled together. From the age of six I was in charge of the household. This meant looking after the younger children—rocking my sister in her cradle and keeping an eye on my brother to see that he didn't misbehave. My other domestic chores were boiling potatoes, washing the dishes, and fetching water from the well.

10   While my father labored on the building site, my mother, a gentle and kind woman by nature, would help relatives and neighbors by sewing clothes. Every night she would sit down with her sewing—never taking money for her work. She was grateful if someone gave her half a loaf of bread or some other morsel of food.

11   My father was rough and quick-tempered, just like my grandfather. No doubt they passed these characteristics on to me. My parents constantly argued about me. My father's chief instrument for teaching good behavior was the strap, and he walloped me good and proper for any lapses. Whatever happened in our neighborhood—if a neighbor's apple tree had been robbed or if someone played a nasty trick on the German teacher in school—my father would not say a word but would reach for the strap. My mother would weep and beg him not to touch me. But he would firmly shut the door and tell me to lie down. I would pull up my shirt and lower my trousers. He would lay into me with great thoroughness. I always clenched my teeth and did not make a sound, which infuriated him; then my mother would burst in, snatch the strap away from him, pushing him aside and standing between us. She always defended me.

12   My father was an inventor, and he was always working on a new idea. One of his ambitions was to invent a machine that would lay bricks. He would sketch it out, rethink it, make calculations, and then produce another set of drawings; it was a kind of will-o'-the-wisp that he was perpetually chasing. Unfortunately, no one has yet invented such a machine, although even now whole research institutes rack their brains over it. He would constantly describe to me what his machine

would be like and how it would work; how it would mix the mortar, lay the bricks, clean off the surface mortar, and move forward. He had worked it all out in his head and drawn the general plan, but he never managed to realize his idea.

We lived in that crowded wooden hut for ten years. Strange as it   13
may seem, the people who lived under those conditions somehow managed to be good, friendly neighbors, especially when one considers that there was no sound insulation. If there was a party in the rooms— a birthday or a wedding—everyone could hear it. There was an old wind-up gramophone with only two or three records, and these were shared by the whole hut; I can still remember one song in particular: "Shchors the Red Commander marches on beneath the standard . . ." which the whole hut used to sing. Conversations, quarrels, rows, se- crets, laughter—the whole hut could hear everything, and everyone knew everyone else's business.

Perhaps it is because I can remember to this day how hard our life   14
was then that I so hate those communal huts. Winter was worst of all. There was nowhere to hide from the cold. Since we had no warm clothes, we would huddle up to the nanny goat to keep warm. We chil- dren survived on her milk. She was also our salvation throughout the war.

We all earned money on the side. Every summer my mother and I   15
would go out to a nearby collective farm. We would be allotted several acres of meadowlands and we scythed the grass, stacked it, and pre- pared the hay, half of which went to the collective farm and the other half to us. We would then sell our half and buy bread at exorbitant prices.

That was how my childhood was spent. It was a fairly joyless time.   16
There were never any sweets, delicacies, or anything of that sort; we had only one aim in life—to survive.

Despite these hardships, I always stood out from the other students—   17
especially because of my energy and drive. From first grade on, I was elected class leader, even though I went to several different schools. I did well at my studies and got top marks in my exams. But my behav- ior was less praiseworthy. In all my years of school I was the ringleader, always devising some mischief. In fifth grade, for instance, I persuaded the whole class to jump out the first-floor window, and when our un- popular teacher came back, the classroom was empty. She immediately went to the watchman at the main entrance, who told her that no one had left the building. We had hidden in a small yard beside the school. When we returned to the classroom we were given a zero for the day. We protested. We said, "Punish us for our bad behavior, but test us on the lesson—we know it." The headmaster arrived, organized a special class, and questioned us for about two hours. We had learned every- thing by heart, and all of us, even the weak pupils, answered every

question correctly. In the end, the zeroes were canceled, although we were given the lowest possible mark for behavior.

18   Another of our adventures took place at the local stream, the Zyryanka. In the spring, it would overflow its banks and become a river, and logs were floated down it. I invented a game to see who could run across floating logs to the far bank. The timber tended to flow in a fairly tight mass, so that if you judged it carefully there was a chance of being able to get across—although to do so you needed to be extremely skillful. Step on a log and if it gave the slightest sign of rolling over and you delayed for a second, you would be under water. So you had to move really fast from one log to another, keeping your balance all the time and leaping briskly in order to reach the far bank. The slightest miscalculation and it was into the icy water, with nothing but logs above you, between which you would have to try to push your head and gulp a lungful of air, not sure if you would come out alive.

19   We also used to have fights, neighborhood against neighborhood, with between sixty and a hundred boys at a time fighting with sticks, cudgels, or fists. I used to take part in these fights, although I always got clobbered. When two solid walls of opponents clashed head-on, however strong you might be, you would always end up with several bumps on your head. I achieved my broken nose, like a boxer's, when someone whacked me with the shaft of a cart. I fell, everything went black, and I thought it was the end. But I came to my senses and was carried home. There were no fatalities in these fights, because although we fought enthusiastically, we observed certain limits.

20   I was expelled from school once. It happened at my primary school graduation. About six hundred people were gathered in the assembly hall—parents, teachers, and pupils—in an atmosphere of cheerfulness and elation. Everyone was solemnly handed his or her diploma. Everything was going according to plan, when I suddenly stood up and asked permission to speak. My exam results had been excellent, nothing but top marks in every subject, and for that reason I was allowed up on the stage. Everyone thought that I would simply say a few gracious words. Naturally I had some kind words to say to those teachers who had given us valuable instruction that would help us in our lives and who had developed in us the habits of reading and thinking. But then I declared that our homeroom teacher had no right to teach children because she crippled them mentally and psychologically.

21   That awful woman might hit you with a heavy ruler, she might stand you in the corner, she might humiliate a boy in front of a girl. She even made us clean her house. Once, the class had to collect food scraps from all over the district to feed her pig. It was endless, and some of the children refused to oblige her, but others submitted.

22   Briefly I described how she mocked her pupils, destroyed their self-confidence, and did everything possible to humiliate every one of us—

I went for her tooth and nail. There was an uproar. The whole event was ruined.

The next day the school board sent for my father to tell him my diploma was being withdrawn and instead I was to be given a so-called wolf's ticket: a little scrap of white paper that testified to my having completed the required seven years of primary schooling but stated below that I was deprived of the right to acquire a secondary education anywhere in the USSR. My father came home furious and reached for the strap—but at that moment, for the first time, I gripped him by the arm and said, "That's enough. From now on I'm going to educate myself." Never again was I made to stand in the corner all night, and no one ever took the strap to me again.   23

I refused to accept the decision of the school board and took my case up the education hierarchy: first to the district and then to the city education department. I learned for the first time what a local party committee was. I succeeded in getting a commission of inquiry set up, which investigated the work of that teacher and dismissed her from the school. She got exactly what she deserved, and I got my diploma back, although under the heading "Discipline," the word "unsatisfactory" glared out from the line of otherwise perfect grades.   24

I decided not to go back to that school and instead entered the eighth grade at Sverdlovsk's Pushkin School, of which I retain the fondest memories. The staff was excellent; and in Angonina Kohonina we had a superb homeroom teacher.   25

It was then that I began participating in sports. I was fascinated by volleyball and was prepared to play it endlessly. I liked the way the ball obeyed me, that I could return even the most difficult volley. At the same time I took up skiing, gymnastics, decathlon, boxing, and wrestling; I wanted to try my hand at them all, to do absolutely everything well. In the end, volleyball prevailed, and I started playing it seriously. I kept a ball with me all the time, even when I went to bed, when I'd sleep with my hand resting on it. As soon as I woke up I would start practicing by myself—spinning the ball on one finger or bouncing it off the wall and the floor. But because I was missing two fingers on my left hand, I had difficulty catching a ball, and I worked out my own unique method of catching.   26

This is the story of how I lost my two fingers: The Second World War had begun, and some of us who were too young to go to the front made our own pistols and rifles and even a cannon. We decided to steal some grenades in order to learn what was inside them. I volunteered to break into the local church, which was being used as an ammunition dump. That night I crept through three layers of barbed wire, and while the sentry was on the other side of the building, I filed through the mesh on a window and climbed inside. There I took two RGD-33 hand grenades with fuses and managed to make my way back unharmed   27 (the sentry would have fired without warning). We went to a forest about forty miles away, and this time I volunteered to take the grenades apart. I told the other boys to take cover a hundred yards off; then I put the grenade on a stone, knelt down, and hit it with a hammer. I didn't realize I had to remove the fuse. There was an explosion—and two of my fingers were mangled. The other boys were unharmed. I kept losing consciousness while they took me to town. Gangrene set in. The hospital surgeons cut off the two fingers.

28 Every summer during my student days I worked to earn pocket money, and I also organized long class hikes. Each trip had a special objective: to find the source of a river, or to get to the mountains. The expeditions usually involved trekking several hundred miles with knapsacks and living in the forest for several weeks.

29 The summer after ninth grade, we decided to find the source of the river Yaiva. We spent a long time climbing up through the forest, knowing that the source was somewhere near the crest of the Urals. The food we had taken with us was soon gone, and we lived on what we could find in the forest, mushrooms and berries. The Urals forest is very fertile; one can survive there for a considerable time. Far from any roads, we tramped for a long time through the virgin woodland. Occasionally we came across a little hut used by hunters, where we would spend the night, but more often we built our own brushwood shelter or simply slept in the open.

30 We did at last find the source of the river—a spring of natural hydrogen sulfide. Turning back, we descended a few miles to the first village, by which time we were pretty worn out. We knew we needed a boat to travel farther. We collected whatever each of us could offer—a knapsack, a shirt, a hat—more or less everything we had to trade for a boat. Then we went to a little cottage and gave our possessions to the owner, in exchange for a small wooden flat-bottomed boat. In this boat we floated downstream; we no longer had the strength to walk. As we were floating along, we suddenly saw a cave in the hillside above us. We decided to stop and explore it. The cave led us on and on, until it suddenly opened out and brought us to a point somewhere deep in the forest. We scouted around but could not figure out where we were. We were lost, and we had lost our boat too. We wandered around for almost a week. We had brought nothing with us from the boat, and since the region turned out to be swampy, with nothing but stunted saplings and undergrowth, it provided us with barely enough to eat, and no fresh water at all. We collected the murky swamp water and sodden moss in a shirt, squeezed it, and drank the liquid that dripped out of the shirt.

31 We finally managed to make our way back to the river, where we found our boat and were able to calculate our position, but the water we had drunk made us all very ill (eventually we were diagnosed as

having typhoid fever). As the expedition leader, I stayed on my feet. I carried all the other boys down to the boat, laid them in the bottom, and, exerting my last ounce of strength to prevent myself from losing consciousness, steered the boat as it drifted downstream. I had only enough energy left to give the others some river water to splash over their faces, which were burning with fever. They lost consciousness, and soon I, too, began to pass out. When we reached a railway bridge that crossed the river, we thought that someone would find us. I moored our boat to the bank and collapsed unconscious. We were seen, picked up, and driven back to town; the school term had begun a month before, and search parties had been looking for us.

Typhoid fever kept us in the hospital for nearly three months. They had no medicines for it. My companions on the expedition had decided not to attend tenth grade—our last—that year and to stay on at school for an extra year. But halfway through the school year I began studying on my own at home. I worked day and night, and when the final exams began, I went to school to take them.

I arrived at school and was told I couldn't take the exams; there was no provision for home study in the final year. Once again, helped by the fact that this path was already familiar to me, I set off on a well-beaten track: all the local education departments and the party committee. By this time I was a member of the city's volleyball team; fortunately, I was also known as the junior champion in several sports and as volleyball champion of Sverdlovsk province. In the end I was allowed to take the exams as an external student. Admittedly I did not get top marks in all subjects; I was given a four in two subjects, a five in all the others. That was my baggage for the onward journey to higher education.

As a boy, I had dreamed of attending an institute of shipbuilding. I had read a number of standard textbooks and tried to understand how ships were built. But gradually I began to be attracted by the profession of civil engineering—no doubt because I had already worked as a building laborer and because my father was in the construction business.

But before I could enter the department of civil engineering at Urals Polytechnic Institute, I had to pass one more test—this one administered by my grandfather. He was over seventy by then, a most impressive man, with a long beard and a quirky, original cast of mind. He said to me, "I won't let you go into the building trade until you have built something with your own hands. You can build me a bathhouse. A small one, in the backyard, complete with a changing room."

We had never had our own bathhouse, though our neighbors did. Circumstances had always prevented us from building one.

My grandfather explained, "You must build it all yourself. My only contribution will be to get the local office of the State Timber Trust to allot you some trees in the forest. From then on you must fell the necessary pine trees, prepare moss for caulking the walls, clean it and dry it; you must carry all the logs from the forest yourself"—it was two miles—"to the place where you're going to build the bathhouse; you must make the foundations and do all the woodworking yourself, all the way up to the roof tree. And I," he said, "will not come anywhere near you." He was a stubborn old man, obstinate as they come, and he never once came within thirty yards of me. Nor did he lift a finger to help me, even though I found the work incredibly hard. When I had finished the bathhouse, my grandfather solemnly announced that I had passed the test and I now had his full permission to enter the department of civil engineering.

✦ Evaluating the Text

1. How is the significance of Yeltsin's Christian name related to the circumstances in which he received it?

2. To what extent does Yeltsin's description of what life was like under communal circumstances, both on the farm and in the city of Berezniki, differ from your conception of the meaning of *communism* (keep in mind the root word *commune*)?

3. What does Yeltsin's decision to publicly castigate a teacher for injurious and unfair treatment of students in front of everyone during the graduation ceremony reveal about him?

4. How was Yeltsin's discovery that he could successfully manipulate the bureaucracy when he was in the seventh grade an important lesson for him?

5. In your opinion, what was Yeltsin's grandfather hoping to achieve by setting such difficult conditions for Boris before allowing him to enroll in a civil engineering program?

✦ Exploring Different Perspectives

1. What insight do you gain from Yeltsin's account about what life is like in a communal setting when compared with Rigoberta Menchú's account in "Birth Ceremonies"?

2. What similarities can you discover in the influence that grandparents had in shaping the lives of Yeltsin and Gayle Pemberton (see "Antidisestablishmentarianism")?

✦ Extending Viewpoints Through Writing

1. Just as Yeltsin nearly drowned during his baptism, people experience events differently because of where their last name comes in the alphabet. How do people whose last names begin with early letters in the alphabet have different experiences than people whose last names begin with letters close to the end? Discuss experiences you have had attributable to where your last name falls in the alphabet.

2. You might want to read the rest of Yeltsin's autobiography *Against the Grain* (1990) to discover how character traits Yeltsin developed in childhood served him in his confrontations with Soviet bureaucracy in general, and Gorbachev in particular, in his rise to being chosen the first freely elected president of Russia.

Rigoberta Menchú

Birth Ceremonies

◆

Rigoberta Menchú, a Quiché Indian, was born in the hamlet of Chimel, in northwestern Guatemala. Her life reflects experiences common to Indian communities throughout Central America. She survived a genocide that destroyed her family and community: Her brother, father, and mother were all killed in acts of savagery after the coming to power of the Garcia Lucas regime in 1978. "Birth Ceremonies" is taken from I, Rigoberta Menchú: An Indian Woman in Guatemala *(1983), translated by Ann Wright, a powerful work that speaks of the struggle to maintain Indian culture and tradition. Menchú received the Nobel Prize for Peace in 1992.*

The republic of Guatemala is located in Central America. After defeating the Quiché (Mayan) Indians in 1523, Spain established a prosperous colony that lasted until Guatemala gained its independence in 1821. The predominantly Roman Catholic population is evenly divided between Mayan Indians and Mestizos (persons of mixed Spanish and Amerindian blood), who Menchú refers to as ladinos. *Politically unstable, Guatemala has been dominated since the 1970s by ruthless military regimes. Violence in the country caused many, including Menchú, to flee and live as exiles. In May of 1993 President Jorge Serrano Elias (who came to power in 1986) dissolved the Congress and Supreme Court and suspended the constitution. An outcry from the public prompted Serrano to resign, and military leaders then installed Ramiro de Leon Carpio to complete Serrano's term as president. A referendum on constitutional reform was held in January 1994, and congressional elections were held in August of that year.*

> *Whoever may ask where we are, tell them what you know of us and nothing more.*
>
> —Popol Vuh

> *Learn to protect yourselves, by keeping our secret.*
>
> —Popol Vuh

1   In our community there is an elected representative, someone who is highly respected. He's not a king but someone whom the community looks up to like a father. In our village, my father and mother were the representatives. Well, then the whole community becomes the children of the woman who's elected. So, a mother, on her first day of pregnancy goes with her husband to tell these elected leaders that she's going to

have a child, because the child will not only belong to them but to the whole community, and must follow as far as he can our ancestors' traditions. The leaders then pledge the support of the community and say: 'We will help you, we will be the child's second parents.' They are known as *abuelos*, 'grandparents' or 'forefathers.' The parents then ask the 'grandparents' to help them find the child some godparents, so that if he's orphaned, he shouldn't be tempted by any of the bad habits our people sometimes fall into. So the 'grandparents' and the parents choose the godparents together. It's also the custom for the pregnant mother's neighbours to visit her every day and take her little things, no matter how simple. They stay and talk to her, and she'll tell them all her problems.

Later, when she's in her seventh month, the mother introduces her baby to the natural world, as our customs tell her to. She goes out in the fields or walks over the hills. She also has to show her baby the kind of life she leads, so that if she gets up at three in the morning, does her chores and tends the animals, she does it all the more so when she's pregnant, conscious that the child is taking all this in. She talks to the child continuously from the first moment he's in her stomach, telling him how hard his life will be. It's as if the mother were a guide explaining things to a tourist. She'll say, for instance; 'You must never abuse nature and you must live your life as honestly as I do.' As she works in the fields, she tells her child all the little things about her work. It's a duty to her child that a mother must fulfill. And then, she also has to think of a way of hiding the baby's birth from her other children.

When her baby is born, the mother mustn't have her other children round her. The people present should be the husband, the village leaders, and the couple's parents. Three couples. The parents are often away in other places, so if they can't be there, the husband's father and the wife's mother can perhaps make up one pair. If one of the village leaders can't come, one of them should be there to make up a couple with one of the parents. If none of the parents can come, some aunts and uncles should come to represent the family on both sides, because the child is to be part of the community. The birth of a new member is very significant for the community, as it belongs to the community not just to the parents, and that's why three couples (but not just anybody) must be there to receive it. They explain that this child is the fruit of communal love. If the village leader is not a midwife as well, another midwife is called (it might be a grandmother) to receive the child. Our customs don't allow single women to see a birth. But it does happen in times of need. For instance, I was with my sister when she went into labour. Nobody else was at home. This was when we were being heavily persecuted. Well, I didn't exactly see, but I was there when the baby was born.

My mother was a midwife from when she was sixteen right up to her death at forty-three. She used to say that a woman hadn't the strength to push the baby out when she's lying down. So what she did with my sister was to hang a rope from the roof and pull her up, because my brother wasn't there to lift her up. My mother helped the baby out with my sister in that position. It's a scandal if an Indian woman goes to hospital and gives birth there. None of our women would agree to that. Our ancestors would be shocked at many of the things which go on today. Family planning, for example. It's an insult to our culture and a way of swindling the people, to get money out of them.

5   This is part of the reserve that we've maintained to defend our customs and our culture. Indians have been very careful not to disclose any details of their communities, and the community does not allow them to talk about Indian things. I too must abide by this. This is because many religious people have come among us and drawn a false impression of the Indian world. We also find a *ladino* using Indian clothes very offensive. All this has meant that we keep a lot of things to ourselves and the community doesn't like us telling its secrets. This applies to all our customs. When the Catholic Action[1] arrived, for instance, everyone started going to mass, and praying, but it's not their only religion, not the only way they have of expressing themselves. Anyway, when a baby is born, he's always baptized within the community before he's taken to church. Our people have taken Catholicism as just another channel of expression, not our one and only belief. Our people do the same with other religions. The priests, monks and nuns haven't gained the people's confidence because so many of their things contradict our own customs. For instance, they say; 'You have too much trust in your elected leaders.' But the village elects them *because* they trust them, don't they? The priests say; 'The trouble is you follow those sorcerers,' and speak badly of them. But for our people this is like speaking ill of their own fathers, and they lose faith in the priests. They say; 'Well, they're not from here, they can't understand our world.' So there's not much hope of winning our people's hearts.

6   To come back to the children, they aren't to know how the baby is born. He's born somewhere hidden away and only the parents know about it. They are told that a baby has arrived and that they can't see their mother for eight days. Later on, the baby's companion, the placenta that is, has to be burned at a special time. If the baby is born at night, the placenta is burned at eight in the morning, and if he's born in the afternoon, it'll be burned at five o'clock. This is out of respect for both the baby and his companion. The placenta is not buried, because the earth is the mother and the father of the child and mustn't be abused by having the placenta buried in it. All these reasons are very

---

[1]Association created in 1945 by Monsignor Rafael Gonzalez, to try and control the Indian fraternities of the *Altiplano*.

important for us. Either the placenta is burned on a log and the ashes left there, or else it is put in the *temascal*. This is a stove which our people use to make vapour baths. It's a small hut made of adobe and inside this hut is another one made of stone, and when we want to have a bath, we light a fire to heat the stones, close the door, and throw water on the stones to produce steam. Well, when the woman is about four months pregnant, she starts taking these baths infused with evergreens, pure natural aromas. There are many plants the community uses for pregnant women, colds, headaches, and things like that. So the pregnant mother takes baths with plants prescribed for her by the midwife or the village leader. The fields are full of plants whose names I don't know in Spanish. Pregnant women use orange and peach leaves a lot for bathing and there's another one we call Saint Mary's leaf which they use. The mother needs these leaves and herbs to relax because she won't be able to rest while she's pregnant since our women go on working just as hard in the fields. So, after work, she takes this calming bath so that she can sleep well, and the baby won't be harmed by her working hard. She's given medicines to take as well. And leaves to feed the child. I believe that in practice (even if this isn't a scientific recommendation) these leaves work very well, because many of them contain vitamins. How else would women who endure hunger and hard work, give birth to healthy babies? I think that these plants have helped our people survive.

The purity with which the child comes into the world is protected for eight days. Our customs say that the new-born baby should be alone with his mother in a special place for eight days, without any of her other children. Her only visitors are the people who bring her food. This is the baby's period of integration into the family; he very slowly becomes a member of it. When the child is born, they kill a sheep and there's a little fiesta just for the family. Then the neighbours start coming to visit, and bring presents. They either bring food for the mother, or something for the baby. The mother has to taste all the food her neighbours bring to show her appreciation for their kindness. After the eight days are over, the family counts up how many visitors the mother had, and how many presents were received; things like eggs or food apart from what was brought for the mother, or clothing, small animals, and wood for the fire, or services like carrying water and chopping wood. If, during the eight days, most of the community has called, this is very important, because it means that this child will have a lot of responsibility towards his community when he grows up. The community takes over all the household expenses for these eight days and the family spends nothing.

After eight days everything has been received, and another animal is killed as recognition that the child's right to be alone with his mother is over. All the mother's clothes, bedclothes, and everything she used during the birth, are taken away by our elected leader and washed. She can't wash them in the well, so no matter how far away the river is, they must be carried and washed there. The baby's purity is washed away and he's ready to learn the ways of humanity. The mother's bed is moved to a part of the house which has first been washed with water and lime. Lime is sacred. It strengthens the child's bones. I believe this really is true. It gives a child strength to face the world. The mother has a bath in the *temascal* and puts on clean clothes. Then, the whole house is cleaned. The child is also washed and dressed and put into the new bed. Four candles are placed on the corners of the bed to represent the four corners of the house and show him that this will be his home. They symbolize the respect the child must have for his community, and the responsibility he must feel towards it as a member of a household. The candles are lit and give off an incense which incorporates the child into the world he must live in. When the baby is born, his hands and feet are bound to show him that they are sacred and must only be used to work or do whatever nature meant them to do. They must never steal or abuse the natural world, or show disrespect for any living thing.

9   After the eight days, his hands and feet are untied and he's now with his mother in the new bed. This means he opens the doors to the other members of the community, because neither the family or the community know him yet. Or rather, they weren't shown the baby when he was born. Now they can all come and kiss him. The neighbours bring another animal, and there's big lunch in the new baby's house for all the community. This is to celebrate his integration 'in the universe,' as our parents used to say. Candles will be lit for him and his candle becomes part of the candle of the whole community, which now has one more person, one more member. The whole community is at the ceremony, or at least, if not all of it, then some of it. Candles are lit to represent all the things which belong to the universe—earth, water, sun, and man—and the child's candle is put with them, together with incense (what we call *pom*) and lime—our sacred lime. Then, the parents tell the baby of the suffering of the family he will be joining. With great feeling, they express their sorrow at bringing a child into the world to suffer. To us, suffering is our fate, and the child must be introduced to the sorrows and hardship, but he must learn that despite his suffering, he will be respectful and live through his pain. The child is then entrusted with the responsibility for his community and told to abide by its rules. After the ceremony comes the lunch, and then the neighbours go home. Now, there is only the baptism to come.

10   When the baby is born, he's given a little bag with a garlic, a bit of lime, salt, and tobacco in it, to hang round his neck. Tobacco is important because it is a sacred plant for Indians. This all means that the child can ward off all the evil things in life. For us, bad things are like spirits, which exist only in our imagination. Something bad, for instance, would

be if the child were to turn out to be a gossip—not sincere, truthful, and respectful, as a child should be. It also helps him collect together and preserve all our ancestors' things. That's more or less the idea of the bag—to keep him pure. The bag is put inside the four candles as well, and this represents the promise of the child when he grows up.

When the child is forty days old, there are more speeches, more 11 promises on his behalf, and he becomes a full member of the community. This is his baptism. All the important people of the village are invited and they speak. The parents make a commitment. They promise to teach the child to keep the secrets of our people, so that our culture and customs will be preserved. The village leaders come and offer their experience, their example, and their knowledge of our ancestors. They explain how to preserve our traditions. Then, they promise to be responsible for the child, teach him as he grows up, and see that he follows in their ways. It's also something of a criticism of humanity, and of the many people who have forsaken their traditions. They say almost a prayer, asking that our traditions again enter the spirits of those who have forsaken them. Then, they evoke the names of our ancestors, like Tecun Umán and others who form part of the ceremony, as a kind of chant. They must be remembered as heroes of the Indian peoples. And then they say (I analyse all this later); 'Let no landowner extinguish all this, nor any rich man wipe out our customs. Let our children, be they workers or servants, respect and keep their secrets.' The child is present for all of this, although he's all wrapped up and can scarcely be seen. He is told that he will eat maize and that, naturally, he is already made of maize because his mother ate it while he was forming in her stomach. He must respect the maize; even the grain of maize which has been thrown away, he must pick up. The child will multiply our race, he will replace all those who have died. From this moment, he takes on this responsibility, and is told to live as his 'grandparents' have lived. The parents then reply that their child promises to accomplish all this. So, the village leaders and the parents both make promises on behalf of the child. It's his initiation into the community.

The ceremony is very important. It is also when the child is consid- 12 ered a child of God, our one father. We don't actually have the word God but that is what it is, because the one father is the only one we have. To reach this one father, the child must love beans, maize, the earth. The one father is the heart of the sky, that is, the sun. The sun is the father and our mother is the moon. She is a gentle mother. And she lights our way. Our people have many notions about the moon, and about the sun. They are the pillars of the universe.

When children reach ten years old, that's the moment when their 13 parents and the village leaders talk to them again. They tell them that they will be young men and women and that one day they will be fathers and mothers. This is actually when they tell the child that he must never abuse his dignity, in the same way his ancestors never abused their dignity. It's also when they remind them that our ancestors were dishonoured by the White Man, by colonization. But they don't tell them the way that it's written down in books, because the majority of Indians can't read or write, and don't even know that they have their own texts. No, they learn it through oral recommendations, the way it has been handed down through the generations. They are told that the Spaniards dishonoured our ancestors' finest sons, and the most humble of them. And it is to honour these humble people that we must keep our secrets. And no-one except we Indians must know. They talk a lot about our ancestors. And the ten-years ceremony is also when our children are reminded that they must respect their elders, even though this is something their parents have been telling them ever since they were little. For example, if an old person is walking along the street, children should cross over to allow him to pass by. If any of us sees an elderly person, we are obliged to bow and greet them. Everyone does this, even the very youngest. We also show respect to pregnant women. Whenever we make food, we always keep some for any of our neighbours who are pregnant.

14   When little girls are born, the midwives pierce their ears at the same time as they tie their umbilical cords. The little bags around their necks and the thread used to tie their umbilical cord are both red. Red is very significant for us. It means heat, strength, all living things. It's linked to the sun, which for us is the channel to the one god, the heart of everything, of the universe. So red gives off heat and fire and red things are supposed to give life to the child. At the same time, it asks him to respect living things too. There are no special clothes for the baby. We don't buy anything special beforehand but just use pieces of *corte* to wrap him in.

15   When a male child is born, there are special celebrations, not because he's male but because of all the hard work and responsibility he'll have as a man. It's not that *machismo* doesn't exist among our people, but it doesn't present a problem for the community because it's so much part of our way of life. The male child is given an extra day alone with his mother. The usual custom is to celebrate a male child by killing a sheep or some chickens. Boys are given more, they get more food because their work is harder and they have more responsibility. At the same time, he is head of the household, not in the bad sense of the word, but because he is responsible for so many things. This doesn't mean girls aren't valued. Their work is hard too and there are other things that are due to them as mothers. Girls are valued because they are part of the earth, which gives us maize, beans, plants and everything we live on. The earth is like a mother which multiplies life. So the girl child will multiply the life of our generation and of our ancestors whom we must respect. The girl and the boy are both integrated into

the community in equally important ways, the two are interrelated and compatible. Nevertheless, the community is always happier when a male child is born and the men feel much prouder. The customs, like the tying of the hands and feet, apply to both boys and girls.

Babies are breast-fed. It's much better than any other sort of food. But the important thing is the sense of community. It's something we all share. From the very first day, the baby belongs to the community, not only to the parents and the baby must learn from all of us . . . in fact, we behave just like bourgeois families in that, as soon as the baby is born, we're thinking of his education, of his well-being. But our people feel that the baby's school must be the community itself, that he must learn to live like all the rest of us. The tying of the hands at birth also symbolizes this; that no-one should accumulate things the rest of the community does not have and he must know how to share, to have open hands. The mother must teach the baby to be generous. This way of thinking comes from poverty and suffering. Each child is taught to live like the fellow members of his community.   16

We never eat in front of pregnant women. You can only eat in front of a pregnant woman if you can offer something as well. The fear is that, otherwise, she might abort the baby or that the baby could suffer if she didn't have enough to eat. It doesn't matter whether you know her or not. The important thing is sharing. You have to treat a pregnant woman differently from other women because she is two people. You must treat her with respect so that she recognizes it and conveys this to the baby inside her. You instinctively think she's the image of the baby about to be born. So you love her. Another reason why you must stop and talk to a pregnant woman is because she doesn't have much chance to rest or enjoy herself. She's always worried and depressed. So when she stops and chats a bit, she can relax and feel some relief.   17

When the baby joins the community, with him in the circle of candles—together with his little red bag—he will have his hoe, his machete, his axe and all the tools he will need in life. These will be his playthings. A little girl will have her washing board and all the things she will need when she grows up. She must learn the things of the house, to clean, to wash, and sew her brothers' trousers, for example. The little boy must begin to live like a man, to be responsible and learn to love the work in the fields. The learning is done as a kind of game. When the parents do anything they always explain what it means. This includes learning prayers. This is very important to our people. The mother may say a prayer at any time. Before getting up in the morning, for instance, she thanks the day which is dawning because it might be a very important one for the family. Before lighting the fire, she blesses the wood because that fire is going to cook food for the whole family. Since it's the little girl who is closest to her mother, she learns all of this. Before washing the *nixtamal,* the woman blows on her hands and puts   18 them in the *nixtamal*. She takes everything out and washes it well. She blows on her hands so that her work will bear fruit. She does it before she does the wash as well. She explains all these little details to her daughter, who learns by copying her. With the men it's the same. Before they start work every day, whatever hour of the morning it is, they greet the sun. They remove their hats and talk to the sun before starting to work. Their sons learn to do it too, taking off their little hats to talk to the sun. Naturally, each ethnic group has its own forms of expression. Other groups have different customs from ours. The meaning of their weaving patterns, for example. We realize the others are different in some things, but the one thing we have in common is our culture. Our people are mainly peasants, but there are some people who buy and sell as well. They go into this after they've worked on the land. Sometimes when they come back from working in the *finca,* instead of tending a little plot of land, they'll start a shop and look for a different sort of life. But if they're used to greeting the sun every morning, they still go on doing it. And they keep all their old customs. Every part of our culture comes from the earth. Our religion comes from the maize and bean harvests which are so vital to our community. So even if a man goes to try and make some money, he never forgets his culture springs from the earth.

19   As we grow up we have a series of obligations. Our parents teach us to be responsible; just as they have been responsible. The eldest son is responsible for the house. Whatever the father cannot correct is up to the eldest son to correct. He is like a second father to us all and is responsible for our upbringing. The mother is the one who is responsible for keeping an account for what the family eats, and what she has to buy. When a child is ill, she has to get medicine. But the father has to solve a lot of problems too. And each one of us, as we grow up, has our own small area of responsibility. This comes from the promises made for the child when he is born, and from the continuity of our customs. The child can make the promise for himself when his parents have taught him to do it. The mother, who is closest to the children, does this, or sometimes the father. They talk to their children explaining what they have to do and what our ancestors used to do. They don't impose it as a law, but just give the example of what our ancestors have always done. This is how we all learn our own small responsibilities. For example, the little girl begins by carrying water, and the little boy begins by tying up the dogs when the animals are brought into the yard at night, or by fetching a horse which has wandered off. Both girls and boys have their tasks and are told the reasons for doing them. They learn responsibility because if they don't do their little jobs, well, their father has the right to scold them, or even beat them. So, they are very careful about learning to do their jobs well, but the parents are also very careful to explain exactly why the jobs have to be done. The little

girl understands the reasons for everything her mother does. For example, when she puts a new earthenware pot on the fire for the first time, she hits it five times with a branch, so that it knows its job is to cook and so that it lasts. When the little girl asks, 'Why did you do that?', her mother says, 'So that it knows what its job is and does it well.' When it's her turn to cook, the little girl does as her mother does. Again this is all bound up with our commitment to maintain our customs and pass on the secrets of our ancestors. The elected fathers of the community explain to us that all these things come down to us from our grandfathers and we must conserve them. Nearly everything we do today is based on what our ancestors did. This is the main purpose of our elected leader—to embody all the values handed down from our ancestors. He is the leader of the community, a father to all our children, and he must lead an exemplary life. Above all, he has a commitment to the whole community. Everything that is done today, is done in memory of those who have passed on.

✦ Evaluating the Text

1. How does the birth of a child represent continuity and the propagation of tradition? In what way is the newborn infant the property of the entire village?

2. How does much of Menchú's narrative depend on the assumption that the *ladino* way of life would represent a denial of nature and tradition?

3. What is the rationale behind the Indian perception of the placenta as a companion to the baby? How does the burning of the placenta rather than its burial reveal a distinctively Guatemalan Indian cultural attitude toward the earth? How is the same attitude expressed in the Indian view of maize?

4. What conflict do you observe between native-Indian beliefs and the belief system of Catholic missionaries? What specific aspects of Indian rituals might missionaries fail to understand? How is the church's attempt to dissuade Indians from electing an elder to lead the village related to their wish to convert Indians to Catholicism?

5. How are the "birth ceremonies" organized around the following stages in the ritual: a community pledge of support for the child, an introduction of the as yet unborn child to the daily regimen, a witnessing of the birth by representatives of the tribe, sequestering of the child for eight days during which the house and baby are washed and purified with lime, candles are lit, the child's hands are bound, and the child is introduced to the community and subsequently baptized? Which one of these rituals struck you as the most unusual and interesting?

✦ *Exploring Different Perspectives*

1. What similarities can you discover between Menchú's account and Colin Turnbull's description in "The Mbuti Pygmies"? How do both cultures impress upon their children the need to live their lives in a way that fulfills obligations to the community, whether defined as the village or the state?

2. What insight do you gain from Menchú's account of what life is like in a communal setting when compared with Boris Yeltsin's account in "Childhood in Russia"?

✦ *Extending Viewpoints Through Writing*

1. Which aspects of Guatemalan Indian life surprised you by presenting a view quite different from the culture in which you were raised?

2. Describe the rituals or "birth ceremonies" of another ethnic community. What objects are used, what prayers are said and what are their significance, and who attends the ceremony and what role do they perform? How is the scene decorated or altered through the use of symbols and what do these symbols mean? How does the ceremony express the specific cultural values of the community?

Nicholas Bornoff

The Marriage Go-Round

◆

Born in London of Anglo–French parentage, Nicholas Bornoff attended school both in England and France. After a year of studying graphic design, he went to film school in Paris, where he lived for a decade. In 1979 his work as a European language translator prompted him to move to Tokyo, where he subsequently lived for eleven years. While in Japan, Bornoff worked as an advertising copywriter, was a film critic for the Japan Times newspaper, and wrote many articles on Japanese society, culture, and business practices. A free-lance journalist, Bornoff now lives in London with his Japanese wife. Pink Samurai: The Pursuit and Politics of Sex in Japan *(1991), from which the following selection is taken, provides an exhaustive travelog and scholarly history of Japanese attitudes toward sex, censorship, courtship, and marriage.*

Known historically as the "land of the rising sun" symbolized in the national flag, Japan is made up of four main islands off the coast of east Asia: Honshu (the largest, where the capital Tokyo and major cities are located), Hokkaido, Shikoku, and Kyushu. Two thirds of Japan's terrain is mountainous, including the most famous peak, Mount Fuji. Earth tremors are a frequent occurrence. Because Japan has few natural resources, and such a small percentage of land is suitable for cultivation, the country must import almost half its food supply and almost all raw materials required for industrial production. Despite this, Japan is one of the most productive industrial nations; its exports of automobiles, electronic equipment, televisions, textiles, chemicals, and machinery have made it an economic superpower. Education is free and compulsory to the age of fifteen, and Japan has an extraordinarily high literacy rate of 99 percent.

According to legend, Japan was founded by Emperor Jimmu in 660 B.C. and has had a line of emperors that continues into the present. The current emperor, Akihito, succeeded to the throne in 1989 following his father, Hirohito, who was emperor from 1926. Actual political control of the country from the twelfth to the late nineteenth century was held by feudal lords, called Shoguns. *In 1854, Commodore Matthew Perry reopened contact with Japan after the Shoguns had expelled all foreigners from the country in the seventeenth century. Subsequently, the Shoguns lost power to the emperor, and with the defeat of China in 1895 and victory over Russia in the Russo–Japanese War ending in 1905, Japan became a global power.*

The Honorable Once-Over

> The fact that two families generally lived in widely separated areas and had no knowledge of each other prompted the use of a go-between initiating the marriage. Needless to say, the marriage partners themselves had little or no previous acquaintance with one another until the day of the wedding.
>
> —*Harumi Befu*, Japan—An Anthropological Introduction *(1971)*

1   The son and heir of the prosperous owner of a large local supermarket, Hiroshi Murakami formally asked his prospective father-in-law for his daughter's hand only days ago. Although he may have lost some sleep over the prospect, there was little chance that Yamashita would refuse him. Such a proposal is nothing more than a ritual involving participants from families who have already agreed on the outcome. Besides, Mayumi had undergone *omiai* (honorable seeing-meetings) or arranged-marriage introductions no less than twenty-three times, so that Shigeru—who likes Hiroshi anyway—was more than relieved at her choice.

2   Obāsan's one and only *omiai* had been for the benefit of her parents and that was that. With her mother and grandmother, it had merely been a pact sealed between families; until fairly recently, that used to set the more educated families apart from the peasants and the poor, who rarely bothered with formal marriage at all. According to ancient custom, too, a family with no sons can "adopt" their daughter's husband. Assuming the role of first son and their family name, he becomes a *yooshi*—a substitute heir assuring the transmission of the patriarchal line. In effect, the formula has also frequently formed a basis for male *marriages de convenance*, since a husband of lower status can thus take a step up the social ladder or enter a lucrative business partnership.

3   *Omiai* still determines roughly half of all marriages today, although the outcome is generally up to the couple concerned. Rather than choosiness, Mayumi's spurning of scores of bachelors might have had more to do with a former sweetheart. That the Yamashitas and his parents did not see eye to eye eventually prompted her to end the affair, which had been permissible as long as all traces of sexuality were concealed and it showed no signs of becoming serious. Shigeru always prides himself on his open mind and progressive spirit. Mayumi, after all, has been an office employee since she left school. She earns her own income, drives her own car and after office hours her time has largely been her own. There was one point, however, about which both her parents had been quite adamant: Mayumi was to be home by ten. A young lady of twenty-five has no business being out too late after dark—the dire consequences of which are stressed in a great many frightening posters hanging outside the country's plentiful police boxes.

That the proliferation of love hotels might allow Mayumi to do what she cannot do at night during the day is neither here nor there to her parents. What really matters is to keep up appearances. Like everyone else in most other contexts too, provided she upholds her own and the family's *tatemae* (front) and keeps her *honne* (true situation) strictly to herself, Mayumi can reasonably do as she pleases. But when it comes to Father, he may well remain remote and aloof as a patriarchical figurehead but, when he puts in a word, reverence for filial piety commands obedience. 4

The defiance underlying the passionate and unconventionally feminist verses of the poet Akiko Yosano (1878–1942) was perhaps instigated by her own past. Infuriated that his firstborn was not a son, her father dumped her with an aunt, until her brilliance prompted him to take her back home. While she was made to manage the family shop when her mother died, at twenty she was expressly forbidden to walk abroad during the day and locked in her bedroom at night. Yosano's leaving home to marry a noted poet marked the beginning of a career; notwithstanding ostensible servitude to a husband, many women see greater freedom in marriage than in protracted spinsterhood. 5

Even when they have passed *tekireiki*—marriageable age—many single women live at home and their parents' words are law. It is not unusual to see a spinster in her thirties hastening home to honor a curfew before the end of a dinner with friends. I recall a 25-year-old office employee living alone who, faced with opposition over a fiancé, found that a noted Tokyo bank had complied with her father's demand to block her account. A painter of the same age was ordered back to the country by her parents in a bid to end her liaison with a noted avant-garde artist. Since they wanted an adoptive *yooshi* to help out on the farm, in 1988 this university graduate did as she was bidden as dutifully as a Sicilian peasant daughter of thirty years ago. 6

When Mayumi was still unmarried at the advanced age of twenty-five, however, the family began to share her mounting anxieties. The successive meetings came to nothing, the round of eligible bachelors began to deplete itself; Mayumi lived in such a state of panic that the strain showed on her face, and she soon feared that the *omiai* photographs sent round to prospects were too flattering. *Omiai* portraiture is one of the mainstays of the photographer's studios found in all but the smallest villages. It keeps them especially busy on 15 January during *Seijin no hi* or Adults Day, a national holiday observed by all young people who have turned twenty during the preceding year. Often displayed in their shop windows, the portraits find the young ladies in traditional attire and the gentlemen in business suits, seated in a chair in the Louis XV style or posed rigidly against a cloudy sylvan backdrop. Nineteenth-century photography—albeit in color—is charmingly alive and well in Japan. 7

8   Relatives or trusted parental friends, who are generally female and can expect a cash contribution for their services, act as *nakodo* (go-between) and present subsequent prints of snapshot size to the prospective family. Informal snapshots are often offered too and, if the girl concerned should have hobbies such as ballet or jazz dancing, skating or aerobics, pictures in accordingly skimpy attire and showing her to her best advantage might work further in her favor. Beach photographs, however, particularly in this age of shrinking swimwear, are out.

9   If expressing interest, the parties will be brought together during an excruciating meeting process, which finds the two families lunching together in a restaurant in a climate of strained conviviality. Both in immaculate tailored suits, the young man and woman in question stare unwaveringly at the tablecloth, hardly daring to exchange a glance— let alone a word. The girl eats practically nothing. The parents talk over their heads. The boy's father reels off his son's academic achievements and his prospects; the girl's father will extol her virtuous nature, schooling, hobbies, housekeeping abilities and fondness for children. At some point, the two will be expected to say something, generally a tremulous and extremely modest version of the already very reticent paternal summary.

10   During the following week, if he doesn't like her, the boy will back out with a range of polite excuses. If he does, he will wipe his sweating palms on the back of his trousers, find his voice and at last grab the telephone to ask her out on a date. If shyness is common among young men in similar circumstances everywhere, its prevalence in Japan is betrayed by the fact that *omiai*, a practice widespread among the rural and the diffident, would otherwise have died out long ago. If mutually impressed, the couple will go out on what might well be a rather painful first date. It may be on a Saturday evening but, where the notion of night holds improper connotations, it might more properly occur on a Sunday afternoon. The scope of activities is pretty much universal, with movies and perhaps amusement parks high on the list, but the culminating meal or cup of coffee is discernible as an *omiai* date at a glance. Facing each other across the table, they are only nominally more comfortable than with their parents the previous week. Their eyes remain glued to their banana sundaes to avoid contact; they are only animated by the sheer relief of a waiter arriving to break the spell. After about a quarter of an hour of awkward silence, one often sees the boy look up with a sudden flash of inspiration, which culminates in his rather overloudly blurting out something such as "Do you like tennis?"

11   If the girl stares with blank embarrassment and gently shakes her head, their future as a couple may well be uncertain. If she happens to like tennis and they warm to each other, they will go from date to date, from restaurant to disco and from hotel to the Shinto altar.

12   The pious might opt for the more austere and less popular Buddhist ceremony and, today, the Christian wedding sometimes offers an

exotic and romantic alternative to non-Christians. The staggering proliferation of posters throughout Japan's trains and subways presents a
wide range of alternative weddings, as do TV commercials and newspaper and magazine advertisements. Some might offer bizarre fantasies such as parading the couple around the wedding hall in a white
and gold Venetian gondola on wheels amidst clouds of dry ice and
whisking them off to their honeymoon aboard a helicopter. There are
underwater weddings for diving enthusiasts and even schemes to have
Christian weddings staged in small, mercenary-minded churches in
Europe. The underlying message is clear: Thou Shalt Get Married. Being considered as "un-adult" at the very least, detractors are viewed
with the gravest suspicion. An eccentric couple of my acquaintance,
living in separate cities but regularly meeting at weekends and spending holidays together, felt that their life was fine just as it was. Both being thirty, however, and pressured by their families, they simply staged
a grand wedding and carried on exactly as before.

With the pull to get married as strong as it is, marriage agencies are   13
a lucrative business. A cheaper alternative for lonely hearts is even to
be found in local government offices, in which matchmaking is conducted by civil servants entering the names and particulars of interested parties in ledgers for a nominal fee. Founded in 1967, the Beauty
Life Association for one had some 6,000 hopefuls on its books by the
mid-seventies, when there were nearly 300 other private agencies catering to all ages and persuasions in Tokyo alone, not a few of which
specialize in companions for the widowed and divorced. One might be
forgiven for assuming that those who drop out of the *omiai* routine in
favor of agencies might be more romantically than practically inclined,
but this is far from being the general rule. Well-advertised on posters
throughout the Tokyo transport system is an agency aptly called the
Magpie Association, which not untypically targets young ladies with
an eye to the main chance: "You can trust us. We arrange introductions
only to the elite: doctors, lawyers, dentists."

Fully computerized, today's thousands of marriage agencies boast   14
of their ability to match data and preferences to come up with perfect
partnerships. Prim middle-aged ladies in business suits aim video
cameras at prospects, providing them with what is only just a more animated alternative to the *omiai* photograph. Individuals pay a flat fee of
150,000 yen to join, couples confront each other over a table on the premises and if the romance—or progenitive business partnership—doesn't
work out, they shell out 10,000 yen for the next time. One Tokyo agency
calling itself Rodin and unabashedly targeting the elite demands a ten
million yen registration fee, degrees and moneyed backgrounds and
stages matchmaking procedures including chaste separate-room weekends in plush resorts, culminating with a grand wedding in New York.

If some women still throw away their lives by respecting their par-   15
ents' wishes rather than their own feelings, the majority of people

welcome *omiai* as a means of meeting members of the opposite sex—whether the outcome is marriage or not. Nevertheless, a grimly humorous phrase for marriage, especially among women, is *jinsei no hakaba*—the cemetery of life. The alternative to an *omiai* wedding procedure is *renai kekkon*—a love marriage. If the new trend still tends to be more of an urban fantasy concocted by the media than a reality, the fact is that girls and boys are nevertheless going out more together and more freely; the *renai* pattern is becoming more common.

16   When Mayumi Yamashita started to pine away reading wedding-wear and honeymoon magazines among the serried ranks of fluffy animals festooning her room, her parents found it difficult to get her out of the house at all. On the rare occasions when she did go out, other than to go to work, she not infrequently drove to Shinto shrines and prayed to the deities most likely to augur a good matrimonial future. Finally, Shigeru resorted to a truly desperate measure: he relaxed the 10 P.M. curfew.

17   So for the few months before Mayumi and Hiroshi were introduced, she went to discos in Nagoya on Saturday nights. She sometimes even came home at two or three in the morning, and, in the meantime, she saw a whole lot of boys. But since wherever she went she was invariably with the same three girlfriends, the operative word here is "saw." The four girls would dance together on the dance floor and giggle as they tippled discreetly in the decotech interiors of fashionable café-bars, taking turns in being the teetotal and driving fourth. In one disco, a couple of boys sauntered up to ask them to dance, which found them raising their hands in front of their faces and giggling all the more as they shook their heads. Crestfallen and sheepishly grinning, the boys soon went back to join their comrades at another table.

18   Mayumi's aunt Etsuko had acted as the *nakodo* or go-between in the *omiai* process; Hiroshi's aunt was one of her colleagues in the administrative office of a neighboring town hall. Before Hiroshi, there had been the son of that Nagoya hotelier whom Mayumi had thought too fat, the young chartered accountant who had talked only of cars and golf in a whiny voice and the boy from the electronics store who suffered from acne. There had been that Yamaguchi boy, too, the one who owned three beauty salons and drove a Porsche. The Yamashitas didn't like him; he had a hairstyle like a gangster and Mayumi's mother pointed out that the signs outside his salons were *purple.* The family hardly needed the sort of fellow who puts up purple signs.

19   In one way or another, everyone agreed. To use purple was presumptuous—for it had once been the color of the mighty Tokugawa shogunate; mauve is precious for having been the dominant color of the effete Heian age. Worse still, as a marriage between red and blue, the color is ambiguous, risqué and thus so very *mizu shobai.*

Tying the Knot

> Statistics weren't available on those who decided to remarry. Could there really be people out there who would be willing to go through it all again? Irish wakes are much more fun.
>
> —*Gail Nakada,* The Tokyo Journal *(June 1984)*

A legacy of rich merchant ostentatiousness from the late Edo pe-   20
riod, weddings are elaborate and expensive. From the exchange of relatively inexpensive symbolic tokens of good luck, the bride's parents
have become increasingly saddled with items such as ruinously expensive suites of furniture and a supply of kimonos considered proper
(though seldom worn) for the married woman's wardrobe. Wedding
expenses thus cover far more than just the ceremony, the cost of which
is shared with the groom's parents. In the Nagoya area, ever a bastion
of conservatism, the parents of one couple of my acquaintance indulged in a curious and ruinous game of one-upmanship in which the
bride's parents, although far less well-off than the groom's, felt obliged
to go all-out to contribute as much as they could to the most ostenta-
tious wedding either could afford. That all this is a venerable custom is
widely believed, although even a cursory glance at history would
prove the notion to be fallacious; the high cost of weddings is upheld
by peer pressure buttressed by the sacrosanct commerce sector, in the
form of companies specializing only in weddings, furniture stores,
clothiers, and the hotel and catering trade.

As "tradition" dictates, Mayumi's and Hiroshi's wedding will be a   21
grand affair. The Yamashitas are comfortably off, but far from wealthy;
it will take ten million yen out of their savings, even if Hiroshi's parents
make substantial contributions. That's life. Besides, all relatives and
wedding guests will place a white envelope on a silver tray at the entrance to the wedding hall. Along with their wishes of goodwill, it will
contain a minimum of 10,000 yen in cash for a more casual guest, and
substantially more for members of the family. In many cases the roster
of guests includes business associates; the cash contributions from
those wishing to curry favor with the groom or his father will be commensurate with their involvement or expectations. As with wedding
presents, the exact value of each contribution will be carefully toted up
afterwards, not through stinginess, but to gauge the effusiveness of
subsequent thanks, the degree of favors owed in return and the value
of presents marking similar occasions later on.

Arriving in a black Nissan limousine of the genus "Cedric" hired   22
for the day, Mayumi will be presented to the groom at a large local
Shinto shrine. She will be wearing majestic bridal finery, which is so as-
tronomically expensive today that all but the wealthiest brides hire it.
Red and white or plain white and for rent at about 100,000 yen, a wedding kimono is intricately embroidered with floral and bird motifs

enhanced with gold and silver thread. On her head, the bride wears a traditional wig made of real human hair spiked with decorative hairpins and combs. A large starched crown in a plain white fabric completes a picture that will have taken a professional dresser almost an hour to prepare. Although she will undoubtedly be lovely, the new wife, with her whitened face and tiny, beestung red lips, will look totally unlike Mayumi Yamashita and very like a standard Japanese bride. Decked out in a black formal kimono and wide *hakama* striped trousers, the groom will meanwhile be processed in only a few minutes.

23　　　　Then there is the Shinto ceremony. As the priest officiates, a *miko* shrine maiden will guide the couple through the proceedings; there is no rehearsal. As a robed *gagaku* ensemble plays instruments imported from China some twelve hundred years ago, the bride and groom ritually exchange cups of sake three times. The groom then reads a document aloud, the gist of which is that he expects his wife to honor and obey. He will complete this by announcing his full name, while his wife announces her forename only, for she has now been adopted by her husband's family.

24　　　　After the ceremony, a photographer freezes the stiffly posing newlyweds in front of their families and principal guests on film for eternity, and then there will be a reception held in one of the capacious wedding halls of a large hotel. Guests will file in over a plush red and yellow carpet in the rococo style beneath a ceiling dripping with shimmering crystal chandeliers. Before entering, Mayumi will have changed into her second kimono (again unlikely to be her own) and enter the room with the groom to the strains of Mendelssohn's Wedding March piped out at deafening volume. Carefully placed around the banqueting hall according to their station, guests sit before round tables impeccably set with flower pieces and a dazzling array of beautifully presented cold delicacies. The bride and groom preside almost invisibly at one end behind a jungle of flowers. Staring rigidly ahead, they might just exchange a few words together out of the corners of their mouths. In the process of becoming bride and groom they relinquish their identities.

25　　　　Guests and family members are specially allotted functional roles essential to the event: one or two masters or mistresses of ceremony and a best man, and many will take turns in playing musical instruments and/or singing songs. Nearly all will rise in turn to deliver lengthy speeches, some extolling the background of the bride and others the groom's. We know what schools they went to, what their work and hobbies are and the names of their best friends who, being present, will soon be delivering speeches of their own. Nothing said will come as any kind of surprise, for had everyone not known all there was to know about the newlyweds, they could hardly be assembled here. One also commonly hears someone reading out a farewell letter from the bride to her parents, thanking them poignantly and profusely for her happy childhood years. Some wedding concerns enhance this with a syrupy musical backing and even a retrospect slide-show; either way, there is hardly a dry eye in the hall.

Many wedding halls offer all-inclusive package deals. A newly built hotel in Okazaki, Aichi prefecture, for instance, typically owes its vastness less to its room capacity than to the fact that it caters over-whelmingly for weddings. The capacious third and fourth floors are devoted to the entire process, which is conducted with conveyor-belt efficiency. The betrothed are encouraged to make plans months before-hand. Some shops on the third floor deploy selections of appropriate gifts, others offering wedding attire for hire or purchase; another handles all the announcements, invitations and banquet place cards and the honeymoon can be organized in an adjacent travel agency. On the day, the bride can be processed in an all-inclusive beauty parlor providing everything from a sauna, through facials and make-up to dressing; a barbershop offers similar facilities for the groom. On the fourth floor are dressing rooms for each, on either side of an antecham-ber in which the guests of both families sit facing each other before the ceremony, which is held in a specially consecrated Shinto shrine a few doors down the corridor. Then everyone troops into the elevators to go down to the capacious banquet halls. Coming as part of the package is a professional wedding supervisor, who steers the couple firmly through their duties like a strict nanny. As does the shrine maiden or priestess during the Shinto ceremony, she will instruct them on how and when to move or speak. Under her guidance, they will ritually hammer open a keg of sake, which is ladled out to guests. 26

Then the bride sometimes dons a third wedding dress. These days it would generally be lacy, expensive and of Western design. While she is away changing, the speeches drone on as the groom's male friends and relatives might treat him to a quick toast; to avoid offending any-one, he will refuse none of the proffered glasses. Although he might find himself downing quite a formidable amount of sake, beer and whisky, this will be one of the very rare occasions when he will be ex-pected to keep his composure when tipsy. 27

During the course of the reception, the bride will have no time to eat; but the sight of one eating would be untoward anyway. A demure doll, she might poke daintily at the delicacies before her with her chop-sticks, perhaps daring to nibble at a shrimp. She will anyway soon be grabbed by the wedding supervisor and posed alongside the groom to allow guests to take photographs. These days there will be much amusement when he is even entreated to kiss the bride. The entire event is formalized and rigorously timed to last some three hours, not one second of which will be left to spontaneity or allow anyone time to themselves. Where timing could have left a gap, it will be filled with *Candoru Sabisu* (Candle Service), a ritual which finds the room plunged 28 in darkness and the newlyweds passing from table to table, lighting candles with a gas taper and bowing low to each guest to express their thanks. These days, urban couples might throw a more informal party for their friends later on, but the practice is rarer in the country.

29   The couple will finally change into street clothes which, befitting the occasion, should in the bride's case be of a recognizable and expensive designer brand. Guests start wending their way home bearing huge white carrier bags and silk *furoshiki* bundles full of presents offered by the bride's family. These presents are often fantastically expensive; at the recent wedding of a renowned kabuki actor, for instance, some 2,000 guests were each presented with a pair of small gilt silver chalices, each set with a ruby and a diamond in the bottom.

30   Glad that the exalting if agonizing ceremony is over, the exhausted couple will finally sink into the back of the limousine which carries them symbolically off to their conjugal life. Next, they will board a train for the nearest airport and on to their honeymoon, which may well take the form of a five-day package tour shuttling dozens of bewildered newlyweds to overcrowded tourist hotels in Hawaii, Guam and—recently capping the list—Australia. In tune with the more intrepid new breed, however, Hiroshi and Mayumi will be going to Europe. She has always wanted to go to Paris, which has the Champs-Élysées, and to London, which has Harrods. Wherever they go, this will be the first and probably the last trip they will make abroad until future progeny, the first of which should ideally be born within the first year of their marriage, grows up.

31   That the bride's parents wave tearfully at the departing car is virtually a universal phenomenon. A cherished bird has flown from the nest, leaving the progenitors facing their declining years. In Japan, however, the wedding was once far more poignant—a girl given into marriage became the property of her husband and his family. A custom observed from early times allowed a pregnant wife to go back to her parents' home to give birth, but among the spartan samurai she often never saw her family again.

✦ *Evaluating the Text*

1. What cultural values and social pressures underlie the practice of arranged marriages in modern-day Japan? How do these practices create and reflect established expectations of how men and women should act?

2. Which case histories did you find the most interesting and effective in illustrating the role arranged marriages play in Japan?

3. What features define Japanese weddings in terms of the expenses incurred, gifts received, pageantry, trousseaus, religious ceremonies, wedding outfits, and so on?

4. What features of traditional Japanese culture are still part of the modern wedding ritual? What does the persistence of these features imply about Japanese society?

✦ Exploring Different Perspectives

1. How do the expectations and customs that precede an arranged marriage in Japan resemble or differ from those described by Serena Nanda in "Arranging a Marriage in India"?

2. How do differences in the cultural values of Japan and Lebanon influence the meaning of marriage in these two countries? (See Shirley Saad's "Amina.")

✦ Extending Viewpoints Through Writing

1. How do Japanese cultural practices resemble or differ from those with which you are familiar that govern under what circumstances the prospective bride and groom meet each other?

2. If you were ever on a blind date, describe your experiences.

3. Write a personal ad describing yourself as you would wish to appear to meet someone suitable.

4. Describe a wedding you attended or in which you participated. Describe the event and mention details that made it memorable.

Serena Nanda

Arranging a Marriage in India

◆

Serena Nanda is professor of anthropology at John Jay College of Criminal Justice, City University of New York. Her fields of interest are visual anthropology, gender, and culture and law. She has carried out field studies in India, in tribal development, and on the social lives of women in urban India. Her published works include Cultural Anthropology, *third edition (1987),* American Cultural Pluralism and Law *(1990), and* Neither Man nor Woman: The Hijras of India *(1990), which won the Ruth Benedict Prize. In the following selection, which first appeared in* The Naked Anthropologist: Tales from Around the World, *edited by Philip R. DeVita (1992), Nanda looks at the cultural forces that have resulted in the practice of arranged marriages in Indian society.*

    India is a republic in southern Asia whose 800 million people make it the second most populous country in the world, after China. Although Indian civilization dates back more than 5,000 years, European traders discovered it only in the sixteenth century. By 1757, Britain had gained control of India from the maharajas (ruling princes). In 1919, Mohandas "Mahatma" (great souled) Gandhi, a lawyer who had worked for Indians in South Africa, launched the movement for India's independence from Britain using techniques of passive resistance and civil disobedience. His dream was realized in 1947 with the dissolution of the British Raj. India was then partitioned into India and Pakistan with hopes of ending the civil war between Hindu and Muslim communities. Gandhi was assassinated the following year. In 1984, Prime Minister Indira Gandhi (no relation to Mohandas) was assassinated by Sikh members of her own bodyguard. She was succeeded by her son, Rajiv Gandhi, who resigned in 1989, and was assassinated himself less than two years later, during a bid for re-election. Congress party leader P. V. Narasimha Rao became prime minister in 1991. The destruction by Hindus of a Muslim mosque in 1992 led to riots and calls for government investigations.

Sister and doctor brother-in-law invite correspondence from North Indian professionals only, for a beautiful, talented, sophisticated, intelligent sister, 5'3", slim, M.A. in textile design, father a senior civil officer. Would prefer immigrant doctors, between 26–29 years. Reply with full details and returnable photo.

A well-settled uncle invites matrimonial correspondence from slim, fair, educated South Indian girl, for his nephew, 25 years, smart, M.B.A., green card holder, 5'6". Full particulars with returnable photo appreciated.

—Matrimonial Advertisements, *India Abroad*

In India, almost all marriages are arranged. Even among the edu- 1
cated middle classes in modern, urban India, marriage is as much a concern of the families as it is of the individuals. So customary is the practice of arranged marriage that there is a special name for a marriage which is not arranged: It is called a "love match."

On my first field trip to India, I met many young men and women 2
whose parents were in the process of "getting them married." In many cases, the bride and groom would not meet each other before the marriage. At most they might meet for a brief conversation, and this meeting would take place only after their parents had decided that the match was suitable. Parents do not compel their children to marry a person who either marriage partner finds objectionable. But only after one match is refused will another be sought.

As a young American woman in India for the first time, I found 3
this custom of arranged marriage oppressive. How could any intelligent young person agree to such a marriage without great reluctance? It was contrary to everything I believed about the importance of romantic love as the only basis of a happy marriage. It also clashed with my strongly held notions that the choice of such an intimate and permanent relationship could be made only by the individuals involved. Had anyone tried to arrange my marriage, I would have been defiant and rebellious!

At the first opportunity, I began, with more curiosity than tact, to 4
question the young people I met on how they felt about this practice. Sita, one of my young informants, was a college graduate with a degree in political science. She had been waiting for over a year while her parents were arranging a match for her. I found it difficult to accept the docile manner in which this well-educated young woman awaited the outcome of a process that would result in her spending the rest of her life with a man she hardly knew, a virtual stranger, picked out by her parents.

"How can you go along with this?" I asked her, in frustration and 5
distress. "Don't you care who you marry?"

"Of course I care," she answered. "This is why I must let my par- 6
ents choose a boy for me. My marriage is too important to be arranged by such an inexperienced person as myself. In such matters, it is better to have my parents' guidance."

I had learned that young men and women in India do not date and 7
have very little social life involving members of the opposite sex.

Although I could not disagree with Sita's reasoning, I continued to pursue the subject.

8   "But how can you marry the first man you have ever met? Not only have you missed the fun of meeting a lot of different people, but you have not given yourself the chance to know who is the right man for you."

9   "Meeting with a lot of different people doesn't sound like any fun at all," Sita answered. "One hears that in America the girls are spending more time worrying about whether they will meet a man and get married. Here we have the chance to enjoy our life and let our parents do this work and worrying for us."

10   She had me there. The high anxiety of the competition to "be popular" with the opposite sex certainly was the most prominent feature of life as an American teenager in the late fifties. The endless worrying about the rules that governed our behavior and about our popularity ratings sapped both our self-esteem and our enjoyment of adolescence. I reflected that absence of this competition in India most certainly may have contributed to the self-confidence and natural charm of so many of the young women I met.

11   And yet, the idea of marrying a perfect stranger, whom one did not know and did not "love," so offended my American ideas of individualism and romanticism, that I persisted with my objections.

12   "I still can't imagine it," I said. "How can you agree to marry a man you hardly know?"

13   "But of course he will be known. My parents would never arrange a marriage for me without knowing all about the boy's family background. Naturally we will not rely only on what the family tells us. We will check the particulars out ourselves. No one will want their daughter to marry into a family that is not good. All these things we will know beforehand."

14   Impatiently, I responded, "Sita, I don't mean know the family, I mean, know the man. How can you marry someone you don't know personally and don't love? How can you think of spending your life with someone you may not even like?"

15   "If he is a good man, why should I not like him?" she said. "With you people, you know the boy so well before you marry, where will be the fun to get married? There will be no mystery and no romance. Here we have the whole of our married life to get to know and love our husband. This way is better, is it not?"

16   Her response made further sense, and I began to have second thoughts on the matter. Indeed, during months of meeting many intelligent young Indian people, both male and female, who had the same ideas as Sita, I saw arranged marriages in a different light. I also saw the importance of the family in Indian life and realized that a couple

who took their marriage into their own hands was taking a big risk, particularly if their families were irreconcilably opposed to the match. In a country where every important resource in life—a job, a house, a social circle—is gained through family connections, it seemed foolhardy to cut oneself off from a supportive social network and depend solely on one person for happiness and success.

Six years later I returned to India to again do fieldwork, this time among the middle class in Bombay, a modern, sophisticated city. From the experience of my earlier visit, I decided to include a study of arranged marriages in my project. By this time I had met many Indian couples whose marriages had been arranged and who seemed very happy. Particularly in contrast to the fate of many of my married friends in the United States who were already in the process of divorce, the positive aspects of arranged marriages appeared to me to outweigh the negatives. In fact, I thought I might even participate in arranging a marriage myself. I had been fairly successful in the United States in "fixing up" many of my friends, and I was confident that my matchmaking skills could be easily applied to this new situation, once I learned the basic rules. "After all," I thought, "how complicated can it be? People want pretty much the same things in a marriage whether it is in India or America."   17

An opportunity presented itself almost immediately. A friend from my previous Indian trip was in the process of arranging for the marriage of her eldest son. In India there is a perceived shortage of "good boys," and since my friend's family was eminently respectable and the boy himself personable, well educated, and nice looking, I was sure that by the end of my year's fieldwork, we would have found a match.   18

The basic rule seems to be that a family's reputation is most important. It is understood that matches would be arranged only within the same caste and general social class, although some crossing of subcastes is permissible if the class positions of the bride's and groom's families are similar. Although dowry is now prohibited by law in India, extensive gift exchanges took place with every marriage. Even when the boy's family do not "make demands," every girl's family nevertheless feels the obligation to give the traditional gifts, to the girl, to the boy, and to the boy's family. Particularly when the couple would be living in the joint family—that is, with the boy's parents and his married brothers and their families, as well as with unmarried siblings—which is still very common even among the urban, upper-middle class in India, the girl's parents are anxious to establish smooth relations between their family and that of the boy. Offering the proper gifts, even when not called "dowry," is often an important factor in influencing the relationship between the bride's and groom's families and perhaps, also, the treatment of the bride in her new home.   19

20   In a society where divorce is still a scandal and where, in fact, the divorce rate is exceedingly low, an arranged marriage is the beginning of a lifetime relationship not just between the bride and groom but between their families as well. Thus, while a girl's looks are important, her character is even more so, for she is being judged as a prospective daughter-in-law as much as a prospective bride. Where she would be living in a joint family, as was the case with my friend, the girl's ability to get along harmoniously in a family is perhaps the single most important quality in assessing her suitability.

21   My friend is a highly esteemed wife, mother, and daughter-in-law. She is religious, soft-spoken, modest, and deferential. She rarely gossips and never quarrels, two qualities highly desirable in a woman. A family that has the reputation for gossip and conflict among its womenfolk will not find it easy to get good wives for their sons. Parents will not want to send their daughter to a house in which there is conflict.

22   My friend's family were originally from North India. They had lived in Bombay, where her husband owned a business, for forty years. The family had delayed in seeking a match for their eldest son because he had been an Air Force pilot for several years, stationed in such remote places that it had seemed fruitless to try to find a girl who would be willing to accompany him. In their social class, a military career, despite its economic security, has little prestige and is considered a drawback in finding a suitable bride. Many families would not allow their daughters to marry a man in an occupation so potentially dangerous and which requires so much moving around.

23   The son had recently left the military and joined his father's business. Since he was a college graduate, modern, and well traveled, from such a good family, and, I thought, quite handsome, it seemed to me that he, or rather his family, was in a position to pick and choose. I said as much to my friend.

24   While she agreed that there were many advantages on their side, she also said, "We must keep in mind that my son is both short and dark; these are drawbacks in finding the right match." While the boy's height had not escaped my notice, "dark" seemed to me inaccurate; I would have called him "wheat" colored perhaps, and in any case, I did not realize that color would be a consideration. I discovered, however, that while a boy's skin color is a less important consideration than a girl's, it is still a factor.

25   An important source of contacts in trying to arrange her son's marriage was my friend's social club in Bombay. Many of the women had daughters of the right age, and some had already expressed an interest in my friend's son. I was most enthusiastic about the possibilities of one particular family who had five daughters, all of whom were pretty, demure, and well educated. Their mother had told my friend, "You can have your pick for your son, whichever one of my daughters appeals to you most."

I saw a match in sight. "Surely," I said to my friend, "we will find one there. Let's go visit and make our choice." But my friend held back; she did not seem to share my enthusiasm, for reasons I could not then fathom. 26

When I kept pressing for an explanation of her reluctance, she admitted, "See, Serena, here is the problem. The family has so many daughters, how will they be able to provide nicely for any of them? We are not making any demands, but still, with so many daughters to marry off, one wonders whether she will even be able to make a proper wedding. Since this is our eldest son, it's best if we marry him to a girl who is the only daughter, then the wedding will truly be a gala affair." I argued that surely the quality of the girls themselves made up for any deficiency in the elaborateness of the wedding. My friend admitted this point but still seemed reluctant to proceed. 27

"Is there something else," I asked her, "some factor I have missed?" "Well," she finally said, "there is one other thing. They have one daughter already married and living in Bombay. The mother is always complaining to me that the girl's in-laws don't let her visit her own family often enough. So it makes me wonder, will she be that kind of mother who always wants her daughter at her own home? This will prevent the girl from adjusting to our house. It is not a good thing." And so, this family of five daughters was dropped as a possibility. 28

Somewhat disappointed, I nevertheless respected my friend's reasoning and geared up for the next prospect. This was also the daughter of a woman in my friend's social club. There was clear interest in this family and I could see why. The family's reputation was excellent; in fact, they came from a subcaste slightly higher than my friend's own. The girl, who was an only daughter, was pretty and well educated and had a brother studying in the United States. Yet, after expressing an interest to me in this family, all talk of them suddenly died down and the search began elsewhere. 29

"What happened to that girl as a prospect?" I asked one day. "You never mention her any more. She is so pretty and so educated, what did you find wrong?" 30

"She is too educated. We've decided against it. My husband's father saw the girl on the bus the other day and thought her forward. A girl who 'roams about' the city by herself is not the girl for our family." My disappointment this time was even greater, as I thought the son would have liked the girl very much. But then I thought, my friend is right, a girl who is going to live in a joint family cannot be too independent or she will make life miserable for everyone. I also learned that if the family of the girl has even a slightly higher social status than the family of the boy, the bride may think herself too good for them, and this too will cause problems. Later my friend admitted to me that this had been an important factor in her decision not to pursue the match. 31

32   The next candidate was the daughter of a client of my friend's husband. When the client learned that the family was looking for a match for their son, he said, "Look no further, we have a daughter." This man then invited my friends to dinner to see the girl. He had already seen their son at the office and decided that "he liked the boy." We all went together for tea, rather than dinner—it was less of a commitment—and while we were there, the girl's mother showed us around the house. The girl was studying for her exams and was briefly introduced to us.

33   After we left, I was anxious to hear my friend's opinion. While her husband liked the family very much and was impressed with his client's business accomplishments and reputation, the wife didn't like the girl's looks. "She is short, no doubt, which is an important plus point, but she is also fat and wears glasses." My friend obviously thought she could do better for her son and asked her husband to make his excuses to his client by saying that they had decided to postpone the boy's marriage indefinitely.

34   By this time almost six months had passed and I was becoming impatient. What I had thought would be an easy matter to arrange was turning out to be quite complicated. I began to believe that between my friend's desire for a girl who was modest enough to fit into her joint family, yet attractive and educated enough to be an acceptable partner for her son, she would not find anyone suitable. My friend laughed at my impatience: "Don't be so much in a hurry," she said. "You Americans want everything done so quickly. You get married quickly and then just as quickly get divorced. Here we take marriage more seriously. We must take all the factors into account. It is not enough for us to learn by our mistakes. This is too serious a business. If a mistake is made we have not only ruined the life of our son or daughter, but we have spoiled the reputation of our family as well. And that will make it much harder for their brothers and sisters to get married. So we must be very careful."

35   What she said was true and I promised myself to be more patient, though it was not easy. I had really hoped and expected that the match would be made before my year in India was up. But it was not to be. When I left India my friend seemed no further along in finding a suitable match for her son than when I had arrived.

36   Two years later, I returned to India and still my friend had not found a girl for her son. By this time, he was close to thirty, and I think she was a little worried. Since she knew I had friends all over India, and I was going to be there for a year, she asked me to "help her in this work" and keep an eye out for someone suitable. I was flattered that my judgment was respected, but knowing now how complicated the process was, I had lost my earlier confidence as a matchmaker. Nevertheless, I promised that I would try.

It was almost at the end of my year's stay in India that I met a family with a marriageable daughter whom I felt might be a good possibility for my friend's son. The girl's father was related to a good friend of mine and by coincidence came from the same village as my friend's husband. This new family had a successful business in a medium-sized city in central India and were from the same subcaste as my friend. The daughter was pretty and chic; in fact, she had studied fashion design in college. Her parents would not allow her to go off by herself to any of the major cities in India where she could make a career, but they had compromised with her wish to work by allowing her to run a small dressmaking boutique from their home. In spite of her desire to have a career, the daughter was both modest and home-loving and had had a traditional, sheltered upbringing. She had only one other sister, already married, and a brother who was in his father's business. 37

I mentioned the possibility of a match with my friend's son. The girl's parents were most interested. Although their daughter was not eager to marry just yet, the idea of living in Bombay—a sophisticated, extremely fashion-conscious city where she could continue her education in clothing design—was a great inducement. I gave the girl's father my friend's address and suggested that when they went to Bombay on some business or whatever, they look up the boy's family. 38

Returning to Bombay on my way to New York, I told my friend of this newly discovered possibility. She seemed to feel there was potential but, in spite of my urging, would not make any moves herself. She rather preferred to wait for the girl's family to call upon them. I hoped something would come of this introduction, though by now I had learned to rein in my optimism. 39

A year later I received a letter from my friend. The family had indeed come to visit Bombay, and their daughter and my friend's daughter, who were near in age, had become very good friends. During that year, the two girls had frequently visited each other. I thought things looked promising. 40

Last week I received an invitation to a wedding: My friend's son and the girl were getting married. Since I had found the match, my presence was particularly requested at the wedding. I was thrilled. Success at last! As I prepared to leave for India, I began thinking, "Now, my friend's younger son, who do I know who has a nice girl for him . . . ?" 41

✦ Evaluating the Text

1. From an Indian perspective, what are the advantages of an arranged marriage?

2. What considerations are taken into account in arranging a marriage in India?

3. What role does Nanda play in helping to find a suitable bride for her friend's son? How would you characterize Nanda's attitude toward arranged marriage and in what way does it change over the course of events?

✦ *Exploring Different Perspectives*

1. What different expectations regarding the role of women emerge from the account by Nanda and Shirley Saad's story "Amina"?

2. Compare the role that families play in arranging marriages in India according to Nanda and in Japan (described by Nicholas Bornoff in "The Marriage Go-Round").

✦ *Extending Viewpoints Through Writing*

1. Would you ever consider allowing your parents to arrange a marriage for you? If so, why would this be more advantageous or disadvantageous than finding someone for yourself?

2. What circumstances led your parents to get married? What considerations, in your opinion, played the most important role?

3. What did this essay add to your understanding of the pressures couples experience when getting married in India? To what extent are these pressures similar to or different from those experienced by couples in the United States?

Shirley Saad

Amina

◆────────────

Shirley Saad was born in Cairo in 1947 to a Lebanese father and a Polish-Rumanian mother. Saad was educated at St. Clare's College by Irish nuns and spoke English, French, and Italian until the 1952 revolution in which Gamal Abdel Nasser gained power, after which the study of Arabic became mandatory in the schools. In 1961 her family moved to Lebanon. Largely self-taught, Saad was influenced by reading the novels of Hanan al-Shaykh and, while she lived in Abu Dhabi, started writing stories about restrictions imposed on women in the Arabic world. "Amina" sympathizes with the plight of a woman who has just given birth to a child and is apprehensive that her husband will take another wife if the child is not a son.

Located on the Mediterranean Sea, Lebanon is a republic in the Middle East bordered to the North and East by Syria and to the South by Israel. The site of the ancient maritime city-state Phoenicia, the region fell to successive Middle Eastern powers. Christianity was introduced under the Roman Empire in the first century and persisted even after the coming of Islam with the Arab conquest in the seventh century. Since independence in 1945, Lebanon has been plagued by civil strife between the Palestine Liberation Organization (PLO), Syrian and Israeli forces, as well as indigenous Christian and Muslim factions. However, under a peace accord reached in 1990, militias representing these different factions withdrew from the capital, Beirut, and the Lebanese Army established control. With the fifteen-year civil war behind them, the Lebanese have begun the process of rebuilding the country's infrastructure.

Amina opened her eyes and for a moment wondered where she was. Then she remembered and a moan escaped her lips. The English nurse hurried over and bent down, "Don't you worry now," she said. "You'll be fine and the baby is all right." 1

Amina asked, not daring to hope, "Is it a boy or a girl?" 2

"A girl," replied the nurse cheerfully. "A beautiful, bouncing, four kilograms girl. *Mabruk*, congratulations." 3

"*Allah yi barek fi omrek*," murmured Amina as she sank back on her pillows. Another girl! 4

What a catastrophe. What would happen to her now? She had brought four girls into the world, four girls in six years of marriage. She felt tears running down her cheeks, and remembered how happy and 5 proud she had been when her mother told her that she was engaged to be married.

6   She had seen Hamid twice, once at her cousin's house when he arrived unexpectedly. The girls all scattered to their quarters to put on their masks and veils. The next time, he came with his father to ask for her hand in marriage. The houseboy serving the coffee told the Indian housegirl who in turn, ran and told her mistress. So, she had gone to peek through the partition between the men's and women's *majlis*. She saw Hamid and his father sipping coffee and being congratulated by all the men in the family. They embraced and rubbed noses, big smiles on everyone's faces.

7   Amina remembered her wedding, the noise and the bustle, her hennaed hands and feet, the whispers among the older women which frightened her and the anticipation. Finally, she found herself alone with this stranger, who had turned out to be very kind and gentle and considerate.

8   Well, there would be no henna and celebration for this girl. God, why couldn't she have a boy? Just one, that's all she wanted, just one little baby boy.

9   She wished the midwife hadn't told her when she had that miscarriage that it had been a boy. The only one in six years, and she had to go and lose it. It was her fault too. She had no business climbing a ladder at five months. She slipped and fell and the doctors kept her in the hospital for a week, then told her she was all right and could go home. But there was no movement, no life, so she went back to the hospital and after two weeks of tests and X-rays and hope and despair, they finally decided the baby was dead.

10   After that, she had two more girls, and now the fourth.

11   Would Hamid divorce her? Would he take a second wife? His older brother had been pressing for two years now, urging him to take a second wife. Hamid loved Amina and his daughters, but he was human. He did have all that money and the social and political position and no boy to leave it to.

12   Her mother came in, then her sisters-in-law. Each one kissed her and said "*Mabruk*," but she could tell they were not really happy. Her mother was especially fearful for her daughter's future and felt that some of the disgrace fell on her and the family too. The sisters-in-law were secretly jubilant, because they had boys. Hamid's social status and half his fortune would revert to their own sons if he never had any boys of his own. Of course, he was still young and he and Amina might try again. But for the moment the in-laws left reassured and falsely commiserated with Amina on her bad luck.

13   "It is God's will," they murmured, smiling under their masks. Their mouths were sad, but Amina could see the twinkle in their eyes. "God's will be done."

Friends started coming into the room. They kissed Amina and said 14
"*Mabruk*," then sat on the floor, cross-legged. Arranging their robes
around them, they sipped coffee from little thimble cups, eating fruits
and sweets.

Her cousin Huda came too. She wore a long, velvet dress, embroi- 15
dered on the sides and bodice, loose and flowing, to conceal her belly.
She was in her sixth month and looked radiantly serene. She sat on the
carpet and sipped her coffee.

Amina thought bitterly, "She already has two daughters and three 16
sons. What does she need another baby for? She's not so young any
more."

As if she had read her thoughts, Huda said, "This is my last baby. It 17
will be the baby for my old age. The others are married or away at
school all day. An empty house is a sad house, You need many sons and
daughters to keep your husband happy. You are still young, Amina.
God has given you four daughters, maybe the next four will be boys.
God's will be done."

"As God wills it, so be it," murmured the other ladies smugly. 18

Hamid came in and the ladies all stood up, saluted him deferen- 19
tially, and hastily went into the next room. The maid served them more
coffee. Hamid looked at his wife, tried to smile and searched for something nice to say. He thought she must be tired, disappointed, ashamed
of having failed him one more time and afraid of being repudiated.

He sat down near the bed and said, "Well, mother of my children, 20
we will just have to try again, won't we?"

Amina burst into tears of sorrow, shame and relief. 21

"Don't cry," he said, distressed. "The important thing is that you 22
and the girls are in good health," smiling. "As long as we are young,
we will try again, eh?"

Amina blushed under her mask and pulled her veil around her 23
face. He patted her hand, got up, and left the room.

The ladies came rushing back in, like a flock of crows, eager for the 24
news, good or bad.

Amina's mother said solicitously, "What did he say, my daughter?" 25

"He said better luck next time, Mother!" 26

The mother let out a sigh of relief. They had another year's re- 27
prieve. The women congratulated Amina and left to spread the news.

Amina sank back on to her pillows and drifted off to sleep. 28

✦ Evaluating the Text

1. What insight do you gain into the kind of societal and personal pressures Amina is under from the reactions of her mother and in-laws?

2. How is the story shaped to build up suspense first as to the sex of the
   child and, second, as to how her husband will react to this news?

3. What does Amina's husband's reaction reveal about him and his feelings for her?

4. How would you characterize the author's attitude toward the events she describes?

✦ Exploring Different Perspectives

1. Compare attitudes toward the birth of girls in Saad's story with those in Rigoberta Menchú's account (see "Birth Ceremonies").

2. To what extent do concepts of marriage differ within the traditional societies of Lebanon and India? (See Serena Nanda's "Arranging a Marriage in India.")

✦ Extending Viewpoints Through Writing

1. How does the conflict between private affection and public obligations reveal the values that govern women's lives in Middle-Eastern society?

2. What recent developments (e.g., ultra-sound clinics in India and genetic screening in the United States) illustrate the pressure on women to produce sons? How has the one-child policy in China and accompanying female infanticide resulted in an imbalance of 70 million more males? What are the social consequences of this policy?

3. Do you consider having children important to your future? Why or why not? What do you think having a family will mean in the future?

Pat Mora

Remembering Lobo

◆

Pat Mora was born in El Paso, Texas, in 1942. She received a bachelor's degree in 1963 from Texas Western College and earned a master's degree from the University of Texas at El Paso in 1967. Her two collections of poems, Chance *(1984) and* Waters *(1986), celebrate the southwest and the desert. Mora's third volume of poetry,* Communion *(1991), explores basic questions of Hispanic identity as she travels to Cuba, New York, and central India. Mora has written books for children, including* A Birthday Present for Tia *(1992) and* Pablo's Tree *(1993). Her commentaries are collected in* Nepantla: Essays from the Land in the Middle *(1993), in which "Remembering Lobo" first appeared. Evoking the image of her aunt, this essay addresses the theme of what it means to be a Chicana in American society and celebrates Mora's cultural identity.*

We called her *Lobo.* The word means "wolf" in Spanish, an odd 1
name for a generous and loving aunt. Like all names it became synonymous with her, and to this day returns me to my childself. Although the name seemed perfectly natural to us and to our friends, it did cause frowns from strangers throughout the years. I particularly remember one hot afternoon when on a crowded streetcar between the border cities of El Paso and Juarez, I momentarily lost sight of her. "Lobo! Lobo!" I cried in panic. Annoyed faces peered at me, disappointed at such disrespect to a white-haired woman.

Actually the fault was hers. She lived with us for years, and when 2
she arrived home from work in the evening, she'd knock on our front door and ask, "*¿Dónde están mis lobitos?*" "Where are my little wolves?"

Gradually she became our *lobo,* a spinster aunt who gathered the 3
four of us around her, tying us to her for life by giving us all she had. Sometimes to tease her we would call her by her real name. "*¿Dónde está Ignacia?*" we would ask. Lobo would laugh and say, "She is a ghost."

To all of us in nuclear families today, the notion of an extended 4
family under one roof seems archaic, complicated. We treasure our private space. I will always marvel at the generosity of my parents, who opened their door to both my grandmother and Lobo. No doubt I am drawn to the elderly because I grew up with two entirely different white-haired women who worried about me, tucked me in at night, made me tomato soup or hot *hierbabuena* (mint tea) when I was ill.

71

5   Lobo grew up in Mexico, the daughter of a circuit judge, my grandfather. She was a wonderful storyteller and over and over told us about the night her father, a widower, brought his grown daughters on a flatbed truck across the Rio Grande at the time of the Mexican Revolution. All their possessions were left in Mexico. Lobo had not been wealthy, but she had probably never expected to have to find a job and learn English.

6   When she lived with us, she worked in the linens section of a local department store. Her area was called "piece goods and bedding." Lobo never sewed, but she would talk about materials she sold, using words I never completely understood, such as *pique* and *broadcloth*. Sometimes I still whisper such words just to remind myself of her. I'll always savor the way she would order "sweet milk" at restaurants. The precision of a speaker new to the language.

7   Lobo saved her money to take us out to dinner and a movie, to take us to Los Angeles in the summer, to buy us shiny black shoes for Christmas. Though she never married and never bore children, Lobo taught me much about one of our greatest challenges as human beings: loving well. I don't think she ever discussed the subject with me, but through the years she lived her love, and I was privileged to watch.

8   She died at ninety-four. She was no sweet, docile Mexican woman dying with perfect resignation. Some of her last words before drifting into semiconsciousness were loud words of annoyance at the incompetence of nurses and doctors.

   "No sirven." "They're worthless," she'd say to me in Spanish.

9   "They don't know what they're doing. My throat is hurting and they're taking X rays. Tell them to take care of my throat first."

10   I was busy striving for my cherished middle-class politeness. "Shh, shh," I'd say. "They're doing the best they can."

11   "Well, it's not good enough," she'd say, sitting up in anger.

12   Lobo was a woman of fierce feelings, of strong opinions. She was a woman who literally whistled while she worked. The best way to cheer her when she'd visit my young children was to ask for her help. Ask her to make a bed, fold laundry, set the table or dry dishes, and the whistling would begin as she moved about her task. Like all of us, she loved being needed. Understandable, then, that she muttered in annoyance when her body began to fail her. She was a woman who found self-definition and joy in visibly showing her family her love for us by bringing us hot *té de canela* (cinnamon tea) in the middle of the night to ease a cough, by bringing us comics and candy whenever she returned home. A life of giving.

13   One of my last memories of her is a visit I made to her on November 2, *El Día de los Muertos,* or All Souls' Day. She was sitting in her rocking chair, smiling wistfully. The source of the smile may seem a bit

bizarre to a U.S. audience. She was fondly remembering past visits to the local cemetery on this religious feast day.

"What a silly old woman I have become," she said. "Here I sit in my rocking chair all day on All Souls' Day, sitting when I should be out there. At the cemetery. Taking good care of *mis muertos,* my dead ones.   14

"What a time I used to have. I'd wake while it was still dark outside. I'd hear the first morning birds, and my fingers would almost itch to begin. By six I'd be having a hot bath, dressing carefully in black, wanting *mis muertos* to be proud of me, proud to have me looking respectable and proud to have their graves taken care of. I'd have my black coffee and plenty of toast. You know the way I like it. Well browned and well buttered. I wanted to be ready to work hard.   15

"The bus ride to the other side of town was a long one, but I'd say a rosary and plan my day. I'd hope that my perfume wasn't too strong and yet would remind others that I was a lady.   16

"The air at the cemetery gates was full of chrysanthemums: that strong, sharp, fall smell. I'd buy tin cans full of the gold and wine flowers. How I liked seeing aunts and uncles who were also there to care for the graves of their loved ones. We'd hug. Happy together.   17

"Then it was time to begin. The smell of chrysanthemums was like a whiff of pure energy. I'd pull the heavy hose and wash the gravestones over and over, listening to the water pelting away the desert sand. I always brought newspaper. I'd kneel on the few patches of grass, and I'd scrub and scrub, shining the gray stones, leaning back on my knees to rest for a bit and then scrubbing again. Finally a relative from nearby would say, '*Ya, ya, Nacha,*' and laugh. Enough. I'd stop, blink my eyes to return from my trance. Slightly dazed, I'd stand slowly, place a can of chrysanthemums before each grave.   18

"Sometimes I would just stand there in the desert sun and listen. I'd hear the quiet crying of people visiting new graves; I'd hear families exchanging gossip while they worked.   19

"One time I heard my aunt scolding her dead husband. She'd sweep his gravestone and say, '*¿Porqué?* Why did you do this, you thoughtless man? Why did you go and leave me like this? You know I don't like to be alone. Why did you stop living?' Such a sight to see my aunt with her proper black hat and her fine dress and her carefully polished shoes muttering away for all to hear.   20

"To stifle my laughter, I had to cover my mouth with my hands."   21

✦ *Evaluating the Text*

1. How does Mora's account of her aunt emphasize attributes that make "Lobo" an apt name? What qualities does Mora's aunt possess that provide a valuable counterbalance to the narrator's own personality?

2. What is the significance of the Mexican custom of visiting the cemetery on All Souls' Day?

3. Why is the shift from the narrator's account to Lobo's own words effective? Why do you think Mora structures her account in this fashion?

✦ *Exploring Different Perspectives*

1. Compare the influence of Gayle Pemberton's grandmother (see "Anti-disestablishmentarianism") with that of Pat Mora's aunt.

2. How do questions of language use and communication play an important role in Pat Mora's account and in John Cheever's story "Reunion"?

✦ *Extending Viewpoints Through Writing*

1. Create a one-page vignette about a relative whom you think of as unusual or striking in some way. Provide descriptive details and examples that will help the reader visualize this person.

2. In what way do you embody the coming together of two diverse ethnic and cultural traditions from your mother's and father's sides of the family? Tell what you know about the past histories of both sides of your family.

Colin Turnbull

The Mbuti Pygmies

◆

Born in 1924 in Harrow, England, Colin Turnbull received a B.A. (1947) and an M.A. (1949) from Magdalen College, Oxford, and his Ph.D. in Social Anthropology from Oxford University in 1964. Turnbull has served as curator of the American Museum of Natural History in New York and has taught at Virginia Commonwealth University, Hunter College, Vassar College, and is currently professor of anthropology at George Washington University. He has written extensively about various peoples in Africa based on years of anthropological field research. His published works include The Mountain People *(1972), an influential study of the* Ik *of northern Uganda,* Tradition and Change in African Life *(1966), and several studies on the pygmies of the Ituri Forest of the Congo with whom he spent four years. His work on the pygmies includes* The Forest People *(1961),* The Mbuti Pygmies: An Ethnographic Survey *(1965),* Wayward Servants: The Two Worlds of the African Pygmies *(1965),* In a Pygmy Camp *(1969), and* The Mbuti Pygmies: Change and Adaptation *(1983), from which the following selection is taken. Turnbull found the pygmies to be a wise people whose society has developed remarkably effective methods for fostering conflict resolution and cooperation.*

The People's Republic of the Congo, in West Central Africa, achieved its independence from France in 1960. Because of its location, the Congo has always played an important role as a center of commerce and transportation connecting inland areas of Africa with the Atlantic Ocean. After a series of coups, a new military regime following socialist policies, led by Colonel Sassou-Nguesso, was installed in 1979. Multiparty democracy was restored in 1992, and Pascal Lissouba was installed as president.

The Educational Process

. . . In the first three years of life every Mbuti alive experiences almost total security. The infant is breast-fed for those three years, and is allowed almost every freedom. Regardless of gender, the infant learns to have absolute trust in both male and female parent. If anything, the father is just another kind of mother, for in the second year the father formally introduces the child to its first solid food. There used to be a beautiful ritual in which the mother presented the child to the father in the middle of the camp, where all important statements are made (anyone speaking from the middle of the camp must be listened to). The father took the child and held it to his breast, and the child would try to suckle, crying "*ema, ema,*" or "mother." The father would shake his head, and say "no, father . . . *eba,*" but like a mother (the Mbuti said), then give the child its first solid food.

2   At three the child ventures out into the world on its own and enters the *bopi,* what we might call a playground, a tiny camp perhaps a hundred yards from the main camp, often on the edge of a stream. The *bopi* were indeed playgrounds, and often very noisy ones, full of fun and high spirits. But they were also rigorous training grounds for eventual economic responsibility. On entry to the *bopi,* for one thing, the child discovers the importance of age as a structural principle, and the relative unimportance of gender and biological kinship. The *bopi* is the private world of the children. Younger youths may occasionally venture in, but if adults or elders try, as they sometimes do when angry at having their afternoon snooze interrupted, they invariably get driven out, taunted, and ridiculed. Children, among the Mbuti, have rights, but they also learn that they have responsibilities. Before the hunt sets out each day it is the children, sometimes the younger youths, who light the hunting fire.

3   Ritual among the Mbuti is often so informal and apparently casual that it may pass unnoticed at first. Yet insofar as ritual involves symbolic acts that represent unspoken, perhaps even unthought, concepts or ideals, or invoke other states of being, alternative frames of mind and reference, then Mbuti life is full of ritual. The hunting fire is one of the more obvious of such rituals. Early in the morning children would take firebrands from the *bopi,* where they always lit their own fire with embers from their family hearths, and set off on the trail by which the hunt was to leave that day (the direction of each day's hunt was always settled by discussion the night before). Just a short distance from the camp they lit a fire at the base of a large tree, and covered it with special leaves that made it give off a column of dense smoke. Hunters leaving the camp, both men and women, and such youths and children as were going with them, had to pass by this fire. Some did so casually, without stopping or looking, but passing through the smoke. Others reached into the smoke with their hands as they passed, rubbing the smoke into their bodies. A few always stopped, for a moment, and let the smoke envelop them, only then almost dreamily moving off.

4   And indeed it *was* a form of intoxication, for the smoke invoked the spirit of the forest, and by passing through it the hunters sought to fill themselves with that spirit, not so much to make the hunt successful as to minimize the sacrilege of killing. Yet they, the hunters, could not light the fire themselves. After all, they were already contaminated by death. Even youths, who daily joined the hunt at the edges, catching any game that escaped the nets, by hand, if they could, were not pure enough to invoke the spirits of forestness. But young children were un-

contaminated, as yet untainted by contact with the original sin of the Mbuti. It was their responsibility to light the fire, and if it was not lit then the hunt would not take place, or, as the Mbuti put it, the hunt *could* not take place.

In this way even the children in Mbuti society, at the first of the four age levels that dominate Mbuti social structure, are given very real social responsibility and see themselves as a part of that structure, by virtue of their purity. After all, they have just been born from the source of all purity, the forest itself. By the same reasoning, the elders, who are about to return to that ultimate source of all being, through death, are at least closer to purity than the adults, who are daily contaminated by killing. Elders no longer go on the hunt. So, like the children, the elders have important sacred ritual responsibilities in the Mbuti division of labor by age.

In the *bopi* the children play, but they have no "games" in the strict sense of the word. Levi-Strauss has perceptively compared games with rituals, suggesting that whereas in a game the players start theoretically equal but end up unequal, in a ritual just the reverse takes place. All are equalized. Mbuti children could be seen every day playing in the *bopi,* but not once did I see a game, not one activity that smacked of any kind of competition, except perhaps that competition that it is necessary for us all to feel from time to time, competition with our own private and personal inadequacies. One such pastime (rather than game) was tree climbing. A dozen or so children would climb up a young sapling. Reaching the top, their weight brought the sapling bending down until it almost touched the ground. Then all the children leapt off together, shrieking as the young tree sprang upright again with a rush. Sometimes one child, male or female, might stay on a little too long, either out of fear, or out of bravado, or from sheer carelessness or bad timing. Whatever the reason, it was a lesson most children only needed to be taught once, for the result was that you got flung upward with the tree, and were lucky to escape with no more than a few bruises and a very bad fright.

Other pastimes taught the children the rules of hunting and gathering. Frequently elders, who stayed in camp when the hunt went off, called the children into the main camp and enacted a mock hunt with them there. Stretching a discarded piece of net across the camp, they pretended to be animals, showing the children how to drive them into the nets. And, of course, the children played house, learning the patterns of cooperation that would be necessary for them later in life. They also learned the prime lesson of egality, other than for purposes of division of labor making no distinction between male and female, this nuclear family or that. All in the *bopi* were *apua'i* to each other, and so they would remain throughout their lives. At every age level—childhood, youth, adulthood, or old age—everyone of that level is *apua'i* to all the others. Only adults sometimes (but so rarely that I think it was only done as a kind of joke, or possibly insult) made the distinction that the Bira do, using *apua'i* for male and *amua'i* for female. Male or female, for the Mbuti, if you are the same age you are *apua'i*, and that means that you share everything equally, regardless of kinship or gender.

Youth and Politics

8   Sometimes before the age of puberty boys or girls, whenever they feel ready, move back into the main camp from the *bopi* and join the youths. This is when they must assume new responsibilities, which for the youths are primarily political. Already, in the *bopi*, the children become involved in disputes, and are sometimes instrumental in settling them by ridicule, for nothing hurts an adult more than being ridiculed by children. The art of reason, however, is something they learn from the youths, and it is the youths who apply the art of reason to the settlement of disputes.

9   When puberty comes it separates them, for the first time in their experience, from each other as *apua'i*. Very plainly girls are different from boys. When a girl has her first menstrual period the whole camp celebrates with the wild *elima* festival, in which the girl, and some of her chosen girl friends, are the center of all attention, living together in a special *elima* house. Male youths sit outside the *elima* house and wait for the girls to come out, usually in the afternoon, for the *elima* singing. They sing in antiphony, the girls leading, the boys responding. Boys come from neighboring territories all around, for this is a time of courtship. But there are always eligible youths within the camp as well, and the *elima* girl may well choose girls from other territories to come and join her, so there is more than enough excuse for every youth to carry on several flirtations, legitimate or illegitimate. I have known even first cousins to flirt with each other, but learned to be prudent enough not to pull out my kinship charts and point this out—well, not in public anyway.

10   The *elima* is more than a premarital festival, more than a joint initiation of youth into adulthood, and more than a rite of passage through puberty, though it is all those things. It is a public recognition of the opposition of male and female, and every *elima* is used to highlight the *potential* for conflict that lies in that opposition. As at other times of crisis, at puberty, a time of change and uncertainty, the Mbuti bring all the major forms of conflict out into the open. And the one that evidently most concerns them is the male/female opposition.

11   The adults begin to play a special form of "tug of war" that is clearly a ritual rather than a game. All the men are on one side, the women on the other. At first it looks like a game, but quickly it becomes

clear that the objective is for *neither* side to win. As soon as the women begin to win, one of them will leave the end of the line and run around to join the men, assuming a deep male voice and in other ways ridiculing manhood. Then, as the men begin to win, a male will similarly join the women, making fun of womanhood as he does so. Each adult on changing sides attempts to outdo all the others in ridiculing the opposite sex. Finally, when nearly all have switched sides, and sexes, the ritual battle between the genders simply collapses into hysterical laughter, the contestants letting go of the rope, falling onto the ground, and rolling over with mirth. Neither side wins, both are equalized very nicely, and each learns the essential lesson, that there should be *no* contest. . . .

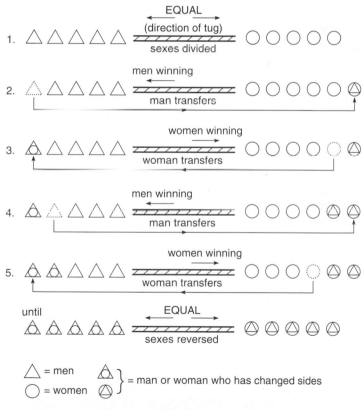

Tug of War. This is one of the Mbuti's many techniques of conflict resolution, involving role reversal and the principle of opposition without hostility.

✦ Evaluating the Text

1. What values do the first rituals in which the child takes part communicate?

2. In what ways is the concept of the age of the peer group the most important determinant of identity for the growing child?

3. Explain the significance of why only young children are allowed to light the fire preceding each day's hunt.

4. What values is the "tug of war" game designed to communicate?

✦ Exploring Different Perspectives

1. Compare how rituals are designed to educate and shape distinctive cultural attitudes in the traditional societies of the Quiché Indians (see Rigoberta Menchú's "Birth Ceremonies") in Guatemala and the Mbuti pygmies. How are these rituals designed to give young children a role to play within their communities?

2. Boris Yeltsin defined himself individualistically in opposition to prevailing societal expectations in sports, education, and leadership (see "Childhood in Russia"). How does this differ from the way children in the Mbuti society define themselves?

✦ Extending Viewpoints Through Writing

1. What games did you play when you were a child? Which, if any, were not competitive? If none were noncompetitive, what can you infer from this?

2. Are you aware of rituals in which the youngest child present performs a role determined solely by his or her age? Describe the ritual, its purpose, and the role the child plays.

John Cheever

Reunion

◆———————◆

John Cheever (1912–1982) was born in Quincy, Massachusetts. His parents had planned for him to attend Harvard, but he was expelled at seventeen from the Thayer Academy for smoking, which marked the end of his formal education. Although he wrote five novels, he is best known for his deftly constructed short stories of suburban affluent America that frequently appeared in The New Yorker. *Collections of his work include* The Enormous Radio *(1953),* The House Breaker of Shady Hill *(1958),* The Brigadier and the Golf Widow *(1964), and* The Stories of John Cheever *(1978), which won a Pulitzer Prize, and from which "Reunion" is reprinted.*

The last time I saw my father was in Grand Central Station. I was going from my grandmother's in the Adirondacks to a cottage on the Cape that my mother had rented, and I wrote my father that I would be in New York between trains for an hour and a half and asked if we could have lunch together. His secretary wrote to say that he would meet me at the information booth at noon, and at twelve o'clock sharp I saw him coming through the crowd. He was a stranger to me—my mother divorced him three years ago, and I hadn't been with him since—but as soon as I saw him I felt that he was my father, my flesh and blood, my future and my doom. I knew that when I was grown I would be something like him; I would have to plan my campaigns within his limitations. He was a big, good-looking man, and I was terribly happy to see him again. He struck me on the back and shook my hand. "Hi, Charlie," he said. "Hi, boy. I'd like to take you up to my club, but it's in the Sixties, and if you have to catch an early train I guess we'd better get something to eat around here." He put his arm around me, and I smelled my father the way my mother sniffs a rose. It was a rich compound of whiskey, after-shave lotion, shoe polish, woolens, and the rankness of a mature male. I hoped that someone would see us together. I wished that we could be photographed. I wanted some record of our having been together.

We went out of the station and up a side street to a restaurant. It was still early, and the place was empty. The bartender was quarreling with a delivery boy, and there was one very old waiter in a red coat down by the kitchen door. We sat down, and my father hailed the waiter in a loud voice. "*Kellner!*" he shouted. "*Garçon! Cameriere! You!*" His boisterousness in the empty restaurant seemed out of place. "Could we have a little service here!" he shouted. "Chop-chop." Then he clapped his hands. This caught the waiter's attention, and he shuffled over to our table.

3   "Were you clapping your hands at me?" he asked.

4   "Calm down, calm down, *sommelier*," my father said. "If it isn't too much to ask of you—if it wouldn't be too much above and beyond the call of duty, we would like a couple of Beefeater Gibsons."

5   "I don't like to be clapped at," the waiter said.

6   "I should have brought my whistle," my father said. "I have a whistle that is audible only to the ears of old waiters. Now, take out your little pad and your little pencil and see if you can get this straight: two Beefeater Gibsons. Repeat after me: two Beefeater Gibsons."

7   "I think you'd better go somewhere else," the waiter said quietly.

8   "That," said my father, "is one of the most brilliant suggestions I have ever heard. Come on, Charlie, let's get the hell out of here."

9   I followed my father out of that restaurant into another. He was not so boisterous this time. Our drinks came, and he cross-questioned me about the baseball season. He then struck the edge of his empty glass with his knife and began shouting again. "*Garçon! Kellner! You!* Could we trouble you to bring us two more of the same."

10   "How old is the boy?" the waiter asked.

11   "That," my father said, "is none of your goddamned business."

12   "I'm sorry, sir," the waiter said, "but I won't serve the boy another drink."

13   "Well, I have some news for you," my father said. "I have some very interesting news for you. This doesn't happen to be the only restaurant in New York. They've opened another on the corner. Come on, Charlie."

14   He paid the bill, and I followed him out of that restaurant into another. Here the waiters wore pink jackets like hunting coats, and there was a lot of horse tack on the walls. We sat down, and my father began to shout again. "Master of the hounds! Tallyhoo and all that sort of thing. We'd like a little something in the way of a stirrup cup. Namely, two Bibson Geefeaters."

15   "Two Bibson Geefeaters?" the waiter asked, smiling.

16   "You know damned well what I want," my father said angrily. "I want two Beefeater Gibsons, and make it snappy. Things have changed in jolly old England. So my friend the duke tells me. Let's see what England can produce in the way of a cocktail."

17   "This isn't England," the waiter said.

18   "Don't argue with me," my father said. "Just do as you're told."

19   "I just thought you might like to know where you are," the waiter said.

20   "If there is one thing I cannot tolerate," my father said, "it is an impudent domestic. Come on, Charlie."

21   The fourth place we went to was Italian. "*Buon giorno,*" my father said. "*Per favore, possiamo avere due cocktail americani, forti, forti. Molto gin, poco vermut.*"

"I don't understand Italian," the waiter said.   22

"Oh, come off it," my father said. "You understand Italian, and you   23
know damned well you do. *Vogliamo due cocktail americani. Subito.*"

The waiter left us and spoke with the captain, who came over to   24
our table and said, "I'm sorry, sir, but this table is reserved."

"All right," my father said. "Get us another table."   25

"All the tables are reserved," the captain said.   26

"I get it," my father said. "You don't desire our patronage. Is that   27
it? Well, the hell with you. *Vada all' inferno.* Let's go, Charlie."

"I have to get my train," I said.   28

"I'm sorry, sonny," my father said. "I'm terribly sorry." He put his   29
arm around me and pressed me against him. "I'll walk you back to the
station. If there had only been time to go up to my club."

"That's all right, Daddy," I said.   30

"I'll get you a paper," he said. "I'll get you a paper to read on the   31
train."

Then he went up to a newsstand and said, "Kind sir, will you be   32
good enough to favor me with one of your goddamned, no-good, ten-
cent afternoon papers?" The clerk turned away from him and stared at
a magazine cover. "Is it asking too much, kind sir," my father said, "is
it asking too much for you to sell me one of your disgusting specimens
of yellow journalism?"

"I have to go, Daddy," I said. "It's late."   33

"Now, just wait a second, sonny," he said. "Just wait a second. I   34
want to get a rise out of this chap."

"Goodbye, Daddy," I said, and I went down the stairs and got my   35
train, and that was the last time I saw my father.

✦ Evaluating the Text

1. What clues tell the reader how much the anticipated meeting with his
   father means to the boy in the story?

2. How would you characterize the father's attitude toward those of
   other nationalities and lower social classes?

3. How does the sequence of episodes that takes place in the story make
   clear why the boy would wish never to see his father again?

✦ Exploring Different Perspectives

1. Both Boris Yeltsin (See "Childhood in Russia") and the boy in John
   Cheever's story are estranged to some extent from their fathers. Compare the reasons for this in both works.

2. Why, in your opinion, does Pat Mora's aunt in "Remembering Lobo"
   make an ally of her niece against the world, whereas the father in John
   Cheever's story alienates his son?

✦ *Extending Viewpoints Through Writing*

1. Has the behavior of a relative or friend toward people of other nationalities or social classes ever caused you to feel shame or embarrassment as the boy does in Cheever's story? Describe the circumstances.

2. In your view, what role does alcoholism play in causing rifts between parents and children? Can it be significant?

Connecting Cultures

◆

Gayle Pemberton, *Antidisestablishmentarianism*

Compare the influence of the grandmother on shaping the outlook of Gayle Pemberton with that of Aunt Susie in Leslie Marmon Silko's essay (see "Language and Literature from a Pueblo Indian Perspective," Chapter 9).

Boris Yeltsin, *Childhood in Russia*

What similarities can you discover in the manner in which Boris Yeltsin and Mary Crow Dog (see "Civilize Them with a Stick," Chapter 5) defend themselves against repressive authorities?

Rigoberta Menchú, *Birth Ceremonies*

Compare the role played by traditional tribal rituals in Rigoberta Menchú's account with the reemergence of an ancient tribal belief in Bessie Head's "Looking for a Rain God" (Chapter 9). How are the attitudes toward children in these two selections connected with superstitions and "magical thinking"?

Nicholas Bornoff, *The Marriage Go-Round*

Compare the factors that serve as a basis for marriage in Nicholas Bornoff's analysis and Feng Jicai's story "The Tall Woman and Her Short Husband" (Chapter 6).

Serena Nanda, *Arranging a Marriage in India*

What insight into the function of the Hindu religion do you get from Serena Nanda's account and Premchand's story "Deliverance" (Chapter 9)?

Shirley Saad, *Amina*

Discuss the cultural pressures that affect the role of a wife in Lebanon and in Mali (see "Her Three Days" by Sembene Ousmane, Chapter 3).

Pat Mora, *Remembering Lobo*

Compare the relationship Pat Mora has with her Aunt Lobo to Leslie Marmon Silko's relationship with her Aunt Susie (see "Language and Literature from a Pueblo Indian Perspective," Chapter 9).

Colin Turnbull, The Mbuti Pygmies

Contrast how Mbuti culture is based on cooperative efforts with the Yąnomamö's reliance on aggression and confrontation (see Napoleon A. Chagnon's "Doing Fieldwork Among the Yąnomamö," Chapter 8).

John Cheever, Reunion

There are a number of works that explore the relationships between fathers and sons. What bond connects fathers and sons in Camara Laye's "The Village Goldsmith" (Chapter 4), Moacyr Scliar's "A Brief History of Capitalism" (Chapter 4), and Mahdokht Kashkuli's "The Button" (Chapter 5)?

2

Turning Points

◆

In virtually every society, certain rites or ceremonies are used to signal
adulthood. Although many of these occasions are informal, some are
quite elaborate and dramatic. This chapter offers a range of perspectives that illustrate how such turning points are marked by informal
and formal rituals across a broad spectrum of cultures. These moments
of insight may be private psychological turning points or ceremonies
that initiate the individual into adulthood within a community. These
crucial moments in which individuals move from childhood innocence
to adult awareness often involve learning a particular society's rules
governing what should or should not be done under different circumstances, values, knowledge, and expectations as to how one should
present oneself in a wide variety of situations.

Turning points often occur during adolescence, when we explore
the limits of what society will and will not allow us to do. This is the
time in which rebellion and defiance against society's rules take place.
We acquire societal norms through imitation, identification, and instruction into what behavior patterns our society deems acceptable or
unacceptable. From internalizing these values we get a sense of personal and social identity. This is often the time when we form our first
voluntary associations or friendships and discover our capacity to trust
and develop relationships, whether strong or fragile, that can lead to
reward or disappointment.

In some cases, belonging to a group, association, fraternity, or sorority involves passing some initiation or test to gain acceptance. Because this chapter is rich in a wide variety of perspectives, it invites you
to make discoveries about turning points in your own life.

The essays and stories in this chapter focus on the psychological
and cultural forces that shape the identity of those who are about
to be initiated into their respective communities. From Ireland, we
read the moving narrative of Christy Brown, who, in "The Letter
'A'," describes his struggle to communicate signs of intelligence by
drawing the letter A with his left foot after having been diagnosed

as hopelessly retarded by cerebral palsy. In the first autobiographical account ever written by a Maasai, Tepilit Ole Saitoti, in "The Initiation of a Maasai Warrior," describes the circumcision ceremony that served as his rite of passage into adulthood. The internationally renowned Egyptian feminist author, Nawal El Saadawi, in "Circumcision of Girls," analyzes the cultural prejudices that still encourage the archaic and damaging practice of female circumcision in many countries. The Lebanese writer Hanan al-Shaykh tells a story, "The Persian Carpet," of a moment of discovery that permanently alters the relationship between a girl and her mother. N. Scott Momaday, in "The Names," describes a crucial moment in his Kiowa background that forever changed his life. The Chinese-American writer Sucheng Chan describes with honesty and humor her struggle to confront her disabilities, in "You're Short, Besides!" The Italian author Dino Buzzati creates a surrealistic parable in "The Falling Girl" that captures the feeling of moving toward adulthood from adolescence. From Finland, Kjell Westö, in his story "Melba, Mallinen and me," describes how a new friend changes a teenager's life.

Christy Brown

The Letter "A"

◆———————

Christy Brown (1932–1981) was born in Dublin, the tenth child in a family of twenty-two. Brown was diagnosed as having cerebral palsy and being hopelessly retarded. An intense personal struggle and the loving attention and faith of his mother resulted in a surprising degree of rehabilitation. Brown's autobiography, My Left Foot *(1954), describing his struggle to overcome his massive handicap, was the basis for the 1989 Academy Award–winning film. Brown is also the author of an internationally acclaimed novel,* Down All the Days *(1970). "The Letter 'A'," from his autobiography, describes the crucial moment when he first communicated signs of awareness and intelligence.*

The Republic of Ireland occupies all but the northeast corner of the island of Ireland, in the British Isles, and has a population of 3.5 million. Cork, founded in the seventh century, is the second-largest city in the Republic of Ireland. A treaty with Great Britain in 1922 partitioned Ireland into the Irish Free State and the six counties of Ulster in the northeast (whose population now numbers 1.5 million) and precipitated a civil war. The anti-treaty forces were identified with the Irish Republican Army (IRA), a nationalist organization that was defeated at the time but has continued to fight for the unification of Ireland. The ongoing conflict between Irish Roman Catholics and Ulster's Protestants stems from Henry VIII's attempt in 1541 to impose the Protestant Church of Ireland on the predominantly Catholic population. To this day, Ulster's Protestants and Catholics are divided over whether to remain under British rule or join the Republic of Ireland. In 1937, a new constitution was put forward, establishing the sovereign state of Ireland within the British Commonwealth. In 1949, the Republic of Ireland was proclaimed, and the country withdrew from the Commonwealth. Discussions with British authorities over the issue of returning Northern Ireland to Irish sovereignty have produced little progress. A high unemployment rate and a poor economy led to the collapse of Ireland's coalition government in 1992. A new coalition was formed under Albert Reynolds, who served as prime minister until 1994. Following his resignation, a new government was formed in April 1995, with John Bruton serving as prime minister.

1   I was born in the Rotunda Hospital,[1] on June 5th, 1932. There were nine children before me and twelve after me, so I myself belong to the middle group. Out of this total of twenty-two, seventeen lived, but four died in infancy, leaving thirteen still to hold the family fort.

2   Mine was a difficult birth, I am told. Both mother and son almost died. A whole army of relations queued up outside the hospital until the small hours of the morning, waiting for news and praying furiously that it would be good.

3   After my birth Mother was sent to recuperate for some weeks and I was kept in the hospital while she was away. I remained there for some time, without name, for I wasn't baptized until my mother was well enough to bring me to church.

4   It was Mother who first saw that there was something wrong with me. I was about four months old at the time. She noticed that my head had a habit of falling backward whenever she tried to feed me. She attempted to correct this by placing her hand on the back of my neck to keep it steady. But when she took it away, back it would drop again. That was the first warning sign. Then she became aware of other defects as I got older. She saw that my hands were clenched nearly all of the time and were inclined to twine behind my back; my mouth couldn't grasp the teat of the bottle because even at that early age my jaws would either lock together tightly, so that it was impossible for her to open them, or they would suddenly become limp and fall loose, dragging my whole mouth to one side. At six months I could not sit up without having a mountain of pillows around me. At twelve months it was the same.

5   Very worried by this, Mother told my father her fears, and they decided to seek medical advice without any further delay. I was a little over a year old when they began to take me to hospitals and clinics, convinced that there was something definitely wrong with me, something which they could not understand or name, but which was very real and disturbing.

6   Almost every doctor who saw and examined me labeled me a very interesting but also a hopeless case. Many told Mother very gently that I was mentally defective and would remain so. That was a hard blow to a young mother who had already reared five healthy children. The doctors were so very sure of themselves that Mother's faith in me seemed almost an impertinence. They assured her that nothing could be done for me.

7   She refused to accept this truth, the inevitable truth—as it then seemed—that I was beyond cure, beyond saving, even beyond hope. She could not and would not believe that I was an imbecile, as the doctors told her. She had nothing in the world to go by, not a scrap of evidence to support her conviction that, though my body was crippled,

---

[1] *Rotunda Hospital,* a hospital in Dublin, Ireland.

my mind was not. In spite of all the doctors and specialists told her, she would not agree. I don't believe she knew why—she just knew, without feeling the smallest shade of doubt.

Finding that the doctors could not help in any way beyond telling   8
her not to place her trust in me, or, in other words, to forget I was a human creature, rather to regard me as just something to be fed and washed and then put away again, Mother decided there and then to take matters into her own hands. I was *her* child, and therefore part of the family. No matter how dull and incapable I might grow up to be, she was determined to treat me on the same plane as the others, and not as the "queer one" in the back room who was never spoken of when there were visitors present.

That was a momentous decision as far as my future life was con-   9
cerned. It meant that I would always have my mother on my side to help me fight all the battles that were to come, and to inspire me with new strength when I was almost beaten. But it wasn't easy for her because now the relatives and friends had decided otherwise. They contended that I should be taken kindly, sympathetically, but not seriously. That would be a mistake. "For your own sake," they told her, "don't look to this boy as you would to the others; it would only break your heart in the end." Luckily for me, Mother and Father held out against the lot of them. But Mother wasn't content just to say that I was not an idiot: she set out to prove it, not because of any rigid sense of duty, but out of love. That is why she was so successful.

At this time she had the five other children to look after besides the   10
"difficult one," though as yet it was not by any means a full house. They were my brothers, Jim, Tony, and Paddy, and my two sisters, Lily and Mona, all of them very young, just a year or so between each of them, so that they were almost exactly like steps of stairs.

Four years rolled by and I was now five, and still as helpless as a   11
newly born baby. While my father was out at bricklaying, earning our bread and butter for us, Mother was slowly, patiently pulling down the wall, brick by brick, that seemed to thrust itself between me and the other children, slowly, patiently penetrating beyond the thick curtain that hung over my mind, separating it from theirs. It was hard, heartbreaking work, for often all she got from me in return was a vague smile and perhaps a faint gurgle. I could not speak or even mumble, nor could I sit up without support on my own, let alone take steps. But I wasn't inert or motionless. I seemed, indeed, to be convulsed with movement, wild, stiff, snakelike movement that never left me, except in sleep. My fingers twisted and twitched continually, my arms twined backwards and would often shoot out suddenly this way and that, and my head lolled and sagged sideways. I was a queer, crooked little fellow.

Mother tells me how one day she had been sitting with me for   12
hours in an upstairs bedroom, showing me pictures out of a great big

storybook that I had got from Santa Claus last Christmas and telling me the names of the different animals and flowers that were in them, trying without success to get me to repeat them. This had gone on for hours while she talked and laughed with me. Then at the end of it she leaned over me and said gently into my ear:

13   "Did you like it, Chris? Did you like the bears and the monkeys and all the lovely flowers? Nod your head for yes, like a good boy."

14   But I could make no sign that I had understood her. Her face was bent over mine hopefully. Suddenly, involuntarily, my queer hand reached up and grasped one of the dark curls that fell in a thick cluster about her neck. Gently she loosened the clenched fingers, though some dark strands were still clutched between them.

15   Then she turned away from my curious stare and left the room, crying. The door closed behind her. It all seemed hopeless. It looked as though there was some justification for my relatives' contention that I was an idiot and beyond help.

16   They now spoke of an institution.

17   "Never!" said my mother almost fiercely, when this was suggested to her. "I know my boy is not an idiot; it is his body that is shattered, not his mind. I'm sure of that."

18   Sure? Yet inwardly, she prayed God would give her some proof of her faith. She knew it was one thing to believe but quite another thing to prove.

19   I was now five, and still I showed no real sign of intelligence. I showed no apparent interest in things except with my toes—more especially those of my left foot. Although my natural habits were clean, I could not aid myself, but in this respect my father took care of me. I used to lie on my back all the time in the kitchen or, on bright warm days, out in the garden, a little bundle of crooked muscles and twisted nerves, surrounded by a family that loved me and hoped for me and that made me part of their own warmth and humanity. I was lonely, imprisoned in a world of my own, unable to communicate with others, cut off, separated from them as though a glass wall stood between my existence and theirs, thrusting me beyond the sphere of their lives and activities. I longed to run about and play with the rest, but I was unable to break loose from my bondage.

20   Then, suddenly, it happened! In a moment everything was changed, my future life molded into a definite shape, my mother's faith in me rewarded, and her secret fear changed into open triumph.

21   It happened so quickly, so simply after all the years of waiting and uncertainty, that I can see and feel the whole scene as if it had happened last week. It was the afternoon of a cold, gray December day. The streets outside glistened with snow, the white sparkling flakes stuck and melted on the windowpanes and hung on the boughs of the trees like molten silver. The wind howled dismally, whipping up little

whirling columns of snow that rose and fell at every fresh gust. And over all, the dull, murky sky stretched like a dark canopy, a vast infinity of grayness.

Inside, all the family were gathered round the big kitchen fire that lit up the little room with a warm glow and made giant shadows dance on the walls and ceiling. 22

In a corner Mona and Paddy were sitting, huddled together, a few torn school primers before them. They were writing down little sums onto an old chipped slate, using a bright piece of yellow chalk. I was close to them, propped up by a few pillows against the wall, watching. 23

It was the chalk that attracted me so much. It was a long, slender stick of vivid yellow. I had never seen anything like it before, and it showed up so well against the black surface of the slate that I was fascinated by it as much as if it had been a stick of gold. 24

Suddenly, I wanted desperately to do what my sister was doing. Then—without thinking or knowing exactly what I was doing, I reached out and took the stick of chalk out of my sister's hand—with my left foot. 25

I do not know why I used my left foot to do this. It is a puzzle to many people as well as to myself, for, although I had displayed a curious interest in my toes at an early age, I had never attempted before this to use either of my feet in any way. They could have been as useless to me as were my hands. That day, however, my left foot, apparently by its own volition, reached out and very impolitely took the chalk out of my sister's hand. 26

I held it tightly between my toes, and, acting on an impulse, made a wild sort of scribble with it on the slate. Next moment I stopped, a bit dazed, surprised, looking down at the stick of yellow chalk stuck between my toes, not knowing what to do with it next, hardly knowing how it got there. Then I looked up and became aware that everyone had stopped talking and was staring at me silently. Nobody stirred. Mona, her black curls framing her chubby little face, stared at me with great big eyes and open mouth. Across the open hearth, his face lit by flames, sat my father, leaning forward, hands outspread on his knees, his shoulders tense. I felt the sweat break out on my forehead. 27

My mother came in from the pantry with a steaming pot in her hand. She stopped midway between the table and the fire, feeling the tension flowing through the room. She followed their stare and saw me in the corner. Her eyes looked from my face down to my foot, with the chalk gripped between my toes. She put down the pot. 28

Then she crossed over to me and knelt down beside me, as she had done so many times before. 29

"I'll show you what to do with it, Chris," she said, very slowly and in a queer, choked way, her face flushed as if with some inner excitement. 30

Taking another piece of chalk from Mona, she hesitated, then very deliberately drew, on the floor in front of me, *the single letter "A."* 31

32   "Copy that," she said, looking steadily at me. "Copy it, Christy."

33   I couldn't.

34   I looked about me, looked around at the faces that were turned towards me, tense, excited faces that were at that moment frozen, immobile, eager, waiting for a miracle in their midst.

35   The stillness was profound. The room was full of flame and shadow that danced before my eyes and lulled my taut nerves into a sort of waking sleep. I could hear the sound of the water tap dripping in the pantry, the loud ticking of the clock on the mantel shelf, and the soft hiss and crackle of the logs on the open hearth.

36   I tried again. I put out my foot and made a wild jerking stab with the chalk which produced a very crooked line and nothing more. Mother held the slate steady for me.

37   "Try again, Chris," she whispered in my ear. "Again."

38   I did. I stiffened my body and put my left foot out again, for the third time. I drew one side of the letter. I drew half the other side. Then the stick of chalk broke and I was left with a stump. I wanted to fling it away and give up. Then I felt my mother's hand on my shoulder. I tried once more. Out went my foot. I shook, I sweated and strained every muscle. My hands were so tightly clenched that my fingernails bit into the flesh. I set my teeth so hard that I nearly pierced my lower lip. Everything in the room swam till the faces around me were mere patches of white. But—I drew it—*the letter "A."* There it was on the floor before me. Shaky, with awkward, wobbly sides and a very uneven center line. But it *was* the letter "A." I looked up. I saw my mother's face for a moment, tears on her cheeks. Then my father stooped and hoisted me onto his shoulder.

39   I had done it! It had started—the thing that was to give my mind its chance of expressing itself. True, I couldn't speak with my lips. But now I would speak through something more lasting than spoken words—written words.

40   That one letter, scrawled on the floor with a broken bit of yellow chalk gripped between my toes, was my road to a new world, my key to mental freedom. It was to provide a source of relaxation to the tense, taut thing that was I, which panted for expression behind a twisted mouth.

✦ *Evaluating the Text*

1. What unusual signs alerted Christy's mother that he might be physically impaired? What did her response to the doctors' diagnosis reveal about her as a person and her attitude toward Christy?

2. What did Christy's mother hope to achieve by showing him pictures of animals and flowers? How did her friends and relatives react to her

decision to treat Christy as if he were capable of mental development? How would Christy's day-to-day treatment have differed if his mother had not treated him as a member of the family?

3. Why does the narrative shift from Christy's mother's perspective to Christy's recollection of the day he was able to form the letter *A* with his left foot?

4. From the point of view of Christy's mother, father, and siblings, how did they know that his forming the letter *A* was a sign of intelligence and not merely an imitative gesture?

5. How does the conclusion of this account suggest that this moment had deeper meaning for Christy than it did even for his family? What did this mean to him?

✦ Exploring Different Perspectives

1. In what way can Brown be considered to be just as courageous in meeting the challenge he faced as Tepilit Ole Saitoti was in exhibiting bravery during his initiation as a Maasai warrior (see "The Initiation of a Maasai Warrior")?

2. What similarities in coping with a disability can you discover in this account by Christy Brown and that of Sucheng Chan in "You're Short, Besides!"?

✦ Extending Viewpoints Through Writing

1. On any given day, how do you think Christy would have been treated if his mother had not made the decision to treat him as a member of the family? Write two brief accounts analyzing why over a period of time the difference in the way he was treated might have been capable of producing the unexpected development Christy describes. Include in your account such everyday events as meals and visits from friends.

2. If you have seen the 1989 Academy Award–winning film *My Left Foot*, based on Christy Brown's autobiography of the same name, discuss which treatment, film or written word, more effectively dramatized the issues at stake and the feelings of Christy and his family at the moment when he drew the letter *A*.

3. If you have ever been temporarily physically incapacitated or have a disability, write an essay that will help your audience understand your plight and the visible and subtle psychological aspects of discrimination that the disabled must endure every day.

Tepilit Ole Saitoti

The Initiation of a Maasai Warrior

◆

Named for the language they speak—Maa, a distinct, but unwritten African tongue—the Maasai of Kenya and Tanzania, a tall, handsome, and proud people, still live much as they always have, herding cattle, sheep, and goats in and around the Great Rift Valley. This personal narrative is unique—the first autobiographical account written by a Maasai, which vividly documents the importance of the circumcision ceremony that serves as a rite of passage into warrior rank. Tepilit Ole Saitoti studied animal ecology in the United States and has returned to Kenya, where he is active in conservation projects. His experiences formed the basis for a National Geographic Society film, Man of Serengeti *(1971). This account first appeared in Saitoti's autobiography,* The Worlds of a Maasai Warrior *(1986).*

The United Republic of Tanzania was formed in 1964 by the union of Tanganyika and Zanzibar. It is bordered on the north by Kenya, Lake Victoria, and Uganda. Fossils discovered by British anthropologist Louis B. Leakey at Olduvai Gorge in northeastern Tanzania have been identified as the remains of a direct ancestor of the human species from 1.75 million years ago. Tanzania contains the famed Mount Kilimanjaro, which at 19,340 feet is the highest point in Africa. Tanzania also boasts the highest literacy rate in Africa. In May of 1992 multiparty democracy was introduced into what had been a one-party state. The current president is Ali Hassan Mwinyi.

1   "Tepilit, circumcision means a sharp knife cutting into the skin of the most sensitive part of your body. You must not budge; don't move a muscle or even blink. You can face only one direction until the operation is completed. The slightest movement on your part will mean you are a coward, incompetent and unworthy to be a Maasai man. Ours has always been a proud family, and we would like to keep it that way. We will not tolerate unnecessary embarrassment, so you had better be ready. If you are not, tell us now so that we will not proceed. Imagine yourself alone remaining uncircumcised like the water youth [white people]. I hear they are not circumcised. Such a thing is not known in

*(For more information on Kenya, see p. 381.)

Maasailand; therefore, circumcision will have to take place even if it means holding you down until it is completed."

My father continued to speak and every one of us kept quiet. "The pain you will feel is symbolic. There is a deeper meaning in all this. Circumcision means a break between childhood and adulthood. For the first time in your life, you are regarded as a grownup, a complete man or woman. You will be expected to give and not just to receive. To protect the family always, not just to be protected yourself. And your wise judgment will for the first time be taken into consideration. No family affairs will be discussed without your being consulted. If you are ready for all these responsibilities, tell us now. Coming into manhood is not simply a matter of growth and maturity. It is a heavy load on your shoulders and especially a burden on the mind. Too much of this—I am done. I have said all I wanted to say. Fellows, if you have anything to add, go ahead and tell your brother, because I am through. I have spoken."

After a prolonged silence, one of my half-brothers said awkwardly, "Face it, man . . . it's painful. I won't lie about it, but it is not the end. We all went through it, after all. Only blood will flow, not milk." There was laughter and my father left.

My brother Lellia said, "Men, there are many things we must acquire and preparations we must make before the ceremony, and we will need the cooperation and help of all of you. Ostrich feathers for the crown and wax for the arrows must be collected."

"Are you *orkirekenyi?*" One of my brothers asked. I quickly replied no, and there was laughter. *Orkirekenyi* is a person who has transgressed sexually. For you must not have sexual intercourse with any circumcised woman before you yourself are circumcised. You must wait until you are circumcised. If you have not waited, you will be fined. Your father, mother, and the circumciser will take a cow from you as punishment.

Just before we departed, one of my closest friends said, "If you kick the knife, you will be in trouble." There was laughter. "By the way, if you have decided to kick the circumciser, do it well. Silence him once and for all." "Do it the way you kick a football in school." "That will fix him," another added, and we all laughed our heads off again as we departed.

The following month was a month of preparation. I and others collected wax, ostrich feathers, honey to be made into honey beer for the elders to drink on the day of circumcision, and all the other required articles.

Three days before the ceremony my head was shaved and I discarded all my belongings, such as my necklaces, garments, spear, and sword. I even had to shave my pubic hair. Circumcision in many ways is similar to Christian baptism. You must put all the sins you have committed during childhood behind and embark as a new person with a different outlook on a new life.

9   The circumciser came the following day and handed the ritual knives to me. He left drinking a calabash of beer. I stared at the knives uneasily. It was hard to accept that he was going to use them on my organ. I was to sharpen them and protect them from people of ill will who might try to blunt them, thus rendering them inefficient during the ritual and thereby bringing shame on our family. The knives threw a chill down my spine; I was not sure I was sharpening them properly, so I took them to my closest brother for him to check out, and he assured me that the knives were all right. I hid them well and waited.

10   Tension started building between me and my relatives, most of whom worried that I wouldn't make it through the ceremony valiantly. Some even snarled at me, which was their way of encouraging me. Others threw insults and abusive words my way. My sister Loiyan in particular was more troubled by the whole affair than anyone in the whole family. She had to assume my mother's role during the circumcision. Were I to fail my initiation, she would have to face the consequences. She would be spat upon and even beaten for representing the mother of an unworthy son. The same fate would befall my father, but he seemed unconcerned. He had this weird belief that because I was not particularly handsome, I must be brave. He kept saying, "God is not so bad as to have made him ugly and a coward at the same time."

11   Failure to be brave during circumcision would have other unfortunate consequences: the herd of cattle belonging to the family still in the compound would be beaten until they stampeded; the slaughtered oxen and honey beer prepared during the month before the ritual would go to waste; the initiate's food would be spat upon and he would have to eat it or else get a severe beating. Everyone would call him Olkasiodoi, the knife kicker.

12   Kicking the knife of the circumciser would not help you anyway. If you struggle and try to get away during the ritual, you will be held down until the operation is completed. Such failure of nerve would haunt you in the future. For example, no one will choose a person who kicked the knife for a position of leadership. However, there have been instances in which a person who failed to go through circumcision successfully became very brave afterwards because he was filled with anger over the incident; no one dares to scold him or remind him of it. His agemates, particularly the warriors, will act as if nothing had happened.

13   During the circumcision of a woman, on the other hand, she is allowed to cry as long as she does not hinder the operation. It is common to see a woman crying and kicking during circumcision. Warriors are usually summoned to help hold her down.

14   For women, circumcision means an end to the company of Maasai warriors. After they recuperate, they soon get married, and often to men twice their age.

The closer it came to the hour of truth, the more I was hated, particularly by those closest to me. I was deeply troubled by the withdrawal of all the support I needed. My annoyance turned into anger and resolve. I decided not to budge or blink, even if I were to see my intestines flowing before me. My resolve was hardened when newly circumcised warriors came to sing for me. Their songs were utterly insulting, intended to annoy me further. They tucked their wax arrows under my crotch and rubbed them on my nose. They repeatedly called me names. 15

By the end of the singing, I was fuming. Crying would have meant I was a coward. After midnight they left me alone and I went into the house and tried to sleep but could not. I was exhausted and numb but remained awake all night. 16

At dawn I was summoned once again by the newly circumcised warriors. They piled more and more insults on me. They sang their weird songs with even more vigor and excitement than before. The songs praised warriorhood and encouraged one to achieve it at all costs. The songs continued until the sun shone on the cattle horns clearly. I was summoned to the main cattle gate, in my hand a ritual cowhide from a cow that had been properly slaughtered during my naming ceremony. I went past Loiyan, who was milking a cow, and she muttered something. She was shaking all over. There was so much tension that people could hardly breathe. 17

I laid the hide down and a boy was ordered to pour ice-cold water, known as *engare entolu* (ax water), over my head. It dripped all over my naked body and I shook furiously. In a matter of seconds I was summoned to sit down. A large crowd of boys and men formed a semicircle in front of me; women are not allowed to watch male circumcision and vice versa. That was the last thing I saw clearly. As soon as I sat down, the circumciser appeared, his knives at the ready. He spread my legs and said, "One cut," a pronouncement necessary to prevent an initiate from claiming that he had been taken by surprise. He splashed a white liquid, a ceremonial paint called *enturoto,* across my face. Almost immediately I felt a spark of pain under my belly as the knife cut through my penis' foreskin. I happened to choose to look in the direction of the operation. I continued to observe the circumciser's fingers working mechanically. The pain became numbness and my lower body felt heavy, as if I were weighed down by a heavy burden. After fifteen minutes or so, a man who had been supporting from behind pointed at something, as if to assist the circumciser. I came to learn later that the circumciser's eyesight had been failing him and that my brothers had been mad at him because the operation had taken longer than was usually necessary. All the same, I remained pinned down until the operation was over. I heard a call for milk to wash the knives, which signaled the end, and soon the ceremony was over. 18

19   With words of praise, I was told to wake up, but I remained seated. I waited for the customary presents in appreciation of my bravery. My father gave me a cow and so did my brother Lellia. The man who had supported my back and my brother-in-law gave me a heifer. In all I had eight animals given to me. I was carried inside the house to my own bed to recuperate as activities intensified to celebrate my bravery.

20   I laid on my own bed and bled profusely. The blood must be retained within the bed, for according to Maasai tradition, it must not spill to the ground. I was drenched in my own blood. I stopped bleeding after about half an hour but soon was in intolerable pain. I was supposed to squeeze my organ and force blood to flow out of the wound, but no one had told me, so the blood coagulated and caused unbearable pain. The circumciser was brought to my aid and showed me what to do, and soon the pain subsided.

21   The following morning, I was escorted by a small boy to a nearby valley to walk and relax, allowing my wound to drain. This was common for everyone who had been circumcised, as well as for women who had just given birth. Having lost a lot of blood, I was extremely weak. I walked very slowly, but in spite of my caution I fainted. I tried to hang on to bushes and shrubs, but I fell, irritating my wound. I came out of unconsciousness quickly, and the boy who was escorting me never realized what had happened. I was so scared that I told him to lead me back home. I could have died without there being anyone around who could have helped me. From that day on, I was selective of my company while I was feeble.

22   In two weeks I was able to walk and was taken to join other newly circumcised boys far away from our settlement. By tradition Maasai initiates are required to decorate their headdresses with all kinds of colorful birds they have killed. On our way to the settlement, we hunted birds and teased girls by shooting them with our wax blunt arrows. We danced and ate and were well treated wherever we went. We were protected from the cold and rain during the healing period. We were not allowed to touch food, as we were regarded as unclean, so whenever we ate we had to use specially prepared sticks instead. We remained in this pampered state until our wounds healed and our headdresses were removed. Our heads were shaved, we discarded our black cloaks and bird headdresses and embarked as newly shaven warriors, Irkeleani.

23   As long as I live I will never forget the day my head was shaved and I emerged a man, a Maasai warrior. I felt a sense of control over my destiny so great that no words can accurately describe it. I now stood with confidence, pride, and happiness of being, for all around me I was desired and loved by beautiful, sensuous Maasai maidens. I could now interact with women and even have sex with them, which I had not been allowed before. I was now regarded as a responsible person.

In the old days, warriors were like gods, and women and men   24
wanted only to be the parent of a warrior. Everything else would be
taken care of as a result. When a poor family had a warrior, they ceased
to be poor. The warrior would go on raids and bring cattle back. The
warrior would defend the family against all odds. When a society respects the individual and displays confidence in him the way the Maasai do their warriors, the individual can grow to his fullest potential.
Whenever there was a task requiring physical strength or bravery, the
Maasai would call upon their warriors. They hardly ever fall short of
what is demanded of them and so are characterized by pride, confidence, and an extreme sense of freedom. But there is an old saying in
Maasai: "You are never a free man until your father dies." In other
words, your father is paramount while he is alive and you are obli-
gated to respect him. My father took advantage of this principle and
held a tight grip on all his warriors, including myself. He always
wanted to know where we all were at any given time. We fought
against his restrictions, but without success. I, being the youngest of
my father's five warriors, tried even harder to get loose repeatedly, but
each time I was punished severely.

Roaming the plains with other warriors in pursuit of girls and ad-   25
venture was a warrior's pastime. We would wander from one settlement to another, singing, wrestling, hunting, and just playing. Often I
was ready to risk my father's punishment for this wonderful freedom.

One clear day my father sent me to take sick children and one of his   26
wives to the dispensary in the Korongoro Highlands. We rode in the
L.S.B. Leakey lorry. We ascended the highlands and were soon attended to in the local hospital. Near the conservation offices I met several acquaintances, and one of them told me of an unusual circumcision
that was about to take place in a day or two. All the local warriors and
girls were preparing to attend it.

The highlands were a lush green from the seasonal rains and the   27
sky was a purple-blue with no clouds in sight. The land was overflowing with milk, and the warriors felt and looked their best, as they always did when there was plenty to eat and drink. Everyone was at
ease. The demands the community usually made on warriors during
the dry season when water was scarce and wells had to be dug were
now not necessary. Herds and flocks were entrusted to youths to look
after. The warriors had all the time for themselves. But my father was
so strict that even at times like these he still insisted on overworking us
in one way or another. He believed that by keeping us busy, he would
keep us out of trouble.

When I heard about the impending ceremony, I decided to remain   28
behind in the Korongoro Highlands and attend it now that the children
had been treated. I knew very well that I would have to make up a
story for my father upon my return, but I would worry about that later.

I had left my spear at home when I boarded the bus, thinking that I would be coming back that very day. I felt lighter but now regretted having left it behind; I was so used to carrying it wherever I went. In gales of laughter resulting from our continuous teasing of each other, we made our way toward a distant kraal. We walked at a leisurely pace and reveled in the breeze. As usual we talked about the women we desired, among other things.

29   The following day we were joined by a long line of colorfully dressed girls and warriors from the kraal and the neighborhood where we had spent the night, and we left the highland and headed to Ingorienito to the rolling hills on the lower slopes to attend the circumcision ceremony. From there one could see Oldopai Gorge, where my parents lived, and the Inaapi hills in the middle of the Serengeti Plain.

30   Three girls and a boy were to be initiated on the same day, an unusual occasion. Four oxen were to be slaughtered, and many people would therefore attend. As we descended, we saw the kraal where the ceremony would take place. All those people dressed in red seemed from a distance like flamingos standing in a lake. We could see lines of other guests heading to the settlements. Warriors made gallant cries of happiness known as *enkiseer.* Our line of warriors and girls responded to their cries even more gallantly.

31   In serpentine fashion, we entered the gates of the settlement. Holding spears in our left hands, we warriors walked proudly, taking small steps, swaying like palm trees, impressing our girls, who walked parallel to us in another line, and of course the spectators, who gazed at us approvingly.

32   We stopped in the center of the kraal and waited to be greeted. Women and children welcomed us. We put our hands on the children's heads, which is how children are commonly saluted. After the greetings were completed, we started dancing.

33   Our singing echoed off the kraal fence and nearby trees. Another line of warriors came up the hill and entered the compound, also singing and moving slowly toward us. Our singing grew in intensity. Both lines of warriors moved parallel to each other, and our feet pounded the ground with style. We stamped vigorously, as if to tell the next line and the spectators that we were the best.

34   The singing continued until the hot sun was overhead. We recessed and ate food already prepared for us by other warriors. Roasted meat was for those who were to eat meat, and milk for the others. By our tradition, meat and milk must not be consumed at the same time, for this would be a betrayal of the animal. It was regarded as cruel to consume a product of the animal that could be obtained while it was alive, such as milk, and meat, which was only available after the animal had been killed.

After eating we resumed singing, and I spotted a tall, beautiful *esian-*   35
kiki (young maiden) of Masiaya whose family was one of the largest and
richest in our area. She stood very erect and seemed taller than the rest.

One of her breasts could be seen just above her dress, which was   36
knotted at the shoulder. While I was supposed to dance generally to
please all the spectators, I took it upon myself to please her especially. I
stared at and flirted with her, and she and I danced in unison at times.
We complemented each other very well.

During a break, I introduced myself to the *esiankiki* and told her I   37
would like to see her after the dance. "Won't you need a warrior to escort you home later when the evening threatens?" I said. She replied,
"Perhaps, but the evening is still far away."

I waited patiently. When the dance ended, I saw her departing with   38
a group of other women her age. She gave me a sidelong glance, and I
took that to mean come later and not now. With so many others
around, I would not have been able to confer with her as I would have
liked anyway.

With another warrior, I wandered around the kraal killing time until   39
the herds returned from pasture. Before the sun dropped out of sight, we
departed. As the kraal of the *esiankiki* was in the lowlands, a place called
Enkoloa, we descended leisurely, our spears resting on our shoulders.

We arrived at the woman's kraal and found that cows were now   40
being milked. One could hear the women trying to appease the cows
by singing to them. Singing calms cows down, making it easier to milk
them. There were no warriors in the whole kraal except for the two of
us. Girls went around into warriors' houses as usual and collected milk
for us. I was so eager to go and meet my *esiankiki* that I could hardly
wait for nightfall. The warriors' girls were trying hard to be sociable,
but my mind was not with them. I found them to be childish, loud,
bothersome, and boring.

As the only warriors present, we had to keep them company and   41
sing for them, at least for a while, as required by custom. I told the
other warrior to sing while I tried to figure out how to approach my
esiankiki. Still a novice warrior, I was not experienced with women and
was in fact still afraid of them. I could flirt from a distance, of course.
But sitting down with a woman and trying to seduce her was another
matter. I had already tried twice to approach women soon after my circumcision and had failed. I got as far as the door of one woman's house
and felt my heart beating like a Congolese drum; breathing became difficult and I had to turn back. Another time I managed to get in the
house and succeeded in sitting on the bed, but then I started trembling
until the whole bed was shaking, and conversation became difficult. I
left the house and the woman, amazed and speechless, and never went
back to her again.

42   Tonight I promised myself I would be brave and would not make any silly, ridiculous moves. "I must be mature and not afraid," I kept reminding myself, as I remembered an incident involving one of my relatives when he was still very young and, like me, afraid of women. He went to a woman's house and sat on a stool for a whole hour; he was afraid to awaken her, as his heart was pounding and he was having difficulty breathing.

43   When he finally calmed down, he woke her up, and their conversation went something like this:

44   "Woman, wake up."

45   "Why should I?"

46   "To light the fire."

47   "For what?"

48   "So you can see me."

49   "I already know who you are. Why don't *you* light the fire, as you're nearer to it than me?"

50   "It's your house and it's only proper that you light it yourself."

51   "I don't feel like it."

52   "At least wake up so we can talk, as I have something to tell you."

53   "Say it."

54   "I need you."

55   "I do not need one-eyed types like yourself."

56   "One-eyed people are people too."

57   "That might be so, but they are not to my taste."

58   They continued talking for quite some time, and the more they spoke, the braver he became. He did not sleep with her that night, but later on he persisted until he won her over. I doubted whether I was as strong-willed as he, but the fact that he had met with success encouraged me. I told my warrior friend where to find me should he need me, and then I departed.

59   When I entered the house of my *esiankiki*, I called for the woman of the house, and as luck would have it, my lady responded. She was waiting for me. I felt better, and I proceeded to talk to her like a professional. After much talking back and forth, I joined her in bed.

60   The night was calm, tender, and loving, like most nights after initiation ceremonies as big as this one. There must have been a lot of courting and lovemaking.

61   Maasai women can be very hard to deal with sometimes. They can simply reject a man outright and refuse to change their minds. Some play hard to get, but in reality are testing the man to see whether he is worth their while. Once a friend of mine while still young was powerfully attracted to a woman nearly his mother's age. He put a bold move on her. At first the woman could not believe his intention, or rather was amazed by his courage. The name of the warrior was Ngengeiya, or Drizzle.

"Drizzle, what do you want?"   62
The warrior stared her right in the eye and said, "You."   63
"For what?"   64
"To make love to you."   65
"I am your mother's age."   66
"The choice was either her or you."   67

This remark took the woman by surprise. She had underestimated   68
the saying "There is no such thing as a young warrior." When you are a
warrior, you are expected to perform bravely in any situation. Your age
and size are immaterial.
"You mean you could really love me like a grownup man?"   69
"Try me, woman."   70
He moved in on her. Soon the woman started moaning with excite-   71
ment, calling out his name. "Honey Drizzle, Honey Drizzle, you *are* a
man." In a breathy, stammering voice, she said, "A real man."
Her attractiveness made Honey Drizzle ignore her relative old age.   72
The Maasai believe that if an older and a younger person have intercourse, it is the older person who stands to gain. For instance, it is believed that an older woman having an affair with a young man starts to
appear younger and healthier, while the young man grows older and
unhealthy.
The following day when the initiation rites had ended, I decided to   73
return home. I had offended my father by staying away from home
without his consent, so I prepared myself for whatever punishment he
might inflict on me. I walked home alone.

✦ Evaluating the Text

1. How is the candidate's life, reputation, and destiny dependent on the
   bravery he shows during the ceremony? What consequences would
   his family have to suffer if he were to flinch or shudder?

2. What is the function of the relentless taunting by warriors and those
   who are newly circumcised prior to the ceremony?

3. What is Tepilit's attitude toward his father? What assumptions about a
   son's responsibilities account for how Tepilit's father treats him?

4. Several Maasai customs reveal the profound symbiotic relationship
   they have with nature and the animal world. For example, what is the
   rationale behind their practice of not eating milk and meat together?
   Why is Tepilit careful not to allow the blood from his wound to spill
   onto the ground as he lies on his bed bleeding from the surgery?

5. What responsibilities does Tepilit assume and what privileges is he allowed upon successful completion of the ceremony?

✦ *Exploring Different Perspectives*

1. Compare the very different objectives that circumcision is designed to achieve among the Maasai and in Middle Eastern cultures, as described by Nawal El Saadawi.

2. How do experiences that are potentially life endangering serve as rites of passage in the accounts by Tepilit Ole Saitoti and N. Scott Momaday? (See "The Names.")

✦ *Extending Viewpoints Through Writing*

1. Every culture or society has some form of initiation that its members must undergo to become part of that society. In what way is the Maasai ritual Tepilit describes intended to deepen the bond between the community and the initiate in ways that are quite similar, allowing for cultural differences, to the Bar or Bat Mitzvah in Judaism and the confirmation ceremony in Christianity? In an essay, explore how any of these rites of passage affirm the culture, unite the candidate with his or her community, and ensure the continuation of traditions.

2. Despite obvious differences between the Maasai society and contemporary American culture, Tepilit's interactions with his friends and the opposite sex are quite typical of those of any teenage boy. Write an essay exploring these similarities.

3. If you had to choose between being initiated as a warrior into the Maasai in East Africa or into the Marine Corps, which would you choose and why? Keep in mind the great differences in the length of time over which the initiation takes place, the respective penalties for not successfully completing the rite of passage, and the privileges and responsibilities that ensue from a successful completion.

4. To what extent do the experiences a pledge in a fraternity or sorority undergoes before being admitted as a member in good standing resemble other rites of passage?

5. Can you remember your first kiss or first sexual experience? Describe your reaction.

Nawal El Saadawi

Circumcision of Girls

—————◆—————

Nawal El Saadawi is an Egyptian physician and feminist writer whose work publicizing the injustices and brutalities to which Arab women are subject is well known throughout the world. Born in the village of Kafr-tahla on the banks of the Nile, in 1931, she began her medical practice in rural areas, then in Cairo, and finally became Egypt's Director of Public Health. The publication of her first nonfiction book, Women and Sex *(1972), resulted in her dismissal from her post by Anwar Sadat, imprisonment, and censorship of her books on the status, psychology, and sexuality of women. Her works are now banned in Egypt, Saudi Arabia, and Libya. The following chapter, "Circumcision of Girls," is from* The Hidden Face of Eve: Women in the Arab World *(1980, translated and edited by Saadawi's husband, Dr. Sherif Hetata), a work depicting the hitherto unpublicized but culturally accepted procedure of female circumcision, a practice to which she herself was subjected at the age of eight.*

Egypt is an Arab republic in northeastern Africa, bordered by the Mediterranean in the north, Israel and the Red Sea to the east, the Sudan to the south, and Libya to the west. Egypt was the site of one of the earliest civilizations that developed in the Nile valley over 5,000 years ago and flourished until it became part of the Roman Empire in 30 B.C. As always, Egypt depends on the Nile River for maintaining arable lands, and its economy, although weakened in the 1980s by earlier Arab–Israeli wars, remains primarily agricultural. Under the leadership of Anwar Sadat, in 1979, Egypt became the first Arab nation to sign a peace treaty with Israel. In 1981, Sadat was assassinated by Muslim fundamentalists, and his successor, Hosni Mubarak, has faced the difficult task of dealing with the resurgence of Islamic fundamentalism while moving Egypt into a position of leadership in the Arab world. Egypt joined the United States and other nations in sending troops to Saudi Arabia after the August 1990 invasion of Kuwait by Iraq. Saadawi's analysis reveals the extent to which women's lives in the Middle East are constrained by age-old Islamic laws and customs. In October of 1993 Hosni Mubarak was sworn in for a third six-year term as president.

The practice of circumcising girls is still a common procedure in a   1
number of Arab countries such as Egypt, the Sudan, Yemen and some
of the Gulf states.

2   The importance given to virginity and an intact hymen in these societies is the reason why female circumcision still remains a very widespread practice despite a growing tendency, especially in urban Egypt,
to do away with it as something outdated and harmful. Behind circumcision lies the belief that, by removing parts of girls external genital organs, sexual desire is minimized. This permits a female who has
reached the 'dangerous age' of puberty and adolescence to protect her
virginity, and therefore her honour, with greater ease. Chastity was imposed on male attendants in the female harem by castration which
turned them into inoffensive eunuchs. Similarly female circumcision is
meant to preserve the chastity of young girls by reducing their desire
for sexual intercourse.

3   Circumcision is most often performed on female children at the age
of seven or eight (before the girl begins to get menstrual periods). On
the scene appears the *daya* or local midwife. Two women members of
the family grasp the child's thighs on either side and pull them apart to
expose the external genital organs and to prevent her from struggling—
like trussing a chicken before it is slain. A sharp razor in the hand of the
daya cuts off the clitoris.

4   During my period of service as a rural physician, I was called upon
many times to treat complications arising from this primitive operation,
which very often jeopardized the life of young girls. The ignorant *daya*
believed that effective circumcision necessitated a deep cut with the razor to ensure radical amputation of the clitoris, so that no part of the
sexually sensitive organ would remain. Severe haemorrhage was therefore a common occurrence and sometimes led to loss of life. The *dayas*
had not the slightest notion of asepsis, and inflammatory conditions as
a result of the operation were common. Above all, the lifelong psychological shock of this cruel procedure left its inprint on the personality of
the child and accompanied her into adolescence, youth and maturity.
Sexual frigidity is one of the after-effects which is accentuated by other
social and psychological factors that influence the personality and mental make-up of females in Arab societies. Girls are therefore exposed to
a whole series of misfortunes as a result of outdated notions and values
related to virginity, which still remains the fundamental criterion of a
girl's honour. In recent years, however, educated families have begun
to realize the harm that is done by the practice of female circumcision.

5   Nevertheless a majority of families still impose on young female
children the barbaric and cruel operation of circumcision. The research
that I carried out on a sample of 160 Egyptian girls and women showed
that 97.5% of uneducated families still insisted on maintaining the custom, but this percentage dropped to 66.2% among educated families.[1]

6   When I discussed the matter with these girls and women it tran-
spired that most of them had no idea of the harm done by circumcision,
and some of them even thought that it was good for one's health and

conducive to cleanliness and 'purity.' (The operation in the common language of the people is in fact called the cleansing or purifying operation.) Despite the fact that the percentage of educated women who have undergone circumcision is only 66.2%, as compared with 97.5% among uneducated women, even the former did not realize the effect that this amputation of the clitoris could have on their psychological and sexual health. The dialogue that occurred between these women and myself would run more or less as follows:

'Have you undergone circumcision?' 7

'Yes.' 8

'How old were you at the time?' 9

'I was a child, about seven or eight years old.' 10

'Do you remember the details of the operation?' 11

'Of course. How could I possibly forget?' 12

'Were you afraid?' 13

'Very afraid. I hid on top of the cupboard [in other cases she would 14 say under the bed, or in the neighbour's house], but they caught hold of me, and I felt my body tremble in their hands.'

'Did you feel any pain?' 15

'Very much so. It was like a burning flame and I screamed. My 16 mother held my head so that I could not move it, my aunt caught hold of my right arm and my grandmother took charge of my left. Two strange women whom I had not seen before tried to keep me from moving my thighs by pushing them as far apart as possible. The *daya* sat between these two women, holding a sharp razor in her hand which she used to cut off the clitoris. I was scared and suffered such great pain that I lost consciousness at the flame that seemed to sear me through and through.'

'What happened after the operation?' 17

'I had severe bodily pains, and remained in bed for several days, 18 unable to move. The pain in my external genital organs led to retention of urine. Every time I wanted to urinate the burning sensation was so unbearable that I could not bring myself to pass water. The wound continued to bleed for some time, and my mother used to change the dressing for me twice a day.'

'What did you feel on discovering that a small organ in your body 19 had been removed?'

'I did not know anything about the operation at the time, except 20 that it was very simple, and that it was done to all girls for purposes of cleanliness, purity and the preservation of a good reputation. It was said that a girl who did not undergo this operation was liable to be talked about by people, her behaviour would become bad, and she would start running after men, with the result that no one would agree to marry her when the time for marriage came. My grandmother told me that the operation had only consisted in the removal of a very small piece of flesh from between my thighs, and that the continued existence of this small piece of flesh in its place would have made me unclean and impure, and would have caused the man whom I would marry to be repelled by me.'

21   'Did you believe what was said to you?'

22   'Of course I did. I was happy the day I recovered from the effects of the operation, and felt as though I was rid of something which had to be removed, and so had become clean and pure.'

23   Those were more or less the answers that I obtained from all those interviewed, whether educated or uneducated. One of them was a medical student from Ein Shams School of Medicine. She was preparing for her final examinations and I expected her answers to be different but in fact they were almost identical to the others. We had quite a long discussion which I reproduce here as I remember it.

24   'You are going to be a medical doctor after a few weeks, so how can you believe that cutting off the clitoris from the body of a girl is a healthy procedure, or at least not harmful?'

25   'This is what I was told by everybody. All the girls in my family have been circumcised. I have studied anatomy and medicine, yet I have never heard any of the professors who taught us explain that the clitoris had any function to fulfil in the body of a woman, neither have I read anything of the kind in the books which deal with the medical subjects I am studying.'

26   'That is true. To this day medical books do not consider the science of sex as a subject which they should deal with. The organs of a woman worthy of attention are considered to be only those directly related to reproduction, namely the vagina, the uterus and the ovaries. The clitoris, however, is an organ neglected by medicine, just as it is ignored and disdained by society.'

27   'I remember a student asking the professor one day about the clitoris. The professor went red in the face and answered him curtly, saying that no one was going to ask him about this part of the female body during examinations, since it was of no importance.'

28   My studies led me to try and find out the effect of circumcision on the girls and women who had been made to undergo it, and to understand what results it had on the psychological and sexual life. The majority of the normal cases I interviewed answered that the operation had no effect on them. To me it was clear that in the face of such questions they were much more ashamed and intimidated than the neurotic cases were. But I did not allow myself to be satisfied with these answers, and would go on to question them closely about their sexual life both before and after the circumcision was done. Once again I will try to reproduce the dialogue that usually occurred.

29   'Did you experience any change of feeling or of sexual desire after the operation?'

30   'I was a child and therefore did not feel anything.'

'Did you not experience any sexual desire when you were a child?' 31

'No, never. Do children experience sexual desire?' 32

'Children feel pleasure when they touch their sexual organs, and 33
some form of sexual play occurs between them, for example, during the
game of bride and bridegroom usually practised under the bed. Have
you never played this game with your friends when still a child?'

At these words the young girl or woman would blush, and her 34
eyes would probably refuse to meet mine, in an attempt to hide her
confusion. But after the conversation had gone on for some time, and
an atmosphere of mutual confidence and understanding had been established, she would begin to recount her childhood memories. She
would often refer to the pleasure she had felt when a man of the family
permitted himself certain sexual caresses. Sometimes these caresses
would be proffered by the domestic servant, the house porter, the private teacher or the neighbour's son. A college student told me that her
brother had been wont to caress her sexual organs and that she used to
experience acute enjoyment. However after undergoing circumcision
she no longer had the same sensation of pleasure. A married woman
admitted that during intercourse with her husband she had never experienced the slightest sexual enjoyment, and that her last memories of
any form of pleasurable sensation went back twenty years, to the age of
six, before she had undergone circumcision. A young girl told me that
she had been accustomed to practise masturbation, but had given it up
completely after removal of the clitoris at the age of ten.

The further our conversations went, and the more I delved into 35
their lives, the more readily they opened themselves up to me and uncovered the secrets of childhood and adolescence, perhaps almost forgotten by them or only vaguely realized.

Being both a woman and a medical doctor I was able to obtain con- 36
fessions from these women and girls which it would be almost impossible, except in very rare cases, for a man to obtain. For the Egyptian
woman, accustomed as she is to a very rigid and severe upbringing
built on a complete denial of any sexual life before marriage, adamantly refuses to admit that she has ever known, or experienced, anything related to sex before the first touches of her husband. She is
therefore ashamed to speak about such things with any man, even the
doctor who is treating her.

My discussions with some of the psychiatrists who had treated a 37
number of the young girls and women in my sample, led me to conclude
that there were many aspects of the life of these neurotic patients that remained unknown to them. This was due either to the fact that the psychiatrist himself had not made the necessary effort to penetrate deeply
into the life of the woman he was treating, or to the tendency of the patient herself not to divulge those things which her upbringing made
her consider matters not to be discussed freely, especially with a man.

38   In fact the long and varied interchanges I had over the years with the majority of practising psychiatrists in Egypt, my close association with a large number of my medical colleagues during the long periods I spent working in health centres and general or specialized hospitals and, finally, the four years I spent as a member of the National Board of the Syndicate of Medical Professions, have all led me to the firm conclusion that the medical profession in our society is still incapable of understanding the fundamental problems with which sick people are burdened, whether they be men or women, but especially if they are women. For the medical profession, like any other profession in society, is governed by the political, social and moral values which predominate, and like other professions is one of the institutions which is utilized more often than not to protect these values and perpetuate them.

39   Men represent the vast majority in the medical profession, as in most professions. But apart from this, the mentality of women doctors differs little, if at all, from that of the men, and I have known quite a number of them who were even more rigid and backward in outlook than their male colleagues.

40   A rigid and backward attitude towards most problems, and in particular towards women and sex, predominates in the medical profession, and particularly within the precincts of the medical colleges in the Universities.

41   Before undertaking my research study on 'Women and Neurosis' at Ein Shams University, I had made a previous attempt to start it at the Kasr El Eini Medical College in the University of Cairo, but had been obliged to give up as a result of the numerous problems I was made to confront. The most important obstacle of all was the overpowering traditionalist mentality that characterized the professors responsible for my research work, and to whom the word 'sex' could only be equated to the word 'shame.' 'Respectable research' therefore could not possibly have sex as its subject, and should under no circumstances think of penetrating into areas even remotely related to it. One of my medical colleagues in the Research Committee advised me not to refer at all to the question of sex in the title of my research paper, when I found myself obliged to shift to Ein Shams University. He warned me that any such reference would most probably lead to fundamental objections which would jeopardize my chances of going ahead with it. I had initially chosen to define my subject as 'Problems that confront the sexual life of modern Egyptian women,' but after prolonged negotiations I was prevailed to delete the word 'sexual' and replace it by 'psychological.' Only thus was it possible to circumvent the sensitivities of the professors at the Ein Shams Medical School and obtain their consent to go ahead with the research.

After I observed the very high percentages of women and girls 42 who had been obliged to undergo circumcision, or who had been exposed to different forms of sexual violation or assault in their childhood, I started to look for research undertaken in these two areas, either in the medical colleges or in research institutes, but in vain. Hardly a single medical doctor or researcher had ventured to do any work on these subjects, in view of the sensitive nature of the issues involved. This can also be explained by the fact that most of the research carried out in such institutions is of a formal and superficial nature, since its sole aim is to obtain a degree or promotion. The path of safety is therefore the one to choose, and safety means to avoid carefully all subjects of controversy. No one is therefore prepared to face difficulties with the responsible academic and scientific authorities, or to engage in any form of struggle against them, or their ideas. Nor is anyone prepared to face up to those who lay down the norms of virtue, morals and religious behaviour in society. All the established leaderships in the area related to such matters suffer from a pronounced allergy to the word 'sex,' and any of its implications, especially if it happens to be linked to the word 'woman.'

Nevertheless I was fortunate enough to discover a small number of 43 medical doctors who had the courage to be different, and therefore to examine some of the problems related to the sexual life of women. I would like to cite, as one of the rare examples, the only research study carried out on the question of female circumcision in Egypt and its harmful effects. This was the joint effort of Dr. Mahmoud Koraim and Dr. Rushdi Ammar, both from Ein Shams Medical College, and which was published in 1965. It is composed of two parts, the first of which was printed under the title *Female Circumcision and Sexual Desire*,[2] and the second, under the title *Complications of Female Circumcision*.[3] The conclusions arrived at as a result of this research study, which covered 651 women circumcised during childhood, may be summarized as follows:

1. Circumcision is an operation with harmful effects on the health 44 of women, and is the cause of sexual shock to young girls. It reduces the capacity of a woman to reach the peak of her sexual pleasure (i.e., orgasm) and has a definite though lesser effect in reducing sexual desire.

2. Education helps to limit the extent to which female circumcision 45 is practised, since educated parents have an increasing tendency to refuse the operation for their daughters. On the other hand, uneducated families still go in for female circumcision in submission to prevailing traditions, or in the belief that removal of the clitoris reduces the sexual desire of the girl, and therefore helps to preserve her virginity and chastity after marriage.

46   3. There is no truth whatsoever in the idea that female circumcision helps in reducing the incidence of cancerous disease of the external genital organs.

47   4. Female circumcision in all its forms and degrees, and in particular the fourth degree known as Pharaonic or Sudanese excision, is accompanied by immediate or delayed complications such as inflammations, haemorrhage, disturbances in the urinary passages, cysts or swellings that can obstruct the urinary flow or the vaginal opening.

48   5. Masturbation in circumcised girls is less frequent than was observed by Kinsey in girls who have not undergone this operation.

49   I was able to exchange views with Dr. Mahmoud Koraim during several meetings in Cairo. I learnt from him that he had faced numerous difficulties while undertaking his research, and was the target of bitter criticism from some of his colleagues and from religious leaders who considered themselves the divinely appointed protectors of morality, and therefore required to shield society from such impious undertakings, which constituted a threat to established values and moral codes.

50   The findings of my research study coincided with some of the conclusions arrived at by my two colleagues on a number of points. There is no longer any doubt that circumcision is the source of sexual and psychological shock in the life of the girl, and leads to a varying degree of sexual frigidity according to the woman and her circumstances. Education helps parents realize that this operation is not beneficial, and should be avoided, but I have found that the traditional education given in our schools and universities, whose aim is simply some certificate, or degree, rather than instilling useful knowledge and culture, is not very effective in combating the long-standing, and established traditions that govern Egyptian society, and in particular those related to sex, virginity in girls, and chastity in women. These areas are strongly linked to moral and religious values that have dominated and operated in our society for hundreds of years.

51   Since circumcision of females aims primarily at ensuring virginity before marriage, and chastity throughout, it is not to be expected that its practice will disappear easily from Egyptian society or within a short period of time. A growing number of educated families are, however, beginning to realize the harm that is done to females by this custom, and are therefore seeking to protect their daughters from being among its victims. Parallel to these changes, the operation itself is no longer performed in the old primitive way, and the more radical degrees approaching, or involving, excision are dying out more rapidly. Nowadays, even in Upper Egypt and the Sudan, the operation is limited to the total, or more commonly the partial, amputation of the clito-

ris. Nevertheless, while undertaking my research, I was surprised to discover, contrary to what I had previously thought, that even in educated urban families over 50% still consider circumcision as essential to ensure female virginity and chastity.

Many people think that female circumcision only started with the advent of Islam. But as a matter of fact it was well known and widespread in some areas of the world before the Islamic era, including in the Arab peninsula. Mahomet the Prophet tried to oppose this custom since he considered it harmful to the sexual health of the woman. In one of his sayings the advice reported as having been given by him to Om Attiah, a woman who did tattooings and circumcision, runs as follows: 'If you circumcise, take only a small part and refrain from cutting most of the clitoris off . . . The woman will have a bright and happy face, and is more welcome to her husband, if her pleasure is complete.'[4]

This means that the circumcision of girls was not originally an Islamic custom, and was not related to monotheistic religions, but was practised in societies with widely varying religious backgrounds, in countries of the East and the West, and among peoples who believed in Christianity, or in Islam, or were atheistic . . . Circumcision was known in Europe as late as the 19th century, as well as in countries like Egypt, the Sudan, Somaliland, Ethiopia, Kenya, Tanzania, Ghana, Guinea and Nigeria. It was also practised in many Asian countries such as Sri Lanka and Indonesia, and in parts of Latin America. It is recorded as going back far into the past under the Pharaonic Kingdoms of Ancient Egypt, and Herodotus mentioned the existence of female circumcision seven hundred years before Christ was born. This is why the operation as practised in the Sudan is called 'Pharaonic excision.'

For many years I tried in vain to find relevant sociological or anthropological studies that would throw some light on the reasons why such a brutal operation is practised on females. However I did discover other practices related to girls and female children which were even more savage. One of them was burying female children alive almost immediately after they were born, or even at a later stage. Other examples are the chastity belt, or closing the aperture of the external genital organs with steel pins and a special iron lock.[5] This last procedure is extremely primitive and very much akin to Sudanese circumcision where the clitoris, external lips and internal lips are completely excised, and the orifice of the genital organs closed with a flap of sheep's intestines leaving only a very small opening barely sufficient to let the tip of the finger in, so that the menstrual and urinary flows are not held back. This opening is slit at the time of marriage and widened to allow penetration of the male sexual organ. It is widened again when a child is born and then narrowed down once more. Complete closure of the aperture is also done on a woman who is divorced, so that she literally

52

53

54

becomes a virgin once more and can have no sexual intercourse except in the eventuality of marriage, in which case the opening is restored.

55   In the face of all these strange and complicated procedures aimed at preventing sexual intercourse in women except if controlled by the husband, it is natural that we should ask ourselves why women, in particular, were subjected to such torture and cruel suppression. There seems to be no doubt that society, as represented by its dominant classes and male structure, realized at a very early stage that sexual desire in the female is very powerful, and that women, unless controlled and subjugated by all sorts of measures, will not submit themselves to the moral, social, legal and religious constraints with which they have been surrounded, and in particular the constraints related to monogamy. The patriarchal system, which came into being when society had reached a certain stage of development and which necessitated the imposition of one husband on the woman whereas a man was left free to have several wives, would never have been possible, or have been maintained to this day, without the whole range of cruel and ingenious devices that were used to keep her sexuality in check and limit her sexual relations to only one man, who had to be her husband. This is the reason for the implacable enmity shown by society towards female sexuality, and the weapons used to resist and subjugate the turbulent force inherent in it. The slightest leniency in facing this 'potential danger' meant that woman would break out of the prison bars to which marriage had confined her, and step over the steely limits of a monogamous relationship to a forbidden intimacy with another man, which would inevitably lead to confusion in succession and inheritance, since there was no guarantee that a strange man's child would not step into the waiting line of descendants. Confusion between the children of the legitimate husband and the outsider lover would mean the unavoidable collapse of the patriarchal family built around the name of the father alone.

56   History shows us clearly that the father was keen on knowing who his real children were, solely for the purpose of handing down his landed property to them. The patriarchal family, therefore, came into existence mainly for economic reasons. It was necessary for society simultaneously to build up a system of moral and religious values, as well as a legal system capable of protecting and maintaining these economic interests. In the final analysis we can safely say that female circumcision, the chastity belt and other savage practices applied to women are basically the result of the economic interests that govern society. The continued existence of such practices in our society today signifies that these economic interests are still operative. The thousands of *dayas*, nurses, paramedical staff and doctors, who make money out of female circumcision, naturally resist any change in these values and practices which are a source of gain to them. In the Sudan there is a veritable army of *dayas* who earn a livelihood out of the series of opera-

tions performed on women, either to excise their external genital organs, or to alternately narrow and widen the outer aperture according to whether the woman is marrying, divorcing, remarrying, having a child or recovering from labour.[6]

Economic factors and, concomitantly, political factors are the basis upon which such customs as female circumcision have grown up. It is important to understand the facts as they really are, the reasons that lie behind them. Many are the people who are not able to distinguish between political and religious factors, or who conceal economic and political motives behind religious arguments in an attempt to hide the real forces that lie at the basis of what happens in society and in history. It has very often been proclaimed that Islam is at the root of female circumcision, and is also responsible for the under-privileged and backward situation of women in Egypt and the Arab countries. Such a contention is not true. If we study Christianity it is easy to see that this religion is much more rigid and orthodox where women are concerned than Islam. Nevertheless, many countries were able to progress rapidly despite the preponderance of Christianity as a religion. This progress was social, economic, scientific and also affected the life and position of women in society.

That is why I firmly believe that the reasons for the lower status of women in our societies, and the lack of opportunities for progress afforded to them, are not due to Islam, but rather to certain economic and political forces, namely those of foreign imperialism operating mainly from the outside, and of the reactionary classes operating from the inside. These two forces cooperate closely and are making a concerted attempt to misinterpret religion and to utilize it as an instrument of fear, oppression and exploitation.

Religion, if authentic in the principles it stands for, aims at truth, equality, justice, love and a healthy wholesome life for all people, whether men or women. There can be no true religion that aims at disease, mutilation of the bodies of female children, and amputation of an essential part of their reproductive organs.

If religion comes from God, how can it order man to cut off an organ created by Him as long as that organ is not diseased or deformed? God does not create the organs of the body haphazardly without a plan. It is not possible that He should have created the clitoris in woman's body only in order that it be cut off at an early stage in life. This is a contradiction into which neither true religion nor the Creator could possibly fall. If God has created the clitoris as a sexually sensitive organ, whose sole function seems to be the procurement of sexual pleasure for women, it follows that He also considers such pleasure for women as normal and legitimate, and therefore as an integral part of mental health. The psychic and mental health of women cannot be complete if they do not experience sexual pleasure.

61   There are still a large number of fathers and mothers who are afraid of leaving the clitoris intact in the bodies of their daughters. Many a time they have said to me that circumcision is a safeguard against the mistakes and deviations into which a girl may be led. This way of thinking is wrong and even dangerous because what protects a boy or a girl from making mistakes is not the removal of a small piece of flesh from the body, but consciousness and understanding of the problems we face, and a worthwhile aim in life, an aim which gives it meaning and for whose attainment we exert our mind and energies. The higher the level of consciousness to which we attain, the closer our aims draw to human motives and values, and the greater our desire to improve life and its quality, rather than to indulge ourselves in the mere satisfaction of our senses and the experience of pleasure, even though these are an essential part of existence. The most liberated and free of girls, in the true sense of liberation, are the least preoccupied with sexual questions, since these no longer represent a problem. On the contrary, a free mind finds room for numerous interests and the many rich experiences of a cultured life. Girls that suffer sexual suppression, however, are greatly preoccupied with men and sex. And it is a common observation that an intelligent and cultured woman is much less engrossed in matters related to sex and to men than is the case with ordinary women, who have not got much with which to fill their lives. Yet at the same time such a woman takes much more initiative to ensure that she will enjoy sex and experience pleasure, and acts with a greater degree of boldness than others. Once sexual satisfaction is attained, she is able to turn herself fully to other important aspects of life.

62   In the life of liberated and intelligent women, sex does not occupy a disproportionate position, but rather tends to maintain itself within normal limits. In contrast, ignorance, suppression, fear and all sorts of limitations exaggerate the role of sex in the life of girls and women, and cause it to swell out of all proportion and to end up by occupying the whole, or almost the whole, of their lives.

Translated and edited by Dr. Sherif Hetata

REFERENCES

1. This research study was carried out in the years 1973 and 1974 in the School of Medicine, Ein Shams University, under the title: *Women and Neurosis.*
2. *Female Circumcision and Sexual Desire,* Mahmoud Koraim and Rushdi Ammar (Ein Shams University Press, Cairo, 1965).
3. *Complications of Female Circumcision,* the same authors (Cairo, 1965).
4. See *Dawlat El Nissa'a,* Abdel Rahman El Barkouky, first edition (Renaissance Bookshop, Cairo, 1945).
5. Desmond Morris, *The Naked Ape* (Corgi, 1967), p. 76.
6. Rose Oldfield, 'Female genital mutilation, fertility control, women's roles, and patrilineage in modern Sudan,' *American Ethnologist,* Vol. II, No. 4, November 1975.

✦ Evaluating the Text

1. How does the fact that El Saadawi herself is a physician who has treated girls suffering the medical complications of circumcision enhance the credibility of her analysis?

2. Why does El Saadawi find it so distressing that, even among the educated (of whom two thirds have undergone the operation), few women have given up the cultural programing that female circumcision is a purifying or cleansing procedure?

3. What are the psychological and economic objectives of female circumcision? How, in El Saadawi's view, does it function as one of the main methods by which the countries of Sudan, Yemen, Saudi Arabia, and Libya keep their social structure intact and ensure the transmission of property from one generation to the next?

4. Do you believe that the 160 interviews she conducted would be a sample sufficiently large to form the basis for generalizations? Why was the interview with the medical student particularly significant? What harmful psychological effects of female circumcision did El Saadawi discover from the interviews she conducted?

5. What prevailing beliefs did Koraim and Ammar's study about the supposed medical efficacy of circumcision disclose to be baseless? How does El Saadawi use the results of their study in her analysis?

6. How does El Saadawi's reference to Mahomet's comment support her claim that female circumcision was not originally an Islamic custom? How is this phase of her argument intended to undercut claims by religious leaders that they are simply upholding Islamic religious values?

✦ Exploring Different Perspectives

1. How is circumcision intended to physically and psychologically restrict girls in Middle Eastern cultures described by El Saadawi and to empower and confer authority onto boys among the Maasai in East Africa (see Tepilit Ole Saitoti's "The Initiation of a Maasai Warrior")? Discuss the different culturally defined values attached to circumcision.

2. How are the cultural values attached to circumcision of girls in Maasai culture (see Tepilit Ole Saitoti's "The Initiation of a Maasai Warrior") similar to, yet different from, the corresponding procedure performed on girls in Middle Eastern countries? How would you distinguish between the underlying social objectives of both cultures?

✦ *Extending Viewpoints Through Writing*

1. Compare and contrast the value placed on female virginity in the cultures El Saadawi is describing with contemporary American society. What factors do you think explain the differences, and how do these differences reflect the different ways women are viewed in these two cultures?

2. Is there any outdated custom or practice that you would like to eliminate in contemporary society? Formulate your response as an argument, making sure that you cite evidence and give cogent reasons to support your views. You should also attempt to anticipate the objections opponents to your views might raise and think of responses to each of these possible objections.

3. Drawing on El Saadawi's essay, explore the relationship between law and custom and women's freedom of choice. How is the societal practice of female circumcision intended to take the power of choice out of the woman's hands as to what she will do with her body? Discuss possible similarities between this practice and issues arising from the continuing abortion debate in America.

Hanan al-Shaykh

The Persian Carpet

◆

Hanan al-Shaykh was born in 1945 in Lebanon and was raised in a tradi-tional Shiite Moslem family. She began her studies at the American Col-lege for Girls in Cairo in 1963 and four years later returned to Beirut where she worked as a journalist and began writing short stories and nov-els. Originally written in Arabic, al-Shaykh's works have been published in Lebanon and have been acclaimed for her capacity to realistically create situations in which her protagonists, often women, gain a new perspective despite the cultural pressures forced upon them. Two of her novels, The Story of Zahra *(1986) and* Women of Sand and Myrrh *(1989), have been translated into English. "The Persian Carpet," translated by Denys Johnson-Davies (1983) from* Arabic Short Stories, *closely observes the behavior and emotions of a girl who is forced to realize that the circum-stances leading to her parents getting divorced were very different from what she had believed as a child.*

When Maryam had finished plaiting my hair into two pigtails, she   1
put her finger to her mouth and licked it, then passed it over my eye-brows, moaning: "Ah, what eyebrows you have—they're all over the place!" She turned quickly to my sister and said: "Go and see if your fa-ther's still praying." Before I knew it my sister had returned and was whispering "He's still at it," and she stretched out her hands and raised them skywards in imitation of him. I didn't laugh as usual, nor did Maryam; instead, she took up the scarf from the chair, put it over her hair and tied it hurriedly at the neck. Then, opening the wardrobe care-fully, she took out her handbag, placed it under her arm and stretched out her hands to us. I grasped one and my sister the other. We under-stood that we should, like her, proceed on tiptoe, holding our breath as we made our way out through the open front door. As we went down the steps, we turned back towards the door, then towards the window. Reaching the last step, we began to run, only stopping when the lane had disappeared out of sight and we had crossed the road and Maryam had stopped a taxi.

Our behaviour was induced by fear, for today we would be seeing   2
my mother for the first time since her separation by divorce from my father. He had sworn he would not let her see us, for, only hours after

*(For information on Lebanon, see p. 67.)

the divorce, the news had spread that she was going to marry a man she had been in love with before her family had forced her into marrying my father.

3   My heart was pounding. This was not from fear or from running but was due to anxiety and a feeling of embarrassment about the meeting that lay ahead. Though in control of myself and my shyness, I knew that I would be incapable—however much I tried—of showing my emotions, even to my mother; I would be unable to throw myself into her arms and smother her with kisses and clasp her head as my sister would do with such spontaneity. I had thought long and hard about this ever since Maryam had whispered in my ear—and in my sister's— that my mother had come from the south and that we were to visit her secretly the following day. I began to imagine that I would make myself act exactly as my sister did, that I would stand behind her and imitate her blindly. Yet I know myself: I have committed myself to myself by heart. However much I tried to force myself, however much I thought in advance about what I should and shouldn't do, once I was actually faced by the situation and was standing looking down at the floor, my forehead puckered into an even deeper frown, I would find I had forgotten what I had resolved to do. Even then, though, I would not give up hope but would implore my mouth to break into a smile; it would none the less be to no avail.

4   When the taxi came to a stop at the entrance to a house, where two lions stood on columns of red sandstone, I was filled with delight and immediately forgot my apprehension. I was overcome with happiness at the thought that my mother was living in a house where two lions stood at the entrance. I heard my sister imitate the roar of a lion and I turned to her in envy. I saw her stretching up her hands in an attempt to clutch the lions. I thought to myself: She's always uncomplicated and jolly, her gaiety never leaves her, even at the most critical moments— and here she was, not a bit worried about this meeting.

5   But when my mother opened the door and I saw her, I found myself unable to wait and rushed forward in front of my sister and threw myself into her arms. I had closed my eyes and all the joints of my body had grown numb after having been unable to be at rest for so long. I took in the unchanged smell of her hair, and I discovered for the first time how much I had missed her and wished that she would come back and live with us, despite the tender care shown to us by my father and Maryam. I couldn't rid my mind of that smile of hers when my father agreed to divorce her, after the religious sheikh had intervened following her threats to pour kerosene over her body and set fire to herself if my father wouldn't divorce her. All my senses were numbed by that smell of her, so well preserved in my memory. I realized how much I had missed her, despite the fact that after she'd hurried off behind her brother to get into the car, having kissed us and started to cry,

we had continued with the games we were playing in the lane outside our house. As night came, and for the first time in a long while we did not hear her squabbling with my father, peace and quiet descended upon the house—except that is for the weeping of Maryam, who was related to my father and had been living with us in the house ever since I was born.

Smiling, my mother moved me away from her so that she could   6
hug and kiss my sister, and hug Maryam again, who had begun to cry. I heard my mother, who was in tears, say to her "Thank you," and she wiped her tears with her sleeve and looked me and my sister up and down, saying: "God keep them safe, how they've sprung up!" She put both arms round me, while my sister buried her head in my mother's waist, and we all began to laugh when we found that it was difficult for us to walk like that. Reaching the inner room, I was convinced her new husband was inside because my mother said, sniffing: "Mahmoud loves you very much and he would like it if your father would give you to me so that you can live with us and become his children too." My sister laughed and answered: "Like that we'd have two fathers." I was still in a benumbed state, my hand placed over my mother's arm, proud at the way I was behaving, at having been able without any effort to be liberated from myself, from my shackled hands, from the prison of my shyness, as I recalled to mind the picture of my meeting with my mother, how I had spontaneously thrown myself at her, something I had thought wholly impossible, and my kissing her so hard I had closed my eyes.

Her husband was not there. As I stared down at the floor I froze. In   7
confusion I looked at the Persian carpet spread on the floor, then gave my mother a long look. Not understanding the significance of my look, she turned and opened a cupboard from which she threw me an embroidered blouse, and moving across to a drawer in the dressing-table, she took out an ivory comb with red hearts painted on it and gave it to my sister. I stared down at the Persian carpet, trembling with burning rage. Again I looked at my mother and she interpreted my gaze as being one of tender longing, so she put her arms round me, saying: "You must come every other day, you must spend the whole of Friday at my place." I remained motionless, wishing that I could remove her arms from around me and sink my teeth into that white forearm. I wished that the moment of meeting could be undone and re-enacted, that she could again open the door and I could stand there—as I should have done—with my eyes staring down at the floor and my forehead in a frown.

The lines and colours of the Persian carpet were imprinted on my   8
memory. I used to lie on it as I did my lessons; I'd be so close to it that I'd gaze at its pattern and find it looking like slices of red water-melon repeated over and over again. But when I sat down on the couch, I

would see that each slice of melon had changed into a comb with thin teeth. The cluster of flowers surrounding its four sides were purple-coloured. At the beginning of summer my mother would put moth-balls on it and on the other ordinary carpets and would roll them up and place them on top of the cupboard. The room would look stark and depressing until autumn came, when she would take them up to the roof and spread them out. She would gather up the mothballs, most of which had dissolved from the summer's heat and humidity, then, having brushed them with a small broom, she'd leave them there. In the evening she'd bring them down and lay them out where they belonged. I would be filled with happiness as their bright colours once again brought the room back to life. This particular carpet, though, had disappeared several months before my mother was divorced. It had been spread out on the roof in the sun and in the afternoon my mother had gone up to get it and hadn't found it. She had called my father and for the first time I had seen his face flushed with anger. When they came down from the roof, my mother was in a state of fury and bewilderment. She got in touch with the neighbours, all of whom swore they hadn't seen it. Suddenly my mother exclaimed: "Ilya!" Everyone stood speechless: not a word from my father or from my sister or from our neighbours Umm Fouad and Abu Salman. I found myself crying out: "Ilya? Don't say such a thing, it's not possible."

9   Ilya was an almost blind man who used to go round the houses of the quarter repairing cane chairs. When it came to our turn, I would see him, on my arrival back from school, seated on the stone bench outside the house with piles of straw in front of him and his red hair glinting in the sunlight. He would deftly take up the strands of straw and, like fishes, they'd slip through the mesh. I would watch him as he coiled them round with great dexterity, then bring them out again until he had formed a circle of straw for the seat of the chair, just like the one that had been there before. Everything was so even and precise: it was as though his hands were a machine and I would be amazed at the speed and nimbleness of his fingers. Sitting as he did with his head lowered, it looked as though he were using his eyes. I once doubted that he could see more than vague shapes in front of him, so I squatted down and looked into his rosy-red face and was able to see his half-closed eyes behind his glasses. They had in them a white line that pricked at my heart and sent me hurrying off to the kitchen, where I found a bag of dates on the table, and I heaped some on a plate and gave them to Ilya.

10   I continued to stare at the carpet as the picture of Ilya, red of face and hair, appeared to me. I was made aware of his hand as he walked up the stairs on his own; of him sitting on his chair, of his bargaining over the price for his work, of how he ate and knew that he had finished everything on the plate, of his drinking from the pitcher, with the

water flowing easily down his throat. Once at midday, having been taught by my father that before entering a Muslim house he should say "Allah" before knocking at the door and entering, as a warning to my mother in case she were unveiled, my mother rushed at him and asked him about the carpet. He made no reply, merely making a sort of sobbing noise. As he walked off, he almost bumped into the table and, for the first time, tripped. I went up to him and took him by the hand. He knew me by the touch of my hand, because he said to me in a half-whisper: "Never mind, child." Then he turned round to leave. As he bent over to put on his shoes, I thought I saw tears on his cheeks. My father didn't let him leave before saying to him: "Ilya, God will forgive you if you tell the truth." But Ilya walked off, steadying himself against the railings. He took an unusually long time as he felt his way down the stairs. Then he disappeared from sight and we never saw him again.

✦ Evaluating the Text

1. What circumstances have made it necessary for the protagonist and her sister to visit their mother in secret?

2. What details suggest how much it means to her to see her mother again? Why is her reaction on first seeing her mother especially poignant and ironic in view of what she discovers subsequently?

3. Why does seeing the Persian carpet cause the young girl to experience such a dramatic change in attitude toward her mother? How does seeing what Ilya, the blind man, meant to her enable the reader to understand her feelings of anger?

✦ Exploring Different Perspectives

1. Contrast the relationship Christy Brown has with his mother in "The Letter 'A'" with the one the young girl has with hers in "The Persian Carpet."

2. Discuss the consequences of the betrayal of trust that the young girls experience in "The Persian Carpet" and in Nawal El Saadawi's "Circumcision of Girls."

✦ Extending Viewpoints Through Writing

1. Did you ever experience a moment of disillusionment with an adult member of your family that represented a turning point in your relationship? Describe your experience.

2. Write about one of your grandparents or parents through an object you connect with him or her. Under what circumstances did you first come across this object? What associations connect this object with your parent or grandparent?

3. Discuss a belief you once held that you no longer hold. What evidence led you to hold the original belief? Was it something you were told, read, or personally experienced? What new experiences raised doubts about this belief? How did you change your attitude in response to these new experiences? What actions have you taken which you would not have taken previously that reflect this changed attitude or revised belief?

N. Scott Momaday

The Names

----◆----

N. Scott Momaday was born in Lawton, Oklahoma, in 1934 and attended Augusta Military Academy. He graduated from the University of New Mexico in 1958 and earned a master's degree in 1960 and a Ph.D. in 1963 from Stanford University. He has been a professor of English at Stanford (1973–82) and is currently professor of English and comparative literature at the University of Arizona in Tucson. Momaday's poetry and prose reflect his Kiowa Indian heritage. He was awarded the Pulitzer Prize for his novel House Made of Dawn *(1968). His next work,* The Way to Rainy Mountain *(1969), presented an imaginative blending of myth, history, and personal recollection. "The Names" is drawn from* The Names: A Memoir *(1976) and focuses on the decisive moment when Momaday left his childhood behind before being sent to military school.*

The Kiowa are North American Indians of the plains. After being forced from the Black Hills in South Dakota by the Cheyenne and the Sioux, they joined the Commanche in raiding parties as far south as Mexico. In the nineteenth century, they actively opposed white settlers until 1874, when the U.S. Army was brought in. Traditionally a nomadic tribe, the largest group of Kiowa (about four thousand) lives in Oklahoma today. The language of the Kiowa is thought to derive from that spoken by the ancient Aztecs.

There was at Jemez a climate of the mind in which we, my parents and I, realized ourselves, understood who we were, not perfectly, it may be, but well enough. It was not our native world, but we appropriated it, as it were, to ourselves; we invested much of our lives in it, and in the end it was the remembered place of our hopes, our dreams, and our deep love.

My father looked after the endless paper work that came down from the many levels of the Bureau of Indian Affairs. In innumerable ways he worked with the people of the village and was their principal contact with the Government of the United States. When a boy or girl wanted to apply for admission to the Santa Fe Indian School or the Albuquerque Indian School, or when a man wanted to find work, or a woman to use the telephone to talk to her daughter in California, it was to my father that the petition was made. But first of all he was the man of the family. It was he who got up before daylight and went out to get wood and coal for the fires on winter mornings; it was he who dealt with the emergencies, great and small, of those years: and it was he who taught me such responsibilities as I learned then. One of these was to myself, and it was to dream. On winter evenings before the fire, or on summer nights on the porch, our home of Jemez was a place to dream, and my father dreamed much of his youth. He told me the stories of the coming-out people, of Mammedaty and of Guipagho, of Saynday, who wandered around and around. And very softly, as to himself, he sang the old Kiowa songs. And in all he went on with his real work, the making of paintings. He saw wonderful things, and he painted them well.

3   My mother has been the inspiration of many people. Certainly she has been mine, and certainly she was mine at Jemez, when inspiration was the nourishment I needed most. I was at that age in which a boy flounders. I had not much sense of where I must go or of what I must do and be in my life, and there were for me moments of great, growing urgency, in which I felt that I was imprisoned in the narrow quarters of my time and place. I wanted, needed to conceive of what my destiny might be, and my mother allowed me to believe that it might be worthwhile. We were so close, she and I, when I was growing up that even now I cannot express the feelings between us. I have great faith in words, but in this there are no words at last; there is only a kind of perfect silence—the stillness of a late autumn afternoon in the village and the valley—in which I listen for the sound of her voice. In a moment she will speak to me; she will speak my name.

4   One day my mother burned her hand. In a way it was my fault, for I had got in her way when she was carrying a hot pan to the table. It was a strange moment. She made a little cry, and I looked to see what was the matter. I stepped out of the way at once, but her hand was already burned. My mother said nothing about it—that was what seemed strange to me—but I had seen the pain in her face.

5   Many times she called me to the kitchen window to see something of interest—horses running on the road, a hen with new chicks in the Tosa's garden, a storm gathering in San Diego Canyon, a sunset. At night we talked about innumerable things at the kitchen table, the innumerable things of our world and of our time. We laughed often together, and we saw eye to eye on the larger issues of our lives. The words we had were the right ones; we were easy and right with each other, as it happened, natural, full of love and trust. "Look," one of us would say to the other, "here is something new, something that we have not seen together." And we would simply take delight in it.

6   In the seasons and among the people of the valley I was content. My spirit was quiet there. The silence was old, immediate, and pervasive, and there was great good in it. The wind of the canyons drew it out; the voices of the village carried and were lost in it. Much was made of the silence; much of the summer and winter was made of it.

At Jemez I came to the end of my childhood. There were no schools within easy reach. I had to go nearly thirty miles to school at Bernalillo, and one year I lived away in Albuquerque. My mother and father wanted me to have the benefit of a sound preparation for college, and so we read through many high school catalogues. After long deliberation we decided that I should spend my last year of high school at a military academy in Virginia.   7

The day before I was to leave I went walking across the river to the red mesa, where many times before I had gone to be alone with my thoughts. And I had climbed several times to the top of the mesa and looked among the old ruins there for pottery. This time I chose to climb the north end, perhaps because I had not gone that way before and wanted to see what it was. It was a difficult climb, and when I got to the top I was spent. I lingered among the ruins for more than an hour, I judge, waiting for my strength to return. From there I could see the whole valley below, the fields, the river, and the village. It was all very beautiful, and the sight of it filled me with longing.   8

I looked for an easier way to come down, and at length I found a broad, smooth runway of rock, a shallow groove winding out like a stream. It appeared to be safe enough, and I started to follow it. There were steps along the way, a stairway, in effect. But the steps became deeper and deeper, and at last I had to drop down the length of my body and more. Still it seemed convenient to follow in the groove of rock. I was more than halfway down when I came upon a deep, funnel-shaped formation in my path. And there I had to make a decision. The slope on either side was extremely steep and forbidding. And yet I thought that I could work my way down on either side. The formation at my feet was something else. It was perhaps ten or twelve feet deep, wide at the top and narrow at the bottom, where there appeared to be a level ledge. If I could get down through the funnel to the ledge, I should be all right; surely the rest of the way down was negotiable. But I realized that there could be no turning back. Once I was down in that rocky chute I could not get up again, for the round wall which nearly encircled the space there was too high and sheer. I elected to go down into it, to try for the ledge directly below. I eased myself down the smooth, nearly vertical wall on my back, pressing my arms and legs outward against the sides. After what seemed a long time I was trapped in the rock. The ledge was no longer there below me: it had been an optical illusion. Now, in this angle of vision, there was nothing but the ground, far, far below, and jagged boulders set there like teeth. I remember that my arms were scraped and bleeding, stretched out against the walls with all the pressure that I could exert. When once I looked down I saw that my legs, also spread out and pressed hard against the walls, were shaking violently. I was in an impossible situation: I could not move in any direction save downward in a fall, and I   9 could not stay beyond another minute where I was. I believed then that I would die there, and I saw with a terrible clarity the things of the valley below. They were not the less beautiful to me. It seemed to me that I grew suddenly very calm in view of that beloved world. And I remember nothing else of that moment. I passed out of my mind, and the next thing I knew I was sitting down on the ground, very cold in the shadows, and looking up at the rock where I had been within an eyelash of eternity. That was a strange thing in my life, and I think of it as the end of an age. I should never again see the world as I saw it on the other side of that moment, in the bright reflection of time lost. There are such reflections, and for some of them I have the names.

✦ *Evaluating the Text*

1. What different facets of Momaday's father emerge from this account?

2. In what way did Momaday's mother serve as an inspiration to him?

3. What was the incident that had such a decisive impact on Momaday's attitude toward his past experiences?

✦ *Exploring Different Perspectives*

1. How does the theme of a fall from a great height figure thematically in both the account by N. Scott Momaday and the story "The Falling Girl" by Dino Buzzati?

2. How does the theme of self-reliance enter into the account by N. Scott Momaday and the story "Melba, Mallinen and me" by Kjell Westö?

✦ *Extending Viewpoints Through Writing*

1. Momaday's account confronts an important change he experienced during a time when he was going to leave home to attend school. If you keep a diary, what observations did you make about the prospect of going away to school? In retrospect, how has this experience changed your attitude toward your home, family, and childhood experiences?

2. Describe a situation in which you were tested to your limits, either physically or mentally or both. What character traits enabled you to meet the challenge?

3. Describe the circumstances underlying the choice of your name. Do you like your given name, or do you prefer to be called by a nickname? If you had a nickname, what would it be?

Sucheng Chan

You're Short, Besides!

——————◆——————

Sucheng Chan graduated from Swarthmore College in 1963 and received an M.A. from the University of Hawaii in 1965. In 1973 she earned a Ph.D. from the University of California at Berkeley, where she subsequently taught for a decade. She is currently professor of history and chair of Asian-American studies at the University of California at Santa Barbara. Her works include Quiet Odyssey: A Pioneer Korean Woman in America *(1990) and the award-winning* The Asian Americans: An Interpretive History *(1991). "You're Short, Besides!" first appeared in* Making Waves: An Anthology of Writing By and About Asian-American Women *(1989).*

When asked to write about being a physically handicapped Asian American woman, I considered it an insult. After all, my accomplishments are many, yet I was not asked to write about any of them. Is being handicapped the most salient feature about me? The fact that it might be in the eyes of others made me decide to write the essay as requested. I realized that the way I think about myself may differ considerably from the way others perceive me. And maybe that's what being physically handicapped is all about.

I was stricken simultaneously with pneumonia and polio at the age of four. Uncertain whether I had polio of the lungs, seven of the eight doctors who attended me—all practitioners of Western medicine—told my parents they should not feel optimistic about my survival. A Chinese fortune teller my mother consulted also gave a grim prognosis, but for an entirely different reason: I had been stricken because my name was offensive to the gods. My grandmother had named me "grandchild of wisdom," a name that the fortune teller said was too presumptuous for a girl. So he advised my parents to change my name to "chaste virgin." All these pessimistic predictions notwithstanding, I hung onto life, if only by a thread. For three years, my body was periodically pierced with electric shocks as the muscles of my legs atrophied. Before my illness, I had been an active, rambunctious, precocious, and very curious child. Being confined to bed was thus a mental agony as great as my physical pain. Living in war-torn China, I received little medical attention; physical therapy was unheard of. But I was determined to walk. So one day, when I was six or seven, I instructed my mother to set up two rows of chairs to face each other so that I could use them as I

131

would parallel bars. I attempted to walk by holding my body up and moving it forward with my arms while dragging my legs along behind. Each time I fell, my mother gasped, but I badgered her until she let me try again. After four nonambulatory years, I finally walked once more by pressing my hands against my thighs so my knees wouldn't buckle.

3   My father had been away from home during most of those years because of the war. When he returned, I had to confront the guilt he felt about my condition. In many East Asian cultures, there is a strong folk belief that a person's physical state in this life is a reflection of how morally or sinfully he or she lived in previous lives. Furthermore, because of the tendency to view the family as a single unit, it is believed that the fate of one member can be caused by the behavior of another. Some of my father's relatives told him that my illness had doubtless been caused by the wild carousing he did in his youth. A well-meaning but somewhat simple man, my father believed them.

4   Throughout my childhood, he sometimes apologized to me for having to suffer retribution for his former bad behavior. This upset me; it was bad enough that I had to deal with the anguish of not being able to walk, but to have to assuage his guilt as well was a real burden! In other ways, my father was very good to me. He took me out often, carrying me on his shoulders or back, to give me fresh air and sunshine. He did this until I was too large and heavy for him to carry. And ever since I can remember, he has told me that I am pretty.

5   After getting over her anxieties about my constant falls, my mother decided to send me to school. I had already learned to read some words of Chinese at the age of three by asking my parents to teach me the sounds and meaning of various characters in the daily newspaper. But between the ages of four and eight, I received no education since just staying alive was a full-time job. Much to her chagrin, my mother found no school in Shanghai, where we lived at the time, which would accept me as a student. Finally, as a last resort, she approached the American School, which agreed to enroll me only if my family kept an *amah* (a servant who takes care of children) by my side at all times. The tuition at the school was twenty U.S. dollars per month—a huge sum of money during those years of runaway inflation in China—and payable only in U.S. dollars. My family afforded the high cost of tuition and the expense of employing a full-time *amah* for less than a year.

6   We left China as the Communist forces swept across the country in victory. We found an apartment in Hong Kong across the street from a school run by Seventh-Day Adventists. By that time I could walk a little, so the principal was persuaded to accept me. An *amah* now had to take care of me only during recess when my classmates might easily knock me over as they ran about the playground.

7   After a year and a half in Hong Kong, we moved to Malaysia, where my father's family had lived for four generations. There I

learned to swim in the lovely warm waters of the tropics and fell in love with the sea. On land I was a cripple; in the ocean I could move with the grace of a fish. I liked the freedom of being in the water so much that many years later, when I was a graduate student in Hawaii, I became greatly enamored with a man just because he called me a "Polynesian water nymph."

As my overall health improved, my mother became less anxious   8
about all aspects of my life. She did everything possible to enable me to lead as normal a life as possible. I remember how once some of her colleagues in the high school where she taught criticized her for letting me wear short skirts. They felt my legs should not be exposed to public view. My mother's response was, "All girls her age wear short skirts, so why shouldn't she?"

The years in Malaysia were the happiest of my childhood, even   9
though I was constantly fending off children who ran after me calling, *"Baikah! Baikah!"* ("Cripple! Cripple!" in the Hokkien dialect commonly spoken in Malaysia). The taunts of children mattered little because I was a star pupil. I won one award after another for general scholarship as well as for art and public speaking. Whenever the school had important visitors my teacher always called on me to recite in front of the class.

A significant event that marked me indelibly occurred when I was   10
twelve. That year my school held a music recital and I was one of the students chosen to play the piano. I managed to get up the steps to the stage without any problem, but as I walked across the stage, I fell. Out of the audience, a voice said loudly and clearly, "Ayah! A *baikah* shouldn't be allowed to perform in public." I got up before anyone could get on stage to help me and, with tears streaming uncontrollably down my face, I rushed to the piano and began to play. Beethoven's "Für Elise" had never been played so fiendishly fast before or since, but I managed to finish the whole piece. That I managed to do so made me feel really strong. I never again feared ridicule.

In later years I was reminded of this experience from time to time.   11
During my fourth year as an assistant professor at the University of California at Berkeley, I won a distinguished teaching award. Some weeks later I ran into a former professor who congratulated me enthusiastically. But I said to him, "You know what? I became a distinguished teacher by *limping* across the stage of Dwinelle 155!" (Dwinelle 155 is a large, cold, classroom that most colleagues of mine hate to teach in.) I was rude not because I lacked graciousness but because this man, who had told me that my dissertation was the finest piece of work he had read in fifteen years, had nevertheless advised me to eschew a teaching career.

"Why?" I asked.   12

"Your leg . . ." he responded.   13

"What about my leg?" I said, puzzled.   14

15   "Well, how would you feel standing in front of a large lecture class?"

16   "If it makes any difference, I want you to know I've won a number of speech contests in my life, and I am not the least bit self-conscious about speaking in front of large audiences. . . . Look, why don't you write me a letter of recommendation to tell people how brilliant I am, and let *me* worry about my leg!"

17   This incident is worth recounting only because it illustrates a dilemma that handicapped persons face frequently: those who care about us sometimes get so protective that they unwittingly limit our growth. This former professor of mine had been one of my greatest supporters for two decades. Time after time, he had written glowing letters of recommendation on my behalf. He had spoken as he did because he thought he had my best interest at heart; he thought that if I got a desk job rather than one that required me to be a visible, public person, I would be spared the misery of being stared at.

18   Americans, for the most part, do not believe as Asians do that physically handicapped persons are morally flawed. But they are equally inept at interacting with those of us who are not able-bodied. Cultural differences in the perception and treatment of handicapped people are most clearly expressed by adults. Children, regardless of where they are, tend to be openly curious about people who do not look "normal." Adults in Asia have no hesitation in asking visibly handicapped people what is wrong with them, often expressing their sympathy with looks of pity, whereas adults in the United States try desperately to be polite by pretending not to notice.

19   One interesting response I often elicited from people in Asia but have never encountered in America is the attempt to link my physical condition to the state of my soul. Many a time while living and traveling in Asia people would ask me what religion I belonged to. I would tell them that my mother is a devout Buddhist, that my father was baptized a Catholic but has never practiced Catholicism, and that I am an agnostic. Upon hearing this, people would try strenuously to convert me to their religion so that whichever God they believed in could bless me. If I would only attend this church or that temple regularly, they urged, I would surely get cured. Catholics and Buddhists alike have pressed religious medallions into my palm, telling me if I would wear these, the relevant deity or saint would make me well. Once while visiting the tomb of Muhammad Ali Jinnah in Karachi, Pakistan, an old Muslim, after finishing his evening prayers, spotted me, gestured toward my legs, raised his arms heavenward, and began a new round of prayers, apparently on my behalf.

20   In the United States adults who try to act "civilized" toward handicapped people by pretending they don't notice anything unusual sometimes end up ignoring handicapped people completely. In the

first few months I lived in this country, I was struck by the fact that whenever children asked me what was the matter with my leg, their adult companions would hurriedly shush them up, furtively look at me, mumble apologies, and rush their children away. After a few months of such encounters, I decided it was my responsibility to educate these people. So I would say to the flustered adults, "It's okay, let the kid ask." Turning to the child, I would say, "When I was a little girl, no bigger than you are, I became sick with something called polio. The muscles of my leg shrank up and I couldn't walk very well. You're much luckier than I am because now you can get a vaccine to make sure you never get my disease. So don't cry when your mommy takes you to get a polio vaccine, okay?" Some adults and their little companions I talked to this way were glad to be rescued from embarrassment; others thought I was strange.

21 Americans have another way of covering up their uneasiness: they become jovially patronizing. Sometimes when people spot my crutch, they ask if I've had a skiing accident. When I answer that unfortunately it is something less glamorous than that they say, "I bet you *could* ski if you put your mind to it!" Alternately, at parties where people dance, men who ask me to dance with them get almost belligerent when I decline their invitation. They say, "Of course you can dance if you *want* to!" Some have given me pep talks about how if I would only develop the right mental attitude, I would have more fun in life.

22 Different cultural attitudes toward handicapped persons came out clearly during my wedding. My father-in-law, as solid a representative of middle America as could be found, had no qualms about objecting to the marriage on racial grounds, but he could bring himself to comment on my handicap only indirectly. He wondered why his son, who had dated numerous high school and college beauty queens, couldn't marry one of them instead of me. My mother-in-law, a devout Christian, did not share her husband's prejudices, but she worried aloud about whether I could have children. Some Chinese friends of my parents, on the other hand, said that I was lucky to have found such a noble man, one who would marry me despite my handicap. I, for my part, appeared in church in a white lace wedding dress I had designed and made myself—a miniskirt!

23 How Asian Americans treat me with respect to my handicap tells me a great deal about their degree of acculturation. Recent immigrants behave just like Asians in Asia; those who have been here longer or who grew up in the United States behave more like their white counterparts. I have not encountered any distinctly Asian American pattern of response. What makes the experience of Asian American handicapped people unique is the duality of responses we elicit.

24 Regardless of racial or cultural background, most handicapped people have to learn to find a balance between the desire to attain

physical independence and the need to take care of ourselves by not overtaxing our bodies. In my case, I've had to learn to accept the fact that leading an active life has its price. Between the ages of eight and eighteen, I walked without using crutches or braces but the effort caused my right leg to become badly misaligned. Soon after I came to the United States, I had a series of operations to straighten out the bones of my right leg; afterwards though my leg looked straighter and presumably better, I could no longer walk on my own. Initially my doctors fitted me with a brace, but I found wearing one cumbersome and soon gave it up. I could move around much more easily—and more important, faster—by using one crutch. One orthopedist after another warned me that using a single crutch was a bad practice. They were right. Over the years my spine developed a double-S curve and for the last twenty years I have suffered from severe, chronic back pains, which neither conventional physical therapy nor a lighter work load can eliminate.

25   The only thing that helps my backaches is a good massage, but the soothing effect lasts no more than a day or two. Massages are expensive, especially when one needs them three times a week. So I found a job that pays better, but at which I have to work longer hours, consequently increasing the physical strain on my body—a sort of vicious circle. When I was in my thirties, my doctors told me that if I kept leading the strenuous life I did, I would be in a wheelchair by the time I was forty. They were right on target; I bought myself a wheelchair when I was forty-one. But being the incorrigible character that I am, I use it only when I am *not* in a hurry!

26   It is a good thing, however, that I am too busy to think much about my handicap or my backaches because pain can physically debilitate as well as cause depression. And there are days when my spirits get rather low. What has helped me is realizing that being handicapped is akin to growing old at an accelerated rate. The contradiction I experience is that often my mind races along as though I'm only twenty while my body feels about sixty. But fifteen or twenty years hence, unlike my peers who will have to cope with aging for the first time, I shall be full of cheer because I will have already fought, and I hope won, that battle long ago.

27   Beyond learning how to be physically independent and, for some of us, living with chronic pain or other kinds of discomfort, the most difficult thing a handicapped person has to deal with, especially during puberty and early adulthood, is relating to potential sexual partners. Because American culture places so much emphasis on physical attractiveness, a person with a shriveled limb, or a tilt to the head, or the inability to speak clearly, experiences great uncertainty—indeed trauma—when interacting with someone to whom he or she is attracted. My problem was that I was not only physically handicapped, small, and short, but worse, I also wore glasses and was smarter than

all the boys I knew! Alas, an insurmountable combination. Yet somehow I have managed to have intimate relationships, all of them with extraordinary men. Not surprisingly, there have also been countless men who broke my heart—men who enjoyed my company "as a friend," but who never found the courage to date or make love with me, although I am sure my experience in this regard is no different from that of many able-bodied persons.

The day came when my backaches got in the way of having an active sex life. Surprisingly that development was liberating because I stopped worrying about being attractive to men. No matter how headstrong I had been, I, like most women of my generation, had had the desire to be alluring to men ingrained into me. And that longing had always worked like a brake on my behavior. When what men think of me ceased to be compelling, I gained greater freedom to be myself.

I've often wondered if I would have been a different person had I not been physically handicapped. I really don't know, though there is no question that being handicapped has marked me. But at the same time I usually do not *feel* handicapped—and consequently, I do not act handicapped. People are therefore less likely to treat me as a handicapped person. There is no doubt, however, that the lives of my parents, sister, husband, other family members, and some close friends have been affected by my physical condition. They have had to learn not to hide me away at home, not to feel embarrassed by how I look or react to people who say silly things to me, and not to resent me for the extra demands my condition makes on them. Perhaps the hardest thing for those who live with handicapped people is to know when and how to offer help. There are no guidelines applicable to all situations. My advice is, when in doubt, ask, but ask in a way that does not smack of pity or embarrassment. Most important, please don't talk to us as though we are children.

So, has being physically handicapped been a handicap? It all depends on one's attitude. Some years ago, I told a friend that I had once said to an affirmative action compliance officer (somewhat sardonically since I do not believe in the head count approach to affirmative action) that the institution which employs me is triply lucky because it can count me as non-white, female and handicapped. He responded, "Why don't you tell them to count you four times? . . . Remember, you're short, besides!"

✦ Evaluating the Text

1. What insight into cross-cultural perceptions of disabilities do you get from Chan's account? Specifically, how do Asian perceptions of disabilities differ from those in America?

2. To what extent did Chan have to overcome the well-meaning advice of family and friends and discount their perception of her diminished potential?

3. Chan has very strongly developed views, that is, she is an agnostic, doesn't believe in affirmative action, is uninhibited about sex, and has an unusual attitude toward the progressive nature of her handicap. Which of her responses toward events made you aware of her unique personality?

4. Do you know anyone who has a sense of irony and detachment similar to Chan's toward a disability or ailment? Write a short account of how this attitude enables them to cope with circumstances that might devastate another person.

✦ *Exploring Different Perspectives*

1. What personal attributes link Sucheng Chan with Christy Brown in confronting disabilities? (See "The Letter 'A'.")

2. How do the accounts by Sucheng Chan and Nawal El Saadawi reveal stereotyped attitudes toward girls in the traditional cultures of China and the Middle East?

✦ *Extending Viewpoints Through Writing*

1. If you have ever been temporarily physically incapacitated or have a disability, write an essay that will help your readers understand your situation, including your experience with both overt and subtle types of discrimination.

Dino Buzzati

The Falling Girl

◆————————◆

Dino Buzzati (1906–1972) spent most of his working life in Milan as an editor and correspondent for Corriere della Sera. *A prolific writer, Buzzati is the author of poems, librettos, a children's book, hundreds of short stories in collections such as* Catastrophe *(1966) and* The Siren *(1984), and novels, including the internationally acclaimed* The Tartar Steppe *(1940). His innovative play,* A Clinical Case *(1955), was translated into French by Albert Camus and performed on stages throughout the world. "The Falling Girl," from his short story collection* Restless Nights *(1983), is a typical Buzzatian mixture of surrealism, journalistic coverage of a human-interest story, and social commentary on the effects of the economic boom in post–World War II Italy.*

Italy is a republic in southern Europe, extending into the Mediterranean sea as a boot-shaped peninsula, bordered to the northwest by France, to the north by Switzerland and Austria, and to the northeast by Slovenia. From the fourth century B.C. *to the fifth century* A.D., *the history of Italy is for the most part that of the Roman empire. The Italian Renaissance, in the fourteenth century, awakened Europe from the Middle Ages and bequeathed countless great works of art and culture to the world. Reacting to Austria's domination in the mid-1800s, Italian nationalism (Risorgimento, or "resurgence") ultimately united different political elements under a parliament and a king. In 1922, Italy came under the Fascist leadership of Benito Mussolini, who later joined Germany and Japan (as the Axis Powers) in World War II until Fascism was overthrown in 1943. In 1946, Italy became a republic and joined NATO (North Atlantic Treaty Organization) in 1949. The post-war era has been a turbulent one politically with a succession of short-lived coalition governments. The issues of class consciousness and social aspiration dramatized in Buzzati's story reflects Italy's rapid industrialization and the emergence of an upwardly striving middle class since the early 1950s. Recent huge budget deficits have curtailed economic growth and forced the government to cut spending in health and education, moves that have resulted in strikes and social unrest. An April 1993 referendum to replace the proportional system of voting by a majority system was approved by over 80 percent of the voters. The prevailing system had led to weak coalition governments coming into power and a breakdown in government services. A new prime minister, Carlo Azeglio Ciampi, committed the government to implementing political reform. He was succeeded as prime minister by Silvio Berlusconi in May 1994 and Lamberto Dini in January 1995.*

1   Marta was nineteen. She looked out over the roof of the skyscraper, and seeing the city below shining in the dusk, she was overcome with dizziness.

2   The skyscraper was silver, supreme and fortunate in that most beautiful and pure evening, as here and there the wind stirred a few fine filaments of cloud against an absolutely incredible blue background. It was in fact the hour when the city is seized by inspiration and whoever is not blind is swept away by it. From that airy height the girl saw the streets and the masses of buildings writhing in the long spasm of sunset, and at the point where the white of the houses ended, the blue of the sea began. Seen from above, the sea looked as if it were rising. And since the veils of the night were advancing from the east, the city became a sweet abyss burning with pulsating lights. Within it were powerful men, and women who were even more powerful, furs and violins, cars glossy and onyx, the neon signs of nightclubs, the entrance halls of darkened mansions, fountains, diamonds, old silent gardens, parties, desires, affairs, and, above all, that consuming sorcery of the evening which provokes dreams of greatness and glory.

3   Seeing these things, Marta hopelessly leaned out over the railing and let herself go. She felt as if she were hovering in the air, but she was falling. Given the extraordinary height of the skyscraper, the streets and squares down at the bottom were very far away. Who knows how long it would take her to get there. Yet the girl was falling.

4   At that hour the terraces and balconies of the top floors were filled with rich and elegant people who were having cocktails and making silly conversation. They were scattered in crowds, and their talk muffled the music. Marta passed before them and several people looked out to watch her.

5   Flights of that kind (mostly by girls, in fact) were not rare in the skyscraper and they constituted an interesting diversion for the tenants; this was also the reason why the price of those apartments was very high.

6   The sun had not yet completely set and it did its best to illuminate Marta's simple clothing. She wore a modest, inexpensive spring dress bought off the rack. Yet the lyrical light of the sunset exalted it somewhat, making it chic.

7   From the millionaires' balconies, gallant hands were stretched out toward her, offering flowers and cocktails. "Miss, would you like a drink? . . . Gentle butterfly, why not stop a minute with us?"

She laughed, hovering, happy (but meanwhile she was falling):   8
"No, thanks, friends. I can't. I'm in a hurry."

"Where are you headed?" they asked her.   9

"Ah, don't make me say," Marta answered, waving her hands in a   10
friendly good-bye.

A young man, tall, dark, very distinguished, extended an arm to   11
snatch her. She liked him. And yet Marta quickly defended herself:
"How dare you, sir?" and she had time to give him a little tap on the
nose.

The beautiful people, then, were interested in her and that filled   12
her with satisfaction. She felt fascinating, stylish. On the flower-filled
terraces, amid the bustle of waiters in white and the bursts of exotic
songs, there was talk for a few minutes, perhaps less, of the young
woman who was passing by (from top to bottom, on a vertical course).
Some thought her pretty, others thought her so-so, everyone found her
interesting.

"You have your entire life before you," they told her, "why are you   13
in such a hurry? You still have time to rush around and busy yourself.
Stop with us for a little while, it's only a modest little party among
friends, really, you'll have a good time."

She made an attempt to answer but the force of gravity had already   14
quickly carried her to the floor below, then two, three, four floors below; in fact, exactly as you gaily rush around when you are just nineteen years old.

Of course, the distance that separated her from the bottom, that is,   15
from street level, was immense. It is true that she began falling just a little while ago, but the street always seemed very far away.

In the meantime, however, the sun had plunged into the sea; one   16
could see it disappear, transformed into a shimmering reddish mush-
room. As a result, it no longer emitted its vivifying rays to light up the
girl's dress and make her a seductive comet. It was a good thing that
the windows and terraces of the skyscraper were almost all illuminated
and the bright reflections completely gilded her as she gradually
passed by.

Now Marta no longer saw just groups of carefree people inside the   17
apartments; at times there were even some businesses where the em-
ployees, in black or blue aprons, were sitting at desks in long rows.
Several of them were young people as old as or older than she, and
weary of the day by now, every once in a while they raised their eyes
from their duties and from typewriters. In this way they too saw her,
and a few ran to the windows. "Where are you going? Why so fast?
Who are you?" they shouted to her. One could divine something akin
to envy in their words.

18　　　"They're waiting for me down there," she answered. "I can't stop. Forgive me." And again she laughed, wavering on her headlong fall, but it wasn't like her previous laughter anymore. The night had craftily fallen and Marta started to feel cold.

19　　　Meanwhile, looking downward, she saw a bright halo of lights at the entrance of a building. Here long black cars were stopping (from the great distance they looked as small as ants), and men and women were getting out, anxious to go inside. She seemed to make out the sparkling of jewels in that swarm. Above the entrance flags were flying.

20　　　They were obviously giving a large party, exactly the kind that Marta dreamed of ever since she was a child. Heaven help her if she missed it. Down there opportunity was waiting for her, fate, romance, the true inauguration of her life. Would she arrive in time?

21　　　She spitefully noticed that another girl was falling about thirty meters above her. She was decidedly prettier than Marta and she wore a rather classy evening gown. For some unknown reason she came down much faster than Marta, so that in a few moments she passed by her and disappeared below, even though Marta was calling her. Without doubt she would get to the party before Marta; perhaps she had a plan all worked out to supplant her.

22　　　Then she realized that they weren't alone. Along the sides of the skyscraper many other young women were plunging downward, their faces taut with the excitement of the flight, their hands cheerfully waving as if to say: look at us, here we are, entertain us, is not the world ours?

23　　　It was a contest, then. And she only had a shabby little dress while those other girls were dressed smartly like high-fashion models and some even wrapped luxurious mink stoles tightly around their bare shoulders. So self-assured when she began the leap, Marta now felt a tremor growing inside her; perhaps it was just the cold; but it may have been fear too, the fear of having made an error without remedy.

24　　　It seemed to be late at night now. The windows were darkened one after another, the echoes of music became more rare, the offices were empty, young men no longer leaned out from the windowsills extending their hands. What time was it? At the entrance to the building down below—which in the meantime had grown larger, and one could now distinguish all the architectural details—the lights were still burning, but the bustle of cars had stopped. Every now and then, in fact, small groups of people came out of the main floor wearily drawing away. Then the lights of the entrance were also turned off.

25　　　Marta felt her heart tightening. Alas, she wouldn't reach the ball in time. Glancing upwards, she saw the pinnacle of the skyscraper in all its cruel power. It was almost completely dark. On the top floors a few windows here and there were still lit. And above the top the first glimmer of dawn was spreading.

In a dining recess of the twenty-eighth floor a man about forty years old was having his morning coffee and reading his newspaper while his wife tidied up the room. A clock on the sideboard indicated 8:45. A shadow suddenly passed before the window.

"Alberto!" the wife shouted. "Did you see that? A woman passed by."

"Who was it?" he said without raising his eyes from the newspaper.

"An old woman," the wife answered. "A decrepit old woman. She looked frightened."

"It's always like that," the man muttered. "At these low floors only falling old women pass by. You can see beautiful girls from the hundred-and-fiftieth floor up. Those apartments don't cost so much for nothing."

"At least down here there's the advantage," observed the wife, "that you can hear the thud when they touch the ground."

"This time not even that," he said, shaking his head, after he stood listening for a few minutes. Then he had another sip of coffee.

Translated by Lawrence Venuti

✦ Evaluating the Text

1. How does the story chart the movement of Marta from naiveté to self-awareness? To what extent does her journey correct the false image she has of herself?

2. How does Buzzati transform the figurative concept of *falling* (as in "falling in love") into the literal premise of the story? Describe the change that takes place in Marta as she falls. Do you find evidence that her initial optimism and idealism gives way to envy, fear, competition, and even despair?

3. To what extent does the phrase *flights of that kind* suggest Marta's story is characteristic of nineteen-year-olds as such? What assumptions and qualities does Marta exhibit that are typical of this age in terms of energy, idealism, and a belief that choices will always be available?

✦ Exploring Different Perspectives

1. Does the metaphor of falling in Dino Buzzati's story have a different meaning than that implied by the prospect of a physical fall in N. Scott Momaday's account, "The Names"?

2. What typical attributes of adolescence underlie the stories by Dino Buzzati and Kjell Westö? (See "Melba, Mallinen and me.")

✦ *Extending Viewpoints Through Writing*

1. Have you known anyone who was prepared to sacrifice everyday
   pleasures to achieve a goal? How did that person's experiences compare with those of Marta in Buzzati's story?

2. In an essay, discuss the way in which you made sense of this story. For
   example, did you see it as a parable of life, youth, and old age; birth
   and death; social striving; psychological change in someone consumed
   by ambition; a parable of an idealist who has a martyr (Marta) complex; or a critical depiction of the class structure of Italian society?

Kjell Westö

Melba, Mallinen and me

———————◆———————

Kjell Westö was born in 1961 in Sweden. The characters in Westö's short stories are generally young men of the urban middle class. He describes their predicaments in ironic narrative that is often at its best when it is directed at the narrator himself. His stories are mostly set in and around Helsinki, Finland, where he lives. "Melba, Mallinen and me" is drawn from his collection of short stories, The Bruus Case *(1992).*

Finland is a republic in northern Europe bounded northwest and north by Norway, east by Russia, south by the Baltic Sea, and west by the Gulf of Bothnia and Sweden. Since the Middle Ages, Finland had been part of the realm of Sweden. In the eighteenth century, sections of southeastern Finland were taken over by Russia, and the rest of the country was ceded to Russia through a treaty of 1809. After the Russian Revolution, Finland declared itself independent on December 6, 1917. On November 30, 1939, Soviet troops invaded Finland, and when Germany attacked the USSR in June 1941, Finland became involved in the war against the USSR. Following the armistice signed in September 1944 in Moscow and a peace treaty signed in Paris, Finland regained its autonomy as a constitutional republic. For much of its history, Finland has sought to remain independent of the cultural, political, and economic dominance of Russia.

After the war Helsingfors began to grow in earnest.   1

Construction started in Mejlans and Brunakärr. People who moved   2
there wondered if all the stone in the country had been damaged by the bombing or if all the competent builders had been killed; if you hammered a nail into a wall you were liable to hammer it right into the back of your neighbour's head and risk getting indicted for manslaughter.

Then the Olympic Village in Kottby was built, and for a few weeks   3
in the summer of 1952 this area of wood-frame houses became a legitimate part of the city that housed such luminaries as the long-legged hop-skip-and-jump champion Da Silva, the runner Emil Zatopek (with the heavily wobbling head), the huge heavyweight boxer Ed Saunders and the somewhat smaller heavyweight Ingemar Johansson who had to run for his life from Saunders.

Before long, the neighbouring area of Esbo started to grow as well,   4
and soon became the town of Esbo. The town of Esbo is a curious metastasis created for people who want to live where the air is clean and in the mornings drive into Helsinki where the air, thanks to people like

145

them, is considerably less than clean. In Esbo the greenbelt town of Hagalund—Tapiola—was built, and it was shown proudly to tourists for decades until the guides got tired of hearing people stage-whispering to each other: 'Why are they taking us to this suburb?'

5   Then people turned their attention to the forests east, north and northwest of Helsinki. Young architects sat in libraries studying Gropius, Le Corbusier and Bauhaus, Russian constructivism and the Finnish planner O.-I. Meurman's views on city planning and greenbelt towns. After they'd misunderstood everything—except Russian constructivism—they were sent out to start designing several northern suburbs. The large construction firms had mastered the technique of building with concrete units, and everything went very fast: the city planners figured that by the turn of the century Helsinki would probably have 1,500,000 inhabitants.

6   But while the young architects were still sitting and studying, the quick mind of Ilmo Malaska, a young city official with an international bent, had time to leave its mark on an area immediately west of the city. Brednäs was on the sea, in an area once owned by the Mattheiszen family. There was a big estate, a defunct school for naval cadets and a hotel. Along the beautiful promenade were luxury villas and a few embassies. Further inland was a long shady avenue or 'allé' with highrises in smudged, unattractive colours.

7   Northwest of Brednäs was a wooded hill so insignificant that it didn't even have a name. Assistant Mayor Malaska contacted the Office of City Planning for the Western District and suggested that a noted foreign architect be given the assignment of planning a suburb on the hill above Brednäs. A commission was appointed, and nine months later it came up with two (or rather three) names. Henry S. Marracott III had studied at MIT and Harvard, worked for Gropius in New York and later was the driving force behind the famous 'housing projects' in Manhattan and St Louis. Marracott's competitors were the famous Russian constructivist couple Pavel Yefimovitch Pavlinsky and Irina Maximovna Pavlinskaya, who'd shortly before created two suburbs for 50,000 people each in the city that everyone thought would be known for the foreseeable future as Leningrad.

8   Two delegations set out. The first, led by Ilmo Malaska, went to Leningrad. Impressed by Pavlinsky & Pavlinskaya's elegance and western habits, they took a look at the suburbs, came back and recommended Marracott. The second, led by Torolf Sundelin, Assistant Chief of the Western District of the Office of City Planning, went to St Louis, met Marracott, took a look at the suburbs, came back and recommended the Pavlinskys.

9   It turned out that Malaska was pulling the strings behind the scene, and Henry S. Marracott got the job in spite of warning grumbles from certain politicians with good contacts in the Soviet Embassy.

Marracott designed a trim little suburb. In spite of heavy pressure   10
from the builder, he avoided concrete as much as possible. Some
houses were built in warm red brick, but most in rough brownish-grey
stone, possibly a tribute to the Brooklyn brownstone where the Marra-
cotts were forced to live during Henry's late childhood after his father
went bankrupt in 1929.

During one phase of the building, private capital also stepped in;   11
Marracott was given the task of designing a few luxury villas along
Brednäs Beach as well as several semi-detached houses a bit further inland. He also drew up plans for a residence for government-invited
VIPs that was only built two decades later adjoining the hotel. This is
where the Finnish government wined and dined the oil billionaire and
weapons broker Adnan Khashoggi in the hope of lucrative contracts
that never materialised.

Ilmo Malaska was pleased. Using the argument that in Stockholm   12
there was a place called Frescati, in Rome the Spanish Steps and in New
York an avenue called De Las Americas, he managed to sell the idea
that the suburb on the hill be called Marracott Hill; Brednäs became
Marracott Beach and Brednäs Allé Marracott Allé. Marracott returned
home, and in 1972 in St Louis became the first architect who dynamited
his own housing development on orders from the authorities.

Work began on a highway which was to make travel between Åbo   13
[Turku] and Helsingfors easier and from Marracott Hill to Marracott
Beach more difficult. The first kilometre became the missing natural
border between the two sections of town, but in time a bridge was built
that became a easily recognisable symbol of the illusory American
Dream of climbing the social ladder by the sweat of one's brow. It must
be said, however, that if the Pavlinskys had been given the assignment,
the villas in Marracott Beach would have been confined in a police-
patrolled, fenced-in area.

One Marracott Hill rumour had it that the schools in Marracott   14
Beach had an especially written first-grade reader which began like
this: 'Father builds his career. The salary is fine. Brother takes drugs.
Mother needs peace and quiet.'

But I never actually saw it with my own eyes.   15

We moved to Marracott Hill while the area still was only half-   16
finished and I was a chubby toddler. On Marracott Hill lived factory
workers—lower middle class and the Upwardly Mobile. There were
Helsinki natives who used words like *buli, snadi, lafka* and *safka* (slang
words of Russian origin: big, small, shop, food). There were people
from the north and east who said *mie, sie, myö, työ* and *hyö* instead of
minä, sinä, me, te and *he* (I, you, we, you, they). There were also some
Finland-Swedes, but not in my building.

17   I remember that the church was made of brick, and was small and compact. Obviously there was no reason to put too much stress on metaphysical questions since the tenets of the New Religion could probably be gleaned from the programmes of the larger political parties.

18   I remember that the shopping centre looked like a fortress, and that inside was a shiny slide, down which one passed through the Black Hole of childhood.

19   I remember that people were strangers to each other and looked it. In the afternoons the adults hurried home as if ticks were pumping them full of fatigue and pallor.

20   Sometimes statisticians visited, burrowing their way through the houses like officious termites.

21   In the evenings a blue light shone out of every fourth window. I remember that it looked like a series of secret laboratories, but that it was actually Bonanza and Maxwell Smart alternating in neat layers with the disciplined objectivity of State-produced programmes.

22   Most of all, I remember Melba: Melba and the Karttunen brothers and the others.

23   I played soccer.

24   Melba didn't. He just sat on the Cliff and watched us.

25   The Cliff was on the side of our yard facing the inner part of Marracott Hill. On the other side was the ring road circling the housing area. Behind the ring road lay the highway.

26   A sandy road went by the Cliff, twisting steeply at its base and then straightening out and continuing down toward the soccer field and the Finnish school. There were no Swedish schools on Marracott Hill; they were all in Marracott Beach.

27   The Cliff was in our yard, but it was part of Melba's territory even though he lived in the neighbouring yard, No. 9. The only people he allowed on the Cliff were the Karttunen brothers. If he ever heard that any unauthorised persons had been up there in his absence, he'd dole out some kind of punishment. I don't know why he was called Melba; there was certainly nothing peach-like about him.

28   Soccer was my admission ticket to the yard. I was slow and deliberate but had a feel for the game. For that I could thank good genes, for my father had played on Vasa IFK. The first thing I learned to say in Finnish was: *Mun-nimi-on-Kenneth* ('My name is Kenneth')—which quickly simplified itself to *Mun-nimi-on-Kenu* ('My name is Kenu'). Later I learned to shout: *Pallo! Tänne! Syötä! Ammu!* and *Ota se!* ('Ball!' 'Here!' 'Pass it!' 'Shoot!' and 'Get it!')

29   But well-executed goals and elegant passes had no effect on Melba. Until Mallinen arrived, my status was always in doubt. Vepsäläinen, who in lieu of figures of the calibre of Melba and the Karttunen brothers was the leader of us kids in No. 11, was polite to me but nothing

more. He had no great love for Finland-Swedes, but since I'd learned a few Finnish phrases fast he tolerated me. But with Melba he was like putty—being only about half his size. Still, he never actually joined up with Melba and the Karttunens, not directly—he just let them do their thing, smiled at their taunts and gratefully took their cigarettes whenever they offered them.

Melba didn't have to try very hard to find fault with me. It was enough to open the door and see the nameplate on Entry F. It was enough to discover that the only Finnish I could really understand was 'Give me the ball!' 'Pass!' 'Shoot!' 'Cover him!'   30

Melba had many opinions about Finland-Swedes, none of them flattering. Quickly he dubbed me Håkan. It was from him that I learned the intimate connection between the Swedish language and pantyhose: according to him, anybody who spoke Swedish was a faggot, a Homo-Håkan, a pantyhose-model.   31

Soon they added to my nickname. For this I could thank Mirva Hovi, who lived in the same entry as me. By the time she was eight she looked like a tougher version of Madame Mim from Donald Duck comics. We were the same age, but I was a stunted version of Feathering Duck, Donald's cousin. It happened that I ski'd a lot that winter; unconsciously I think I already knew that I had to develop into a Physical Specimen. That, combined with the fact that Melba's territory didn't extend to the ski trails.   32

One January afternoon when I got home to the yard, I noticed that something was wrong with my bindings; I couldn't get my skis off. Mirva Hovi saw her chance, rushed out and began pummelling me. To fight with skis on turned out to be difficult, and all I could do was protect myself with my ski-poles. Melba saw this, came down from the Cliff and grabbed the poles. Then he let Mirva Hovi continue beating me up.   33

It took me an hour to get inside the stairwell. It was pure hell getting into the elevator with my skis on and a furious Mirva Hovi on my back. By then Melba had had plenty of time to tell me what a wimp I was for not being able to defend myself against a girl. That's how I became Wimp-Håkan.   34

Melba had a habit of spitting at any small, objectionable creature as they walked beneath the Cliff on their way between the yard and the field. He was content with that for a long time. But after the incident with Mirva he thought he'd sniffed out weakness.   35

Then one afternoon he made his move. I was on my way home from the Swedish school in Marracott Beach, and I'd already turned into the yard from the ring road when I saw him sitting on the Cliff with his back turned toward me. I tried to speed along the parked cars and make myself invisible in a way that had already become second nature. Suddenly he turned around and saw me. I looked to the left   36 and saw that I'd only gotten as far as Entry B, so I started taking slightly longer steps.

37   When I reached Entry C he stood up and started strolling slowly in my direction. It was no more than twenty metres from the Cliff to Entry F, and he knew that he could make it even if I started running. I tried to think up some errand that I had to do in Entry D or E, but I didn't know anybody who lived there. And the path down to the shopping centre was next to my entryway, so he could block that too.

38   When I arrived he was nonchalantly sitting on the steps, hunched over. I started going in, trying to pretend that I'd just noticed him.

39   'Greetings!' I said in Finnish.

40   'Greetings, Wimp-Håkan,' said Melba.

41   'My-name-is-Kenu,' I said. I could hear that my voice was light and squeaky. Feverishly I tried to figure out a way to get past him and inside the entryway. He wouldn't dare make too much trouble there because there were lots of old ladies who stuck their heads out the door at the slightest noise.

42   'Where you heading, Wimp-Håkan?' asked Melba.

43   'Home. And my-name-is-Kenu,' I said again. I hated that my voice was cracking, and became trembly and small.

44   'Gotanycigs?'

45   'I-don't-smoke.'

46   'Meantosayyouhaven'tgotasmoke?' he replied with reptilian quickness.

47   'I-don't-smoke,' I repeated. It was a good way to practice Finnish, but I didn't like the way it was being taught.

48   'Wouldn'thurttostart,' said Melba, and his hand came flying at me and I fell over the railing into the rose bed. He came after me, sat on top of me, twisted my right arm behind my back and asked: 'Andsowhat'syourname?'

49   'My-name-is-Kenu,' I said.

50   'Whatdidyousayyournamewas?' he repeated, twisting my arm a little more. We kept on that way until I said, 'My-name-is-Wimp-Håkan.'

51   While I struggled to my feet I watched Melba stroll calmly across the lawn with the tall pines and bushes that separated No. 11's yard from No. 9's.

52   I wondered why I couldn't imagine what his parents were like.

53   I began to feel Melba's eyes on the back of my neck when we played soccer down on the field. That made me play worse.

54   Secretly I was furious at the world in general and my situation in particular. I'd quickly learned the important Finnish curse words and sex words, and I went around mumbling a mantra: *Mulkku-Melba, Pillu-Mirva, Paska-Pasi* ('Fuck my Melba, Suck my Mirva, Prick my Pasi') (the younger Karttunen brother was Pasi). Probably I hoped that a mantra would somehow erase my own humiliating nickname.

We all looked totally alike, and I've often wondered what kind of a 55 person I would have become had I grown up with the feeling of belonging to a majority and having the indisputable right to live where I did live.

We all had ugly windbreakers and woollen caps pulled down over 56 our foreheads. Gradually we got rid of the caps because it was cooler to go around bareheaded, and it made us look more like individuals. Our faces were still smooth and our voices shrill—except for Melba. He couldn't have been more than two to three years older than Vepsäläinen, Mirva Hovi and I, but his voice and face were already rough, and he was inordinately big and tough-looking. He let his hair grow early, and soon wisps of dirty-blonde hair were falling down over his face. His voice was a little hoarse and deceptively neutral, but anyone who'd spoken to him once never mistook the threat behind it.

No one had ever seen his parents, and he seemed to be free to roam 57 his territory anytime he felt like it.

The Karttunen brothers were Melba's bodyguards. The older one 58 was tall, taller than Melba, but skinny. He had glasses and jet black, almost slicked-down hair. He might have looked sympathetic, but there was something asymmetrical in his face that made one uneasy. He didn't say much.

Pasi was a year younger than I, very short—and otherwise a car- 59 bon copy of his brother. Alone he would have been harmless, but he was never alone.

The Karttunen brothers lived in one of the twelve-storey buildings 60 on the other side of Marracott Hill, behind a grove of trees. But after they'd become Melba's pals, they had the right to hang out in his territory. Most likely they were uncomfortable in their own home territory, which was run by Killer, a legendary teenager whose cruelty made Melba and the Karttunen brothers look like choirboys.

I wasn't the only kid who walked around with a vague feeling that 61 the sky could fall any minute. There was a slightly crazy, nervous boy named Sunila who was ambushed frequently by Melba and his henchmen. Vepsäläinen himself was never completely at ease, and not even the Sonetti kids with the cherubic curls who lived in Entry A at a comfortable distance from the Cliff could feel completely out of harm's way.

But I was the favourite. Even if I had certain Male Attributes that, 62 for example, Sunila and Sonetti didn't have, I was being judged by factors beyond my control and understanding. So I decided that it had to be my mother tongue that was the problem, and that my role as Wimp-Håkan made me irresistible to them.

Therefore, I was very surprised when the Mallinen family moved 63 into an apartment near me. Mallinen was undoubtedly a Finnish name, and the tall, stringy-looking boy with the short dark hair was clearly Finnish-speaking.

But he started in my class at the Swedish school in Marracott Beach. 64

65   Mallinen's father, an engineer, had built the country's first highway, but that didn't help his son; sooner or later he had to be introduced to the hierarchy of the yard.

66   It happened one afternoon when we were playing soccer—Mallinen
(who'd quickly proved to be a player with good technique), Vepsäläinen,
I and Tamminen and Nylund, two kids who lived in a building on the
other side of the Finnish school. For a long time Melba just sat on the Cliff
and watched us. He sat there until the Karttunen brothers came; then
he stood up, walked down the Cliff and headed toward us along the
sandy road, accompanied by the two others.

67   I could see what was about to happen. I can still remember the cold
autumn air—it was the end of October—there was a strong wind, and
brown and yellow leaves whirled down the grassy embankments, the
tall pines sighed, the temperature was almost at the freezing point and
the puddles crunched—and a girl named Tea Alanne had arrived some
days earlier from the centre of the city to join our class. She had Finnish-
speaking parents, too, so Mallinen was no longer unique.

68   Melba went up to Vepsäläinen, who stopped playing and stood
there, surprised, with the ball at his feet. Melba picked it up and
handed it to the elder Karttunen, who kicked it away as far as he could.

69   'Gimmesomecash,' said Melba to Vepsäläinen. Vepsäläinen began
nervously to dig around in his pockets, and smiled a crooked smile to
Mallinen and me. Melba glanced quickly at me and said:

70   'GetthefuckoutofherefuckingSwede.'

71   Mallinen said:

72   'Let him be. And tell the jerk with the glasses to get the ball.'

73   Melba looked up. For years he hadn't heard that tone of voice from
anyone in No. 9 or No. 11. He was already very close to the age where
even mild-mannered grown-ups were intimidated by him. His gaze
met Mallinen's. Mallinen was younger, but almost as tall. However,
there was a weight difference between them of ten to fifteen kilos.

74   Vepsäläinen, Tamminen, Nylund and I gaped. We looked at
Mallinen as if he were a kamikaze pilot.

75   'What'djusay?' asked Melba in a drawling, nonchalant way that
we'd learned to recognise; it made us shudder.

76   'Tell your friend to move his ass and get the ball—now!' repeated
Mallinen insistently, staring into Melba's eyes.

77   'You're the traitor who goes to the fucking Swedish school,' said
Melba in a factual, almost thoughtful tone of voice. I watched as he and
Mallinen both hunched slightly and tensed their muscles.

78   'What's it to you?' said Mallinen, and at the same moment Melba's
foot came flying.

79   With time I came to understand that Mallinen's secret lay in his
quickness. That first time Melba tried to surprise him with a kick instead of a punch, but Mallinen had time to jump out of the way, grab

Melba's wrist and twist it. A second later there was a cracking sound, and Melba was lying with his face in a pool of shattered ice and muddy water.

Mallinen had never taken any course—either in boxing, wrestling, or judo. He just had a natural talent for protecting himself by violent means if it was necessary. For many, many years I was to admire and envy that talent.

Melba cursed and tried to heave Mallinen off. But Mallinen was sitting on his back with one of Melba's arms twisted behind him; it looked like he could twist it off whenever he wanted.

'FuckingcocksuckerI'llkillyou!' hissed Melba. Mallinen twisted the arm a little more, at the same time pushing Melba's face deeper into the water. There was a bubbling, spitting sound. The Karttunen brothers looked anxiously at Vepsäläinen, Tamminen, Nylund and me. Vepsäläinen had quickly allied himself with Mallinen, and there was something in his face that made the elder Karttunen look at the younger and shake his head.

'Tell your friends to go get the ball,' repeated Mallinen.

Melba writhed like a snake in his grip, but said nothing. The elder Karttunen brother nodded to the younger, who ran after the ball. He gave it to Vepsäläinen. Mallinen looked up; he let go of Melba, and at the same time hopped two steps backward, waiting with clenched fists.

Melba got up. He was soaking wet, and his light-coloured jacket was covered with dark spots. His hair was matted and wet. He looked from Mallinen to Vepsäläinen to me and back to Mallinen. He didn't say a thing, just looked for a long time. Vepsäläinen and I swallowed. Then they left—Melba and the brothers. We stood there watching them. Then Mallinen said, 'Let's keep playing.'

After ten minutes I looked up toward the Cliff. No one was there. It felt liberating to run in the cold, clear autumn air.

Translated by George Blecher and Lone Thygesen Blecher

✦ Evaluating the Text

1. How do the title and the use of capital and lowercase letters reinforce the events of the story in terms of the narrator's need to become more assertive?

2. How is the narrator's problematic status related to his being from Sweden, living in Finland, and not being able to speak Finnish very well?

3. Describe the narrator and the role soccer plays in enabling him to cope with Melba's bullying tactics. How does Mallinen's arrival change the dynamics of the whole situation? In what way were the events in the story a turning point for the narrator during his adolescence?

✦ *Exploring Different Perspectives*

1. Explain the group dynamics in the story by Kjell Westö and in the account by Tepilit Ole Saitoti (see "Initiation of a Maasai Warrior").

2. What role does the desire for acceptance play in the stories by Dino Buzzati (see "The Falling Girl") and Kjell Westö?

✦ *Extending Viewpoints Through Writing*

1. Were you ever bullied at school during your adolescence? Describe your experience and its outcome, including how you reacted and how it changed your life.

2. If you have ever been a member of a gang, describe the significance of your street name. What were the advantages and disadvantages of being a member of this gang?

3. How do the sports or pastimes of a culture express its dominant values? Examples include bullfighting in Spain, cricket in the West Indies, ice hockey and lacrosse in Canada, football in the United States, polo in Argentina, and soccer in Brazil.

Connecting Cultures

———————◆———————

Christy Brown, The Letter "A"

What different attitudes toward disabilities emerge from Christy Brown's account and Lennard J. Davis's analysis (see "Visualizing the Disabled Body," Chapter 3)?

Tepilit Ole Saitoti, The Initiation of a Maasai Warrior

How are the initiation rituals described by Tepilit Ole Saitoti and Rigoberta Menchú (see "Birth Ceremonies," Chapter 1) designed to integrate the individual into the community?

Nawal El Saadawi, Circumcision of Girls

After reading Kim Chernin's "The Flesh and the Devil" (Chapter 3), write an essay exploring how cultural pressure created by manipulating body images of women in contemporary America is as damaging, psychologically and physically, as female circumcision is in the Middle East. To what extent are female circumcision and dieting to the point of anorexia culturally conditioned? How do these two phenomena stem from culturally reinforced stereotypes governing women's bodies? How are these stereotypes related to the status of women in Middle-Eastern and American cultures?

Hanan al-Shaykh, The Persian Carpet

In what sense do both Hanan al-Shaykh's and John Cheever's stories (see "Reunion," Chapter 1) hinge on the disillusionment of the narrators?

N. Scott Momaday, The Names

What cultural values characteristic of the Kiowa are revealed in the accounts by N. Scott Momaday and Gretel Ehrlich (see "To Live in Two Worlds," Chapter 8)?

Sucheng Chan, You're Short, Besides!

What contrasting attitudes toward disabilities emerge from Sucheng Chan's account and Lennard J. Davis's analysis (see "Visualizing the Disabled Body," Chapter 3)?

Dino Buzzati, The Falling Girl

Compare how the reader has to interpret and participate, when the surreal displaces the real, in the stories by Dino Buzzati and Naguib Mahfouz (see "Half a Day," Chapter 9).

Kjell Westö, Melba, Mallinen and me

What insights into the psychology of gang allegiance do you get from Kjell Westö's story and Alonso Salazar's interview (see "The Lords of Creation," Chapter 5)?

3

How Culture Shapes Gender Roles

◆

Culture plays an enormous part in shaping our expectations attached to sex roles. This process, sometimes called *socialization,* determines how each of us assimilates our culture's ideas of what it means to act as a male or female. We tend to acquire a sense of our own sexual identity in conjunction with societal expectations. Yet, these expectations differ strikingly from culture to culture. For example, in male-dominated Islamic Middle Eastern societies, the gender roles and relationships between men and women are very different from those in modern industrial societies.

The characteristics that define gender roles have varied widely throughout history in cultures as diverse as those in Europe, the Orient, South Pacific, Africa, and the Americas. The responsibilities and obligations that collectively define what it means to be a woman or a man in different societies have changed dramatically in those societies, which have themselves changed in recent times. The movement toward equality between the sexes—a transformation that has been only partially realized—has allowed women to assume positions of leadership and perform tasks in the workplace, the professions, and in society that were traditionally reserved for men. The works in this chapter address the changing cultural expectations attached to being a man or a woman as well as the psychological and social stresses produced by these changes in redrawing the boundaries of gender roles, marriage, and parenthood.

How you see yourself is determined in large part by the social meanings attached to specific behavior for men and women in your culture—beginning with the fairy tales told to children, extending through the conceptions of masculinity and femininity promulgated by the media, and including opportunities available in the workplace.

The authors in this chapter provide insight into the way in which we acquire specific sexual identities, because of the cultural expectations, pressures, and values that shape the choices we make. How we

157

feel about ourselves and our life experiences reveals the powerful role gender stereotypes play in shaping our personal development. Some writers in this chapter speak out against the constricting effects of these rigid cultural expectations that enforce inflexible images of masculine and feminine behavior. These restrictive stereotypes legitimize and perpetuate gender inequality.

The writers in this chapter address the question of how males and females learn the sex roles they are to play in their respective societies, and conceive of possibilities beyond the limitations of gender restrictions. Kim Chernin, in "The Flesh and the Devil," perceptively analyzes the cultural pressures that compel women to starve themselves to be thin.

Judith Ortiz Cofer, in "The Myth of the Latin Woman," describes how different cultural expectations in her native Puerto Rico and the United States led her to be stereotyped as a "hot-blooded Latina." From Mali, Sembene Ousmane, in "Her Three Days," reveals the plight of a third wife waiting for her husband's visit. Deborah Tannen, in "Talk in the Intimate Relationship," explores reasons why men and women fail to communicate. Lennard J. Davis, in "Visualizing the Disabled Body," looks at the paradoxical double standard applied to physical imperfection in works of art and in human beings who are disabled. Andrew Sullivan's "What Are Homosexuals For?" explores the differences in lifestyle, perception, and culture that separate homosexuals from heterosexuals. Rosa Liksom, in her story "One Night Stands," looks at the impact of having an abortion through the eyes of a cynical and jaded fourteen-year-old.

Kim Chernin

The Flesh and the Devil

---◆---

Kim Chernin, born in 1940, is a freelance writer, editor, and self-described "feminist humanist." "The Flesh and the Devil" is a chapter from The Obsession: Reflections on the Tyranny of Slenderness *(1981). In this essay, Chernin draws on her personal experiences as well as surveys, research studies, and life stories of friends to support her incisive analysis of the extent to which cultural stereotypes dominate women's lives.*

> *We know that every woman wants to be thin. Our images of womanhood are almost synonymous with thinness.*
>
> —Susie Orbach

> *. . . I must now be able to look at my ideal, this ideal of being thin, of being without a body, and to realize: "it is a fiction."*
>
> —Ellen West

> *When the body is hiding the complex, it then becomes our most immediate access to the problem.*
>
> —Marian Woodman

The locker room of the tennis club. Several exercise benches, two old-fashioned hair dryers, a mechanical bicycle, a treadmill, a reducing machine, a mirror, and a scale. 1

A tall woman enters, removes her towel; she throws it across a bench, faces herself squarely in the mirror, climbs on the scale, looks down. 2

A silence. 3

"I knew it," she mutters, turning to me. "I knew it." 4

And I think, before I answer, just how much I admire her, for this courage beyond my own, this daring to weigh herself daily in this way. And I sympathize. I know what she must be feeling. Not quite candidly, I say: "Up or down?" I am hoping to suggest that there might be people and cultures where gaining weight might not be considered a disaster. Places where women, stepping on scales, might be horrified to notice that they had reduced themselves. A mythical, almost unimaginable land. 5

"Two pounds," she says, ignoring my hint. "Two pounds." And then she turns, grabs the towel and swings out at her image in the mirror, 6 smashing it violently, the towel spattering water over the glass. "Fat pig," she shouts at her image in the glass. "You fat, fat pig. . . ."

7   Later, I go to talk with this woman. Her name is Rachel and she becomes, as my work progresses, one of the choral voices that shape its vision.

8   Two girls come into the exercise room. They are perhaps ten or eleven years old, at that elongated stage when the skeletal structure seems to be winning its war against flesh. And these two are particularly skinny. They sit beneath the hair dryers for a moment, kicking their legs on the faded green upholstery; they run a few steps on the eternal treadmill, they wrap the rubber belt of the reducing machine around themselves and jiggle for a moment before it falls off. And then they go to the scale.

9   The taller one steps up, glances at herself in the mirror, looks down at the scale. She sighs, shaking her head. I see at once that this girl is imitating someone. The sigh, the headshake are theatrical, beyond her years. And so, too, is the little drama enacting itself in front of me. The other girl leans forward, eager to see for herself the troubling message imprinted upon the scale. But the older girl throws her hand over the secret. It is not to be revealed. And now the younger one, accepting this, steps up to confront the ultimate judgment. "Oh God," she says, this growing girl. "Oh God," with only a shade of imitation in her voice: "Would you believe it? I've gained five pounds."

10   These girls, too, become a part of my work. They enter, they perform their little scene again and again; it extends beyond them and in it I am finally able to behold something that would have remained hidden— for it does not express itself directly, although we feel its pressure— almost every day of our lives. Something, unnamed as yet, struggling against our emergence into femininity. This is my first glimpse of it, out there. And the vision ripens.

11   I return to the sauna. Two women I have seen regularly at the club arc sitting on the bench above me. One of them is very beautiful, the sort of woman Renoir would have admired. The other, who is probably in her late sixties, looks, in the twilight of this sweltering room, very much an adolescent. I have noticed her before, with her tan face, her white hair, her fashionable clothes, her slender hips and jaunty walk. But the effect has not been soothing. A woman of advancing age who looks like a boy.

12   "I've heard about that illness, anorexia nervosa," the plump one is saying, "and I keep looking around for someone who has it. I want to go sit next to her. I think to myself, maybe I'll catch it. . . ."

13   "Well," the other woman says to her, "I've felt the same way myself. One of my cousins used to throw food under the table when no one was looking. Finally, she got so thin they had to take her to the hospital. . . . I always admired her."

What am I to understand from these stories? The woman in the   14
locker room who swings out at her image in the mirror, the little girls
who are afraid of the coming of adolescence to their bodies, the woman
who admires the slenderness of the anorexic girl. Is it possible to miss
the dislike these women feel for their bodies?

And yet, an instant's reflection tells us that this dislike for the body   15
is not a biological fact of our condition as women—we do not come
upon it by nature, we are not born to it, it does not arise for us because
of anything predetermined in our sex. We know that once we loved the
body, delighting in it the way children will, reaching out to touch our
toes and count over our fingers, repeating the game endlessly as we
come to knowledge of this body in which we will live out our lives. No
part of the body exempt from our curiosity, nothing yet forbidden, we
know an equal fascination with the feces we eliminate from ourselves,
as with the ear we discover one day and the knees that have become
bruised and scraped with falling and that warm, moist place between
the legs from which feelings of indescribable bliss arise.

From that state to the condition of the woman in the locker room is   16
a journey from innocence to despair, from the infant's naive pleasure in
the body, to the woman's anguished confrontation with herself. In this
journey we can read our struggle with natural existence—the loss of
the body as a source of pleasure. But the most striking thing about this
alienation from the body is the fact that we take it for granted. Few of
us ask to be redeemed from this struggle against the flesh by overcoming our antagonism toward the body. We do not rush about looking for
someone who can tell us how to enjoy the fact that our appetite is large,
or how we might delight in the curves and fullness of our own natural
shape. We hope instead to be able to reduce the body, to limit the urges
and desires it feels, to remove the body from nature. Indeed, the suffering we experience through our obsession with the body arises precisely
from the hopeless and impossible nature of this goal.

Cheryl Prewitt, the 1980 winner of the Miss America contest, is a   17
twenty-two-year-old woman, "slender, bright-eyed, and attractive."[1] If
there were a single woman alive in America today who might feel comfortable about the size and shape of her body, surely we would expect
her to be Ms. Prewitt? And yet, in order to make her body suitable for
the swimsuit event of the beauty contest she has just won, Cheryl Prewitt
"put herself through a grueling regimen, jogging long distances down
back-country roads, pedaling for hours on her stationary bicycle." The
bicycle is still kept in the living room of her parents' house so that she
can take part in conversation while she works out. This body she has
created, after an arduous struggle against nature, in conformity with
her culture's ideal standard for a woman, cannot now be left to its own
desires. It must be perpetually shaped, monitored, and watched. If you
were to visit her at home in Ackerman, Mississippi, you might well

find her riding her stationary bicycle in her parents' living room, "working off the calories from a large slice of homemade coconut cake she has just had for a snack."

18   And so we imagine a woman who will never be Miss America, a next-door neighbor, a woman down the street, waking in the morning and setting out for her regular routine of exercise. The eagerness with which she jumps up at six o'clock and races for her jogging shoes and embarks upon the cold and arduous toiling up the hill road that runs past her house. And yes, she feels certain that her zeal to take off another pound, tighten another inch of softening flesh, places her in the school of those ancient wise men who formulated that vision of harmony between mind and body. "A healthy mind in a healthy body," she repeats to herself and imagines that it is love of the body which inspires her this early morning. But now she lets her mind wander and encounter her obsession. First it had been those hips, and she could feel them jogging along there with their own rhythm as she jogged. It was they that had needed reducing. Then, when the hips came down it was the thighs, hidden when she was clothed but revealing themselves every time she went to the sauna, and threatening great suffering now that summer drew near. Later, it was the flesh under the arms—this proved singularly resistant to tautness even after the rest of the body had become gaunt. And finally it was the ankles. But then, was there no end to it? What had begun as a vision of harmony between mind and body, a sense of well-being, physical fitness, and glowing health, had become now demonic, driving her always to further exploits, running farther, denying herself more food, losing more weight, always goaded on by the idea that the body's perfection lay just beyond her present achievement. And then, when she began to observe this driven quality in herself, she also began to notice what she had been thinking about her body. For she would write down in her notebook, without being aware of the violence in what she wrote: "I don't care how long it takes. One day I'm going to get my body to obey me. I'm going to make it lean and tight and hard. I'll succeed in this, even if it kills me."

19   But what a vicious attitude this is, she realizes one day, toward a body she professes to love. Was it love or hatred of the flesh that inspired her now to awaken even before it was light, and to go out on the coldest morning, running with bare arms and bare legs, busily fantasizing what she would make of her body? Love or hatred?

20   "You know perfectly well we hate our bodies," says Rachel, who calls herself the pig. She grabs the flesh of her stomach between her hands. "Who could love this?"

21   There is an appealing honesty in this despair, an articulation of what is virtually a universal attitude among women in our culture today. Few women who diet realize that they are confessing to a dislike for the body when they weigh and measure their flesh, subject it to rig-

orous fasts or strenuous regimens of exercise. And yet, over and over again, as I spoke to women about their bodies, this antagonism became apparent. One woman disliked her thighs, another her stomach, a third the loose flesh under her arms. Many would grab their skin and squeeze it as we talked, with that grimace of distaste language cannot translate into itself. One woman said to me: "Little by little I began to be aware that the pounds I was trying to 'melt away' were my own flesh. Would you believe it? It never occurred to me before. These 'ugly pounds' which filled me with so much hatred were my body."

The sound of this dawning consciousness can be heard now and again among the voices I have recorded in my notebook, heralding what may be a growing awareness of how bitterly the women of this culture are alienated from their bodies. Thus, another woman said to me: "It's true, I never used to like my body." We had been looking at pictures of women from the nineteenth century; they were large women, with full hips and thighs. "What do you think of them?" I said. "They're like me," she answered, and then began to laugh. "Soft, sensual, and inviting."

22

The description is accurate; the women in the pictures, and the woman looking at them, share a quality of voluptuousness that is no longer admired by our culture:

23

> When I look at myself in the mirror I see that there's nothing wrong with me—now! Sometimes I even think I'm beautiful. I don't know why this began to change. It might have been when I started going to the YWCA. It was the first time I saw so many women naked. I realized it was the fuller bodies that were more beautiful. The thin women, who looked so good in clothes, seemed old and worn out. Their bodies were gaunt. But the bodies of the larger women had a certain natural mystery, very different from the false illusion of clothes. And I thought, I'm like them; I'm a big woman like they are and perhaps my body is beautiful. I had always been trying to make my body have the right shape so that I could fit into clothes. But then I started to look at myself in the mirror. Before that I had always looked at parts of myself. The hips were too flabby, the thighs were too fat. Now I began to see myself as a whole. I stopped hearing my mother's voice, asking me if I was going to go on a diet. I just looked at what was really there instead of what should have been there. What was wrong with it? I asked myself. And little by little I stopped disliking my body.[2]

This is the starting point. It is from this new way of looking at an old problem that liberation will come. The very simple idea that an obsession with weight reflects a dislike and uneasiness for the body can have a profound effect upon a woman's life.

24

> I always thought I was too fat. I never liked my body. I kept trying to lose weight. I just tortured myself. But if I see pictures of myself from a year or two ago I discover now that I looked just fine.

I remember recently going out to buy Häagen Dazs ice cream. I had decided I was going to give myself something I really wanted to eat. I had to walk all the way down to the World Trade Center. But on my way there I began to feel terribly fat. I felt that I was being punished by being fat. I had lost the beautiful self I had made by becoming thinner. I could hear these voices saying to me: "You're fat, you're ugly, who do you think you are, don't you know you'll never be happy?" I had always heard these voices in my mind but now when they would come into consciousness I would tell them to shut up. I saw two men on the street. I was eating the Häagen Dazs ice cream. I thought I heard one of them say "heavy." I thought they were saying: "She's so fat." But I knew that I had to live through these feelings if I was ever to eat what I liked. I just couldn't go on tormenting myself any more about the size of my body.

One day, shortly after this, I walked into my house. I noticed the scales, standing under the sink in the bathroom. Suddenly, I hated them. I was filled with grief for having tortured myself for so many years. They looked like shackles. I didn't want to have anything more to do with them. I called my boyfriend and offered him the scales. Then, I went into the kitchen. I looked at my shelves. I saw diet books there. I was filled with rage and hatred of them. I hurled them all into a box and got rid of them. Then I looked into the ice box. There was a bottle of Weight Watchers dressing. I hurled it into the garbage and watched it shatter and drip down the plastic bag. Little by little, I started to feel better about myself. At first I didn't eat less, I just worried less about my eating. I allowed myself to eat whatever I wanted. I began to give away the clothes I couldn't fit into. It turned out that they weren't right for me anyway. I had bought them with the idea of what my body should look like. Now I buy clothes because I like the way they look on me. If something doesn't fit it doesn't fit. I'm not trying to make myself into something I'm not. I weigh more than I once considered my ideal. But I don't seem fat to myself. Now, I can honestly say that I like my body.[3]

25   Some weeks ago, at a dinner party, a woman who had recently gained weight began to talk about her body.

26   "I was once very thin," she said, "but I didn't feel comfortable in my body. I fit into all the right clothes. But somehow I just couldn't find myself any longer."

27   I looked over at her expectantly; she was a voluptuous woman, who had recently given birth to her first child.

28   "But now," she said as she got to her feet, "now, if I walk or jog or dance, I feel my flesh jiggling along with me." She began to shake her shoulders and move her hips, her eyes wide as she hopped about in front of the coffee table. "You see what I mean?" she shouted over to me. "I love it."

This image of a woman dancing came with me when I sat down to   29
write. I remembered her expression. There was in it something secretive, I thought, something knowing and pleased—the look of a woman
who has made peace with her body. Then I recalled the faces of women
who had recently lost weight. The haggard look, the lines of strain
around the mouth, the neck too lean, the tendons visible, the head too
large for the emaciated body. I began to reason:

There must be, I said, for every woman a correct weight, which   30
cannot be discovered with reference to a weight chart or to any statisti-
cal norm. For the size of the body is a matter of highly subjective individual preferences and natural endowments. If we should evolve an
aesthetic for women that was appropriate to women it would reflect
this diversity, would conceive, indeed celebrate and even love, slenderness in a woman intended by nature to be slim, and love the rounded
cheeks of another, the plump arms, broad shoulders, narrow hips, full
thighs, rounded ass, straight back, narrow shoulders or slender arms,
of a woman made that way according to her nature, walking with head
high in pride of her body, however it happened to be shaped. And then
Miss America, and the woman jogging in the morning, and the woman
swinging out at her image in the mirror might say, with Susan Griffin
in *Woman and Nature:*

> And we are various, and amazing in our variety, and our differences
> multiply, so that edge after edge of the endlessness of possibility is
> exposed . . . none of us beautiful when separate but all exquisite as we
> stand, each moment heeded in this cycle, no detail unlovely. . . .[4]

NOTES

1. Sally Hegelson, *TWA Ambassador,* July 1980.
2. Private communication.
3. Private communication.
4. Susan Griffin, *Woman and Nature: The Roaring Inside Her,* New York, 1978.

✦ Evaluating the Text

1. How do the kinds and range of examples Kim Chernin presents serve
   as evidence for her thesis?

2. According to Chernin, what kind of role do cultural values play in de-
   termining how women see themselves? What is her attitude toward
   these values?

3. What alternative value system does Chernin present to replace the prevailing cultural norms?

✦ *Exploring Different Perspectives*

1. How do Kim Chernin and Lennard J. Davis (see "Visualizing the Disabled Body") deal with questions of the stereotyping of the female body image in western cultures?

2. How do Kim Chernin and Judith Ortiz Cofer (see "The Myth of the Latin Woman") deal with the psychological effects of stereotyping based on appearance?

✦ *Extending Viewpoints Through Writing*

1. To what extent has your own self-image been determined by prevailing cultural expectations of the kind described by Chernin? What parts of your body or aspects of your appearance would you change and why?

2. Analyze some of the cultural messages in ads or other media that communicate socially desirable values having to do with how you look. To what extent do these messages conflict with your own values regarding appearance?

Judith Ortiz Cofer

The Myth of the Latin Woman

---◆---

Judith Ortiz Cofer, a poet and novelist, was born in 1952 in Hormigueros, Puerto Rico. After her father, a career navy officer, retired, the family settled in Georgia where Cofer attended Augusta College. During college she married and, with her husband and daughter, moved to Florida where she finished a master's degree in English at Florida Atlantic University. A fellowship allowed her to pursue graduate work at Oxford University, after which she returned to Florida and began teaching English and writing poetry. Her first volume of poetry, Peregrina *(1985), won the Riverstone International Poetry Competition and was followed by two more poetry collections,* Reaching for the Mainland *(1987) and* Terms of Survival *(1988). Her first novel,* The Line of the Sun *(1989), was listed as one of 1989's "twenty-five books to remember" of 1989 by the New York City Public Library System. In the following essay, drawn from her collection* The Latin Deli: Prose and Poetry *(1993), Cofer explores the destructive effects of the Latina stereotype.*

On a bus trip to London from Oxford University where I was earning some graduate credits one summer, a young man, obviously fresh from a pub, spotted me and as if struck by inspiration went down on his knees in the aisle. With both hands over his heart he broke into an Irish tenor's rendition of "Maria" from *West Side Story*. My politely amused fellow passengers gave his lovely voice the round of gentle applause it deserved. Though I was not quite as amused, I managed my version of an English smile: no show of teeth, no extreme contortions of the facial muscles—I was at this time of my life practicing reserve and cool. Oh, that British control, how I coveted it. But "Maria" had followed me to London, reminding me of a prime fact of my life: you can leave the island, master the English language, and travel as far as you can, but if you are a Latina, especially one like me who so obviously belongs to Rita Moreno's gene pool, the island travels with you.

This is sometimes a very good thing—it may win you that extra minute of someone's attention. But with some people, the same things can make *you* an island—not a tropical paradise but an Alcatraz, a place nobody wants to visit. As a Puerto Rican girl living in the United States and wanting like most children to "belong," I resented the stereotype that my Hispanic appearance called forth from many people I met.

3   Growing up in a large urban center in New Jersey during the 1960s, I suffered from what I think of as "cultural schizophrenia." Our life was designed by my parents as a microcosm of their *casas* on the island. We spoke in Spanish, ate Puerto Rican food bought at the *bodega*, and practiced strict Catholicism at a church that allotted us a one-hour slot each week for mass, performed in Spanish by a Chinese priest trained as a missionary for Latin America.

4   As a girl I was kept under strict surveillance by my parents, since my virtue and modesty were, by their cultural equation, the same as their honor. As a teenager I was lectured constantly on how to behave as a proper *senorita*. But it was a conflicting message I received, since the Puerto Rican mothers also encouraged their daughters to look and act like women and to dress in clothes our Anglo friends and their mothers found too "mature" and flashy. The difference was, and is, cultural; yet I often felt humiliated when I appeared at an American friend's party wearing a dress more suitable to a semi-formal than to a playroom birthday celebration. At Puerto Rican festivities, neither the music nor the colors we wore could be too loud.

5   I remember Career Day in our high school, when teachers told us to come dressed as if for a job interview. It quickly became obvious that to the Puerto Rican girls "dressing up" meant wearing their mothers' ornate jewelry and clothing, more appropriate (by mainstream standards) for the company Christmas party than as daily office attire. That morning I had agonized in front of my closet, trying to figure out what a "career girl" would wear. I knew how to dress for school (at the Catholic school I attended, we all wore uniforms), I knew how to dress for Sunday mass, and I knew what dresses to wear for parties at my relatives' homes. Though I do not recall the precise details of my Career Day outfit, it must have been a composite of these choices. But I remember a comment my friend (an Italian American) made in later years that coalesced my impressions of that day. She said that at the business school she was attending, the Puerto Rican girls always stood out for wearing "everything at once." She meant, of course, too much jewelry, too many accessories. On that day at school we were simply made the negative models by the nuns, who were themselves not credible fashion experts to any of us. But it was painfully obvious to me that to the others, in their tailored skirts and silk blouses, we must have seemed "hopeless" and "vulgar." Though I now know that most adolescents feel out of step much of the time, I also know that for the Puerto Rican girls of my generation that sense was intensified. The way our teachers and classmates looked at us that day in school was just a taste of the cultural clash that awaited us in the real world, where prospective employers and men on the street would often misinterpret our tight skirts and jingling bracelets as a "come-on."

Mixed cultural signals have perpetuated certain stereotypes—for example, that of the Hispanic woman as the "hot tamale" or sexual firebrand. It is a one-dimensional view that the media have found easy to promote. In their special vocabulary, advertisers have designated "sizzling" and "smoldering" as the adjectives of choice for describing not only the foods but also the women of Latin America. From conversations in my house I recall hearing about the harassment that Puerto Rican women endured in factories where the "boss-men" talked to them as if sexual innuendo was all they understood, and worse, often gave them the choice of submitting to their advances or being fired. 6

It is custom, however, not chromosomes, that leads us to choose scarlet over pale pink. As young girls, it was our mothers who influenced our decisions about clothes and colors—mothers who had grown up on a tropical island where the natural environment was a riot of primary colors, where showing your skin was one way to keep cool as well as to look sexy. Most important of all, on the island, women perhaps felt freer to dress and move more provocatively since, in most cases, they were protected by the traditions, mores, and laws of a Spanish/Catholic system of morality and machismo whose main rule was: *You may look at my sister, but if you touch her I will kill you.* The extended family and church structure could provide a young woman with a circle of safety in her small pueblo on the island; if a man "wronged" a girl, everyone would close in to save her family honor. 7

My mother has told me about dressing in her best party clothes on Saturday nights and going to the town's plaza to promenade with her girlfriends in front of the boys they liked. The males were thus given an opportunity to admire the women and to express their admiration in the form of *piropos:* erotically charged street poems they composed on the spot. (I have myself been subjected to a few *piropos* while visiting the island, and they can be outrageous, although custom dictates that they must never cross into obscenity.) This ritual, as I understand it, also entails a show of studied indifference on the woman's part; if she is "decent," she must not acknowledge the man's impassioned words. So I do understand how things can be lost in translation. When a Puerto Rican girl dressed in her idea of what is attractive meets a man from the mainstream culture who has been trained to react to certain types of clothing as a sexual signal, a clash is likely to take place. I remember the boy who took me to my first formal dance leaning over to plant a sloppy, over-eager kiss painfully on my mouth; when I didn't respond with sufficient passion, he remarked resentfully: "I thought you Latin girls were supposed to mature early," as if I were expected to *ripen* like a fruit or vegetable, not just grow into womanhood like other girls. 8

It is surprising to my professional friends that even today some people, including those who should know better, still put others "in 9 their place." It happened to me most recently during a stay at a classy metropolitan hotel favored by young professional couples for weddings. Late one evening after the theater, as I walked toward my room with a colleague (a woman with whom I was coordinating an arts program), a middle-aged man in a tuxedo, with a young girl in satin and lace on his arm, stepped directly into our path. With his champagne glass extended toward me, he exclaimed "Evita!"[1]

10   Our way blocked, my companion and I listened as the man half-recited, half-bellowed "Don't Cry for Me, Argentina." When he finished, the young girl said: "How about a round of applause for my daddy?" We complied, hoping this would bring the silly spectacle to a close. I was becoming aware that our little group was attracting the attention of the other guests. "Daddy" must have perceived this too, and he once more barred the way as we tried to walk past him. He began to shout-sing a ditty to the tune of "La Bamba"—except the lyrics were about a girl named Maria whose exploits rhymed with her name and gonorrhea. The girl kept saying "Oh, Daddy" and looking at me with pleading eyes. She wanted me to laugh along with the others. My companion and I stood silently waiting for the man to end his offensive song. When he finished, I looked not at him but at his daughter. I advised her calmly never to ask her father what he had done in the army. Then I walked between them and to my room. My friend complimented me on my cool handling of the situation, but I confessed that I had really wanted to push the jerk into the swimming pool. This same man—probably a corporate executive, well-educated, even worldly by most standards—would not have been likely to regale an Anglo woman with a dirty song in public. He might have checked his impulse by assuming that she could be somebody's wife or mother, or at least *somebody* who might take offense. But, to him, I was just an Evita or a Maria: merely a character in his cartoon-populated universe.

11   Another facet of the myth of the Latin woman in the United States is the menial, the domestic—Maria the housemaid or countergirl. It's true that work as domestics, as waitresses, and in factories is all that's available to women with little English and few skills. But the myth of the Hispanic menial—the funny maid, mispronouncing words and cooking up a spicy storm in a shiny California kitchen—has been perpetuated by the media in the same way that "Mammy" from *Gone with the Wind* became America's idea of the black woman for generations. Since I do not wear my diplomas around my neck for all to see, I have on occasion been sent to that "kitchen" where some think I obviously belong.

12   One incident has stayed with me, though I recognize it as a minor offense. My first public poetry reading took place in Miami, at a restau-

---

[1]A musical about Eva Duarte de Peron, the former first lady of Argentina.

rant where a luncheon was being held before the event. I was nervous and excited as I walked in with notebook in hand. An older woman motioned me to her table, and thinking (foolish me) that she wanted me to autograph a copy of my newly published slender volume of verse, I went over. She ordered a cup of coffee from me, assuming that I was the waitress. (Easy enough to mistake my poems for menus, I suppose.) I know it wasn't an intentional act of cruelty. Yet of all the good things that happened later, I remember that scene most clearly, because it reminded me of what I had to overcome before anyone would take me seriously. In retrospect I understand that my anger gave my reading fire. In fact, I have almost always taken any doubt in my abilities as a challenge, the result most often being the satisfaction of winning a convert, of seeing the cold, appraising eyes warm to my words, the body language change, the smile that indicates I have opened some avenue for communication. So that day as I read, I looked directly at that woman. Her lowered eyes told me she was embarrassed at her faux pas, and when I willed her to look up at me, she graciously allowed me to punish her with my full attention. We shook hands at the end of the reading and I never saw her again. She has probably forgotten the entire incident, but maybe not.

Yet I am one of the lucky ones. There are thousands of Latinas without the privilege of an education or the entrees into society that I have. For them life is a constant struggle against the misconceptions perpetuated by the myth of the Latina. My goal is to try to replace the old stereotypes with a much more interesting set of realities. Every time I give a reading, I hope the stories I tell, the dreams and fears I examine in my work, can achieve some universal truth that will get my audience past the particulars of my skin color, my accent, or my clothes. 13

I once wrote a poem in which I called all Latinas "God's brown daughters." This poem is really a prayer of sorts, offered upward, but also, through the human-to-human channel of art, outward. It is a prayer for communication and for respect. In it, Latin women pray "in Spanish to an Anglo God/ with a Jewish heritage," and they are "fervently hoping/ that if not omnipotent,/ at least He be bilingual." 14

✦ Evaluating the Text

1. What characteristics define, from Cofer's perspective, the "Maria" stereotype in terms of style, clothes, and behavior? How has this stereotype been a source of harassment for Cofer?

2. How has the desire to destroy this stereotype and its underlying attitudes motivated Cofer to write the kinds of works she has?

3. How does Cofer use her personal experiences as a springboard to understanding sexual stereotyping of Latinas?

4. Restate in your own words Cofer's explanation of the cultural basis for the Latina stereotype as a cross-cultural misperception. How persuasive did you find her explanation?

✦ *Exploring Different Perspectives*

1. How do Cofer and Andrew Sullivan (see "What Are Homosexuals For?") seek to replace sexual stereotypes with realistic portraits?

2. In what ways do Judith Ortiz Cofer and Sembene Ousmane, in "Her Three Days," treat questions of differing cultural expectations about appropriate behavior for women?

✦ *Extending Viewpoints Through Writing*

1. Were you ever perceived in a stereotyped way? What behavioral cues or customs did others use to form their perception of you? What, if anything, did you do to set them straight?

2. Were you ever in a situation in which someone who was unaware of your ethnic, racial, or religious background disparaged the group to which you belong? What did you do?

3. Create a character sketch of a male chauvinist.

Sembene Ousmane

Her Three Days

———◆———

Sembene Ousmane was born in Senegal, North Africa, in 1923. Essentially self-educated, he became a fisherman like his father, then moved to Dakar until the outbreak of World War II, when he was drafted into the French Army and saw action in Italy and Germany. After the war, he went to Marseille where he worked as a docker, joined the French Communist party, and became a union organizer. After his fourth novel, Ousmane studied at the Moscow Film School and wrote and directed several films including The Money Order, *which won a prize at the Venice Film Festival.* Zala, *based on his 1973 novel, went on to become one of a series of successful films that established his reputation as a director. Ousmane's latest novel,* Niiwam and Taaw, *was published in 1992. "Her Three Days," translated by Len Ortzen, is taken from Ousmane's 1974 collection of short stories,* Tribal Scars. *In this compassionate and realistic account of the plight of a third wife waiting for her husband to return, Ousmane dramatizes the rules governing Muslim life in Mali under which, according to the Koran, "every wife of a Muslim is entitled to three days of her husband's company each month."*

The Republic of Mali is the largest country in West Africa, bordered by Algeria to the north, Niger to the east, Burkina Faso and the Ivory Coast to the south, and Guinea, Senegal, and Mauritania to the west. The Muslim influence in Mali (where today about 90 percent of the people are Sunni Muslims) began in 700 A.D. with the Arab conquest of North Africa. During medieval times, Mali was a powerful state, and the city of Timbuktu served as a commercial and cultural center for several centuries. Subsequent invasions by Morocco in 1591 shattered the empire into a series of smaller states dominated by nomadic tribes, including the Tuareg. The French began exercising sovereignty over this area and in 1898 Mali, then called the French Sudan, became part of French West Africa. Nationalist movements that began between the two World Wars led to full independence and to the formation of the new Republic of Mali in 1960. Famines and periodic border conflicts between Mali and Burkina Faso from 1974 through 1985 have slowed economic progress. The country had been led since 1969 by General Moussa Traore, but, in 1991 when popular demonstrations erupted and Traore ordered his soldiers to shoot civilians, key army officers staged a coup and Traore was arrested. Since then a new constitution was drafted, and a national assembly was elected under the leadership of President Alpha Oumar Konare, whose multiparty democracy faces serious challenges if it is to survive. As reflected in "Her Three Days," polygamy is still practiced but has increasingly been seen as an economic burden. Currently, a Moslem man who wishes to take another wife must first gain the approval of his first wife and then must provide for all wives (up to four) equally. In urban areas, many women no longer accept the status of being second, third, or fourth wife.

1   She raised her haggard face, and her far-away look ranged beyond the muddle of roofs, some tiled, others of thatch or galvanized-iron; the wide fronds of the twin coconut-palms were swaying slowly in the breeze, and in her mind she could hear their faint rustling. Noumbe was thinking of "her three days." Three days for her alone, when she would have her husband Mustapha to herself . . . It was a long time since she had felt such emotion. To have Mustapha! The thought comforted her. She had heart trouble and still felt some pain, but she had been dosing herself for the past two days, taking more medicine than was prescribed. It was a nice syrup that just slipped down, and she felt the beneficial effects at once. She blinked; her eyes were like two worn buttonholes, with lashes that were like frayed thread, in little clusters of fives and threes; the whites were the colour of old ivory.

2   "What's the matter, Noumbe?" asked Aida, her next-door neighbour, who was sitting at the door of her room.

3   "Nothing," she answered, and went on cutting up the slice of raw meat, helped by her youngest daughter.

4   "Ah, it's your three days," exclaimed Aida, whose words held a meaning that she could not elaborate on while the little girl was present. She went on: "You're looking fine enough to prevent a holy man from saying his prayers properly!"

5   "Aida, be careful what you say," she protested, a little annoyed.

6   But it was true; Noumbe had plaited her hair and put henna on her hands and feet. And that morning she had got the children up early to give her room a thorough clean. She was not old, but one pregnancy after another—and she had five children—and her heart trouble had aged her before her time.

7   "Go and ask Laity to give you five francs' worth of salt and twenty francs' worth of oil," Noumbe said to the girl. "Tell him I sent you. I'll pay for them as soon as your father is here, at midday." She looked disapprovingly at the cut-up meat in the bottom of the bowl.

8   The child went off with the empty bottle and Noumbe got to her feet. She was thin and of average height. She went into her one-room shack, which was sparsely furnished; there was a bed with a white cover, and in one corner stood a table with pieces of china on display. The walls were covered with enlargements and photos of friends and strangers framed in passe-partout.

When she came out again she took the Moorish stove and set about   9
lighting it.

Her daughter had returned from her errand.   10

"He gave them to you?" asked Noumbe.   11

"Yes, mother."   12

A woman came across the compound to her. "Noumbe, I can see   13
that you're preparing a delicious dish."

"Yes," she replied. "It's my three days. I want to revive the feasts of   14
the old days, so that his palate will retain the taste of the dish for many
moons, and he'll forget the cooking of his other wives."

"Ah-ha! So that his palate is eager for dishes to come," said the   15
woman, who was having a good look at the ingredients.

"I'm feeling in good form," said Noumbe, with some pride in her   16
voice. She grasped the woman's hand and passed it over her loins.

"*Thieh, souya dome!* I hope you can say the same tomorrow   17
morning . . ."

The woman clapped her hands; as if it were a signal or an invita-   18
tion, other women came across, one with a metal jar, another with a
saucepan, which they beat while the woman sang:

> *Sope dousa rafetail,*
> *Sopa nala dousa rafetail*
> *Sa yahi n'diguela.*
> (Worship of you is not for your beauty,
> I worship you not for your beauty
> But for your backbone.)

In a few moments, they improvised a wild dance to this chorus. At   19
the end, panting and perspiring, they burst out laughing. Then one of
them stepped into Noumbe's room and called the others.

"Let's take away the bed! Because tonight they'll wreck it!"   20

"She's right. Tomorrow this room will be . . ."   21

Each woman contributed an earthy comment which set them all   22
laughing hilariously. Then they remembered they had work to do,
and brought their amusement to an end; each went back to her family
occupations.

Noumbe had joined in the laughter; she knew this boisterous "rag-   23
ging" was the custom in the compound. No one escaped it. Besides, she
was an exceptional case, as they all knew. She had a heart condition
and her husband had quite openly neglected her. Mustapha had not
been to see her for a fortnight. All this time she had been hoping that he
would come, if only for a moment. When she went to the clinic for
mothers and children she compelled her youngest daughter to stay at
home, so that—thus did her mind work—if her husband turned up the
child could detain him until she returned. She ought to have gone to

the clinic again this day, but she had spent what little money she possessed on preparing for Mustapha. She did not want her husband to esteem her less than his other wives, or to think her meaner. She did not neglect her duty as a mother, but her wifely duty came first—at certain times.

24   She imagined what the next three days would be like; already her "three days" filled her whole horizon. She forgot her illness and her baby's ailments. She had thought about these three days in a thousand different ways. Mustapha would not leave before the Monday morning. In her mind she could see Mustapha and his henchmen crowding into her room, and could hear their suggestive jokes. "If she had been a perfect wife . . ." She laughed to herself. "Why shouldn't it always be like that for every woman—to have a husband of one's own?" She wondered why not.

25   The morning passed at its usual pace, the shadows of the coconut-palms and the people growing steadily shorter. As midday approached, the housewives busied themselves with the meal. In the compound each one stood near her door, ready to welcome her man. The kids were playing around, and their mothers' calls to them crossed in the air. Noumbe gave her children a quick meal and sent them out again. She sat waiting for Mustapha to arrive at any moment . . . he wouldn't be much longer now.

26   An hour passed, and the men began going back to work. Soon the compound was empty of the male element; the women, after a long siesta, joined one another under the coconut-palms and the sounds of their gossiping gradually increased.

27   Noumbe, weary of waiting, had finally given up keeping a lookout. Dressed in her mauve velvet, she had been on the watch since before midday. She had eaten no solid food, consoling herself with the thought that Mustapha would appear at any moment. Now she fought back the pangs of hunger by telling herself that in the past Mustapha had a habit of arriving late. In those days, this lateness was pleasant. Without admitting it to herself, those moments (which had hung terribly heavy) had been very sweet; they prolonged the sensual pleasure of anticipation. Although those minutes had been sometimes shot through with doubts and fears (often, very often, the thought of her coming disgrace had assailed her; for Mustapha, who had taken two wives before her, had just married another), they had not been too hard to bear. She realized that those demanding minutes were the price she had to pay for Mustapha's presence. Then she began to reckon up the score, in small ways, against the *veudieux*, the other wives. One washed his *boubous* when it was another wife's turn, or kept him long into the night; another sometimes held him in her embrace a whole day, knowing quite well that she was preventing Mustapha from carrying out his marital duty elsewhere.

She sulked as she waited; Mustapha had not been near her for a 28
fortnight. All these bitter thoughts brought her up against reality: four
months ago Mustapha had married a younger woman. This sudden realization of the facts sent a pain to her heart, a pain of anguish. The additional pain did not prevent her heart from functioning normally,
rather was it like a sick person whose sleep banishes pain but who once
awake again finds his suffering is as bad as ever, and pays for the relief
by a redoubling of pain.

She took three spoonfuls of her medicine instead of the two pre- 29
scribed, and felt a little better in herself.

She called her youngest daughter. "Tell Mactar I want him." 30

The girl ran off and soon returned with her eldest brother. 31

"Go and fetch your father," Noumbe told him. 32

"Where, mother?" 33

"Where? Oh, on the main square or at one of your other mothers'." 34

"But I've been to the main square already, and he wasn't there." 35

"Well, go and have another look. Perhaps he's there now." 36

The boy looked up at his mother, then dropped his head again and 37
reluctantly turned to go.

"When your father has finished eating, I'll give you what's left. It's 38
meat. Now be quick, Mactar."

It was scorching hot and the clouds were riding high. Mactar was 39
back after an hour. He had not found his father. Noumbe went and
joined the group of women. They were chattering about this and that;
one of them asked (just for the sake of asking), "Noumbe, has your uncle
(darling) arrived?" "Not yet," she replied, then hastened to add, "Oh,
he won't be long now. He knows it's my three days." She deliberately
changed the conversation in order to avoid a long discussion about the
other three wives. But all the time she was longing to go and find Mustapha. She was being robbed of her three days. And the other wives
knew it. Her hours alone with Mustapha were being snatched from her.
The thought of his being with one of the other wives, who was feeding
him and opening his waistcloth when she ought to be doing all that,
who was enjoying those hours which were hers by right, so numbed
Noumbe that it was impossible for her to react. The idea that Mustapha
might have been admitted to hospital or taken to a police station never
entered her head.

She knew how to make tasty little dishes for Mustapha which cost 40
him nothing. She never asked him for money. Indeed, hadn't she got
herself into debt so that he would be more comfortable and have better
meals at her place? And in the past, when Mustapha sometimes arrived
unexpectedly—this was soon after he had married her—hadn't she
hastened to make succulent dishes for him? All her friends knew this.

A comforting thought coursed through her and sent these aggres- 41
sive and vindictive reflections to sleep. She told herself that Mustapha

was bound to come to her this evening. The certainty of his presence stripped her mind of the too cruel thought that the time of her dis-favour was approaching; this thought had been as much a burden to her as a heavy weight dragging a drowning man to the bottom. When all the bad, unfavourable thoughts besetting her had been dispersed, like piles of rubbish on waste land swept by a flood, the future seemed brighter, and she joined in the conversation of the women with childish enthusiasm, unable to hide her pleasure and her hopes. It was like something in a parcel; questioning eyes wondered what was inside, but she alone knew and enjoyed the secret, drawing an agreeable strength from it. She took an active part in the talking and brought her wit into play. All this vivacity sprang from the joyful conviction that Mustapha would arrive this evening very hungry and be hers alone.

42   In the far distance, high above the tree-tops, a long trail of dark-grey clouds tinged with red was hiding the sun. The time for the *tacou-sane*, the afternoon prayer, was drawing near. One by one, the women withdrew to their rooms, and the shadows of the trees grew longer, wider and darker.

43   Night fell; a dark, starry night.

44   Noumbe cooked some rice for the children. They clamoured in vain for some of the meat. Noumbe was stern and unyielding: "The meat is for your father. He didn't eat at midday." When she had fed the children, she washed herself again to get rid of the smell of cooking and touched up her toilette, rubbing oil on her hands, feet and legs to make the henna more brilliant. She intended to remain by her door, and sat down on the bench; the incense smelt strongly, filling the whole room. She was facing the entrance to the compound and could see the other women's husbands coming in.

45   But for her there was no one.

46   She began to feel tired again. Her heart was troubling her, and she had a fit of coughing. Her inside seemed to be on fire. Knowing that she would not be going to the dispensary during her "three days," in order to economize, she went and got some wood-ash which she mixed with water and drank. It did not taste very nice, but it would make the medicine last longer, and the drink checked and soothed the burning within her for a while. She was tormenting herself with the thoughts passing through her mind. Where can he be? With the first wife? No, she's quite old. The second then? Everyone knew that she was out of favour with Mustapha. The third wife was herself. So he must be with the fourth. There were puckers of uncertainty and doubt in the answers she gave herself. She kept putting back the time to go to bed, like a lover who does not give up waiting when the time of the rendezvous is long past, but with an absurd and stupid hope waits still longer, self-torture and the heavy minutes chaining him to the spot. At each step Noumbe took, she stopped and mentally explored the town, prying

into each house inhabited by one of the other wives. Eventually she went indoors.

So that she would not be caught unawares by Mustapha nor lose   47
the advantages which her make-up and good clothes gave her, she lay down on the bed fully dressed and alert. She had turned down the lamp as far as possible, so the room was dimly lit. But she fell asleep despite exerting great strength of mind to remain awake and saying repeatedly to herself, "I shall wait for him." To make sure that she would be standing there expectantly when he crossed the threshold, she had bolted the door. Thus she would be the devoted wife, always ready to serve her husband, having got up at once and appearing as elegant as if it were broad daylight. She had even thought of making a gesture as she stood there, of passing her hands casually over her hips so that Mustapha would hear the clinking of the beads she had strung round her waist and be incited to look at her from head to foot.

Morning came, but there was no Mustapha.   48

When the children awoke they asked if their father had come. The   49
oldest of them, Mactar, a promising lad, was quick to spot that his mother had not made the bed, that the bowl containing the stew was still in the same place, by a dish of rice, and the loaf of bread on the table was untouched. The children got a taste of their mother's anger. The youngest, Amadou, took a long time over dressing. Noumbe hurried them up and sent the youngest girl to Laity's to buy five francs' worth of ground coffee. The children's breakfast was warmed-up rice with a meagre sprinkling of gravy from the previous day's stew. Then she gave them their wings, as the saying goes, letting them all out except the youngest daughter. Noumbe inspected the bottle of medicine and saw that she had taken a lot of it; there were only three spoonfuls left. She gave herself half a spoonful and made up for the rest with her mixture of ashes and water. After that she felt calmer.

"Why, Noumbe, you must have got up bright and early this morn-   50
ing, to be so dressed up. Are you going off on a long journey?"

It was Aida, her next-door neighbour, who was surprised to see her   51
dressed in such a manner, especially for a woman who was having "her three days." Then Aida realized what had happened and tried to rectify her mistake.

"Oh, I see he hasn't come yet. They're all the same, these men!"   52

"He'll be here this morning, Aida." Noumbe bridled, ready to de-   53
fend her man. But it was rather her own worth she was defending, wanting to conceal what an awful time she had spent. It had been a broken night's sleep, listening to harmless sounds which she had taken for Mustapha's footsteps, and this had left its mark on her already haggard face.

"I'm sure he will! I'm sure he will!" exclaimed Aida, well aware of   54
this comedy that all the women played in turn.

55   "Mustapha is such a kind man, and so noble in his attitude," added another woman, rubbing it in.

56   "If he weren't, he wouldn't be my master," said Noumbe, feeling flattered by this description of Mustapha.

57   The news soon spread round the compound that Mustapha had slept elsewhere during Noumbe's three days. The other women pitied her. It was against all the rules for Mustapha to spend a night elsewhere. Polygamy had its laws, which should be respected. A sense of decency and common dignity restrained a wife from keeping the husband day and night when his whole person and everything connected with him belonged to another wife during "her three days." The game, however, was not without its underhand tricks that one wife played on another; for instance, to wear out the man and hand him over when he was incapable of performing his conjugal duties. When women criticized the practice of polygamy they always found that the wives were to blame, especially those who openly dared to play a dirty trick. The man was whitewashed. He was a weakling who always ended by falling into the enticing traps set for him by woman. Satisfied with this conclusion, Noumbe's neighbours made common cause with her and turned to abusing Mustapha's fourth wife.

58   Noumbe made some coffee—she never had any herself, because of her heart. She consoled herself with the thought that Mustapha would find more things at her place. The bread had gone stale; she would buy some more when he arrived.

59   The hours dragged by again, long hours of waiting which became harder to bear as the day progressed. She wished she knew where he was . . . The thought obsessed her, and her eyes became glazed and searching. Every time she heard a man's voice she straightened up quickly. Her heart was paining her more and more, but the physical pain was separate from the mental one; they never came together, alternating in a way that reminded her of the acrobatic feat of a man riding two speeding horses.

60   At about four o'clock Noumbe was surprised to see Mustapha's second wife appear at the door. She had come to see if Mustapha was there, knowing that it was Noumbe's three days. She did not tell Noumbe the reason for her wishing to see Mustapha, despite being pressed. So Noumbe concluded that it was largely due to jealousy, and was pleased that the other wife could see how clean and tidy her room was, and what a display of fine things she had, all of which could hardly fail to make the other think that Mustapha had been (and still was) very generous to her, Noumbe. During the rambling conversation her heart thumped ominously, but she bore up and held off taking any medicine.

61   Noumbe remembered only too well that when she was newly married she had usurped the second wife's three days. At that time she had

been the youngest wife. Mustapha had not let a day pass without coming to see her. Although not completely certain, she believed she had conceived her third child during this wife's three days. The latter's presence now and remarks that she let drop made Noumbe realize that she was no longer the favourite. This revelation, and the polite, amiable tone and her visitor's eagerness to inquire after her children's health and her own, to praise her superior choice of household utensils, her taste in clothes, the cleanliness of the room and the lingering fragrance of the incense, all this was like a stab in cold blood, a cruel reminder of the perfidy of words and the hypocrisy of rivals; and all part of the world of women. This observation did not get her anywhere, except to arouse a desire to escape from the circle of polygamy and to cause her to ask herself—it was a moment of mental aberration really—"Why do we allow ourselves to be men's playthings?"

The other wife complimented her and insisted that Noumbe's children should go and spend a few days with her own children (in this she was sincere). By accepting in principle, Noumbe was weaving her own waist-cloth of hypocrisy. It was all to make the most of herself, to set tongues wagging so that she would lose none of her respectability and rank. The other wife casually added—before she forgot, as she said—that she wanted to see Mustapha, and if mischief-makers told Noumbe that "their" husband had been to see her during Noumbe's three days, Noumbe shouldn't think ill of her, and she would rather have seen him here to tell him what she had to say. To save face, Noumbe dared not ask her when she had last seen Mustapha. The other would have replied with a smile, "The last morning of my three days, of course. I've only come here because it's urgent." And Noumbe would have looked embarrassed and put on an air of innocence. "No, that isn't what I meant. I just wondered if you had happened to meet him by chance."

Neither of them would have lost face. It was all that remained to them. They were not lying, to their way of thinking. Each had been desired and spoilt for a time, then the man, like a gorged vulture, had left them on one side and the venom of chagrin at having been mere playthings had entered their hearts. They quite understood, it was all quite clear to them, that they could sink no lower; so they clung to what was left to them, that is to say, to saving what dignity remained to them by false words and gaining advantages at the expense of the other. They did not indulge in this game for the sake of it. This falseness contained all that remained of the flame of dignity. No one was taken in, certainly not themselves. Each knew that the other was lying, but neither could bring herself to further humiliation, for it would be the final crushing blow.

The other wife left. Noumbe almost propelled her to the door, then stood there thoughtful for a few moments. Noumbe understood the reason for the other's visit. She had come to get her own back. Noumbe felt absolutely sure that Mustapha was with his latest wife. The visit meant in fact: "You stole those days from me because I am older than you. Now a younger woman than you is avenging me. Try as you might to make everything nice and pleasant for him, you have to toe the line with the rest of us now, you old carcass. He's slept with someone else—and he will again."

65   The second day passed like the first, but was more dreadful. She ate no proper food, just enough to stave off the pangs of hunger.

66   It was Sunday morning and all the men were at home; they nosed about in one room and another, some of them cradling their youngest in their arms, others playing with the older children. The draught-players had gathered in one place, the card-players in another. There was a friendly atmosphere in the compound, with bursts of happy laughter and sounds of guttural voices, while the women busied themselves with the housework.

67   Aida went to see Noumbe to console her, and said without much conviction, "He'll probably come today. Men always seem to have something to do at the last minute. It's Sunday today, so he'll be here."

68   "Aida, Mustapha doesn't work," Noumbe pointed out, hard-eyed. She gave a cough. "I've been waiting for him now for two days and nights! When it's my three days I think the least he could do is to be here—at night, anyway. I might die . . ."

69   "Do you want me to go and look for him?"

70   "No."

71   She had thought "yes." It was the way in which Aida had made the offer that embarrassed her. Of course she would like her to! Last night, when everyone had gone to bed, she had started out and covered quite some distance before turning back. The flame of her dignity had been fanned on the way. She did not want to abase herself still further by going to claim a man who seemed to have no desire to see her. She had lain awake until dawn, thinking it all over and telling herself that her marriage to Mustapha was at an end, that she would divorce him. But this morning there was a tiny flicker of hope in her heart: "Mustapha will come, all the same. This is my last night."

72   She borrowed a thousand francs from Aida, who readily lent her the money. And she followed the advice to send the children off again, to Mustapha's fourth wife.

73   "Tell him that I must see him at once, I'm not well!"

74   She hurried off to the little market near by and bought a chicken and several other things. Her eyes were feverishly, joyfully bright as she carefully added seasoning to the dish she prepared. The appetizing smell of her cooking was wafted out to the compound and its Sunday

atmosphere. She swept the room again, shut the door and windows, but the heady scent of the incense escaped through the cracks between the planks.

The children returned from their errand.   75

"Is he ill?" she asked them.   76

"No, mother. He's going to come. We found him with some of his   77
friends at Voulimata's (the fourth wife). He asked about you."

"And that's all he said?"   78

"Yes, mother."   79

"Don't come indoors. Here's ten francs. Go and play somewhere   80
else."

A delicious warm feeling spread over her. "He was going to come."   81
Ever since Friday she had been harbouring spiteful words to throw in
his face. He would beat her, of course . . . But never mind. Now she
found it would be useless to utter those words. Instead she would do
everything possible to make up for the lost days. She was happy, much
too happy to bear a grudge against him, now that she knew he was
coming—he might even be on the way with his henchmen. The only
means of getting her own back was to cook a big meal . . . then he
would stay in bed.

She finished preparing the meal, had a bath and went on to the rest   82
of her toilette. She did her hair again, put antimony on her lower lip,
eyebrows and lashes, then dressed in a white starched blouse and a
hand-woven waist-cloth, and inspected her hands and feet. She was
quite satisfied with her appearance.

But the waiting became prolonged.   83

No one in the compound spoke to her for fear of hurting her feel-   84
ings. She had sat down outside the door, facing the entrance to the
compound, and the other inhabitants avoided meeting her sorrowful
gaze. Her tears overflowed the brim of her eyes like a swollen river its
banks; she tried to hold them back, but in vain. She was eating her
heart out.

The sound of a distant tom-tom was being carried on the wind.   85
Time passed over her, like the seasons over monuments. Twilight came
and darkness fell.

On the table were three plates in a row, one for each day.   86

"I've come to keep you company," declared Aida as she entered the   87
room. Noumbe was sitting on the foot of the bed—she had fled from
the silence of the others. "You mustn't get worked up about it," went
on Aida. "Every woman goes through it. Of course it's not nice! But I
don't think he'll be long now."

Noumbe raised a moist face and bit her lips nervously. Aida saw   88
that she had made up her mind not to say anything. Everything was

shrouded in darkness; no light came from her room. After supper, the children had refrained from playing their noisy games.

89   Just when adults were beginning to feel sleepy and going to bed, into the compound walked Mustapha, escorted by two of his lieutenants. He was clad entirely in white. He greeted the people still about in an oily manner, then invited his companions into Noumbe's hut.

90   She had not stirred.

91   "Wife, where's the lamp?"

92   "Where you left it this morning when you went out."

93   "How are you?" inquired Mustapha when he had lit the lamp. He went and sat down on the bed, and motioned to the two men to take the bench.

94   "God be praised," Noumbe replied to his polite inquiry. Her thin face seemed relaxed and the angry lines had disappeared.

95   "And the children?"

96   "They're well, praise be to God."

97   "Our wife isn't very talkative this evening," put in one of the men.

98   "I'm quite well, though."

99   "Your heart isn't playing you up now?" asked Mustapha, not unkindly.

100   "No, it's quite steady," she answered.

101   "God be praised! Mustapha, we'll be off," said the man, uncomfortable at Noumbe's cold manner.

102   "Wait," said Mustapha, and turned to Noumbe. "Wife, are we eating tonight or tomorrow?"

103   "Did you leave me something when you went out this morning?"

104   "What? That's not the way to answer."

105   "No, uncle (darling). I'm just asking . . . Isn't it right?"

106   Mustapha realized that Noumbe was mocking him and trying to humiliate him in front of his men.

107   "You do like your little joke. Don't you know it's your three days?"

108   "Oh, uncle, I'm sorry, I'd quite forgotten. What an unworthy wife I am!" she exclaimed, looking straight at Mustapha.

109   "You're making fun of me!"

110   "Oh, uncle, I shouldn't dare! What, I? And who would help me into Paradise, if not my worthy husband? Oh, I would never poke fun at you, neither in this world nor the next."

111   "Anyone would think so."

112   "Who?" she asked.

113   "You might have stood up when I came in, to begin with . . ."

114   "Oh, uncle, forgive me. I'm out of my mind with joy at seeing you again. But whose fault is that, uncle?"

115   "And just what are these three plates for?" said Mustapha with annoyance.

"These three plates?" She looked at him, a malicious smile on her   116
lips. "Nothing. Or rather, my three days. Nothing that would interest
you. Is there anything here that interests you . . . uncle?"

As if moved by a common impulse, the three men stood up.   117

Noumbe deliberately knocked over one of the plates. "Oh, uncle,   118
forgive me . . ." Then she broke the other two plates. Her eyes had gone
red; suddenly a pain stabbed at her heart, she bent double, and as she
fell to the floor gave a loud groan which roused the whole compound.

Some women came hurrying in. "What's the matter with her?"   119

"Nothing . . . only her heart. Look what she's done, the silly   120
woman. One of these days her jealousy will suffocate her. I haven't
been to see her—only two days, and she cries her eyes out. Give her
some ash and she'll be all right," gabbled Mustapha, and went off.

"Now these hussies have got their associations, they think they're   121
going to run the country," said one of his men.

"Have you heard that at Bamako they passed a resolution con-   122
demning polygamy?" added the other. "Heaven preserve us from having only one wife. "

"They can go out to work then," pronounced Mustapha as he left   123
the compound.

Aida and some of the women lifted Noumbe on to the bed. She was   124
groaning. They got her to take some of her mixture of ash and water . . .

✦ Evaluating the Text

1. How do the preparations she makes provide important insights into
   Noumbe's character that explain her relationships with Mustapha, his
   other wives, and her friends and neighbors?

2. How do Noumbe's memories of how she behaved when she was the
   "new" wife add an ironic dimension to the story? How does it make
   you feel about her?

3. What changes can you observe in Noumbe's character from the beginning of the story through its conclusion? What does she do or say at
   the end of the story that implies she will never be the same person she
   was at the beginning of the story?

✦ Exploring Different Perspectives

1. Compare the selections by Sembene Ousmane and Kim Chernin (see
   "The Flesh and the Devil") to discover differences in what their respective cultures consider to be beautiful.

2. Using Deborah Tannen's hypothesis about "metamessages," analyze Noumbé's conversations in Sembene Ousmane's story.

✦ *Extending Viewpoints Through Writing*

1. In a short essay, discuss the author's attitude toward polygamy and its effect on the relationship between men and women as it emerges in this story.

2. Describe someone who initially had very little self-esteem and who gained self-confidence.

Deborah Tannen

Talk in the
Intimate Relationship

———————◆———————

Deborah Tannen is a professor of linguistics at Georgetown University. She is the author of many books, including You Just Don't Understand: Men and Women in Conversation *(1990),* That's Not What I Meant!: How Conversational Style Makes or Breaks Relationships *(1986), and* Talking from 9 to 5: How Women's and Men's Conversational Styles Affect Who Gets Heard and Who Gets Credit and What Gets Done at Work *(1994). The following essay is drawn from the second of these studies.*

Male-female conversation is cross-cultural communication. Culture is simply a network of habits and patterns gleaned from past experience, and women and men have different past experiences. From the time they're born, they're treated differently, talked to differently, and talk differently as a result. Boys and girls grow up in different worlds, even if they grow up in the same house. And as adults they travel in different worlds, reinforcing patterns established in childhood. These cultural differences include different expectations about the role of talk in relationships and how it fulfills that role.

Everyone knows that as a relationship becomes long-term, its terms change. But women and men often differ in how they expect them to change. Many women feel, "After all this time, you should know what I want without my telling you." Many men feel, "After all this time, we should be able to tell each other what we want."

These incongruent expectations capture one of the key differences between men and women. Communication is always a matter of balancing conflicting needs for involvement and independence. Though everyone has both these needs, women often have a relatively greater need for involvement, and men a relatively greater need for independence. Being understood without saying what you mean gives a payoff in involvement, and that is why women value it so highly.

If you want to be understood without saying what you mean explicitly in words, you must convey meaning somewhere else—in how words are spoken, or by metamessages. Thus it stands to reason that women are often more attuned than men to the metamessages of talk. When women surmise meaning in this way, it seems mysterious to men, who call it "women's intuition" (if they think it's right) or "reading things in" (if they think it's wrong). Indeed, it could be wrong, since metamessages are not on record. And even if it is right, there is still the question of scale: How significant are the metamessages that are there?

5   Metamessages are a form of indirectness. Women are more likely to be indirect, and to try to reach agreement by negotiation. Another way to understand this preference is that negotiation allows a display of solidarity, which women prefer to the display of power (even though the aim may be the same—getting what you want). Unfortunately, power and solidarity are bought with the same currency: Ways of talking intended to create solidarity have the simultaneous effect of framing power differences. When they think they're being nice, women often end up appearing deferential and unsure of themselves or of what they want.

6   When styles differ, misunderstandings are always rife. As their differing styles create misunderstandings, women and men try to clear them up by talking things out. These pitfalls are compounded in talks between men and women because they have different ways of going about talking things out, and different assumptions about the significance of going about it.

7   Sylvia and Harry celebrated their fiftieth wedding anniversary at a mountain resort. Some of the guests were at the resort for the whole weekend, others just for the evening of the celebration: a cocktail party followed by a sit-down dinner. The manager of the dining room approached Sylvia during dinner. "Since there's so much food tonight," he said, "and the hotel prepared a fancy dessert and everyone already ate at the cocktail party anyway, how about cutting and serving the anniversary cake at lunch tomorrow?" Sylvia asked the advice of the others at her table. All the men agreed: "Sure, that makes sense. Save the cake for tomorrow." All the women disagreed: "No, the party is tonight. Serve the cake tonight." The men were focusing on the message: the cake as food. The women were thinking of the metamessage: Serving a special cake frames an occasion as a celebration.

8   Why are women more attuned to metamessages? Because they are more focused on involvement, that is, on relationships among people, and it is through metamessages that relationships among people are established and maintained. If you want to take the temperature and check the vital signs of a relationship, the barometers to check are its metamessages: what is said and how.

9   Everyone can see these signals, but whether or nor we pay attention to them is another matter—a matter of being sensitized. Once you are sensitized, you can't roll your antennae back in; they're stuck in the extended position.

10   When interpreting meaning, it is possible to pick up signals that weren't intentionally sent out, like an innocent flock of birds on a radar screen. The birds are there—and the signals women pick up are there—

but they may not mean what the interpreter thinks they mean. For example, Maryellen looks at Larry and asks, "What's wrong?" because his brow is furrowed. Since he was only thinking about lunch, her expression of concern makes him feel under scrutiny.

The difference in focus on messages and metamessages can give   11
men and women different points of view on almost any comment. Harriet complains to Morton, "Why don't you ask me how my day was?" He replies, "If you have something to tell me, tell me. Why do you have to be invited?" The reason is that she wants the metamessage of interest: evidence that he cares how her day was, regardless of whether or not she has something to tell.

A lot of trouble is caused between women and men by, of all   12
things, pronouns. Women often feel hurt when their partners use "I" or "me" in a situation in which they would use "we" or "us." When Morton announces, "I think I'll go for a walk," Harriet feels specifically uninvited, though Morton later claims she would have been welcome to join him. She felt locked out by his use of "I" and his omission of an invitation: "Would you like to come?" Metamessages can be seen in what is not said as well as what is said.

It's difficult to straighten out such misunderstandings because each   13
one feels convinced of the logic of his or her position and the illogic—or irresponsibility—of the other's. Harriet knows that she always asks Morton how his day was, and that she'd never announce, "I'm going for a walk," without inviting him to join her. If he talks differently to her, it must be that he feels differently. But Morton wouldn't feel unloved if Harriet didn't ask about his day, and he would feel free to ask, "Can I come along?," if she announced she was taking a walk. So he can't believe she is justified in feeling responses he knows he wouldn't have.

These processes are dramatized with chilling yet absurdly amusing   14
authenticity in Jules Feiffer's play *Grown Ups*. To get a closer look at what happens when men and women focus on different levels of talk in talking things out, let's look at what happens in this play.

Jake criticizes Louise for not responding when their daughter,   15
Edie, called her. His comment leads to a fight even though they're both aware that this one incident is not in itself important.

> *Jake:* Look, I don't care if it's important or not, when a kid calls its   16
>   mother the mother should answer.
> *Louise:* Now I'm a bad mother.   17
> *Jake:* I didn't say that.   18
> *Louise:* It's in your stare.   19
> *Jake:* Is that another thing you know? My stare?   20

Louise ignores Jake's message—the question of whether or not she re-   21
sponded when Edie called—and goes for the metamessage: his

implication that she's a bad mother, which Jake insistently disclaims. When Louise explains the signals she's reacting to, Jake not only discounts them but is angered at being held accountable not for what he said but for how he looked—his stare.

22   As the play goes on, Jake and Louise replay and intensify these patterns:

23   *Louise:* If I'm such a terrible mother, do you want a divorce?
24   *Jake:* I do not think you're a terrible mother and no, thank you, I do not want a divorce. Why is it that whenever I bring up any difference between us you ask me if I want a divorce?

25   The more he denies any meaning beyond the message, the more she blows it up, the more adamantly he denies it, and so on:

26   *Jake:* I have brought up one thing that you do with Edie that I don't think you notice that I have noticed for some time but which I have deliberately not brought up before because I had hoped you would notice it for yourself and stop doing it and also— frankly, baby, I have to say this—I knew if I brought it up we'd get into exactly the kind of circular argument we're in right now. And I wanted to avoid it. But I haven't and we're in it, so now, with your permission, I'd like to talk about it.
27   *Louise:* You don't see how that puts me down?
28   *Jake:* What?
29   *Louise:* If you think I'm so stupid why do you go on living with me?
30   *Jake: Dammit! Why can't anything ever be simple around here?!*

31   It can't be simple because Louise and Jake are responding to different levels of communication. As in Bateson's example of the dual-control electric blanket with crossed wires, each one intensifies the energy going to a different aspect of the problem. Jake tries to clarify his point by overelaborating it, which gives Louise further evidence that he's condescending to her, making it even less likely that she will address his point rather than his condescension.

32   What pushes Jake and Louise beyond anger to rage is their different perspectives on metamessages. His refusal to admit that his statements have implications and overtones denies her authority over her own feelings. Her attempts to interpret what he didn't say and put the metamessage into the message makes him feel she's putting words into his mouth—denying his authority over his own meaning.

33   The same thing happens when Louise tells Jake that he is being manipulated by Edie:

Louise: Why don't you ever make her come to see you? Why do 34
you always go to her?

Jake: You want me to play power games with a nine year old? I 35
want her to know I'm interested in her. Someone around here
has to show interest in her.

Louise: You love her more than I do. 36

Jake: I didn't say that. 37

Louise: Yes, you did. 38

Jake: You don't know how to listen. You have never learned how to 39
listen. It's as if listening to you is a foreign language.

Again, Louise responds to his implication—this time, that he loves 40
Edie more because he runs when she calls. And yet again, Jake cries literal meaning, denying he meant any more than he said.

Throughout their argument, the point to Louise is her feelings— 41
that Jake makes her feel put down—but to him the point is her actions—that she doesn't always respond when Edie calls:

Louise: You talk about what I do to Edie, what do you think you do 42
to me?

Jake: This is not the time to go into what we do to each other. 43

Since she will talk only about the metamessage, and he will talk only 44
about the message, neither can get satisfaction from their talk, and they
end up where they started—only angrier:

Jake: That's not the point! 45

Louise: It's my point. 46

Jake: It's hopeless! 47

Louise: Then get a divorce. 48

American conventional wisdom (and many of our parents and English 49
teachers) tell us that meaning is conveyed by words, so men who tend
to be literal about words are supported by conventional wisdom. They
may not simply deny but actually miss the cues that are sent by how
words are spoken. If they sense something about it, they may nonetheless discount what they sense. After all, it wasn't said. Sometimes that's
a dodge—a plausible defense rather than a gut feeling. But sometimes
it is a sincere conviction. Women are also likely to doubt the reality of
what they sense. If they don't doubt it in their guts, they nonetheless
may lack the arguments to support their position and thus are reduced
to repeating, "You said it. You did so." Knowing that metamessages are
a real and fundamental part of communication makes it easier to understand and justify what they feel.

50   An article in a popular newspaper reports that one of the five most common complaints of wives about their husbands is "He doesn't listen to me anymore." Another is "He doesn't talk to me anymore." Political scientist Andrew Hacker noted that lack of communication, while high on women's lists of reasons for divorce, is much less often mentioned by men. Since couples are parties to the same conversations, why are women more dissatisfied with them than men? Because what they expect is different, as well as what they see as the significance of talk itself.

51   First, let's consider the complaint "He doesn't talk to me."

52   One of the most common stereotypes of American men is the strong silent type. Jack Kroll, writing about Henry Fonda on the occasion of his death, used the phrases "quiet power," "abashed silences," "combustible catatonia," and "sense of power held in check." He explained that Fonda's goal was not to let anyone see "the wheels go around," not to let the "machinery" show. According to Kroll, the resulting silence was effective on stage but devastating to Fonda's family.

53   The image of a silent father is common and is often the model for the lover or husband. But what attracts us can become flypaper to which we are unhappily stuck. Many women find the strong silent type to be a lure as a lover but a lug as a husband. Nancy Schoenberger begins a poem with the lines "It was your silence that hooked me,/ so like my father's." Adrienne Rich refers in a poem to the "husband who is frustratingly mute." Despite the initial attraction of such quintessentially male silence, it may begin to feel, to a woman in a long-term relationship, like a brick wall against which she is banging her head.

54   In addition to these images of male and female behavior—both the result and the cause of them—are differences in how women and men view the role of talk in relationships as well as how talk accomplishes its purpose. These differences have their roots in the settings in which men and women learn to have conversations: among their peers, growing up.

55   Children whose parents have foreign accents don't speak with accents. They learn to talk like their peers. Little girls and little boys learn how to have conversations as they learn how to pronounce words: from their playmates. Between the ages of five and fifteen, when children are learning to have conversations, they play mostly with friends of their own sex. So it's not surprising that they learn different ways of having and using conversations.

56   Anthropologists Daniel Maltz and Ruth Borker point out that boys and girls socialize differently. Little girls tend to play in small groups or, even more common, in pairs. Their social life usually centers around a best friend, and friendships are made, maintained, and broken by talk—especially "secrets." If a little girl tells her friend's secret to another little girl, she may find herself with a new best friend. The secrets themselves may or may not be important, but the fact of telling them is

all-important. It's hard for newcomers to get into these tight groups, but anyone who is admitted is treated as an equal. Girls like to play co-operatively; if they can't cooperate, the group breaks up.

Little boys tend to play in larger groups, often outdoors, and they   57
spend more time doing things than talking. It's easy for boys to get into the group, but not everyone is accepted as an equal. Once in the group, boys must jockey for their status in it. One of the most important ways they do this is through talk: verbal display such as telling stories and jokes, challenging and sidetracking the verbal displays of other boys, and withstanding other boys' challenges in order to maintain their own story—and status. Their talk is often competitive talk about who is best at what.

Feiffer's play is ironically named *Grown Ups* because adult men and   58
women struggling to communicate often sound like children: "You said so!" "I did not!" The reason is that when they grow up, women and men keep the divergent attitudes and habits they learned as children— which they don't recognize as attitudes and habits but simply take for granted as ways of talking,

Women want their partners to be a new and improved version of a   59
best friend. This gives them a soft spot for men who tell them secrets. As Jack Nicholson once advised a guy in a movie: "Tell her about your troubled childhood—that always gets 'em." Men expect to *do* things together—and don't feel anything is missing if they don't have heart-to-heart talks all the time.

If they do have heart-to-heart talks, the meaning of those talks   60
may be opposite for men and women. To many women, the relation-ship is working as long as they can talk things out. To many men, the relationship isn't working out if they have to keep working it over. If she keeps trying to get talks going to save the relationship, and he keeps trying to avoid them because he sees them as weakening it, then each one's efforts to preserve the relationship appear to the other as reckless endangerment.

If talks (of any kind) do get going, men's and women's ideas about   61
how to conduct them may be very different. For example, Dora is feel-ing comfortable and close to Tom. She settles into a chair after dinner and begins to tell him about a problem at work. She expects him to ask questions to show he's interested; reassure her that he understands and that what she feels is normal; and return the intimacy by telling her a problem of his. Instead, Tom sidetracks her story, cracks jokes about it, questions her interpretation of the problem, and gives her advice about how to solve it and avoid such problems in the future.

All of these responses, natural to men, are unexpected to women,   62
who interpret them in terms of their own habits—negatively. When Tom comments on side issues or cracks jokes, Dora thinks he doesn't care about what she's saying and isn't really listening. If he challenges

her reading of what went on, she feels he is criticizing her and telling her she's crazy, when what she wants is to be reassured that she's not. If he tells her how to solve the problem, it makes her feel as if she's the patient to his doctor—a metamessage of condescension, echoing male one-upmanship compared to the female etiquette of equality. Because he doesn't volunteer information about his problems, she feels he's implying he doesn't have any.

63   His way of responding to her bid for intimacy makes her feel distant from him. She tries harder to regain intimacy the only way she knows how—by revealing more and more about herself. He tries harder by giving more insistent advice. The more problems she exposes, the more incompetent she feels, until they both see her as emotionally draining and problem-ridden. When his efforts to help aren't appreciated, he wonders why she asks for his advice if she doesn't want to take it. . . .

64   When women talk about what seems obviously interesting to them, their conversations often include reports of conversations. Tone of voice, timing, intonation, and wording are all re-created in the telling in order to explain—dramatize, really—the experience that is being reported. If men tell about an incident and give a brief summary instead of recreating what was said and how, the women often feel that the essence of the experience is being omitted. If the woman asks, "What exactly did he say?," and "How did he say it?," the man probably can't remember. If she continues to press him, he may feel as if he's being grilled.

65   All these different habits have repercussions when the man and the woman are talking about their relationship. He feels out of his element, even one down. She claims to recall exactly what he said, and what she said, and in what sequence, and she wants him to account for what he said. He can hardly account for it since he has forgotten exactly what was said—if not the whole conversation. She secretly suspects he's only pretending not to remember, and he secretly suspects that she's making up the details.

66   One woman reported such a problem as being a matter of her boyfriend's poor memory. It is unlikely, however, that his problem was poor memory in general. The question is what types of material each person remembers or forgets.

67   Frances was sitting at her kitchen table talking to Edward, when the toaster did something funny. Edward began to explain why it did it. Frances tried to pay attention, but very early in his explanation, she realized she was completely lost. She felt very stupid. And indications were that he thought so too.

68   Later that day they were taking a walk. He was telling her about a difficult situation in his office that involved a complex network of interrelationships among a large number of people. Suddenly he stopped and said, "I'm sure you can't keep track of all these people." "Of course

I can," she said, and she retraced his story with all the characters in place, all the details right. He was genuinely impressed. She felt very smart.

How could Frances be both smart and stupid? Did she have a good   69
memory or a bad one? Frances's and Edward's abilities to follow, re-member, and recount depended on the subject—and paralleled her parents' abilities to follow and remember. Whenever Frances told her parents about people in her life, her mother could follow with no prob-lem, but her father got lost as soon as she introduced a second charac-ter. "Now who was that?" he'd ask. "Your boss?" "No, my boss is Susan. This was my friend." Often he'd still be in the previous story. But whenever she told them about her work, it was her mother who would get lost as soon as she mentioned a second step: "That was your tech report?" "No, I handed my tech report in last month. This was a special project."

Frances's mother and father, like many other men and women, had   70
honed their listening and remembering skills in different arenas. Their experience talking to other men and other women gave them practice in following different kinds of talk.

Knowing whether and how we are likely to report events later in-   71
fluences whether and how we pay attention when they happen. As women listen to and take part in conversations, knowing they may talk about them later makes them more likely to pay attention to exactly what is said and how. Since most men aren't in the habit of making such reports, they are less likely to pay much attention at the time. On the other hand, many women aren't in the habit of paying attention to sci-entific explanations and facts because they don't expect to have to per-form in public by reciting them—just as those who aren't in the habit of entertaining others by telling jokes "can't" remember jokes they've heard, even though they listened carefully enough to enjoy them.

So women's conversations with their women friends keep them in   72
training for talking about their relationships with men, but many men come to such conversations with no training at all—and an uncomfort-able sense that this really isn't their event.

Most of us place enormous emphasis on the importance of a pri-   73
mary relationship. We regard the ability to maintain such relationships as a sign of mental health—our contemporary metaphor for being a good person.

Yet our expectations of such relationships are nearly—maybe in   74
fact—impossible. When primary relationships are between women and men, male-female differences contribute to the impossibility. We expect partners to be both romantic interests and best friends. Though women and men may have fairly similar expectations for romantic interests, obscuring their differences when relationships begin, they have very different ideas about how to be friends, and these are the differences that mount over time.

75   In conversations between friends who are not lovers, small misunderstandings can be passed over or diffused by breaks in contact. But in the context of a primary relationship, differences can't be ignored, and the pressure cooker of continued contact keeps both people stewing in the juice of accumulated minor misunderstandings. And stylistic differences are sure to cause misunderstandings—not, ironically, in matters such as sharing values and interests or understanding each other's philosophies of life. These large and significant yet palpable issues can be talked about and agreed on. It is far harder to achieve congruence—and much more surprising and troubling that it is hard—in the simple day-to-day matters of the automatic rhythms and nuances of talk. Nothing in our backgrounds or in the media (the present-day counterpart to religion or grandparents' teachings) prepares us for this failure. If two people share so much in terms of point of view and basic values, how can they continually get into fights about insignificant matters?

76   If you find yourself in such a situation and you don't know about differences in conversational style, you assume something's wrong with your partner, or you for having chosen your partner. At best, if you are forward thinking and generous minded, you may absolve individuals and blame the relationship. But if you know about differences in conversational style, you can accept that there are differences in habits and assumptions about how to have conversation, show interest, be considerate, and so on. You may not always correctly interpret your partner's intentions, but you will know that if you get a negative impression, it may not be what was intended—and neither are your responses unfounded. If he says he really is interested even though he doesn't seem to be, maybe you should believe what he says and not what you sense.

77   Sometimes explaining assumptions can help. If a man starts to tell a woman what to do to solve her problem, she may say, "Thanks for the advice but I really don't want to be told what to do. I just want you to listen and say you understand." A man might want to explain, "If I challenge you, it's not to prove you wrong; it's just my way of paying attention to what you're telling me." Both may try either or both to modify their ways of talking and to try to accept what the other does. The important thing is to know that what seem like bad intentions may really be good intentions expressed in a different conversational style. We have to give up our conviction that, as Robin Lakoff put it, "Love means never having to say 'What do you mean?'"

◆ *Evaluating the Text*

1. How does the contrast between "involvement" and "independence" help explain difficulties that men and women have in communicating with each other? In what way do men understand messages literally while women understand them contextually?

2. How does Tannen's theory of "metamessages" help explain how misunderstandings between men and women arise and develop? Evaluate the range of evidence Tannen brings in to support her thesis.

✦ Exploring Different Perspectives

1. Drawing upon Deborah Tannen's analysis, analyze the narrator's language style in Rosa Liksom's story "One Night Stands." Does she speak more like a man or a woman?

2. What do both Deborah Tannen and Kim Chernin (see "The Flesh and the Devil") reveal about gender stereotyping (in language and appearance) in American culture?

✦ Extending Viewpoints Through Writing

1. What instances from your own experience illustrate the kinds of clashing expectations that Tannen has identified between men and women? How do these experiences reveal the conflict between the female desire for "solidarity" and the male desire for "power"?

2. Do you believe there is such a thing as men's language or women's language? How do they differ? What examples from different sections of your local newspaper can you find that illustrate these differences?

3. To discover whether you can decode what men and women say to each other, discuss what the following statements by men speaking to women really mean. Explain your choices.

   A. If a man says "You're really a great person," he means:
      1. I like you as more than a friend.
      2. I'm sorry, but I'm really just not attracted to you.
      3. I'm glad we're such good friends.

   B. A woman invites a man over for dinner, and he asks, "Is your sister going to be there?" He really means:
      1. Are we going to be alone?
      2. I'm psyched to meet the rest of your family.
      3. I have a serious crush on your sister.

Lennard J. Davis

Visualizing the Disabled Body

———————◆———————

Lennard J. Davis is assistant professor of English at Binghamton University. He has written on disability for the Nation. *His previous books include* Factual Fictions: The Origins of the English Novel *(1983) and* Resisting Novels: Ideology and Fiction *(1987). Although not hearing impaired himself, Davis was born to deaf parents and uttered his first word in sign language. "Visualizing the Disabled Body" is drawn from* Enforcing Normalcy: Disability, Deafness, and the Body *(1995).*

> *A human being who is first of all an invalid is* all *body, therein lies his inhumanity and his debasement. In most cases he is little better than a carcass—.*
>
> —Thomas Mann, *The Magic Mountain*

> *. . . the female is as it were a deformed male.*
>
> —Aristotle, *Generation of Animals*

> *When I begin to wish I were crippled—even though I am perfectly healthy—or rather that I would have been better off crippled, that is the first step towards* butoh.
>
> —Tatsumi Hijikata, co-founder of the Japanese performance art/dance form *butoh.*

1   She has no arms or hands, although the stump of her upper right arm extends just to her breast. Her left foot has been severed, and her face is badly scarred, with her nose torn at the tip, and her lower lip gouged out. Fortunately, her facial mutilations have been treated and are barely visible, except for minor scarring visible only up close. The big toe of her right foot has been cut off, and her torso is covered with scars, including a particularly large one between her shoulder blades, one that covers her shoulder, and one covering the tip of her breast where her left nipple was torn out.

2   Yet she is considered one of the most beautiful female figures in the world. When the romantic poet Heinrich Heine saw her he called her 'Notre-Dame de la Beauté.'

3   He was referring to the Venus de Milo.

4   Consider too Pam Herbert, a quadriplegic with muscular dystrophy, writing her memoir by pressing her tongue on a computer keyboard, who describes herself at twenty-eight years old:

I weigh about 130 pounds; I'm about four feet tall. It's pretty hard to get an accurate measurement on me because both of my knees are permanently bent and my spine is curved, so 4' is an estimate. I wear size two tennis shoes and strong glasses; my hair is dishwater blonde and shoulder length. (Browne et al., eds, 1985, 147)

In this memoir, she describes her wedding night: 5

We got to the room and Mark laid me down on the bed because I was so tired from sitting all day. Anyway, I hadn't gone to the bathroom all day so Mark had to catheterize me. I had been having trouble going to the bathroom for many years, so it was nothing new to Mark, he had done it lots of times before.

It was time for the biggest moment of my life, making love. Of course, I was a little nervous and scared. Mark was very gentle with me. He started undressing me and kissing me. We tried making love in the normal fashion with Mark on top and me on the bottom. Well, that position didn't work at all, so then we tried laying on our sides coming in from behind. That was a little better. Anyway, we went to sleep that night a little discouraged because we didn't have a very good love-making session. You would have thought that it would be great, but sometimes things don't always go the way we want them to. We didn't get the hang of making love for about two months. It hurt for a long time. (ibid., 155)

I take the liberty of bringing these two women's bodies together.   6
Both have disabilities. The statue is considered the ideal of Western beauty and eroticism, although it is armless and disfigured. The living woman might be considered by many 'normal' people to be physically repulsive, and certainly without erotic allure. The question I wish to ask is why does the impairment of the Venus de Milo in no way prevent 'normal' people from considering her beauty, while Pam Herbert's disability becomes the focal point for horror and pity?

In asking this question, I am really raising a complex issue. On a   7
social level, the question has to do with how people with disabilities are seen and why, by and large, they are de-eroticized. If, as I mentioned earlier, disability is a cultural phenomenon rooted in the senses, one needs to inquire how a disability occupies a field of vision, of touch, of hearing; and how that disruption or distress in the sensory field translates into psycho-dynamic representations. This is more a question about the nature of the subject than about the qualities of the object, more about the observer than the observed. The 'problem' of the disabled has been put at the feet of people with disabilities for too long.

Normalcy, rather than being a degree zero of existence, is more ac-   8
curately a location of bio-power, as Foucault would use the term. The 'normal' person (clinging to that title) has a network of traditional ableist assumptions and social supports that empowers the gaze and

interaction. The person with disabilities, until fairly recently, had only his or her own individual force or will. Classically, the encounter has been, and remains, an uneven one. Anne Finger describes it in strikingly visual terms by relating an imagined meeting between Rosa Luxemburg and Antonio Gramsci, each of whom was a person with disabilities, although Rosa is given the temporary power of the abled gaze:

> We can measure Rosa's startled reaction as she glimpses him the misshapen dwarf limping towards her in a second-hand black suit so worn that the cuffs are frayed and the fabric is turning green with age, her eye immediately drawn to this disruption in the visual field; the unconscious flinch; the realization that she is staring at him, and the too-rapid turning away of the head. And then, the moment after, the consciousness that the quick aversion of the gaze was as much of an insult as the stare, so she turns her head back but tries to make her focus general, not a sharp gape. Comrade Rosa, would you have felt a slight flicker of embarrassment? shame? revulsion? dread? of a feeling that can have no name?

In this encounter what is suppressed, at least in this moment, is the fact that Rosa Luxemburg herself is physically impaired (she walked with a limp for her whole life). The emphasis then shifts from the cultural norm to the deviation; Luxemburg, now the gazing subject, places herself in the empowered position of the norm, even if that position is not warranted.

9   Disability, in this and other encounters, is a disruption in the visual, auditory, or perceptual field as it relates to the power of the gaze. As such, the disruption, the rebellion of the visual, must be regulated, rationalized, contained. Why the modern binary—normal/abnormal—must be maintained is a complex question. But we can begin by accounting for the desire to split bodies into two immutable categories: whole and incomplete, abled and disabled, normal and abnormal, functional and dysfunctional.

10   In the most general sense, cultures perform an act of splitting (*Spaltung,* to use Freud's term). These violent cleavages of consciousness are as primitive as our thought processes can be. The young infant splits the good parent from the bad parent—although the parent is the same entity. When the child is satisfied by the parent, the parent is the good parent; when the child is not satisfied, the parent is bad. As a child grows out of the earliest phases of infancy, she learns to combine those split images into a single parent who is sometimes good and sometimes not. The residue of *Spaltung* remains in our inner life, personal and collective, to produce monsters and evil stepmothers as well as noble princes and fairy godmothers.

11   In this same primitive vein, culture tends to split bodies into good and bad parts. Some cultural norms are considered good and others bad. Everyone is familiar with the 'bad' body: too short or tall, too fat

or thin, not masculine or feminine enough, not enough or too much hair on the head or other parts of the body, penis or breasts too small or (excepting the penis) too big. Furthermore, each individual assigns good and bad labels to body parts—good: hair, face, lips, eyes, hands; bad: sexual organs, excretory organs, underarms.

The psychological explanation may provide a reason why it is imperative for society at large to engage in *Spaltung*. The divisions whole/incomplete, able/disabled neatly cover up the frightening writing on the wall that reminds the hallucinated whole being that its wholeness is in fact a hallucination, a developmental fiction. *Spaltung* creates the absolute categories of abled and disabled, with concomitant defenses against the repressed fragmented body.   12

But a psychological explanation alone is finally insufficient. Historical specificity makes us understand that disability is a social process with an origin. So, why certain disabilities are labeled negatively while others have a less negative connotation is a question tied to complex social forces (some of which I have tried to lay out in earlier chapters). It is fair to say, in general, that disabilities would be most dysfunctional in postindustrial countries, where the ability to perambulate or manipulate is so concretely tied to productivity, which in itself is tied to production. The body of the average worker, as we have seen, becomes the new measure of man and woman. Michael Oliver, citing Ryan and Thomas (1980), notes: 13

> With the rise of the factory . . . [during industrialization] many more disabled people were excluded from the production process for 'The speed of factory work, the enforced discipline, the time-keeping and production norms—all these were a highly unfavourable change from the slower, more self-determined and flexible methods of work into which many handicapped people had been integrated.' (1990, 27)

Both industrial production and the concomitant standardization of the human body have had a profound impact on how we split up bodies.

We tend to group impairments into the categories either of 'disabling' (bad) or just 'limiting' (good). For example, wearing a hearing aid is seen as much more disabling than wearing glasses, although both serve to amplify a deficient sense. But loss of hearing is associated with aging in a way that nearsightedness is not. Breast removal is seen as an impairment of femininity and sexuality, whereas the removal of a foreskin is not seen as a diminution of masculinity. The coding of body parts and the importance attached to their selective function or dysfunction is part of a much larger system of signs and meanings in society, and is constructed as such.   14

'Splitting' may help us to understand one way in which disability is seen as part of a system in which value is attributed to body parts. The disabling of the body part or function is then part of a removal of   15 value. The gradations of value are socially determined, but what is striking is the way that rather than being incremental or graduated, the assignment of the term 'disabled,' and the consequent devaluation are total. That is, the concept of disabled seems to be an absolute rather than a gradient one. One is either disabled or not. Value is tied to the ability to earn money. If one's body is productive, it is not disabled. People with disabilities continue to earn less than 'normal' people and, even after the passage of the Americans with Disabilities Act, 69 percent of Americans with disabilities were unemployed (*New York Times*, 27 October 1994, A:22). Women and men with disabilites are seen as less attractive, less able to marry and be involved in domestic production.

16   The ideology of the assigning of value to the body goes back to pre-industrial times. Myths of beauty and ugliness have laid the foundations for normalcy. In particular, the Venus myth is one that is dialectically linked to another. This embodiment of beauty and desire is tied to the story of the embodiment of ugliness and repulsion. So the appropriate mythological character to compare the armless Venus with is Medusa. Medusa was once a beautiful sea goddess who, because she had sexual intercourse with Poseidon at one of Athene's temples, was turned by Athene into a winged monster with glaring eyes, huge teeth, protruding tongue, brazen claws, and writhing snakes for hair. Her hideous appearance has the power to turn people into stone, and Athene eventually completes her revenge by having Perseus kill Medusa. He finds Medusa by stealing the one eye and one tooth shared by the Graiae until they agree to help him. Perseus then kills Medusa by decapitating her while looking into his brightly polished shield, which neutralizes the power of her appearance; he then puts her head into a magic wallet that shields onlookers from its effects. When Athene receives the booty, she uses Medusa's head and skin to fashion her own shield.

17   In the Venus tradition, Medusa is a poignant double. She is the necessary counter in the dialectic of beauty and ugliness, desire and repulsion, wholeness and fragmentation. Medusa is the disabled woman to Venus's perfect body. The story is a kind of allegory of a 'normal' person's intersection with the disabled body. This intersection is marked by the power of the visual. The 'normal' person sees the disabled person and is turned to stone, in some sense, by the visual interaction. In this moment, the normal person suddenly feels self-conscious, rigid, unable to look but equally drawn to look. The visual field becomes problematic, dangerous, treacherous. The disability becomes a power derived from its otherness, its monstrosity, in the eyes of the 'normal' person. The disability must be decapitated and then contained in a variety of magic wallets. Rationality, for which Athene stands, is one of the devices for containing, controlling, and reforming the disabled body so that it no longer has the power to terrorize. And the issue of mutilation comes up as well because the disabled body is always the

reminder of the whole body about to come apart at the seams. It provides a vision of, a caution about, the body as a construct held together willfully, always threatening to become its individual parts—cells, organs, limbs, perceptions—like the fragmented, shared eye and tooth that Perseus ransoms back to the Graiae.

I have been concentrating on the physical body, but it is worth considering for a moment the issue of madness. While mental illness is by definition not related to the intactness of the body, nevertheless, it shows up as a disruption in the visual field. We 'see' that someone is insane by her physical behavior, communication, and so on. Yet the fear is that the mind is fragmenting, breaking up, falling apart, losing itself—all terms we associate with becoming mad. With the considerable information we have about the biological roots of mental illness, we begin to see the disease again as a breaking up of 'normal' body chemistry: amino acid production gone awry, depleted levels of certain polypeptide chains or hormones. Language production can become fragmentary, broken, in schizophrenic speech production. David Rothman points out that in eighteenth- and nineteenth-century America, insanity was seen as being caused by the fragmented nature of 'modern' life—particularly the pressures brought to bear on people by a society in which economic boundaries were disappearing. This fragmenting of society produced a fragmentation of the individual person. So the asylums that sprung up during this period recommended a cure that involved a removal from the urban, alienated, fragmented environment to rural hospitals in which order and precision could be restored. 'A precise schedule and regular work became the two characteristics of the best private and public institutions. . . . The structure of the mental hospital would counteract the debilitating influences of the community' (Rothman 1971, 144). As Rothman notes, 'Precision, certainty, regularity, order' were the words that were seen as embodying the essence of cure (ibid., 145). The mind would be restored to 'wholeness' by restoring the body through manual labor. However, needless to add, one had to have a whole body to have a whole mind. The general metaphor here continues to be a notion of wholeness, order, clean boundaries, as opposed to fragmentations, disordered bodies, messy boundaries.

If people with disabilities are considered anything, they are or have been considered creatures of disorder—monsters, monstrous. Leslie Fieldler has taken some pains to show this in his book *Freaks*. If we look at Mary Shelley's *Frankenstein*, we find some of the themes we have been discussing emerge in novelistic form. First, we might want to note that we have no name for the creation of Dr Frankenstein other than 'monster.' (This linguistic lapsus is usually made up for in popular culture by referring to the creature itself as 'Frankenstein,' a terminology that confuses the creator with the created.) In reading the novel, or

18

19

speaking about it, we can only call the creature 'the monster.' This linguistic limitation is worth noting because it encourages the reader to consider the creature a monster rather than a person with disabilities.

20   We do not often think of the monster in Mary Shelley's work as disabled, but what else is he? The characteristic of his disability is a difference in appearance. He is more than anything a disruption in the visual field. There is nothing else different about him—he can see, hear, talk, think, ambulate, and so on. It is worth noting that in popular culture, largely through the early film versions of the novel, the monster is inarticulate, somewhat mentally slow, and walks with a kind of physical impairment. In addition, the film versions add Ygor, the hunchbacked criminal who echoes the monster's disability in his own. Even in the recent film version by Kenneth Branagh, the creature walks with a limp and speaks with an impediment. One cannot dismiss this filtering of the creature through the lens of multiple disability. In order for the audience to fear and loathe the creature, he must be made to transcend the pathos of a single disability. Of course, it would be unseemly for a village to chase and torment a paraplegic or a person with acromegaly. Disabled people are to be pitied and ostracized; monsters are to be destroyed; audiences must not confuse the two.

21   In the novel, it is clear that Dr Frankenstein cannot abide his creation for only one reason—its hideous appearance. Indeed, the creature's only positive human contact is with the blind old man De Lacey, who cannot see the unsightly features. When De Lacey's family catches a glimpse of the creature, the women faint or run, and the men beat and pursue him. His body is a zone of repulsion; the reaction he evokes is fear and loathing. The question one wants to ask is why does a physical difference produce such a profound response?

22   The answer, I believe, is twofold. First, what is really hideous about the creature is not so much his physiognomy as what that appearance suggests. The *corps morcelé* makes its appearance immediately in the construction of the monster. Ironically, Dr Frankenstein adapts Zeuxis's notion of taking ideal parts from individuals to create the ideal whole body. As he says, 'I collected bones from charnel houses. . . . The dissecting room and the slaughter-house furnished many of my materials' (Shelley 1990, 54–5). From these fragments, seen as loathsome and disgusting, Frankenstein assembles what he wishes to create—a perfect human. It is instructive in this regard to distinguish the Boris Karloff incarnation of the creature—with the bolt through his neck—or Branagh's grotesquely sewn creature, from the image that Mary Shelley would have us imagine. Dr Frankenstein tells us:

> His limbs were in proportion, and I had selected his features as beautiful. Beautiful!—Great God! His yellow skin scarcely covered the work

of muscles and arteries beneath; his hair was of a lustrous black and flowing; his teeth of a pearly whiteness; but these luxuriances only formed a more horrid contrast with his watery eyes, that seemed almost of the same colour as the dun white sockets in which they were set, his shrivelled complexion and straight black lips. (ibid., 57)

What then constitutes the horror? If we add up the details, what we see is a well-proportioned man with long black hair, pearly white teeth, whose skin is somewhat deformed—resulting in jaundice and perhaps a tightness or thinness of the skin, a lack of circulation perhaps causing shriveling, watery eyes and darkened lips. This hardly seems to constitute horror rather than, say, pathos.   23

What is found to be truly horrifying about Frankenstein's creature is its composite quality, which is too evocative of the fragmented body. Frankenstein's reaction to this living *corps morcelé* is repulsion: 'the beauty of the dream vanished, and breathless horror and disgust filled my heart' (ibid., 57). Frankenstein attempted to create a unified nude, an object of beauty and harmony—a Venus, in effect. He ended up with a Medusa whose existence reveals the inhering and enduring nature of the archaic endlessly fragmented body, endlessly repressed but endlessly reappearing.   24

✦ *Evaluating the Text*

1. How does the contrast between the Venus de Milo and Pam Herbert draw attention to the paradox governing cultural perceptions of people with disabilities?

2. How does the phenomenon known as "splitting" help explain the stereotyped perception of people with disabilities?

3. How does Davis's example of an imagined meeting between Rosa Luxemburg and Antonio Gramsci help illustrate important issues of control and power?

4. How does Davis broaden his discussion to include Mary Shelley's *Frankenstein* and issues of mythology and madness?

5. How does each of the examples tie in with Davis's theory that "disability is a cultural phenomenon rooted in the senses"?

✦ *Exploring Different Perspectives*

1. How are Lennard J. Davis's and Judith Ortiz Cofer's analyses based on messages communicated through the perception of physical appearance?

2. Using Lennard J. Davis's concept of "splitting," analyze Andrew Sullivan's depiction of how homosexuals are defined (see "What Are Homosexuals For?").

✦ Extending Viewpoints Through Writing

1. Recently, the terms "differently abled" or "person with disabilities"
have been preferred to the term "disabled person." Earlier, the term
"disabled" was used to replace "handicapped." To what extent did
Davis's analysis make you realize how the category of disability is a
relative rather than an absolute term? For example, what if one were to
include dyslexia, myopia, learning impairments, arthritis, or obesity?
Discuss how attempts to control these terms reflect a desire to control
public perceptions of these states.

2. Select a film you have seen in recent years and discuss the treatment of
the central character in terms of the filmmaker's depiction of the "disabled." For example, Disney's 1996 release of *The Hunchback of Notre
Dame, Forrest Gump, Rain Man, Mask, Nell, Immortal Beloved,* or *Lorenzo's
Oil.* In your opinion, why are films depicting the disabled made so frequently, and why are they so popular?

Andrew Sullivan

What Are Homosexuals For?

———————◆———————

Andrew Sullivan was educated at Reigate Grammar School and Oxford University, where he was president of the Union. He holds a master's degree in public administration and a Ph.D. in political science from Harvard. From 1991 to 1996 he was the editor of the New Republic. *He currently analyzes American politics for the* Sunday Times *of London.*

> *Reason has so many shapes we don't know what to seize hold of; experience has just as many. What we infer from the similarity of events is uncertain, because they are always dissimilar: there is no quality so universal here as difference.*
>
> —Michel de Montaigne

The discovery of one's homosexuality is for many people the same experience as acting upon it. For me, alas, this was not the case. Maybe, in some respects, this was intellectually salutary: I was able, from an early age, to distinguish, as my Church taught, the condition of homosexuality from its practice. But in life, nothing is as easily distinguished. Even disavowing homosexuality is a response to it; and the response slowly, subtly alters who you are. The sublimation of sexual longing can create a particular form of alienated person: a more ferocious perfectionist, a cranky individual, an extremely brittle emotionalist, an ideological fanatic. This may lead to some brilliant lives: witty, urbane, subtle, passionate. But it also leads to some devastating loneliness. The abandonment of intimacy and the rejection of one's emotional core are, I have come to believe, alloyed evils. All too often, they preserve the persona at the expense of the person.

I remember a man, a university figure, who knew everyone in a distant avuncular fashion. I suppose we all understood that somewhere he was a homosexual; he had few women friends, and no emotional or sexual life to speak of. He lived in a carefully constructed world of university gossip, intellectual argument, and intense, platonic relationships with proteges and students. He was immensely fat. One day, he told me, in his mid-forties, he woke up in a room at the Harvard Club in New York and couldn't move. He stayed there immobile for the morning and much of the afternoon. He realized at that moment that there was no honesty at the core of his life, and no love at its center. The recognition of this emptiness literally paralyzed him. He was the lucky one. He set about re-ordering his life; in his late middle age, he began to have adolescent affairs; he declared his sexuality loudly and somewhat crudely to anyone who could hear; he unloaded himself to his friends and loved ones. In one of those ultimately unintelligible tragedies, he died of a swift and deadly cancer three years later. But at his funeral, I couldn't help but reflect that he had at least tasted a few years of life. He had regained himself before he lost himself forever.

3   Others never experience such dreadful epiphanies. There was a time when I felt that the closeted homosexual was a useful social creature, and possibly happier than those immersed in what sometimes seems like a merciless and shallow subculture. But the etiolation of the heart which this self-abnegation requires is enormous. For many of us, a shared love is elusive anyway, a goal we rarely achieve and, when we do, find extremely hard to maintain. But to make the lack of such an achievement a condition of one's existence is to remove from a human life much that might propel it forward. Which is why I cannot forget the image of that man in a bed. He could not move. For him, there was no forward, no future to move into.

4   This is how the world can seem to many adolescent homosexuals; and I was no exception. Heterosexual marriage is perceived as the primary emotional goal for your peers; and yet you know this cannot be your fate. It terrifies and alarms you. While its form comforts, its content appalls. It requires a systematic dishonesty; and this dishonesty either is programmed into your soul and so warps your integrity, or is rejected in favor of—what? You scan your mind for an alternative. You dream grandiose dreams, construct a fantasy of a future, pour your energies into some massive distraction, pursue a consuming career to cover up the lie at the center of your existence. You are caught between escape and the constant daily wrench of self-denial. It is a vise from which many teenagers and young adults never emerge.

5   I was lucky. I found an escape, an escape into a world of ideas, into a career, and into another country. America provided an excuse for a new beginning, as it had done for millions of immigrants before me. I often wonder, had I stayed in the place which reminded me so much of where I was from, whether I would have found a way to construct a measurably honest life. I don't know. But I do know that in this as well I was not alone. So many homosexuals find it essential to move away from where they are before they can regain themselves. Go to any major city and you'll find thousands of exiles from the heartland, making long-distance phone calls which echo with the same euphemisms of adolescence, the same awkward pauses, the same banal banter. These city limits are the equivalent of the adolescent's bedroom door: a barrier where two lives can be maintained with some hope of success and a minimal amount of mutual embarrassment.

It was in the safety of this exile that I could come home. I remem-   6
ber my first kiss with another man, the first embrace, the first love affair. Many metaphors have been used to describe this delayed
homecoming—I was twenty-three—but to me, it was like being in a
black-and-white movie that suddenly converted to color. The richness
of experience seemed possible for the first time; the abstractions of
dogma, of morality, of society, dissolved into the sheer, mysterious
pleasure of being human. Perhaps this is a homosexual privilege: for
many heterosexuals, the pleasures of intimacy and sexuality are stumbled upon gradually when young; for many homosexuals, the entire
experience can come at once, when an adult, eclipsing everything, humiliating the developed person's sense of equilibrium, infantilizing
and liberating at the same time. Sometimes I wonder whether some homosexuals' addiction to constant romance, to the thrill of the new lover,
to the revelation of a new and obliviating desire, is in fact an attempt to
relive this experience, again and again.

What followed over the years was not without its stupidity, excess,   7
and hurt. But it was far realler than anything I had experienced before.
I was never really "in the closet" in this sense. Until my early twenties, I
was essentially heterosexual in public disclosure and emotionless in private life. Within a year, I was both privately and publicly someone who
attempted little disguise of his emotional orientation. In this, I was convinced I was entering finally into normal life. I was the equal of heterosexuals, deserving of exactly the same respect, attempting to construct
in the necessarily contrived world of the gay subculture the mirror image of the happy heterosexuality I imagined around me. Like many in
my generation, I flattered myself that this was a first: a form of pioneer-
ing equality, an insistence on one's interchangeability with the dominant culture, on one's radical similarity with the heterosexual majority.

And in a fundamental sense, as I have tried to explain, this was   8
true. The homosexual's emotional longings, his development, his dreams
are human phenomena. They are, I think, instantly recognizable to any
heterosexual, in their form if not their content. The humanity of homosexuals is clear everywhere. Perhaps nothing has illustrated this more
clearly than the AIDS epidemic. Gay people have to confront grief and
shock and mortality like anybody else. They die like all people die.

Except, of course, that they don't. Homosexuals in contemporary   9
America tend to die young; they sometimes die estranged from their
families; they die among friends who have become their new families;
they die surrounded by young death, and by the arch symbols of cultural otherness. Growing up homosexual was to grow up normally but
displaced; to experience romantic love, but with the wrong person; to
entertain grand ambitions, but of the unacceptable sort; to seek a gradual self-awakening, but in secret, not in public.

10   But to live as an adult homosexual is to experience something else again. By the simple fact of one's increasing cultural separation, the human personality begins to develop differently. As an adolescent and child you are surrounded by the majority culture: so your concerns and habits and thoughts become embedded in the familiar and communicable. But slowly, and gradually, in adulthood, your friends and acquaintances become increasingly gay or lesbian. Lesbian women can find themselves slowly distanced from the company of men; gay men can find themselves slowly disentangled from women. One day, I glanced at my log of telephone calls: the ratio of men to women, once roughly even, had become six-to-one male. The women I knew and cared about had dwindled to a small but intimate group of confidantes and friends, women who were able to share my homosexual life and understand it. The straight men, too, had fallen in number. And both these groups tended to come from people I had met *before* I had fully developed an openly gay life.

11   These trends reinforced each other. Of course, like most gay people, I worked in a largely heterosexual environment and still maintained close links with my heterosexual family. But the environmental incentives upon me were clearly in another direction. I naturally gravitated toward people who were similar. Especially in your twenties, when romantic entanglement assumes a dominant role in life, you naturally socialize with prospective partners. Before you know where you are, certain patterns develop. Familiarity breeds familiarity; and, by no conscious process, your inculturation is subtly and powerfully different than that of your heterosexual peers.

12   In the world of emotional and sexual life, there were no clear patterns to follow: homosexual culture offered a gamut of possibilities, from anonymous sex to bourgeois coupling. But its ease with sexual activity, its male facility with sexual candor, its surprising lack of formal, moral stricture—all these made my life subtly and slowly more different than my straight male (let alone my straight female) peers'. In my late twenties, the difference became particularly acute. My heterosexual male friends became married; soon, my straight peers were having children. Weddings, babies, career couples, engagements: the calendar began to become crowded with the clatter of heterosexual bonding. And yet in my gay life, something somewhat different was occurring.

13   I remember vividly one Labor Day weekend. I had two engagements to attend. The first was a gay friend's thirtieth birthday party. It was held in the Deep South, in his family's seaside home. He had told his family he was gay the previous winter; he had told them he had AIDS that Memorial Day. His best friends had come to meet the family for the first time—two straight women, his boyfriend, his ex-boyfriend, and me. That year, we had all been through the trauma of his illness, and he was visibly thinner now than he had been even a month before.

Although we attended to the typical family functions—dinners, beach trips, photo ops—there was a strained air of irony and sadness about the place. How could we explain what it was like to live in one's twenties and thirties with such a short horizon, to face mortality and sickness and death, to attend funerals when others were attending weddings? And yet, somehow the communication was possible. He was their son, after all. And after they had acclimatized to our mutual affection, and humor, and occasional diffidence, there was something of an understanding. His father took me aside toward the end of the trip to thank me for taking care of his son. I found it hard to speak any words of reply.

I flew directly from that event to another family gathering of another thirty-year-old friend of mine. This one was heterosexual; and he and his fiancee were getting married surrounded by a bevy of beaming acquaintances and family. In the Jewish ceremony, there was an unspoken, comforting rhythm of rebirth and life. The event was not untouched by tragedy: my friend's father had died earlier that year. But the wedding was almost an instinctive response to that sadness, a reaffirmation that the cycles and structures that had made sense of most of the lives there would be making sense of another two in the years ahead. I did not begrudge it at all; it is hard not to be moved by the sight of a new life beginning. But I could not help also feeling deeply, powerfully estranged.   14

AIDS has intensified a difference that I think is inherent between homosexual and heterosexual adults. The latter group is committed to the procreation of a new generation. The former simply isn't. Yes, there are major qualifications to this—gay men and lesbians are often biological fathers and mothers—but no two lesbians and no two homosexual men can be parents in the way that a heterosexual man and a heterosexual woman with a biological son or daughter can be. And yes, many heterosexuals neither marry nor have children and many have adopted children. But in general, the difference holds. The timeless, necessary, procreative unity of a man and a woman is inherently denied homosexuals; and the way in which fatherhood transforms heterosexual men, and motherhood transforms heterosexual women, and parenthood transforms their relationship, is far less common among homosexuals than among heterosexuals.   15

AIDS has only added a bitter twist to this state of affairs. My straight peers in their early thirties are engaged in the business of births; I am largely engaged in the business of deaths. Both experiences alter people profoundly. The very patterns of life of mothers and fathers with young children are vastly different than those who have none; and the perspectives of those who have stared death in the face in their twenties are bound to be different than those who have stared into cribs. Last year, I saw my first nephew come into the world, the   16 first new life in my life to whom I felt physically, emotionally connected. I wondered which was the deeper feeling: the sense of excruciating pain seeing a member of my acquired family die, or the excruciating joy of seeing a member of my given family born. I am at a loss to decide; but I am not at a loss to know that they are different experiences: equally human, but radically different.

17   In a society more and more aware of its manifold cultures and subcultures, we have been educated to be familiar and comfortable with what has been called "diversity": the diversity of perspective, culture, meaning. And this diversity is usually associated with what are described as cultural constructs: race, gender, sexuality, and so on. But as the obsession with diversity intensifies, the possibility of real difference alarms and terrifies all the more. The notion of collective characteristics—of attributes more associated with blacks than with whites, with Asians than with Latinos, with gay men than with straight men, with men than with women—has become anathema. They are marginalized as "stereotypes." The acceptance of diversity has come to mean the acceptance of the essential sameness of all types of people, and the danger of generalizing among them at all. In fact, it has become virtually a definition of "racist" to make any substantive generalizations about a particular ethnicity, and a definition of "homophobic" to make any generalizations about homosexuals.

18   What follows, then, is likely to be understood as "homophobic." But I think it's true that certain necessary features of homosexual life lead to certain unavoidable features of homosexual character. This is not to say that they define any random homosexual: they do not. As with any group or way of life, there are many, many exceptions. Nor is it to say that they define the homosexual life: it should be clear by now that I believe that the needs and feelings of homosexual children and adolescents are largely interchangeable with those of their heterosexual peers. But there are certain generalizations that can be made about adult homosexuals and lesbians that have the ring of truth.

19   Of course, in a culture where homosexuals remain hidden and wrapped in self-contempt, in which their emotional development is often stunted and late, in which the closet protects all sorts of self-destructive behavior that a more open society would not, it is still very hard to tell what is inherent in a homosexual life that makes it different, and what is simply imposed upon it. Nevertheless, it seems to me that even in the most tolerant societies, some of the differences that I have just described would inhere.

20   The experience of growing up profoundly different in emotional and psychological makeup inevitably alters a person's self-perception, tends to make him or her more wary and distant, more attuned to appearance and its foibles, more self-conscious and perhaps more reflective. The presence of homosexuals in the arts, in literature, in

architecture, in design, in fashion could be understood, as some have, as a simple response to oppression. Homosexuals have created safe professions within which to hide and protect each other. But why these professions? Maybe it's also that these are professions of appearance. Many homosexual children, feeling distant from their peers, become experts at trying to figure out how to disguise their inner feelings, to "pass." They notice the signs and signals of social interaction, because they do not come instinctively. They develop skills early on that help them notice the inflections of a voice, the quirks of a particular movement, and the ways in which meaning can be conveyed in code. They have an ear for irony and for double meanings. Sometimes, by virtue of having to suppress their natural emotions, they find formal outlets to express themselves: music, theater, art. And so their lives become set on a trajectory which reinforces these trends.

As a child I remember, as I suppressed the natural emotions of an adolescent, how I naturally turned in on myself—writing, painting, and participating in amateur drama. Or I devised fantasies of future exploits—war leader, parliamentarian, famous actor—that could absorb those emotions that were being diverted from meeting other boys and developing natural emotional relationships with them. And I developed mannerisms, small ways in which I could express myself, tiny revolts of personal space—a speech affectation, a ridiculous piece of clothing—that were, in retrospect, attempts to communicate something in code which could not be communicated in language. In this homosexual archness there was, of course, much pain. And it came as no surprise that once I had become more open about my homosexuality, these mannerisms declined. Once I found the strength to be myself, I had no need to act myself. So my clothes became progressively more regular and slovenly; I lost interest in drama; my writing moved from fiction to journalism; my speech actually became less affected. 21

This, of course, is not a universal homosexual experience. Many homosexuals never become more open, and the skills required to survive the closet remain skills by which to earn a living. And many homosexuals, even once they no longer need those skills, retain them. My point is simply that the universal experience of self-conscious difference in childhood and adolescence—common, but not exclusive, to homosexuals—develops identifiable skills. They are the skills of mimesis; and one of the goods that homosexuals bring to society is undoubtedly a more highly developed sense of form, of style. Even in the most open of societies, I think, this will continue to be the case. It is not something genetically homosexual; it is something environmentally homosexual. And it begins young. 22

Closely connected to this is a sense of irony. Like Jews who have developed ways to resist, subvert, and adopt a majority culture, so homosexuals have found themselves ironizing their difference. Because, 23 in many cases, they have survived acute periods of emotion, they are more likely to appreciate—even willfully celebrate—its more over-wrought and melodramatic depictions. They have learned to see the funny side of etiolation. This, perhaps, is the true origin of camp. It is the ability to see agony and enjoy its form while ignoring its content, the ability to watch emotional trauma and not see its essence but its appearance. It is the aestheticization of pain.

24   This role in the aestheticization of the culture is perhaps enhanced by another unavoidable fact about most homosexuals and lesbians: their childlessness. This generates two related qualities: the relative freedom to procreate in a broader, structural sense, and to experiment with human relationships that can be instructive for the society as a whole.

25   The lack of children is something some homosexuals regard as a curse; and it is the thing which many heterosexuals most pity (and some envy) about their homosexual acquaintances. But it is also an opportunity. Childless men and women have many things to offer a society. They can transfer their absent parental instincts into broader parental roles: they can be extraordinary teachers and mentors, nurses and doctors, priests, rabbis, and nuns; they can throw themselves into charity work, helping the needy and the lonely; they can care for the young who have been abandoned by others, through adoption. Or they can use all their spare time to forge an excellence in their field of work that is sometimes unavailable to the harried mother or burdened father. They can stay late in the office, be the most loyal staffer in an election campaign, work round the clock in a journalistic production, be the lawyer most able and willing to meet the emerging deadline.

26   One of their critical roles in society has also often been in the military. Here is an institution which requires dedication beyond the calling to the biological, nuclear family, that needs people prepared to give all their time to the common endeavor, that requires men and women able to subsume their personal needs into the formal demands of military discipline. Of all institutions in our society, the military is perhaps the most naturally homosexual, which is part of the reason, of course, why it is so hostile to their visible presence. The displacement of family affection onto a broader community also makes the homosexual an ideal person to devote him- or herself to a social institution: the university, the school, the little league, the Boy Scouts, the church, the sports team. Scratch most of these institutions and you'll find a homosexual or two sustaining many of its vital functions.

27   But the homosexual's contribution can be more than nourishing the society's aesthetic and institutional life. It has become a truism that in the field of emotional development, homosexuals have much to learn from the heterosexual culture. The values of commitment, of monogamy, of marriage, of stability are all posited as models for homosexual existence. And, indeed, of course, they are. Without an architectonic

institution like that of marriage, it is difficult to create the conditions for nurturing such virtues, but that doesn't belie their importance.

It is also true, however, that homosexual relationships, even in their current, somewhat eclectic form, may contain features that could nourish the broader society as well. Precisely because there is no institutional model, gay relationships are often sustained more powerfully by genuine commitment. The mutual nurturing and sexual expressiveness of many lesbian relationships, the solidity and space of many adult gay male relationships, are qualities sometimes lacking in more rote, heterosexual couplings. Same-sex unions often incorporate the virtues of friendship more effectively than traditional marriages; and at times, among gay male relationships, the openness of the contract makes it more likely to survive than many heterosexual bonds. Some of this is unavailable to the male-female union: there is more likely to be greater understanding of the need for extramarital outlets between two men than between a man and a woman; and again, the lack of children gives gay couples greater freedom. Their failures entail fewer consequences for others. But something of the gay relationship's necessary honesty, its flexibility, and its equality could undoubtedly help strengthen and inform many heterosexual bonds.

In my own sometimes comic, sometimes passionate attempts to construct relationships, I learned something of the foibles of a simple heterosexual model. I saw how the network of gay friendship was often as good an emotional nourishment as a single relationship, that sexual candor was not always the same as sexual license, that the kind of supportive community that bolsters many gay relationships is something many isolated straight marriages could benefit from. I also learned how the subcultural fact of gay life rendered it remarkably democratic: in gay bars, there was far less socioeconomic stratification than in heterosexual bars. The shared experience of same-sex desire cut through class and race; it provided a humbling experience, which allowed many of us to risk our hearts and our friendships with people we otherwise might never have met. It loosened us up, and gave us a keener sense, perhaps, that people were often difficult to understand, let alone judge, from appearances. My heterosexual peers, through no fault of their own, were often denied these experiences. But they might gain from understanding them a little better, and not simply from a position of condescension.

As I've just argued, I believe strongly that marriage should be made available to everyone, in a politics of strict public neutrality. But within this model, there is plenty of scope for cultural difference. There is something baleful about the attempt of some gay conservatives to educate homosexuals and lesbians into an uncritical acceptance of a stifling model of heterosexual normality. The truth is, homosexuals are not entirely normal; and to flatten their varied and complicated lives

28

29

30

into a single, moralistic model is to miss what is essential and exhilarating about their otherness.

31   This need not mean, as some have historically claimed, that homosexuals have no stake in the sustenance of a society, but rather that their role is somewhat different; they may be involved in procreation in a less literal sense: in a society's cultural regeneration, its entrepreneurial or intellectual rejuvenation, its religious ministry, or its professional education. Unencumbered by children, they may be able to press the limits of the culture or the business infrastructure, or the boundaries of intellectual life, in a way that heterosexuals, by dint of a different type of calling, cannot. Of course, many heterosexuals perform similar roles; and many homosexuals prefer domesticity to public performance; but the inevitable way of life of the homosexual provides an opportunity that many intuitively seem to grasp and understand.

32   Or perhaps their role is to have no role at all. Perhaps it is the experience of rebellion that prompts homosexual culture to be peculiarly resistant to attempts to guide it to be useful or instructive or productive. Go to any march for gay rights and you will see the impossibility of organizing it into a coherent lobby: such attempts are always undermined by irony, or exhibitionism, or irresponsibility. It is as if homosexuals have learned something about life that makes them immune to the puritanical and flattening demands of modern politics. It is as if they have learned that life is fickle; that there are parts of it that cannot be understood, let alone solved; that some things lead nowhere and mean nothing; that the ultimate exercise of freedom is not a programmatic journey but a spontaneous one. Perhaps it requires seeing one's life as the end of a biological chain, or seeing one's deepest emotions as the object of detestation, that provides this insight. But the seeds of homosexual wisdom are the seeds of human wisdom. They contain the truth that order is in fact a euphemism for disorder; that problems are often more sanely enjoyed than solved; that there is reason in mystery; that there is beauty in the wild flowers that grow randomly among our wheat.

✦ Evaluating the Text

1. How does Sullivan's account of the two engagements he attended one Labor Day weekend bring into focus the vast cultural differences that separate the homosexual and heterosexual worlds?

2. How does Sullivan use his own experience of concealing his homosexuality for many years before "coming out of the closet" as evidence to support his analysis of homosexual culture?

3. In Sullivan's view, how does the increasing cultural separation homosexuals experience from childhood onward produce a way of looking

at the world quite different from that of the straight world? What, in his view, are the advantages and disadvantages of seeing the world from this perspective?

✦ Exploring Different Perspectives

1. How do the accounts by Andrew Sullivan and Judith Ortiz Cofer (see "The Myth of the Latin Woman") seek to replace sexual stereotypes with realistic portraits?

2. How does the definition of homosexuals present a dichotomy like that involved in "splitting," as described by Lennard J. Davis in "Visualizing the Disabled Body"?

✦ Extending Viewpoints Through Writing

1. In your view, was the military correct in adopting a "don't ask, don't tell" policy toward gays in 1995? Explain your reasons.

2. When you first started college and became part of a new social group in which you were free to present yourself in any way you chose, did your reinvention compel you to hide aspects of yourself in ways that proved stressful?

Rosa Liksom

One Night Stands

———————◆———————

Rosa Liksom (the pseudonym of Anni Ylavaara) was born in Lapland in 1958. She is the author of six books and has attracted attention as a painter as well. Her short prose includes laconic passages in which a depersonalized urban reality appears in a harsh, macabre, or ridiculous light. She is among the most translated of contemporary Finnish writers. She currently resides in Helsinki, where she works as a bartender. "One Night Stands" is taken from her 1993 collection of the same name.

1   I got knocked up. Shit, it really happened. I still can't see how it was possible, I'd been screwing guys for years without any precautions. I guess I thought I was lucky enough to be barren.

2   Wham, no period, and then this thing started growing in my belly.

3   I waited for almost three months, I was almost a mother. It was really a drag, everything tasted like shit, and gunk started dripping out of my tits. I even had to buy a bra, my titties got so tender.

4   About three months after that screw I lay on a table in an operating room, spreading my legs. It didn't feel like much anything. At that point all I wanted was for the lady in the white coat to push the anesthetic button and for the doctor to stick his tongs in there and get the whole thing over with.

5   It was one of those typical black-and-white Friday afternoons when I ran into Misty at the mall and she invited me for a drink at her place. I can always use a drink and besides, that Misty's a dish.

6   I think that was the day I was knocked up. That's my theory, at least.

7   We went to Misty's place. Her mom and dad had gone out to lunch at the neighborhood tavern to celebrate their fifteenth anniversary, so it was just the two of us. We talked and had a couple of stiff drinks. I took a shower and put my cruddy clothes back on. We put some make-up on in front of the hall mirror. It must've taken us a couple of hours, our hands were none too steady. Then we took off, really feeling the buzz by now, and went down eight floors in the elevator to the cool sidewalk down below.

*(For information on Finland, see p. 145.)

Of course we knew where we were going. At that time, Misty had   8
had a fight with Pige, and I had just given Kaide his walking papers. I
guess I got drunk to drown my sorrows. Or something, I don't know. I
guess Misty just got drunk for the hell of it, she really had the hots for
Pige.

We took the bus to the railroad station, but our trip got off to a bad   9
start: we got kicked out after two stops. Just because we started laying
some shit on this guy with a fat neck. We hadn't even got started, really,
before he blew his top. He grabbed Misty by the neck and was about to
strangle her. I yelled and screamed, and finally the driver slammed on
the brakes. He saved Misty's life by throwing us out.

So there we were, incredibly smashed, somewhere in the sticks in   10
the middle of a lot of trees. We walked to the next stop and amused
ourselves a little. It was cold and windy, so we decided to perform a
little lesbian number. We kissed each other so our lipstick smeared, and
Misty pushed her hand into my jeans. It looked really heavy, especially
to the idiots who were standing at the stop. Their eyes were popping
out of their heads. Then we really started to make out. We were a big
hit with those guys.

The next bus took us to the station. We didn't mean to hang around   11
there, shit, we had promised each other fifteen times that we wouldn't
even slow down at the station. But, once again, it proved fateful.

Just as we got off the bus, Ike and Rami showed up. And that was   12
that. Misty forgot Pige, I forgot my sorrows, and off we went.

At some point, the guys remembered a party in Käpylä, so we took   13
the bus out there. People at the party were downing beers, and they
had New York Dolls and Alice Cooper on the stereo.

So we partied for hours, and finally I just blacked out. I babbled on   14
for a while, then I crashed. The first thing I noticed after that was that I
was flat on my back in some really dark place, and also that someone
was shoving himself into me. I remember closing my eyes tight and
trying to forget everything.

But as soon as I managed to get things into focus a little I realized   15
that it was Ike who was humping me. It was a relief, in a way. At least I
knew the guy. But then my blood sugar went up when I realized that
this asshole was banging me although he could see that I was off somewhere in the happy hunting grounds. I tried to push him off me, but he
didn't budge. I gave up and let him get on with it.

Much later I realized that it wasn't just Ike who was screwing.   16
Misty and Rami were doing it next to us, and a few more couples were
at it over by the other wall. I gulped and tried to flush all the mud out
of my head, but it was more than I could manage. OK, it could have
been a blast if there had been some feeling involved, but there wasn't
any. I still don't understand what fun Ike could have had screwing
someone who had passed out. But I have to admit that it was quite a

jolt when I realized that the guy screwing me that night was Ike and no one else. Ike isn't just anybody. Ike is The King.

17   So I lay there on the cold floor next to the rattling boiler. My legs were fucking cold, and I could see my breath in the air.

18   It was the same old story. Ike had been drunk for two months and smelled like it, too. He hadn't been anywhere near water for weeks, and his breath stank like the plague. Even though I can't say I'm all that different, at least I remember to wash once in a while.

19   What else to say. I tried to think of something totally else while Ike kept pumping. I could tell from the window up by the ceiling that a nice fall day was about to begin out there.

20   After Ike was done, Misty and I took off. The guys followed us but got off at the railroad station. I didn't feel too good but not too pissed-off either. Our make-up was a mess, and my head felt like a parrot house. We went to Misty's to sleep it off.

21   It was Misty who first realized that I was pregnant. She took me to a doctor, and her mother paid for the deal. Shit, if it weren't for Misty, I might have twins. Without her, I might not have realized that it was time to get my womb cleaned out. Missing a period or two wasn't that unusual, it had happened before, but then everything had been all right.

22   It was pretty amazing when they called from the health center and said well, it seems like the seed has fallen on fertile ground. But then they were pretty quick when they found out that I was only fourteen years old.

23   I said all right when can you take care of it? I had decided before-hand that if the test turned out positive I would just get rid of it without further ado. I didn't even want to start counting to figure out who its father might be, since it would land in the garbage anyway.

24   At the health center they really got heavy about the paternity question. They claimed that it was my civic duty to reveal the identity of the child's father. I told them it was my private affair, and they should butt out.

25   They conducted about a dozen interrogations on my lifestyle, wanted to know what I do and think and so on. They couldn't really catch me out on anything, because I manage to keep up with my schoolwork in spite of everything, and my mom and dad are in the upper income bracket. They managed, nevertheless, to make me feel disgusted and sorry for myself and all that.

26   Now when I run into Ike, he acts just like before. He doesn't even say hello to me. I haven't said a word to him about the whole thing, and I don't give a shit. I know how to take care of this kind of stuff. I wouldn't want any jerks to help me out. Come to think of it, even if I had wanted to tell Ike about it, I wouldn't have dared. I can't even imagine what he'd look like if I told him. Or, yes, I can. He would have

forced me to have that kid. Then he could have bragged to the other guys about having added another little Ike to the world's population. As far as I know, it would have been his third, and he would have been the champ. Twenty years old, and the dad of three miserable kids.

I had goose bumps on my thighs. Finally the lady in the white coat 27
stuck the needle in my arm, and I drifted off into a deep sleep.

✦ *Evaluating the Text*

1. What characteristics of this story would explain why Liksom's work is often characterized as "post-punk" writing?

2. To what extent does this story portray an alienated generation without time to wallow in self-pity, for whom paradise consists of drugs and liquor? How does Liksom communicate this tone of hopelessness?

✦ *Exploring Different Perspectives*

1. How do the narrators in the stories by Rosa Liksom and Sembene Ousmane (see "Her Three Days") free themselves from male societal expectations?

2. What different forms does alienation take in Liksom's story and in Andrew Sullivan's account (see "What Are Homosexuals For?")?

✦ *Extending Viewpoints Through Writing*

1. What cultural, class, and generational values does the main character in the story embody?

2. How does the matter-of-fact tone of Liksom's story, given the age of the narrator, make the events of the "One Night Stands" all the more shocking?

3. Did you ever "put someone on" in order to confirm their worst fears about you? What story did you invent? What reactions did you elicit? Did you tell the person later what you had done?

Connecting Cultures

◆

Kim Chernin, The Flesh and the Devil

In what way is the concept of how society judges your appearance analyzed by Kim Chernin and Alison Lurie (see "The Language of Clothes," Chapter 8)?

Judith Ortiz Cofer, The Myth of the Latin Woman

What common societal attitude toward Hispanics do Judith Ortiz Cofer and Ron Maydon (see "Ron Maydon," Chapter 4) assail?

Sembene Ousmane, Her Three Days

How do the stories by Sembene Ousmane and Shirley Saad (see "Amina," Chapter 1) shed light on the predicament of women under the system of polygamy common to the Islamic cultures they portray?

Deborah Tannen, Talk in the Intimate Relationship

How do Deborah Tannen's analysis and John Cheever's story, "Reunion" (Chapter 1), turn on questions of poor communication?

Lennard J. Davis, Visualizing the Disabled Body

What differing attitudes toward disabilities emerge from Lennard J. Davis's analysis and Sucheng Chan's account (see "You're Short, Besides!", Chapter 2)?

Andrew Sullivan, What Are Homosexuals For?

How does Andrew Sullivan's account illustrate, albeit in a different context, the psychology of those who are exiled from society (see Edward Said's "Reflections on Exile," Chapter 7)?

Rosa Liksom, One Night Stands

What insights into the psychology of young women are offered in the stories by Rosa Liksom and Dino Buzzati (see "The Falling Girl," Chapter 2)?

4

How Work Creates Identity

◆

The way we identify ourselves in terms of the work we do is far-reaching. Frequently, the first question we ask when we meet someone is, "What do you do?" Through work we define ourselves and others; yet, cultural values also play a part in influencing how we feel about the work we do.

In addition to providing a means to live, work has an important psychological meaning in our culture. Some societies value work more than leisure; in other cultures, the reverse is true and work is viewed as something you do just to provide the necessities of life. In the United States, the work you perform is intertwined with a sense of identity and self-esteem.

Work in most societies involves the exchange of goods and services. In tribal cultures, as distinct from highly industrialized cultures, there is little job specialization, although age and gender determine what tasks one performs. Economies may range from the barter system where goods are traded to more complex market economies based on the reciprocal exchange of goods and services for money.

The attitude people have toward the work they do varies within and between cultures. For example, think of the momentous change in attitude toward the work women do in terms of equal opportunity and equal pay.

Lesley Hazleton, in "Confessions of a Fast Woman," describes the challenges and rewards of being an auto mechanic. Camara Laye offers an autobiographical account, "The Village Goldsmith," describing the awe with which he viewed his father's vocation as a goldsmith in Guinea. An interview with Anton Vassilievich, in "Radiation Expert," offers an extraordinary insight into the measures needed to cope with high levels of radiation following the Chernobyl disaster. An American teacher in China, Mark Salzman, describes (in "Lessons") the unusual bargain he struck with the renowned martial arts master Pan Qingfu to exchange English lessons for instruction in the Chinese martial arts.

223

The Thai writer Kon Krailet dramatizes the anguish of a young man in Bangkok who must conceal his profession from his family in the poignant story "In the Mirror." Studs Terkel's interview with Ron Maydon provides an eye-opening account of how Hispanics feel caught between the Anglo and African-American communities. Indian writer R. K. Narayan describes, in "Misguided 'Guide'," the comedy of errors that resulted from trying to make a film from one of his novels. The Brazilian writer Moacyr Scliar, in "A Brief History of Capitalism," presents an ironic portrait of an idealistic communist in a new capitalistic society.

Lesley Hazleton

Confessions of a Fast Woman

———————◆———————

Lesley Hazleton was born in 1945 in Reading, England, received a B.A. in 1966 from Manchester University, and an M.A. in 1971 from the Hebrew University in Jerusalem. She immigrated to the United States in 1979. She has worked as a feature writer for the Jerusalem Post, *1968–1973, and as a reporter for Time-Life, Inc., Jerusalem, 1973–1976. She has been a distinguished writer in residence at Pacific Lutheran University, Tacoma, Washington, 1986, and has taught creative nonfiction writing at Pennsylvania State University, University Park, 1989. Her writings include* Israeli Women *(1978),* Where Mountains Roar: A Personal Report from the Sinai and Negev Desert *(1980). Hazleton's dramatic reporting from the Middle East has been published in the award-winning* Jerusalem, Jerusalem *(1986). She has also written* England, Bloody England *(1989) and* Confessions of a Fast Woman *(1992). Since 1989, she has written the car column for* Lear's *magazine and has also written about cars and driving for* The New York Times, Connoisseur, Penthouse, *and* Newsday. *"Confessions of a Fast Woman," from her 1992 book of that name, tells how her lifelong passion for racing survived a stint working as an auto mechanic in upstate Vermont.*

I loved working at the sink. Harvey thought this was perverse of   1
me. He was probably right. It was one of the dirtiest jobs in the shop.

The sink was a neatly self-enclosed system: a steel tub set atop a   2
barrel containing parts cleaner, a small pump sucking the cleaner up
from the barrel into a tube with a thick steel brush at the end, and a fil-
ter to clean the used fluid before it drained back into the barrel to be
used again.

Working there, I'd stand with my back to everything else in the   3
shop, concentrated entirely on the mass of gunked parts before me. The
gunk was thick, black. The parts were so filthy they seemed almost
anonymous, just so many interchangeable relics of the mechanical age.
Even thinking of cleaning them at first seemed pointless.

But leave something to soak in that sink for a while, then come   4
back to it and start scrubbing, and a kind of magic happened. What had
been anonymous began to reveal form and personality. Vague shapes
achieved particularity.

Black paled, gleamed here and there, turned slowly to silver. An   5
ancient alchemy took place right under my hands as I hosed and

scrubbed. Years of baked grease and oil and road dirt gave way to the corrosiveness of the parts cleaner, and as I worked, it seemed that here, under my very hands, I was rediscovering the original form, the bright gleaming essence of each part. Old melted gaskets disappeared under the brush. Flywheel teeth became sharp and effective. Clutch plates became intricate pieces of sculpture. I had a distinct sense of creating each part anew, of restoring its form and function.

6   And all the time, of course, I was breathing in the fumes of the parts cleaner, so that I am still not sure if the work itself was really that satisfying, or if I was simply so high that it seemed that way.

7   All the cleaners began to smell good—a seductive, chemical smell that seemed to enter my head, clear my sinuses, clean up all the synapses of my brain. There was the 5-56, so much like dry-cleaning fluid that I sometimes thought if I just stood in the path of its fumes, it would clean the clothes right on me. Oddly, I'd always hated that smell before. Then there was the Carb Clean, for gummed-up carbs; the Brakleen brakes cleaner, each can with a thin red straw laid horizontally across its black cap like the headgear of a Japanese geisha; and the Gunk—a registered trademark name for heavy-duty engine cleaner.

8   I had no idea just how addictive the fumes were until a few weeks into my apprenticeship, on our Monday off. I was driving past another repair shop that was open on Mondays. The windows of my car were wide open, and as I went by, I recognized the smells of parts cleaner, gasoline, lubricants—all the acids and oils with which I now worked five days a week. I slowed way down, breathed in deep, and was suffused with an immense sense of well-being.

9   After a month, the shop and the smells and the work were in my dreams. They were good dreams, but I'd wake with the fumes still in my nostrils, wondering how smells from a dream could spill over into the first moments of waking. Was the sense of smell independent of reality? Was my brain so addicted that it could create the smell by itself, without any external stimulus?

10   No matter how seductive the fumes, however, there was no doubt as to the corrosiveness of the parts cleaner: it turned my tanned hands a whitish hue and made the skin parchment dry. I began to use rubber gloves when working at the sink, but even then the chemicals seemed to work their way through the rubber, and my hands still paled.

11   Meanwhile, the blackened asbestos dust from the brake pads was just plain hazardous. It was caked onto the calipers and the whole of the brake assembly. Cleaning it out demanded a screwdriver and a rag and copious amounts of Brakleen. It was close-up work, so that however careful I was, I still inhaled the dust.

12   You take all the precautions you can in a repair shop. You keep as many doors and windows open as possible. You keep fans going. You back out cars and bikes to start them up, or if you have to start them in-

side, you attach a hose to the exhaust pipe and run the fumes outside. You could, of course, wear a mask, but few mechanics do. Most know they should, but the masks are hot and stuffy and they get in the way. And besides, the truth is that most mechanics do not worry about fumes. They have bigger things to worry about: a jack or a hoist giving way, a fire, a loose part spinning off. Auto mechanics is not a safe profession.

Despite all the protestations of writers and researchers that intel- 13 lectual work is hard and exhausting, physical work is harder. Like any-one who's done it day in and day out, I now know this in my bones.

For years, I argued that intellectual work was exhausting, as indeed 14 it can be. After a few hours at the typewriter, there is little I can do for a while. All my energy has been consumed, poured onto the page. Some-times I do some physical work for a change—scythe an overgrown gar-den, for instance, or clean the oven. In such circumstances, physical work seems a pleasure and a relief, something that produces a healthy kind of exhaustion instead of the enervating overload of the mind that I am escaping.

This kind of short-term excursion into physical work can indeed 15 make it seem attractive. But when you do it for a living, it exacts a heavy toll. The long-term effects of fumes and asbestos dust working their way into the body's cells are one thing, but the short term can be riskier still. With all due respect to the physical strain on hands, eyes, back, and brain from working at a keyboard all day, in physical work you can literally break your back.

I was lucky. I only sprained mine. 16

The culprit was a Datsun 240Z. It arrived on a truck with a note 17 that read, "It went to Woodstock, and while there, the gears went." Just that, and a signature.

It hadn't been cruising the idyllic scenery of Woodstock. It had 18 been drag racing. The owners had put a six-cylinder 260 engine into it, with triple carbs and a psi gauge. There'd been a big pop, it seemed, and then—nothing. No motion.

"We'll have to pull out the transmission and replace it," said Carl. 19

I was delighted. The heavier the work—the more it got down to the 20 basics, into the actual drive mechanisms—the happier I was because the more I'd learn. Better still, if we had to replace the transmission, I could take the broken one apart. I already knew from the exploded di-agrams in my textbook that there's nothing like taking things apart to understand how they work. Putting them back together again, I had still to discover, is yet another level of understanding.

The Z-car rode so low to the ground that we had to jack it up just to 21 get the arms of the hydraulic lift underneath it. Harvey removed the bolt at the bottom of the transmission case so we could drain the trans-mission fluid—foul-smelling stuff—and found a small chunk of metal sitting on top of the bolt. "Bad sign," he said. "Something's come loose and ripped through the gears."

22   The next stage was to get the exhaust system off. That should have been simple enough, but there was so much gunk and rust that even after we'd loosened all the bolts, nothing moved. So Harvey stood up front and yanked, and I stood toward the back, pulling and yanking at the pipe above my head.

23   I felt something go inside me. Somewhere in my abdomen, it seemed. But I was focused on that exhaust pipe, eyes half-closed against flecks of grit and rust, and paid no attention. Harvey finally managed to loosen the front end, then we swapped places, me steadying as he pulled, and finally, lo and behold, the pipe slid off. We disconnected the fuel and oil lines, and then faced the really tough part.

24   When you're deeply involved in hard work, you simply don't notice pain. By the time we got the transmission case down from its mountings and into the yard, and then dismantled the clutch, it was late afternoon, and it was clear that this was going to be a long, drawn-out job. The drive plate and flywheel were so badly worn that they too would have to be replaced.

25   I went home that night exhausted. That was nothing unusual. Most evenings I'd flop down in an armchair with a beer in one hand, and find myself unable to move. It was the kind of deep exhaustion that comes only from hard physical work, the kind that you can feel in every muscle of your body, that seems to reach into your bones and sit there, making them feel both incredibly heavy and weightless at the same time. There is a strange kind of floating feeling to this exhaustion, yet at the same time you are convinced that you must weigh twice what you usually weigh.

26   If someone had shouted "Fire!" right then, I'd have nodded, said "Fine," and not moved an inch.

27   This stage of exhaustion would usually last a good half-hour or so, and in that half hour, I'd hold my hands up in front of my face and wonder where all those cuts and burns and scrapes had come from. From the repair shop, obviously, but what car, what movement, what moment? I never knew. Cuts and burns and scrapes and other minor injuries were just part of the job, so much so that I never noticed them at the time. Only later, in another place and time, in a comfortable armchair as the sun was setting, did they begin to seem remarkable. And then I'd feel an odd pride in them. They were proof of my work, small badges of my apprenticeship.

28   That Z-car had been a tougher job than most. We'd been working on it nearly the whole of the ten-hour day, and now, as I sat still, I realized my abdomen was really hurting, and that the pain was spreading to my back. A pulled muscle, I thought. We had three days off now for the Fourth of July weekend, and I was glad: my body needed it.

29   The next morning, I picked up a loaded wheelbarrow of split wood, turned it to the right, and could almost swear that I heard some-

thing go pop in my lower back, just like the gears of that Z-car. For the first time in my life, I understood what crippling pain was. By the time I got to a chiropractor in Barre, the only one around who'd see me on a holiday weekend, I couldn't walk without a crutch.

Half an hour later, I walked out carrying the crutch—still in pain, but mobile. The chiro, young and gentle, merely smiled tolerantly when I compared him to Christ.   30

"This back has forty-eight hours to heal," I told him.   31

"It will probably take four or five weeks," he said.   32

I shook my head. "It can't," I said. "I've got to go to work."   33

He studied my face. "Come on in tomorrow and the next day," he said, "and we'll see what we can do."   34

That included the Fourth of July itself. Rob Borowske became more and more Christ-like in my mind. Forty-eight hours of cold compresses, gentle stretching, electrical stimulation, aspirin, and chiropractic adjustments did not make for the happiest of weekends, but on the morning of July 5, I was there at Just Imports, a compress strapped to my lower back, cautiously mobile.   35

It wasn't macho that made me so determined. Partly it was the awareness that if I lay in bed and played invalid, my back would "freeze" and take far longer to heal. But more than that, it was the knowledge that Harvey and Bud would have to literally break their backs before they'd stay away from work. A mere "subluxation" simply did not rank. Not alongside what Harvey had been through.   36

The back healed quickly. Between Rob's four or five weeks and my forty-eight hours, it compromised on two weeks, although by the middle of the first week I was working as I had been. Being on my feet all day helped. Besides, I had to take apart that transmission case, discovering in the process that Harvey had been right: ball bearings had come loose and torn through the gears. No wonder nothing would move.   37

Harvey asked after the back a couple of times, but after that it was business as usual. Neither he nor Bud nor Carl thought it at all odd that I should turn up for work. Injuries were just part of the job. My back, the left foot I bruised badly when I moved a motorcycle the wrong way, the concussion I'd get of couple of weeks later when I'd stand up and hit my head on the strut of the hydraulic lift ("Every apprentice has to do it at least once," said Harvey)—these were just par for the course. As one injury healed and another replaced it, I began to think of them as rites of passage: stages in my evolution as an apprentice.   38

✦ Evaluating the Text

1. Describe the tasks Hazleton confronted in her everyday work as an auto mechanic.

2. What explains her unwillingness to let her back injury incapacitate her?

3. In your opinion, what does being an apprentice in an auto repair shop mean to her? What satisfactions does she seem to be getting from it?

✦ Exploring Different Perspectives

1. Compare the satisfactions that Hazleton and Camara Laye's father, in "The Village Goldsmith," derive from repairing or creating physical objects using materials that are hard to work with and under grueling conditions.

2. What different perspectives on being an auto mechanic are offered by Lesley Hazleton and Moacyr Scliar (see "A Brief History of Capitalism")? How are the narrators' attitudes toward work influenced by differences in gender, class, and culture?

✦ Extending Viewpoints Through Writing

1. Compare the demands of hard physical work with the stresses of hard intellectual work. Which did you find more exhausting and why?

2. Have you ever had a job where you performed work traditionally associated with the opposite gender? Did you find it to be a pleasant or unpleasant experience?

3. Have you ever had the experience of trying to get a job and thinking that your gender, ethnicity, or race was a factor in your prospective employer's decision whether or not to hire you?

Camara Laye

The Village Goldsmith

◆

Camara Laye (1928–1980) was born in Kouroussa, French Guinea (now Guinea), West Africa. All of Laye's books affirm traditional African life and culture. Raised as a Moslem in the countryside, Laye left his family's village to attend high school, after which he accepted a scholarship to study engineering in Paris. To ease the tension and loneliness of student life, Laye began to write down remembrances of his childhood. These writings became his first book, The Dark Child *(1953), a work that has been widely praised for its quiet restraint in depicting traditional ways of life in Guinea. The book's success enabled Laye to devote his full time to writing. Laye served as a diplomat for the government of Guinea in Liberia and Ghana and was a university professor in Senegal, where he died in 1980. His other published novels include* The Radiance of the King *(1956),* A Dream of Africa *(1968), and* The Guardian of the Word, *published posthumously in 1984. From Laye's account of his father's work as a goldsmith we can understand the laws, customs, and manners that prevailed in the village of his childhood.*

The territory of the present-day republic of Guinea in West Africa belonged to the kingdom of Mandingo and the medieval empire of Ghana. Portuguese exploration of the Guinea coast in the mid-fifteenth century led to the development of a slave trade involving the French, the British, and Arab slave traders. The country became a French colony in 1891 and, under the name French Guinea, became part of French West Africa. Guinea became independent in 1958 under the leadership of Sekou Toure, who remained in power until his death in 1984 when the military took power. General Lansana Conte has declared his intention to restore democracy and return the country to a civilian regime. Although poor transportation has hampered industrialization, Guinea possesses some of the world's largest bauxite deposits as well as substantial quantities of iron ore, gold, and diamonds. Presidential elections were held on December 19, 1993, and President Conte was reelected.

Of all the different kinds of work my father engaged in, none fascinated me so much as his skill with gold. No other occupation was so noble, no other needed such a delicate touch. And then, every time he worked in gold it was like a festival—indeed it *was* a festival—that broke the monotony of ordinary working days.

1

2   So, if a woman, accompanied by a go-between, crossed the threshold of the workshop, I followed her in at once. I knew what she
wanted: she had brought some gold, and had come to ask my father to
transform it into a trinket. She had collected it in the placers of Siguiri
where, crouching over the river for months on end, she had patiently
extracted grains of gold from the mud.

3   These women never came alone. They knew my father had other
things to do than make trinkets. And even when he had the time, they
knew they were not the first to ask a favor of him, and that, consequently, they would not be served before others.

4   Generally they required the trinket for a certain date, for the festival of Ramadan or the Tabaski or some other family ceremony or dance.

5   Therefore, to enhance their chances of being served quickly and to
more easily persuade my father to interrupt the work before him, they
used to request the services of an official praise-singer, a go-between,
arranging in advance the fee they were to pay him for his good offices.

6   The go-between installed himself in the workshop, tuned up his
cora, which is our harp, and began to sing my father's praises. This was
always a great event for me. I heard recalled the lofty deeds of my father's ancestors and their names from the earliest times. As the cou-
plets were reeled off it was like watching the growth of a great
genealogical tree that spread its branches far and wide and flourished
its boughs and twigs before my mind's eye. The harp played an accompaniment to this vast utterance of names, expanding it with notes that
were now soft, now shrill.

7   I could sense my father's vanity being inflamed, and I already
knew that after having sipped this milk-and-honey he would lend a fa-
vorable ear to the woman's request. But I was not alone in my knowledge. The woman also had seen my father's eyes gleaming with
contented pride. She held out her grains of gold as if the whole matter
were settled. My father took up his scales and weighed the gold.

8   "What sort of trinket do you want?" he would ask.

9   "I want. . . ."

10   And then the woman would not know any longer exactly what she
wanted because desire kept making her change her mind, and because
she would have liked all the trinkets at once. But it would have taken a
pile of gold much larger than she had brought to satisfy her whim, and
from then on her chief purpose in life was to get hold of it as soon as
she could.

11   "When do you want it?"

12   Always the answer was that the trinket was needed for an occasion
in the near future.

13   "So! You are in that much of a hurry? Where do you think I shall
find the time?"

14   "I am in a great hurry, I assure you."

"I have never seen a woman eager to deck herself out who wasn't in a great hurry! Good! I shall arrange my time to suit you. Are you satisfied?"

He would take the clay pot that was kept specially for smelting gold, and would pour the grains into it. He would then cover the gold with powdered charcoal, a charcoal he prepared by using plant juices of exceptional purity. Finally, he would place a large lump of the same kind of charcoal over the pot.

As soon as she saw that the work had been duly undertaken, the woman, now quite satisfied, would return to her household tasks, leaving her go-between to carry on with the praise-singing which had already proved so advantageous.

At a sign from my father the apprentices began working two sheepskin bellows. The skins were on the floor, on opposite sides of the forge, connected to it by earthen pipes. While the work was in progress the apprentices sat in front of the bellows with crossed legs. That is, the younger of the two sat, for the elder was sometimes allowed to assist. But the younger—this time it was Sidafa—was only permitted to work the bellows and watch while waiting his turn for promotion to less rudimentary tasks. First one and then the other worked hard at the bellows: the flame in the forge rose higher and became a living thing, a genie implacable and full of life.

Then my father lifted the clay pot with his long tongs and placed it on the flame.

Immediately all activity in the workshop almost came to a halt. During the whole time that the gold was being smelted, neither copper nor aluminum could be worked nearby, lest some particle of these base metals fall into the container which held the gold. Only steel could be worked on such occasions, but the men, whose task that was, hurried to finish what they were doing, or left it abruptly to join the apprentices gathered around the forge. There were so many, and they crowded so around my father, that I, the smallest person present, had to come near the forge in order not to lose track of what was going on.

If he felt he had inadequate working space, my father had the apprentices stand well away from him. He merely raised his hand in a simple gesture: at that particular moment he never uttered a word, and no one else would: no one was allowed to utter a word. Even the go-between's voice was no longer raised in song. The silence was broken only by the panting of the bellows and the faint hissing of the gold. But if my father never actually spoke, I know that he was forming words in his mind. I could tell from his lips, which kept moving, while, bending over the pot, he stirred the gold and charcoal with a bit of wood that kept bursting into flame and had constantly to be replaced by a fresh one.

What words did my father utter? I do not know. At least I am not certain what they were. No one ever told me. But could they have been anything but incantations? On these occasions was he not invoking the genies of fire and gold, of fire and wind, of wind blown by the blast-pipes of the forge, of fire born of wind, of gold married to fire? Was it not their assistance, their friendship, their espousal that he besought? Yes. Almost certainly he was invoking these genies, all of whom are equally indispensable for smelting gold.

23   The operation going on before my eyes was certainly the smelting of gold, yet something more than that: a magical operation that the guiding spirits could regard with favor or disfavor. That is why, all around my father, there was absolute silence and anxious expectancy. Though only a child, I knew there could be no craft greater than the goldsmith's. I expected a ceremony; I had come to be present at a cere-mony; and it actually was one, though very protracted. I was still too young to understand why, but I had an inkling as I watched the almost religious concentration of those who followed the mixing process in the clay pot.

24   When finally the gold began to melt I could have shouted aloud—and perhaps we all would have if we had not been forbidden to make a sound. I trembled, and so did everyone else watching my father stir the mixture—it was still a heavy paste—in which the charcoal was gradu-ally consumed. The next stage followed swiftly. The gold now had the fluidity of water. The genies had smiled on the operation!

25   "Bring me the brick!" my father would order, thus lifting the ban that until then had silenced us.

26   The brick, which an apprentice would place beside the fire, was hollowed out, generously greased with Galam butter. My father would take the pot off the fire and tilt it carefully, while I would watch the gold flow into the brick, flow like liquid fire. True, it was only a very sparse trickle of fire, but how vivid, how brilliant! As the gold flowed into the brick, the grease sputtered and flamed and emitted a thick smoke that caught in the throat and stung the eyes, leaving us all weep-ing and coughing.

27   But there were times when it seemed to me that my father ought to turn this task over to one of his assistants. They were experienced, had assisted him hundreds of times, and could certainly have performed the work well. But my father's lips moved and those inaudible, secret words, those incantations he addressed to one we could not see or hear, was the essential part. Calling on the genies of fire, of wind, of gold and exorcising the evil spirits—this was a knowledge he alone possessed.

28   By now the gold had been cooled in the hollow of the brick, and my father began to hammer and stretch it. This was the moment when his work as a goldsmith really began. I noticed that before embarking on it he never failed to stroke the little snake stealthily as it lay coiled up un-der the sheepskin. I can only assume that this was his way of gathering strength for what remained to be done, the most trying part of his task.

But was it not extraordinary and miraculous that on these occa-   29
sions the little black snake was always coiled under the sheepskin? He
was not always there. He did not visit my father every day. But he was
always present whenever there was gold to be worked. His presence
was no surprise to *me*. After that evening when my father had spoken
of the guiding spirit of his race I was no longer astonished. The snake
was there intentionally. He knew what the future held. Did he tell my
father? I think that he most certainly did. Did he tell him everything? I
have another reason for believing firmly that he did.

The craftsman who works in gold must first of all purify himself.   30
That is, he must wash himself all over and, of course, abstain from all
sexual commerce during the whole time. Great respecter of ceremony
as he was, it would have been impossible for my father to ignore these
rules. Now, I never saw him make these preparations. I saw him address himself to his work without any apparent preliminaries. From
that moment it was obvious that, forewarned in a dream by his black
guiding spirit of the task which awaited him in the morning, my father
must have prepared for it as soon as he arose, entering his workshop in
a state of purity, his body smeared with the secret potions hidden in his
numerous pots of magical substances; or perhaps he always came into
his workshop in a state of ritual purity. I am not trying to make him out
a better man than he was—he was a man and had his share of human
frailties—but he was always uncompromising in his respect for ritual
observance.

The woman for whom the trinket was being made, and who had   31
come often to see how the work was progressing, would arrive for the
final time, not wanting to miss a moment of this spectacle—as marvelous to her as to us—when the gold wire, which my father had succeeded in drawing out from the mass of molten gold and charcoal, was
transformed into a trinket.

There she would be. Her eyes would devour the fragile gold wire,   32
following it in its tranquil and regular spiral around the little slab of
metal which supported it. My father would catch a glimpse of her and
I would see him slowly beginning to smile. Her avid attention delighted him.

"Are you trembling?" he would ask.   33

"Am I trembling?"   34

And we would all burst out laughing at her. For she would be   35
trembling! She would be trembling with covetousness for the spiral
pyramid in which my father would be inserting, among the convolu-
tions, tiny grains of gold. When he had finally finished by crowning the
pyramid with a heavier grain, she would dance in delight.

No one—no one at all—would be more enchanted than she as my   36
father slowly turned the trinket back and forth between his fingers to
display its perfection. Not even the praise-singer whose business it was

to register excitement would be more excited than she. Throughout this metamorphosis he did not stop speaking faster and ever faster, increasing his tempo, accelerating his praises and flatteries as the trinket took shape, shouting to the skies my father's skill.

37   For the praise-singer took a curious part—I should say rather that it was direct and effective—in the work. He was drunk with the joy of creation. He shouted aloud in joy. He plucked his *cora* like a man inspired. He sweated as if he were the trinket-maker, as if he were my father, as if the trinket were his creation. He was no longer a hired censer-bearer, a man whose services anyone could rent. He was a man who created his song out of some deep inner necessity. And when my father, after having soldered the large grain of gold that crowned the summit, held out his work to be admired, the praise-singer would no longer be able to contain himself. He would begin to intone the *douga,* the great chant which is sung only for celebrated men and which is danced for them alone.

38   But the *douga* is a formidable chant, a provocative chant, a chant which the praise-singer dared not sing, and which the man for whom it is sung dared not dance before certain precautions had been taken. My father had taken them as soon as he woke, since he had been warned in a dream. The praise-singer had taken them when he concluded his arrangements with the woman. Like my father he had smeared his body with magic substances and had made himself invulnerable to the evil genies whom the *douga* inevitably set free; these potions made him invulnerable also to rival praise-singers, perhaps jealous of him, who awaited only this song and the exaltation and loss of control which attended it, in order to begin casting their spells.

39   At the first notes of the *douga* my father would arise and emit a cry in which happiness and triumph were equally mingled; and brandishing in his right hand the hammer that was the symbol of his profession and in his left a ram's horn filled with magic substances, he would dance the glorious dance.

40   No sooner had he finished, than workmen and apprentices, friends and customers in their turn, not forgetting the woman for whom the trinket had been created, would flock around him, congratulating him, showering praises on him and complimenting the praise-singer at the same time. The latter found himself laden with gifts—almost his only means of support, for the praise-singer leads a wandering life after the fashion of the troubadours of old. Aglow with dancing and the praises he had received, my father would offer everyone cola nuts, that small change of Guinean courtesy.

41   Now all that remained to be done was to redden the trinket in a little water to which chlorine and sea salt had been added. I was at liberty to leave. The festival was over! But often as I came out of the work-

shop my mother would be in the court, pounding millet or rice, and she would call to me:

"Where have you been?" although she knew perfectly well where I had been.   42

"In the workshop."   43

"Of course. Your father was smelting gold. Gold! Always gold!"   44

And she would beat the millet or rice furiously with her pestle.   45

"Your father is ruining his health!"   46

"He danced the *douga*."   47

"The *douga!* The *douga* won't keep him from ruining his eyes. As for you, you would be better off playing in the courtyard instead of breathing dust and smoke in the workshop."   48

My mother did not like my father to work in gold. She knew how dangerous it was: a trinket-maker empties his lungs blowing on the blow-pipe and his eyes suffer from the fire. Perhaps they suffer even more from the microscopic precision which the work requires. And even if there had been no such objections involved, my mother would scarcely have relished this work. She was suspicious of it, for gold can not be smelted without the use of other metals, and my mother thought it was not entirely honest to put aside for one's own use the gold which the alloy had displaced. However, this was a custom generally known, and one which she herself had accepted when she took cotton to be woven and received back only a piece of cotton cloth half the weight of the original bundle.   49

✦ Evaluating the Text

1. What is the function of the praise-singer?

2. What can you infer about the value attached to the father's craftsmanship?

3. Describe the process by which the father makes the trinket, including those who help him, the tools he uses, the layout of the shop, and what he does step by step.

4. What cultural values and assumptions are revealed in the incantations the father speaks while working with the gold and the role played by the black snake?

✦ Exploring Different Perspectives

1. Compare the boys' attitudes toward their fathers' vocations in Camara Laye's account and in Moacyr Scliar's "A Brief History of Capitalism."

2. How do the accounts by Camara Laye and Anton Vassilievich deal with the relationship between expertise and the value of the worker?

✦ Extending Viewpoints Through Writing

1. Invent a short announcement you would make as a praise-singer for a worker who provides a needed and valuable service; that is, your dentist, car mechanic, hair stylist, or teacher, for example.

2. Describe a process with which you are familiar, specifying the place where it is done, the tools used if any, what needs to be done step by step, and the results.

Anton Vassilievich

Radiation Expert

———◆———

This interview with Anton Vassilievich appears in Russian Voices *(1991) by Tony Parker, a gifted interviewer who spent five months in Moscow interviewing a broad range of Russian citizens to produce a fascinating cross section of contemporary Russia. Tony Parker's many books include* Lighthouse *(1986),* Red Hill: A Mining Community *(1987),* Life After Life: Interviews with Twelve Murderers *(1987), and* Bird, Kansas *(1989). He lives with his wife in Suffolk, England. The following account provides unequalled insight into the world's worst nuclear accident at Chernobyl by a firsthand observer who risked his life and volunteered his services as a radiation expert. In 1993, the World Health Organization reported that it had recorded an unprecedented number of genetic abnormalities in children born within a radius of ten miles from Chernobyl.*

He was a tall distinguished-looking man in a dark suit, with a white shirt and a burgundy-coloured tie. He talked quietly, fluently and authoritatively. 1

I am forty-eight years in age, I am married, and my wife and I have two children. One is a boy of twenty who is a history student at Moscow University, and our daughter of sixteen, she is at school in the eleventh grade. I think it is her intention to be a chemist, I hope so, I would like that. 2

At the time of the disaster at Chernobyl we were living in the Gorky region, which is about five hundred kilometres to the east of Moscow. I was head of the department in a large factory which manufactures what are called dosimeters. These are precise instruments which measure the amount of radiation present in a small or large given area, depending on their type. All workers in the atomic-power industry wear such a one here on the pocket of their overall; larger ones are placed at eye-level in rooms and along corridors throughout every atomic-power plant. I am a highly qualified specialist in this subject, if I may be permitted to say so. 3

For the people at Chernobyl when the disaster happened, there was insufficient knowledge to know how serious it was. There was one 4

———

*(For information on Russia, see p. 26.)

simple reason for this: the leakage of radiation was so great there were no instruments capable of measuring it. You will hear different stories: either that the authorities did not want to admit this because they thought it would cause panic, or they themselves were incapable of imagining such a thing. They refused to believe the evidence which was in front of their own eyes. It is generally taught, you see, both within the atomic-power industry itself, and also in the information about it given to the press and other media for dissemination, that some things are so unlikely ever to happen that mention of them can be ignored. The chances against them are so high—perhaps one in one million, one in five million or ten million or whatever number is calculated—that the risks are completely negligible. It is one of the greatest dangers of those concerned with our atomic industry, that the first people they have to persuade of this are themselves: when they have done this, they can then convincingly persuade others, with less knowledge, that some such thing is unthinkable. Then if it is unthinkable, they no longer think of it; nor what to do if it should occur.

5   What happened at Chernobyl was such an occurrence: the unthinkable occurred. Perhaps it is true that the suppression of information about it at the beginning did, as the authorities hoped, prevent widespread public panic. They themselves were in a panic, because they did not know what to think or how to act; but they could not admit this. But among those who knew more thoroughly about the subject, information was soon making itself known. Scientists talk: they talk among themselves and with other scientists, even when they are long distances apart, by means of a scientific invention called the telephone. So it was so that soon many scientists knew. I was one of those who quickly learned what had really happened: and what I learned was that because their metering equipment could not give them enough measurement, therefore they could not know dosages of radiation and estimate what steps should be taken to give protection to their personnel.

6   I went at once to my superiors, and asked could I have permission to go to Chernobyl, to offer my specialised knowledge, and it was immediately given. I then talked with my wife and children, and explained to them that although the situation was one in which danger was present, I had the necessary knowledge to assist, and felt it was my duty to go. They too immediately agreed. And so within less than two weeks necessary formalities were completed, and I arrived at the power station at Pripyet at the end of May, four weeks after the explosion had occurred.

7   When I arrived, I have to say that the situation was in fact worse than I had imagined it to be. The whole of the town of Pripyet had been evacuated: every single person had gone who had not been detained as a worker of essential necessity. Of those who remained, few had qualifications high enough to be able to perform the task I had already de-

fined in my mind as the first essential. This was somehow to discover the amount of radiation present everywhere in the plant, even in the smallest and least accessible areas. By calculation it had to be decided where would be safe, and where would be unsafe, and for what period of time. Of course an aspect of radiation is that it is not visible: its presence can only be detected and measured in some instances by instruments of higher sophistication than those in this day we possess. So we constantly had to make calculations which in many cases could be not more than guesses, and hope that always we were over-cautious rather than over-optimistic.

Another fact we found, but we still do not know the reason for it, was that in some places as little as two metres apart, there would be in one a dangerously high level of radioactivity, and in another no radioactivity at all. This is what causes for example the situation where two people are in close proximity to each other, and one later is found to be irradiated and the other not. We simply do not understand properly yet the behaviour of radiation. In the plant we were able, but only very slowly and gradually, to identify the radiation present at all points. It led for example to situations where notices were posted along corridors which said HERE YOU MAY WALK, and then only a few metres on would be another saying HERE YOU MUST RUN.

I worked with a team of sixteen scientifically qualified men I had selected from those made available to me: some inevitably were those whose qualifications were not perhaps as high as could have been wished. But without exception all of them were volunteers, and had to work in circumstances where it was often not known if they were dangerous, or lethal, or perfectly safe. All of them were heroes, and the same also must be said of the ordinary soldiers who worked with us, often in the most dangerous place of all. This was on what was left of the roof covering of Reactor Number 4: that was the one which had exploded and burst into flames. There still remained an extensive flat surface, and on it was lying a huge amount of smouldering debris, which it was necessary to clear, to prevent further spreading of fire which would have caused more explosions.

We were not willing to send any man, no matter what type or amount of protective clothing he was wearing, up on to the roof until we had at least an approximate idea of how radioactive it was. Among the great amount of assistance which we had received from many countries in the world, there was from Germany a highly sophisticated machine to measure levels of radioactivity. It was a robot, it was operated by remote control. This machine was lifted by crane on to the roof, where we had constructed a thick concrete bunker for shelter, and it was sent forward from there. But after a short distance it stopped: it had become embedded in debris. When eventually we retrieved it by helicopter, we found its measuring instruments had not been able to withstand the radiation level, and it had failed. We therefore had to fall back again on our own calculations. These were initially that it was not safe for a person to spend a longer period on the roof than twenty seconds. In several weeks' time the permitted period was able to be extended to sixty seconds; and then later, at its maximum, it was extended to two minutes. The longest period I myself ever spent on the roof was sixty seconds, which I did on the afternoon of Saturday 27th September at 4.30 p.m.

11   It was always a matter of great priority that this roof debris should be cleared. This was eventually achieved by a large team of brave soldiers and as I have said, each of them was a volunteer. Every man in turn, wearing a lead jacket and a respirator, would run out on to the roof with his shovel, fill it with debris, and run to the edge and throw it over, down to the ground. From there it was then cleared by remote-control tractors. No soldier was allowed to do this more than once, and when he returned from the roof to the ground he was then immediately tested to find the amount of radiation he had received. If it was above a certain level, he was sent instantly to hospital. So you see these were all men of very great bravery.

12   I remained at Pripyet from May until December, a total of 199 days. During that period I went twice back to my home to see my family, on one occasion for four days and on another for five. We did not talk about the situation, and I am grateful to my wife for that. She knew that the work had to be done, and that few other people had the knowledge of the subject which I did. She knew also, if I may say so, that because I was a professional I would approach the danger in a sensible way, and teach others to do so similarly. She accepted that it was my duty to be there, and so it was as simple as that.

13   After the disaster, there are many things to be reflected upon. We still do not have the full answer to its cause or causes, or what happened and why it did so. I am sorry to say I cannot assert with confidence such a thing could never occur again, either in the Soviet Union or elsewhere in the world. Indeed I would assert the contrary, that with the proliferation in number of the building of atomic-power stations, the likelihood of such a thing can only be increasing. If such an accident should again take place, I am not confident either that the necessary lessons have been learned from Chernobyl as to what actions should be taken to limit the damage. Seventy-one people died there at the time of the accident: some were workers killed in the explosion itself, some were firemen trying to control the fire, and others were members of staff who were not injured in any way but were victims of heart attacks. But this number of seventy-one in no way relates to those who died later from radiation sickness, or from radiation-induced illness such as leukaemia and other forms of cancer. It is not a matter of hundreds or thousands, but of a far greater figure; and because of the long-lasting

after-effects, as we speak this figure is still increasing day by day. A total of 432 towns in surrounding areas were contaminated, and more than one million people have been evacuated from them. Undoubtedly babies yet unborn will be malformed, or will die at an early age, as a result of Chernobyl; and I mean not in Russia only, but in many other places in the world.

✦ Evaluating the Text

1. What special training, background, or experience has qualified Vassilievich for the job he performs?

2. What circumstances and personal motivation led Vassilievich to go to Chernobyl?

3. What work did the volunteer soldiers perform, and why was the most accurate information on radiation absolutely indispensable as part of this process?

✦ Exploring Different Perspectives

1. What insight into the methods of interviewers do you get from Studs Terkel's interview with Ron Maydon and Tony Parker's interview with Anton Vassilievich? How do their methods differ?

2. How are the skills involved in Camara Laye's description of his father in "The Village Goldsmith" as specialized as those described in Vassilievich's account?

✦ Extending Viewpoints Through Writing

1. Describe what in your view would be defined as a dangerous occupation, identifying the work involved and what makes it hazardous.

2. If you were in the same situation as Vassilievich, would you have gone? Why or why not?

Mark Salzman

Lessons

———————◆———————

Mark Salzman graduated Phi Beta Kappa, summa cum laude from Yale in 1982 with a degree in Chinese language and literature. From 1982 to 1984, he lived in Chang-sha, Hunan, in the People's Republic of China, where he taught English at Hunan Medical College. There he studied under Pan Qingfu, one of China's greatest traditional boxers and martial arts masters. In October 1985, he was invited back to China to participate in the National Martial Arts Competition and Conference in Tianjin. Iron and Silk *(1986) recounts his adventures and provides a fascinating behind-the-scenes glimpse into the workings of Chinese society. His experiences also formed the basis for a 1991 film of the same name starring the author. He also has written three novels:* Eclipse *(1991),* The Laughing Sutra *(1992), and* The Soloist *(1994). "Lessons," from* Iron and Silk, *describes the extraordinary opportunity that studying martial arts with Pan Qingfu offered, along with the comic misunderstandings produced by their being from such different cultures.*

The People's Republic of China is ruled by a government established in 1949 after the victory of Mao Zedong (Tse-tung) and his communist forces against the Nationalist forces of Chiang Kai-Chek, who fled to Taiwan and set up a government in exile. Under Mao's leadership, industry was nationalized and a land reform program, based on collectivization, was introduced. China entered the Korean War against United Nations forces between 1950 and the Armistice of 1953. China's modern history has been characterized by cycles of liberalization followed by violent oppression. In 1957, reaction against the so-called "let a hundred flowers bloom" period led to a crackdown against intellectuals. In 1966, Mao launched the Cultural Revolution to purge the government and society of liberal elements. After Mao's death in 1976, a backlash led to the imprisoning of Mao's wife, Jiang Qing, and three colleagues (the "Gang of Four"). A period of liberalization once again followed, as Deng Xiaoping came to power in 1977 and adopted more conciliatory economic, social, and political policies. The United States recognized the People's Republic of China as a valid government on January 1, 1979. The pattern reemerged in June 1989, when government troops were sent into Tiananmen Square to crush the prodemocracy movement. Zhao Ziyang, who had shown sympathy toward the students, was ousted and replaced by hardliner Jing Zemin. The June events, in which thousands are reported to have died, led to a crackdown and execution of sympathizers throughout

China, despite widespread international condemnation. A behind-the-scenes power struggle in 1992 by Deng Xiaoping has led to some economic market style reforms although political liberalization still is not allowed.

The period when Salzman was in China coincided with liberal developments within the society, under the leadership of Zhan Ziyang as prime minister, and a more conciliatory relationship with the United States. President Reagan visited China in April 1984 and signed an agreement on nuclear cooperation in nonmilitary areas. In September 1984, China and Britain signed accords designed to facilitate the return of Hong Kong (a British crown colony leased in 1898 for ninety-nine years) to Chinese control in 1997.

I was to meet Pan at the training hall four nights a week, to receive   1
private instruction after the athletes finished their evening workout. Waving and wishing me good night, they politely filed out and closed the wooden doors, leaving Pan and me alone in the room. First he explained that I must start from scratch. He meant it, too, for beginning that night, and for many nights thereafter, I learned how to stand at attention. He stood inches away from me and screamed, "Stand straight!" then bored into me with his terrifying gaze. He insisted that I maintain eye contact for as long as he stood in front of me, and that I meet his gaze with one of equal intensity. After as long as a minute of this silent torture, he would shout "At ease!" and I could relax a bit, but not smile or take my eyes away from his. We repeated this exercise countless times, and I was expected to practice it four to six hours a day. At the time, I wondered what those staring contests had to do with wushu, but I came to realize that everything he was to teach me later was really contained in those first few weeks when we stared at each other. His art drew strength from his eyes; this was his way of passing it on.

After several weeks I came to enjoy staring at him. I would break   2
into a sweat and feel a kind of heat rushing up through the floor into my legs and up into my brain. He told me that when standing like that, I must at all times be prepared to duel, that at any moment he might attack, and I should be ready to defend myself. It exhilarated me to face off with him, to feel his power and taste the fear and anticipation of the blow. Days and weeks passed, but the blow did not come.

One night he broke the lesson off early, telling me that tonight was   3
special. I followed him out of the training hall, and we bicycled a short distance to his apartment. He lived with his wife and two sons on the fifth floor of a large, anonymous cement building. Like all the urban housing going up in China today, the building was indistinguishable from its neighbors, mercilessly practical and depressing in appearance.

*(For more background on China, see p. 401.)

Pan's apartment had three rooms and a small kitchen. A private bathroom and painted, as opposed to raw, cement walls in all the rooms identified it as the home of an important family. The only decoration in the apartment consisted of some silk banners, awards and photographs from Pan's years as the national wushu champion and from the set of *Shaolin Temple*. Pan's wife, a doctor, greeted me with all sorts of homemade snacks and sat me down at a table set for two. Pan sat across from me and poured two glasses of baijiu. He called to his sons, both in their teens, and they appeared from the bedroom instantly. They stood in complete silence until Pan asked them to greet me, which they did, very politely, but so softly I could barely hear them. They were handsome boys, and the elder, at about fourteen, was taller than me and had a moustache. I tried asking them questions to put them at ease, but they answered only by nodding. They apparently had no idea how to behave toward something like me and did not want to make any mistakes in front of their father. Pan told them to say good night, and they, along with his wife, disappeared into the bedroom. Pan raised his glass and proposed that the evening begin.

4   He told me stories that made my hair stand on end, with such gusto that I thought the building would shake apart. When he came to the parts where he vanquished his enemies, he brought his terrible hand down on the table or against the wall with a crash, sending our snacks jumping out of their serving bowls. His imitations of cowards and bullies were so funny I could hardly breathe for laughing. He had me spellbound for three solid hours; then his wife came in to see if we needed any more food or baijiu. I took the opportunity to ask her if she had ever been afraid for her husband's safety when, for example, he went off alone to bust up a gang of hoodlums in Shenyang. She laughed and touched his right hand. "Sometimes I figured he'd be late for dinner." A look of tremendous satisfaction came over Pan's face, and he got up to use the bathroom. She sat down in his chair and looked at me. "Every day he receives tens of letters from all over China, all from people asking to become his student. Since he made the movie, it's been almost impossible for him to go out during the day." She refilled our cups, then looked at me again. "He has trained professionals for more than twenty-five years now, but in all that time he has accepted only one private student." After a long pause, she gestured at me with her chin. "You." Just then Pan came back into the room, returned to his seat and started a new story. This one was about a spear:

5   While still a young man training for the national wushu competition, Pan overheard a debate among some of his fellow athletes about the credibility of an old story. The story described a famous warrior as being able to execute a thousand spear-thrusts without stopping to rest. Some of the athletes felt this to be impossible: after fifty, one's shoulders ache, and by one hundred the skin on the left hand, which

guides the spear as the right hand thrusts, twists and returns it, begins
to blister. Pan had argued that surely this particular warrior would not
have been intimidated by aching shoulders and blisters, and soon a
challenge was raised. The next day Pan went out into a field with a
spear, and as the other athletes watched, executed one thousand and
seven thrusts without stopping to rest. Certain details of the story as
Pan told it—that the bones of his left hand were exposed, and so
forth—might be called into question, but the number of thrusts I am
sure is accurate, and the scar tissue on his left palm indicates that it was
not easy for him.

One evening later in the year, when I felt discouraged with my
progress in a form of Northern Shaolin boxing called "Changquan," or
"Long Fist," I asked Pan if he thought I should discontinue the training. He frowned, the only time he ever seemed genuinely angry with
me, and said quietly, "When I say I will do something, I do it, exactly as
I said I would. In my whole life I have never started something without
finishing it. I said that in the time we have, I would make your wushu
better than you could imagine, and I will. Your only responsibility to
me is to practice and to learn. My responsibility to you is much greater!
Every time you think your task is great, think how much greater mine
is. Just keep this in mind: if you fail"—here he paused to make sure I
understood—"I will lose face." 6

Though my responsibility to him was merely to practice and to
learn, he had one request that he vigorously encouraged me to fulfill—
to teach him English. I felt relieved to have something to offer him, so I
quickly prepared some beginning materials and rode over to his house
for the first lesson. When I got there, he had a tape recorder set up on a
small table, along with a pile of oversized paper and a few felt-tip pens
from a coloring set. He showed no interest at all in my books, but sat
me down next to the recorder and pointed at the pile of paper. On each
sheet he had written out in Chinese dozens of phrases, such as "We'll
need a spotlight over there," "These mats aren't springy enough," and
"Don't worry—it's just a shoulder dislocation." He asked me to write
down the English translation next to each phrase, which took a little
over two and a half hours. When I was finished, I asked him if he could
read my handwriting, and he smiled, saying that he was sure my handwriting was fine. After a series of delicate questions, I determined that
he was as yet unfamiliar with the alphabet, so I encouraged him to
have a look at my beginning materials. "That's too slow for me," he
said. He asked me to repeat each of the phrases I'd written down five
times into the recorder, leaving enough time after each repetition for
him to say it aloud after me. "The first time should be very slow—one
word at a time, with a pause after each word so I can repeat it. The second time should be the same. The third time you should pause after every other word. The fourth time read it through slowly. The fifth time 7

you can read it fast." I looked at the pile of phrase sheets, calculated how much time this would take, and asked if we could do half today and half tomorrow, as dinner was only three hours away. "Don't worry!" he said, beaming. "I've prepared some food for you here. Just tell me when you get hungry." He sat next to me, turned on the machine, then turned it off again. "How do you say, 'And now, Mark will teach me English'?" I told him how and he repeated it, at first slowly, then more quickly, twenty or twenty-one times. He turned the machine on. "And now, Mark will teach me English." I read the first phrase, five times as he had requested, and he pushed a little note across the table. "Better read it six times," it read, "and a little slower."

8   After several weeks during which we nearly exhausted the phrasal possibilities of our two languages, Pan announced that the time had come to do something new. "Now I want to learn routines." I didn't understand. "Routines?" "Yes. Everything, including language, is like wushu. First you learn the basic moves, or words, then you string them together into routines." He produced from his bedroom a huge sheet of paper made up of smaller pieces taped together. He wanted me to write a story on it. The story he had in mind was a famous Chinese folk tale, "How Yu Gong Moved the Mountain." The story tells of an old man who realized that, if he only had fields where a mountain stood instead, he would have enough arable land to support his family comfortably. So he went out to the mountain with a shovel and a bucket and started to take the mountain down. All his neighbors made fun of him, calling it an impossible task, but Yu Gong disagreed: it would just take a long time, and after several tens of generations had passed, the mountain would at last become a field and his family would live comfortably. Pan had me write this story in big letters, so that he could paste it up on his bedroom wall, listen to the tape I was to make and read along as he lay in bed.

9   Not only did I repeat this story into the tape recorder several dozen times—at first one word at a time, and so on—but Pan invited Bill, Bob and Marcy over for dinner one night and had them read it a few times for variety. After they had finished, Pan said that he would like to recite a few phrases for them to evaluate and correct. He chose some of his favorite sentences and repeated each seven or eight times without a pause. He belted them out with such fierce concentration we were all afraid to move lest it disturb him. At last he finished and looked at me, asking quietly if it was all right. I nodded and he seemed overcome with relief. He smiled, pointed at me and said to my friends, "I was very nervous just then. I didn't want him to lose face."

10   While Pan struggled to recite English routines from memory, he began teaching me how to use traditional weapons. He would teach me a single move, then have me practice it in front of him until I could do it ten times in a row without a mistake. He always stood about five feet

away from me, with his arms folded, grinding his teeth, and the only time he took his eyes off me was to blink. One night in the late spring I was having a particularly hard time learning a move with the staff. I was sweating heavily and my right hand was bleeding, so the staff had become slippery and hard to control. Several of the athletes stayed on after their workout to watch and to enjoy the breeze that sometimes passed through the training hall. Pan stopped me and indicated that I wasn't working hard enough. "Imagine," he said, "that you are partic-ipating in the national competition, and those athletes are your com-petitors. Look as if you know what you are doing! Frighten them with your strength and confidence." I mustered all the confidence I could, under the circumstances, and flung myself into the move. I lost control of the staff, and it whirled straight into my forehead. As if in a dream, the floor raised up several feet to support my behind, and I sat staring up at Pan while blood ran down across my nose and a fleshy knob grew between my eyebrows. The athletes sprang forward to help me up. They seemed nervous, never having had a foreigner knock himself out in their training hall before, but Pan, after asking if I felt all right, seemed positively inspired. "Sweating and bleeding. Good."

* * *

Every once in a while, Pan felt it necessary to give his students 11
something to think about, to spur them on to greater efforts. During one morning workout two women practiced a combat routine, one armed with a spear, the other with a *dadao,* or halberd. The dadao stands about six feet high and consists of a broadsword attached to a thick wooden pole, with an angry-looking spike at the far end. It is heavy and difficult to wield even for a strong man, so it surprised me to see this young woman, who could not weigh more than one hundred pounds, using it so effectively. At one point in their battle the woman with the dadao swept it toward the other woman's feet, as if to cut them off, but the other woman jumped up in time to avoid the blow. The first woman, without letting the blade of the dadao stop, brought it around in another sweep, as if to cut the other woman in half at the waist. The other woman, without an instant to spare, bent straight from the hips so that the dadao slashed over her back and head, barely an inch away. This combination was to be repeated three times in rapid succession before moving on to the next exchange. The women prac-ticed this move several times, none of which satisfied Pan. "Too slow, and the weapon is too far away from her. It should graze her back as it goes by." They tried again, but still Pan growled angrily. Suddenly he got up and took the dadao from the first woman. The entire training hall went silent and still. Without warming up at all, Pan ordered the woman with the spear to get ready, and to move fast when the time came. His body looked as though electricity had suddenly passed

through it, and the huge blade flashed toward her. Once, twice the dadao flew beneath her feet, then swung around in a terrible arc and rode her back with flawless precision. The third time he added a little twist at the end, so that the blade grazed up her neck and sent a little decoration stuck in her pigtails flying across the room.

12   I had to sit down for a moment to ponder the difficulty of sending an object roughly the shape of an oversized shovel, only heavier, across a girl's back and through her pigtails, without guide ropes or even a safety helmet. Not long before, I had spoken with a former troupe member who, when practicing with this instrument, had suddenly found himself on his knees. The blade, unsharpened, had twirled a bit too close to him and passed through his Achilles' tendon without a sound. Pan handed the dadao back to the woman and walked over to me. "What if you had made a mistake?" I asked. "I never make mistakes," he said, without looking at me.

✦ Evaluating the Text

1. What is the relevance of the Chinese folk tale "How Yu Gong Moved the Mountain" to Salzman's apprenticeship?

2. What evidence can you cite to show that Pan applies the same standard (based on fear of "losing face") to Mark as he does to himself? What part does the concept of "losing face" play in Chinese culture, and what values are expressed through this term?

3. What similarities can you discover between Pan's approach to learning English and his methods of teaching Chinese martial arts?

4. What factors do you believe might explain why Pan chooses Mark to be the only private student he has ever had? Why is this especially significant because Mark is an American and Pan has never taken one private student within China in twenty-five years?

5. What conclusions can you draw about the standard of living in China from the way in which Pan and his family live? Keep in mind that being a champion in martial arts is comparable to being an outstanding baseball, football, or basketball player and that Pan's wife is a physician.

✦ Exploring Different Perspectives

1. Compare and contrast the impression you get of the father in Camara Laye's "The Village Goldsmith" with that of Pan. What common features can you discover in terms of the goals they set for themselves and how they go about reaching these goals? In what respects are they different from one another?

2. What common elements can you discover between the self-imposed discipline of Lesley Hazleton in "Confessions of a Fast Woman" and of Pan in Salzman's "Lessons"?

✦ Extending Viewpoints Through Writing

1. Describe an experience, including martial arts instruction, that you have had that gave you insight into Salzman's experiences.

2. If you could master anything you wished, what would it be, and who would you want to be your teacher? Would you want to learn from someone like Pan?

3. To what extent does the concept of shame, or "losing face," play an important role in Chinese culture? What part does this idea play in Mark Salzman's account?

Kon Krailet

In the Mirror

◆

Kon Krailet is the nom-de-plume of Pakon Phongwarapha, who was born to an immigrant Chinese family in Thailand in 1947. His first published story appeared when he was sixteen. He moved to Bangkok to pursue a literary career, worked as a proofreader, and then with his wife, the writer Khwan Phiangphuthai, published Youth *magazine. Four short story collections of Krailet's have been published in Thailand:* Fire of Life, Golden Flowers, Report from the Pung Clan, *and most recently,* We Are Not Flowers, We Are Life. *"In the Mirror," translated by Benedict R. O'G. Anderson and Ruchira Chinnapongse Mendiones, was first published in* Waves of the Chao Praya, *an anthology edited by Sujit Wong Thet (1978). This story depicts a poignant conflict generated by a clash between new urban and traditional cultural values.*

The kingdom of Thailand (formerly Siam) is a constitutional monarchy in Southeast Asia bordered by Burma to the west and northwest, Laos to the north and east, Cambodia to the southeast, and Malaysia and the Gulf of Siam to the south. Although there are large Chinese, Malay, Khmer, and Vietnamese minorities, Thais, who are ethnically related to the Shan of Burma and the Lao of Laos, constitute 75 percent of the population. Migrating to the area from China in the thirteenth century, the Thais established kingdoms at Sukhothai in 1238 and Ayutthaya in 1350. The arrival of Portuguese traders in the sixteenth century marked the beginning of Siam's relations with the West. During the Vietnam War Thailand strongly supported the United States and was the site of American air bases until 1976. The influx of tens of thousands of Vietnamese and Cambodian refugees in the 1970s and 1980s severely strained the Thai economy. The present king, Bhumibol Adulyadej, known as Rama IX, has ruled since 1946, has few executive responsibilities but is highly respected. The sex show industry described by Kon Krailet in his story "In the Mirror" reflects in part the role Thailand has played as a rest and recreation (R & R) stop for American G.I.s during the Vietnam War and Japanese businessmen since then. As a result Thailand has the highest rate of HIV infection in Southeast Asia.

1   Chiwin[1] sits quietly in a dark corner, waiting for his moment to come. . . .

---

[1]The name Chiwin, hardly chosen at random, also means "life."

Tonight the place is packed, since it's the beginning of the month   2
and people still have enough cash to go out and enjoy themselves. Chiwin lights up a cigarette and inhales listlessly. It's very strange, but this
evening he feels lonely, moody, not himself. He's got a lot of complicated problems on his mind, among them a letter from his mother.
*"Win, my dear son, your father isn't very well. The rice planting season's al-
ready here, but there's no one at home. How are things going for you in
Bangkok? Have you found a job yet or not? We haven't heard from you at
all. . . ."* Parts of the letters Mother wrote usually went like this. In fact,
of course, she hadn't written them at all. She was illiterate, so she must
have asked someone in the neighborhood to write them for her.

Actually, it's only now that Chiwin takes cognizance of how long   3
it's been since he left home. Days turned into years before he was
aware of it. In this city, where he now lives, night and day are unlike
night and day anywhere else. . . . They rush by so rapidly that he
doesn't have time to think about things as they happen. . . . If he does
think about them, it's only cursorily, for a moment or so. . . . like a brief
gust of wind which merely rustles the leaves and then vanishes without a trace. . . .

His mother's letter brings to his mind images of various people,   4
but heaped up on one another in such confusion that he feels dizzy and
disoriented. And Chiwin inhales cigarette smoke, puff after puff, one
after the other. . . .

It's so dark in that corner that people can't see each other's faces.   5
The customers sitting at the tables loom up only as obscure silhouettes.
The waitresses move back and forth, some holding flashlights to guide
new arrivals in search of empty tables. On the tiny stage a naked girl is
dancing to the pounding rhythm of a song. Her name is Latda. She has
two children, plus a do-nothing husband drunk day in day out. So
she's had to come and work as a go-go girl, stripping her body for
people to have a look. She'd told him all about it one day, not long after
they'd got to know each other. . . . The Tale of Latda . . . cracked in
pieces like the lives of all the women in this place, full of knots and
problems. If one had a good and happy life, who would ever want to
bare every inch of one's body for any Tom, Dick, or Harry to stare at?
Chiwin reflects, like someone who thinks he understands pretty well
how the people working here tick.

The last strains of the song die away. Latda steps down from the   6
stage. There's some halfhearted clapping from a few of the customers,
none of whom know why they clap. Utter silence for a second, as
though the spectators sense that the moment they've been waiting for
has finally arrived. The lights on the stage turn pale pink. A slow, soft
melody . . . láa-laa-láa-laa-laa-laa-laa . . . strikes up. . . . Another girl,
dressed in black underwear, takes her turn on the stage. She makes her
appearance slowly and silently.

7   And now they're playing Chiwin's musical cue. He stubs out his cigarette and pushes himself to his feet. He steps out of the dark corner into the pink glow, with the lithe movements of a young man of twenty-four. Some of the male spectators who remember him stare at him now, half in scorn, half wanting to do it themselves.

8   "You know, it's not easy at all," Chiwin had once told one of those who spoke to him in this tone. "It's only when you're on stage that you realize it's really no piece of cake."

9   No one has much of an idea about the music that's now being played, and it seems as if no one has the slightest interest in finding out. Most of the spectators simply know that when it's played it's time for the house's "special program" to begin. The words, accompanied by rhythmic sighs, most likely describe the mood of a young woman on a lonely night. The girl on the stage stretches out on her back and begins to writhe and quiver as though her flesh were burning with desire. Then she slowly removes the two little bits of clothing from her body.

10   Her name is Wanphen. . . .

11   Chiwin has now stepped up onto the stage. The play of spotlight moves back and forth between purple, blue, and red. Wanphen's act is so well done that it makes some of the young men close by the stage almost forget to breathe. Chiwin slowly unbuttons his shirt, then shakes his head two or three times. His eyes are getting used to the lights, which keep changing color like a magic show.

12   A moment later and Chiwin has nothing left to himself but his bared body. It's a handsome, well-proportioned body, full of young flesh and blood. He throws his clothes in a heap in one corner. Everything takes place with the utmost slowness, as if in this piece of life time has ceased to exist. At this moment no one can think of anything else—even if the country should meanwhile collapse in ruins.

13   Chiwin stretches his body out alongside Wanphen and embraces her, while caressing her naked flesh with his hands. He kisses her once, and she kisses him in turn, then turns her face away and snuggles it into the hollow of his neck.

14   "How many times have I told you, Elder Brother Win!" he hears her whisper. "Please don't smoke before doing the show with me. It smells horrible. I can't stand the stink, and I lose the mood. . . ."

15   "I'm sorry," he whispers back, as he rolls his body back and forth over hers. "Something's been bothering me. I've been in a bad mood, so I forgot. . . ."

16   How many times now had he partnered this woman! . . . Chiwin thinks about the man with the unremarkable face who comes to wait for her every night when the bar closes. He can't imagine what the man's real feelings are. He comes to wait here in silence, and he goes home in silence. He must feel something. How could one man not understand another? But the two of us don't even know each other. And

we both suffer. At least the man had once stared at Chiwin with a strange, cold gleam in his eye.

"He's my husband," Wanphen had once explained, "a real hus- 17 band, you know; we're properly registered and all."

"How can he stand having you come here and do this kind of show 18 with me?" He couldn't put the gleam in the man's eye out of his mind.

"What can you do?" she'd answered seriously. "It's a job. It's a way 19 to make a living. If you live with a woman like me, you have to be able to take it."

She's right. That's what it is, a job. O.K. At least it's a job for me too 20 right now. Chiwin has the feeling that he won't be able to perform well tonight. He doesn't feel prepared at all. The young man rolls over and down. Wanphen knows the signs very well, so she presses her body tightly to him. Deploying all her skills, using everything she has, she begins, with intense concentration, to arouse his desire. The play of the lights halts for a moment at pink, bathing the bodies of the couple and bringing out their beauty.

Chiwin stretches out full length and closes his eyes. The whole 21 world darkens before his vision. The air-conditioning makes the air cold and moist, but he feels the sweat beginning to ooze from some of his pores. His ears catch the soft music . . . when the song comes to an end, it starts up again, in an endless, indolent cycle, making his thoughts drift far away, to the past, to broad rice fields and to days and nights long gone.

. . . By now the rains must have started back home. . . . Sometimes 22 one could see the gray-white rain pouring down, moving in over the rice fields from the horizon, blurring everything in sight. The nights would be chilly and damp, and filled with the loud croaking of big and little frogs. And mornings, if the sun shone at all, its beams would be soft and tender, soon to vanish as the thick rain clouds piled up once more. In the rainy season, the earth would be turned over once again with the plow. And it wouldn't be long before the rice plants came up green, ripening later to a brilliant yellow throughout the pad- dies. But this isn't his work anymore. He abandoned it a long time ago. It's hard work, backbreakingly hard. Worse still, the harder you work, the poorer you get. He'd been so utterly, indescribably tired of that way of life that he'd struggled to get a better education, and with every ounce of will turned his face and headed toward Bangkok to find a new life. . . .

. . . And my little brother Wang. . . . I wonder if he's out of the 23 monkhood yet? Mother doesn't mention him in her letter. He's been in since last Lent.[2] Does he really want to study in the temple to become a

---

[2]The Buddhist "Lent," which runs from mid-July to mid-October, is a time designated for religious retreat and for the ordination of new monks.

Maha?[3] Doesn't he know these days there's no road to Nirvana anymore? And what about my little sister Wan? She must be buckling down to look after the kids she produces year in year out, giving her almost no breathing space for anything else. She got married to a boy from another subdistrict before she was even eighteen. Everyone's left the family home. Only Father and Mother still remain, and how much can they do on their own? And now Father's sick too. . . .

24   Last night he'd had a terrible dream. It seemed that Father was in it somehow, but he couldn't arrange the images of the dream properly. All he knew was that it was so horrible that when he woke up his heart was pounding with fear. And then he remembered that it was a long time since he'd dreamed at all. Every night he fell into a deep sleep, as though his body'd been picked up and laid casually down on the bed, feeling nothing, till a new day dawned and the time came for him to get up once again. And when the next night fell, he'd be picked up and laid down once again in the same old place. Dreams are the travels of one's soul. It's no good if one lives without dreams. It shows that there's no soul left inside. So it's a good thing he dreamed last night, even if the dream was a nightmare. . . .

25   Chiwin feels Wanphen's body arching up and pressing tightly to him almost all over. As she rains kisses over his chest and in the hollow of his neck, she whispers. . . .

26   "What's the matter with you tonight . . . huh?"

27   "I told you, I'm really feeling down. . . ." Chiwin embraces her in turn, mechanically. "I keep thinking about my father. . . ."

28   "You crazy? This is no time to think about your father. . . . If you go on like this, how can we do the show? In no time at all, the crowd'll be booing us!"

29   Chiwin shakes his head once. Some sort of realization makes him push his body up from hers on outstretched arms. If only this night were over! The spectators are dead quiet, each pair of eyes glued to the stage. He puts everything out of his mind, draws Wanphen's body onto his, and begins to go through all the acts he usually performs on this stage.

30   Many of the people up front move closer and closer. Some of them even poke their faces in, right close up—as though this were the single most extraordinary thing in life, something they'd never seen from the day they were born. Some of the customers who have girls sitting with them begin to grope them obscenely. His gaze meets their eyes and in a flash he senses that in some things men may not understand other men at all. In their eyes glitter a thousand and one things—pleasure and desire. Some of the men pretend to be unaffected by the scene, though in fact their souls are seething through every vein.

[3]Maha is a title awarded to any monk who has passed at least the lowest of the seven grades of the ecclesiastical examination system for the study of Pali texts.

"What have I become?" Chiwin asks himself. He feels like a male 31
animal in the rutting season, brutishly copulating with a female animal,
right before the eyes of a group of studmasters. The more powerfully he
performs, and the more varied the couplings, the more they're satisfied.

He glances down at Wanphen for a moment. He is now fully 32
astride her body. She is sighing and groaning, twisting and writhing
her body as if she's being aroused to the limit, even though actually she
experiences nothing from what she's doing. This is the first time that
Chiwin understands her life clearly, and he feels a heartrending pity for
her. He wants to ask her just one question: how much does she suffer
from living this way? Having intercourse with a man she doesn't love
in front of a crowd. Pretending to experience so much pleasure to
arouse all these people . . . in exchange for no more than a hundred
baht a night. Do her children back home know what's going on? Isn't
there a night when she goes back home, lies down, and cries? After all,
she still has feelings, doesn't she?

Chiwin lifts his head and stares once again at the audience, as if 33
searching for even one person with some understanding of the things
that go on in the stories of the people working here. But he sees nothing
but faces burning more hotly than ever with satisfaction and excitement. In fact, it looks like some of them have even reached a climax.

Chiwin begins to see the truth. . . . 34

All of us here are simply victims . . . Latda . . . Wanphen . . . me . . . 35
even those people sitting there watching with such satisfied expressions. All of them feel the pressure of society outside. So they come
here for emotional compensation, to build up a superiority complex.
They come to eat and drink. They come to sit and watch others expose
their genitals and perform every variety of sexual intercourse. This allows them to feel contempt for people they can then regard as lower
than themselves. Man has a deep abiding instinct to shove his way up
over his fellow men. The truth is that we're all animals of the city, who
live lives of pain and suffering in the midst of a demented society. The
only difference between us is that those who have greater advantages
stand on top of those who have less, and so on down the line.

"Give it to her! All the way, kid . . . !" comes a roaring cheer from a 36
table to the left, mixed with delighted laughter from a group of friends.
Wanphen clutches him still more tightly to her body. I wonder what
she's thinking about now. Chiwin stares at her, but can't see her clearly.
In her eyes there's an expression of entreaty. He grits his teeth, swallows his saliva down his dry throat, and gasps for breath. The sweat
oozes from his forehead, back, and shoulders. A stinging drop trickles
down into one eye, blurring his vision. Feeling a numb rage, Chiwin is
almost at the point of jumping up and kicking out in the direction of
those voices. But in fact he doesn't dare do anything, not even respond
with words.

37   Wanphen's hands, still clasped around his back, give him a stealthy pinch. "Take it easy, Elder Brother Win." Her voice is barely audible. "Don't listen to those crazy people. I'm not a cow or a water buffalo, you know. . . ."

38   So that's it! He's turned Wanphen herself into a victim of his own oppression. He comes to himself at the nip of her nails and the sound of her voice. Suddenly the tears well up in his eyes, mixed with drops of sweat. He pushes his body up, leaning on his outstretched arms, and stares Wanphen full in the eyes. When he bends over and gives her a kiss, she's surprised by a touch she's never felt from him before. Just then the song ends and the stage lights dim to darkness.

39   Chiwin goes into the bathroom, his shirt still unbuttoned. He turns on the tap, washes his hands, and scoops up some water to rub in the hollow of his neck. As he lifts his head, he encounters his own face reflected in the little mirror above the basin.

40   Indeed man encounters his real self when he stands before a mirror. . . .

41   In the bare, empty bathroom the faint sound of music filters in. He leans on his hands, gripping the basin's edge, and stares at that face for a long time, in silent questioning.

42   He thinks back to his mother's letter. "*How are things going for you in Bangkok? Have you found a job yet?*" How can he possibly tell his mother about the kind of work that he has found? She would faint dead away. And he himself can't really say why he's struggled so hard to make a living this way. The easy answer is probably because he was hungry and had reached a dead end.

43   When he'd set off for Bangkok, carrying his teacher's certificate with him, who could have known that for months he'd be clutching at straws, trying to compete with tens of thousands, hundreds of thousands, of others, taking test after test? And then go home, waiting to learn the results of his applications, place after place, day after day. At first his hopes had still been bright and clear. But, as time passed, they'd faded, like a candle that melts itself completely away, dimming down to his last baht. Then a friend of his, who worked as a bartender in a go-go club, had invited him along to try this line of work.

44   "Don't worry . . . at first you feel a bit shy. . . . But you get used to it after a while. . . . A good-looking guy with a nice build like yours is just what these people are looking for. You get a hundred a night, two or three thousand a month. It's far better than being a teacher. You talk yourself blue in the face for nothing but a few pennies a month." His friend had patted him on the shoulder and said, "OK? Give it a go, to tide you over while you wait to hear about your job applications. You want to starve? You don't have to worry about getting picked up. The

police don't make any trouble, the people there have got connections high up."

Is this the true image of a man who's studied to become a teacher?   45
Chiwin stares at his reflection with a feeling of nausea. His hair's a mess, his eyes dry and lifeless, with a sad, evasive look. The skin on his face and lips is parched and wan with strain. Not a shred of dignity left, though he's still young and strong. How did a man with clear, firm hopes and goals end up as someone who doesn't have the courage to confront even his own face?

Suddenly he feels a terrible churning deep in his abdomen. It   46
surges up through his insides to his throat. Chiwin clings tightly to the washbasin, hiccups once, and then, before being conscious of it, doubles over, arches his neck, and vomits in a torrent. All the different foods he ate earlier in the evening, accumulated in his belly, spout out in streams, splattering the washbasin. Once, twice, three times. Sounds of retching follow quickly, one after the other. Each time, he spits out what he'd swallowed earlier, till he's gasping with exhaustion. Snot and tears join together in a dirty stream. Chiwin lifts one forearm to wipe his mouth, and smells the sour stink pervading everything.

The reflection in the mirror is now a murky blur, because of the   47
tears which well up and fill the sockets of his eyes. He feels so dizzy that he almost cannot stay on his feet. Chiwin swallows his viscous saliva and hiccups once again. This time what he vomits up is a thick, clear liquid. It spouts out so violently that it seems to carry with it his liver, kidneys, and intestines.

✦ Evaluating the Text

1. What can you infer about the differences in values between rural Thailand and main urban areas like Bangkok in terms of the kinds of work Chiwin would be performing at home as opposed to what he now does?

2. How would you characterize Chiwin? How do his feelings about his co-workers' lives help explain how he feels about what he does?

3. How do Wanphen's comments to Chiwin during the course of their performance emphasize the fact that it is a staged performance? How do their real feelings contrast with what they are doing on the stage?

✦ Exploring Different Perspectives

1. Compare the attitude toward work in Lesley Hazleton's "Confessions of a Fast Woman" with that of Kon Krailet's main character.

2. How do both the account by R. K. Narayan in "Misguided 'Guide'" and Kon Krailet's story deal with the creation of a theatrical illusion?

✦ Extending Viewpoints Through Writing

1. What is the most unpleasant job you ever had to do to make money? Describe your experiences.

2. Did you ever have a job that appeared enviable to others that you knew was not what it appeared to be? Describe the job and why it looked appealing to others but was not to you.

Studs Terkel

Ron Maydon

———————◆———————

Studs (Louis) Terkel was born in 1912 in New York City. He changed his name to "Studs" after Studs Lonigan, the central character in James T. Farrell's novels about the Chicago working-class Irish. He received a law degree from the University of Chicago in 1932 and has served as moderator for several radio programs and "Studs' Place," a television show broadcast from Chicago. His interviews with ordinary people in everyday settings include Hard Times: An Oral History of the Great Depression *(1970),* Working: People Talk about What They Do All Day and How They Feel about What They Do *(1974), and* The Good War: An Oral History of World War II, *which received the Pulitzer Prize for nonfiction in 1985. More recently he has written* Race: How Blacks and Whites Think and Feel About the American Obsession *(1992) and* Coming of Age *(1995).*

"I'm a forty-two-year-old Mexican-American, born and raised on the Southeast side of Chicago. I have worked since I was sixteen. I lied about my age, so I could make some money. While going to college, I worked summers in the steel mill, side by side with my late father."

His father's flight from Mexico, across the border, is a walking, hitchhiking saga; town to town; odd jobs picking cotton in Texas, peeling potatoes at the Rice Hotel; gandy-dancing for the railroads; water boy in a Chicago steel mill.

"We are a Godfearing, religious family. Every Sunday we're in church, my mother, my sister and me. 'You take a few knocks coming up,' my mother used to say. 'That's why God gave you more padding in the butt, so it could be spanked.' She and my father both worked hard."

He is fair-complexioned and could easily pass for an Anglo, if he wished. He does not. "Throughout my life, I've been a proud nationalistic Mexican-American."

Hispanics are used as a buffer, and also a wedge, between white and black communities. Show me a white community and a black community and I'll show you an adjoining community between both. We're kind of a geographic Ping-Pong ball. Whites may let us move into their neighborhood because they've got a choice. "We'll take the lesser of the two evils," they say. They make it seem like they're doing us a big favor.

1

2   I call him a dumb Hispanic, the one who moves into a white community and is not even greeted as a neighbor. He thinks it's a miracle from God that he was let in. Or he did it on his own. "Oh wonderful! I've been accepted." He thinks he's moved up the ladder socially. I tell him, "Look, dummy, the only reason you're here is because right behind you are the blacks about to move in. They'll use you to hold off the blacks, and when they move, you'll stay here as the buffer." They're under the illusion that they're accepted. Of course they're not.

3   Because I could pass for Anglo, I got a bird's-eye view, an inside view of a racist country. I kind of snuck behind enemy lines. A kamikaze. When I was playing football in high school, they thought I was Italian or Greek. I got to hear comments about Mexicans. I'd immediately stand up, and the next thing I'm in a fistfight. "Oh, Ron, I'm sorry, I didn't mean you." "Who the fuck did you mean?" I've heard it all and it has gotten me angry and inspired and determined to keep fighting. I know how they really feel.

4   When my name confused the other kids, they'd ask me what I was. I said, "I'm an American." Today I'd say, "I'm an American of Mexican descent."

5   I don't like the word Hispanic. It sounds nice and says nothing. Which Hispanic? Mexican? Cuban? Puerto Rican? Every ten years, the United States government census gives us a new label. Spanish-Americans. Latinos. Chicanos. It's a lot like black labels.

6   Economically, the Puerto Rican is the lowest-income, least educated of the Hispanic community. They are our blacks. We look on the Mexican-Americans as the Polacks, the Polish-Americans. Family-oriented, hard-working, Catholic. The white Cubans are our Jews: the professionals, pharmacists, doctors, lawyers. Know why? After Batista lost, Castro sent them here. They were the elite, the landlords, the robber barons, the well-to-do. They were the ones with the money. They didn't like to identify with the Indians or the racially mixed Cubans. They came here with skills, education, and money they had socked away. They took over Florida. They're successful up and down the coast. They don't like black Cubans. There's racism in the Spanish community as anywhere else.

7   I would get into some arguments with dark-complected Latinos. They'd make racist remarks about blacks: "Niggers are getting everything." I'd say, "Look, you so-and-so, black as you are, you got a lot of nerve talking about blacks. You've been a victim of discrimination as much as blacks. You're the new niggers, you dummies."

8   I guess you'd call me a community activist, working for a black-Latino coalition. Our own people were calling us nigger-lovers. We had to let them know the police were beating the shit out of us, too. We organized the first Mexican-American march on police brutality in 1971.

9   I'm a strong believer in minority coalitions. Whatever gains the Hispanic community has made, we have piggy-backed on the black

movement. I say every time the blacks make political, economic, and social gains, hooray for them, because we get some of the fallout. They sneeze, we catch cold. They make inroads, we get hired. There are also problems in the black-Hispanic coalition. It's really a mixed bag.

The black community says they haven't made any progress. But   10
the Hispanic sees the blacks as moving up and taking over. It's piggy-move-up. We're on the bottom of the totem pole. We're the busboys, the new ditchdiggers, the new laborers. We see Hispanics on the assembly line with a black supervisor, a black boss.

Historically, it's always been so. The Irish dumped on the Italians.   11
The last one in gets the shit. So we're the latest. The Asians are behind us, but they're intellectually making the greatest gains. The Japanese may be getting lazy and the Koreans, the Jews of the Asian community, are working hard round the clock.

There are two kinds of Hispanics: the ethnic and the racial. The first   12
identify with the whites and act, think, and try to be like them. But there are those who say: "We don't have a low self-esteem. We know where we stand. We know we're not black or white. We're in the middle and not trying to be either."

The Hispanics who believe they are white often try interracial mar-   13
riages. Personally, I'm against that. When I get married, it will be to a Mexican woman. My kids will be one-hundred-percent Mexican. I'll be frank with you, I don't want to see halfbreeds. It's a personal prefer-ence. When I wake up Sunday morning, I want *menudo* or *carnitas* or *chorizo* and eggs. I don't want to have to go through a historical expla-nation to my Anglo wife of what I want. We're going to dance to the same tune. I'm not nationalistic to the point of being blind to the cul-tures of others. But what I want you to know we're definitely Mexican-American and proud.

This is not a melting pot. It's more of a layer cake. I believe we're a   14
pluralistic society. This city is divided by viaducts, railroad crossings, thoroughfares. We say: This is Polish, this is Italian, this is Jewish, this is a Mexican community. Live and let live, but we must maintain our identity.

Once you lose your identity, your whole psyche is twisted. You're   15
at the whim of anything that occurs in a society. I don't want to be a Mexican Fritz Mondale, who wanted to be everything to everybody and wound up being nothin' to no one.

In our country at this time, there is latent and blatant racism. You   16
meet these closet racists who are condescending and patronizing, but deep inside they don't really want us.

This is part of the racism between Hispanics and blacks. I know   17
some nationalistic black activists. I understand where they're coming from. I have no problems with them. I ask myself, Are blacks capable of racism? Of course. Are Hispanics capable of racism? Of course. I think

these two extremes are going to have some kind of come-together. There has to be some serious coalition-building if we're going to live side by side.

18   We'll have to work on the Hispanic Uncle Toms, who do everything they can to ingratiate themselves, to please their white racist neighbors. Tio Tacos we call them. A Tio Taco is worse than an Uncle Tom.

19   You don't find many Hispanics living in black areas, period. If they do, they're residual, the last ones left. I know this city like the back of my hand. I was a paramedic for three years and a building inspector for three.

20   We have Hispanic huppies, urban professionals. The huppies, the buppies, and the yuppies are living alongside one another on the lakefront. Junior execs. It's a real paradox they find themselves in, the Hispanics and the blacks. On the one hand, we say: Get an education, get that degree, make a better life. But when they leave the old neighborhood, they're sell-outs. Uncle Toms, Tio Tacos. The rest of the people say, "You're too good, you don't come around anymore. You've made it now and you can't talk to us."

21   This is the crisis of the black and Hispanic professional. They're in two worlds. Some talk of depression and suicide. Should we say: "Don't make any progress and stay put?"

22   As for role models, we have very few. Up until recently, we haven't had a Martin Luther King or a Harold Washington. We don't have people breaking the ice. We have a few unrecognized, unsung heroes anonymously chipping away. Mostly in the neighborhoods.

23   The only time you see Hispanics on TV, it's a street gang, an immigration raid, a drug bust. If I landed here from Mars and turned on the TV, I'd say, "All these people named Sánchez, Gómez, Rodríguez and García are troublemakers. You better get them out of this country. Every time I turn around, they're taking away a job and they're illegal."

24   On the lowest rung of the Mexican society is the illegal. He, she cannot surface. He had come here to earn a living, to send money back home to mom. They're terrified of exposure. They will go to the supermercado to buy their Mexican food products. They will listen to Mexican radio and watch Mexican TV and stay in hiding.

25   To Hispanics, the word "minorities" is a code word for blacks. I fault both communities. The blacks were too exclusive and didn't try to recruit us, get us involved. The Hispanics were not aggressive enough, didn't say, "Cut us in or cut it out." I blame the Church for our fault. It's always been, "Whatever your plight is, accept it. God will take care of you later." Look at its history in Mexico.

26   The Mexican loves the authoritarian personality. He loves to be told what to do. The strong church, the strong father figure. But there's a contradiction here, too. It's still the mother who holds the family to-

gether. The father gives the appearance: "I wear the pants. I'm the *chingón*, the bad so-and-so." His perception is that he must be assertive. Yet the little Anglo supervisor calls him every dirty name in the book: wetback, illegal, spic, greaser. He chews him out. And he meekly says, "Yes, sir, no, sir, I'm sorry." He comes home and asserts himself as the main man.

His kids and wife are thinking, "You could have beat the shit out of the little Anglo, but you didn't say nothin'. You come home and take it out on us." That's what's happening right now in Hispanic families. But the father is just finding out you can't talk tough at night and be a sissy during the day. If you're going to be a man, be a man twenty-four hours a day, not part-time. Now the mother and kids are saying: To hell with the damn job. Your self-respect is worth more than that four-dollar-an-hour job. You should have grabbed him and kicked the shit out of him. 27

It's a new sign. It's one of the first indications that we're going to make serious attempts to break down the barriers of racism. We're seeing this at college and high-school levels. 28

But we're also seeing Hispanic street gangs fight black street gangs. This may go on for years. The guy will say, "I fought with this black kid twenty years ago. He came into our neighborhood. I just don't like niggers now." He'll remember, "It was a black kid shot at me." The black kid will remember, "It was a Mexican cracked me over the head. I just don't like grease balls." 29

The fights are over drugs and turf and money and gang signs. We're having trouble in four high schools right now. That is what's happening in this country now. We're turning on each other. Whites will blame the blacks. Blacks will blame the Hispanics and vice-versa. Hispanics will say of affirmative action, "They hired seventeen blacks and one Hispanic." They're using us against them. 30

In the sixties, everyone was more aware. We always lived next door and worked with blacks. We were car-pooling because we didn't have any money. We shared lunches together. We went to school together. We worked in the stockyards together. We worked in the steel mills together. We worked in the fields together, migrant workers, side by side. We were in the same boat and it was sinking. 31

Now because of racial consciousness, groups are trying to assert their identity and get their share of the American pie. The economic pie is not big enough for anybody, not the way it's divided. Now we're competitors. We're not allies, we're adversaries. We're on a collision course. 32

I don't know if many Hispanics view affirmative action as a program to benefit them. The don't really identify with it. Many Hispanics believe affirmative action is a black program. We don't aggressively apply, seek out. I've heard that from every college recruiter: "Send me Hispanics." How many get their degree and do something about it? 33

Few. I see signs of change. The kids are becoming more aggressive and are not going to take the bullshit their mom and dad did.

34   Our women have never been recognized. Mexican-American women have never received their just due. They've held our family together, period. Our women have taken the abuse, kept their mouths shut: "Don't tell anybody." Dad comes home drunk. He's a real man now. The boss has told him off and he's taking it out on his wife. We have a saying: "When Anglos drink, they drink to forget. When Mexicans drink, they drink to remember."

35   I see a duality in the Mexican community. The wedding, the Christmas ceremony, the stores, the music, the food, the art, the culture. We must never lose our identity. But I also want assimilation. We can't carry it off alone, separately.

36   We're at a crucial period in black-Hispanic relations. Do we want to be identified with whites or blacks? I think we're schizophrenic now. We really don't have a sense of where we fit. We're the buffer.

✦ Evaluating the Text

1. In what way, according to Maydon, are Hispanics used as a "buffer," and also a wedge, between white and black communities?

2. What is the purpose of Maydon's analysis of different groups of Hispanics?

3. What are the causes of black-versus-Mexican antagonisms within the community? Why is it important, according to Maydon, for blacks and Latinos to establish a coalition?

✦ Exploring Different Perspectives

1. How does being forced to take whatever job you can get become an important theme in Maydon's account and Kon Krailet's story?

2. How do the narrator's father in Moacyr Scliar's story "A Brief History of Capitalism" and Ron Maydon both depend on an identification with the labor movement for a sense of self?

✦ Extending Viewpoints Through Writing

1. In an essay, evaluate Maydon's explanation for "macho" behavior. Do you agree with his analysis? Why or why not?

2. If you could interview anyone in the world, who would it be and what would you ask them? Create a short interview with this person.

R. K. Narayan

Misguided 'Guide'

◆

*R. K. Narayan was born in 1906 in Madras, in southern India, and edu-
cated there and at Maharaja's College in Mysore. His first novel,* Swami
and Friends *(1935), and its successor,* The Bachelor of Arts *(1937), are
set in the fictional village of Malgudi, which Narayan created as a microcosm for all of life in India. His other "Malgudi" novels include* A Tiger
for Malgudi *(1983) and* Talkative Man *(1986). His novel* The Guide
*(1958) received the National Prize of the Indian Literary Academy, his
country's highest literary honor, and was adapted for the stage and produced as an off-Broadway show in New York City in 1968. He has also published numerous collections of short stories and two travel books, as well as
collections of essays and a volume of memoirs. "Misguided 'Guide'" is
drawn from* A Writer's Nightmare: Selected Essays *(1958–1988).*

The letter came by airmail from Los Angeles. 'I am a producer and   1
actor from Bombay,' it read. 'I don't know if my name is familiar to you.'

He was too modest. Millions of young men copied his screen im-   2
age, walking as he did, slinging a folded coat over the shoulder carelessly, buffing up a lock of hair over the right temple, and assuming
that the total effect would make the girls sigh with hopeless longing.
My young nephews at home were thrilled at the sight of the handwriting of Dev Anand.

The Letter went on to say, 'I was in London and came across your   3
novel *The Guide.* I am anxious to make it into a film. I can promise you
that I will keep to the spirit and quality of your writing. My plans are to
make both a Hindi and an English film of this story.' He explained how
he had arranged with an American film producer for collaboration. He
also described how he had flown from London to New York in search
of me, since someone had told him I lived there, and then across the
whole continent before he could discover my address. He was ready to
come to Mysore if I should indicate the slightest willingness to consider
his proposal.

I cabled him an invitation, already catching the fever of hurry char-   4
acteristic of the film world. He flew from Los Angeles to Bombay to Bangalore, and motored down a hundred miles without losing a moment.

*(For information on India, see p. 58.)

5   A small crowd of autograph-hunters had gathered at the gate of my house in Yadava Giri. He expertly eluded the inquisitive crowd, and we were soon closeted in the dining room, breakfasting on *idli, dosai,* and other South Indian delicacies, my nephews attending on the star in a state of elation. The talk was all about *The Guide* and its cinematic merits. Within an hour we had become so friendly that he could ask without embarrassment, 'What price will you demand for your story?' The checkbook was out and the pen poised over it. I had the impression that if I had suggested that the entire face of the check be covered with closely knit figures, he would have obliged me. But I hemmed and hawed, suggested a slight advance, and told him to go ahead. I was sure that if the picture turned out to be a success he would share with me the glory and the profits. "Oh, certainly," he affirmed, "if the picture, by God's grace, turns out to be a success, we will be on top of the world, and the sky will be the limit!"

6   The following months were filled with a sense of importance: Long Distance Calls, Urgent Telegrams, Express Letters, sudden arrivals and departures by plane and car. I received constant summonses to be present here or there. "PLEASE COME TO DELHI. SUIT RESERVED AT IMPERIALL HOTEL. URGENTLY NEED YOUR PRESENCE."

7   Locking away my novel-in-progress, I fly to Delhi. There is the press conference, with introductions, speeches and overflowing conviviality. The American director explains the unique nature of their present effort: for the first time in the history of Indian movie-making, they are going to bring out a hundred-percent-Indian story, with a hundred-percent-Indian cast, and a hundred-percent-Indian setting, for an international audience. And mark this: actually in colour-and-wide-screen-first-time-in-the-history-of-this-country.

8   A distinguished group of Americans, headed by the Nobel Prize winner Pearl Buck, would produce the film. Again and again I heard the phrase: "Sky is the limit", and the repeated assurances: "We will make the picture just as Narayan has written it, with his co-operation at every stage." Reporters pressed me for a statement. It was impossible to say anything but the pleasantest things in such an atmosphere of overwhelming optimism and good fellowship.

9   Soon we were assembled in Mysore. They wanted to see the exact spots which had inspired me to write *The Guide.* Could I show them the locations? A photographer, and some others whose business with us I never quite understood, were in the party. We started out in two cars. The American director, Tad Danielewski, explained that he would direct the English version first. He kept discussing with me the finer points of my novel. "I guess your hero is a man of impulsive plans? Self-made, given to daydreaming?" he would ask, and add, before I could muster an answer, "Am I not right?" Of course he had to be right. Once or twice when I attempted to mitigate his impressions, he brushed

aside my comments and went on with his own explanation as to what I must have had in mind when I created such-and-such a character.

I began to realize that monologue is the privilege of the film maker,   10
and that it was futile to try butting in with my own observations. But for some obscure reason, they seemed to need my presence, though not my voice. I must be seen and not heard.

We drove about 300 miles that day, during the course of which I   11
showed them the river steps and a little shrine overshadowed by a banyan on the banks of Kaveri, which was the actual spot around which I wrote *The Guide*. As I had recalled, nothing more needed to be done than put the actors there and start the camera. They uttered little cries of joy at finding a "set" so readily available. In the summer, when the river dried up, they could shoot the drought scenes with equal ease. Then I took them to the tiny town of Nanjangud, with its little streets, its shops selling sweets and toys and ribbons, and a pilgrim crowd bathing in the holy waters of the Kabini, which flowed through the town. The crowd was colourful and lively around the temple, and in a few weeks it would increase a hundredfold when people from the surrounding villages arrived to participate in the annual festival—the sort of crowd described in the last pages of my novel. If the film makers made a note of the date and sent down a cameraman at that time, they could secure the last scene of my novel in an authentic manner and absolutely free of cost.

The producer at once passed an order to his assistant to arrange for   12
an outdoor unit to arrive here at the right time. Then we all posed at the portals of the ancient temple, with arms encircling each other's necks and smiling. This was but the first of innumerable similar scenes in which I found myself posing with the starry folk, crushed in the friendliest embrace.

From Nanjangud we drove up mountains and the forests and photo-   13
graphed our radiant smiles against every possible background. It was a fatiguing business on the whole, but the American director claimed that it was nothing to what he was used to. He generally went 5,000 miles in search of locations, exposing hundreds of rolls of film on the way.

After inspecting jungles, mountains, village streets, hamlets and   14
huts, we reached the base of Gopalaswami Hill in the afternoon, and drove up the five-mile mud track; the cars had to be pushed up the steep hill after encroaching vegetation had been cleared from the path. This was a part of the forest country where at any bend of the road one could anticipate a tiger or a herd of elephants; but, luckily for us, they were out of view today.

At the summit I showed them the original of the "Peak House" in   15
my novel, a bungalow built 50 years ago, with glassed in verandas affording a view of wildlife at night, and a 2,000-foot drop to a valley beyond. A hundred yards off, a foot-track wound through the undergrowth, leading on to an ancient temple whose walls were crumbling

and whose immense timber doors moved on rusty hinges with a groan. Once again I felt that here everything was ready-made for the film. They could shoot in the bright sunlight, and for the indoor scenes they assured me that it would be a simple matter to haul up a generator and lights.

16   Sitting under a banyan tree and consuming sandwiches and lemonade, we discussed and settled the practical aspects of the expedition: where to locate the base camp and where the advance units consisting of engineers, mechanics, and truck drivers, in charge of the generator and lights. All through the journey back the talk involved schedules and arrangements for shooting the scenes in this part of the country. I was impressed with the ease they displayed in accepting such mighty logistical tasks. Film executives, it seemed to me, could solve mankind's problems on a global scale with the casual confidence of demi-gods, if only they could take time off their illusory pursuits and notice the serious aspects of existence.

17   Then came total silence, for many weeks. Finally I discovered that they were busy searching for their locations in Northern India.

18   This was a shock. I had never visualized my story in that part of India, where costumes, human types and details of daily life are different. They had settled upon Jaipur and Udaipur in Rajaputana, a thousand miles away from my location for the story.

19   Our next meeting was in Bombay, and I wasted no time in speaking of this problem. "My story takes place in south India, in Malgudi, an imaginary town known to thousands of my readers all over the world", I explained. "It is South India in costume, tone and contents. Although the whole country is one, there are diversities, and one has to be faithful in delineating them. You have to stick to my geography and sociology. Although it is a world of fiction there are certain inner veracities."

20   One of them replied: "We feel it a privilege to be doing your story." This sounded irrelevant as an answer to my statement.

21   We were sitting under a gaudy umbrella beside a blue swimming pool on Juhu Beach, where the American party was housed in princely suites in a modern hotel. It was hard to believe that we were in India. Most of our discussions took place somewhat amphibiously, on the edge of the swimming pool, in which the director spent a great deal of his time.

22   This particular discussion was interrupted as a bulky European tourist in swimming briefs fell off the diving plank, hit the bottom and had to be hauled out and rendered first aid. After the atmosphere had cleared, I resumed my speech. They listened with a mixture of respect and condescension, evidently willing to make allowances for an author's whims.

23   "Please remember", one of them tried to explain, "that we are shooting, for the first time in India, in wide screen and Eastman Colour, and we must shoot where there is spectacle. Hence Jaipur."

"In that case", I had to ask, "Why all that strenuous motoring near   24
my home? Why my story at all, if what you need is a picturesque spectacle?"

I was taken aback when their reply came! "How do you know that   25
Malgudi is where you think it is?"

Somewhat bewildered, I said, with what I hoped was proper humility, "I suppose I know because I have imagined it, created it and   26
have been writing novel after novel set in the area for the last 30 years."

"We are out to expand the notion of Malgudi", one of them explained. "Malgudi will be where we place it, in Kashmir, Rajasthan,   27
Bombay, Delhi, even Ceylon."

I could not share the flexibility of their outlook or the expanse of   28
their vision. It seemed to me that for their purpose a focal point was unnecessary. They appeared to be striving to achieve mere optical effects.

I recalled a talk with Satyajit Ray, the great director, some years earlier, when I met him in Calcutta. He expressed his admiration for *The*   29
Guide but also his doubts as to whether he could ever capture the tone
and atmosphere of its background. He had said, "Its roots are so deep
in the soil of your part of our country that I doubt if I could do justice to
your book, being unfamiliar with its milieu . . . " Such misgivings did
not bother the American director. I noticed that though he was visiting
India for the first time, he never paused to ask what was what in this
bewildering country.

Finally he solved the whole problem by declaring, "Why should   30
we mention where the story takes place? We will avoid the name
'Malgudi.'" Thereafter the director not only avoided the word Malgudi
but fell foul of anyone who uttered that sound.

My brother, an artist who has illustrated my stories for 25 years,   31
tried to expound his view. At a dinner in his home in Bombay, he mentioned the forbidden word to the director. Malgudi, he explained,
meant a little town, not so picturesque as Jaipur, of a neutral shade,
with characters wearing dhoti and jibba when they were not barebodied. The Guide himself was a man of charm, creating history and archaeology out of thin air for his clients, and to provide him with solid,
concrete monuments to talk about would go against the grain of the
tale. The director listened and firmly said, "There is no Malgudi, and
that is all there is to it."

But my brother persisted. I became concerned that the controversy   32
threatened to spoil our dinner. The director replied, in a sad tone, that
they could as well have planned a picture for black and white and narrow screen if all one wanted was what he contemptuously termed a
"Festival Film", while he was planning a million-dollar spectacle to
open simultaneously in 2,000 theaters in America. I was getting used to
arguments everyday over details. My story is about a dancer in a small
town, an exponent of the strictly classical tradition of South Indian

Bharat Natyam. The film makers felt this was inadequate. They therefore engaged an expensive, popular dance director with a troupe of a
hundred or more dancers, and converted my heroine's performances
into an extravaganza in delirious, fruity colours and costumes. Their
dancer was constantly traveling hither and thither in an Air India Boe-
ing no matter how short the distance to be covered. The moviegoer, too,
I began to realize, would be whisked all over India. Although he would
see none of the countryside in which the novel was set, he would see
the latest U.S. Embassy building in New Delhi, Parliament House, the
Ashoka Hotel, the Lake Palace, Elephanta Caves and whatnot. Unity of
place seemed an unknown concept for a film maker. (Later Mrs. Indira
Gandhi, whom I met after she had seen a special showing of the film,
asked, "Why should they have dragged the story all over as if it were a
travelogue, instead of confining themselves to the simple background
of your book?" She added as an afterthought, and in what seemed to
me an understatement: "Perhaps they have other considerations."

33   The co-operation of many persons was needed in the course of the
film making, and anyone whose help was requested had to be given a
copy of *The Guide.* Thus there occurred a shortage, and an inevitable
black market, in copies of the book. A production executive searched
the bookshops in Bombay, and cornered all the available copies at any
price. He could usually be seen going about like a scholar with a
bundle of books under his arm. I was also intrigued by the intense
study and pencil-marking that the director was making on his copy of
the book; it was as if he were studying it for a doctoral thesis. Not until
I had a chance to read his "treatment" did I understand what all his
penciling meant: he had been marking off passages and portions that
were to be avoided in the film.

34   When the script came, I read through it with mixed feelings. The
director answered my complaints with "I have only exteriorized what
you have expressed. It is all in your book."

35   'In which part of my book' I would ask without any hope of an
answer.

36   Or he would say, "I could give you two hundred reasons why this
change should be so." I did not feel up to hearing them all. If I still
proved truculent he would explain away "This is only a first draft. We
could make any change you want in the final screenplay."

37   The screenplay was finally presented to me with a great flourish
and expressions of fraternal sentiments at a hotel in Bangalore. But I
learned at this time that they had already started shooting and had
even completed a number of scenes. Whenever expressed my views,
the answer would be either, "Oh, it will all be rectified in the editing",
or, "We will deal with it when we decide about the retakes. But please
wait until we have a chance to see the rushes". By now a bewildering
number of hands were behind the scenes, at laboratories, workshops,

carpentries, editing rooms and so forth. It was impossible to keep track of what was going on, or get hold of anyone with a final say. Soon I trained myself to give up all attempts to connect the film with the book of which I happened to be the author.

But I was not sufficiently braced for the shock that came the day when the director insisted upon the production of two tigers to fight and destroy each other over a spotted deer. He wished to establish the destructive animality of two men clashing over one woman: my heroine's husband and lover fighting over her. The director intended a tiger fight to portray depths of symbolism. It struck me as obvious. Moreover it was not in the story. But he asserted that it was; evidently I had intended the scene without realizing it.

The Indian producer, who was financing the project, groaned at the thought of the tigers. He begged me privately, "Please do something about it. We have no time for tigers; and it will cost hell of a lot to hire them, just for a passing fancy." I spoke to the director again, but he was insistent. No tiger, no film, and two tigers or none.

Scouts were sent out through the length and breadth of India to explore the tiger possibilities. They returned to report that only one tiger was available. It belonged to a circus and the circus owner would under no circumstance consent to have the tiger injured or killed. The director decreed, "I want the beast to die, otherwise the scene will have no meaning." They finally found a man in Madras, living in the heart of the city with a full-grown Bengal tiger which he occasionally lent for jungle pictures, after sewing its lips and pulling out its claws.

The director examined a photograph of the tiger, in order to satisfy himself that they were not trying to palm off a pi-dog in tiger clothing, and signed it up. Since a second tiger was not available, he had to settle for its fighting a leopard. It was an easier matter to find a deer for the sacrifice. What they termed a "second unit" was dispatched to Madras to shoot the sequence. Ten days later the unit returned, looking forlorn.

The tiger had shrunk at the sight of the leopard, and the leopard had shown no inclination to maul the deer, whose cries of fright had been so heart-rending that they had paralyzed the technicians. By prodding, kicking and irritating the animals, they had succeeded in producing a spectacle gory enough to make them retch. "The deer was actually lifted and fed into the jaws of the other two", said an assistant cameraman. (This shot passes on the screen, in the finished film, in the winking of an eye as a bloody smudge, to the accompaniment of a lot of wild uproar.)

Presently another crisis developed. The director wanted the hero to kiss the heroine, who of course rejected the suggestion as unbecoming an Indian woman. The director was distraught. The hero, for his part, was willing to obey the director, but he was helpless, since kissing is a co-operative effort. The American director realized that it is against

38

39

40

41

42

43

Indian custom to kiss in public; but he insisted that the public in his country would boo if they missed the kiss. I am told that the heroine replied: "There is enough kissing in your country at all times and places, off and on the screen, and your public, I am sure, will flock to a picture where, for a change, no kissing is shown." She stood firm. Finally, the required situation was apparently faked by tricky editing.

44   Next: trouble at the governmental level. A representation was made to the Ministry dealing with films, by an influential group, that *The Guide* glorified adultery, and hence was not fit to be presented as a film, since it might degrade Indian womanhood. The dancer in my story, to hear their arguments, has no justification for preferring Raju the Guide to her legally wedded husband. The Ministry summoned the movie principals to Delhi and asked them to explain how they proposed to meet the situation. They promised to revise the film script to the Ministry's satisfaction.

45   In my story the dancer's husband is a preoccupied archaeologist who has no time or inclination for marital life and is not interested in her artistic aspirations. Raju the Guide exploits the situation and weans her away from her husband. That is all there is to it—in my story. But now a justification had to be found for adultery.

46   So the archaeological husband was converted into a drunkard and womanizer who kicks out his wife when he discovers that another man has watched her dance in her room and has spoken encouragingly to her. I knew nothing about this drastic change of my characters until I saw the 'rushes' some months later. This was the point at which I lamented most over my naivete: the contract that I had signed in blind faith, in the intoxication of cheques bonhomie, and backslapping, empowered them to do whatever they pleased with my story, and I had no recourse.

47   Near the end of the project I made another discovery: the extent to which movie producers will go to publicize a film. The excessive affability to pressmen, the entertaining of V.I.P.s, the button-holding of ministers and officials in authority, the extravagant advertising campaigns, seem to me to drain off money, energy and ingenuity that might be reserved for the creation of an honest and sensible product.

48   On one occasion Lord Mountbatten was passing through India, and someone was seized with the sudden idea that he could help make a success of the picture. A banquet was held at Raj Bhavan in his honor, and the Governor of Bombay, Mrs. Vijayalaxmi Pandit, was kind enough to invite us to it. I was home in Mysore as Operation Mountbatten was launched, so telegrams and long-distance telephone calls poured in on me to urge me to come to Bombay at once. I flew in just in time to dress and reach Raj Bhavan. It was red-carpeted, crowded and gorgeous. When dinner was over, leaving the guests aside, our hostess managed to isolate his Lordship and the 'Guide'-makers on a side veranda of this noble building. His Lordship sat on a sofa surrounded by

us; close to him sat Pearl Buck, who was one of the producers and who, by virtue of her seniority and standing, was to speak for us. As she opened the theme with a brief explanation of the epoch-making effort that was being made in India, in colour and wide-screen, with a hundred-percent-Indian cast, story and background, his Lordship displayed no special emotion. Then came the practical demand: in order that this grand, stupendous achievement might bear fruit, would Lord Mountbatten influence Queen Elizabeth to preside at the world premiere of the film in London in due course?

Lord Mountbatten responded promptly, "I don't think it is possible. Anyway what is the story?" 49

There was dead silence for a moment, as each looked at the other 50
wondering who was to begin. I was fully aware that they ruled me out; they feared that I might take 80,000 words to narrate the story, as I had in the book. The obvious alternative was Pearl Buck, who was supposed to have written the screenplay.

Time was running out and his Lordship had others to talk to. Pearl 51
Buck began.

"It is the story of a man called Raju. He was a tourist guide. . . ." 52

"Where does it take place?" 53

I wanted to shout, "Malgudi, of course." But they were explaining, 54
"We have taken the story through many interesting locations—Jaipur, Udaipur."

"Let me hear the story." 55

"Raju was a guide", began Pearl Buck again. 56

"In Jaipur?" asked his Lordship. 57

"Well, no. Anyway he did not remain a guide because when Rosie 58
came . . . "

"Who is Rosie" 59

"A dancer . . . but she changed her name when she became a . . . 60
a . . . dancer. . . ."

"But the guide? What happened to him?" 61

"I am coming to it. Rosie's husband . . . " 62

"Rosie is the dancer?" 63

'Yes, of course . . . ' Pearl Buck struggled on, but I was in no mood 64
to extricate her.

Within several minutes Lord Mountbatten said, "Most interest- 65
ing." His deep bass voice was a delight to the ear, but it also had a ring of finality and discouraged further talk. "Elizabeth's appointments are complicated these days. Anyway her private secretary Lord—must know more about it than I do. I am rather out of touch now. Anyway, perhaps I could ask Philip." He summoned an aide and said, "William, please remind me when we get to London. . . ." Our Producers went home feeling that a definite step had been taken to establish the film in proper quarters. As for myself, I was not so sure.

66   Elaborate efforts were made to shoot the last scene of the story, in which the saint fasts on the dry river's edge, in hopes of bringing rain, and a huge crowd turns up to witness the spectacle. For this scene the director selected a site at a village called Okla, outside Delhi on the bank of the Jamuna river, which was dry and provided enormous stretches of sand. He had, of course, ruled out the spot we had visited near Mysore, explaining that two coconut trees were visible a mile away on the horizon and might spoil the appearance of unrelieved desert which he wanted. Thirty truckloads of property, carpenters, lumber, painters, artisans and art department personnel arrived at Okla to erect a two-dimensional temple beside a dry river, at a cost of 80,000 rupees. As the director kept demanding, "I must have 100,000 people for a helicopter shot", I thought of the cost: five rupees per head for extras, while both the festival crowd at Nanjangud and the little temple on the river would cost nothing.

67   The crowd had been mobilized, the sets readied and lights mounted, and all other preparations completed for shooting the scene next morning when, at midnight, news was brought to the chiefs relaxing at the Ashoka Hotel that the Jamuna was rising dangerously as a result of unexpected rains in Simla. All hands were mobilized and they rushed desperately to the location to save the equipment. Wading in knee-deep water, they salvaged a few things. But I believe the two-dimensional temple was carried off in the floods.

68   Like a colony of ants laboriously building up again, the carpenters and artisans rebuilt, this time at a place in Western India called Limdi, which was reputed to have an annual rainfall of a few droplets. Within one week the last scene was completed, the hero collapsing in harrowing fashion as a result of his penance. The director and technicians paid off the huge crowd and packed up their cameras and sound equipment, and were just leaving the scene when a storm broke—an unknown phenomenon in that part of the country—uprooting and tearing off everything that stood. Those who had lingered had to make their exit with dispatch.

69   This seemed to me an appropriate conclusion for my story, which, after all, was concerned with the subject of rain, and in which Nature, rather than film makers, acted in consonance with the subject. I remembered that years ago when I was in New York City on my way to sign the contract, before writing *The Guide,* a sudden downpour caught me on Madison Avenue and I entered the Viking Press offices dripping wet. I still treasure a letter from Keith Jennison, who was then my editor. "Somehow I will always, from now on", he wrote, "associate the rainiest days in New York with you. The afternoon we officially became your publishers was wet enough to have made me feel like a fish ever since."

✦ *Evaluating the Text*

1. What change in attitude did Narayan experience between the beginning and the end of the "project"? What key steps or incidents can you discover en route to his change of perspective?

2. What features of "Bollywood" (that is, the Bombay version of Hollywood, where hundreds of films are made each week) does Narayan satirize in his account?

3. In what way would an authentic film made from Narayan's novel differ from the one actually made? Based on your answer, evaluate whether the film producers were correct in their decisions concerning locations, story line, and other aspects of the project.

✦ *Exploring Different Perspectives*

1. What different cultural attitudes are revealed in how celebrities are treated in China and India, as described by R. K. Narayan and Mark Salzman (see "Lessons")?

2. What similarities in village life can you discover when comparing R. K. Narayan's "Malgudi" to the goldsmith's village as described by Camara Laye in "The Village Goldsmith"?

✦ *Extending Viewpoints Through Writing*

1. In a short essay, discuss some of the ways in which an Indian movie differs from a Hollywood picture in terms of the cultural values of each society.

2. Have you ever counted on something as a sure thing, only to have it subsequently never materialize—an event, a trip, a material possession, a relationship? How is counting on something that never came about more dispiriting than never having believed it could happen at all? How did this experience help you understand R. K. Narayan's feelings in "Misguided 'Guide'"?

Moacyr Scliar

A Brief History of Capitalism

◆

Moacyr Scliar was born in 1937 in Russia but grew up among the Russian-Jewish emigrés living in the southern Brazilian city of Porto Alegere. Scliar is a physician working in public health whose writing concentrates on the absurdity of modern urban life. His works include The Strange Nation of Rafael Mendes *(1987),* The Volunteers *(1988), and* The Enigmatic Eye *(1989), in which his story "A Brief History of Capitalism" first appeared.*

1   My father was a Communist and a car mechanic. A good Communist, according to his comrades, but a lousy mechanic according to consensus. As a matter of fact, so great was his inability to handle cars that people wondered why he had chosen such an occupation. He used to say it had been a conscious choice on his part; he believed in manual work as a form of personal development, and he had confidence in machines and in their capability to liberate man and launch him into the future, in the direction of a freer, more desirable life. Roughly, that's what he meant.

2   I used to help my father in his car repair shop. Since I was an only son, he wanted me to follow in his footsteps. There wasn't, however, much that I could do; at that time I was eleven years old, and almost as clumsy as he was at using tools. Anyhow, for the most part, there was no call for us to use them since there wasn't much work coming our way. We would sit talking and thus while away the time. My father was a great storyteller; enthralled, I would listen to his accounts of the uprising of the Spartacists, and of the rebellion led by the fugitive slave Zambi. In those moments his eyes would glitter. I would listen, deeply affected by his stories; often, my eyes would fill with tears.

3   Once in awhile a customer appeared. Usually a Party sympathizer (my father's comrades didn't own cars), who came to Father more out of a desire to help than out of need. These customers played it safe, though: It was always some minor repair, like fixing the license plate securely, or changing the blades of the windshield wipers. But even such simple tasks turned out to be extraordinarily difficult for Father to perform; sometimes it would take him a whole day to change a distrib-

---

*(For information on Brazil, see p. 514.)

utor point. And the car would drive away with the engine misfiring (needless to say, its owner would never set foot in our repair shop again). If it weren't for the financial problems (my mother had to support us by taking in sewing), I wouldn't have minded the lack of work too much. I really enjoyed those rap sessions with my father. In the morning I would go to school; but as soon as I came home, I would run to the repair shop, which was near our house. And there I would find Father reading. Upon my arrival, he would set his book aside, light his pipe, and start telling me his stories. And there we would stay until Mother came to call us for dinner.

One day when I arrived at our repair shop, there was a car there, a huge, sparkling, luxury car. None of the Party sympathizers, not even the wealthiest among them, owned a car like that. Father told me that the monster car had stalled right in front of the shop. The owner then left it there, under his care, saying he would be back late in the afternoon. And what's wrong with it? I asked, somewhat alarmed, sensing a foul-up in the offing. 4

"I wish I knew." Father sighed. "Frankly, I don't know what's wrong with it. I already took a look but couldn't find the defect. It must be something minor, probably the carburetor is clogged up, but . . . I don't know, I just don't know what it is." 5

Dejected, he sat down, took a handkerchief out of his pocket, and wiped his forehead. Come on, I said, annoyed at his passivity, it's no use your sitting there. 6

He got up and the two of us took a look at the enormous engine, so clean, it glittered. Isn't it a beauty? remarked my father with the pleasure of an owner who took pride in his car. 7

Yes, it was a beauty—except that he couldn't open the carburetor. I had to give him a hand; three hours later, when the man returned, we were still at it. 8

He was a pudgy, well-dressed man. He got out of a taxi, his face already displaying annoyance. I expected him to be disgruntled, but never for a moment did I imagine what was to happen next. 9

At first the man said nothing. Seeing that we weren't finished yet, he sat down on a stool and watched us. A moment later he stood up; he examined the stool on which he had sat. 10

"Dirty. This stool is dirty. Can't you people even offer your customers a decent chair to sit on?" 11

We made no reply. Neither did we raise our heads. The man looked around him. 12

"A real dump, this place. A sty. How can you people work amid such filth?" 13

We, silent. 14

"But that's the way everything is," the man went on. "In this country that's the way it is. Nobody wants to do any work, nobody wants to 15 get his act together. All people ever think of is booze, women, the Carnival, soccer. But to get down to work? Never."

16 Where's the wrench? asked Father in a low, restrained voice. Over there, by your side, I said. Thanks, he said, and resumed fiddling with the carburetor.

17 "You people want nothing to do with a regular, steady job." The man sounded increasingly more irritated. "You people will never get out of this filth. Now, take me, for instance. I started at the bottom. But nowadays I'm a rich man. Very rich. And do you know why? Because I was clean, well organized, hardworking. This car here, do you think it's the only one I own? Do you?"

18 Tighten the screw, said Father, tighten it really tight.

19 "I'm talking to you!" yelled the man, fuming. "I'm asking you a question! Do you think this is the only car I own? That's what you think, isn't it? Well, let me tell you something, I own two other cars. Two other cars! They are in my garage. I don't use them. Because I don't want to. If I wanted, I could abandon this car here in the middle of the street and get another one. Well, I wouldn't get it myself; I would have someone get it for me. Because I have a chauffeur, see? That's right. I drive because I enjoy driving, but I have a chauffeur. I don't *have* to drive, I don't *need* this car. If I wanted to, I could junk this fucking car, you hear me?"

20 Hand me the pipe wrench, will you? said Father. The small one.

21 The man was now standing quite close to us. I didn't look at him, but I could feel his breath on my arm.

22 "Do you doubt my word? Do you doubt that I can smash up this car? Do you?"

23 I looked at the man. He was upset. When his eyes met mine, he seemed to come to his senses; only for a moment, though; he opened his eyes wide.

24 "Do you doubt it? That I can smash up this fucking car? Give me a hammer. Quick! Give me a hammer!"

25 He searched for a hammer but couldn't find one (it would have been a miracle had he found one; even we could never find the tools in our shop). Without knowing what he was doing, he gave the car door a kick; soon followed by another, then another.

26 "That's what I've been telling you," he kept screaming. "That I'll smash up this fucking car! That's what I've been telling you."

27 Ready, said Father. I looked at him; he was pale, beads of sweat were running down his face. Ready? I asked, not getting it. Ready, he said. You can now start the engine.

28 The man, panting, was looking at us. Opening the car door, I sat at the steering wheel and turned on the ignition. Incredible: The engine started. I revved it up. The shop was filled with the roar of the engine.

29 My father stood mopping his face with his dirty handkerchief. The man, silent, kept looking at us. How much I owe you? finally he asked.

Nothing, said my father. What do you mean, nothing? Suspicious, the man frowned. Nothing, said my father, it costs you nothing, it's on the house. Then the man, opening his wallet, pulled out a bill.

"Here, for a shot of rum."   30

"I don't drink," said my father without touching the money.   31

The man replaced the bill in his wallet, which he then put into his   32
pocket. Without a word he got into his car, and, revving the engine, drove away.

For a moment Father stood motionless, in silence. Then he turned   33
to me.

"This," he said in a hoarse voice, a voice that wasn't his, "is capital-   34
ism."

No, it wasn't. That wasn't capitalism. I wished it were capitalism—   35
but it was not. Unfortunately not. It was something else. Something I didn't even dare to think about.

✦ Evaluating the Text

1. What has motivated the father to become a car mechanic even though he is clumsy with tools and cannot solve automotive problems?

2. How does the boy's attitude toward his father change as a result of the encounter described in the story?

3. In what way might the story be understood as a satire on the emergence of capitalism in what had been a communist country? How do the conversations between the father and the customer express differences in ideology and class? What is at stake for the father that makes him miraculously able to fix the car?

✦ Exploring Different Perspectives

1. What different kinds of things does working on cars mean to the father, the son, and the capitalist in Moacyr Scliar's story compared to its meaning in Lesley Hazleton's account, "Confessions of a Fast Woman"?

2. How is being a worker in a communist system tested in different ways when machinery goes awry in Moacyr Scliar's story and in Anton Vassilievich's account (see "Radiation Expert)"?

✦ Extending Viewpoints Through Writing

1. How do you interpret the boy's last statement that what has taken place deals with something other than capitalism that he "didn't even dare to think about"?

Connecting Cultures

◆

Lesley Hazleton, Confessions of a Fast Woman

In what respects is becoming an apprentice auto mechanic a rite of passage similar to those described by Tepilit Ole Saitoti (see "The Initiation of a Maasai Warrior," Chapter 2)?

Camara Laye, The Village Goldsmith

How do the accounts by Camara Laye and by Colin Turnbull (see "The Mbuti Pgymies," Chapter 1) suggest the importance of initiation into the mysteries of adult life for children in traditional African cultures?

Anton Vassilievich, Radiation Expert

Discuss how the accounts by Anton Vassilievich and by Boris Yeltsin (see "Childhood in Russia," Chapter 1) reveal the importance of individuals taking the initiative when faced with characteristic Russian bureaucracy.

Mark Salzman, Lessons

Compare Mark Salzman's narrative with that of David R. Counts in terms of the lessons learned from the cultures in which they are living (see "Too Many Bananas," Chapter 8).

Kon Krailet, In the Mirror

How is the commercialization of sexuality a feature of both Kim Chernin's account (see "The Flesh and the Devil," Chapter 3) and Kon Krailet's story?

Studs Terkel, Ron Maydon

What attitude toward Cubans does Ron Maydon display, and is it borne out by Joan Didion's analysis (see "Miami: The Cuban Presence," Chapter 7)?

R. K. Narayan, Misguided 'Guide'

To what extent would R. K. Narayan's "Malgudi" look like the village in Premchand's story "Deliverance" (Chapter 9)? To what extent do you think the producers were correct in not filming in a "Malgudi"-type village?

Moacyr Scliar, A Brief History of Capitalism

What attitude toward workers, displayed in Moacyr Scliar's story, is also reflected in Constance Classen's analysis of class conflicts (see "The Odour of the Other," Chapter 5)?

5

Class Conflicts

◆

Every society can be characterized in terms of social class. Although the principles by which class is identified vary widely from culture to culture, from the amount of money you earn in the United States to what kind of accent you speak with in England to what religious caste you are born into in India, class serves to set boundaries around individuals in terms of opportunities and possibilities. The concept of class in its present form has been in force for only a few hundred years in Western cultures. In prior times, for example, in medieval Europe, your position and chances in life were determined at birth by the *estate* into which you were born, whether that of peasant, clergy, or noble.

Conflicts based on inequalities of social class are often intertwined with those of race, because minorities usually receive the least education, have the least political clout, earn the least income, and find work in occupations considered menial without the possibility of advancement. In some societies, such as that in South Africa, for example, an oppressive caste system based on ethnicity had been until recently officially sanctioned by the government under an apartheid policy.

Class conditions our entire lives by setting limitations that determine, more than we might like to admit, who we can be friends with, what our goals are, and even who we can marry.

Class reflects the access one has to important resources, social privileges, choices, and a sense of control over one's own life. For example, in a traditional culture like India, the caste into which one is born is something one cannot change. By contrast, social stratification in the United States is less rigid and upward mobility is possible through a variety of means such as work, financial success, marriage, and education. More frequently, however, a de facto class system can be said to exist in terms of health care, salaries, housing, and opportunities for education that varies greatly for the rich and the poor.

The writers in this chapter explore many of the less obvious connections between social class and the control people exercise over their lives. Roland Barthes looks beneath the veneer of flashy food ads to discover the social realities of class distinctions in "Ornamental Cookery." In "What Is Poverty?" Jo Goodwin Parker brings home the day-to-day consequences of being poverty stricken in the southern United States. Mahdokht Kashkuli, in "The Button," describes the circumstances of a family in modern-day Iran that force them to place one of their children in an orphanage. Alonso Salazar, in "The Lords of Creation," provides a first-hand account of a teenage contract killer's life in the underworld of Colombia's drug capital, Medellín. Jamaica Kincaid, in "A Small Place," offers an ironic perspective on tourism in Antigua. Mary Crow Dog and Richard Erdoes, in "Civilize Them with a Stick," recount the racism experienced by Native-Americans attending a government-run boarding school. In "The Odour of the Other," Constance Classen analyzes how olfactory symbolism expresses class values in different cultures. From Singapore, Catherine Lim, in "Paper," explores the tragic consequences of greed in this tale of a middle-class couple's entanglement with the Singapore Stock Exchange.

Roland Barthes

Ornamental Cookery

◆

Roland Barthes (1915–1980), considered by many to have been the great-est thinker since Jean-Paul Sartre, was born in Cherbourg, France. Al-though he did not receive his first post in a university until he was in his fifties, he subsequently taught at institutions in France, Egypt, Romania, and the United States, including the Sorbonne, the University of Paris, and Johns Hopkins University. He is widely regarded as the father of semi-otic theory, a field of study which investigates and interprets the meaning of signs in many contexts, including those of culture, linguistics, and lit-erature. "Ornamental Cookery" is drawn from Mythologies *(1972).*

Traditionally an ally of the United States, France was a world power and cultural center in Europe during the reign of Louis XIV (1653–1715). The French absolute monarchy was brought to an end during the French Revolution, a tumultuous period that set the stage for Napoleon's rise to power during the late eighteenth century. France emerged from the Napoleonic Wars as a modern bureaucratic state dominated by the bour-geoisie (middle class), a social structure that endures to the present. In the twentieth century, France has endured two world wars fought on its ter-ritory and has been involved in colonial wars in Indochina and Algeria. The difficulty of governing a people so exasperating and stimulating was perhaps best stated by Charles de Gaulle (president from 1959 to 1969), who returned France to a position of prestige in world affairs: "How can you be expected to govern a country that has 246 kinds of cheese?" In 1981 François Mitterrand, a socialist, was elected president of the repub-lic and served in that capacity until his death in 1995. After his death, Jacques Chirac became the president of the republic and brought in a con-servative government headed by Edouard Balladur as prime minister.

1   The weekly *Elle* (a real mythological treasure) gives us almost every week a fine colour photograph of a prepared dish: golden partridges studded with cherries, a faintly pink chicken chaudfroid, a mould of crayfish surrounded by their red shells, a frothy charlotte prettified with glacé fruit designs, multicoloured trifle, etc.

2   The 'substantial' category which prevails in this type of cooking is that of the smooth coating: there is an obvious endeavour to glaze sur-faces, to round them off, to bury the food under the even sediment of sauces, creams, icing and jellies. This of course comes from the very fi-nality of the coating, which belongs to a visual category, and cooking

286

according to *Elle* is meant for the eye alone, since sight is a genteel sense. For there is, in this persistence of glazing, a need for gentility. *Elle* is a highly valuable journal, from the point of view of legend at least, since its role is to present to its vast public which (market-research tells us) is working-class, the very dream of smartness. Hence a cookery which is based on coatings and alibis, and is for ever trying to extenuate and even to disguise the primary nature of foodstuffs, the brutality of meat or the abruptness of sea-food. A country dish is admitted only as an exception (the good family boiled beef), as the rustic whim of jaded city-dwellers.

But above all, coatings prepare and support one of the major developments of genteel cookery: ornamentation. Glazing, in *Elle,* serves as background for unbridled beautification: chiselled mushrooms, punctuation of cherries, motifs of carved lemon, shavings of truffle, silver pastilles, arabesques of glacé fruit: the underlying coat (and this is why I called it a sediment, since the food itself becomes no more than an indeterminate bed-rock) is intended to be the page on which can be read a whole rococo cookery (there is a partiality for a pinkish colour).

Ornamentation proceeds in two contradictory ways, which we shall in a moment see dialectically reconciled: on the one hand, fleeing from nature thanks to a kind of frenzied baroque (sticking shrimps in a lemon, making a chicken look pink, serving grapefruit hot), and on the other, trying to reconstitute it through an incongruous artifice (strewing meringue mushrooms and holly leaves on a traditional log-shaped Christmas cake, replacing the heads of crayfish around the sophisticated bechamel which hides their bodies). It is in fact the same pattern which one finds in the elaboration of petit-bourgeois trinkets (ashtrays in the shape of a saddle, lighters in the shape of a cigarette, terrines in the shape of a hare).

This is because here, as in all petit-bourgeois art, the irrepressible tendency towards extreme realism is countered—or balanced—by one of the eternal imperatives of journalism for women's magazines: what is pompously called, at *L'Express, having ideas.* Cookery in *Elle* is, in the same way, an 'idea'-cookery. But here inventiveness, confined to a fairy-land reality, must be applied only to *garnishings,* for the genteel tendency of the magazine precludes it from touching on the real problems concerning food (the real problem is not to have the idea of sticking cherries into a partridge, it is to have the partridge, that is to say, to pay for it).

This ornamental cookery is indeed supported by wholly mythical economics. This is an openly dream-like cookery, as proved in fact by the photographs in *Elle,* which never show the dishes except from a high angle, as objects at once near and inaccessible, whose consumption can perfectly well be accomplished simply by looking. It is, in the fullest meaning of the word, a cuisine of advertisement, totally magical, especially when one remembers that this magazine is widely read in small-income groups. The latter, in fact, explains the former: it is because *Elle* is addressed to a genuinely working-class public that it is very careful not to take for granted that cooking must be economical. Compare with *L'Express*, whose exclusively middle-class public enjoys a comfortable purchasing power: its cookery is real, not magical. *Elle* gives the recipe of fancy partridges, *L'Express* gives that of *salad niçoise*. The readers of *Elle* are entitled only to fiction; one can suggest real dishes to those of *L'Express*, in the certainty that they will be able to prepare them.

✦ Evaluating the Text

1. According to Barthes, what is the relationship between how food is depicted in the magazine *Elle* and the social class of its readers?

2. Why don't the readers of *L'Express* require similar depictions of food?

✦ Exploring Different Perspectives

1. How do Roland Barthes and Jamaica Kincaid, in "A Small Place," deal with the issue of appearance versus reality? What place does irony play in both accounts?

2. How do Roland Barthes and Jamaica Kincaid, in "A Small Place," deal with the issue of what is affordable and what is not, and for whom?

✦ Extending Viewpoints Through Writing

1. In which contemporary magazines can you find the same relationship between advertisements and readership as Barthes identifies? Analyze one of these ads in a short essay and discuss how the depiction serves as a vehicle for class aspirations.

Jo Goodwin Parker

What Is Poverty?

◆————

Jo Goodwin Parker's poignant and realistic account of the shame, humiliation, and outrage of being poor was first given as a speech in Deland, Florida, on December 27, 1965, and was published in America's Other Children: Public Schools Outside Suburbia, *edited by George Henderson (1971). Parker reveals in graphic detail the hard choices she was forced to make in an ever-losing battle to preserve the health of her three children.*

You ask me what is poverty? Listen to me. Here I am, dirty, smelly, and with no "proper" underwear on and with the stench of my rotting teeth near you. I will tell you. Listen to me. Listen without pity. I cannot use your pity. Listen with understanding. Put yourself in my dirty, worn out, ill-fitting shoes, and hear me.

Poverty is getting up every morning from a dirt- and illness-stained mattress. The sheets have long since been used for diapers. Poverty is living in a smell that never leaves. This is a smell of urine, sour milk, and spoiling food sometimes joined with the strong smell of long-cooked onions. Onions are cheap. If you have smelled this smell, you did not know how it came. It is the smell of the outdoor privy. It is the smell of young children who cannot walk the long dark way in the night. It is the smell of the mattresses where years of "accidents" have happened. It is the smell of the milk which has gone sour because the refrigerator long has not worked, and it costs money to get it fixed. It is the smell of rotting garbage. I could bury it, but where is the shovel? Shovels cost money.

Poverty is being tired. I have always been tired. They told me at the hospital when the last baby came that I had chronic anemia caused from poor diet, a bad case of worms, and that I needed a corrective operation. I listened politely—the poor are always polite. The poor always listen. They don't say that there is no money for iron pills, or better food, or worm medicine. The idea of an operation is frightening and costs so much that, if I had dared, I would have laughed. Who takes care of my children? Recovery from an operation takes a long time. I have three children. When I left them with "Granny" the last time I had a job, I came home to find the baby covered with fly specks, and a diaper that had not been changed since I left. When the dried diaper came off, bits of my baby's flesh came with it. My other child was

289

playing with a sharp bit of broken glass, and my oldest was playing alone at the edge of a lake. I made twenty-two dollars a week, and a good nursery school costs twenty dollars a week for three children. I quit my job.

4   Poverty is dirt. You say in your clean clothes coming from your clean house, "Anybody can be clean." Let me explain about housekeeping with no money. For breakfast I give my children grits with no oleo or cornbread without eggs and oleo. This does not use up many dishes. What dishes there are, I wash in cold water and with no soap. Even the cheapest soap has to be saved for the baby's diapers. Look at my hands, so cracked and red. Once I saved for two months to buy a jar of Vaseline for my hands and the baby's diaper rash. When I had saved enough, I went to buy it and the price had gone up two cents. The baby and I suffered on. I have to decide every day if I can bear to put my cracked, sore hands into the cold water and strong soap. But you ask, why not hot water? Fuel costs money. If you have a wood fire it costs money. If you burn electricity, it costs money. Hot water is a luxury. I do not have luxuries. I know you will be surprised when I tell you how young I am. I look so much older. My back has been bent over the wash tubs every day for so long, I cannot remember when I ever did anything else. Every night I wash every stitch my school age child has on and just hope her clothes will be dry by morning.

5   Poverty is staying up all night on cold nights to watch the fire, knowing one spark on the newspaper covering the walls means your sleeping children die in flames. In summer poverty is watching gnats and flies devour your baby's tears when he cries. The screens are torn and you pay so little rent you know they will never be fixed. Poverty means insects in your food, in your nose, in your eyes, and crawling over you when you sleep. Poverty is hoping it never rains because diapers won't dry when it rains and soon you are using newspapers. Poverty is seeing your children forever with runny noses. Paper handkerchiefs cost money and all your rags you need for other things. Even more costly are antihistamines. Poverty is cooking without food and cleaning without soap.

6   Poverty is asking for help. Have you ever had to ask for help, knowing your children will suffer unless you get it? Think about asking for a loan from a relative, if this is the only way you can imagine asking for help. I will tell you how it feels. You find out where the office is that you are supposed to visit. You circle that block four or five times. Thinking of your children, you go in. Everyone is very busy. Finally, someone comes out and you tell her that you need help. That never is the person you need to see. You go see another person, and after spilling the whole shame of your poverty all over the desk between you, you find that this isn't the right office after all—you must repeat the whole process, and it never is any easier at the next place.

You have asked for help, and after all it has a cost. You are again   7
told to wait. You are told why, but you don't really hear because of the
red cloud of shame and the rising black cloud of despair.

Poverty is remembering. It is remembering quitting school in jun-   8
ior high because "nice" children had been so cruel about my clothes
and my smell. The attendance officer came. My mother told him I was
pregnant. I wasn't, but she thought that I could get a job and help out. I
had jobs off and on, but never long enough to learn anything. Mostly I
remember being married. I was so young then. I am still young. For a
time, we had all the things you have. There was a little house in another town, with hot water and everything. Then my husband lost his
job. There was unemployment insurance for a while and what few jobs
I could get. Soon, all our nice things were repossessed and we moved
back here. I was pregnant then. This house didn't look so bad when we
first moved in. Every week it gets worse. Nothing is ever fixed. We now
had no money. There were a few odd jobs for my husband, but everything went for food then, as it does now. I don't know how we lived
through three years and three babies, but we did. I'll tell you something, after the last baby I destroyed my marriage. It had been a good
one, but could you keep on bringing children in this dirt? Did you ever
think how much it costs for any kind of birth control? I knew my husband was leaving the day he left, but there were no good-bys between
us. I hope he has been able to climb out of this mess somewhere. He
never could hope with us to drag him down.

That's when I asked for help. When I got it, you know how much it   9
was? It was, and is, seventy-eight dollars a month for the four of us; that
is all I ever can get. Now you know why there is no soap, no needles
and thread, no hot water, no aspirin, no worm medicine, no hand
cream, no shampoo. None of these things forever and ever and ever. So
that you can see clearly, I pay twenty dollars a month rent, and most of
the rest goes for food. For grits and cornmeal, and rice and milk and
beans. I try my best to use only the minimum electricity. If I use more,
there is that much less for food.

Poverty is looking into a black future. Your children won't play   10
with my boys. They will turn to other boys who steal to get what they
want. I can already see them behind the bars of their prison instead of
behind the bars of my poverty. Or they will turn to the freedom of alcohol or drugs, and find themselves enslaved. And my daughter? At best,
there is for her a life like mine.

But you say to me, there are schools. Yes, there are schools. My chil-   11
dren have no extra books, no magazines, no extra pencils, or crayons,
or paper and the most important of all, they do not have health. They
have worms, they have infections, they have pink-eye all summer.
They do not sleep well on the floor, or with me in my one bed. They do
not suffer from hunger, my seventy-eight dollars keeps us alive, but

they do suffer from malnutrition. Oh yes, I do remember what I was taught about health in school. It doesn't do much good. In some places there is a surplus commodities program. Not here. The county said it cost too much. There is a school lunch program. But I have two children who will already be damaged by the time they get to school.

12   But, you say to me, there are health clinics. Yes, there are health clinics and they are in the towns. I live out here eight miles from town. I can walk that far (even if it is sixteen miles both ways), but can my little children? My neighbor will take me when he goes; but he expects to get paid, *one way or another.* I bet you know my neighbor. He is that large man who spends his time at the gas station, the barbershop, and the corner store complaining about the government spending money on the immoral mothers of illegitimate children.

13   Poverty is an acid that drips on pride until all pride is worn away. Poverty is a chisel that chips on honor until honor is worn away. Some of you say that you would do *something* in my situation, and maybe you would, for the first week or the first month, but for year after year after year?

14   Even the poor can dream. A dream of a time when there is money. Money for the right kinds of food, for worm medicine, for iron pills, for toothbrushes, for hand cream, for a hammer and nails and a bit of screening, for a shovel, for a bit of paint, for some sheeting, for needles and thread. Money to pay *in money* for a trip to town. And, oh, money for hot water and money for soap. A dream of when asking for help does not eat away the last bit of pride. When the office you visit is as nice as the offices of other governmental agencies, when there are enough workers to help you quickly, when workers do not quit in defeat and despair. When you have to tell your story to only one person, and that person can send you for other help and you don't have to prove your poverty over and over again.

15   I have come out of my despair to tell you this. Remember I did not come from another place or another time. Others like me are all around you. Look at us with an angry heart, anger that will help you help me. Anger that will let you tell of me. The poor are always silent. Can you be silent too?

✦ *Evaluating the Text*

1. What hard choices confront Parker when she tries to decide whether she should work and send her three children to nursery school or leave them with her mother?

2. What are the obstacles Parker faces in simply trying to keep her three children clean and fed? What trade-offs is she constantly forced to consider because she does not have enough money?

3. Explain why being poor and knowing your children will suffer if you do not get help from state or government agencies is a source of shame and humiliation. What does Parker mean when she says the poor are very polite and good listeners? Why is this so?

4. How does Parker answer critics who suggest how she might improve her situation? For example, what does she reveal about the amount of money she receives from public relief, what it will buy, the opportunities offered by public schools, food give-away programs, school-lunch programs, and health clinics? How, in each case, does she answer the objections that well-meaning people might raise?

5. What damaging consequences for her children does Parker foresee because of her inability to help them in the present?

6. What evidence does Parker offer to illustrate that being poor and a woman means that you are in constant danger of being exploited by men?

✦ Exploring Different Perspectives

1. Compare the circumstances Parker is in with those of the family in Mahdokht Kashkuli's "The Button." How are their circumstances very similar but their reactions quite different?

2. What different set of cultural dynamics might explain the choices made by Antonio in "The Lords of Creation" when compared with those facing Parker?

✦ Extending Viewpoints Through Writing

1. How did reading this article change preconceptions you may have had about the poor?

2. If you or anyone you know ever had to rely on public assistance such as welfare, unemployment compensation, or disability compensation, were the experiences similar to or different from those described by Parker? Are there any details that Parker does not mention that you could add?

3. To discover what you really value, consider the following hypothetical situation. You can only save one item from a raging fire. What would you save and why?

Mahdokht Kashkuli

The Button

◆

Mahdokht Kashkuli was born in 1950 in Teheran, Iran. She was married at age fourteen and, unlike similar marriages, hers did not prevent her from pursuing an education. She succeeded in obtaining her bachelor of arts in performing literature from Teheran University. By 1982 she had completed two master's degrees, one in library science and one in linguistics, and a doctorate in the language, culture, and religion of ancient Iran from the same university. She started her career first as a researcher for Iranian Educational Television from 1975 to 1985 and then as a professor of performing literature at Teheran University. Her short stories, including "The Fable of Rain in Iran," "The Fable of Creation in Iran," "Our Customs, Our Share," "The Pearl and the Moon," and "Tears and Water," have won her national recognition. She is presently working on a novel. "The Button," translated by Soraya Sullivan, was first published in the summer of 1978 in the periodical Arash. *This short story explores the heartbreaking consequences of a family's poverty in contemporary Iran.*

Iran, known as Persia until 1935, is an Islamic republic south of Russia and northeast of Saudi Arabia. Shiite Islam has been the state religion since the 1500s. Iran has the largest population of Shiite Moslems in the world. The Qur'an (Koran), the scripture of the Moslems, is made up of revelations delivered to Mohammed by the Angel Gabriel and also includes revelations to other prophets (Adam, Noah, Abraham, Isaac, Jacob, Joseph, Moses, and Jesus). The discovery of oil in Iran in the early 1900s made the country the object of British and Russian attempts at domination. Between 1925 and 1979, Iran was ruled by the Shahs (father and son), whose regime was supported by the United States, until Muhammad Reza Shah Pahlevi was ousted by popular opposition and replaced by the aged Moslem leader Ayatollah Ruhollah Khomeini. Since this time, the clergy (Mullahs) have carried out a conservative and fundamentalist interpretation of Islam. In 1979, Iranian militants seized the U.S. embassy in Teheran and held the occupants hostage until a negotiated agreement freed them in 1981. Concurrently, a full-scale border war with Iraq began in 1980 and ended eight years later, with casualties estimated at 1 million. In June 1989, Khomeini died, four months after exhorting the Moslem world to assassinate British author Salman Rushdie for writing The Satanic Verses *(1988), a novel perceived as blasphemous to Islam. Hashemi Rafsanjani first came to power as president in 1989 and, despite opposition from fundamentalist clerics, was reelected in June 1993.*

My sister was perched in the doorway, sobbing bitterly; her curly, russet hair was stuck to her sweaty forehead. My mother was doing her wash by the pond, paying no attention to my sister's sobs or my father's shouts, "Hurry up Reza! Move it!" I was holding on to the edge of the mantle shelf tightly, wishing that my hand would remain glued there permanently. It was only a few nights ago that I had heard, with my own ears, my father's voice whispering to my mother, "Woman, stop grumbling! God knows that my heart is aching too, but we don't have a choice. I can't even provide them with bread. What else can I do? This way, we'll have one less mouth to feed." I had cocked my ears to hear who that "one less mouth to feed" was. I remained frozen, holding my breath for a few minutes; then I heard my father say, "Reza is the naughtiest of all; the most restless. Akbar and Asghar are more tame, and we can't send the girls away. It's not wise." Suddenly a dry cough erupted from my mouth. My father called out, "Reza! Reza! Are you awake?" I did not answer him. He fell silent, and then my mother's snorts followed the awkward silence. My father went on, "Woman, who said the orphanage is a bad place? They teach the kids, they feed them, they clothe them. At least this one will have a chance to live a good life." My mother's snorts stopped. She groaned, "I don't know. I don't know anything. Just do what you think is best." And then there was silence.

Why are they going to make me the "one less mouth to feed"? What is an orphanage? I wish I hadn't nibbled the bread on my way home from the bakery; I wish I hadn't quarreled with Asghar; I wish I hadn't messed around with my mother's yarn, as if it were a ball; I wish I hadn't pulled the bottle out of Kobra's mouth, and drunk her milk; I wish I could stay still, like the mannequin in the clothing store at the corner. Then they wouldn't make me the "one less mouth to feed." My pillow was soaked with tears.

I ran outside with puffy eyes the next morning. Ahmad was standing at the other end of the alley, keeping watch for Husain so he could pick a fight with him. I yelled, "Ahmad, Ahmad! What's an orphanage?" Keeping his eyes still on the door to Husain's house, Ahmad said, "It's a place where they put up poor people's children." "Have you been there?" I asked. He shouted indignantly, "Listen to this goddamn wretch! You can't be nice to anyone these days!" I ran back to the house, scared. If Ahmad hadn't been waiting for Husain, he surely would have beaten me up.

My father's screams shot up again, "Are you deaf? Hurry up, it's late!" I released my grip on the shelf and went down the stairs. The saltiness of my tears burned my face. My father said, "What's wrong? Why are you crying? Come, my boy! Come wash your face!" Then he took my hand and led me to the pond and splashed a handful of the murky water on my face. He wiped my face with his coat lining. I became uneasy. My father seldom showed signs of affection; I suspected that he was being affectionate because he had decided to make me the "one less mouth to feed." We walked towards the door. He pulled aside the old cotton rug hanging before the door with his bony hands. Then he said, in a tone as if he were talking to himself, "One thousand . . . God knows, I had to pull a thousand strings before they agreed to admit you."

5   I asked, while I kept my head down, "Why?" My father screamed angrily, "He asks why again! Because!" I lowered my head. My eyes met his shoes. They were strangely crooked and worn out; maybe he had them on wrong. . . . The lower part of his long underwear showed from beneath his pants. He was wearing a belt to hold his loose pants up, and they creased like my mother's skirt. "I'm telling you, Reza, a thousand strings," he repeated. "You must behave when you get there." I didn't look at him but said grudgingly, "I don't want to behave!"

6   He threw a darting glance at me and raved, his hand rising to cuff me on the back of the neck but he changed his mind and said instead, "They'll teach you how to behave yourself." Indignantly I said, "I don't want to go to an orphanage, and if you take me there, I'll run away." I pulled my hand out of his quickly and ran ahead, knowing that he'd hit me this time. But he didn't. He only said, "You think they admit everyone? I've been running around for a year, resorting to everyone I know." I said, "Dad, I don't want to go to the orphanage. They keep poor children there." "What, do you think you are, rich?" my father said. "Listen to him use words bigger than his mouth!" And he broke out laughing. When he laughed I saw his gold teeth. There were two of them. I thought to myself, "What does it take to be rich? My father has gold teeth, my mother has gold teeth, and my brother has a fountain pen." I looked at his face. He wasn't laughing anymore; his face had turned gray. I said spontaneously, "Dad, is the landlord rich?" He didn't hear me, or it seemed he didn't, and said absentmindedly, "What?" I said, "Nothing."

7   I thought about the landlord. He sends his oldest son or his young daughter to collect the rent two weeks before the rent is due. His oldest son enters my father's shop and stands in the front of the mirror, scrutinizing himself, resting one hand on his waist. My father rushes to him and says, "Do you want a haircut?" The landlord's son responds, "No. You just gave me one on Thursday." My father says politely, "What can I do for you, then?" The landlord's son says, "Is the rent ready?" My father answers, "Give me a few more days. Tell Haji Agha I'll pay before the due date." And the next day his young daughter shows up in the shop. She is so small that she can hardly see herself in the mirror. She holds her veil tightly under her chin with those tiny, delicate hands, and says, "Hello!" My father smiles and says, "Hello, cutie pie! What can I do for you?" The girl laughs cheerfully and says, "My father sent me after the rent. If it's ready, give it to me." My father picks a sugar

cube out of the sugar bowl, puts it gently in her palm, and says, "Tell Haji Agha, fine!"

We reached the intersection. My father held my hand in his tightly   8
and stopped to look around. We then crossed the street. He was mumbling to himself, "The damn thing is so far away. . . ."

I felt sick. I said, "Wait a minute!" He eyed me curiously and said,   9
"Why, what's wrong?" I said, "I'm tired; I don't want to go to the orphanage." He mimicked me, pursing his lips, and said, "You don't understand! You were always dumb, dense!"

I remembered that my father was always unhappy with me, al-   10
though I swept the shop every day and watered the China roses he had planted in front of the shop. I would take my shirt off on hot summer afternoons and jump in the brook with my underpants. The elastic of my pants was always loose and I always tried to tie it into a knot, never succeeding to make it tight enough to stay. In the brook, I held my pants with one hand while I watered the China roses with a small bowl. It felt nice and cool there. Flies would gather around my shoulders and arms. Grandmother used to say, "God made flies out of wax." But I didn't understand why they didn't melt in the hot sun; they flew off my body and landed on the China rose flowers and I shook the branches with my bowl to disperse them. The flowers were my father's and no fly was allowed to sit on them. In spite of all my efforts, my father was always unhappy with me; he was unhappy with my mother, with my sisters and brothers, with the landlord, and with the neighbors. But he was happy with one person: God. He would sigh, tap himself hard on the forehead, and say, "Thank God!"

I said to him one day, "Why are you thanking God, Dad?" Sud-   11
denly, he hit me in the mouth with the back of his hand. My upper lip swelled and my mouth tasted bloody. I was used to the taste of blood because whenever I bled in the nose, I tasted blood in my mouth. I covered my mouth, walked to the garden and spat in the dirt. I looked at the bubbles on my spittle, tapped myself on the forehead and said, "Thank God!" Then I picked up a piece of watermelon skin lying on the brook and smacked it on the head of a yellow dog that always used to nap by the electric post. The yellow dog only opened its eyes, looked at me indifferently, and shut its eyes again, thanking God, perhaps.

We passed another street before we got to the bus station. A few   12
people were waiting in line; one of them was sitting at the edge of the brook. My father took my hand and led me to the front of the bus line. Someone said, "This is not the end of the line, old man!" I only looked at my father.

He said to me, "Ignore him. Just stay right here!" The bus came and   13
my father pushed me towards it. I tore my feet off the ground and jumped on the coach-stop, feeling as if I were floating in the air. Someone said, "Old man, the end of the line is on the other side! Look how

people give you a headache on a Monday morning!" My father didn't hear him; he pushed me forward. I was stuck between a seat and the handle bar. . . . So, today is Monday. . . . Every week on Monday my mother does her wash. The clothesline spread around the entire yard. I liked the smell of damp clothes. In spite of my mother's curses, I liked cupping my hands underneath the dripping clothes so that the water that dripped could tickle my palms. Every Monday we had yogurt soup for lunch. My brother and I would take a bowl to the neighborhood dairy store to buy yogurt. On the way back, we took turns licking the surface of the yogurt. When we handed the bowl to my mother, she would scream at us and beat the first one of us she could get her hands on. . . . I felt depressed. I wished I could jump out the window.

14   The bus stopped at a station and we got off. My father walked ahead of me while I dragged my feet along behind him.

15   He waited for me to catch up, then he said, "Move it! He walks like a corpse. Hurry up, it's late!" I stopped momentarily and said, "Dad, I don't want to go. I don't want to go to the orphanage." My father froze in his spot. He said incredulously, "What did you say? You think you know what's good for you? Don't you want to become a decent human being some day? They have rooms, there. They have food, and they'll teach you everything you need to learn to get a decent job." I sobbed, "To hell with anyone who has a decent job. To hell with decent jobs. I don't want one! I like staying home. I like playing with Asghar and Akbar. I want to sell roasted corn with the kids from the neighborhood in the summer. I want to help you out in the shop. I don't want to go."

16   My father sprang towards me, but suddenly retreated and became affectionate. He said, "Let's go, good boy! We're almost there." I felt sorry for him because every time he was kind he looked miserable. My father was walking ahead of me and I was following him, dragging my feet on the street like that yellow dog. On the next street, we stopped in front of a big metal door. A chair was placed inside the door to keep it ajar. A man was sitting on the chair, playing with a ring of prayer beads. He had on a navy blue coat with metal buttons. His eyes were half-closed and his mouth was open. His cheeks were puffy, as if he had a toothache. My father greeted him and said, "Mr. Guard!" The man opened his eyes. Strands of blood ran through the white of his eyes. He said with a gloomy voice, "What is it, what do you want?" My father thrust his hand in both his pockets, took out an envelope and extended it toward the guard with both hands. The man looked at my father, then threw a threatening glance at me. He yawned, stared at the envelope for a while (I didn't believe he could read), shook his head, coughed, and said, "They won't leave you alone; one leaves, another comes!" Then he pushed the door with the tip of his shoes. The door opened just enough to let me in.

After my father walked through the doorway behind me, the guard gave him the envelope and said, "The first door!" My father was walking fast, and when he opened the hallway door, my heart started beating violently and I started to cry. He said, "My boy, my sweet Reza, this is a nice place. The people here are nice, the kids are all your own age. . . ." 17

He didn't finish his sentence. He pushed on the door. The door opened and I saw a woman inside the room. I wished she were my mother, but she was heavier than my mother, with a deep vertical wrinkle between her eyebrows. She wore a blue uniform and her hair was a bleached blonde. 18

My father pushed me further in and said, "Greet her, Reza! Greet her!" I didn't feel like greeting anyone. 19

My father handed the woman the envelope. She opened it, pulled the letter out halfway, and started reading it. Then she turned to my father and said, "Go to the office so they can complete his file." 20

My father leaped and ran out the door. Then, as though he had remembered something, he returned and stood in front of the door, rubbing his hand on the wood frame of the door. He raised one hand to tap on his forehead and say, "Thank God," but stopped, rubbed his forehead gently and sighed. His eyes were as moist and shiny as the eyes of the yellow dog hanging around his shop. Her head still lowered on the letter, the woman said, "Go, old man! What are you waiting for? Go to the office!" Father took a few steps backwards, then tore himself from the door and disappeared into the corridor. 21

The woman looked at me, then turned her gaze toward the window and fixed it there. While she had her back to me, she said, "Don't cry, boy! Please don't, I'm not in the mood!" Then she turned around and put her hands on my shoulders. Her hands were as heavy as my mother's but not as warm. She took my hand and walked me toward the door. We passed one corridor, and entered another. Then we entered a room, then another corridor and another room. There were a few people in the room. One was sitting in the doorway, whistling; one was leaning against the desk; one was sitting in a chair writing something. Although the room was furnished with chairs and desks, it was not warm. The woman said, "Say hello to these people!" I looked at her but didn't say anything. I didn't feel like talking to them. I didn't hear what they said to each other, either. I only wanted to sit still and look at them. We left that room and went into another. There was another woman there. I wished she were my mother. She was wearing a blue uniform and had a red scarf around her neck. I think she had a cold because she sniffled constantly. As soon as she saw me, she checked me out thoroughly and spoke with a nasal voice, "Is he new here? I don't know where we're going to put him." She then opened a closet, took out a uniform and said to me, "Take your jacket off and wear this!" 22

Then she continued, "Take your shirt off, too. How long has it been since your last shower?" I didn't answer. Her words hit my ears and bounced right off. She went toward the closet again and asked, "Are you done?" I looked around and then looked at myself, my eyes becoming fixed on my jacket. It had only one button. The button had belonged to my mother's jacket before she used it to replace my missing button. The woman's voice went on, "Quit stalling, boy! Hurry up, I have tons of work to do!"

23   I put my hand on the button and pulled it out, then hid it in my palm. The woman said, "Are you done?" I said, "Yes!"

24   I thrust the button in my uniform pocket and wiped my tears with the back of my hand.

✦ Evaluating the Text

1. Of what imagined crimes does the narrator accuse himself that might explain why he is the one to be sent to an orphanage instead of one of his three siblings?

2. How would you characterize the boy's relationship with his father? In your view, what has caused the father to choose him to be the one out of his four children to be sent to an orphanage?

3. How does Reza's attitude toward the button reveal his feelings and emotions?

✦ Exploring Different Perspectives

1. Discuss this story in terms of how parents who live in poverty (see "What Is Poverty?") have to face hard choices, find themselves in "no-win" situations, and are forced to make sacrifices.

2. How do both Mahdokht Kashkuli's "The Button" and Mary Crow Dog's "Civilize Them with a Stick" deal with the issue of what happens to children who are handed over to the state to raise?

✦ Extending Viewpoints Through Writing

1. What insight does this story provide into the prevailing economic and social conditions in modern Iranian society?

2. Write about one of your grandparents or parents through an object you connect with him or her. Under what circumstances did you first come across this object? What associations connect this object with your parent or grandparent?

Alonso Salazar

The Lords of Creation

◆

Alonso Salazar is a leading Colombian journalist and social scientist. Salazar journeyed into the jails, hospitals, and shantytowns of Medellín, Colombia's second largest city and drug capital, to interview teenage contract killers, their families, priests, and self-defense vigilantes. His book, Born to Die in Medellín *(1990), provides a graphic exploration of one of the most violent societies in the world. "The Lords of Creation," translated by Nick Caistor, taken from this book, provides riveting insight into the world of Medellín's youth gangs.*

The only South American country with both Pacific and Caribbean coastlines, the republic of Colombia is bordered by Panama to the northwest, Venezuela to the northeast, Ecuador and Peru to the south, and Brazil to the southeast. After being conquered by the Spanish in the 1530s Colombia's struggle for independence from Spain began in 1810, lasted nine years, and ended with the victory of Simón Bolívar in 1819. From its inception, the republic of New Granada, as it was then called (which originally included Venezuela, Ecuador, and Panama) was torn by the opposition between federalist liberals and centralist conservatives. As many as 100,000 people were killed in a civil war that raged from 1899 to 1903. Civil war again erupted in 1948, and orderly government was restored as a result of compromise between liberals and conservatives in 1958. Widespread poverty and a political climate destabilized by guerilla warfare in urban areas led to a precarious economy ostensibly dependent on coffee, its major legal crop, but even more dependent on the illegal growth and trafficking in marijuana and cocaine. After several rounds of elections, Ernesto Samper was elected president in August 1994 for a four-year term.

Silhouetted against the full moon, the shape of a headless cat strung up by its paws. Its blood has been collected in a bowl on the floor. Only a few drops continue to fall. As each one hits the bowl it makes tiny ripples, which grow until the whole surface seems full of tossing waves. Waves that shake to the noise of heavy rock being played at full blast. The cat's head is in the corner, its luminous green eyes staring sightlessly. Fifteen people are taking part in the silent ritual. The city is spread below them.

Warm blood is mixed with wine in a glass. The blood of a cat that climbs walls, leaps nonchalantly from fence to fence, walks on the silent

1

2

301

pads of its paws across rooftops, vanishes effortlessly into the shadows of night. Cat's blood, full of the urge to pounce unerringly on its prey. Blood that conjures up strange energies, that speeds the brain.

3   Antonio recalls in a jumble of images the moment of his own initiation into one of the teenage gangs in a neighbourhood on the hills of north-east Medellín. In his feverish dreams as he fights for life, he sees himself on the streets again. Strange shapes appear in the sea of city lights. They raise the cup to seal their pact. There is no need for words, they all know what they are committing themselves to, what the laws are, the rewards and the punishment. From now on they will be all for one and one for all, they will be as one. They'll be the lords of creation.

4   But now Antonio is in the San Rafael Ward of the Saint Vincent de Paul hospital. A military ward, full of the wounded and the dying, the victims of an unequal war waged day and night along undefined fronts on the streets of Medellín. One Tuesday, three months earlier, Antonio was blasted with a shotgun as he boarded a bus in his neighbourhood. The shot perforated his stomach, leaving him hovering between life and death. Although only twenty, Antonio has often faced death, but has never felt it so close to him. He knows, even though he won't admit it, that he's not going to make it. He has a skinny body, a face drained of colour, dark eyes sunk in huge sockets. He begins to tell me his life story in a calm voice, searching inside himself, as if taking stock for reasons of his own.

Antonio

5   When I was a kid I used to get a bit of money using a home-made pistol. Then Lunar and Papucho—they're both dead now—let me have proper guns, so I started to steal and kill for real. You get violent because there are a lot of guys who want to tell you what to do, to take you over, just because you're a kid. You've got to keep your wits about you, to spread your own wings. That's what I did, and off I flew; anybody who got in my way paid for it.

6   I learned that lesson from my family. From the old woman, who's tough as nails. She's with me whatever I do. She might not look much, but she's always on my side. The only regret I have in quitting this earth is leaving her on her own. To know she might be all alone in her old age. She's fought hard all her life, and she doesn't deserve that.

7   My old man died about 14 years ago. He was a hard case too, and taught me a lot, but he was always at the bottle, and left us in the lurch. That was why I had to fend for myself, to help my ma and my brothers and sisters. That's how I started in a gang—but also because it was something inside me, I was born with this violent streak.

8   Lunar, the leader of the gang, was only a teenager but he was tough all right. He'd been in the business for years already. He lived in

Bello for a while and knew the people from Los Monjes. He learned a lot from them, so when he came to live here he started up his own gang. He had a birthmark or *lunar* on his cheek, that's how he got the nickname. It was thanks to him and Papucho, the other leader, that I learned how to do things properly.

I'll never forget the first time I had to kill someone. I had already   9
shot a few people, but I'd never seen death close up. It was in Copaca-bana, a small place near Medellín. We were breaking into a farmhouse one morning when the watchman suddenly appeared out of nowhere. I was behind a wall, he ran in front of me, I looked up and was so star-tled I emptied my revolver into him. He was stone dead. That was tough, I won't lie, it was tough for me to take. For two weeks I couldn't eat a thing because I saw his face even in my food . . . but after that it got easy. You learn to kill without it disturbing your sleep.

Now it's me who's the gang leader. Papucho was killed by the guys   10
up on the hill there. They set a trap for him and he fell for it. They asked him to do a job for them, then shot him to pieces. A friend of his was behind it, who'd sold out. Lunar made me second-in-command be-cause we understood each other almost without speaking —we didn't need words.

Lunar didn't last much longer; he was never one to back down   11
from a fight, never a chicken. He really enjoyed life; he always said we were all playing extra time anyway. And he was enjoying himself when he died: he was at a dance about three blocks down the hill when they shot him three times in the back. He was on his own because he reck-oned there were no skunks down there. The kid who shot him died al-most before he could blink. We tracked him down that same night, and sent him on his trip to the stars.

After Lunar's death another wise guy thought he'd take over the   12
gang. I had to get tough and show him who was boss. For being such a smart ass now he's pushing up the dirt as well. It's me who gives the orders round here, I say what we do and don't do. There were about fifty of us to begin with, but a lot of them have been killed or put inside, and others have grassed. There's only twenty of us real hard cases left. They're all teenagers, between 15 and 18. I'm the oldest. A lot get killed or caught, but more always want to join, to get some action.

Whenever anyone wants to join I ask around: 'Who is this kid? Can   13
I trust him?' Then I decide if he can join or not. They're all kids who see things as they are; they know they won't get anywhere by working or studying, but if they join us they'll have ready money. They join be-cause they want to, not because we force them. We don't tell anybody they have to. Not all of them are really poor, some do it for their fami-lies, others because they want to live in style.

Before we finally choose someone we give him a test: to take some-   14
thing somewhere, to carry guns and to keep them hidden. Then finally

we give them a job to do. If the kid shows he can do it, then he's one of us. But if he ever grasses on us, if he shoots his mouth off, if he gets out of line, then he's dead meat. Everyone understands that. Then again, we support each other all we can; 'If you haven't got something and I have, take it, friend—as a gift, not a loan.' We also help if someone's in trouble. We look after each other, but nobody can double-cross us.

15   We take good care of our guns, because they're hard to come by. The last kid I shot died because of that.

16   'Antonio, help me out will you brother? Lend me a gun for a job I have to do,' he said to me.

17   'I'll let you have this .38, but be sure you give it back tomorrow; you know the rules.'

18   I lent it to him because the kid had always been straight with us, but this time he wasn't. So I went to talk to him, and he came up with a really strange excuse. He said the law had taken it from him. I gave him another two days, and when he didn't show up I passed the death sentence. He knew he was a marked man, so he didn't make any attempt to hide. It was easy for me.

19   The thing is, it's hard to find guns. You either have to shoot a guy to get his, or buy them, and a good weapon costs. We nearly always buy them from the police, and they sell us the ammo too. I've also bought grenades from a retired army guy. We've had T-55s, 32-shot mini-Uzis, 9mm Ingrands, but we usually use sawn-off shotguns, pistols and revolvers. We're all good shots.

20   We practise late at night, two, three in the morning, in some woods over at Rionegro. We set up a line of bottles and fire at them. I smash the lot. You have to keep a steady hand when you're on a job, you only have one chance to kill someone, you can't afford to miss. You only have a few seconds so you have to know what you're doing: if the dummy doesn't die, you could. You have to know how to handle your weapon, to shoot straight, and how to make your get-away. We learn a lot from films. We get videos of people like Chuck Norris, Black Cobra, Commando, or Stallone, and watch how they handle their weapons, how they cover each other, how they get away. We watch the films and discuss tactics.

21   We learn to ride motor bikes on the hills round here. They're all souped up, really quick. Most of them are stolen; we buy papers for them for 20,000 pesos[1] down at the traffic police. Our territory is from the bus terminal down to the school. People who don't mess with us have no problems, but anyone who tries to muscle in either gets out or dies. We help the people in our neighbourhood, they come to us and say: 'we've got nothing to eat,' so we help them and keep them happy. And when we've done a job that pays well, we make sure they get some. We look after them so that they're on our side. Whenever some-

[1] £1 = 545 pesos (1990).

one tries to move in on our territory, I personally go and kneecap them as a warning they should never come back.

Lots of kids in the neighbourhood want to be in a gang. All I tell them is if that's what they want to do they have to be serious about it, but I don't force them to join. Most of them start by stealing cars, then they save up to buy a shotgun, which is the cheapest weapon around. We give them cartridges so they can get started.   22

I reckon I've killed 13 people. That's 13 I've killed personally, I don't count those we've shot when we're out as a gang. If I die now, I'll die happy. Killing is our business really, we do other jobs, but mostly we're hired to kill people.   23

People from all sorts of places contract us: from Bellavista jail, from El Poblado, from Itagüí. People who don't want to show their faces, and take you on to get rid of their problem for them. I try to work out whether our client means business, if he can pay us. We charge according to who we have to hit: if he's important, we charge more. We're putting our lives, our freedom, our guns on the line. If we have to leave the city to deal with some big shot, our price is anything up to three million. Here in Medellín the lowest we go is half a million.   24

We don't care who we have to give it to, we know it has to be done, that's all there is to it. Whoever it may be: I have no allegiances. I'll drive the bike and gun anyone down myself, no problem. Sometimes we don't even know who it is we have to kill. You hear later who the hit was, from the news on the radio. It's all the same to us, we've done our job, that's all.   25

Whenever I have to kill someone, all I think is: too bad for him he crossed my path. If their back is towards me, I call out, so I can make sure I've got the right guy, and when he turns round, I give it to him. I don't worry about it, I don't worry about running into the law, or that things will go wrong, nothing like that. I only hope I don't kill a woman or a child in a shoot-out. If I'm going to kill, there has to be a reason for it.   26

Once we went out to a small town to deal with a local councillor. We don't usually know who is giving us the contract, but in this case it was more or less direct contact, and we realised that the guy who wanted him dead was the leader of a political party. We kept well away from him after that, because you can be the ones who end up paying. They can easily have you rubbed out as well to get rid of witnesses. We made a million on that job.   27

The week before, we went to the town to see the lie of the land. We were shown the client, we took a look at where the police were, worked out how to get out afterwards. On the Saturday, I went back with a girlfriend. She was carrying the weapon—a submachine gun—in her bag. We took a room in the best hotel, pretending we were a honeymoon couple. We took our time checking out the town, making sure nothing could go wrong.   28

29   On the Sunday, two of the gang stole a car in Medellín, and kept the owner in a room in Guayaquil until the job was done. One of them drove to the town and parked where we'd agreed, right on time. The councillor always liked to have a coffee in a corner bar after his meetings. My girlfriend showed up with the gun around two in the afternoon. I took it and waited for the action. Waiting like that really gets you down. You get real nervous. I've found a trick which always helps me: I get a bullet, take out the lead, and pour the gunpowder into a hot black coffee. I drink the lot, and that steadies my nerves.

30   At ten to six I left the hotel and sat waiting in the bar. It was a hot evening, and there were a lot of people on the street. I saw our car arrive and park a few metres away. The target came in a couple of minutes later. On the dot as promised.

31   It was beginning to get dark, which is always useful. I took another good look round to make sure there was nothing unusual going on, then paid for my drink. When the waiter was giving me my change, I pulled out the submachine gun and started firing. Everybody hit the floor. When something like that happens in a small town, they all stay well out of it, no one is expecting it. I went over and put a final bullet in him, because some of these guys are really tough and you have to make sure of your money. It was all over in seconds. While I had been firing, they had started the car, so I walked to it as calm as could be, and got in. We made sure we didn't drive too fast out of town. We made as if we were going out on the main highway, but then headed off down a side road. We drove for about a quarter of an hour, then left the car by the roadside. We walked for an hour, until we came to a safe house on a farm owned by a friend of the politician who had hired us. We caught a bus back to Medellín about five o'clock the next morning. They sent the gun back to us a few days later. Everything had been well planned and worked like clockwork.

32   That night we had a huge party. We'd already had the pay-off, so as the saying goes: 'the dead to their graves, the living to the dance.' It was like Christmas. We bought a pig, crates of beer and liquor, set up a sound system in the street, and gave it all we'd got 'til morning.

33   The bus struggles up the hill, along narrow twisting streets full of people and shops. From this main road you have to walk another two blocks up a narrow alley-way, then climb a gully before you reach the Montoya family's house. The roof is made of corrugated iron and cardboard; the walls are not plastered, just painted with a blue wash. Red geraniums flower outside. The house is three tiny rooms. Posters of movie stars and rock musicians cover the walls. Lost in one corner under a layer of cobwebs is a small picture of the Virgin of El Carmen. A horseshoe and a piece of aloe vera hang over the front door to bring good luck.

Doña Azucena, Antonio's mother, is a small, thin woman. Her face   34
shows the marks of all she has been through in her life. Two children,
aged four and six, whom she had by her second husband, cling to her
legs. She works in a cafe in the centre of Medellín. A few years ago,
when she still had legs worth showing off, she worked in the Porteño
bar in Guayaquil. The kind of bar where men go to drink liquor and
pick up women. Doña Azucena takes some photos out of an old album
which show her in high heels, a mini skirt, and wearing bright scarlet
lipstick. She would never dream of showing them to her children. It
was in that bar, to the sound of music from Olimpo Cárdenas and Julio
Jaramillo, that her second husband fell in love with her. A much older
man, she lived with him for four years until one weekend, she never
knew why, he walked out and didn't come back. She didn't miss him,
because her older children had never got on with him, and because she
herself had lost all her affection for him.

Doña Azucena

In the bar there's a big picture of a man hanging from a branch. A   35
tiger is trying to climb the tree, there's a rattlesnake in the tree-top, and
under the branch is a pool full of crocodiles. I used to look at that picture and think my life was exactly like that. Wherever I've been, I've
lost out.

I can remember it like it was yesterday. I was at a rural school in Li-   36
borina, a beautiful part of the country. It was May, the month of the
Holy Virgin, and we were preparing to celebrate. Our teacher, who was
called Petronilla, asked me to pick some roses for the altar, and said I
should make sure to cut all the thorns off. I went down a path below
the school where there were some lovely rose bushes. I picked them
and sat down to snip the thorns off. Then I went back to the school and
gave them to the teacher. She took them, but a splinter got caught in her
finger, so suddenly she drew back her hand and slapped me across the
face. Without even thinking about it, I slashed at her with the knife, the
one I'd used to cut the roses. She was badly wounded, but they managed to save her life. That was the end of school for me.

I've always had a quick temper, I've never let anyone put anything   37
over on me. That's how my family was, that's how my children are. I
was born in Urrao, but we had to leave there when I was still little because of the political violence. My father, whose name was Antonio
too, was a die-hard Liberal, every weekend he'd go into town, get
drunk, and start shouting 'Up with the Liberals!' for everyone to hear.
As soon as the violence started, we began to get death threats.

Once my father and his brothers had to take on a bunch of Conser-   38
vative thugs who were terrorising the area. We knew they'd come up after us. So the men borrowed some shotguns and took up their positions

on a bit of a hill just below the house. When they saw the Conservatives arrive, they fired at them and they ran off.

39   That same evening Don Aquileo, a neighbour who was a Conservative too, but who got on well with us, came up to see us. He told us that down in town everyone was saying they'd get together and come up and finish us off. There'd already been other tremendous massacres in the countryside, so we decided to get out that same night and go to Liborina, where we had family. Later some Liberal guerrillas got organised in Urrao, led by Captain Franco. But that was after we left. We had a dreadful time there, I can remember passing lots of mutilated bodies by the roadsides, those are things you never forget.

40   A few years later, I was a teenager by then, we moved on to Chigorodó, in Urabá, because they said the land was fertile there. We began to clear a farm in the jungle, about two hours from the nearest town. That was where my mother María died. The climate killed her. The weather was impossible. Up there the heat is hellish, and it can rain the whole day long. It was a struggle to clear the jungle, but eventually we were able to plant bananas and maize.

41   The good times didn't last long. We'd just begun to harvest our crops, when the violence began there too. Not between Conservatives and Liberals, but just between people for no reason at all. There was a store where we all used to go at weekends to talk and drink. But soon people began to fight with machetes. The men got drunk and killed each other without ever knowing why, or rather, at the slightest excuse.

42   My brothers have always been difficult, they've fought with almost everyone. But above all they got into trouble with a family called García, who came from Dabeiba. There were about ten of them, all dangerous men. It was when they started threatening us that we decided to sell up and come to Medellín.

43   We settled in the Barrio Popular. We built a place up on this hill, just when people had started moving in. Soon everywhere was full of shacks. People who had lost their land in the country because of the violence, and had come to the city to escape.

44   I can remember the day when Don Polo was out laying the floor for his place. He'd come from Andes with his family. The police on horseback turned up, and wanted to take him away. We all used to help each other, to protect ourselves, so I went out and started to shout at them.

45   'You can't take him if you haven't got an arrest warrant.'

46   'You're not the law, you bitch, we are, and we know what we're doing,' one of them shouted back, pointing his rifle at me.

47   I was really angry by then, and I thought well, if I'm going to die then so be it, may God forgive me all my sins but this injustice shouldn't be allowed to happen. Other people began pouring out of their houses. Then a police car arrived. We were still arguing, and one of the police hit me with the butt of his rifle.

'Come on, it's you we're going to arrest for causing an obstruction,'   48
he said, pushing me into the car.

I began to kick out, and my neighbours all closed round the car,   49
saying: 'You've no right to take Doña Azucena.'

'Drive off,' the captain told his driver.   50

'Which way? D'you want me to kill all these people?'   51

They all crowded closer and closer round the car, and finally   52
pulled me out. The other policemen on horseback were shouting insults all the time. Then a young fellow hit one of them with a stick, and
they all fired at him. The rest of us ran off. They picked up his body and
left. They took him to the hospital, but he died. Things like that happened all the time, the police would come up to destroy our houses,
but we'd all stand firm. A lot of lives were lost. That's why we've never
liked the law, it seems they're always out to get the poor.

It was around that time that I married Diego Montoya. He was a   53
young man who had just moved to Medellín from Puerto Berrío. I went
with him against my family's wishes; they didn't like him because he
was black. We went to live with one of his sisters over in Santa Cruz.
For a few years it was good, he looked after me and remembered all the
little details—everything was fine. We had five children, almost one after the other: Claudia, Diego, Antonio, Orlando, and Nelly.

But gradually Diego went downhill. He became a tremendous   54
drinker and would give me almost nothing for the kids, so I had to go
and find work, first of all in houses over in Laureles, then in a bar in
Guayaquil. One day when I came back from work I found my eldest
daughter Claudia with her leg all bloody. Diego's sister's eldest son
had sliced her with a saw because she had picked up something he
was working with. I took my belt off, went to find the boy, and gave
him a good thrashing. His mother tried to defend him, so I started on
her too. When Diego came back later that night, I told him what had
happened. His sister went whining to him, and told him he should
teach me a lesson.

'He's not going to teach me any lesson, you do it if you want to,' I   55
told her.

'But he's your husband,' she replied.   56

'That he may be, but if I have to show him what's what, I will.'   57

Diego got really angry and left. By the time he returned I was in   58
bed, reading a magazine by candlelight.

'I'm leaving, thanks for everything. All your things are on the   59
table,' I told him.

I'd put his revolver and some money he'd given me on the table by   60
the bed. He didn't say a word, but got into bed. At about five in the
morning, he got up again. He stood there for a minute staring at me,
then went over to our daughter's bed, stroked her hair, gave her a kiss,
and began to cry.

61   'Wake up sweetheart, wake up so we can talk about it,' he said to me, shaking me gently by the shoulder.

62   'There's nothing for us to talk about. I've already given you back all your things, what more do I owe you?'

63   'Can't you wait 'til Saturday so I can sort things out?'

64   'When did you ever sort things out? All you do is make one promise after another, then spend every cent you earn on whores and booze.'

65   'Just wait, in the next few days I'm expecting a big note, I promise I'll hand it over to you,' he begged, and my heart softened.

66   'OK, let's see; if you love your children and want to stay with them, then buy us somewhere to live, that's the only condition. I'll give you all day today to think about it, if you don't come up with something by tonight, I'm off.'

67   He didn't come back to sleep that night, but the next day, Saturday, he arrived very early. He took me and the children to look at a plot of land in the Barrio Popular. We did the deal there and then, and the following week had already built a place. We've been living in this gully ever since.

68   This is where I brought up my children. Diego died 14 years ago, a few months after he had an accident that crippled him. While he was at home sick he told people's fortunes for them. He knew a lot. Just by looking at the palm of someone's hand he could tell what was wrong, what their illness was, if they had been smoking too much dope, if a woman had the evil eye on them. Then he'd give them a cure or take the spell off them. He learned from his father, who practised these things down in Puerto Berrío. I asked him to teach me, but he always said: 'You're too black-hearted, if you learned this, you'd use it to harm people.'

69   It's true that in some ways I can be hard. I wouldn't harm a soul, but if anyone crosses me, they're for it. That's what I've always taught my children, that they've got to make people respect them. They've got it in their blood, they were born as rebellious as me. My eldest worked for a while in the building trade, but then he fell in with some friends and began to go wrong. At first they dealt in marijuana, then they started with robberies. At the moment he's doing three years in Acacías, Meta, for assault.

70   Ever since he was little, Antonio's been the wildest of the lot. The same thing happened to him at school as me, although I've never told them my story. In his third year at primary school they had a teacher who used to punish them terribly, so one day Antonio and a friend waited for him outside the school and stabbed him with a knife. Since then, Antonio's been on the streets.

71   It was Diego, his older brother, who got him started in crime. Antonio was only eleven when he was sent to a remand home, in Floresta. He'd had a fight with a neighbour's boy, Doña Blanca's son, a kid's quarrel. But then Alberto, her older son, threatened to give him a hid-

ing. I spoke to them and said that if anyone was going to give him a
hiding it would be me. In return they insulted me, and that drove my
kids wild. Without my knowing it, Diego gave Antonio a gun.

'If you let that Alberto lay a finger on you, I'll give you another hid-   72
ing myself. You have to show you're a Montoya,' Diego told him.

One day soon after, I was making lunch when I heard some shots   73
and a terrific row outside. I ran out and saw Alberto lying on the pave-
ment. Antonio had shot him five times. Fortunately he didn't die, but
since then it's been war between our two families. Two of them have
died, and my sons have been wounded several times.

After Antonio got out of the remand home he studied plumbing   74
and electrics at the San José school. But that didn't last long, he was
soon back on the streets. A few days later I saw him with a couple of
boys who were a good bit older than him, Papucho and Lunar, both of
them dead now. They were the ones who sealed his fate. People began
to be afraid of them, grassed on them to the police, and they came looking for them.

All I can say is that he's been a good son to me. I've had to work in   75
bars all these years to earn enough to keep my family. It's hard for a
woman on her own. Antonio is the one who's helped me the most. He's
never drunk a lot, and whenever he's done a job he always brings
something back for the house.

I've been with him through thick and thin. Whenever he's inside I   76
always go and visit him. I've often had to struggle with the police, but
I've made sure they respect me as a woman. I've made a vow to the
Fallen Christ of Girardota to make sure my boy gets well quickly.
That's what I want, I want him to get well and go and find the coward
who shot him, things can't stay like this. None of my family is going to
feel safe with that fellow around.

Antonio knew they wanted to kill him, that's why he left home.   77
That Tuesday, he came up here in the morning and was chatting with
the girls, playing with the dog. I went down to the main street to buy
things for lunch. As I was coming back I saw two of the Capucho gang
on the corner. That scared me, but I walked past them calmly, as if I
hadn't even seen them.

'Antonio, get away from here, they're out to get you,' I told him   78
when I reached home.

'Don't worry, ma, the day I die I'll have my bags packed and ready,   79
but today isn't the day,' he said laughing, lying back on the bed.

In the afternoon he went round to his girlfriend Claudia's house   80
next door. He was still joking about, listening to music as if nothing
was wrong. At six I saw the others again, they were at the bottom of the
gully. They had their hands in their pockets, and were staring up our
way. The worst of it was that Antonio didn't have any protection. I
went and found him and told him what was going on.

81   'It looks bad out there, I think you should find some way to get away.'

82   'Cool it, ma, I'll be off in a minute. Go round to Gitano's place and tell him to bring a couple of guns up here, that there's going to be some action.'

83   I sneaked out the back way and went to find Gitano.

84   'Doña Azucena, he's not back from town, and anyway he hasn't got any guns either,' they told me.

85   When I told Antonio that Gitano wasn't around, he looked worried, but pretended everything was all right.

86   'I'm going over the wall at the back here,' he said. 'You two go out the front and act normal, while I get away.'

87   We went out and sat on the front porch to chat. The Capucho boys were still down at the bottom of the gully, so I relaxed a bit. But then 15 minutes later I got a call from the hospital.

88   'We have your boy Antonio Montoya here, he's in a bad way.'

89   In the three months since then I've been down there every afternoon between two and five, when you can visit them. Every week the hospital is full of wounded kids, they come and go, new ones take the place of those who get better, but Antonio is still there. I don't know how all this is going to end.

90   The priest went to give him confession yesterday, I've no idea what Antonio told him about his life. When the priest came out he greeted me very formally. 'Don't worry, he has repented and is at peace with God,' he told me. And that did bring me peace of mind. Even though I'm not much of a believer it's always better to know you're at peace with God.

Antonio

91   I'd like to be out on the streets of my neighbourhood again, that's my territory. I love walking down them. I've always got my wits about me of course, my eyes wide open and my gun in my pocket, because I've got as many enemies as friends. You never know where you might get shot from. A lot of people are after me, I've got a lot of admirers in other gangs. The law is also on my tail. If I get out of here, I'm going to be real careful.

92   There've always been gangs in our neighbourhood: the Nachos, the Montañeros, Loco Uribe's gang, the Calvos . . . and as the song says: 'this bed ain't big enough for everyone.' You have to be on the lookout, if you're not careful one of the other gangs muscles in and people start leaving you. You have to make sure of your territory, that's the main thing. The biggest war we ever had was with the Nachos, who were hired killers like us. When they first showed up we did nothing, but then they started throwing their weight around, upsetting people. Until

one day Martín, one of our gang, told them where to get off, and they shot him. That same night we went up to their place and taught them a lesson. Six of us went up there in groups of two: we met up on the street corner where they hung out, and took them completely by surprise. We shot two of them. They thought they were such tough guys they never even imagined anyone would come for them.

A few days later they came for us. We were waiting for them. I put   93
a handkerchief over my face, put on a baseball cap, and went out with my submachine gun. Others from the gang were covering me, watching what would happen.

'We want peace, not war,' one of the Nachos shouted.   94

'We don't want peace, what we want is war,' Lunar shouted back,   95
and fired off a volley into the air.

Of course they didn't really want peace, what they were trying to   96
do was to see all our faces so they could pick us off. In the end they retreated back up the gully. 'Get them to start making your coffins,' they shouted from up top.

From then on it was war. They would come down into the gully,   97
we'd go and raid them, both sides would try to ambush each other . . . it was a real shootin' war that left a lot of people dead.

The Nachos went to pieces after the police got their leader in a raid.   98
Even I have to admit that the guy was a real man: he and this other guy were fighting it out with the pigs for hours. They say that when Nacho had only one bullet left he shut himself in the bathroom of the house they were holed up in and shot himself in the head. After that his gang was nothing, they had no stomach for a fight. A few days later the law arrested about twenty of them, and now they're all in Bellavista for a good long while.

The gang wars have been tough. whole families have been wiped   99
out in vendettas. What happens is if one of the gang or one of your relatives gets killed, you go out and get the bastard who did it, or one of his family; but we never touch women. If you don't react, they walk all over you.

We also fight police, but it's easier with them. They're shit scared   100
when they come up here, and we know our own territory. Of course they've caught me twice, and I ended up in Bellavista as well.

The first time was the hardest. I'd been holed up in a house in a   101
nearby neighbourhood. About midnight I woke up to hear them knocking the door down.

'Open up, this is the police,' they shouted.   102

I tried to escape out the back, but the place was surrounded. Before   103
I could do a thing, the police were everywhere. They put me into the patrol car without even letting me get dressed, and took me off to the F-2 headquarters. All they found in the house were three guns we had stashed there.

104 　　At the station they put me in a tub with water up to my neck. They left me there all night freezing my balls off, and ran electric current through me too. They kept asking me about the others in the gang, who the leaders were, but I didn't say a word.

105 　　'Think you're a real tough guy, don't you, you fairy,' they shouted, kicking me as hard as they could in the stomach.

106 　　I didn't think I was tough at all, but to grass on people is the lowest you can go. They asked me about enemies of mine, but I didn't even give them away, although I knew where they hung out. It's like Cruz Medina sings in the tango: 'Don't anyone ask who wounded me so, you're wasting your time, you'll never know. Let me die here in peace, and don't be surprised at that, when a man is a man, he won't squeal like a rat.'

107 　　I was sent to Bellavista prison for illegal possession of firearms. I didn't have a record, and they couldn't get anything out of me, so they got mad. They even tried to get people from the neighbourhood to testify against me, but nobody would. There may be people who hate your guts, but they know that if they start blabbing, they're signing their own death warrants. Either you get them once you're out, or one of the gang does it for you.

108 　　I was three months in the slammer. That was only about long enough to get over the beating the pigs had given me. I met several of the gang in the jail. I was lucky that the boss man on our block was an old guy I'd done a job for, who liked me. If you end up in Bellavista with no one to look after you, you're done for. You get kicked from block to block until you end up in the worst hole, where they steal everything you've got, even your sex.

109 　　That's why I was lucky, because I had someone to look out for me. Of course I met up with a few of my old enemies too, some of the Nachos and others. But the worst was a guy called Pepe, whose brother I had shot. I told the boss man about him, and he said: 'Tell him to get out of here, and if he cuts up rough about it, send him to the funeral parlour.'

110 　　I sent the message to Pepe, and a few days later he changed blocks. Whatever the boss man says goes. Nobody in there can do anything without his permission.

111 　　Once I got into a fight. I had some air-cushion Nike running shoes, the ones that cost 20,000 pesos. Two guys came up to me: 'Listen, sweetheart, get those shoes off, they've been sold,' one of them said, a switchblade in his hand.

112 　　'You listen. Tell whoever bought them to come and take them off, I'm too tired,' I said, pulling out a metal bar I had hidden in my jacket.

113 　　Three of my gang appeared out of nowhere, and we set on them. I ended up stabbing one right in the heart. He died on the way to the infirmary. The other one got away. One of us was wounded too, but noth-

ing serious. In Bellavista they don't even bother to make any enquiries, they know no one will say a word. Anyone who's been hit gets his own back if he can, if not, he chokes on it.

I paid my way out of Bellavista. There are people who act as go-   114
betweens with the judges. My case was easy, because it wasn't a serious charge and nobody came forward to accuse me of anything else. I paid around 250,000 pesos. Or rather, some associates of the gang who'd just done a job paid it for me.

After that I went back to my patch, to my normal life. Half the time   115
I'm happy, the other half I'm worked up. When I haven't got anything to do, I get up late, it's almost dark by the time I hit the streets. I hang around the street corners listening to rock music with the gang or I go to a bar with my girl to listen to love songs or country music.

My girl is called Claudia. I know I can trust her, she knows what I   116
do, and backs me up, but she doesn't want to get involved at all. She works in a dress factory and comes home early every day. She's got expensive tastes: she likes new clothes, jewels, all the fancy stuff, and I give her everything she wants. At the weekend either we go out to bars in Bello, or dance salsa, or go down into Manrique to listen to some smoochy music. She's a good-looker, but what I most like about her is that she's serious. Because there's a lot of girls who make your eyes pop, but most of them are just good for a quick lay, a one night stand. Sometimes we like to party at the houses we hide up in, and we get girls in. Fabulous women, but they're only out for what they can get from you. The only real girlfriend I've had is Claudia.

Things have got very difficult. This gang's appeared called the Ca-   117
puchos, they're killing people all over the place. It was them who shot me. I knew they were after me, that's why I split from home. But then I got it into my head to go up and say hello to the old woman and Claudia I thought everything was quiet because the police were snooping around the neighbourhood a lot at the time. I didn't want any trouble, so I went up there without a weapon. Ma soon told me that they were out looking for me. I wasn't worried, I knew they wouldn't dare come up to the house. It's in a narrow gully, so long as you're under cover you can take on anyone.

I was waiting for some of the gang to arrive with the guns so we   118
could get rid of those guys. By the time night fell and they hadn't arrived, I realised things were getting serious. So I climbed out of the back of the house and made for the road up top. I walked about a block, and saw a bus coming down, so I waved it to stop. Just as I was getting on, I saw a kid about two metres from me with a shotgun. Then I felt this heat spreading all through my body, and that was the last I knew. I was out for four days before I came round. What got me most was that a lot of people in the neighbourhood knew what was going on but

didn't warn me. The Capuchos had every exit staked. I guess it's everyone's turn sometime, and that day it was mine.

119   What I wish is that they had killed me there and then, without time for me to let out a sigh or feel any pain, or even to say 'they've got me.' I'd have preferred that to this feeling that my body and my mind are being torn apart. Having to stare death in the face all day long, grinning and beckoning at me, but not daring to come any closer. Better to die straight off, so you don't get to see how all your so-called friends abandon you. In here you realise that people are only with you in the good times. As Don Olimpo sings: 'When you're on top of the world, you can have friends galore, but when fate trips you up, you'll see it's all lies, they won't want you any more.' I don't care about dying, we were all born to die. But I want to die quickly, without all this pain and loneliness.

120   Last night Antonio had his final dream. He dreamt he was up again on the flat roof of the house in the gully where he'd been happiest, blowing his mind with all his gang to the music of drums and electric guitars.

Antonio

121   The city at night is fabulous, it's all light and darkness. I feel just like one of those dots, lost in a sea of light. That's what we are, a tiny light, or maybe a patch of darkness. In the end, we're all or nothing. We can do great things, but we're all mortal. Look closely at the yellow lights, and they turn into all colours, they spread upwards until they make a rainbow in the night. Then they're like a huge cascade of white water that is falling and falling into a deep, invisible well. Then the water gushes out again, this time like a giant flame, making a great bonfire that devours everything. Afterwards there are only red embers and ashes, which are blown everywhere. Now everything is a desert, nothing grows, nothing blooms. The city at night is a screen, a lot of images that flash in front of your eyes. Take a good look at the buildings in the centre. They're pointed-headed monsters. You can see their long arms stretching out, trying to catch something. It's us they're trying to grab. But we're as high and as far away as a cloud. We're on the heights where we can look down on everything, where nothing can touch us. We're the lords of all creation.

✦ Evaluating the Text

1. What picture do you get of Antonio, his relationship with other gang members, and the reasons for his life of violence?

2. What insight does this interview give you into the values of being a member of a gang?

3. Describe the circumstances that surround recruitment, weapons used, training, role models, and the nature of the jobs performed.

4. What insight do you get from learning about Antonio's mother, Doña Azucena, that sheds light on the direction his life has taken?

✦ Exploring Different Perspectives

1. How do the different cultural factors explain the reactions of Antonio's mother in this account and the reactions of the mother in Jo Goodwin Parker's "What Is Poverty?"

2. What insight do the accounts by Alonso Salazar and Mary Crow Dog (see "Civilize Them with a Stick") provide into rebellion against mainstream society?

✦ Extending Viewpoints Through Writing

1. Have you ever belonged to a gang or club? Describe your experiences emphasizing the advantages and disadvantages you found in being a member.

2. Describe the role popular music and films play in Antonio's life. Are there songs or movies that you have seen that have had as strong an effect in shaping your outlook as those mentioned by Antonio?

Jamaica Kincaid

A Small Place

---◆---

Jamaica Kincaid was born in St. John's, Antigua, in 1949, and educated there at the Princess Margaret School. She is a staff writer for the New Yorker. *Her work has appeared in* Rolling Stone *magazine and in* The Paris Review. *She is the author of a highly praised collection of stories,* At the Bottom of the River *(1984), which won the Morton Dauwen Zabel Award of the American Academy and Institute of Arts and Letters, and a book of related stories,* Annie John *(1985), an autobiographical account of a girl's coming of age in the West Indies. Her most recent book, a novel,* Lucy *(1990), is based on her experiences of beginning a new life in the United States. "A Small Place," from the 1988 book of that name, is an impassioned diatribe on the sweeping corruption, dilapidated schools, inadequately staffed hospital, and shameful legacy of Antigua's colonial past, which tourists, absorbed in their self-centered pleasures, fail to recognize.*

Antigua, a small island in the Antilles, was discovered by Christopher Columbus in 1493, on his second voyage to the Americas. He named the island after the Church of Santa Maria de la Antigua of Seville in Spain. The British occupied and colonized Antigua (and two smaller islands, Barbuda and Redonda) in 1632 and set up sugar plantations, which flourished until the abolition of slavery in 1834. Antigua achieved full independence in 1981 as a member of the commonwealth, with Queen Elizabeth II as head of state. The tourist industry described by Kincaid (averaging 275,000 visitors each year) brings in approximately $225 million each year, or over half of the island's yearly gross national product. Elections of March 1994 saw the Antigua Labor Party gain a majority of seats with Lester Bird at the helm as prime minister.

1   If you go to Antigua as a tourist, this is what you will see. If you come by aeroplane, you will land at the V. C. Bird International Airport. Vere Cornwall (V. C.) Bird is the Prime Minister of Antigua. You may be the sort of tourist who would wonder why a Prime Minister would want an airport named after him—why not a school, why not a hospital, why not some great public monument? You are a tourist and you have not yet seen a school in Antigua, you have not yet seen the hospital in Antigua, you have not yet seen a public monument in Antigua. As your plane descends to land, you might say, What a beautiful island Antigua is—more beautiful than any of the other islands you have seen, and they were very beautiful, in their way, but they were

much too green, much too lush with vegetation, which indicated to you, the tourist, that they got quite a bit of rainfall, and rain is the very thing that you, just now, do not want, for you are thinking of the hard and cold and dark and long days you spent working in North America (or, worse, Europe), earning some money so that you could stay in this place (Antigua) where the sun always shines and where the climate is deliciously hot and dry for the four to ten days you are going to be staying there; and since you are on your holiday, since you are a tourist, the thought of what it might be like for someone who had to live day in, day out in a place that suffers constantly from drought, and so has to watch carefully every drop of fresh water used (while at the same time surrounded by a sea and an ocean—the Caribbean Sea on one side, the Atlantic Ocean on the other), must never cross your mind.

You disembark from your plane. You go through customs. Since you are a tourist, a North American or European—to be frank, white— and not an Antiguan black returning to Antigua from Europe or North America with cardboard boxes of much needed cheap clothes and food for relatives, you move through customs swiftly, you move through customs with ease. Your bags are not searched. You emerge from customs into the hot, clean air: immediately you feel cleansed, immediately you feel blessed (which is to say special); you feel free. You see a man, a taxi driver; you ask him to take you to your destination; he quotes you a price. You immediately think that the price is in the local currency, for you are a tourist and you are familiar with these things (rates of exchange) and you feel even more free, for things seem so cheap, but then your driver ends by saying, "In U.S. currency." You may say, "Hmmmm, do you have a formal sheet that lists official prices and destinations?" Your driver obeys the law and shows you the sheet, and he apologises for the incredible mistake he has made in quoting you a price off the top of his head which is so vastly different (favouring him) from the one listed. You are driven to your hotel by this taxi driver in his taxi, a brand-new Japanese-made vehicle. The road on which you are travelling is a very bad road, very much in need of repair. You are feeling wonderful, so you say, "Oh, what a marvellous change these bad roads are from the splendid highways I am used to in North America." (Or, worse, Europe.) Your driver is reckless; he is a dangerous man who drives in the middle of the road when he thinks no other cars are coming in the opposite direction, passes other cars on blind curves that run uphill, drives at sixty miles an hour on narrow, curving roads when the road sign, a rusting, beat-up thing left over from colonial days, says 40 MPH. This might frighten you (you are on your holiday; you are a tourist); this might excite you (you are on your holiday; you are a tourist), though if you are from New York and take taxis you are used to this style of driving: most of the taxi drivers in New York are from places in the world like this. You are looking out the window (because you want to get your money's worth); you notice that all the cars you see are brand-new, or almost brand-new, and that they are all Japanese-made. There are no American cars in Antigua—no new ones, at any rate; none that were manufactured in the last ten years. You continue to look at the cars and you say to yourself, Why, they look brand-new, but they have an awful sound, like an old car—a very old, dilapidated car. How to account for that? Well, possibly it's because they use leaded gasoline in these brand-new cars whose engines were built to use non-leaded gasoline, but you mustn't ask the person driving the car if this is so, because he or she has never heard of unleaded gasoline. You look closely at the car; you see that it's a model of a Japanese car that you might hesitate to buy; it's a model that's very expensive; it's a model that's quite impractical for a person who has to work as hard as you do and who watches every penny you earn so that you can afford this holiday you are on. How do they afford such a car? And do they live in a luxurious house to match such a car? Well, no. You will be surprised, then, to see that most likely the person driving this brand-new car filled with the wrong gas lives in a house that, in comparison, is far beneath the status of the car; and if you were to ask why you would be told that the banks are encouraged by the government to make loans available for cars, but loans for houses not so easily available; and if you ask again why, you will be told that the two main car dealerships in Antigua are owned in part or outright by ministers in government. Oh, but you are on holiday and the sight of these brand-new cars driven by people who may or may not have really passed their driving test (there was once a scandal about driving licenses for sale) would not really stir up these thoughts in you. You pass a building sitting in a sea of dust and you think, It's some latrines for people just passing by, but when you look again you see the building has written on it PIGOTT'S SCHOOL. You pass the hospital, the Holberton Hospital, and how wrong you are not to think about this, for though you are a tourist on your holiday, what if your heart should miss a few beats? What if a blood vessel in your neck should break? What if one of those people driving those brand-new cars filled with the wrong gas fails to pass safely while going uphill on a curve and you are in the car going in the opposite direction? Will you be comforted to know that the hospital is staffed with doctors that no actual Antiguan trusts; that Antiguans always say about the doctors, "I don't want them near me"; that Antiguans refer to them not as doctors but as "the three men" (there are three of them); that when the Minister of Health himself doesn't feel well he takes the first plane to New York to see a real doctor; that if any one of the ministers in government needs medical care he flies to New York to get it?

3   It's a good thing that you brought your own books with you, for you couldn't just go to the library and borrow some. Antigua used to

have a splendid library, but in The Earthquake (everyone talks about it that way—The Earthquake; we Antiguans, for I am one, have a great sense of things, and the more meaningful the thing, the more meaningless we make it) the library building was damaged. This was in 1974, and soon after that a sign was placed on the front of the building saying, THIS BUILDING WAS DAMAGED IN THE EARTHQUAKE OF 1974. REPAIRS ARE PENDING. The sign hangs there, and hangs there more than a decade later, with its unfulfilled promise of repair, and you might see this as a sort of quaintness on the part of these islanders, these people descended from slaves—what a strange, unusual perception of time they have. REPAIRS ARE PENDING, and here it is many years later, but perhaps in a world that is twelve miles long and nine miles wide (the size of Antigua) twelve years and twelve minutes and twelve days are all the same. The library is one of those splendid old buildings from colonial times, and the sign telling of the repairs is a splendid old sign from colonial times. Not very long after The Earthquake Antigua got its independence from Britain, making Antigua a state in its own right, and Antiguans are so proud of this that each year, to mark the day, they go to church and thank God, a British God, for this. But you should not think of the confusion that must lie in all that and you must not think of the damaged library. You have brought your own books with you, and among them is one of those new books about economic history, one of those books explaining how the West (meaning Europe and North America after its conquest and settlement by Europeans) got rich: the West got rich not from the free (free—in this case meaning got-for-nothing) and then undervalued labour, for generations, of the people like me you see walking around you in Antigua but from the ingenuity of small shopkeepers in Sheffield and Yorkshire and Lancashire, or wherever; and what a great part the invention of the wristwatch played in it, for there was nothing noble-minded men could not do when they discovered they could slap time on their wrists just like that (isn't that the last straw; for not only did we have to suffer the unspeakableness of slavery, but the satisfaction to be had from "We made you bastards rich" is taken away, too), and so you needn't let that slightly funny feeling you have from time to time about exploitation, oppression, domination develop into full-fledged unease, discomfort; you could ruin your holiday. They are not responsible for what you have; you owe them nothing; in fact, you did them a big favour, and you can provide one hundred examples. For here you are now, passing by Government House. And here you are now, passing by the Prime Minister's Office and the Parliament Building, and overlooking these, with a splendid view of St. John's Harbour, the American Embassy. If it were not for you, they would not have Government House, and Prime Minister's Office, and Parliament Building and embassy of powerful country. Now you are passing a mansion, an extraordinary house painted the colour of old cow dung, with more aerials and antennas attached to it than you will see even at the American Embassy. The people who live in this house are a merchant family who came to Antigua from the Middle East less than twenty years ago. When this family first came to Antigua, they sold dry goods door to door from suitcases they carried on their backs. Now they own a lot of Antigua; they regularly lend money to the government, they build enormous (for Antigua), ugly (for Antigua), concrete buildings in Antigua's capital, St. John's, which the government then rents for huge sums of money; a member of their family is the Antiguan Ambassador to Syria; Antiguans hate them. Not far from this mansion is another mansion, the home of a drug smuggler. Everybody knows he's a drug smuggler, and if just as you were driving by he stepped out of his door your driver might point him out to you as the notorious person that he is, for this drug smuggler is so rich people say he buys cars in tens—ten of this one, ten of that one—and that he bought a house (another mansion) near Five Islands, contents included, with cash he carried in a suitcase: three hundred and fifty thousand American dollars, and, to the surprise of the seller of the house, lots of American dollars were left over. Overlooking the drug smuggler's mansion is yet another mansion, and leading up to it is the best paved road in all of Antigua—even better than the road that was paved for the Queen's visit in 1985 (when the Queen came, all the roads that she would travel on were paved anew, so that the Queen might have been left with the impression that riding in a car in Antigua was a pleasant experience). In this mansion lives a woman sophisticated people in Antigua call Evita. She is a notorious woman. She's young and beautiful and the girlfriend of somebody very high up in the government. Evita is notorious because her relationship with this high government official has made her the owner of boutiques and property and given her a say in cabinet meetings, and all sorts of other privileges such a relationship would bring a beautiful young woman.

4   Oh, but by now you are tired of all this looking, and you want to reach your destination—your hotel, your room. You long to refresh yourself; you long to eat some nice lobster, some nice local food. You take a bath, you brush your teeth. You get dressed again; as you get dressed, you look out the window. That water—have you ever seen anything like it? Far out, to the horizon, the colour of the water is navy-blue; nearer, the water is the colour of the North American sky. From there to the shore, the water is pale, silvery, clear, so clear that you can see its pinkish-white sand bottom. Oh, what beauty! Oh, what beauty! You have never seen anything like this. You are so excited. You breathe shallow. You breathe deep. You see a beautiful boy skimming the water, godlike, on a Windsurfer. You see an incredibly unattractive, fat, pastrylike-fleshed woman enjoying a walk on the beautiful sand, with a man, an incredibly unattractive, fat, pastrylike-fleshed man; you see

the pleasure they're taking in their surroundings. Still standing, looking out the window, you see yourself lying on the beach, enjoying the amazing sun (a sun so powerful and yet so beautiful, the way it is always overhead as if on permanent guard, ready to stamp out any cloud that dares to darken and so empty rain on you and ruin your holiday; a sun that is your personal friend). You see yourself taking a walk on that beach, you see yourself meeting new people (only they are new in a very limited way, for they are people just like you). You see yourself eating some delicious, locally grown food. You see yourself, you see yourself . . . You must not wonder what exactly happened to the contents of your lavatory when you flushed it. You must not wonder where your bathwater went when you pulled out the stopper. You must not wonder what happened when you brushed your teeth. Oh, it might all end up in the water you are thinking of taking a swim in; the contents of your lavatory might, just might, graze gently against your ankle as you wade carefree in the water, for you see, in Antigua, there is no proper sewage-disposal system. But the Caribbean Sea is very big and the Atlantic Ocean is even bigger; it would amaze even you to know the number of black slaves this ocean has swallowed up. When you sit down to eat your delicious meal, it's better that you don't know that most of what you are eating came off a plane from Miami. And before it got on a plane in Miami, who knows where it came from? A good guess is that it came from a place like Antigua first, where it was grown dirt-cheap, went to Miami, and came back. There is a world of something in this, but I can't go into it right now.

The thing you have always suspected about yourself the minute   5
you become a tourist is true: A tourist is an ugly human being. You are not an ugly person all the time; you are not an ugly person ordinarily; you are not an ugly person day to day. From day to day, you are a nice person. From day to day, all the people who are supposed to love you on the whole do. From day to day, as you walk down a busy street in the large and modern and prosperous city in which you work and live, dismayed, puzzled (a cliché but only a cliché can explain you) at how alone you feel in this crowd, how awful it is to go unnoticed, how awful it is to go unloved, even as you are surrounded by more people than you could possibly get to know in a lifetime that lasted for millennia, and then out of the corner of your eye you see someone looking at you and absolute pleasure is written all over that person's face, and then you realise that you are not as revolting a presence as you think you are (for that look just told you so). And so, ordinarily, you are a nice person, an attractive person, a person capable of drawing to yourself the affection of other people (people just like you), a person at home in your own skin (sort of; I mean, in a way; I mean, your dismay and puzzlement are natural to you, because people like you just seem to be like

that, and so many of the things people like you find admirable about
yourselves—the things you think about, the things you think really define you—seem rooted in these feelings): a person at home in your own
house (and all its nice house things), with its nice back yard (and its
nice back-yard things), at home on your street, your church, in community activities, your job, at home with your family, your relatives, your
friends—you are a whole person. But one day, when you are sitting
somewhere, alone in that crowd, and that awful feeling of displaced-
ness comes over you, and really, as an ordinary person you are not well
equipped to look too far inward and set yourself aright, because being
ordinary is already so taxing, and being ordinary takes all you have out
of you, and though the words "I must get away" do not actually pass
across your lips, you make a leap from being that nice blob just sitting
like a boob in your amniotic sac of the modern experience to being a
person visiting heaps of death and ruin and feeling alive and inspired
at the sight of it; to being a person lying on some faraway beach, your
stilled body stinking and glistening in the sand, looking like something
first forgotten, then remembered, then not important enough to go
back for; to being a person marvelling at the harmony (ordinarily, what
you would say is the backwardness) and the union these other people
(and they are other people) have with nature. And you look at the
things they can do with a piece of ordinary cloth, the things they fashion out of cheap, vulgarly colored (to you) twine, the way they squat
down over a hole they have made in the ground, the hole itself is something to marvel at, and since you are being an ugly person this ugly but
joyful thought will swell inside you: their ancestors were not clever in
the way yours were and not ruthless in the way yours were, for then
would it not be you who would be in harmony with nature and backwards in that charming way? An ugly thing, that is what you are when
you become a tourist, an ugly, empty thing, a stupid thing, a piece of
rubbish pausing here and there to gaze at this and taste that, and it will
never occur to you that the people who inhabit the place in which you
have just paused cannot stand you, that behind their closed doors they
laugh at your strangeness (you do not look the way they look); the
physical sight of you does not please them; you have bad manners (it is
their custom to eat their food with their hands; you try eating their
way, you look silly; you try eating the way you always eat, you look
silly); they do not like the way you speak (you have an accent); they
collapse helpless from laughter, mimicking the way they imagine you
must look as you carry out some everyday bodily function. They do
not like you. *They do not like me!* That thought never actually occurs to
you. Still, you feel a little uneasy. Still, you feel a little foolish. Still, you
feel a little out of place. But the banality of your own life is very real to
you; it drove you to this extreme, spending your days and your nights
in the company of people who despise you, people you do not like re-

ally, people you would not want to have as your actual neighbour. And so you must devote yourself to puzzling out how much of what you are told is really, really true (Is ground-up bottle glass in peanut sauce really a delicacy around here, or will it do just what you think ground-up bottle glass will do? Is this rare, multicoloured, snout-mouthed fish really an aphrodisiac, or will it cause you to fall asleep permanently?). Oh, the hard work all of this is, and is it any wonder, then, that on your return home you feel the need of a long rest, so that you can recover from your life as a tourist?

That the native does not like the tourist is not hard to explain. For every native of every place is a potential tourist, and every tourist is a native of somewhere. Every native everywhere lives a life of over-whelming and crushing banality and boredom and desperation and depression, and every deed, good and bad, is an attempt to forget this. Every native would like to find a way out, every native would like a rest, every native would like a tour. But some natives—most natives in the world—cannot go anywhere. They are too poor. They are too poor to go anywhere. They are too poor to escape the reality of their lives; and they are too poor to live properly in the place where they live, which is the very place you, the tourist, want to go—so when the natives see you, the tourist, they envy you, they envy your ability to leave your own banality and boredom, they envy your ability to turn their own banality and boredom into a source of pleasure for yourself.

6

✦ Evaluating the Text

1. How does the fact that tourists do not know that the "local" food is imported from Miami illustrate the artificially created impression of Antigua tourists have?

2. How do vacations create an atmosphere in which tourists apply very different standards than they would if the same "exciting" events happened back home? How do their expectations differ from people who must live there all the time?

3. What inferences might you draw about the government's attitude toward tourists (compared with their concern about Antiguans) from the sight of the dilapidated schools and hospital alongside brand new taxicabs and fine government buildings?

4. Why is it significant, according to Kincaid, that most history books omit the extent to which the wealth of Great Britain was derived by exploiting the labor of natives in their colonial possessions? Why is it ironic that history books credit England's wealth to the ingenuity of British shopkeepers?

5. How did the kind of treatment given to the Queen of England (the ultimate "tourist" to Antigua) suggest the local government's double standard?

6. Evaluate Kincaid's argument that nice people are transformed into ugly people when they become tourists. Do you agree that tourists travel to places where they can enjoy a master-slave relationship to reaffirm an impaired sense of self-worth? Explain your reasons.

✦ Exploring Different Perspectives

1. How do Roland Barthes (see "Ornamental Cookery") and Jamaica Kincaid use the idea of a veneer disguising reality and develop this theme in different contexts?

2. How do both Jamaica Kincaid and Catherine Lim, in "Paper," criticize the complacency and delusions of the rich and would-be rich?

✦ Extending Viewpoints Through Writing

1. To what extent was your perception of yourself as a tourist changed by reading Kincaid's account? Describe how you would have appeared from the perspective of any of the people who live where you took your last vacation.

2. Write a counterargument to Kincaid's position from a native Antiguan who believes tourism is beneficial to the island.

3. Before traveling to a place, did you ever construct a mental picture of what the place would be like only to discover that it did not match your expectations? In what ways were your expectations unrealistic?

Mary Crow Dog
and Richard Erdoes

Civilize Them with a Stick

◆

Mary Crow Dog (who later took the name Mary Brave Bird) was born in 1956 and grew up on a South Dakota reservation in a one-room cabin without running water or electricity. She joined the new movement of tribal pride sweeping Native American communities in the 1960s and 1970s and was at the siege of Wounded Knee, South Dakota, in 1973. She married the American Indian Movement (AIM) leader Leonard Crow Dog, the movement's chief medicine man. Her powerful autobiography La-kota Woman, written with Richard Erdoes, one of America's leading writers on Native American affairs and the author of eleven books, became a national bestseller and won the American Book Award for 1991. In it she describes what it was like to grow up a Sioux in a white-dominated society. Her second book, Ohitka Woman (1993), also written with Richard Er-does, continues the story of a woman whose struggle for a sense of self and freedom is a testament to her will and spirit. In "Civilize Them with a Stick," from Lakota Woman, the author recounts her personal struggle as a young student at a boarding school run by the Bureau of Indian Affairs.

> . . . *Gathered from the cabin, the wickiup, and the tepee,*
> *partly by cajolery and partly by threats;*
> *partly by bribery and partly by force,*
> *they are induced to leave their kindred*
> *to enter these schools and take upon themselves*
> *the outward appearance of civilized life.*
>
> —Annual report of the Department of Interior, 1901

It is almost impossible to explain to a sympathetic white person 1
what a typical old Indian boarding school was like; how it affected the Indian child suddenly dumped into it like a small creature from another world, helpless, defenseless, bewildered, trying desperately and instinctively to survive and sometimes not surviving at all. I think such children were like the victims of Nazi concentration camps trying to tell average, middle-class Americans what their experience had been like. Even now, when these schools are much improved, when the buildings are new, all gleaming steel and glass, the food tolerable, the teachers well trained and well intentioned, even trained in child psychology—unfortunately the psychology of white children, which is different from

327

ours—the shock to the child upon arrival is still tremendous. Some just seem to shrivel up, don't speak for days on end, and have an empty look in their eyes. I know of an eleven-year-old on another reservation who hanged herself, and in our school, while I was there, a girl jumped out of the window, trying to kill herself to escape an unbearable situation. That first shock is always there. . . .

2   The mission school at St. Francis was a curse for our family for generations. My grandmother went there, then my mother, then my sisters and I. At one time or other every one of us tried to run away. Grandma told me once about the bad times she had experienced at St. Francis. In those days they let students go home only for one week every year. Two days were used up for transportation, which meant spending just five days out of three hundred and sixty-five with her family. And that was an improvement. Before grandma's time, on many reservations they did not let the students go home at all until they had finished school. Anybody who disobeyed the nuns was severely punished. The building in which my grandmother stayed had three floors, for girls only. Way up in the attic were little cells, about five by five by ten feet. One time she was in church and instead of praying she was playing jacks. As punishment they took her to one of those little cubicles where she stayed in darkness because the windows had been boarded up. They left her there for a whole week with only bread and water for nourishment. After she came out she promptly ran away, together with three other girls. They were found and brought back. The nuns stripped them naked and whipped them. They used a horse buggy whip on my grandmother. Then she was put back into the attic—for two weeks.

3   My mother had much the same experiences but never wanted to talk about them, and then there I was, in the same place. The school is now run by the BIA—the Bureau of Indian Affairs—but only since about fifteen years ago. When I was there, during the 1960s, it was still run by the Church. The Jesuit fathers ran the boys' wing and the Sisters of the Sacred Heart ran us—with the help of the strap. Nothing had changed since my grandmother's days. I have been told recently that even in the '70s they were still beating children at that school. All I got out of school was being taught how to pray. I learned quickly that I would be beaten if I failed in my devotions or, God forbid, prayed the wrong way, especially prayed in Indian to Wakan Tanka, the Indian Creator.

4   The girls' wing was built like an F and was run like a penal institution. Every morning at five o'clock the sisters would come into our large dormitory to wake us up, and immediately we had to kneel down at the sides of our beds and recite the prayers. At six o'clock we were herded into the church for more of the same. I did not take kindly to the discipline and to marching by the clock, left-right, left-right. I was never one to like being forced to do something. I do something because I feel like doing it. I felt this way always, as far as I can remember, and

my sister Barbara felt the same way. An old medicine man once told me: "Us Lakotas are not like dogs who can be trained, who can be beaten and keep on wagging their tails, licking the hand that whipped them. We are like cats, little cats, big cats, wildcats, bobcats, mountain lions. It doesn't matter what kind, but cats who can't be tamed, who scratch if you step on their tails." But I was only a kitten and my claws were still small.

Barbara was still in the school when I arrived and during my first   5 year or two she could still protect me a little bit. When Barb was a seventh-grader she ran away together with five other girls, early in the morning before sunrise. They brought them back in the evening. The girls had to wait for two hours in front of the mother superior's office. They were hungry and cold, frozen through. It was wintertime and they had been running the whole day without food, trying to make good their escape. The mother superior asked each girl, "Would you do this again?" She told them that as punishment they would not be allowed to visit home for a month and that she'd keep them busy on work details until the skin on their knees and elbows had worn off. At the end of her speech she told each girl, "Get up from this chair and lean over it." She then lifted the girls' skirts and pulled down their underpants. Not little girls either, but teenagers. She had a leather strap about a foot long and four inches wide fastened to a stick, and beat the girls, one after another, until they cried. Barb did not give her that satisfaction but just clenched her teeth. There was one girl, Barb told me, the nun kept on beating and beating until her arm got tired.

I did not escape my share of the strap. Once, when I was thirteen   6 years old, I refused to go to Mass. I did not want to go to church because I did not feel well. A nun grabbed me by the hair, dragged me upstairs, made me stoop over, pulled my dress up (we were not allowed at the time to wear jeans), pulled my panties down, and gave me what they called "swats"—twenty-five swats with a board around which Scotch tape had been wound. She hurt me badly.

My classroom was right next to the principal's office and almost   7 every day I could hear him swatting the boys. Beating was the common punishment for not doing one's homework, or for being late to school. It had such a bad effect upon me that I hated and mistrusted every white person on sight, because I met only one kind. It was not until much later that I met sincere white people I could relate to and be friends with. Racism breeds racism in reverse.

The routine at St. Francis was dreary. Six A.M., kneeling in church for   8 an hour or so; seven o'clock, breakfast; eight o'clock, scrub the floor, peel spuds, make classes. We had to mop the dining room twice every day and scrub the tables. If you were caught taking a rest, doodling on the bench with a fingernail or knife, or just rapping, the nun would come up with a dish towel and just slap it across your face, saying,

"You're not supposed to be talking, you're supposed to be working!" Monday mornings we had cornmeal mush, Tuesday oatmeal, Wednesday rice and raisins, Thursday cornflakes, and Friday all the leftovers mixed together or sometimes fish. Frequently the food had bugs or rocks in it. We were eating hot dogs that were weeks old, while the nuns were dining on ham, whipped potatoes, sweet peas, and cranberry sauce. In winter our dorm was icy cold while the nuns' rooms were always warm.

9　　I have seen little girls arrive at the school, first-graders, just fresh from home and totally unprepared for what awaited them, little girls with pretty braids, and the first thing the nuns did was chop their hair off and tie up what was left behind their ears. Next they would dump the children into tubs of alcohol, a sort of rubbing alcohol, "to get the germs off." Many of the nuns were German immigrants, some from Bavaria, so that we sometimes speculated whether Bavaria was some sort of Dracula country inhabited by monsters. For the sake of objectivity I ought to mention that two of the German fathers were great linguists and that the only Lakota-English dictionaries and grammars which are worth anything were put together by them.

10　　At night some of the girls would huddle in bed together for comfort and reassurance. Then the nun in charge of the dorm would come in and say, "What are the two of you doing in bed together? I smell evil in this room. You girls are evil incarnate. You are sinning. You are going to hell and burn forever. You can act that way in the devil's frying pan." She would get them out of bed in the middle of the night, making them kneel and pray until morning. We had not the slightest idea what it was all about. At home we slept two and three in a bed for animal warmth and a feeling of security.

11　　The nuns and the girls in the two top grades were constantly battling it out physically with fists, nails, and hair-pulling. I myself was growing from a kitten into an undersized cat. My claws were getting bigger and were itching for action. About 1969 or 1970 a strange young white girl appeared on the reservation. She looked about eighteen or twenty years old. She was pretty and had long, blond hair down to her waist, patched jeans, boots, and a backpack. She was different from any other white person we had met before. I think her name was Wise. I do not know how she managed to overcome our reluctance and distrust, getting us into a corner, making us listen to her, asking us how we were treated. She told us that she was from New York. She was the first real hippie or Yippie we had come across. She told us of people called the Black Panthers, Young Lords, and Weathermen. She said, "Black people are getting it on. Indians are getting it on in St. Paul and California. How about you?" She also said, "Why don't you put out an underground paper, mimeograph it. It's easy. Tell it like it is. Let it all hang out." She spoke a strange lingo but we caught on fast.

Charlene Left Hand Bull and Gina One Star were two full-blood   12
girls I used to hang out with. We did everything together. They were
willing to join me in a Sioux uprising. We put together a newspaper
which we called the *Red Panther*. In it we wrote how bad the school
was, what kind of slop we had to eat—slimy, rotten, blackened potatoes for two weeks—the way we were beaten. I think I was the one who
wrote the worst article about our principal of the moment, Father
Keeler. I put all my anger and venom into it. I called him a goddam
wasičun son of a bitch. I wrote that he knew nothing about Indians and
should go back to where he came from, teaching white children whom
he could relate to. I wrote that we knew which priests slept with which
nuns and that all they ever could think about was filling their bellies
and buying a new car. It was the kind of writing which foamed at the
mouth, but which also lifted a great deal of weight from one's soul.

On Saint Patrick's Day, when everybody was at the big powwow,   13
we distributed our newspapers. We put them on windshields and bul-
letin boards, in desks and pews, in dorms and toilets. But someone saw
us and snitched on us. The shit hit the fan. The three of us were taken
before a board meeting. Our parents, in my case my mother, had to
come. They were told that ours was a most serious matter, the worst
thing that had ever happened in the school's long history. One of the
nuns told my mother, "Your daughter really needs to be talked to."
"What's wrong with my daughter?" my mother asked. She was given
one of our *Red Panther* newspapers. The nun pointed out its name to
her and then my piece, waiting for mom's reaction. After a while she
asked, "Well, what have you got to say to this? What do you think?"

My mother said, "Well, when I went to school here, some years   14
back, I was treated a lot worse then these kids are. I really can't see how
they can have any complaints, because we was treated a lot stricter. We
could not even wear skirts halfway up our knees. These girls have it
made. But you should forgive them because they are young. And it's
supposed to be a free country, free speech and all that. I don't believe
what they done is wrong." So all I got out of it was scrubbing six flights
of stairs on my hands and knees, every day. And no boy-side privileges.

The boys and girls were still pretty much separated. The only time   15
one could meet a member of the opposite sex was during free time, between four and five-thirty, in the study hall or on benches or the volleyball court outside, and that was strictly supervised. One day Charlene
and I went over to the boys' side. We were on the ball team and they
had to let us practice. We played three extra minutes, only three minutes more than we were supposed to. Here was the nuns' opportunity
for revenge. We got twenty-five swats. I told Charlene, "We are getting
too old to have our bare asses whipped that way. We are old enough to
have babies. Enough of this shit. Next time we fight back." Charlene
only said, "Hoka-hay!"

16   We had to take showers every evening. One little girl did not want to take her panties off and one of the nuns told her, "You take those underpants off—or else!" But the child was ashamed to do it. The nun was getting her swat to threaten the girl. I went up to the sister, pushed her veil off, and knocked her down. I told her that if she wanted to hit a little girl she should pick on me, pick one her own size. She got herself transferred out of the dorm a week later.

17   In a school like this there is always a lot of favoritism. At St. Francis it was strongly tinged with racism. Girls who were near-white, who came from what the nuns called "nice families," got preferential treatment. They waited on the faculty and got to eat ham or eggs and bacon in the morning. They got the easy jobs while the skins, who did not have the right kind of background—myself among them—always wound up in the laundry room sorting out ten bushel baskets of dirty boys' socks every day. Or we wound up scrubbing the floors and doing all the dishes. The school therefore fostered fights and antagonism between whites and breeds, and between breeds and skins. At one time Charlene and I had to iron all the robes and vestments the priests wore when saying Mass. We had to fold them up and put them into a chest in the back of the church. In a corner, looking over our shoulders, was a statue of the crucified Savior, all bloody and beaten up. Charlene looked up and said, "Look at that poor Indian. The pigs sure worked him over." That was the closest I ever came to seeing Jesus.

18   I was held up as a bad example and didn't mind. I was old enough to have a boyfriend and promptly got one. At the school we had an hour and a half for ourselves. Between the boys' and the girls' wings were some benches where one could sit. My boyfriend and I used to go there just to hold hands and talk. The nuns were very uptight about any boy-girl stuff. They had an exaggerated fear of anything having even the faintest connection with sex. One day in religion class, an all-girl class, Sister Bernard singled me out for some remarks, pointing me out as a bad example, an example that should be shown. She said that I was too free with my body. That I was holding hands which meant that I was not a good example to follow. She also said that I wore unchaste dresses, skirts which were too short, too suggestive, shorter than regulations permitted, and for that I would be punished. She dressed me down before the whole class, carrying on and on about my unchastity.

19   I stood up and told her, "You shouldn't say any of those things, miss. You people are a lot worse than us Indians. I know all about you, because my grandmother and my aunt told me about you. Maybe twelve, thirteen years ago you had a water stoppage here in St. Francis. No water could get through the pipes. There are water lines right under the mission, underground tunnels and passages where in my grandmother's time only the nuns and priests could go, which were off-limits to everybody else. When the water backed up they had to go through all the water lines and clean them out. And in those huge pipes they

found the bodies of newborn babies. And they were white babies. They weren't Indian babies. At least when our girls have babies, they don't do away with them that way, like flushing them down the toilet, almost.

"And that priest they sent here from Holy Rosary in Pine Ridge be-   20
cause he molested a little girl. You couldn't think of anything better than dump him on us. All he does is watch young women and girls with that funny smile on his face. Why don't you point him out for an example?"

Charlene and I worked on the school newspaper. After all we had   21
some practice. Every day we went down to Publications. One of the priests acted as the photographer, doing the enlarging and developing. He smelled of chemicals which had stained his hands yellow. One day he invited Charlene into the darkroom. He was going to teach her developing. She was developed already. She was a big girl compared to him, taller too. Charlene was nicely built, not fat, just rounded. No sharp edges anywhere. All of a sudden she rushed out of the darkroom, yelling to me, "Let's get out of here! He's trying to feel me up. That priest is nasty." So there was this too to contend with—sexual harassment. We complained to the student body. The nuns said we just had a dirty mind.

We got a new priest in English. During one of his first classes he   22
asked one of the boys a certain question. The boy was shy. He spoke poor English, but he had the right answer. The priest told him, "You did not say it right. Correct yourself. Say it over again." The boy got flustered and stammered. He could hardly get out a word. But the priest kept after him: "Didn't you hear? I told you to do the whole thing over. Get it right this time." He kept on and on.

I stood up and said, "Father, don't be doing that. If you go into an   23
Indian's home and try to talk Indian, they might laugh at you and say, 'Do it over correctly. Get it right this time!'"

He shouted at me, "Mary, you stay after class. Sit down right now!"   24

I stayed after class, until after the bell. He told me, "Get over here!"   25

He grabbed me by the arm, pushing me against the blackboard,   26
shouting, "Why are you always mocking us? You have no reason to do this."

I said, "Sure I do. You were making fun of him. You embarrassed   27
him. He needs strengthening, not weakening. You hurt him. I did not hurt you."

He twisted my arm and pushed real hard. I turned around and hit   28
him in the face, giving him a bloody nose. After that I ran out of the room, slamming the door behind me. He and I went to Sister Bernard's office. I told her, "Today I quit school. I'm not taking any more of this, none of this shit anymore. None of this treatment. Better give me my diploma. I can't waste any more time on you people."

Sister Bernard looked at me for a long, long time. She said, "All   29
right, Mary Ellen, go home today. Come back in a few days and get

your diploma." And that was that. Oddly enough, that priest turned out okay. He taught a class in grammar, orthography, composition, things like that. I think he wanted more respect in class. He was still young and unsure of himself. But I was in there too long. I didn't feel like hearing it. Later he became a good friend of the Indians, a personal friend of myself and my husband. He stood up for us during Wounded Knee and after. He stood up to his superiors, stuck his neck way out, became a real people's priest. He even learned our language. He died prematurely of cancer. It is not only the good Indians who die young, but the good whites, too. It is the timid ones who know how to take care of themselves who grow old. I am still grateful to that priest for what he did for us later and for the quarrel he picked with me—or did I pick it with him?—because it ended a situation which had become unendurable for me. The day of my fight with him was my last day in school.

✦ Evaluating the Text

1. What aspects of life at the government boarding school most clearly illustrate the government's desire to transform Native-Americans?

2. How did Mary Crow Dog react to the experiences to which she was subjected at the government-run school?

3. What historical insight did the experiences of Mary Crow Dog's mother and grandmother provide into those of Mary Crow Dog herself?

4. Why was the incident of the underground newspaper a crucial one for Mary Crow Dog?

✦ Exploring Different Perspectives

1. How do both Mary Crow Dog's account and Mahdokht Kashkuli's story "The Button" dramatize the effects of being raised by the state?

2. How is the way in which the nuns in "Civilize Them with a Stick" react to Mary Crow Dog similar to the phenomena described by Constance Classen in "The Odour of the Other"?

✦ Extending Viewpoints Through Writing

1. What experiences have you had that made you aware of institutionalized racism?

2. How did this essay give you insight into the vast difference between the traditional culture of Native-Americans and their lives in the present?

Constance Classen

The Odour of the Other

◆

Constance Classen is senior fellow at the Center for the Study of World Religions at Harvard University, where she specializes in cross-cultural studies of sensory symbolism. Her previous publications include Inca Cosmology and the Human Body *(1993). "The Odour of the Other" is drawn from* Worlds of Sense: Exploring the Senses in History and Across Cultures *(1993).*

By exploring the ways in which olfactory symbolism is used to express themes of identity and difference in diverse cultures, including that of the West, I hope to show here the extent to which olfactory codes pervade classificatory thought, not only in 'exotic' highly olfactory-conscious societies, but even in our own, rather 'deodorized' society. To this end I will bring together examples of such symbolism from a wide variety of cultures. At the same time, the examination of how odours are used to categorize 'others' in different societies, provides an important insight, or better, 'inscent', into the construction of concepts of 'oneness' and 'otherness', and their basic similarities and differences across cultures.

Odours and Class

The ascription of different characteristic odours to different races and different social groups is a universal trait and one which has a certain empirical basis: body odours can differ among ethnic groups, due partly to the different foods consumed and partly to genetic factors. While all peoples give off odours, however, most people are so accustomed to their own personal and group scents as to not be aware of them and only notice the odours of others. Edmund Carpenter, for instance, reports the following interchange from his anthropological fieldwork among the Inuit:

> One day when Kowanerk [an Inuit woman] and I were alone, she looked up from the boot she was mending to ask, without preamble, 'Do we smell?'
> 'Yes.'
> 'Does the odor offend you?'
> 'Yes.'

She sewed in silence for a while, then said, 'You smell and it's offensive to us. We wondered if we smelled and if it offended you.'

The widespread role of odour as a marker of social identity and difference led one early twentieth-century scientist to hypothesize that olfactory affinities and antipathies are an important means of group preservation. Whether this is true or not, the odour of the other does in fact often serve as a scapegoat for certain antipathies towards the other. This principle can be found to operate when members of one culture attribute an exaggeratedly offensive odour to members of another culture for whom they feel an animosity for unrelated reasons. In the anti-Semitic Europe of the Middle Ages, for example, it was believed by many that Jews emitted a reek so horrible that they could only rid themselves of it by Christian baptism or by drinking the blood of a Christian child!

3   Blacks have also traditionally been assigned a foul odour by mainstream Western culture, evidenced both in descriptions by early European anthropologists of the 'stench' of Africans, and in white stereotypes of 'repulsive-smelling' blacks in the American South. John Dollard writes in *Caste and Class in a Southern Town*:

> Among beliefs which profess to show that Negro and white people cannot intimately participate in the same civilization is the perennial one that Negroes have a smell extremely disagreeable to white people . . . White people generally regard this argument as a crushing final proof of the impossibility of close association between the races.

White Westerners, in turn, are often, to their surprise, perceived as foul-smelling by members of other cultures and races.

4   It is evident in most such cases that the stench ascribed to the other is far less a response to an actual perception of the odour of the other than a potent metaphor for the social decay it is feared the other, often simply by virtue of its being 'other', will cause in the established order. On a small scale we say that something or someone 'stinks' when it or they disagree with our notion of propriety, on a large scale we apply this metaphor to whole groups of people. Therefore, while we may feel an antipathy towards something or someone because its or their odour offends us, we may equally ascribe an offensive odour to something because we feel an antipathy for it (or indeed the two elements may operate simultaneously so as to reinforce each other).

5   The use of olfactory symbolism as a means of expressing and regulating cultural identity and difference is found in a great many societies. A particularly well-elaborated example of the olfactory classification of different social groups is provided by the Tukano-speaking tribes of the Colombian Amazon. According to this Amazonian culture, all mem-

bers of a tribe share the same general body odour which is said to mark the territory of the tribe in the same way that animals mark their territories through odour. This territorial odour is called *mahsá sëríri,* and has the metaphorical meaning of 'sympathy' or 'tribal feeling'.

The specific odour of each tribal group is considered to be caused 6 by the different foods it customarily eats. Thus, it is said of the intermarrying Desana, Pira-Tapuya and Tukano tribes that the Desana, who are hunters, smell of meat, the Pira-Tapuya, associated with fishing, smell of fish, and the Tukano, associated with agriculture, of roots. It is held to be possible to recognize the distinct 'odour trails' laid down by these different exogamic groups within the general communal territory. Indeed, when travelling from one region to another, members of these tribes continually sniff the air and remark on the different territorial and tribal odours. These distinct group odours all have different symbolic associations which serve to order the interaction between one tribe and another. Odour thus functions in this Amazonian society as a marker of tribal identity and territory, and as a regulator of intertribal relations.

The establishment of social boundaries through recourse to olfac- 7 tory markers can take place within communities as well as between them. It is common, for instance, for the dominant class in a society to characterize itself as pleasant-smelling, or inodorate, and the subordinate class as foul-smelling. In ancient Greece, for example, Socrates opposed the use of perfume by men on the principle that it masked the natural olfactory distinctions between freemen and slaves: 'If you perfume a slave and a freeman, the difference of their birth produces none in the smell; and the scent is perceived as soon in the one as in the other.'

In nineteenth- and early twentieth-century Europe, the principal 8 olfactory distinction was between the upper class, who lived in a clean, inodorate or fragrant environment and used light delicate scents, and the working class, who lived in a dirty, foul-smelling environment, and used heavy coarse scents. Somerset Maugham wrote in 1927:

> In the West we are divided from our fellows by our sense of smell . . . I do not blame the working man because he stinks, but stink he does. It makes social intercourse difficult to persons of a sensitive nostril.

George Orwell likewise argued that the 'real secret of class distinctions in the West' could be 'summed up in four frightful words . . . *The lower classes smell'*. It is odour, according to Orwell, which serves to make the class barrier impassable:

> Race-hatred, religious hatred, differences of education, of temperament, of intellect, even differences of moral code, can be got over; but physical repulsion cannot.

The social hierarchy of smell described by Maugham and Orwell is also evidenced in the imaginative literature of the period. In *My Lady Ludlow* by Elizabeth Gaskell, for example, the superfine sensibility of an aristocrat is described in terms of her olfactory preferences:

> The choice of odours was what my lady piqued herself upon, saying nothing showed birth like a keen susceptibility of smell. We never named musk in her presence . . . her opinion on the subject was believed to be, that no scent derived from an animal could ever be of a sufficiently pure nature to give pleasure to any person of good family.

Indeed, even musky-scented flowers were suspect. If a suitor of one of Lady Ludlow's maids appeared wearing an offending sprig in his buttonhole, 'she was afraid that he liked coarse pleasures, and I am not sure if she did not think that his preference for this coarse sweetness did not imply a probability that he would take to drinking'.

9   If the olfactory delicacy of the upper class was due to the fineness of its sense of smell, the olfactory promiscuity indulged in by the working class was reputed to be the result of a dull sense of smell. As a Victorian perfumer explains:

> Among the lower orders, bad smells are little heeded; in fact, 'noses have they, but they smell not'; and the result is, a continuance to live in an atmosphere laden with poisonous odours, whereas anyone with the least power of smelling retained shuns such odours, as they would anything else that is vile or pernicious.

As these citations make plain, the working classes' apparent proclivity for 'disreputable' odours was considered an index of their propensity for all else that was disreputable. As is also evident, these olfactory class distinctions were not thought to be based on mere social circumstance, but rather on fundamental differences in the quality of the sense of smell itself between the classes.

10   The odour of the proletarian other in nineteenth-century Europe was often real enough: many workers did reek of the filthy conditions in which they lived and worked. The disapprobation accorded this reek by the middle and upper classes, however, was as much a product of certain social sensibilities as of natural olfactory sensibilities. Orwell, for example, admits as much by saying that 'even "lower class" people whom you knew to be quite clean—servants, for instance—were faintly unappetising. The smell of their sweat, the very texture of their skins, were mysteriously different from yours.'

11   Indeed, in previous centuries members of the European aristocracy had reeked just as much as anyone. The typical stench of the elaborate wigs affected by the eighteenth-century nobility, for instance, led one English writer of the time to comment that he had had 'the honour of smell-

ing in the most unsavoury manner very many heads of the first rank', 'rank' wittily conveying here both class and reek. So closely associated were certain 'foul' odours with the nobility of the day, that, according to the contemporary playwright, Sebastien Chamfort, one provincial gentleman, on returning home from Versailles, ordered his servants to urinate around his manor so that his home would acquire the same aristocratic aroma as that famed court. Thus while certain odours, such as that of urine, tend to be universally disliked, cultural norms can make these odours a matter of indifference or even of appeal. Just as 'beauty is in the eye of the beholder', so 'fragrance is in the nose of the smeller'.

With this in mind, let us turn to the rigorous olfactory class division [12] effected by the Dasseneton of Southwestern Ethiopia. The Dassanetch divide themselves into cattle-raising pastoralists and fishermen. As cattle are of pre-eminent practical and symbolic importance for the Dassanetch, pastoralists are regarded as greatly superior to fishermen. Each of these two social groups is identified with the odour of the species of animal it depends on for its livelihood. The Dassanetch, in fact, believe that humans are naturally inodorate and that their odours are acquired through contact with their particular environments.

The value accorded cattle by the Dassanetch is such that the smell [13] of everything associated with cattle is considered good, and the pastoralists do all they can to augment their identification with this prestigious odour:

> They often wash their hands in cattle urine; men smear manure on their bodies to advertise the fertility of their herds; and nubile girls and fertile women smear *ghee* [liquid butter] on their shoulders, heads, hair and bosoms to ensure fertility . . . The Dassanetch explicitly say that the smell of *ghee* serves to attract men and is the 'perfume', so to speak, of women.

While other odours, such as those of flowers, are also considered good by the Dassanetch, the odour of cattle has the added characteristic of serving as a marker of group identity for the pastoralists.

As pastoralists are identified with the odour of cattle in Dassanetch [14] society, so fishermen and their families are identified with the odour of fish. Unlike cattle, however, fish are symbolically suspect: they are considered to exist outside the natural cycles of weather and sexuality, so fundamental to the well-being and procreation of cattle. Fish, and the fishermen who are associated with them, are therefore said by the pastoralists to be foul-smelling. The supposed acyclical nature of fish makes their odour particularly noxious for, 'unlike other bad smells, which come and go, stimulate awareness, and evaporate, the bad smell of fish is a kind of stagnation and is permanently connected with [fishermen]'. This belief in the foul odour of fishermen is so strongly held by the 'upper-class' pastoralists that they will hold their noses when walking by fishermen's huts. Although a certain amount of inter-change takes place between the two groups, usually to the advantage of the pastoralists, the social and olfactory barriers between them are so rigidly established as to prevent any merging of identities.

15   It is noteworthy that for most outsiders the smell of the Dassanetch pastoralists, perfumed with butter, manure and cattle urine, would probably be more repellent than that of the fishermen, who apparently do not make any special effort to give themselves a piscine odour. Nonetheless, the social and olfactory codes of Dassanetch society state definitively that pastoralists are good-smelling and fishermen bad-smelling. Evidently, here again the standards of olfactory classification are being strongly influenced by cultural considerations. The odour of cattle is held to be superior to that of fish by the Dassanetch because cattle are considered superior to fish. The odour of pastoralists, who are identified with cattle and form the elite within Dassanetch society, is therefore considered good, while that of fishermen, who are identi-fied with the inferior fish, is considered bad.

16   The odour of the fisherman other is classified as foul by the domi-nant pastoralists, however, not only because fish and fishermen consti-tute an 'inferior' and 'alien' group, but also—as seems to be the rule in such cases—because the pastoralists perceive them as threatening de-cay within their own community. For the pastoralists, the world of fish and fishermen, independent as it apparently is from periodic cycles, represents a world without order which can disrupt the orderly cycles on which their own bovine world depends. The pastoralists' repug-nance to the odour of fish and fishermen is thus above all a repugnance to the disorder which it represents. This repugnance is heightened by the fear that disorder, like odour, has the ability to transgress bound-aries. The pastoralists, for example, believe that 'the bad smell of fisher-men can infect the cattle'.

17   The fact that the two groups are not entirely separate but constitute one interdependent community probably only increases the pastoral-ists' concern to safeguard their own identity and social structure from external forces of corruption. Even within the general order of a society, therefore, certain peoples can represent disorder from the perspective of the dominant class and as a result be attributed the foul smell of decay.

When One Becomes Other

18   In *Gulliver's Travels*, when Gulliver returns home from his voyages, he finds that he cannot abide the odour of his family. Even after having been home for five years, Gulliver can still barely tolerate the smell of other humans. He states:

> I began last week to permit my wife to sit at dinner with me, at the far-thest end of a long table . . . Yet the smell of a [human] continuing very

offensive, I always keep my nose well stopped with rue, lavender, or tobacco leaves.

This olfactory antipathy was instilled in Gulliver during his stay in a land in which human-like creatures, called Yahoos, manifested all the coarsest vices, and horse-like creatures, called Houyhnhmns, the highest virtues. On returning home after this experience Gulliver found that his cultural and olfactory antipodes had become inverted: he felt at odds with his own kind, and at one with horses:

> The first money I laid out [on returning] was to buy two young stone-horses, which I keep in a good stable, and next to them the groom is my greatest favourite; for I feel my spirits revived by the smell he contracts in the stable. My horses understand me tolerably well; I converse with them at least four hours every day. They are strangers to bridle or saddle; they live in great amity with me, and friendship to each other.

For Gulliver humans had become the threatening other, dangerous 'brutes' who leave the earth 'reeking with the blood of its inhabitants', while nature had come to represent harmony and order. The olfactory consequence of this was that the odour of humans became repulsive to Gulliver, and the odour of horses attractive.

The olfactory reversal described so strikingly in *Gulliver's Travels*   19 can be found in actual tales of journeys in which travellers are assimilated into other cultures and odours. One such case deals with a young white man, Manuel Cordova, who was captured by an Amazonian tribe in the early twentieth century. Cordova's first olfactory impression of his captors was that they had a strange, musky odour. In turn, the Amazonians apparently did not consider Cordova to have quite the right 'odour of culture', for, as part of their rite of tribal initiation, they brushed Cordova's body with fragrant leaves and bathed him with a fragrant liquid.

After a period of living with the tribe, Cordova became 'attuned' to   20 its olfactory traits. Eventually, however, he began to long to return to his own people. 'It was at this time', he states, 'that I began to notice again the smell of these people, a strange, persistent musky odor that I began to dislike.' As his dissatisfaction with tribal life grew, Cordova found that the 'overpowering musky smell' of the tribe 'nauseated' him. The Indians had once more become 'other' for Cordova and he returned to the world of whites. One can imagine that, without the cultural and olfactory re-reversal that Cordova experienced before returning to his own people, he would have found himself in a similar predicament to Gulliver on his return home.

A similar 'olfactory reversal' is sometimes described as occurring   21 after a journey to the world of the supernatural. An example of this is found in the legend of the twelfth-century Dutch mystic, Christina Mirabilis. Christina, on resurrecting shortly after her death, found that her experience of the divine fragrance had rendered her unable to abide the odour of humans. It was only after she immersed herself in a baptismal fount and was symbolically born again that she was once again able to tolerate the odour of humans and live among them.

22   One's own odour is also often altered through association with the supernatural in the traditions of different cultures. In the West holy persons were believed to manifest an 'odour of sanctity', signalling the presence of the Holy Spirit, while the wicked manifested the stench of the Devil. Similarly, among the Warao of Venezuela, the bad breath of the sorcerer indicates that he has recently returned from a journey to the foul underworld.

23   Those persons who come into the presence of supernatural beings without undergoing the correct olfactory transformation are experienced as 'other' by such beings. In a legend of the Andes the daughter of a mountain deity falls in love with a human and tries to hide him in her home. Her parents discover the man by his foul odour, however, and he is forced to leave the supernatural abode. In ancient Egypt the dead king had to be perfumed with incense in order to be accepted by the gods:

> The use of [incense] in assuring the divinity of the dead king is important, for when he goes to the Horizon or the West he is most easily accepted by the gods when he is like them, and being like them means among other things that 'your scent is as their scent . . .'

For the ancient Egyptians, incense was the scent of the gods. By acquiring this scent, the king affirmed his basic identity with the gods: 'My sweat is the sweat of Horus, my odour is the odour of Horus.'

24   One can become other not only through contact with others, but also through a change in one's social status, which often produces a corresponding change in one's olfactory status (and vice versa). In Bororo society, for instance, new parents, who constitute a particularly anomalous class, are surrounded by olfactory taboos: they are not supposed to engage in strenuous labour because the odour of their sweat would be harmful to them, and they are not supposed to engage in sexual relations because the odours of sexual fluids would be harmful to their child. New mothers are not allowed to prepare food for others for their 'stench' would be communicated through the food and harm those who ate it. In parts of Southern Europe, the anomalous nature of couples who contracted what was considered a socially inappropriate marriage was traditionally signalled by incensing the couple's house with foul smoke. In such cases, olfactory symbolism is used to mark a person's separation, temporary or permanent, from cultural norms.

Significantly, individuals who feel themselves to be cut off from so- 25
ciety can sometimes attribute a foul odour to themselves. Such persons
imagine that their bodies give off putrid emanations, often as a result of
an inherent fault or evil within themselves, which cause them to be socially isolated. Interestingly, this disorder is particularly found in Japan. The sufferers tend to be timid young men, who believe that the
odours they emit are so repugnant that they avoid contact with others,
and constantly wash and deodorize themselves. This disorder would
seem to be a literal actualization of the expression 'to be in ill odour',
meaning to be in a state of social disfavour. One feels that, in some in-
trinsic way, one is 'other' within one's society, and one imagines that
this 'otherness' is communicated to one's fellows through a distinguishing evil odour.

*   *   *

Odours are symbolically employed by many cultures to serve as 26
identifying marks of different classes of beings. The attractive/repul-
sive nature of olfactory experience makes odour a particularly useful
symbolic vehicle for categorizing different groups according to cultural
values, as it invests classificatory systems with a strong emotive power.
The inhalation of a foul odour, for instance, produces the immediate
physical repugnance a society might demand its members feel in response to a particular class of people. To characterize a certain group as
foul-smelling, therefore, is to render it repellent at a very basic physical
and emotional level, and not simply at a cognitive level. Likewise, to
characterize a group as fragrant is to render it attractive, although this
attractiveness may be tempered by connotations of underlying danger.

Such categorizations are not always absolute, for the same group 27
may sometimes be characterized as fragrant, and sometimes as foul. In
the West, for example, a woman may be a fragrant maiden in one context, and a foul witch in another. Similarly, among the Tukano, deer are
sometimes seen as 'clean, sleek forest maidens, sweet scented and seductive', and sometimes as 'repulsive bitches in heat'. This ambivalence of
odour indicates the ambivalent attitudes of the dominant group towards
those others it finds attractive on one level and repellent on another.

As a rule, the dominant group in a society ascribes to itself a pleas- 28
ant or neutral smell within this system of olfactory classification. What
constitutes a 'pleasant' (or 'unpleasant') odour is by no means universally agreed upon, however. For the Dassanetch of Ethopia, the odour
of cow manure is 'pleasant' and serves as the identifying olfactory
mark of the dominant group. In the West, where the odour of manure is
considered 'unpleasant', to identify a group as smelling of manure
would be to place it in a position of exclusion and inferiority. Fragrance
and foulness must therefore always be understood within a specific
cultural context.

29   It is not only the strong emotional appeal of smell which makes odours useful for classifying others, but also the fact that it can be perceived at a distance and does not require intimate contact to be experienced. Thus, to label a group 'foul', one does not need to have had any close association with it. At the same time, the ability of odours to travel through space renders them capable of crossing barriers.

30   This transitive character of odour symbolically expresses the ability of different classes of beings to transcend class boundaries. The foul other can invade one; the fragrant other, absorb one. Odour therefore comes to symbolize not only the qualities of the other, but also the ability of the other to disrupt one's own order. The disintegrative power of the odour of the other can be controlled through practices of strict separation of groups with different olfactory and cultural values, or through the use of powerful opposing odours—a classic example of the latter practice being the widespread use of fragrance to ward off evil spirits.

31   The very ability of odour to break down barriers, which renders it so dangerous in one regard, also makes it, however, a powerful force for integration. The incense employed in a religious ritual, for instance, serves not only to unite humans and gods, but also to unite the participants in the rite. With regard to this characteristic of odour, a shared smell can give the partakers a strong 'we' feeling, while an interchange of personal or other odours between individuals and groups, such as takes place in many forms of greetings, can serve as a basis for the recognition and mediation of mutual differences.

✦ Evaluating the Text

1. Which of the examples presented by Classen did you find most effective in clarifying the extent to which olfactory codes are shaped by and express cultural values?

2. Why are the concepts of identity and difference important in understanding how different cultures have strikingly different ways of making sense of the world?

3. How do considerations of social class enter into Classen's analysis?

✦ Exploring Different Perspectives

1. What insights can you discover in Jo Goodwin Parker's account (see "What Is Poverty?") that confirm Constance Classen's observations about the olfactory symbolism of smell?

2. To what extent is the use of perfume an olfactory veneer similar to veneers used in visual depictions of food, as described by Roland Barthes

in "Ornamental Cookery"? Are the associated class aspirations similar, and if so, in what way?

✦ *Extending Viewpoints Through Writing*

1. Discuss some examples of how olfactory symbolism operates in contemporary American culture and analyze the values that are attached to certain smells (for example, the smell inserts advertisers use in magazines or the choice of air fresheners available at carwashes, such as the "new car smell").

2. Analyze any horror tale in terms of its traditional elements that pit a righteous hero or heroine against an inhuman foe (for example, Von Helsing versus Dracula). To what extent is the horror of the story based on the fear that the hero or heroine will become contaminated by contact with the "monster"? How is this similar to Constance Classen's explanation, in "The Odour of the Other," of the fear the "other" engenders, as reflected in olfactory symbolism?

Catherine Lim

Paper

---◆---

Catherine Lim is one of Singapore's foremost writers. She currently works for the Curriculum Development Institute of Singapore, writing English language instructional materials for use in the primary schools. Her widely praised collections of short stories include Little Ironies—Stories of Singapore *(1978), from which "Paper" is taken,* Or Else, The Lightning God and Other Stories *(1980), and* The Shadow of a Shadow of a Dream—Love Stories of Singapore *(1981). She is also the author of two novels,* They Do Return *(1982) and* The Serpent's Tooth *(1983). Her short stories have been compared to those of Guy de Maupassant for their accuracy of observation, clarity in presentation of character, and precise detail. Lim's stories reveal a wealth of information about the forces, customs, and pressures that shape the lives of the Chinese community in Singapore, a densely populated metropolis in which Chinese, Malay, and Indian cultures coexist and thrive. "Paper" is set against the turbulent background of the Singapore Stock Exchange, a volatile financial market reflecting the seemingly limitless possibilities of one of the world's most productive financial, industrial, and commercial centers. This story dramatically explores how the lure of easy money leads a man and his wife to tragic consequences.*

The city of Singapore (in Malay, "City of Lions") and about sixty islets make up the Republic of Singapore, at the southern tip of the Malay peninsula. The British East India Company purchased it in 1819 through the efforts of Sir T. S. Raffles. After occupation by the Japanese in World War II, Singapore became a British colony in 1946 and an independent self-governing state in 1959. Although it is the smallest country in Southeast Asia, Singapore has the second highest standard of living in eastern Asia, second only to Japan.

1   He wanted it, he dreamed of it, he hankered after it, as an addict after his opiate. Once the notion of a big beautiful house had lodged itself in his imagination, Tay Soon nurtured it until it became the consuming passion of his life. A house. A dream house such as he had seen on his drives with his wife and children along the roads bordering the prestigious housing estates on the island, and in the glossy pages of *Homes* and *Modern Living*. Or rather, it was a house which was an amalgam of the best, the most beautiful aspects of the houses he had seen. He knew every detail of his dream house already, from the aluminum sliding doors to the actual shade of the dining room carpet to the shape of the

346

swimming pool. Kidney. He rather liked that shape. He was not ashamed of the enthusiasm with which he spoke of the dream house, an enthusiasm that belonged to women only, he was told. Indeed, his enthusiasm was so great that it had infected his wife and even his children, small though they were. Soon his wife Yee Lian was describing to her sister Yee Yeng, the dream house in all its perfection of shape and decor, and the children were telling their cousins and friends,"My daddy says that when our house is ready . . ."

They talked of the dream house endlessly. It had become a reality   2
stronger than the reality of the small terrace house which they were sharing with Tay Soon's mother, to whom it belonged. Tay Soon's mother, whose little business of selling bottled curries and vegetable preserves which she made herself, left her little time for dreams, clucked her tongue and shook her head and made sarcastic remarks about the ambitiousness of young people nowadays.

"What's wrong with this house we're staying in?" she asked petu-   3
lantly. "Aren't we all comfortable in it?"

Not as long as you have your horrid ancestral altars all over the   4
place, and your grotesque sense of colour—imagine painting the kitchen wall bright pink. But Yee Lian was tactful enough to keep the remarks to herself, or to make them only to her sister Yee Yeng, otherwise they were sure to reach the old lady, and there would be no end to her sharp tongue.

The house—the dream house—it would be a far cry from the little   5
terrace house in which they were all staying now, and Tay Soon and Yee Lian talked endlessly about it, and it grew magnificently in their imaginations, this dream house of theirs with its timbered ceiling and panelled walls and sunken circular sitting room which was to be carpeted in rich amber. It was no empty dream, for there was much money in the bank already. Forty thousand dollars had been saved. The house would cost many times that, but Tay Soon and Yee Lian with their good salaries would be able to manage very well. Once they took care of the down payment, they would be able to pay back monthly over a period of ten years—fifteen, twenty—what did it matter how long it took as long as the dream house was theirs? It had become the symbol of the peak of earthly achievement, and all of Tay Soon's energies and devotion were directed towards its realisation. His mother said,"You're a show-off; what's so grand about marble flooring and a swimming pool? Why don't you put your money to better use?" But the forty thousand grew steadily, and after Tay Soon and Yee Lian had put in every cent of their annual bonuses, it grew to forty eight thousand, and husband and wife smiled at the smooth way their plans were going.

It was a time of growing interest in the stock market. The quota-   6
tions for stocks and shares were climbing the charts, and the crowds in the rooms of the broking houses were growing perceptibly. Might we

not do something about this? Yee Lian said to her husband. Do you know that Dr. Soo bought Rustan Banking for four dollars and today the shares are worth seven dollars each? The temptation was great. The rewards were almost immediate. Thirty thousand dollars' worth of NBE became fifty-five thousand almost overnight. Tay Soon and Yee Lian whooped. They put their remaining eighteen thousand in Far East Mart. Three days later the shares were worth twice that much. It was not to be imagined that things could stop here. Tay Soon secured a loan from his bank and put twenty thousand in OHTE. This was a particularly lucky share; it shot up to four times its value in three days.

7 "Oh, this is too much, too much," cried Yee Lian in her ecstasy, and she sat down with pencil and paper, and found after a few minutes' calculation that they had made a cool one hundred thousand in a matter of days.

8 And now there was to be no stopping. The newspapers were full of it, everybody was talking about it, it was in the very air. There was plenty of money to be made in the stock exchange by those who had guts—money to be made by the hour, by the minute, for the prices of stocks and shares were rising faster than anyone could keep track of them! Dr. Soo was said—he laughingly dismissed it as a silly rumour—Dr. Soo was said to have made two million dollars already. If he sold all his shares now, he would be a millionaire twice over. And Yee Yeng, Yee Lian's sister, who had been urged with sisterly goodwill to come join the others make money, laughed happily to find that the shares she had bought for four twenty on Tuesday had risen to seven ninety-five on Friday—she laughed and thanked Yee Lian who advised her not to sell yet, it was going further, it would hit the ten dollar mark by next week. And Tay Soon both laughed and cursed—cursed that he had failed to buy a share at nine dollars which a few days later had hit seventeen dollars! Yee Lian said reproachfully, "I thought I told you to buy it, darling," and Tay Soon had beaten his forehead in despair and said, "I know, I know, why didn't I! Big fool that I am!" And he had another reason to curse himself—he sold five thousand West Parkes at sixteen twenty-three per share, and saw, to his horror, West Parkes climb to eighteen ninety the very next day!

9 "I'll never sell now," he vowed. "I'll hold on. I won't be so foolish." And the frenzy continued. Husband and wife couldn't talk or think of anything else. They thought fondly of their shares—going to be worth a million altogether soon. A million! In the peak of good humour, Yee Lian went to her mother-in-law, forgetting the past insults, and advised her to join the others by buying some shares; she would get her broker to buy them immediately for her, there was sure money in it. The old lady refused curtly, and to her son later, she showed great annoyance, scolding him for being so foolish as to put all his money in those worthless shares. "Worthless!" exploded Tay Soon. "Do you know, Mother, if

I sold all my shares today, I would have the money to buy fifty terrace houses like the one you have?"

His wife said,"Oh, we'll just leave her alone. I was kind enough to offer to help her make money. But since she's so nasty and ungrateful, we'll leave her alone." The comforting, triumphant thought was that soon, very soon, they would be able to purchase their dream house; it would be even more magnificent than the one they had dreamt of, since they had made almost a—Yee Lian preferred not to say the sum. There was the old superstitious fear of losing something when it is too often or too directly referred to, and Yee Lian had cautioned her husband not to make mention of their gains.

"Not to worry, not to worry," he said jovially, not superstitious like his wife. "After all, it's just paper gains so far."

The downward slide, or the bursting of the bubble as the newspapers dramatically called it, did not initially cause much alarm. For the speculators all expected the shares to bounce back to their original strength and thence continue the phenomenal growth, but that did not happen. The slide continued.

Tay Soon said nervously,"Shall we sell? Do you think we should sell?" but Yee Lian said stoutly, "There is talk that this decline is a technical thing only—it will be over soon, and then the rise will continue. After all, see what is happening in Hong Kong and London and New York. Things are as good as ever."

"We're still making, so not to worry," said Yee Lian after a few days. Their gains were pared by half. A few days later, their gains were pared to marginal.

There is talk of a recovery, insisted Yee Lian. Do you know, Tay Soon, Dr. Soo's wife is buying up some OHTE and West Parkes now? She says these two are sure to rise. She has some inside information that these two are going to climb past the forty-dollar mark—

Tay Soon sold all his shares and put the money in OHTE and West Parkes. OHTE and West Parkes crashed shortly afterwards. Some began to say the shares were not worth the paper of the certificates.

"Oh, I can't believe, I can't believe it," gasped Yee Lian, pale and sick. Tay Soon looked in mute horror at her.

"All our money was in OHTE and West Parkes," he said, his lips dry.

"That stupid Soo woman!" shrieked Yee Lian. "I think she deliberately led me astray with her advice! She's always been jealous of me—ever since she knew we were going to build a house grander than hers!"

"How are we going to get our house now?" asked Tay Soon in deep distress, and for the first time he wept. He wept like a child, for the loss of all his money, for the loss of the dream house that he had never stopped loving and worshipping.

21   The pain bit into his very mind and soul, so that he was like a mad-man, unable to go to his office to work, unable to do anything but haunt the broking houses, watching with frenzied anxiety for the OHTE and West Parkes to show him hope. But there was no hope. The decline continued with gleeful rapidity. His broker advised him to sell, before it was too late, but he shrieked angrily, "What! Sell at a fraction at which I bought them! How can this be tolerated!"

22   And he went on hoping against hope.

23   He began to have wild dreams in which he sometimes laughed and sometimes screamed. His wife Yee Lian was afraid and she ran sobbing to her sister who never failed to remind her curtly that all her savings were gone, simply because when she had wanted to sell, Yee Lian had advised her not to.

24   "But what is your sorrow compared to mine," wept Yee Lian,"see what's happening to my husband. He's cracking up! He talks to him-self, he doesn't eat, he has nightmares, he beats the children. Oh, he's finished!"

25   Her mother-in-law took charge of the situation, while Yee Lian, wide-eyed in mute horror at the terrible change that had come over her husband, shrank away and looked to her two small children for com-fort. Tight-lipped and grim, the elderly woman made herbal medicines for Tay Soon, brewing and straining for hours, and got a Chinese med-icine man to come have a look at him.

26   "There is a devil in him," said the medicine man, and he proceeded to make him a drink which he mixed with the ashes of a piece of prayer paper. But Tay Soon grew worse. He lay in bed, white, haggard and de-lirious, seeming to be beyond the touch of healing. In the end, Yee Lian, on the advice of her sister and friends, put him in hospital.

27   "I have money left for the funeral," whimpered the frightened Yee Lian only a week later, but her mother-in-law sharply retorted,"You leave everything to me! I have the money for his funeral, and I shall give him the best! He wanted a beautiful house all his life; I shall give him a beautiful house now!"

28   She went to the man who was well-known on the island for his beautiful houses, and she ordered the best. It would come to nearly a thousand dollars, said the man, a thin, wizened fellow whose funereal gauntness and pallor seemed to be a concession to his calling.

29   That doesn't matter, she said, I want the best. The house is to be made of superior paper, she instructed, and he was to make it to her specifications. She recollected that he, Tay Soon, had often spoken of marble flooring, a timbered ceiling and a kidney-shaped swimming pool. Could he simulate all these in paper?

30   The thin, wizened man said,"I've never done anything like that be-fore. All my paper houses for the dead have been the usual kind—I can put in paper furniture and paper cars, paper utensils for the kitchen

and paper servants, all that the dead will need in the other world. But I shall try to put in what you've asked for. Only it will cost more."

The house when it was ready, was most beautiful to see. It stood 31 seven feet tall, a delicate framework of wire and thin bamboo strips covered with finely worked paper of a myriad colours. Little silver flowers, scattered liberally throughout the entire structure, gave a carnival atmosphere. There was a paper swimming pool (round, as the man had not understood "kidney") which had to be fitted inside the house itself, as there was no provision for a garden or surrounding grounds. Inside the house were paper figures; there were at least four servants to attend to the needs of the master who was posed beside two cars, one distinctly a Chevrolet and the other a Mercedes.

At the appointed time, the paper house was brought to Tay Soon's 32 grave and set on fire there. It burned brilliantly, and in three minutes was a heap of ashes on the grave.

✦ Evaluating the Text

1. To what extent are Tay Soon and his wife and children caught up in the idea of buying a magnificent dream house? How does the elaborate nature of the house Tay Soon wishes to own symbolize the peak of achievement?

2. How does Lim establish that Tay Soon's mother (with whom Tay Soon and his wife live) is indifferent to and even critical of their dream house? How would you characterize the difference in values of Tay Soon and his wife as compared with those of his mother?

3. What is Lim's attitude toward the events she describes in her story? How do you think she feels toward her characters—Tay Soon, Yee Lian, and Tay Soon's mother?

4. Why doesn't Tay Soon sell his shares and capitalize on his first remarkable gains instead of staying in the market in hopes of being able to build an even more magnificent house? What in Tay Soon's nature makes him his own worst enemy?

5. What role does Tay Soon's wife, Yee Lian, play in contributing to the entire disaster? You might examine her actions both at the beginning of the story and later when the disastrous outcome might still have been averted.

6. How does the recurrent mention of the word *paper* (paper profits, certificates of paper, prayer paper, a paper house, and shares not worth the paper they are printed on) focus the reader's attention on one of the story's central themes?

7. Analyze the structure of the story, and follow its development through the four separate scenes of ever-rising tension and final resolution. How would you describe the action in each of these scenes?

8. How does the miniature paper house that Tay Soon's mother has constructed for him after his death contrast ironically to the magnificent dream house Tay Soon had envisioned? How does the contrast of these two houses (the miniature paper version of his dream house) dramatize the story's central theme?

✦ *Exploring Different Perspectives*

1. In a strange way, the paper house burned at Tay Soon's grave is more representative of Tay Soon's desires for material gratification than anything he had achieved in life. Compare the fantasy function of this image with Roland Barthes's analysis of the symbolism of how things look in "Ornamental Cookery."

2. How does the contrast between Jo Goodwin Parker and Tay Soon illustrate the difference between genuine needs and illusory wants and desires? How does the function of "paper" in the two selections illustrate this contrast between the two?

✦ *Extending Viewpoints Through Writing*

1. If you have ever been involved in a gambling venture in which the psychological dynamics of greed and fear were operating, describe the experiences.

2. What is your attitude toward deferring material gratification? Did you find yourself valuing the fantasies you had about a vacation, car, clothes, jewelry, or whatever, in ways comparable to the feelings of Tay Soon?

3. To discover what you really value, consider the following hypothetical situation: a raging fire has started where you live. You can only save one item other than another person or a pet. What item would you save? How does the value of this item (material, sentimental, or both) imply what is really important to you? Discuss your reactions.

Connecting Cultures

◆

Roland Barthes, Ornamental Cookery

What insights into the symbolic function of food emerge from the analyses of Roland Barthes and Nick Fiddes (see "The Power of Meat," Chapter 8)?

Jo Goodwin Parker, What Is Poverty?

Discuss the devastating effects of poverty on the human spirit, drawing on the accounts by Jo Goodwin Parker and Luis Alberto Urrea (see "Border Story," Chapter 7).

Mahdokht Kashkuli, The Button

How is the use of the button in Mahdokht Kashkuli's story and the Persian carpet in Hanan al-Shaykh's story (see "The Persian Carpet," Chapter 2) made to symbolize the respective emotional states of the protagonists?

Alonso Salazar, The Lords of Creation

What similarities and differences can you discover in the reactions to the horrifying conditions in Medellín and Tijuana (see Luis Alberto Urrea's "Border Story," Chapter 7)?

Jamaica Kincaid, A Small Place

How does the voluntary displacement characteristic of the tourist encourage perceptions that are very different from those of exiles who are forced to emigrate to a strange land? You may wish to draw on the discussion in Edward Said's "Reflections on Exile" (Chapter 7).

Mary Crow Dog and Richard Erdoes, Civilize Them with a Stick

How does the phenomenon of diminished self-esteem as a result of propaganda by those in power enter into the account by Mary Crow Dog and that of Ngũgĩ wa Thiong'o (see "Decolonising the Mind," Chapter 6)?

Constance Classen, *The Odour of the Other*

How does Constance Classen's theory of the "other" help explain the concept of *marimé* (see William M. Kephart's "The Gypsies," Chapter 7)?

Catherine Lim, *Paper*

In what way do Catherine Lim and Dino Buzzati (see "The Falling Girl," Chapter 2) treat the theme of a fatal attraction to wealth and social status using the very different approaches of realism and surrealism?

6

Power and Politics

$\blacklozenge$

No conflicts between different points of view are more dramatic than those between individual citizens and the nation-states to which they relinquish a certain degree of freedom in exchange for the benefits that can be achieved only through collective political and social institutions, such as the military and the legal, health care, and educational systems. The allegiance individuals owe their governments and the protection of individual rights that citizens expect in return have been the subject of intense analysis through the ages by such figures as Socrates in Plato's *Apology* and *Crito,* Henry David Thoreau in *Civil Disobedience,* and Martin Luther King, Jr., in "A Letter From Birmingham Jail." The readings that follow continue this debate by providing accounts drawn from many different societies and revealing assumptions and expectations very different, in many cases, from those that characterize our own democratic form of government.

The concept of the state includes those political processes and organizations that serve as the means through which individuals and groups obtain and employ power. Political organization in different cultures may take a variety of forms, whether that of a chieftain in a tribal culture or more complex distributions of power and authority in societies like that of the United States, with two parties, an electoral college, judges, courts, prisons, armed forces, a state department, and other institutions designed to maintain and regulate order.

In theory, the legal processes of a society exist to enforce that society's concept of justice and its accompanying norms, laws, and customs. In practice, however, penalties and fines, imprisonment, torture, ostracism, and even death are meted out in many cultures in far more arbitrary ways.

In the former Yugoslavia, for example, the use of the phrase *ethnic cleansing* has served to conceal a genocidal policy in which state power was employed to destroy entire groups of people on grounds of presumed ethnicity. In South Africa, for many years, the bureaucratic machinery of the state served the purpose of implementing a repressive theory of apartheid.

A politicized environment within a state has an intensely corrosive effect on personal relationships when individual loyalties clash with officially decreed allegiances. Authors in many countries and cultures describe the seductive and persuasive powers the state can mobilize through propaganda and the threat of force to manipulate its citizens. Regimes also remain in power by channeling the frustrations of one group against another. Many of the following selections explore the predicaments of ordinary citizens trying to survive oppression.

Golda Meir, a former prime minister of Israel, describes the creation of a country in "We Have Our State." Albert Camus, in his classic story "The Guest," projects the no-win situation of a Frenchman living in Algeria during a civil war. A Croatian journalist, Slavenka Drakulić, in "The Balkan Express," reflects on the horrors of the Serbo-Croatian war during her journey to Zagreb. Speaking from a postcolonial perspective in Kenya, Ngũgĩ wa Thiong'o, in "Decolonising the Mind," analyzes the damaging psychological consequences of having been forbidden by the British rulers to write or speak his native language while in school. Jon Swain, in "The Eyes of Vietnam," communicates the atrocities inflicted on boat people following the war in Vietnam. The Chinese writer Nien Cheng describes what happened to her in Shanghai during the Cultural Revolution in "The Red Guards." Also from China, Feng Jicai creates a moving story, "The Tall Woman and Her Short Husband," that depicts the impact of political repression on village life during the same period. In Cyprus, Panos Ioannides explores the question of conscience during wartime in his startling story, "Gregory," which is based on a true incident.

Golda Meir

We Have Our State

———◆———

Golda Meir (1898–1978) was born in Russia, and after a teaching career in the United States, she settled in Palestine in 1921. She later served as Israel's minister of labor and foreign affairs before becoming prime minister in 1969. She sought peace between Israel and the Arab nations through diplomacy but was forced to resign in 1974 after Arab forces launched an unexpected onslaught on Israel a year before. "We Have Our State" is drawn from her autobiography, My Life *(1975), and recounts the circumstances surrounding the moment when Israel became a state on May 14, 1948.*

Formerly part of Palestine, the state of Israel, a homeland for Jews worldwide, was proclaimed in 1948. Israel is bordered by Lebanon to the north, Syria and Jordan to the east, the Mediterranean Sea to the west, and the Gulf of Aqaba (an extension of the Red Sea) to the south. Since its inception, conflict has arisen because of opposition by the surrounding Arab nations to the formation of a Jewish state. In 1979, President Jimmy Carter met with Israeli Prime Minister Menachem Begin and Egyptian President Anwar Sadat to sign a peace treaty. Agreements signed by representatives of Israel and the Palestine Liberation Organization (PLO) in 1993 and 1994 began a process of accommodation that has been periodically undermined by provocations on both sides. The current prime minister is Benjamin Netanyahu, a conservative who was elected following the assassination in 1995 of the Labor Party's prime minister, Yitzhak Rabin.

On the morning of May 14, I participated in a meeting of the People's Council at which we were to decide on the name of the state and on the final formulation of the declaration. The name was less of a problem than the declaration because there was a last-minute argument about the inclusion of a reference to God. Actually the issue had been brought up the day before. The very last sentence, as finally submitted to the small subcommittee charged with producing the final version of the proclamation, began with the words "With trust in the Rock of Israel, we set our hands in witness to this Proclamation. . . ." Ben-Gurion had hoped that the phrase "Rock of Israel" was sufficiently ambiguous to satisfy those Jews for whom it was inconceivable that the document which established the Jewish state should not contain any reference to God, as well as those who were certain to object strenuously to even the least hint of clericalism in the proclamation.

2   But the compromise was not so easily accepted. The spokesman of the religious parties, Rabbi Fishman-Maimon, demanded that the reference to God be unequivocal and said that he would approve of the "Rock of Israel" only if the words "and its Redeemer" were added, while Aaron Zisling of the left wing of the Labor Party was just as determined in the opposite direction. "I cannot sign a document referring in any way to a God in whom I do not believe," he said. It took Ben-Gurion most of the morning to persuade Maimon and Zisling that the meaning of the "Rock of Israel" was actually twofold: While it signified "God" for a great many Jews, perhaps for most, it could also be considered a symbolic and secular reference to the "strength of the Jewish people." In the end Maimon agreed that the word "Redeemer" should be left out of the text, though, funnily enough, the first English-language translation of the proclamation, released for publication abroad that day, contained no reference at all to the "Rock of Israel" since the military censor had struck out the entire last paragraph as a security precaution because it mentioned the time and place of the ceremony.

3   The argument itself, however, although it was perhaps not exactly what one would have expected a prime minister-designate to be spending his time on only a few hours before proclaiming the independence of a new state—particularly one threatened by immediate invasion—was far from being just an argument about terminology. We were all deeply aware of the fact that the proclamation not only spelled the formal end to 2,000 years of Jewish homelessness, but also gave expression to the most fundamental principles of the State of Israel. For this reason, each and every word mattered greatly. Incidentally, my good friend Zeev Sharef, the first secretary of the government-to-be (who laid the foundations for the machinery of government), even found time to see to it that the scroll we were about to sign that afternoon should be rushed to the vaults of the Anglo-Palestine Bank after the ceremony, so that it could at least be preserved for posterity—even if the state and we ourselves did not survive for very long.

4   At about 2 P.M. I went back to my hotel on the seashore, washed my hair and changed into my best black dress. Then I sat down for a few minutes, partly to catch my breath, partly to think—for the first time in the past two or three days—about the children. Menachem was in the United States then—a student at the Manhattan School of Music. I knew that he would come back now that war was inevitable, and I wondered when and how we would meet again. Sarah was in Revivim, and although not so very far away, as the crow flies, we were quite cut off from each other. Months ago, gangs of Palestinian Arabs and armed infiltrators from Egypt had blocked the road that connected the Negev to the rest of the country and were still systematically blowing up or cutting most of the pipelines that brought water to the twenty-seven Jewish settlements that then dotted the Negev. The Haganah had done

its best to break the siege. It had opened a dirt track, parallel to the main road, on which convoys managed, now and then, to bring food and water to the 1,000-odd settlers in the south. But who knew what would happen to Revivim or any other of the small, ill-armed ill-equipped Negev settlements when the full-scale Egyptian invasion of Israel began, as it almost certainly would, within only a few hours? Both Sarah and her Zechariah were wireless operators in Revivim, and I had been able to keep in touch with them up till then. But I hadn't heard about or from either of them for several days, and I was extremely worried. It was on youngsters like them, their spirit and their courage, that the future of the Negev and, therefore, of Israel depended, and I shuddered at the thought of their having to face the invading troops of the Egyptian army.

I was so lost in my thoughts about the children that I can remember being momentarily surprised when the phone rang in my room and I was told that a car was waiting to take me to the museum. It had been decided to hold the ceremony at the Tel Aviv museum on Rothschild Boulevard, not because it was such an imposing building (which it wasn't), but because it was small enough to be easily guarded. One of the oldest buildings in Tel Aviv, it had originally belonged to the city's first mayor, who had willed it to the citizens of Tel Aviv for use as an art museum. The grand total of about $200 had been allocated for decorating it suitably for the ceremony; the floors had been scrubbed, the nude paintings on the walls modestly draped, the windows blacked out in case of an air raid and a large picture of Theodor Herzl hung behind the table at which the thirteen members of the provisional government were to sit. Although supposedly only the 200-odd people who had been invited to participate knew the details, a large crowd was already waiting outside the museum by the time I arrived there.

A few minutes later, at exactly 4 P.M., the ceremony began. Ben-Gurion, wearing a dark suit and tie, stood up and rapped a gavel. According to the plan, this was to be the signal for the orchestra, tucked away in a second floor gallery, to play "Hatikvah." But something went wrong, and there was no music. Spontaneously, we rose to our feet and sang our national anthem. Then Ben-Gurion cleared his throat and said quietly, "I shall now read the Scroll of Independence." It took him only a quarter of an hour to read the entire proclamation. He read it slowly and very clearly, and I remember his voice changing and rising a little as he came to the eleventh paragraph:

> Accordingly we, the members of the National Council, representing the Jewish people in the Land of Israel and the Zionist movement, have assembled on the day of the termination of the British mandate for Palestine, and, by virtue of our natural and historic right and of the resolution of the General Assembly of the United Nations, do hereby

proclaim the establishment of a Jewish state in the Land of Israel—the State of Israel.

7   The State of Israel! My eyes filled with tears, and my hands shook. We had done it. We had brought the Jewish state into existence—and I, Golda Mabovitch Meyerson, had lived to see the day. Whatever happened now, whatever price any of us would have to pay for it, we had recreated the Jewish national home. The long exile was over. From this day on we would no longer live on sufferance in the land of our forefathers. Now we were a nation like other nations, master—for the first time in twenty centuries—of our own destiny. The dream had come true—too late to save those who had perished in the Holocaust, but not too late for the generations to come. Almost exactly fifty years ago, at the close of the First Zionist Congress in Basel, Theodor Herzl had written in his diary: "At Basel, I founded the Jewish state. If I were to say this today, I would be greeted with laughter. In five years perhaps, and certainly in fifty, everyone will see it." And so it had come to pass.

8   As Ben-Gurion read, I thought again about my children and the children that they would have, how different their lives would be from mine and how different my own life would be from what it had been in the past, and I thought about my colleagues in besieged Jerusalem, gathered in the offices of the Jewish Agency, listening to the ceremony through static on the radio, while I, by sheer accident, was in the museum itself. It seemed to me that no Jew on earth had ever been more privileged than I was that Friday afternoon.

9   Then, as though a signal had been given, we rose to our feet, crying and clapping, while Ben-Gurion, his voice breaking for the only time, read: "The State of Israel will be open to Jewish immigration and the ingathering of exiles." This was the very heart of the proclamation, the reason for the state and the point of it all. I remember sobbing out loud when I heard those words spoken in that hot, packed little hall. But Ben-Gurion just rapped his gavel again for order and went on reading:

10   "Even amidst the violent attacks launched against us for months past, we call upon the sons of the Arab people dwelling in Israel to keep the peace and to play their part in building the state on the basis of full and equal citizenship and due representation in all its institutions, provisional and permanent."

11   And: "We extend the hand of peace and good neighborliness to all the states around us and to their peoples, and we call upon them to cooperate in mutual helpfulness with the independent Jewish nation in its land. The State of Israel is prepared to make its contribution in a concerted effort for the advancement of the entire Middle East."

12   When he finished reading the 979 Hebrew words of the proclamation, he asked us to stand and "adopt the scroll establishing the Jewish state," so once again we rose to our feet. Then, something quite un-

scheduled and very moving happened. All of a sudden Rabbi Fishman-Maimon stood up, and, in a trembling voice, pronounced the traditional Hebrew prayer of thanksgiving. "Blessed be Thou, O Lord our God, King of the Universe, who has kept us alive and made us endure and brought us to this day. Amen." It was a prayer that I had heard often, but it had never held such meaning for me as it did that day.

Before we came up, each in turn, in alphabetical order, to sign the proclamation, there was one other point of "business" that required our attention. Ben-Gurion read the first decrees of the new state. The White Paper was declared null and void, while, to avoid a legal vacuum, all the other mandatory rules and regulations were declared valid and in temporary effect. Then the signing began. As I got up from my seat to sign my name to the scroll, I caught sight of Ada Golomb, standing not far away. I wanted to go over to her, take her in my arms and tell her that I knew that Eliahu and Dov should have been there in my place, but I couldn't hold up the line of the signatories, so I walked straight to the middle of the table, where Ben-Gurion and Sharett sat with the scroll between them. All I recall about my actual signing of the proclamation is that I was crying openly, not able even to wipe the tears from my face, and I remember that as Sharett held the scroll in place for me, a man called David Zvi Pincus, who belonged to the religious Mizrachi Party, came over to try and calm me. "Why do you weep so much, Golda?" he asked me. [13]

"Because it breaks my heart to think of all those who should have been here today and are not," I replied, but I still couldn't stop crying. [14]

Only twenty-five members of the People's Council signed the proclamation on May 14. Eleven others were in Jerusalem, and one was in the States. The last to sign was Moshe Sharett. He looked very controlled and calm compared to me as though he were merely performing a standard duty. Later, when once we talked about that day, he told me that when he wrote his name on the scroll, he felt as though he were standing on a cliff with a gale blowing up all around him and nothing to hold on to except his determination not to be blown over into the raging sea below—but none of this showed at the time. [15]

After the Palestine Philharmonic Orchestra played "Hatikvah," Ben-Gurion rapped his gavel for the third time. "The State of Israel is established. This meeting is ended." We all shook hands and embraced each other. The ceremony was over. Israel was a reality. [16]

✦ Evaluating the Text

1. What details in Meir's account communicate the conflict and compromise that would allow Israel to exist as both a religious and secular state? What role did terminology play in the resolution of this problem?

2. What historical events in the immediate and distant past gave this moment its particular significance?

3. What considerations were uppermost in Meir's mind during this crucial time?

4. What details are effective in communicating the precariousness of the fledgling state?

✦ *Exploring Different Perspectives*

1. Compare the opposite ends of the spectrum in terms of the creation of a state and the disintegration of a nation, as depicted by Golda Meir and by Slavenka Drakulić in "The Balkan Express."

2. In what way does Golda Meir reveal the benefits of personally identifying with the political process in ways that are diametrically opposite to the feelings of Albert Camus's protagonist in "The Guest"?

✦ *Extending Viewpoints Through Writing*

1. Describe where you were and what you thought and felt at the moment an important political event took place in the nation, the town or region where you live, or on your campus.

Albert Camus

The Guest

◆

Albert Camus (1913–1960) was born in Mondavi, Algeria (then a colony of France), in 1913 to Breton and Spanish parents. Despite the hardships of poverty and his bouts with tuberculosis, Camus excelled as both an athlete and scholarship student at the University of Algiers. Camus lived and worked as a journalist in Algeria until 1940 when he traveled to France and became active in the Resistance, serving as editor of the clandestine paper Combat. *Internationally recognized for his essays and novels, Camus received the Nobel Prize for Literature in 1957, a few years before he was killed in an automobile accident. Camus was closely associated with Jean-Paul Sartre and the French existentialist movement, but broke with Sartre and developed his own concept of the absurd that asserts the importance of human solidarity as the only value capable of redeeming a world without meaning. Although Camus began as a journalist, his work soon extended far beyond journalism to encompass novels, such as* The Stranger *(1942), the play* Caligula *(1944), and a lengthy essay defining his concept of the "absurd" hero, in* The Myth of Sisyphus *(1942). Camus's second novel,* The Plague *(1947), uses the description of a plague in a quarantined city to depict the human struggle against physical and spiritual evil in all its forms, a position Camus outlined in great detail in his nonfiction work* The Rebel *(1951). "The Guest," translated by Justin O'Brien, is drawn from his last collection of short stories,* Exile and the Kingdom *(1957). In this story, Camus returns to the landscape of his native Algeria to depict the poignant dilemma of his protagonist, Daru, a rural schoolteacher who resists being forced into complicity with the French during the war between France and Algeria, which lasted from 1954 to 1962. Set against the background of the Algerian struggle for independence, the story masterfully explores all the important themes of the burdens of freedom, brotherhood, responsibility, moral ambiguity, and the inevitability of choice that Camus grappled with throughout his life.*

Algeria is a republic in northwest Africa bordered to the north by the Mediterranean Sea, to the east by Tunisia and Libya, to the south by Niger and Mali, and to the west by Mauritania and Morocco. Algeria was colonized by France in the nineteenth century and only gained its independence after a long and bloody battle with France in the 1960s under circumstances reflected in Albert Camus's "The Guest." After a round of elections in 1991 that were won by the Islamic Party but subsequently nullified by a court order, a movement toward Moslem fundamentalism was launched that resulted in the assassination of the head of state in July of 1992. The future of the country is uncertain.

1   The schoolmaster was watching the two men climb toward him. One was on horseback, the other on foot. They had not yet tackled the abrupt rise leading to the schoolhouse built on the hillside. They were toiling onward, making slow progress in the snow, among the stones, on the vast expanse of the high, deserted plateau. From time to time the horse stumbled. Without hearing anything yet, he could see the breath issuing from the horse's nostrils. One of the men, at least, knew the region. They were following the trail although it had disappeared days ago under a layer of dirty white snow. The schoolmaster calculated that it would take them half an hour to get onto the hill. It was cold; he went back into the school to get a sweater.

2   He crossed the empty frigid classroom. On the blackboard the four rivers of France, drawn with four different colored chalks, had been flowing toward their estuaries for the past three days. Snow had suddenly fallen in mid-October after eight months of drought without the transition of rain, and the twenty pupils, more or less, who lived in the villages scattered over the plateau had stopped coming. With fair weather they would return. Daru now heated only the single room that was his lodging, adjoining the classroom and giving also onto the plateau to the east. Like the class windows, his window looked to the south too. On that side the school was a few kilometers from the point where the plateau began to slope toward the south. In clear weather could be seen the purple mass of the mountain range where the gap opened onto the desert.

3   Somewhat warmed, Daru returned to the window from which he had first seen the two men. They were no longer visible. Hence they must have tackled the rise. The sky was not so dark, for the snow had stopped falling during the night. The morning had opened with a dirty light which had scarcely become brighter as the ceiling of clouds lifted. At two in the afternoon it seemed as if the day were merely beginning. But still this was better than those three days when the thick snow was falling amidst unbroken darkness with little gusts of wind that rattled the double door of the classroom. Then Daru had spent long hours in his room, leaving it only to go to the shed and feed the chickens or get some coal. Fortunately the delivery truck from Tadjid, the nearest village to the north, had brought his supplies two days before the blizzard. It would return in forty-eight hours.

4   Besides, he had enough to resist a siege, for the little room was cluttered with bags of wheat that the administration left as a stock to distribute to those of his pupils whose families had suffered from the drought. Actually they had all been victims because they were all poor. Every day Daru would distribute a ration to the children. They had

missed it, he knew, during these bad days. Possibly one of the fathers or big brothers would come this afternoon and he could supply them with grain. It was just a matter of carrying them over to the next harvest. Now shiploads of wheat were arriving from France and the worst was over. But it would be hard to forget that poverty, that army of ragged ghosts wandering in the sunlight, the plateaus burned to a cinder month after month, the earth shriveled up little by little, literally scorched, every stone bursting into dust under one's foot. The sheep had died then by thousands and even a few men, here and there, sometimes without anyone's knowing.

In contrast with such poverty, he who lived almost like a monk in   5
his remote schoolhouse, nonetheless satisfied with the little he had and with the rough life, had felt like a lord with his whitewashed walls, his narrow couch, his unpainted shelves, his well, and his weekly provision of water and food. And suddenly this snow, without warning, without the foretaste of rain. This is the way the region was, cruel to live in, even without men—who didn't help matters either. But Daru had been born here. Everywhere else, he felt exiled.

He stepped out onto the terrace in front of the schoolhouse. The   6
two men were now halfway up the slope. He recognized the horseman as Balducci, the old gendarme he had known for a long time. Balducci was holding on the end of a rope an Arab who was walking behind him with hands bound and head lowered. The gendarme waved a greeting to which Daru did not reply, lost as he was in contemplation of the Arab dressed in a faded blue jellaba, his feet in sandals but covered with socks of heavy raw wool, his head surmounted by a narrow, short *chèche*. They were approaching. Balducci was holding back his horse in order not to hurt the Arab, and the group was advancing slowly.

Within earshot, Balducci shouted: "One hour to do the three kilo-   7
meters from El Ameur!" Daru did not answer. Short and square in his thick sweater, he watched them climb. Not once had the Arab raised his head. "Hello" said Daru when they got up onto the terrace. "Come in and warm up." Balducci painfully got down from his horse without letting go the rope. From under his bristling mustache he smiled at the schoolmaster. His little dark eyes, deep-set under a tanned forehead, and his mouth surrounded with wrinkles made him look attentive and studious. Daru took the bridle, led the horse to the shed, and came back to the two men, who were now waiting for him in the school. He led them into his room. "I am going to heat up the classroom," he said. "We'll be more comfortable there." When he entered the room again, Balducci was on the couch. He had undone the rope tying him to the Arab, who had squatted near the stove. His hands still bound, the *chèche* pushed back on his head, he was looking toward the window. At first Daru noticed only his huge lips, fat, smooth, almost Negroid; yet his nose was straight, his eyes were dark and full of fever. The *chèche*

revealed an obstinate forehead and, under the weathered skin now rather discolored by the cold, the whole face had a restless and rebellious look that struck Daru when the Arab, turning his face toward him, looked him straight in the eyes. "Go into the other room," said the schoolmaster, "and I'll make you some mint tea." "Thanks," Balducci said. "What a chore! How I long for retirement." And addressing his prisoner in Arabic: "Come on, you." The Arab got up and, slowly, holding his bound wrists in front of him, went into the classroom.

8   With the tea, Daru brought a chair. But Balducci was already enthroned on the nearest pupil's desk and the Arab had squatted against the teacher's platform facing the stove, which stood between the desk and the window. When he held out the glass of tea to the prisoner, Daru hesitated at the sight of his bound hands. "He might perhaps be untied." "Sure," said Balducci, "that was for the trip." He started to get to his feet. But Daru, setting the glass on the floor, had knelt beside the Arab. Without saying anything, the Arab watched him with his feverish eyes. Once his hands were free, he rubbed his swollen wrists against each other, took the glass of tea, and sucked up the burning liquid in swift little sips.

9   "Good," said Daru. "And where are you headed?"

10   Balducci withdrew his mustache from the tea. "Here, son."

11   "Odd pupils! And you're spending the night?"

12   "No. I'm going back to El Ameur. And you will deliver this fellow to Tinguit. He is expected at police headquarters."

13   Balducci was looking at Daru with a friendly little smile.

14   "What's this story?" asked the schoolmaster. "Are you pulling my leg?"

15   "No, son. Those are the orders."

16   "The orders? I'm not . . ." Daru hesitated, not wanting to hurt the old Corsican. "I mean, that's not my job."

17   "What! What's the meaning of that? In wartime people do all kinds of jobs."

18   "Then I'll wait for the declaration of war!"

19   Balducci nodded.

20   "O.K. But the orders exist and they concern you too. Things are brewing, it appears. There is talk of a forthcoming revolt. We are mobilized, in a way."

21   Daru still had his obstinate look.

22   "Listen, son," Balducci said. "I like you and you must understand. There's only a dozen of us at El Ameur to patrol throughout the whole territory of a small department and I must get back in a hurry. I was told to hand this guy over to you and return without delay. He couldn't be kept there. His village was beginning to stir; they wanted to take him back. You must take him to Tinguit tomorrow before the day is

over. Twenty kilometers shouldn't faze a husky fellow like you. After that, all will be over. You'll come back to your pupils and your comfortable life."

Behind the wall the horse could be heard snorting and pawing the earth. Daru was looking out the window. Decidedly, the weather was clearing and the light was increasing over the snowy plateau. When all the snow was melted, the sun would take over again and once more would burn the fields of stone. For days, still, the unchanging sky would shed its dry light on the solitary expanse where nothing had any connection with man.

"After all," he said, turning around toward Balducci, "what did he do?" And, before the gendarme had opened his mouth, he asked: "Does he speak French?"

"No, not a word. We had been looking for him for a month, but they were hiding him. He killed his cousin."

"Is he against us?"

"I don't think so. But you can never be sure."

"Why did he kill?"

"A family squabble, I think. One owed the other grain, it seems. It's not at all clear. In short, he killed his cousin with a billhook. You know, like a sheep, *kreezk*!"

Balducci made the gesture of drawing a blade across his throat and the Arab, his attention attracted, watched him with a sort of anxiety. Daru felt a sudden wrath against the man, against all men with their rotten spite, their tireless hates, their blood lust.

But the kettle was singing on the stove. He served Balducci more tea, hesitated, then served the Arab again, who, a second time, drank avidly. His raised arms made the jellaba fall open and the schoolmaster saw his thin, muscular chest.

"Thanks, kid," Balducci said. "And now, I'm off."

He got up and went toward the Arab, taking a small rope from his pocket.

"What are you doing?" Daru asked dryly.

Balducci, disconcerted, showed him the rope.

"Don't bother."

The old gendarme hesitated. "It's up to you. Of course, you are armed?"

"I have my shotgun."

"Where?"

"In the trunk."

"You ought to have it near your bed."

"Why? I have nothing to fear."

"You're crazy, son. If there's an uprising, no one is safe, we're all in the same boat."

23

24

25

26

27

28

29

30

31

32

33

34

35

36

37

38

39

40

41

42

43

44 "I'll defend myself. I'll have time to see them coming."

45 Balducci began to laugh, then suddenly the mustache covered the white teeth.

46 "You'll have time? O.K. That's just what I was saying. You have always been a little cracked. That's why I like you, my son was like that."

47 At the same time he took out his revolver and put it on the desk.

48 "Keep it; I don't need two weapons from here to El Ameur."

49 The revolver shone against the black paint of the table. When the gendarme turned toward him, the schoolmaster caught the smell of leather and horseflesh.

50 "Listen, Balducci," Daru said suddenly, "every bit of this disgusts me, and first of all your fellow here. But I won't hand him over. Fight, yes, if I have to. But not that."

51 The old gendarme stood in front of him and looked at him severely.

52 "You're being a fool," he said slowly. "I don't like it either. You don't get used to putting a rope on a man even after years of it, and you're even ashamed—yes, ashamed. But you can't let them have their way."

53 "I won't hand him over," Daru said again.

54 "It's an order, son, and I repeat it."

55 "That's right. Repeat to them what I've said to you: I won't hand him over."

56 Balducci made a visible effort to reflect. He looked at the Arab and at Daru. At last he decided.

57 "No, I won't tell them anything. If you want to drop us, go ahead; I'll not denounce you. I have an order to deliver the prisoner and I'm doing so. And now you'll just sign this paper for me."

58 "There's no need. I'll not deny that you left him with me."

59 "Don't be mean with me. I know you'll tell the truth. You're from hereabouts and you are a man. But you must sign, that's the rule."

60 Daru opened his drawer, took out a little square bottle of purple ink, the red wooden penholder with the "sergeant-major" pen he used for making models of penmanship, and signed. The gendarme carefully folded the paper and put it into his wallet. Then he moved toward the door.

61 "I'll see you off," Daru said.

62 "No," said Balducci. "There's no use being polite. You insulted me."

63 He looked at the Arab, motionless in the same spot, sniffed peevishly, and turned away toward the door. "Good-by, son," he said. The door shut behind him. Balducci appeared suddenly outside the window and then disappeared. His footsteps were muffled by the snow. The horse stirred on the other side of the wall and several chickens fluttered in fright. A moment later Balducci reappeared outside the window leading the horse by the bridle. He walked toward the little rise without turning around and disappeared from sight with the horse following him. A big stone could be heard bouncing down. Daru walked

back toward the prisoner, who, without stirring, never took his eyes off him. "Wait," the schoolmaster said in Arabic and went toward the bedroom. As he was going through the door, he had a second thought, went to the desk, took the revolver, and stuck it in his pocket. Then, without looking back, he went into his room.

For some time he lay on his couch watching the sky gradually close 64 over, listening to the silence. It was this silence that had seemed painful to him during the first days here, after the war. He had requested a post in the little town at the base of the foothills separating the upper plateaus from the desert. There, rocky walls, green and black to the north, pink and lavender to the south, marked the frontier of eternal summer. He had been named to a post farther north, on the plateau itself. In the beginning, the solitude and the silence had been hard for him on these wastelands peopled only by stones. Occasionally, furrows suggested cultivation, but they had been dug to uncover a certain kind of stone good for building. The only plowing here was to harvest rocks. Elsewhere a thin layer of soil accumulated in the hollows would be scraped out to enrich paltry village gardens. This is the way it was: bare rock covered three quarters of the region. Towns sprang up, flourished, then disappeared; men came by, loved one another or fought bitterly, then died. No one in this desert, neither he nor his guest, mattered. And yet, outside this desert neither of them, Daru knew, could have really lived.

When he got up, no noise came from the classroom. He was 65 amazed at the unmixed joy he derived from the mere thought that the Arab might have fled and that he would be alone with no decision to make. But the prisoner was there. He had merely stretched out between the stove and the desk. With eyes open, he was staring at the ceiling. In that position, his thick lips were particularly noticeable, giving him a pouting look. "Come," said Daru. The Arab got up and followed him. In the bedroom, the schoolmaster pointed to a chair near the table under the window. The Arab sat down without taking his eyes off Daru.

"Are you hungry?" 66
"Yes," the prisoner said. 67
Daru set the table for two. He took flour and oil, shaped a cake in a 68 frying-pan and lighted the little stove that functioned on bottled gas. While the cake was cooking, he went out to the shed to get cheese, eggs, dates, and condensed milk. When the cake was done he set it on the window sill to cool, heated some condensed milk diluted with water, and beat up the eggs into an omelette. In one of his motions he knocked against the revolver stuck in his right pocket. He set the bowl down, went into the classroom, and put the revolver in his desk drawer. When he came back to the room, night was falling. He put on the light and served the Arab. "Eat," he said. The Arab took a piece of the cake, lifted it eagerly to his mouth, and stopped short.

69   "And you?" he asked.

70   "After you. I'll eat too."

71   The thick lips opened slightly. The Arab hesitated, then bit into the cake determinedly.

72   The meal over, the Arab looked at the schoolmaster. "Are you the judge?"

73   "No, I'm simply keeping you until tomorrow."

74   "Why do you eat with me?"

75   "I'm hungry."

76   The Arab fell silent. Daru got up and went out. He brought back a folding bed from the shed, set it up between the table and the stove, perpendicular to his own bed. From a large suitcase which, upright in a corner, served as a shelf for papers, he took two blankets and arranged them on the camp bed. Then he stopped, felt useless, and sat down on his bed. There was nothing more to do or to get ready. He had to look at this man. He looked at him, therefore, trying to imagine his face bursting with rage. He couldn't do so. He could see nothing but the dark yet shining eyes and the animal mouth.

77   "Why did you kill him?" he asked in a voice whose hostile tone surprised him.

78   The Arab looked away.

79   "He ran away. I ran after him."

80   He raised his eyes to Daru again and they were full of a sort of woeful interrogation. "Now what will they do to me?"

81   "Are you afraid?"

82   He stiffened, turning his eyes away.

83   "Are you sorry?"

84   The Arab stared at him openmouthed. Obviously he did not understand. Daru's annoyance was growing. At the same time he felt awkward and self-conscious with his big body wedged between the two beds.

85   "Lie down there," he said impatiently. "That's your bed."

86   The Arab didn't move. He called to Daru:

87   "Tell me!"

88   The schoolmaster looked at him.

89   "Is the gendarme coming back tomorrow?"

90   "I don't know."

91   "Are you coming with us?"

92   "I don't know. Why?"

93   The prisoner got up and stretched out on top of the blankets, his feet toward the window. The light from the electric bulb shone straight into his eyes and he closed them at once.

94   "Why?" Daru repeated, standing beside the bed.

95   The Arab opened his eyes under the blinding light and looked at him, trying not to blink.

96   "Come with us," he said.

In the middle of the night, Daru was still not asleep. He had gone   97
to bed after undressing completely; he generally slept naked. But when
he suddenly realized that he had nothing on, he hesitated. He felt vulnerable and the temptation came to him to put his clothes back on.
Then he shrugged his shoulders; after all, he wasn't a child and, if need
be, he could break his adversary in two. From his bed he could observe
him, lying on his back, still motionless with his eyes closed under the
harsh light. When Daru turned out the light, the darkness seemed to
coagulate all of a sudden. Little by little, the night came back to life in
the window where the starless sky was stirring gently. The schoolmaster soon made out the body laying at his feet. The Arab still did not
move, but his eyes seemed open. A faint wind was prowling around
the schoolhouse. Perhaps it would drive away the clouds and the sun
would reappear.

During the night the wind increased. The hens fluttered a little   98
and then were silent. The Arab turned over on his side with his back to
Daru, who thought he heard him moan. Then he listened for his
guest's breathing, become heavier and more regular. He listened to
that breath so close to him and mused without being able to go to
sleep. In this room where he had been sleeping alone for a year, this
presence bothered him. But it bothered him also by imposing on him a
sort of brotherhood he knew well but refused to accept in the present
circumstances. Men who share the same rooms, soldiers or prisoners,
develop a strange alliance as if, having cast off their armor with their
clothing, they fraternized every evening, over and above their differences, in the ancient community of dream and fatigue. But Daru shook
himself; he didn't like such musings, and it was essential to sleep.

A little later, however, when the Arab stirred slightly, the school-   99
master was still not asleep. When the prisoner made a second move, he
stiffened, on the alert. The Arab was lifting himself slowly on his arms
with almost the motion of a sleepwalker. Seated upright in bed, he
waited motionless without turning his head toward Daru, as if he were
listening attentively. Daru did not stir, it had just occurred to him that
the revolver was still in the drawer of his desk. It was better to act at
once. Yet he continued to observe the prisoner, who, with the same
slithery motion, put his feet on the ground, waited again, then began to
stand up slowly. Daru was about to call out to him when the Arab began to walk, in a quite natural but extraordinarily silent way. He was
heading toward the door at the end of the room that opened into the
shed. He lifted the latch with precaution and went out, pushing the
door behind him but without shutting it. Daru had not stirred. "He is
running away," he merely thought. "Good riddance!" Yet he listened
attentively. The hens were not fluttering; the guest must be on the plateau. A faint sound of water reached him, and he didn't know what it
was until the Arab again stood framed in the doorway, closed the door

carefully, and came back to bed without a sound. Then Daru turned his back on him and fell asleep. Still later he seemed, from the depths of his sleep, to hear furtive steps around the schoolhouse. "I'm dreaming! I'm dreaming!" he repeated to himself. And he went on sleeping.

100   When he awoke, the sky was clear; the loose window let in a cold, pure air. The Arab was asleep, hunched up under the blankets now, his mouth open, utterly relaxed. But when Daru shook him, he started dreadfully, staring at Daru with wild eyes as if he had never seen him and such a frightened expression that the schoolmaster stepped back. "Don't be afraid. It's me. You must eat." The Arab nodded his head and said yes. Calm had returned to his face, but his expression was vacant and listless.

101   The coffee was ready. They drank it seated together on the folding bed as they munched their pieces of the cake. Then Daru led the Arab under the shed and showed him the faucet where he washed. He went back into the room, folded the blankets and the bed, made his own bed and put the room in order. Then he went through the classroom and out onto the terrace. The sun was already rising in the blue sky; a soft, bright light was bathing the deserted plateau. On the ridge the snow was melting in spots. The stones were about to reappear. Crouched on the edge of the plateau, the schoolmaster looked at the deserted expanse. He thought of Balducci. He had hurt him, for he had sent him off in a way as if he didn't want to be associated with him. He could still hear the gendarme's farewell and, without knowing why, he felt strangely empty and vulnerable. At that moment, from the other side of the schoolhouse, the prisoner coughed. Daru listened to him almost despite himself and then, furious, threw a pebble that whistled through the air before sinking into the snow. That man's stupid crime revolted him, but to hand him over was contrary to honor. Merely thinking of it made him smart with humiliation. And he cursed at one and the same time his own people who had sent him this Arab and the Arab too who had dared to kill and not managed to get away. Daru got up, walked in a circle on the terrace, waited motionless, and then went back into the schoolhouse.

102   The Arab, leaning over the cement floor of the shed, was washing his teeth with two fingers. Daru looked at him and said: "Come." He went back into the room ahead of the prisoner. He slipped a hunting-jacket on over his sweater and put on walking-shoes. Standing, he waited until the Arab had put on his *chèche* and sandals. They went into the classroom and the schoolmaster pointed to the exit, saying: "Go ahead." The fellow didn't budge. "I'm coming," said Daru. The Arab went out. Daru went back into the room and made a package of pieces of rusk, dates, and sugar. In the classroom, before going out, he hesitated a second in front of his desk, then crossed the threshold and locked the door. "That's the way," he said. He started toward the east,

followed by the prisoner. But, a short distance from the schoolhouse, he thought he heard a slight sound behind them. He retraced his steps and examined the surroundings of the house; there was no one there. The Arab watched him without seeming to understand. "Come on," said Daru.

They walked for an hour and rested beside a sharp peak of lime- 103
stone. The snow was melting faster and faster and the sun was drink- ing up the puddles at once, rapidly cleaning the plateau, which gradually dried and vibrated like the air itself. When they resumed walking, the ground rang under their feet. From time to time a bird rent the space in front of them with a joyful cry. Daru breathed in deeply the fresh morning light. He felt a sort of rapture before the vast familiar ex- panse, now almost entirely yellow under its dome of blue sky. They walked an hour more, descending toward the south. They reached a level height made up of crumbly rocks. From there on, the plateau sloped down, eastward, toward a low plain where there were a few spindly trees and, to the south, toward outcroppings of rock that gave the landscape a chaotic look.

Daru surveyed the two directions. There was nothing but the sky 104
on the horizon. Not a man could be seen. He turned toward the Arab, who was looking at him blankly. Daru held out the package to him. "Take it," he said. "There are dates, bread, and sugar. You can hold out for two days. Here are a thousand francs too." The Arab took the pack- age and the money but kept his full hands at chest level as if he didn't know what to do with what was being given him. "Now look," the schoolmaster said as he pointed in the direction of the east, "there's the way to Tinguit. You have a two-hour walk. At Tinguit you'll find the administration and the police. They are expecting you." The Arab looked toward the east, still holding the package and the money against his chest. Daru took his elbow and turned him rather roughly toward the south. At the foot of the height on which they stood could be seen a faint path. "That's the trail across the plateau. In a day's walk from here you'll find pasturelands and the first nomads. They'll take you in and shelter you according to their law." The Arab had now turned toward Daru and a sort of panic was visible in his expression. "Listen," he said. Daru shook his head: "No, be quiet. Now I'm leaving you." He turned his back on him, took two long steps in the direction of the school, looked hesitantly at the motionless Arab, and started off again. For a few minutes he heard nothing but his own step resounding on the cold ground and did not turn his head. A moment later, however, he turned around. The Arab was still there on the edge of the hill, his arms hang- ing now, and he was looking at the schoolmaster. Daru felt something rise in his throat. But he swore with impatience, waved vaguely, and started off again. He had already gone some distance when he again stopped and looked. There was no longer anyone on the hill.

105   Daru hesitated. The sun was now rather high in the sky and was beginning to beat down on his head. The schoolmaster retraced his steps, at first somewhat uncertainly, then with decision. When he reached the little hill, he was bathed in sweat. He climbed it as fast as he could and stopped, out of breath, at the top. The rock-fields to the south stood out sharply against the blue sky, but on the plain to the west a steamy heat was already rising. And in that slight haze, Daru, with heavy heart, made out the Arab walking slowly on the road to prison.

106   A little later, standing before the window of the classroom, the schoolmaster was watching the clear light bathing the whole surface of the plateau, but he hardly saw it. Behind him on the blackboard, among the winding French rivers, sprawled the clumsily chalked-up words he had just read: "You handed over our brother. You will pay for this." Daru looked at the sky, the plateau, and, beyond, the invisible lands stretching all the way to the sea. In his vast landscape he had loved so much, he was alone.

✦ Evaluating the Text

1. What do you know about Daru's background that would explain why in his present circumstances he does not wish to step outside of his role as teacher to enforce the rulings of the authorities? Between what conflicting loyalties is Daru torn?

2. What can you infer about Daru's past relationship with Balducci from his reaction to Balducci's request?

3. What is the crime of which the Arab has been accused? How is it related to the food shortage afflicting the community?

4. How do the descriptions of the physical environment (the stones, the sudden snow and melting that follows) underscore the human drama?

5. How does Daru's feeling of common humanity make it increasingly difficult for him to turn the Arab over to the authorities? How does Daru try to avoid the responsibility for turning in the Arab?

6. How are Daru's actions toward the Arab misunderstood by the local populace who are spying on him? What is the significance of the message written on the blackboard?

7. What outside sources of knowledge about historical and literary contexts would be useful in interpreting this story? Why would it be helpful to know something about existentialism, the history of the Algerian revolt, or Camus's own childhood growing up as a non-Arab French citizen in Algeria?

8. Why, in your opinion, does the Arab choose to go to the place where he will be imprisoned or even executed although he now has money, food, and the freedom to go wherever he wants?

✦ Exploring Different Perspectives

1. How do the stories by Albert Camus and Panos Ioannides ("Gregory") dramatize the conflict between loyalty to a cause and compassion for another human being?

2. How do both Albert Camus's story and the account by Slavenka Drakulić ("The Balkan Express") dramatize the dehumanizing effects of being forced to take sides politically?

✦ Extending Viewpoints Through Writing

1. Describe the last time a guest stayed with you or your family, or a time when you were a guest in someone else's home. What insight did these experiences give you into Camus's story?

2. Just as the protagonist in the story finds he cannot live a private life outside of public events, do you remember where you were and what you thought immediately before and after you heard the news of an historical event?

3. Describe your expectations about what constitutes a good story. For example, do you want a story that will surprise you or one that is predictable? What are some of your favorite works of fiction, and how do they fulfill your expectations?

Slavenka Drakulić

The Balkan Express

◆

Slavenka Drakulić is a leading Croatian journalist and novelist. Her insightful commentary on East European affairs first appeared in her columns in the magazine Danas, *published in Zagreb. She is a regular contributor to* The Nation, The New Republic, *and* The New York Times Magazine. *Drakulić is the author of a novel,* Holograms of Fear *(1992), and several works of nonfiction, including* How We Survived Communism and Even Laughed *(1991). This chapter is from her recent book of essays,* The Balkan Express *(1993), and presents a heartfelt account of the war involving Serbia, Croatia, and Bosnia-Herzegovina from which she escaped to live in New York.*

Croatia is about the size of West Virginia and is situated along the eastern coast of the Adriatic Sea, extending inland to the slopes of the Julian Alps in Slovenia and into the Pannonian Valley to the banks of the Drava and Danube Rivers. The capital, Zagreb, lies on the Sava River, and many famous cities including the medieval port of Dubrovnik are found along the extended coastline. Although Slavs began settling the Balkan peninsula as early as the sixth century A.D., *Croatians were first united into a single state by King Tomislav in 925. The Croats accepted Roman Catholicism in the eleventh century, and by the 1500s, Croatia and Hungary became part of the Hapsburg Empire. In 1914 the assassination of Austria's crown prince in Sarajavo (Bosnia) embroiled the entire Balkans into World War I. For decades, Croatia was part of Yugoslavia under the socialist federation led by Josip Broz Tito. When Tito died in 1980, his authority was transferred to a collective state presidency, which had a rotating chairman. With the fall of communism and the weakening of the federation, Yugoslavia declared its independence in June 1991 and was recognized by the international community in January 1992. Opposition from the Yugoslav Army and the Serbian government, which strongly opposed independence, led to fierce fighting and the destruction of entire cities, which created a serious refugee problem. Various ceasefires brokered by the United Nations produced an uneasy peace that did not last long, as fighting between the Croats, Serbs, and Muslims broke out again in 1993. Additionally, Croatian irregulars became involved in the more serious civil war in Bosnia-Herzegovina. The current president of Croatia is Franjo Tudjman. United Nations peacekeeping forces played an active role in creating circumstances under which elections could take place in 1996.*

Early Sunday morning a mist hovered over the Vienna streets like   1
whipped cream, but the sunshine piercing the lead-grey clouds promised a beautiful autumn day, a day for leafing through magazines at the
Museum Kaffe, for taking a leisurely walk along the Prater park and
enjoying an easy family lunch. Then perhaps a movie or the theatre—
several films were premiering.

But when I entered the Südbanhof, the South Station, the milky Vi-   2
ennese world redolent with café au lait, fresh rolls and butter or apple
strudel and the neat life of the ordinary Viennese citizens was far behind me. As soon as I stepped into the building I found myself in another world; a group of men cursed someone's mother in Serbian, their
greasy, sodden words tumbling to the floor by their feet, and a familiar
slightly sour odour, a mixture of urine, beer and plastic-covered seats in
second-class rail compartments, wafted through the stale air of the station. Here in the heart of Vienna I felt as if I were already on territory occupied by another sort of people, a people now second-class. Not only
because they had come from a poor socialist country, at least not any
more. Now they were second-class because they had come from a country collapsing under the ravages of war. War is what made them distinct
from the sleepy Viennese, war was turning these people into ghosts of
the past—ghosts whom the Viennese are trying hard to ignore. They'd
rather forget the past, they cannot believe that history is repeating itself,
that such a thing is possible: bloodshed in the Balkans, TV images of
burning buildings and beheaded corpses, a stench of fear spreading
from the south and east through the streets, a stench brought here by
refugees. War is like a brand on the brows of Serbs who curse Croat
mothers, but it is also a brand on the faces of Croats leaving a country
where all they had is gone. The first are branded by hatred, the second
by the horror that here in Vienna no one really understands them. Every
day more and more refugees arrive from Croatia. Vienna is beginning to
feel the pressure from the Südbanhof and is getting worried. Tormented
by days spent in bomb shelters, by their arduous journey and the destruction they have left behind, the exiles are disembarking—those who
have the courage and the money to come so far—stepping first into the
vast hall of the warehouse-like station. From there they continue out
into the street, but once in the street they stop and stare at the fortress-
like buildings, at the bolted doors and the doormen. They stand there
staring at this metropolis, this outpost of Western Europe, helplessly
looking on as Europe turns its back on them indifferently behind the
safety of closed doors. The exiles feel a new fear now: Europe is the enemy, the cold, rational, polite and fortified enemy who still believes
that the war in Croatia is far away, that it can be banished from sight,
that the madness and death will stop across the border.

But it's too late. The madness will find its way, and with it, death.   3
Standing on the platform of the Karlsplatz subway, I could hardly

believe I was still in the same city: here at the very nerve centre of the city, in the trams, shops, at 'Kneipe,' German was seldom heard. Instead everyone seems to speak Croatian or Serbian (in the meantime, the language has changed its name too), the languages of people at war. One hundred thousand Yugoslavs are now living in Vienna, or so I've heard. And seventy thousand of them are Serbs. In a small park near Margaretenstrasse I came across a carving on a wooden table that read 'This is Serbia.' Further along, on a main street, I saw the graffiti 'Red Chetniks,' but also 'Fuck the Red Chetniks' scrawled over it. War creeps out of the cheap apartments near the Gurtel and claims its victims.

4   I am one of a very few passengers, maybe twenty, heading southeast on a train to Zagreb. I've just visited my daughter who, after staying some time in Canada with her father, has come to live in Vienna. There are three of us in the compartment. The train is already well on its way, but we have not yet spoken to one another. The only sound is the rattling of the steel wheels, the rhythmic pulse of a long journey. We are wrapped in a strange, tense silence. All three of us are from the same collapsing country (betrayed by the tell-tale, 'Excuse me, is this seat taken?' 'No, it's free'), but we feel none of the usual camaraderie of travel when passengers talk or share snacks and newspapers to pass the time. Indeed, it seems as if we are afraid to exchange words which might trap us in that small compartment where our knees are so close they almost rub. If we speak up, our languages will disclose who is a Croat and who a Serb, which of us is the enemy. And even if we are all Croats (or Serbs) we might disagree on the war and yet there is no other topic we could talk about. Not even the landscape because even the landscape is not innocent any more. Slovenia has put real border posts along the border with Croatia and has a different currency. This lends another tint to the Slovenian hills, the colour of sadness. Or bitterness. Or anger. If we three strike up a conversation about the green woods passing us by, someone might sigh and say, 'Only yesterday this was my country too.' Perhaps then the other two would start in about independence and how the Slovenes were clever while the Croats were not, while the Serbs, those bastards . . .

5   The war would be there, in our words, in meaningful glances, and in the faces reflecting our anxiety and nausea. In that moment the madness we are travelling towards might become so alive among us that we wouldn't be able perhaps to hold it back. What if one of us is a Serb? What if he says a couple of ordinary, innocent words? Would we pretend to be civilized or would we start to attack him? What if the hypothetical Serb among us keeps silent because he is not really to blame? Are there people in this war, members of the aggressor nation, who are not to blame? Or maybe he doesn't want to hurt our feelings, thinking that we might have family or friends in Vukovar, Osijek, Šibenik, Dubrovnik, those cities under the heaviest fire? Judging from our silence,

growing more and more impenetrable as we approach the Croatian border, I know that we are more than mere strangers—surly, unfamiliar, fellow passengers—just as one cannot be a mere bank clerk. In war one loses all possibility of choice. But for all that, I think the unbearable silence between us that verges on a scream is a good sign, a sign of our unwillingness to accept the war, our desire to distance ourselves and spare each other, if possible.

So we do not talk to each other. The man on my left stares out of the window, the woman opposite sleeps with her mouth half open. From time to time she wakes up and looks around, confused; then she closes her eyes again, thinking that this is the best she can do, close her eyes and pretend the world doesn't exist. I pick up a newspaper, risking recognition—one betrays oneself by the newspapers one reads—but my fellow travellers choose not to see it. At the Südbanhof newspaper stand there were no papers from Croatia, only *Borba*, one of the daily papers published in Serbia. As I leaf through the pages I come across a description of an atrocity of war, supposedly committed by the Ustashe—the Croatian Army—which freezes the blood in my veins. When you are forced to accept war as a fact, death becomes something you have to reckon with, a harsh reality that mangles your life even if it leaves you physically unharmed. But the kind of death I met with on the second page of the *Borba* paper was by no means common and therefore acceptable in its inevitability: . . . *and we looked down the well in the back yard. We pulled up the bucket—it was full of testicles, about 300 in all.* An image as if fabricated to manufacture horror. A long line of men, hundreds of them, someone's hands, a lightning swift jab of a knife, then blood, a jet of thick dark blood cooling on someone's hands, on clothing, on the ground. Were the men alive when it happened, I wondered, never questioning whether the report was true. The question of truth, or any other question for that matter, pales next to the swirling pictures, the whirlpool of pictures that sucks me in, choking me. At that moment, whatever the truth, I can imagine nothing but the bucket full of testicles, slit throats, bodies with gory holes where hearts had been, gouged eyes—death as sheer madness. As I rest my forehead on the cold windowpane I notice that there is still a little light outside, and other scenes are flitting by, scenes of peaceful tranquillity. I don't believe in tranquillity any more. It is just a thin crust of ice over a deadly treacherous river. I know I am travelling towards a darkness that has the power, in a single sentence in a newspaper, to shatter in me the capacity to distinguish real from unreal, possible from impossible. Hardly anything seems strange or dreadful now—not dismembered bodies, not autopsy reports from Croatian doctors, claiming that the victims were forced by Serbians to eat their own eyes before they were killed.

Only on the train heading southeast, on that sad 'Balkan Express' did I understand what it means to report bestialities as the most ordinary facts. The gruesome pictures are giving birth to a gruesome reality; a man who, as he reads a newspaper, forms in his mind a picture of the testicles being drawn up from the well will be prepared to do the same tomorrow, closing the circle of death.

8   I fold the paper. I don't need it for any further 'information.' Now I'm ready for what awaits me upon my return. I have crossed the internal border of the warring country long before I've crossed the border outside, and my journey with the two other silent passengers, the newspaper and the seed of madness growing in each of us is close to its end. Late that night at home in Zagreb I watch the news on television. The anchor man announces that seven people have been slaughtered in a Slavonian village. I watch him as he utters the word 'slaughtered' as if it were the most commonplace word in the world. He doesn't flinch, he doesn't stop, the word slips easily from his lips. The chill that emanates from the words feels cold on my throat, like the blade of a knife. Only then do I know that I've come home, that my journey has ended here in front of the TV screen, plunged in a thick, clotted darkness, a darkness that reminds me of blood.

✦ *Evaluating the Text*

1. In what ways, overt and subtle, has the war affected the relationships of the passengers traveling on the train to Zagreb?

2. In what ways is Drakulić a different person at the end of the journey from the way she was at the beginning?

3. How has reading about the atrocities changed her?

✦ *Exploring Different Perspectives*

1. How do the accounts by Slavenka Drakulić and Jon Swain ("The Eyes of Vietnam") focus on the atrocities people are capable of and subject to in wartime?

2. How do the accounts by Slavenka Drakulić and Nien Cheng ("The Red Guards") dramatize the consequences of politicization on everyday life?

✦ *Extending Viewpoints Through Writing*

1. Have you ever known anyone who became inflamed with political passions by which they themselves were never really affected?

2. Explain your understanding of the present situation in what used to be Yugoslavia.

Ngũgĩ wa Thiong'o

Decolonising the Mind

———————◆———————

Ngũgĩ wa Thiong'o is regarded as one of the most important contemporary writers on the African continent. He wrote his first novels, Weep Not, Child *(1964) and* The River Between *(1965), in English, and* Caitaani Mũtharava-Ini *(translated as* Devil on the Cross, *1982) in his native language, Gĩkũyũ. He was chairman of the department of literature at the University of Nairobi until his detention without trial by the Kenyan authorities in 1977, an account of which appeared under the title* Detained: A Writer's Prison Diary *(1981). The international outcry over his imprisonment eventually produced his release. This selection comes from* Decolonising the Mind: The Politics of Language in African Literature *(1986), a work that constitutes, says Ngũgĩ, "my farewell to English as a vehicle for any of my writings." Subsequently, he has written novels and plays in Gĩkũyũ.*

Kenya is a republic in East Africa. Discoveries by anthropologists and archaeologists in the Great Rift Valley in Kenya have unearthed remains of what may be the earliest known humans, believed to be some 2 million years old. German missionaries were the first Europeans to make their way into Kenya in 1844, making contact with the then-ruling Maasai (for more background on the Maasai, see p. 96) and Kĩkũyũ tribes. The Imperial British East Africa Company wrested political control from Germany, and Kenya became a British protectorate in 1890 and a Crown Colony in 1920. Increasingly violent confrontations between European settlers and the Kĩkũyũs reached a crisis in the 1950s during the terror campaign of the Mau Mau rebellion. In response, the British declared a state of emergency, which was not lifted until 1960.

Originally a leader of the Mau Mau uprising, Jomo Kenyatta became Kenya's first president in 1964, on the first anniversary of Kenya's independence, and served until his death in 1978. Continuing opposition and unrest prompted Kenyatta's government to imprison political dissidents, including Ngugi wa Thiong'o. Kenyatta's successor, Daniel T. arap Moi, has yielded to pressure to open the country to an open-party democracy. National elections were held in December 1992, which returned Moi to power amid tensions threatening the democratization process.

Black Africans of forty different ethnic groups make up 97 percent of the population. The official languages are Swahili and English. The situation described by Thiong'o has changed to the extent that children are now taught in their native languages for the first three years of school, after which instruction is exclusively in English.

1   I was born into a large peasant family: father, four wives and about twenty-eight children. I also belonged, as we all did in those days, to a wider extended family and to the community as a whole.

2   We spoke Gĩkũyũ as we worked in the fields. We spoke Gĩkũyũ in and outside the home. I can vividly recall those evenings of story-telling around the fireside. It was mostly the grown-ups telling the children but everybody was interested and involved. We children would re-tell the stories the following day to other children who worked in the fields picking the pyrethrum flowers, tea-leaves or coffee beans of our European and African landlords.

3   The stories, with mostly animals as the main characters, were all told in Gĩkũyũ. Hare, being small, weak but full of innovative wit and cunning, was our hero. We identified with him as he struggled against the brutes of prey like lion, leopard, hyena. His victories were our victories and we learnt that the apparently weak can outwit the strong. We followed the animals in their struggle against hostile nature—drought, rain, sun, wind—a confrontation often forcing them to search for forms of co-operation. But we were also interested in their struggles amongst themselves, and particularly between the beasts and the victims of prey. These twin struggles, against nature and other animals, reflected real-life struggles in the human world.

4   Not that we neglected stories with human beings as the main characters. There were two types of characters in such human-centred narratives: the species of truly human beings with qualities of courage, kindness, mercy, hatred of evil, concern for others; and a man-eat-man two-mouthed species with qualities of greed, selfishness, individualism and hatred of what was good for the larger co-operative community. Co-operation as the ultimate good in a community was a constant theme. It could unite human beings with animals against ogres and beasts of prey, as in the story of how dove, after being fed with castor-oil seeds, was sent to fetch a smith working far away from home and whose pregnant wife was being threatened by these man-eating two-mouthed ogres.

5   There were good and bad story-tellers. A good one could tell the same story over and over again, and it would always be fresh to us, the listeners. He or she could tell a story told by someone else and make it more alive and dramatic. The differences really were in the use of words and images and the inflexion of voices to effect different tones.

6   We therefore learnt to value words for their meaning and nuances. Language was not a mere string of words. It had a suggestive power well beyond the immediate and lexical meaning. Our appreciation of the suggestive magical power of language was reinforced by the games

we played with words through riddles, proverbs, transpositions of syllables, or through nonsensical but musically arranged words.[1] So we learnt the music of our language on top of the content. The language, through images and symbols, gave us a view of the world, but it had a beauty of its own. The home and the field were then our pre-primary school but what is important, for this discussion, is that the language of our evening teach-ins, and the language of our immediate and wider community, and the language of our work in the fields were one.

And then I went to school, a colonial school, and this harmony was broken. The language of my education was no longer the language of my culture. I first went to Kamaandura, missionary run, and then to another called Maanguuũ run by nationalists grouped around the Gĩkũyũ Independent and Karinga Schools Association. Our language of education was still Gĩkũyũ. The very first time I was ever given an ovation for my writing was over a composition in Gĩkũyũ. So for my first four years there was still harmony between the language of my formal education and that of the Limuru peasant community. 7

It was after the declaration of a state of emergency over Kenya in 1952 that all the schools run by patriotic nationalists were taken over by the colonial regime and were placed under District Education Boards chaired by Englishmen. English became the language of my formal education. In Kenya, English became more than a language: it was *the* language, and all the others had to bow before it in deference. 8

Thus one of the most humiliating experiences was to be caught speaking Gĩkũyũ in the vicinity of the school. The culprit was given corporal punishment—three to five strokes of the cane on bare buttocks— or was made to carry a metal plate around the neck with inscriptions such as I AM STUPID or I AM A DONKEY. Sometimes the culprits were fined money they could hardly afford. And how did the teachers catch the culprits? A button was initially given to one pupil who was supposed to hand it over to whoever was caught speaking his mother tongue. Whoever had the button at the end of the day would sing who had given it to him and the ensuing process would bring out all the culprits of the day. Thus children were turned into witch-hunters and in the process were being taught the lucrative value of being a traitor to one's immediate community. 9

The attitude to English was the exact opposite: any achievement in spoken or written English was highly rewarded; prizes, prestige, applause; the ticket to higher realms. English became the measure of 10

---

[1]Example from a tongue twister: 'Kaana ka Nikoora koona koora koora: na ko koora koona kaana ka Nikoora koora koora.' I'm indebted to Wangui wa Goro for this example. 'Nichola's child saw a baby frog and ran away: and when the baby frog saw Nichola's child it also ran away.' A Gĩkũyũ-speaking child has to get the correct tone and length of vowel and pauses to get it right. Otherwise it becomes a jumble of *k*'s and *r*'s and *na*'s [Author's note].

intelligence and ability in the arts, the sciences, and all the other branches of learning. English became *the* main determinant of a child's progress up the ladder of formal education.

11   As you may know, the colonial system of education in addition to its apartheid racial demarcation had the structure of a pyramid: a broad primary base, a narrowing secondary middle, and an even narrower university apex. Selections from primary into secondary were through an examination, in my time called Kenya African Preliminary Examination, in which one had to pass six subjects ranging from Maths to Nature Study and Kiswahili. All the papers were written in English. Nobody could pass the exam who failed the English language paper no matter how brilliantly he had done in the other subjects. I remember one boy in my class of 1954 who had distinctions in all subjects except English, which he had failed. He was made to fail the entire exam. He went on to become a turn boy in a bus company. I who had only passes but a credit in English got a place at the Alliance High School, one of the most elitist institutions for Africans in colonial Kenya. The requirements for a place at the University, Makerere University College, were broadly the same: nobody could go on to wear the undergraduate red gown, no matter how brilliantly they had performed in all the other subjects unless they had a credit—not even a simple pass!—in English. Thus the most coveted place in the pyramid and in the system was only available to the holder of an English language credit card. English was the official vehicle and the magic formula to colonial elitedom.

12   Literary education was now determined by the dominant language while also reinforcing that dominance. Orature (oral literature) in Kenyan languages stopped. In primary school I now read simplified Dickens and Stevenson alongside Rider Haggard. Jim Hawkins, Oliver Twist, Tom Brown—not Hare, Leopard, and Lion—were now my daily companions in the world of imagination. In secondary school, Scott and G. B. Shaw vied with more Rider Haggard, John Buchan, Alan Paton, Captain W. E. Johns. At Makerere I read English: from Chaucer to T. S. Eliot with a touch of Graham Greene.

13   Thus language and literature were taking us further and further from ourselves to other selves, from our world to other worlds.

14   What was the colonial system doing to us Kenyan children? What were the consequences of, on the one hand, this systematic suppression of our languages and the literature they carried, and on the other the elevation of English and the literature it carried? To answer those questions, let me first examine the relationship of language to human experience, human culture, and the human perception of reality.

15   Language, any language, has a dual character: it is both a means of communication and a carrier of culture. Take English. It is spoken in Brit-

ain and in Sweden and Denmark. But for Swedish and Danish people English is only a means of communication with non-Scandinavians. It is not a carrier of their culture. For the British, and particularly the English, it is additionally, and inseparably from its use as a tool of communication, a carrier of their culture and history. Or take Swahili in East and Central Africa. It is widely used as a means of communication across many nationalities. But it is not the carrier of a culture and history of many of those nationalities. However in parts of Kenya and Tanzania, and particularly in Zanzibar, Swahili is inseparably both a means of communication and a carrier of the culture of those people to whom it is a mother-tongue.

*   *   *

Culture transmits or imparts those images of the world and reality through the spoken and the written language, that is through a specific language. In other words, the capacity to speak, the capacity to order sounds in a manner that makes for mutual comprehension between human beings is universal. This is the universality of language, a quality specific to human beings. It corresponds to the universality of the struggle against nature and that between human beings. But the particularity of the sounds, the words, the word order into phrases and sentences, and the specific manner, or laws, of their ordering is what distinguishes one language from another. Thus a specific culture is not transmitted through language in its universality but in its particularity as the language of a specific community with a specific history. Written literature and orature are the main means by which a particular language transmits the images of the world contained in the culture it carries.   16

Language as communication and as culture are then products of each other. Communication creates culture: culture is a means of communication. Language carries culture, and culture carries, particularly through orature and literature, the entire body of values by which we come to perceive ourselves and our place in the world. How people perceive themselves affects how they look at their culture, at their politics and at the social production of wealth, at their entire relationship to nature and to other beings. Language is thus inseparable from ourselves as a community of human beings with a specific form and character, a specific history, a specific relationship to the world.   17

So what was the colonialist imposition of a foreign language doing to us children?   18

The real aim of colonialism was to control the people's wealth: what they produced, how they produced it, and how it was distributed; to control, in other words, the entire realm of the language of real life. Colonialism imposed its control of the social production of wealth   19 through military conquest and subsequent political dictatorship. But its most important area of domination was the mental universe of the colonised, the control, through culture, of how people perceived themselves and their relationship to the world. Economic and political control can never be complete or effective without mental control. To control a people's culture is to control their tools of self-definition in relationship to others.

20   For colonialism this involved two aspects of the same process: the destruction or the deliberate undervaluing of a people's culture, their art, dances, religions, history, geography, education, orature and literature, and the conscious elevation of the language of the coloniser. The domination of a people's language by the languages of the colonising nations was crucial to the domination of the mental universe of the colonised.

21   Take language as communication. Imposing a foreign language, and suppressing the native languages as spoken and written, were already breaking the harmony previously existing between the African child and the three aspects of language. Since the new language as a means of communication was a product of and was reflecting the 'real language of life' elsewhere, it could never as spoken or written properly reflect or imitate the real life of that community. This may in part explain why technology always appears to us as slightly external, *their* product and not *ours.* The word 'missile' used to hold an alien faraway sound until I recently learnt its equivalent in Gĩkũyũ, *ngurukuhĩ*, and it made me apprehend it differently. Learning, for a colonial child, became a cerebral activity and not an emotionally felt experience.

22   But since the new, imposed languages could never completely break the native languages as spoken, their most effective area of domination was the third aspect of language as communication, the written. The language of an African child's formal education was foreign. The language of the books he read was foreign. The language of his conceptualisation was foreign. Thought, in him, took the visible form of a foreign language. So the written language of a child's upbringing in the school (even his spoken language within the school compound) became divorced from his spoken language at home. There was often not the slightest relationship between the child's written world, which was also the language of his schooling, and the world of his immediate environment in the family and the community. For a colonial child, the harmony existing between the three aspects of language as communication was irrevocably broken. This resulted in the disassociation of the sensibility of that child from his natural and social environment, what we might call colonial alienation. The alienation became reinforced in the teaching of history, geography, music, where bourgeois Europe was always the centre of the universe.

This disassociation, divorce, or alienation from the immediate en-   23
vironment becomes clearer when you look at colonial language as a
carrier of culture.

Since culture is a product of the history of a people which it in turn   24
reflects, the child was now being exposed exclusively to a culture that
was a product of a world external to himself. He was being made to
stand outside himself to look at himself. *Catching Them Young* is the title
of a book on racism, class, sex, and politics in children's literature by
Bob Dixon. 'Catching them young' as an aim was even more true of a
colonial child. The images of this world and his place in it implanted in
a child take years to eradicate, if they ever can be.

Since culture does not just reflect the world in images but actually,   25
through those very images, conditions a child to see that world in a certain way, the colonial child was made to see the world and where he
stands in it as seen and defined by or reflected in the culture of the language of imposition.

And since those images are mostly passed on through orature and   26
literature it meant the child would now only see the world as seen in
the literature of his language of adoption. From the point of view of
alienation, that is of seeing oneself from outside oneself as if one was
another self, it does not matter that the imported literature carried the
great humanist tradition of the best in Shakespeare, Goethe, Balzac,
Tolstoy, Gorky, Brecht, Sholokhov, Dickens. The location of this great
mirror of imagination was necessarily Europe and its history and culture and the rest of the universe was seen from the centre.

But obviously it was worse when the colonial child was exposed to   27
images of his world as mirrored in the written languages of his coloniser. Where his own native languages were associated in his impres-
sionable mind with low status, humiliation, corporal punishment, slow-
footed intelligence and ability or downright stupidity, non-intelligibility
and barbarism, this was reinforced by the world he met in the works of
such geniuses of racism as a Rider Haggard or a Nicholas Monsarrat;
not to mention the pronouncement of some of the giants of western intellectual and political establishment, such as Hume ('. . . the negro is
naturally inferior to the whites . . .'),[2] Thomas Jefferson ('. . . the
blacks . . . are inferior to the whites on the endowments of both body
and mind . . .'),[3] or Hegel with his Africa comparable to a land of childhood still enveloped in the dark mantle of the night as far as the development of self-conscious history was concerned. Hegel's statement that
there was nothing harmonious with humanity to be found in the African

[2]Quoted in Eric Williams *A History of the People of Trinidad and Tobago,* London 1964, p. 32
[Author's note].
[3]Eric Williams, ibid, p. 31 [Author's note].

character is representative of the racist images of Africans and Africa such a colonial child was bound to encounter in the literature of the colonial languages.[4] The results could be disastrous.

28   In her paper read to the conference on the teaching of African literature in schools held in Nairobi in 1973,[5] entitled 'Written Literature and Black Images,' the Kenyan writer and scholar Professor Mīcere Mūgo related how a reading of the description of Gagool as an old African woman in Rider Haggard's *King Solomon's Mines* had for a long time made her feel mortal terror whenever she encountered old African women. In his autobiography *This Life* Sydney Poitier describes how, as a result of the literature he had read, he had come to associate Africa with snakes. So on arrival in Africa and being put up in a modern hotel in a modern city, he could not sleep because he kept on looking for snakes everywhere, even under the bed. These two have been able to pinpoint the origins of their fears. But for most others the negative image becomes internalised and it affects their cultural and even political choices in ordinary living.

✦ Evaluating the Text

1. In what way would stories involving animals as heroes be especially important to the children to whom they were told? How might the nature of the conflicts in the animal stories better prepare children to deal with conflicts in real life? To what extent do these stories transmit cultural values by stressing the importance of resourcefulness, high self-esteem, a connection to the past, and a pride in one's culture?

2. In addition to transmitting cultural values, how did hearing these stories, along with riddles and proverbs, imbue the children with a love of the language of Gīkūyū and enhance their responsiveness to and skill with features of narrative, imagery, inflection, and tone? How did hearing different people tell the same stories contribute to their devel-

---

[4]In references to Africa in the introduction to his lectures in *The Philosophy of History,* Hegel gives historical, philosophical, rational expression and legitimacy to every conceivable European racist myth about Africa. Africa is even denied her own geography where it does not correspond to the myth. Thus Egypt is not part of Africa; and North Africa is part of Europe. Africa proper is the especial home of ravenous beasts, snakes of all kinds. The African is not part of humanity. Only slavery to Europe can raise him, possibly, to the lower ranks of humanity. Slavery is good for the African. 'Slavery is in and for itself *injustice,* for the essence of humanity is *freedom;* but for this man must be matured. The gradual abolition of slavery is therefore wiser and more equitable than its sudden removal.' (Hegel, *The Philosophy of History,* Dover edition, New York: 1956, pp. 91–9.) Hegel clearly reveals himself as the nineteenth-century Hitler of the intellect [Author's note].

[5]The paper is now in Akivaga and Gachukiah's *The Teaching of African Literature in Schools,* published by Kenya Literature Bureau [Author's note].

opment of critical abilities in distinguishing whether a given story was told well or poorly?

3. Describe the disruption Thiong'o experienced when he first attended a colonial school, where he was forbidden to speak the language of the community from which he came. How do the kinds of punishments meted out for speaking Gĩkũyũ give you some insight into how psychologically damaging such an experience could be for a child? Which of the examples Thiong'o gives, in your opinion, most clearly reveals the extent to which speaking English was rewarded? In what way was the knowledge of English the single most important determinant of advancement?

4. Explain how the British as colonizers of Kenya sought to achieve dominance by (1) devaluing native speech, dance, art, and traditions and (2) promoting the worth of everything British, including the speaking of English.

5. How does changing the language a people are allowed to speak change the way they perceive themselves and their relationship to those around them? Why did the British try to make it impossible for Kenyans to draw on the cultural values and traditions embodied in their language, Gĩkũyũ? Why was it also in the British interest to encourage and even compel Kenyans to look at themselves only through a British perspective? How was this view reinforced by teaching Kenyans British literature?

✦ *Exploring Different Perspectives*

1. Compare the accounts by Thiong'o and Nien Cheng ("The Red Guards") in terms of reprogramming citizens to accept a "correct" ideology, whether that of British colonialism or Mao Tse-tung's Cultural Revolution.

2. In what way can the account by Thiong'o and Albert Camus's story "The Guest" be understood as documents of resistance to colonial powers (the British in Kenya and the French in Algeria)?

✦ *Extending Viewpoints Through Writing*

1. For a research project, you might compare Thiong'o's discussion of the stories he heard as a child with Bruno Bettleheim's study *The Uses of Enchantment: The Meaning and Importance of Fairy Tales* (1976). Bettleheim suggests that these traditional forms of storytelling help children build inner strength by acknowledging that real evil exists and can be

dangerous while offering hope that those who are resourceful can overcome the evil.

2. Discuss the extent to which Thiong'o's argument expresses a rationale similar to that advanced by proponents of bilingualism. You might also wish to consider the similarities and differences in political terms between the situation Thiong'o describes and that of a Hispanic or Chinese child in the United States.

3. If you come from a culture where English was not your first language, to what extent did your experiences match Thiong'o's when you entered a school where English was the required language?

Jon Swain

The Eyes of Vietnam

———————◆———————

Jon Swain is on the staff of the Sunday Times *of London. After a brief stint in the French foreign legion, he became a journalist and reported from Vietnam and Cambodia. He was captured by the Khmer Rouge and saved from execution through the intervention of Dith Pran, a New York* Times *interpreter, whose story is among those told in the film* The Killing Fields *(1984). "The Eyes of Vietnam" is drawn from Swain's memoir* River of Time *(1996).*

Bordered by Cambodia and Laos to the west, China to the north, and the South China Sea to the east and south, Vietnam was first visited by European traders in the early sixteenth century. After the French captured Saigon in 1859, Vietnam was under the control of France until World War II, when the Viet Minh, a coalition of nationalists and communists, established a republic headed by Ho Chi Minh. France's attempts to reassert control resulted in the French Indochina War (1946–1954), in which the French were defeated. In the Geneva Conference of 1954, Vietnam was divided, pending nationwide free elections, into North Vietnam, controlled by communists, and South Vietnam, controlled by nationalists. Ngo Dinh Diem's refusal to hold these elections, out of fear of a communist victory, precipitated the Vietnam War of 1954–1975, in which South Vietnam, aided by the United States, fought communist insurgents, who were supported by North Vietnam. United States troops were withdrawn in 1973, after a cease-fire, and in 1975 the communists overran the south. The country was reunified as the Socialist Republic of Vietnam in 1976. In 1978, Vietnam invaded Cambodia, deposed the genocidal Pol Pot regime, and installed a government that remained until the Vietnamese withdrew in 1989. Since 1989, Vietnam has been committed to a policy of doi moi *(renovation), which includes private enterprise and trade, an interest in tourism, and better relations with the United States. Some economic sanctions have been lifted since 1993 and the United States has opened a diplomatic office in Hanoi. Swain offers insight into the lives of great numbers of Vietnamese who fled the country during and after the war.*

The unification of North and South Vietnam into the Socialist Republic of Vietnam took place formally in July 1976. Between 1975 and 1984, approximately 550,000 "boat people" found refuge abroad. By 1989, 57,000 in Hong Kong would be forcibly repatriated following agreements reached in 1992 between the Communist Party of Vietnam and the

United Kingdom. Market-oriented reforms in recent years have begun a process of shifting the economy to one based on free-enterprise principles.

1   Little by little, a curtain now began to rise on a new Indo-Chinese horror. The war in Vietnam was over. The Americans and the army of South Vietnam had been defeated. The country was unified. The killing had stopped. But in a sense there was something more murderous than gunfire. Many people, indeed many ordinary people, ignorant of politics, were in despair. They were suffering greatly, their spirits crushed by the creed of communism and a continuous rotting of the system. A dark hopelessness filled their souls. And so first hundreds, then thousands of Vietnamese put to sea in small fishing boats from the heavily guarded shores of Vietnam.

2   Each boatload was representative of Vietnam's unhappy post-war society: there were teachers, writers, lawyers, students, former soldiers and young men of draft age. There were aircraft mechanics and shopkeepers and single mothers who fled because of official discrimination against their Amerasian children, the offspring of American GIs. There were whores; there were farmers and fishermen and, sometimes, there were disillusioned former Viet Cong fleeing the regime they fought so fiercely to install. The communist government often encouraged them to leave, regarding them as potential troublemakers. Many of the refugees were ethnic Chinese, former businessmen from Cholon, Saigon's Chinatown, who were being persecuted by Vietnam's vociferously anti-Chinese post-war government.

3   After a special UN conference, Hanoi was forced to abandon its policy of evicting its unwanted Chinese and to adopt a programme of 'orderly departures' by air. But there were also numerous disenchanted Vietnamese who regarded escape, preferably to the United States, as the only hope the future held. Desperately they put to sea in unseaworthy boats.

4   Many did not live to taste the freedom they sought. Just hours after they sailed from little fishing ports in the Mekong Delta of southern Vietnam, they found rape, robbery and a watery death in the Gulf of Thailand.

5   The pirates who attacked them were Thai fishermen. Piracy has prospered in the waters of the Gulf of Thailand for centuries, but falling fish catches, rising fuel costs, and the presence of gold and of defenceless and attractive women turned these law-abiding fishermen into monsters. The suffering of the Vietnamese boat people was almost beyond imagination; it consumed anyone who came into contact with it; for years after the war was over, I found myself coming back again and again to the subject and visiting the camps, principally in Thailand, where they were held. World opinion was slow to react to the horrors of piracy, however. The camps were controlled by the Thai

army and visitors needed an official pass and an escort. But sometimes it was possible to sneak in, in the guise of an aid worker; then the Vietnamese would open their hearts, secure in the knowledge that they were not being eavesdropped on by the Thais.

I was astonished to find boat people who appeared to have come to terms with the horror of their flight and could talk dispassionately about their ordeals even to a complete stranger like myself. However, one day I met a mother who had virtually lost the will to live, a tragic representative of all their suffering. A Thai policeman had pulled her by the hair from the hold of a boat where she was hiding and had deliberately thrown her baby son into the water to drown when she resisted. And I still think back with sorrow to sixteen-year-old La Kieu Ly, soft-faced and graceful; she was the sole survivor of a boat raided by pirates.

I met her in a dead-end refugee camp in Thailand near the Cambodian border. Her desperation and grief were reflected in the candle she was offering up at the camp's makeshift Catholic church. 'It is for Kim,' she said. Kim was her sister. Though barely ten years old, she was raped repeatedly by the pirates and was presumed to have drowned. Then Ly told me what had happened. One night, she said, she had slipped out of the Vietnamese fishing village of An Giang in a twenty-four foot fishing boat. Altogether, there were twenty-two people tucked out of sight below decks, including her aunt and a younger sister. A few hours out to sea, the boat ran into some Vietnamese fishermen, who confiscated their money and gold in return for allowing them to proceed. Thirty-six hours later, they met a Thai fishing boat whose crew gave them canned fish and sweets. A few hours afterwards they were attacked by another Thai fishing boat, this time with a crew of pirates aboard. It rammed their boat twice until it sank. The pirates plucked six girls, including Ly, her aunt and Kim, out of the sea. Everyone else they left to drown, including the men, whom they drove off with knives.

Then the terror began. The girls became the pirates' playthings, repeatedly raped and terrorised with fists, hammers and knives. After tiring of them, the pirates threw the three older girls overboard. They clubbed and beat Ly. And Kim, her little sister, was raped by three fishermen in succession. Ly could hear her screams. Her last memory of Kim was of a sobbing, pain-racked little bundle of humanity, begging for life. No trace of Kim was ever found.

Ly struggled so hard that the pirates threw her, too, into the sea. Naked but for a pirate's shirt and a shawl, she kept afloat for nine hours until another Thai fishing boat rescued her. The immense generosity of these men matched the immense cruelty of the pirates. They nursed her back to life, and when they landed at the southern Thai port of Nakhon Si Thammarat, they handed Ly over to the police who sent her to the Vietnamese boat people camp at Ban Thad.

10   I met her there one sad Sunday morning in a small comfortless room next to the church, through Joakim Dao, president of the camp's Catholic community, and heard her story. She told me that even now, and throughout her life, she would be looking out of the window for her little sister Kim, though she knew in her heart that Kim would never be coming home. As I left the church, apologising for my unwarranted intrusion, I remember thinking with humility how she reflected the special dignity of Vietnamese women and their instinct of survival.

11   But when I looked into her eyes they were expressionless. They were dead. They were the eyes of Vietnam—the eyes of someone who had born the unbearable.

12   On another occasion, travelling along the coast of southern Thailand, I came across a group of ten men, women and children, wading ashore on the beach at Ya Ring. Shocked and physically exhausted after repeated pirate attacks, they collapsed in a huddle on the sand, all that remained of a boatload of thirty-seven refugees raided by pirates. They were all wet through and looked like drowned rats. But something about one girl was different and yet disturbingly familiar. With a jolt of recognition and sadness, I realised why she had caught my attention. She had blue eyes and brown hair. She was an Amerasian. Her name was Chung Thi Ai Ngoc. She was thirteen, and she needed urgent medical treatment; the pirates had thought her western features were a prize to be fought over, and she had been repeatedly raped.

13   In due course I asked Ngoc about her American father, and how she felt about going to America. She looked down at her bare feet in the sand and said nothing. Then she begin to cry. She had never known her father, she said; he had gone away a few months before she was born. At the end of his Vietnam tour, he had gone home leaving her pregnant mother to fend for herself and his baby. Her mother had raised her as best she could and had only one dream, getting to America. So they had escaped by boat. And her mother? Ngoc was sobbing like a baby now, her shoulders shaking uncontrollably and her hands clenched tightly. 'I don't know where she is,' she said. The pirates had put her mother on a different boat. During the night the two boats had become separated at sea; her mother was lost to her.

14   In the cruel roulette of life Ngoc seemed to be an especially tragic loser. More than an innocent victim, she was a metaphor for America's intervention in Vietnam, made for the best of motives but which brought about terrible death and destruction and in the end more tragedy than it can possibly have been worth. The Americans courted the south Vietnamese assiduously; they made them dependent, then abandoned them to their fate. That is precisely what happened to Ngoc's mother; her GI boyfriend made her pregnant, then one day—like America—he jilted her and went away. When I looked into Ngoc's tear-filled eyes I saw that they, too, were the eyes of Vietnam.

I had been hearing sinister stories about the goings on at Koh Kra,   15
an island in the Gulf of Thailand much frequented by Thai fishermen-
turned-pirates. On this jagged finger of jungle-capped rock forty miles
from the Thai coast and directly on the route from Vietnam to Thailand,
the pirates committed their worst atrocities.

When I got to Koh Kra, it was deserted, having been cleaned up by   16
the United Nations and Thai police raids. I quickly saw though that it
stood out as a monument to all the suffering of the boat people. The evidence of the pirates' occupation remained on its sandy beach; the
charred carcasses of two wooden refugee boats, women's hair, a girl's
shoe, bloodstained clothing and a torn bra. There were charcoal inscriptions in Vietnamese on the walls of the white hut, the only shelter
on the island, and more poignant messages in paint on the rocks.

'When your boat reaches the island, immediately send all the   17
women to hide in the bushes and caves. Don't let the Thai pirates see
them. If they do they will rape them,' said one inscription. 'They will
give you something to eat, but they will take everything you own, even
your clothes,' said another. 'They will rape you, one boat after another,
one hundred boats altogether, taking turns coming to the girls.'

In the face of such horrors, a singular man set an epic example.   18
Theodore Schweitzer, a Missouri-born American was for a while the
UN field officer at Songkhla refugee camp in the south of Thailand—a
job which need not have demanded much initiative. But he saw piracy
as a curse, its eradication a challenge, and in twenty-seven daring missions to Kra he rescued nearly 1500 stranded Vietnamese refugees at
great risk to himself.

In his first dramatic rescue, Schweitzer swam the best part of a mile   19
from his boat to the island at two in the morning. In the best Hollywood tradition, he rose from the sea and confronted a group of pirates
gang-raping refugee women on the beach. He had only a commando
knife with which to defend himself against this ruthless bunch. But his
unexpected arrival and tough air of authority unnerved the pirates and
probably saved his life. That night, he rescued 157 distraught refugees.
One was a badly burned woman who had been hiding from the pirates
in high grass when they poured petrol on it and set it alight. Another
woman was so terrified of being gang-raped again that she stood in sea
water up to her knees in a rock cave and stifled her screams of pain as
giant crabs bit at her legs. Claude Bordes, a French doctor who treated
her, told me she would bear the scars for life.

One of the most barbaric pirate attacks on Kra happened a few   20
days before I arrived when more than 200 fishermen-turned-pirates attacked and towed Vietnamese refugee boats to the island. The fishermen raped more than fifty women and teenage girls and killed sixteen
of them. Such incidents affected the tough American deeply. In a moving interview, he described the death in hospital of a Vietnamese girl in

her early teens shortly after he had rescued her from Kra. 'She died of shock and convulsion,' he said. 'Her jaw locked open. She died from fear. She was just totally scared to death. She was a very beautiful little girl and the pirates picked on her every time.'

21   Nothing better captures the sorrow in the souls of these victims than the simple message I saw scrawled in charcoal on a hut wall on Kra. It read: 'Moment of remembering father and mother,' and was signed Tran Van Sang. Another said: 'Remembering twenty-one days' suffering of three sisters.'

22   More than ten years later, to international indifference, Vietnamese in their thousands were still putting to sea in small boats to escape poverty and oppression at home. And so, not very long ago, I spent two unforgettable days with a group of boat people whose thirty-seven-day struggle for survival in a drifting boat was as harrowing as any I have ever encountered, and quite beyond the range of most people's experiences.

23   I met them at Puerto Princesa on the lovely Philippines island of Palawan, where an asylum camp for boat people waiting to be resettled in the West had been established. It was not Vietnam; it might have been. A frenzy of green trees tumbled down to a sandy beach and a turquoise sea. The air was scented with the smell of woodsmoke and cooking. There was a little Catholic church, there were dimly lit noodle shops and masses of ragged children, laughing and tumbling in the mud, for it was the rainy season. There were pretty women, generous with their smiles. There were boy scout groups, lovers sitting on a bench and ageing men with wispy beards and wrinkled faces and sad, watery eyes. It had the chaotic intimacy of a fishing port on the Mekong.

24   Early in the morning in a quiet corner of the camp, I sat down with Dinh Thong Hai, a thirty-year-old tailor from Saigon, and Vo Thi Bach Yen, a seamstress from the Mekong Delta As we drank *cà phê sũa*, filtered coffee sweetened with condensed milk, out of grimy glasses, I was struck by how sad they were. Both had left Vietnam desperately looking forward to a future in America. It was Hai's fifteenth escape attempt. He had been jailed several times for trying to flee. Yen's husband, a former captain in the defeated Saigon army, and her two older children had been in California for more than a year and she had escaped from Vietnam with her four-year-old daughter to join them. Now, in front of me, they blurted out the story of their barbaric voyage in a drifting boat.

25   Their forty-five foot long riverboat had left Ben Tre, in the Mekong Delta, in chaos, overloaded with 110 men, women and children crammed on board with only enough food and water for a few days. It was bound for Malaysia, six days away across the ocean. But after barely two days a storm had blown up, the boat sprang a leak, the motor

failed. The passengers rigged a makeshift sail and prayed for deliverance. Day after day, they were passed by merchant ships, some within hailing distance. They scrawled an SOS with toothpaste on a piece of wood and held it up; at night they made bonfires of their clothes. One night, a Japanese freighter came within a hundred yards. Several refugees, maddened by hunger and thirst, jumped into the water and swam towards it but the ship sailed on, leaving them to drown.

Panic set in as they ran out of food. Phung Quang Minh, a former corporal in the Saigon air force, forcibly established his leadership in the drifting boat. He surrounded himself with a group of followers, mostly teenagers, and they armed themselves with sticks and knives and carried out his orders in return for extra food and water seized from the weaker passengers. Even the captain of the fishing boat deferred to Minh's authority. One dawn, he jumped over the side with his daughter and three relatives and vanished in the ocean swell. 26

On the fourteenth day a twenty-two-year-old man died of thirst and his body was committed to the deep. On the fifteenth day, Yen's daughter died. She was one of seven small children to perish that day and was the focus of Yen's life. 'She did not say anything. She just stopped breathing,' Yen said quietly. 'The next day I asked two passengers in the boat to help me to put her little body into the sea.' 27

During the next days, several people began drinking sea water and their own urine, which hastened their deaths. Others toppled into the sea, jumped overboard and swam away, or clung to pieces of wood or oil drums, convinced by the seagulls circling overhead that land was nearby. 28

A few days later, their spirits rose when they were spotted by the USS *Dubuque*. As the 8800-ton American amphibious landing ship circled, four refugees jumped into the sea and swam towards it. One drowned; the others reached the ship only to be rebuffed by the sailors, who leaned over the side to tell them it was on a secret mission (to the Arabian Gulf) and they could not come aboard. They threw down three life-jackets and told the refugees to swim back to the boat. 29

In full view of the American ship, the body of a refugee who had died was thrown overboard. Sailors photographed the corpse floating in the water. One Vietnamese-speaking American told them, 'We will never let anyone on your boat die again.' The Americans gave them six cases of tinned meat, boxes of apples, plastic containers of fresh water and a map with directions to the Philippines, 250 miles away. Although the Vietnamese explained to the sailor that the boat had broken down no one offered to repair the engine. Two hours later the *Dubuque* sailed away, leaving them to their fate. 30

The suffering now became unendurable. Minh confiscated the American food. He beat Yen about the head with a shoe to stop her giving water to dying children. Then, twelve days after the encounter with 31 the *Dubuque,* he and his gang turned on the others and began to murder them, one by one.

32   The first victim to be killed and eaten was Dao Cuong, the best friend of Hai and one of the feeblest on the boat. The refugees were dying at the rate of one or two a day; but Minh's gang preferred to kill rather than feast on the corpses of those who had died. Two children, aged eleven and fourteen, and a twenty-two-year-old woman, were his other victims. One of the children was Hai's cousin.

33   For the first time in almost an hour Hai and Yen were both silent for a moment. I thought they did not want to talk about it any more, because the memories of the cannibalism were too painful to recall, especially to a stranger. But then Yen took a deep breath, sighed and went on: 'It was horrible, but we did not have the strength to stop him.'

34   Another difficult pause, then Hai was saying: 'Two days before it happened, Cuong was so driven by hunger that he gave Minh a gold ring in exchange for an apple. But Minh's group came with knives and sticks and said they needed my friend for food to help the others to survive. I said, "No, Cuong is still alive. I cannot let you kill and eat him. You can use him if he dies." Cuong overheard the conversation. He said he did not agree to be killed. He still believed we would be rescued the next day. But the men had made up their minds. We were too weak to resist. "Kill him, kill him," one said. "Quickly, quickly, it's almost night." And when I saw the two men grab Cuong by the feet and realised they were about to kill him, I asked them to allow us a few minutes in private. Cuong had told me before we had left Vietnam he wanted to be a Catholic. I scooped up some sea water, poured it over his head and read the Bible. Then the men pushed Cuong's head under the water until he drowned, before eating his body.'

35   A silence intervened. Hai's face was suddenly very pale. But the whole story was not yet out, for he said that an eleven-year-old boy— his cousin—was Minh's last victim, killed the day before their rescue by Filipino fishermen. The boy still had the strength to move and understood what was happening. 'I don't want to die. I don't want to die,' he screamed and hid in the cabin. Minh dragged him out and handed him over to his men. They held him over the side of the boat while he struggled and screamed and kicked; it took them about three minutes to drown him. Then they took out a knife, cut off the head, dismembered the body, cooked the flesh and distributed it.

36   Hai stopped talking. The whole story was out. A terrible sadness filled the air. I saw the shame in their faces and felt guilty that I had made them relive their experience. The significance of what Hai had been saying suddenly dawned on me. Probably they had all become cannibals to survive that terrible voyage; perhaps some of the people on that boat had, in desperation, eaten the flesh of Minh's victims and not just some part of the naturally dead. There have been reports before of cannibalism at sea; starving boat people who ate the dead. But never

before, as far as I know, had there been a case of boat people murdering and eating each other to survive.

I sought to talk to Minh but UN refugee officials responsible for the camp would not allow it. He and six members of his gang were shut in a locked building guarded by Filipino soldiers and out of bounds to the rest of the camp's 4800 inmates, while their future was decided. Some of the best legal brains of the Philippines were arguing whether they should be prosecuted. Clearly it was not a normal case of murder. The desperate circumstances raised complex questions. The refugee status of the Vietnamese and the fact that the deaths had occurred at sea compounded the issue. Minh's defence was the plea of necessity. He argued that twelve days after the *Dubuque* had steamed off and left them helplessly adrift in a leaking and disabled boat, the refugees had lost all semblance of sanity and were driven by desperation to killing and cannibalism.

As I got up to go, I looked into Hai's eyes. They were black pools of horror. The eyes of the dead. This man too had eyes I cannot forget. The eyes of Vietnam.

Of the 110 refugees who left Vietnam fifty-eight died en route, *most by drowning and starvation. After investigating whether the* Dubuque *should have given more help to the refugees, the US navy suspended Captain Alexander Balian from his command and later court-martialled him. Hai and Yen have left the Philippines and are learning to live with their memories in their new lives.*

✦ Evaluating the Text

1. What circumstances led Swain to encounter La Kieu Ly at the refugee camp in Thailand?

2. How do the experiences of Ly and of Chung Thi Ai Ngoc reflect those undergone by tens of thousands of other refugees after the war in Vietnam was over?

3. How does the treatment of boat people as described by Swain reveal the kinds of overwhelming obstacles they had to overcome in order to survive long enough to even get to the refugee asylum camps? How do the experiences Swain reports as having taken place on the riverboat present a legal and moral dilemma?

✦ Exploring Different Perspectives

1. How do the accounts by Jon Swain and Slavenka Drakulić ("The Balkan Express") reveal the extent to which atrocities can become part of everyday life?

2. What sense do you get of the need to assume ethical responsibility in the account by Jon Swain and in "The Guest" by Albert Camus?

✦ *Extending Viewpoints Through Writing*

1. In a short essay, describe what effects these narratives had on Swain personally and explain the meaning of the title "The Eyes of Vietnam."

Nien Cheng

The Red Guards

───────◆───────

Nien Cheng (b. 1915) was raised in Shanghai within the traditional Chinese culture. In the 1930s she received an unparalleled opportunity to pursue an education at the London School of Economics, where she mastered English and met her husband. They had a daughter, Meiping. After the communists took over in 1949, they chose to remain in China, and with the approval of the new government, Cheng's husband became the general manager of the Shanghai branch of Shell Oil Company. After his death in 1957, Nien Cheng went to work at the same company. In August of 1966, at the beginning of the Cultural Revolution, a group of fanatical Red Guards invaded her home and sent her to prison, where she was subjected to relentless interrogations. The record of her imprisonment is contained in an extraordinary book, Life and Death in Shanghai *(1988), from which the following selection is taken.*

The Cultural Revolution of 1966–1969 was a massive campaign begun by Mao Tse-tung to renew the nation's revolutionary spirit by purging society of its liberal elements. Revolutionary Red Guards composed of ideologically motivated young men and women acted with the army to attack so-called bourgeois elements in the government and in the culture at large. Mao's wife, Jing Quing, played an active role and was caught in the backlash to this violent and oppressive movement when Mao died in 1976.

As the tempo of the Proletarian Cultural Revolution gathered momentum, all-night sessions of political indoctrination were often held in different organizations. On the evening of August 30, when the Red Guards came to loot my house, my daughter was at her film studio attending one of these meetings. I was sitting alone in my study reading *The Rise and Fall of the Third Reich,* which had come in the last batch of books from a bookshop in London with which I had an account. Throughout the years I worked for Shell, I managed to receive books from this shop by having the parcels sent to the office. Since the Shanghai censors always passed unopened all parcels addressed to organizations, and since Shell received an enormous amount of scientific literature for distribution to Chinese research organizations, my small parcel attracted no undue attention.

1

*(For additional information about China, see p. 245.)

2   The house was very quiet. I knew Lao-zhao was sitting in the pantry as he had done day after day. Chen-ma was in her room, probably lying in bed wide awake. There was not the slightest sound or movement anywhere, almost as if everything in the house were holding its breath waiting helplessly for its own destruction.

3   The windows of my study were open. The bittersweet perfume of the magnolia in the garden and the damp smell of the cool evening air with a hint of autumn pervaded the atmosphere. From the direction of the street, faint at first but growing louder, came the sound of a heavy motor vehicle slowly approaching. I listened and waited for it to speed up and pass the house. But it slowed down, and the motor was cut off. I knew my neighbor on the left was also expecting the Red Guards. Dropping the book on my lap and sitting up tensely, I listened, wondering which house was to be the target.

4   Suddenly the doorbell began to ring incessantly. At the same time, there was furious pounding of many fists on my front gate, accompanied by the confused sound of hysterical voices shouting slogans. The cacophony told me that the time of waiting was over and that I must face the threat of the Red Guards and the destruction of my home. Lao-zhao came up the stairs breathlessly. Although he had known the Red Guards were sure to come eventually and had been waiting night after night just as I had, his face was ashen.

5   "They have come!" His unsteady voice was a mixture of awe and fright.

6   "Please keep calm, Lao-zhao! Open the gate but don't say anything. Take Chen-ma with you to your room and stay there," I told him.

7   Lao-zhao's room was over the garage. I wanted both of them out of the way so that they would not say anything to offend the Red Guards out of a sense of loyalty to me.

8   Outside, the sound of voices became louder. "Open the gate! Open the gate! Are you all dead? Why don't you open the gate?" Someone was swearing and kicking the wooden gate. The horn of the truck was blasting too.

9   Lao-zhao ran downstairs. I stood up to put the book on the shelf. A copy of the Constitution of the People's Republic caught my eye. Taking it in my hand and picking up the bunch of keys I had ready on my desk, I went downstairs.

10   Although in my imagination I had already lived through this moment many times, my heart was pounding. However, lifelong discipline enabled me to maintain a calm appearance. By the time I had reached the bottom of the staircase, I was the epitome of Chinese fatalism.

11   At the same moment, the Red Guards pushed open the front door and entered the house. There were thirty or forty senior high school students, aged between fifteen and twenty, led by two men and one woman much older. Although they all wore the armband of the Red

Guard, I thought the three older people were the teachers who generally accompanied the Red Guards when they looted private homes. As they crowded into the hall, one of them knocked over a pot of jasmine on a *fencai* porcelain stool. The tiny white blooms scattered on the floor, trampled by their impatient feet.

The leading Red Guard, a gangling youth with angry eyes, stepped forward and said to me, "We are the Red Guards. We have come to take revolutionary action against you!"   12

Though I knew it was futile, I held up the copy of the Constitution and said calmly, "It's against the Constitution of the People's Republic of China to enter a private house without a search warrant."   13

The young man snatched the document out of my hand and threw it on the floor. With his eyes blazing, he said, "The Constitution is abolished. It was a document written by the Revisionists within the Communist Party. We recognize only the teachings of our Great Leader Chairman Mao."   14

"Only the People's Congress has the power to change the Constitution," I said.   15

"We have abolished it. What can you do about it?" he said aggressively while assuming a militant stance with feet apart and shoulders braced.   16

A girl came within a few inches of where I stood and said, "What trick are you trying to play? Your only way out is to bow your head in submission. Otherwise you will suffer." She shook her fist in front of my nose and spat on the floor.   17

Another young man used a stick to smash the mirror hanging over the blackwood chest facing the front door. A shower of glass fell on the blue-and-white Kangxi vase on the chest, but the carved frame of the mirror remained on the hook. He tore the frame off and hurled it against the banister. Then he took from another Red Guard a small blackboard, which he hung up on the hook. On it was written a quotation from Mao Zedong. It said, "When the enemies with guns are annihilated, the enemies without guns still remain. We must not belittle these enemies."   18

The Red Guards read the quotation aloud as if taking a solemn oath. Afterwards, they told me to read it. Then one of them shouted to me, "An enemy without gun! That's what you are. Hand over the keys!"   19

I placed my bunch of keys on the chest amidst the fragments of glass. One of them picked it up. All the Red Guards dispersed into various parts of the house. A girl pushed me into the dining room and locked the door.   20

I sat down by the dining table and looked around the room. It was strange to realize that after this night I would never see it again as it was. The room had never looked so beautiful as it did at that moment. The gleam of the polished blackwood table was richer than ever. The   21 white lacquered screen with its inlaid ivory figures stood proudly in one corner, a symbol of fine craftsmanship. The antique porcelain plates and vases on their blackwood stands were placed at just the right angle to show off their beauty. Even the curtains hung completely evenly, not a fraction out of line. In the glass cabinet were white jade figures, a rose quartz incense burner, and ornaments of other semiprecious stones that I had lovingly collected over the years. They had been beautifully carved in intricate designs by the hands of skilled artists. Now my eyes caressed them to bid them farewell. Having heard from Winnie that the painter Lin Fengmian was in serious trouble, I knew that his painting of a lady in blue hanging over the sideboard would be ruthlessly destroyed. But what about the other ink-and-brush painting by Qi Baishi? He was a great artist of the traditional style. Because of his having been a carpenter in early life, he was honored by the Communist Party. Would the Red Guards know the facts of Qi Baishi's life and spare this painting? I looked at it carefully, my eyes lingering over each stroke of his masterful brush. It was a picture of the lotus, a favorite subject for Chinese artists because the lotus symbolized purity. The poet Tao Yuanming (A.D. 376–427) used the lotus to represent a man of honor in a famous poem, saying that the lotus rose out of mud but remained unstained.

22   I recited the poem to myself and wondered whether it was really possible for anyone to remain unstained by his environment. It was an idea contrary to Marxism, which held that the environment molded the man. Perhaps the poet was too idealistic, I thought as I listened to the laughter of the Red Guards overhead. They seemed to be blissfully happy in their work of destruction because they were sure they were doing something to satisfy their God, Mao Zedong. Their behavior was the result of their upbringing in Communist China. The propaganda they had absorbed precluded their having a free will of their own.

23   A heavy thud overhead stopped my speculations. I could hear the sound of many people walking up and down the stairs, glasses breaking, and heavy knocking on the wall. The noise intensified. It sounded almost as if the Red Guards were tearing the house down rather than merely looting its contents. I became alarmed and decided to try to secure my release by deception.

24   I knocked on the door. There was such a din in the house that no one heard me. I knocked harder and harder. When I heard a movement outside the door, I called out, "Open up!"

25   The handle was turned slowly, and the door opened a narrow gap. A girl Red Guard in pigtails asked what I wanted. I told her I had to go to the bathroom. She let me out after cautioning me not to interfere with their revolutionary activities.

26   The Red Guards had taken from the storeroom the crates containing my father's books and papers and were trying to open them with

pliers. Through the open drawing room door, I saw a girl on a ladder removing the curtains. Two bridge tables were in the middle of the room. On them was a collection of cameras, watches, clocks, binoculars, and silverware that the Red Guards had gathered from all over the house. These were the "valuables" they intended to present to the state.

Mounting the stairs, I was astonished to see several Red Guards taking pieces of my porcelain collection out of their padded boxes. One young man had arranged a set of four Kangxi winecups in a row on the floor and was stepping on them. I was just in time to hear the crunch of delicate porcelain under the sole of his shoe. The sound pierced my heart. Impulsively I leapt forward and caught his leg just as he raised his foot to crush the next cup. He toppled. We fell in a heap together. My eyes searched for the other winecups to make sure we had not broken them in our fall, and, momentarily distracted, I was not able to move aside when the boy regained his feet and kicked me right in my chest. I cried out in pain. The other Red Guards dropped what they were doing and gathered around us, shouting at me angrily for interfering in their revolutionary activities. One of the teachers pulled me up from the floor. His face flushed in anger, the young man waved his fist, threatening me with a severe beating. The teacher raised her voice to restore order. She said to me, "What do you think you are doing? Are you trying to protect your possessions?" 27

"No, no, you can do whatever you like with my things. But you mustn't break these porcelain treasures. They are old and valuable and cannot be replaced," I said rather breathlessly. My chest throbbed with pain. 28

"Shut up! Shut up!" A chorus of voices drowned my words. 29

"Our Great Leader said, 'Lay out the facts; state the reasons.'" I summoned all my strength and yelled at the top of my voice to be heard. 30

The teacher raised her hand to silence the Red Guards and said, "We will allow you to lay out the facts and state the reasons." The Red Guards glared at me. 31

I picked up one of the remaining winecups and cradled it in my palm. Holding my hand out, I said, "This winecup is nearly three hundred years old. You seem to value the cameras, watches, and binoculars, but better cameras, better watches, and more powerful binoculars are being made every year. No one in this world can make another winecup like this one again. This is a part of our cultural heritage. Every Chinese should be proud of it." 32

The young man whose revolutionary work of destruction I had interrupted said angrily, "You shut up! These things belong to the old culture. They are the useless toys of the feudal emperors and the modern capitalist class and have no significance to us, the proletarian class. They cannot be compared to cameras and binoculars, which are useful 33 for our struggle in time of war. Our Great Leader Chairman Mao taught us, 'If we do not destroy, we cannot establish.' The old culture must be destroyed to make way for the new socialist culture."

34   Another Red Guard said, "The purpose of the Great Proletarian Cultural Revolution is to destroy the old culture. You cannot stop us!"

35   I was trembling with anxiety and frantically searching my mind for some convincing argument to stop this senseless destruction. But before I could utter another futile word, I saw another young man coming down the stairs from the third floor with my blanc de chine Goddess of Mercy, Guanyin, in his hand. I turned to him and asked uneasily, "What are you going to do with that figure?"

36   He swung the arm holding the Guanyin carelessly in the air and declared, "This is a figure of Buddhist superstition. I'm going to throw it in the trash."

37   The Guanyin was a perfect specimen and a genuine product of the Dehua kiln in Fujian province. It was the work of the famous seventeenth-century Ming sculptor Chen Wei and bore his seal on the back. The beauty of the creamy-white figure was beyond description. The serene expression of the face was so skillfully captured that it seemed to be alive. The folds of the robe flowed so naturally that one forgot it was carved out of hard biscuit. The glaze was so rich and creamy that the whole figure looked as if it were soft to the touch. This figure of Guanyin I always kept in its padded box, deeming it too valuable to be displayed. I took it out only when knowledgeable friends interested in porcelain asked to look at it.

38   "No, no, please! You mustn't do that! I beg you." I was so agitated that my voice was shrill. The Red Guard just fixed me with a stony stare and continued to swing his arm casually, holding the Guanyin now with only two fingers.

39   Pleading was not going to move the Red Guards. If I wanted to communicate, I must speak their language. The time had come to employ diplomacy, it seemed to me. If the Red Guards thought I opposed them, I would never succeed in saving the treasures. By this time, I no longer thought of them as my own possessions. I did not care to whom they belonged after tonight as long as they were saved from destruction.

40   "Please, Red Guards! Believe me, I'm not opposed to you. You have come here as representatives of our Great Leader. How could I oppose the representatives of Chairman Mao? I understand the purpose of the Cultural Revolution. Did I not surrender the keys willingly when you asked for them?" I said.

41   "Yes, you did," conceded the teacher with a nod. The Red Guards gathered around us seemed to relax a little.

42   Somewhat encouraged, I went on. "All these old things belong to the past era. The past is old. It must go to make way for the new culture

of socialism. But they could be taken away without immediate destruction. Remember, they were not made by members of the capitalist class. They were made by the hands of the workers of a bygone age. Should you not respect the labor of those workers?"

A Red Guard at the back of the group shouted impatiently, "Don't 43 listen to her flowery words. She is trying to confuse us. She is trying to protect her possessions."

I quickly turned to him and said, "No, no! Your being in my house 44 has already improved my socialist awareness. It was wrong of me to have kept all these beautiful and valuable things to myself. They rightly belong to the people. I beg you to take them to the Shanghai Museum. You can consult their experts. If the experts advise you to destroy them, there will still be time to do so."

A girl said, "The Shanghai Museum is closed. The experts there are 45 being investigated. Some of them are also class enemies. In any case, they are intellectuals. Our Great Leader has said, 'The capitalist class is the skin; the intellectuals are the hairs that grow on the skin. When the skin dies, there will be no hair.' The capitalist class nourishes the intellectuals, so they belong to the same side. Now we are going to destroy the capitalist class. Naturally the intellectuals are to be destroyed too."

The quotation of Mao she mentioned was new to me, but this was 46 no time to think of that. I pursued my purpose by saying, "In that case, consult someone you can trust, someone in a position of authority. Perhaps one of the vice-mayors of Shanghai. Surely there are many private collections in the city. There must be some sort of policy for dealing with them."

"No, no! You are a stupid class enemy! You simply do not under- 47 stand. You are arguing and advising us to consult either other class enemies or the revisionist officials of the government. You talk about official policy. The only valid official policy is in this book." The young man took his book of Mao's quotations from his pocket and held it up as he continued, "The teachings of our Great Leader Chairman Mao are the only valid official policy."

Changing the direction of my argument, I said, "I saw a placard 48 saying, 'Long Live World Revolution.' You are going to carry the red flag of our Great Leader Chairman Mao all over the world, aren't you?"

"Of course we are! What has that got to do with you? You are only 49 a class enemy," a girl sneered. She turned to the others and warned, "She is a tricky woman. Don't listen to her nonsense!"

Getting really desperate, I said, "Don't you realize all these things 50 are extremely valuable? They can be sold in Hong Kong for a large sum of money. You will be able to finance your world revolution with that money."

At last, what I said made an impression. The Red Guards were lis- 51 tening. The wonderful prospect of playing a heroic role on the broad world stage was flattering to their egos, especially now that they were getting intoxicated with a sense of power.

52   I seized the psychological moment and went on. "Please put all these porcelain pieces back in their boxes and take them to a safe place. You can sell them or give them to the museum, whatever you consider right, according to the teachings of our Great Leader."

53   Perhaps, being an older person, the teacher felt some sense of responsibility. She asked me, "Are you sure your collection is valuable? How much would you say it is worth?"

54   "You will find a notebook with the date of purchase and the sum of money I spent on each item. Their price increases every month, especially on the world market. As a rough estimate, I think they are worth at least a million yuan," I told her.

55   Although members of the proletarian class did not appreciate value, they understood price. The Red Guards were impressed by the figure "one million." The teacher was by now just as anxious as I was to save the treasures, but she was afraid to put herself in the wrong with the Red Guards. However, she found a way for the Red Guards to back down without loss of face.

56   "Little revolutionary generals! Let's have a meeting and talk over this matter." She was flattering the Red Guards by calling them "little revolutionary generals," a title coined by the Maoists to encourage the Red Guards to do their bidding. The Red Guards were obviously pleased and readily agreed to her suggestion. She led them down the stairs to the dining room.

57   I knelt down to pick up the remaining winecups and put them in the box. The Guanyin had been left on the table. I took it and went upstairs to the large cupboard on the landing of the third floor, where I normally kept my collection. I saw that all the boxes had been taken out. On the floor there were fragments of porcelain in colors of oxblood, imperial yellow, celadon green, and blue-and-white. My heart sank at the realization that whatever my desperate effort might now achieve, it was already too late. Many of the boxes were empty.

58   The third-floor rooms resembled a scene after an earthquake except for the absence of corpses. But the red wine spilled out of broken bottles on white sheets and blankets was the same color as blood.

59   Because we lived in a permanent state of shortage, every household with enough living space had a store cupboard in which we hoarded reserves of such daily necessities as flour, sugar, and canned meat. Each time I went to Hong Kong I also brought back cases of food and soap to supplement our meager ration, even though the import duty was astronomical. The Red Guards had emptied my store cupboard. Flour, sugar, and food from cans they had opened lay on top of heaps of clothing they had taken out of cupboards, trunks, and drawers. Some suitcases remained undisturbed, but I could see that they

had already dealt with my fur coats and evening dresses with a pair of scissors. The ceiling fan was whirling. Bits of fur, silk, and torn sheets of tissue paper were flying around.

Every piece of furniture was pulled out of its place. Tables and chairs were overturned, some placed on top of others to form a ladder. As it was summer, my carpets had been cleaned, sprinkled with camphor powder, rolled up, and stored in an empty bedroom on the third floor. Behind the largest roll of carpet, I found a shopping bag stuffed with two of my cashmere cardigans and several sets of new underwear. It seemed a thoughtful Red Guard had quietly put them away for personal use.

In the largest guest room, where the Red Guards had carried out most of their destructive labor of cutting and smashing, a radio set was tuned to a local station broadcasting revolutionary songs based on Mao's quotations. A female voice was singing, "Marxism can be summed up in one sentence: revolution is justifiable." There was a note of urgency in her voice that compelled the listener's attention. This song was to become the clarion call not only for the Red Guards but also for the Proletarian Revolutionaries when they were organized later on. I thought of switching off the radio, but it was out of my reach unless I climbed over the mountain of debris in the middle of the room.

I looked at what had happened to my things hopelessly but indifferently. They belonged to a period of my life that had abruptly ended when the Red Guards entered my house. Though I could not see into the future, I refused to look back. I supposed the Red Guards had enjoyed themselves. Is it not true that we all possess some destructive tendencies in our nature? The veneer of civilization is very thin. Underneath lurks the animal in each of us. If I were young and had had a working-class background, if I had been brought up to worship Mao and taught to believe him infallible, would I not have behaved exactly as the Red Guards had done?

✦ Evaluating the Text

1. What is the objective of the Red Guards when they invade and ransack Nien Cheng's home? What Maoist political ideology guides their activities?

2. What does Nien Cheng's reaction to the systematic attempts to intimidate and humiliate her reveal about her as a person? How does she attempt to manipulate the Red Guards so they will not destroy irreplaceable artifacts?

3. Why is it significant that she is able to project herself into their situation and understand the appeal that Maoism has for them?

✦ *Exploring Different Perspectives*

1. Compare Nien Cheng's account with Jicai Feng's story "The Tall Woman and Her Short Husband" in terms of the extent to which everyday citizens can seize on questions of ideology as a pretext for acting on their personal enmities, jealousies, and other emotions.

2. Compare Nien Cheng's account with that of Ngũgĩ wa Thiong'o ("Decolonising the Mind") in terms of the attitude of those in power toward traditional culture.

✦ *Extending Viewpoints Through Writing*

1. Is there any idea or belief so important to you that you would undergo imprisonment and/or torture to defend it?

Feng Jicai

The Tall Woman and Her Short Husband

———————◆———————

Feng Jicai, one of China's best-known writers, was born and brought up in Tianjin. He started out as an athlete but after an injury was transferred to work in a Chinese traditional painting press, where he began to paint and write. In 1974, he started teaching Chinese traditional painting at the Tianjin Worker's College of Decorative Art and continued to write in his spare time. Since 1976 he has published three novels and six collections of novelettes and short stories. "The Tall Woman and Her Short Husband" appeared in Best Chinese Stories: 1949–1989 *(1989).*

1

Say you have a small tree in your yard and are used to its smooth trunk. If one day it turns twisted and gnarled it strikes you as awkward. As time goes by, however, you grow to like it, as if that was how this tree should always have been. Were it suddenly to straighten out again you would feel indescribably put out. A trunk as dull and boring as a stick! In fact it would simply have reverted to its original form, so why should you worry?

Is this force of habit? Well, don't underestimate "habit". It runs through everything done under the sun. It is not a law to be strictly observed, yet flouting it is simply asking for trouble. Don't complain though if it proves so binding that sometimes, unconsciously, you conform to it. For instance, do you presume to throw your weight about before your superiors? Do you air your views recklessly in front of your seniors? When a group photograph is taken, can you shove celebrities aside to stand swaggering and chortling in the middle? You can't, of course you can't. Or again, would you choose a wife ten years older than you, heftier than you or a head taller than you? Don't be in a rush to answer. Here's an instance of such a couple.

2

She was seventeen centimetres taller than he.

(For information about China, see p. 401.)

411

4   One point seven five metres in height, she towered above most of her sex like a crane over chickens. Her husband, a bare 1.58 metres, had been nicknamed Shorty at college. He came up to her earlobes but actually looked two heads shorter.

5   And take their appearances. She seemed dried up and scrawny with a face like an unvarnished ping-pong bat. Her features would pass, but they were small and insignificant as if carved in shallow relief. She was flat-chested, had a ramrod back and buttocks as scraggy as a scrubbing-board. Her husband on the other hand seemed a rubber rolypoly: well-fleshed, solid and radiant. Everything about him—his calves, insteps, lips, nose and fingers—were like pudgy little meatballs. He had soft skin and a fine complexion shining with excess fat and ruddy because of all the red blood in his veins. His eyes were like two high-voltage little light bulbs, while his wife's were like glazed marbles. The two of them just did not match, and formed a marked contrast. But they were inseparable.

6   One day some of their neighbours were having a family reunion. After drinking his fill the grandfather put a tall, thin empty wine bottle on the table next to a squat tin of pork.

7   "Who do these remind you of?" he asked. Before anyone could guess he gave the answer, "That tall woman downstairs and that short husband of hers."

8   Everyone burst out laughing and went on laughing through the meal.

9   What had brought such a pair together?

10   This was a mystery to the dozens of households living in Unity Mansions. Ever since this couple moved in, the old residents had eyed them curiously. Some registered a question mark in their minds, while others put their curiosity into words. Tongues started wagging, especially in wet weather when the two of them went out and it was always Mrs Tall who held the umbrella. If anything dropped to the ground, though, it was simpler for Mr Short to pick it up. Some old ladies at a loose end would gesticulate, finding this comic, and splutter with laughter. This set a bad example for the children who would burst out laughing at sight of the pair and hoot, "Long carrying-pole; big, low stool!" The husband and wife pretended not to hear and kept their tempers, paying no attention. Maybe for this reason their relations with their neighbours remained rather cool. The few less officious ones simply nodded a greeting when they met. This made it hard for those really intrigued by them to find out more about them. For instance, how did they hit it off? Why had they married? Which gave way to the other? They could only speculate.

11   This was an old-fashioned block of flats with large sunny rooms and wide, dark corridors. It stood in a big courtyard with a small gatehouse. The man who lived there was a tailor, a decent fellow. His wife, who brimmed over with energy, liked to call on her neighbours and

gossip. Most of all she liked to ferret out their secrets. She knew exactly how husbands and wives got on, why sisters-in-law quarrelled, who was lazy, who hard-working, and how much everyone earned. If she was unclear about anything she would leave no stone unturned to get at the truth. The thirst for knowledge makes even the ignorant wise. In this respect she was outstanding. She analyzed conversations, watched expressions, and could even tell what people were secretly thinking. Simply by using her nose, she knew which household was eating meat or fish, and from that could deduce their income. For some reason or other, ever since the sixties each housing estate had chosen someone like this as a "neighbourhood activist," giving legal status to these nosey-parkers so that their officiousness could have full play. It seems the Creator will never waste any talent.

Though the tailor's wife was indefatigable she failed to discover   12
how this incongruous couple who passed daily before her eyes had come to marry. She found this most frustrating; it posed a formidable challenge. On the base of her experience, however, and by racking her brains she finally came up with a plausible explanation: either husband or wife must have some physiological deficiency. Otherwise no one would marry someone a whole head taller or shorter. Her grounds for this reasoning were that after three years of marriage they still had no children. The residents of Unity Mansions were all convinced by this brilliant hypothesis.

But facts are merciless. The tailor's wife was debunked and lost   13
face when Mrs Tall appeared in the family way. Her womb could be seen swelling from day to day, for being relatively far from the ground it was all too evident. Regardless of their amazement, misgivings or embarrassment, she gave birth to a fine baby. When the sun was hot or it rained and the couple went out, Mrs Tall would carry the baby while Mr Short held the umbrella. He plodded along comically on his plump legs, the umbrella held high, keeping just behind his wife. And the neighbours remained as intrigued as at the start by this ill-assorted, in-separable couple. They went on making plausible conjectures, but could find no confirmation for any of them.

The tailor's wife said, "They must have something to hide, those   14
two. Why else should they keep to themselves? Well, it's bound to come to light some day, just wait and see."

One evening, sure enough, she heard the sound of breaking glass   15
in their flat. On the pretext of collecting money for sweeping the yard she rushed to knock on their door, sure that their long hidden feud had come to a head and avid to watch the confrontation between them. The door opened. Mrs Tall asked her in with a smile. Mr Short was smiling too at a smashed plate on the floor—that was all the tailor's wife saw. She hastily collected the money and left to puzzle over what had hap-pened. A plate had been smashed, yet instead of quarrelling they had treated it as a joke. How very strange!

16   Later the tailor's wife became the residents' representative for Unity Mansions. When she helped the police check up on living permits, she at last found the answer to this puzzle. A reliable and irrefutable answer. The tall woman and her short husband both worked in the Research Institute of the Ministry of Chemical Industry. He was chief engineer, with a salary of over 180 yuan! She was an ordinary laboratory technician earning less than sixty yuan, and her father was a hardworking low-paid postman. So that explained why she had married a man so much shorter. For status, money and an easy life. Right! The tailor's wife lost no time in passing on this priceless information to all the bored old ladies in Unity Mansions. Judging others by themselves, they believed her. At last this riddle was solved. They saw the light. Rich Mr Short was congenitally deficient while poor Mrs Tall was a money-grabber on the make. When they discussed the good luck of this tall woman who looked like a horse, they often voiced resentment—especially the tailor's wife.

3

17   Sometimes good luck turns into bad.

18   In 1966, disaster struck China. Great changes came into the lives of all the residents in Unity Mansions, which was like a microcosm of the whole country. Mr Short as chief engineer was the first to suffer. His flat was raided, his furniture moved out, he was struggled against and confined in his institute. And worse was to come. He was accused of smuggling out the results of his research to write up at home in the evenings, with a view to fleeing the country to join a wealthy relative abroad. This preposterous charge of passing on scientific secrets to foreign capitalists was widely believed. In that period of lunacy people took leave of their senses and cruelly made up groundless accusations in order to find some Hitler in their midst. The institute kept a stranglehold on its chief engineer. He was threatened, beaten up, put under all kinds of pressure; his wife was ordered to hand over that manuscript which no one had ever seen. But all was to no effect. Someone proposed holding a struggle meeting against them both in the courtyard of Unity Mansions. As everyone dreads losing face in front of relatives and friends, this would put more pressure on them. Since all else had failed, it was at least worth trying. Never before had Unity Mansions been the scene of such excitement.

19   In the afternoon the institute sent people to fix up ropes between two trees in the yard, on which to hang a poster with the name of Mr Short on it—crossed out. Inside and outside the yard they pasted up threatening slogans, and on the wall put eighteen more posters listing the engineer's "crimes". As the meeting was to be held after supper, an

electrician was sent to fix up four big 500-watt bulbs. By now the tailor's wife, promoted to be the chairman of the neighbourhood's Public Security Committee, was a powerful person, full of self-importance, and much fatter than before. She had been busy all day bossing the other women about, helping to put up slogans and make tea for the revolutionaries from the institute. The wiring for the lights had been fixed up from her gatehouse as if she were celebrating a wedding!

After supper the tailor's wife assembled all the residents in the   20
yard, lit up as brilliantly as a sportsground at night. Their shadows, magnified ten-fold, were thrown on the wall of the building. These shadows stayed stock-still, not even the children daring to play about. The tailor's wife led a group also wearing red armbands, in those days most awe-inspiring, to guard the gate and keep outsiders out. Presently a crowd from the institute, wearing armbands and shouting slogans, marched in the tall woman and her short husband. He had a placard hung round his neck, she had none. The two of them were marched in front of the platform, and stood there side by side with lowered heads.

The tailor's wife darted forward. "This wretch is too short for the   21
revolutionary masses at the back to see," she cried. "I'll soon fix that." She dashed into the gatehouse, her fat shoulders heaving, to fetch a soapbox which she turned upside down. Mr Short standing on this was the same height as his wife. But at this point little attention was paid to the relative heights of this couple facing disaster.

The meeting followed the customary procedure. After slogans had   22
been shouted, passionate accusations were made, punctuated by more slogans. The pressure built up. First Mrs Tall was ordered to come clean, to produce that "manuscript". Questions and denunciations were fired at her, hysterical screams, angry shouts and threatening growls. But she simply shook her head gravely and sincerely. What use was sincerity? To believe in her would have made the whole business a farce.

No matter what bullies sprang forward to shake their fists at her, or   23
what tricky questions were asked to try to trap her, she simply shook her head. The members of the institute were at a loss, afraid that if this went on the struggle meeting would fizzle out and end up a fiasco.

The tailor's wife had listened with mounting exasperation. Being   24
illiterate she took no interest in the "manuscript" they wanted, and felt these research workers were too soft-spoken. All of a sudden she ran to the platform. Raising her right arm with its red armband she pointed accusingly at Mrs Tall.

"Say!" she screeched. "Why did you marry him?"   25

The members of the institute were staggered by this unexpected   26
question. What connection had it with their investigation?

Mrs Tall was staggered too. This wasn't the sort of question asked   27
these days. She looked up with surprise on her thin face which showed the ravages of the last few months.

28   "So you don't dare answer, eh?" The tailor's wife raised her voice. "I'll answer for you! You married this scoundrel, didn't you, for his money? If he hadn't had money who'd want such a short fellow!" She sounded rather smug, as if she alone had seen through Mrs Tall.

29   Mrs Tall neither nodded nor shook her head. She had seen through the tailor's wife too. Her eyes glinted with derision and contempt.

30   "All right, you won't admit it. This wretch is done for now, he's a broken reed. Oh, I know what you're thinking." The tailor's wife slapped her chest and brandished one hand gloatingly. Some other women chimed in.

31   The members of the institute were flummoxed. A question like this was best ignored. But though these women had strayed far from the subject, they had also livened up the meeting. So the institute members let them take the field. The women yelled:

32   "How much has he paid you? What has he bought you? Own up!"

33   "Two hundred a month isn't enough for you, is it? You have to go abroad!"

34   "Is Deng Tuo* behind you?"

35   "That day you made a long-distance call to Beijing, were you ringing up the Three Family Village?**"

36   The success of a meeting depends on the enthusiasm worked up. The institute members who had convened this meeting saw that the time was ripe now to shout a few more slogans and conclude it. They then searched Mrs Tall's flat, prizing up floorboards and stripping off wallpaper. When they discovered nothing, they marched her husband away, leaving her behind.

37   Mrs Tall stayed in all the next day but went out alone after dark, unaware that though the light in the gatehouse was out the tailor's wife was watching her from the window. She trailed her out of the gate and past two crossroads till Mrs Tall stopped to knock softly on a gate. The tailor's wife ducked behind a telegraph pole and waited, holding her breath, as if to pounce on a rabbit when it popped out of its burrow.

38   The gate creaked open. An old woman led out a child.

39   "All over, is it?" she asked.

40   Mrs Tall's answer was inaudible.

41   "He's had his supper and a sleep," the old woman said. "Take him home quickly now."

42   The tailor's wife realized that this was the woman who minded their little boy. Her excitement died down as Mrs Tall turned back to

*Deng Tuo (1912–1966), historian, poet and essayist, was the Party secretary of Beijing in charge of cultural and educational work, who was considered a counter-revolutionary after the start of the "cultural revolution" in 1966.

**In 1961 Deng Tuo, Wu Han (a historian) and Liao Mosha (a writer) started a magazine column "Notes from the Three Family Village" and published many essays which were well received. During the "cultural revolution" the three writers were falsely charged as "The Three Family Village".

lead her son home. All was silence apart from the sound of their footsteps. The tailor's wife stood motionless behind the telegraph pole till they had gone, then scurried home herself.

The next morning when Mrs Tall led her son out, her eyes were red. 43
No one would speak to her, but they all saw her red, swollen eyes. Those who had denounced her the previous day had a strange feeling of guilt. They turned away so as not to meet her eyes.

4

After the struggle meeting Mr Short was not allowed home again. 44
The tailor's wife, who was in the know, said he had been imprisoned as an active counter-revolutionary. That made Mrs Tall the lowest of the low, naturally unfit to live in a roomy flat. She was forced to change places with the tailor's wife and moved into the little gatehouse. This didn't worry her, as it meant she could avoid the other residents who snubbed her. But they could look through her window and see her all alone there. Where she had sent her son, they didn't know, for he only came home for a few days at a time. Ostracized by all, she looked older than a woman in her thirties.

"Mark my words," the tailor's wife said, "she can only keep this up 45
for at most a year. Then if Shorty doesn't get out she'll have to remarry. If I were her I'd get a divorce and remarry. Even if he's let out his name will be mud, and he won't have any money."

A year went by. Mr Short still didn't come back and Mrs Tall kept 46
to herself. In silence she went to work, came back, lit her stove and went out with a big shabby shopping basket. Day after day she did this, the whole year round. . . . But one day in autumn Mr Short reappeared—thinly clad, his head shaved, and his whole appearance changed. He seemed to have shrunk and his skin no longer gleamed with health. He went straight to his old flat. Its new master, the honest tailor, directed him to the gatehouse. Mrs Tall was squatting in the doorway chopping firewood. At the sound of his voice she sprang up to stare at him. After two years' separation both were appalled by the change in the other. One was wrinkled, the other haggard; one looked taller than before, the other shorter. After gazing at each other they hastily turned away, and Mrs Tall ran inside. When finally she came out again he had picked up the axe and squatted down to chop firewood, until two big boxes of wood had been chopped into kindling, as if he feared some new disaster might befall them at any moment. After that they were inseparable again, going to work together and coming back together just as before. The neighbours, finding them unchanged, gradually lost interest in them and ignored them.

One morning Mrs Tall had an accident. Her husband rushed franti- 47
cally out and came back with an ambulance to fetch her. For days the

gatehouse was empty and dark at night. After three weeks Mr Short returned with a stranger. They were carrying her on a stretcher. She was confined to her room. He went to work as usual, hurrying back at dusk to light the stove and go out with the shopping basket. This was the same basket she had used every day. In his hand it looked even bigger and nearly reached the ground.

48 When the weather turned warmer Mrs Tall came out. After so long in bed her face was deathly white, and she swayed from side to side. She held a cane in her right hand and kept her left elbow bent in front of her. Her half-paralysed left leg made walking difficult. She had obviously had a stroke. Every morning and every evening Mr Short helped her twice round the yard, painfully and slowly. By hunching up his shoulders he was able to grip her crooked arm in both hands. It was hard for him, but he smiled to encourage her. As she couldn't raise her left foot, he tied a rope round it and pulled this up when she wanted to take a step forward. This was a pathetic yet impressive sight, and the neighbours were touched by it. Now when they met the couple they nodded cordially to them.

5

49 Mrs Tall's luck had run out: she was not to linger long by the side of the short husband who loved her so dearly. Death and life were equally cruel to her. Life had struck her down and now death carried her off. Mr Short was left all alone.

50 But after her death fortune smiled on him again. He was rehabilitated, his confiscated possessions were returned, and he received all his back pay. Only his flat, occupied by the tailor's wife, was not given back to him. The neighbours watched to see what he would do. It was said that some of his colleagues had proposed finding him another wife, but he had declined their offers.

51 "I know the kind of woman he wants," said the tailor's wife. "Just leave it to me!"

52 Having passed her zenith she had become more subdued. Stripped of her power she had to wear a smile. With a photograph of a pretty girl in her pocket she went to the gatehouse to find Mr Short. The girl in the picture was her niece.

53 She sat in the gatehouse sizing up its furnishing as she proposed this match to rich Mr Short. Smiling all over her face she held forth with gusto until suddenly she realized that he had said not a word, his face was black, and behind him hung a picture of him and Mrs Tall on their wedding day. Then she beat a retreat without venturing to produce the photograph of her niece.

54 Since then several years have passed. Mr Short is still a widower, but on Sundays he fetches his son home to keep him company. At the

sight of his squat, lonely figure, his neighbours recall all that he has been through and have come to understand why he goes on living alone. When it rains and he takes an umbrella to go to work, out of force of habit perhaps he still holds it high. Then they have the strange sensation that there is a big empty space under that umbrella, a vacuum that nothing on earth can fill.

January 16, 1982
Translated by Gladys Yang

✦ Evaluating the Text

1. How does the characterization of the tall woman and her short husband encourage the reader to become sympathetic toward them and unsympathetic toward the town busybodies who speculate about their marriage?

2. In what way are the events that take place in the village a microcosm of the effects produced by the Cultural Revolution under Mao Tse-tung? In which phrases and events can you most clearly see the effect of political ideology in everyday life?

3. How does the characterization of the tailor's wife illustrate the way vendettas and other personal agendas can be carried out under the guise of political zeal?

✦ Exploring Different Perspectives

1. How does Feng Jicai create a fictional reflection of the kind of personal and political turmoil Nien Cheng describes in "The Red Guards"? Which form, the story or the essay, did you find more effective in communicating the reality of these events that took place during the Cultural Revolution?

2. How do the stories by both Feng Jicai and Panos Ioannides ("Gregory") dramatize how people who are apolitical may be turned into scapegoats during times of political turmoil?

✦ Extending Viewpoints Through Writing

1. Have you ever had occasion to notice the effect of political beliefs on personal relationships? Do you know any people whose "speculations" have undermined or even destroyed a relationship? Was the strategy used similar to that used by the tailor's wife in the story, in terms of disguising personal malice under the guise of advancing the public good?

Panos Ioannides

Gregory

◆

Panos Ioannides was born in Cyprus in 1935 and was educated in Cyprus, the United States, and Canada. He has been the head of TV programs at Cyprus Broadcasting Corporation. Ioannides is the author of many plays, which have been staged or telecast internationally, and has written novels, short stories, and radio scripts. "Gregory" was written in 1963 and first appeared in The Charioteer, a Review of Modern Greek Literature *(1965). The English translation is by Marion Byron and Catherine Raisiz. This compelling story is based on a true incident that took place during the Cypriot Liberation struggle against the British in the late 1950s. Ioannides takes the unusual approach of letting the reader experience the torments of a soldier ordered to shoot a prisoner, Gregory, who had saved his life and was his friend.*

Cyprus is an island republic with a population of nearly 700,000 situated in the eastern Mediterranean south of Turkey and west of Syria and has been inhabited since 6500 B.C. Seventy-seven percent of the people are of Greek origin, living mainly in the south, and the remaining population, situated in the north, is of Turkish descent. Cyprus came under British administration in 1878 and was annexed by Britain in 1914. The quest among Greek Cypriots for self-rule and union with Greece has been a source of continuous civil discord, erupting in 1955 into a civil war. The conflict was aggravated by Turkish support of Turkish Cypriot demands for partition of the island. A settlement was reached in 1959 including provisions for both union with Greece and partition. In 1960, Makarios III, leader of the Greek Cypriot Nationalists, was elected president, a development that did not prevent continued fighting. A United Nations peacekeeping force was sent to Cyprus in 1965. In 1974, in response to the overthrow by Greek Army officers of the Makarios regime, Turkey invaded Cyprus. Since then, Cyprus has remained a divided state, and little progress has been made toward reunification.

1   My hand was sweating as I held the pistol. The curve of the trigger was biting against my finger.

2   Facing me, Gregory trembled.

3   His whole being was beseeching me, "Don't!"

4   Only his mouth did not make a sound. His lips were squeezed tight. If it had been me, I would have screamed, shouted, cursed.

5   The soldiers were watching . . .

The day before, during a brief meeting, they had each given their   6
opinions: "It's tough luck, but it has to be done. We've got no choice."

The order from Headquarters was clear: "As soon as Lieutenant   7
Rafel's execution is announced, the hostage Gregory is to be shot and
his body must be hanged from a telegraph pole in the main street as an
exemplary punishment."

It was not the first time that I had to execute a hostage in this war. I   8
had acquired experience, thanks to Headquarters which had kept en-
trusting me with these delicate assignments. Gregory's case was precisely the sixth.

The first time, I remember, I vomited. The second time I got sick   9
and had a headache for days. The third time I drank a bottle of rum.
The fourth, just two glasses of beer. The fifth time I joked about it, "This
little guy, with the big pop-eyes, won't be much of a ghost!"

But why, dammit, when the day came did I have to start thinking   10
that I'm not so tough, after all? The thought had come at exactly the
wrong time and spoiled all my disposition to do my duty.

You see, this Gregory was such a miserable little creature, such a   11
puny thing, such a nobody, damn him.

That very morning, although he had heard over the loudspeakers   12
that Rafel had been executed, he believed that we would spare his life
because we had been eating together so long.

"Those who eat from the same mess tins and drink from the same   13
water canteen," he said, "remain good friends no matter what."

And a lot more of the same sort of nonsense.   14

He was a silly fool—we had smelled that out the very first day   15
Headquarters gave him to us. The sentry guarding him had got dead
drunk and had dozed off. The rest of us with exit permits had gone
from the barracks. When we came back, there was Gregory sitting by
the sleeping sentry and thumbing through a magazine.

"Why didn't you run away, Gregory?" we asked, laughing at him,   16
several days later.

And he answered, "Where would I go in this freezing weather? I'm   17
O.K. here."

So we started teasing him.   18

"You're dead right. The accommodations here are splendid . . ."   19

"It's not so bad here," he replied. "The barracks where I used to be   20
are like a sieve. The wind blows in from every side . . ."

We asked him about his girl. He smiled.   21

"Maria is a wonderful person," he told us. "Before I met her she   22
was engaged to a no-good fellow, a pig. He gave her up for another
girl. Then nobody in the village wanted to marry Maria. I didn't miss
my chance. So what if she is second-hand. Nonsense. Peasant ideas, my
friend. She's beautiful and good-hearted. What more could I want?
And didn't she load me with watermelons and cucumbers every time I

passed by her vegetable garden? Well, one day I stole some cucumbers and melons and watermelons and I took them to her. 'Maria,' I said, 'from now on I'm going to take care of you.' She started crying and then me, too. But ever since that day she has given me lots of trouble—jealousy. She wouldn't let me go even to my mother's. Until the day I was recruited, she wouldn't let me go far from her apron strings. But that was just what I wanted . . ."

23   He used to tell this story over and over, always with the same words, the same commonplace gestures. At the end he would have a good laugh and start gulping from his water jug.

24   His tongue was always wagging! When he started talking, nothing could stop him. We used to listen and nod our heads, not saying a word. But sometimes, as he was telling us about his mother and family problems, we couldn't help wondering, "Eh, well, these people have the same headaches in their country as we've got."

25   Strange, isn't it!

26   Except for his talking too much, Gregory wasn't a bad fellow. He was a marvelous cook. Once he made us some apple tarts, so delicious we licked the platter clean. And he could sew, too. He used to sew on all our buttons, patch our clothes, darn our socks, iron our ties, wash our clothes . . .

27   How the devil could you kill such a friend?

28   Even though his name was Gregory and some people on his side had killed one of ours, even though we had left wives and children to go to war against him and his kind—but how can I explain? He was our friend. He actually liked us! A few days before, hadn't he killed with his own bare hands a scorpion that was climbing up my leg? He could have let it send me to hell!

29   "Thanks, Gregory!" I said then, "Thank God who made you . . ."

30   When the order came, it was like a thunderbolt. Gregory was to be shot, it said, and hanged from a telegraph pole as an exemplary punishment.

31   We got together inside the barracks. We sent Gregory to wash some underwear for us.

32   "It ain't right."

33   "What is right?"

34   "Our duty!"

35   "Shit!"

36   "If you dare, don't do it! They'll drag you to court-martial and then bang-bang . . ."

37   Well, of course. The right thing is to save your skin. That's only logical. It's either your skin or his. His, of course, even if it was Gregory, the fellow you've been sharing the same plate with, eating with your fingers, and who was washing your clothes that very minute.

38   What could I do? That's war. We had seen worse things.

39   So we set the hour.

We didn't tell him anything when he came back from the washing.   40
He slept peacefully. He snored for the last time. In the morning, he
heard the news over the loudspeaker and he saw that we looked
gloomy and he began to suspect that something was up. He tried talking to us, but he got no answers and then he stopped talking.

He just stood there and looked at us, stunned and lost . . .   41

Now, I'll squeeze the trigger. A tiny bullet will rip through his
chest. Maybe I'll lose my sleep tonight but in the morning I'll wake
up alive.

Gregory seems to guess my thoughts. He puts out his hand
and asks, "You're kidding, friend! Aren't you kidding?"

What a jackass! Doesn't he deserve to be cut to pieces? What a
thing to ask at such a time. Your heart is about to burst and he's asking if you're kidding. How can a body be kidding about such a thing?
Idiot! This is no time for jokes. And you, if you're such a fine friend,
why don't you make things easier for us? Help us kill you with fewer
qualms? If you would get angry—curse our Virgin, our God—if
you'd try to escape it would be much easier for us and for you.

So it is *now.*

Now, Mr. Gregory, you are going to pay for your stupidities
wholesale. Because you didn't escape the day the sentry fell asleep;
because you didn't escape yesterday when we sent you all alone to
the laundry—we did it on purpose, you idiot! Why didn't you let
me die from the sting of the scorpion?

So now don't complain. It's all your fault, nitwit.

Eh? What's happening to him now?

Gregory is crying. Tears flood his eyes and trickle down over
his cleanshaven cheeks. He is turning his face and pressing his
forehead against the wall. His back is shaking as he sobs. His
hands cling, rigid and helpless, to the wall.

Now is my best chance, now that he knows there is no other solution and turns his face from us.

I squeeze the trigger.

Gregory jerks. His back stops shaking up and down.

I think I've finished him! How easy it is . . . But suddenly he
starts crying out loud, his hands claw at the wall and try to pull it
down. He screams, "No, no . . ."

I turn to the others. I expect them to nod, "That's enough."

They nod, "What are you waiting for?"

I squeeze the trigger again.

The bullet smashed into his neck. A thick spray of blood spurts
out.

Gregory turns. His eyes are all red. He lunges at me and starts
punching me with his fists.

"I hate you, hate you . . ." he screams.

I emptied the barrel. He fell and grabbed my leg as if he wanted to hold on.

42   He died with a terrible spasm. His mouth was full of blood and so were my boots and socks.

43   We stood quietly, looking at him.

44   When we came to, we stooped and picked him up. His hands were frozen and wouldn't let my legs go.

45   I still have their imprints, red and deep, as if made by a hot knife.

46   "We will hang him tonight," the men said.

47   "Tonight or now?" they said.

48   I turned and looked at them one by one.

49   "Is that what you all want?" I asked.

50   They gave me no answer.

51   "Dig a grave," I said.

Headquarters did not ask for a report the next day or the day after. The top brass were sure that we had obeyed them and had left him swinging from a pole.

52   They didn't care to know what happened to that Gregory, alive or dead.

Translated by Marion Byron Raizis and Catherine Raizis

✦ *Evaluating the Text*

1. Discuss Ioannides's use of framing techniques in his choice of how to open and close his story. How does his choice of opening the story as Gregory is about to be shot and his use of flashbacks to explore the narrator's relationship with Gregory enhance the effectiveness of the story?

2. Much of the story's action takes place during the few seconds when the narrator must decide whether to pull the trigger. Why do you think Ioannides chooses to tell the story from the executioner's point of view rather than from Gregory's?

3. What in the narrator's past leads his superiors (and the narrator himself) to conclude he is the one best-suited to kill Gregory?

4. What details illustrate that Gregory has become a friend to the narrator and other soldiers rather than just a prisoner? In what way does Gregory embody the qualities of humanity, decency, and domestic life that the soldiers were forced to leave behind? Why is his innocence a source of both admiration and irritation?

5. How does Gregory's decision to marry Maria suggest the kind of person he is and answer the question as to why he doesn't try to escape when he is told he is going to be killed?

6. Discuss the psychological process that allows the narrator to convert his anguish at having to shoot Gregory into a justification to do so.

7. Why didn't Gregory take the opportunity to escape that the soldiers gave him? What insight does Ioannides give the reader into Gregory's character that would explain why he doesn't perceive the real threat to his life even at the moment the narrator is pointing a gun at his head?

8. How does the question *"Why didn't you let me die from the sting of the scorpion?"* reveal the anguish the narrator feels as he is faced with the order to kill his friend Gregory?

9. When the narrator fires the first shot, why does he hope the other soldiers will stop him from firing again; why don't they stop him?

10. At the end, how does the narrator's order not to hang Gregory's body reveal his distress after shooting Gregory? Why is it ironic that the higher-ups never inquire whether their orders have been carried out? What does this imply and why does it make the narrator feel even worse?

✦ Exploring Different Perspectives

1. In what ways does Daru's choice in Albert Camus's "The Guest" evoke the choice facing the narrator in "Gregory"?

2. In what ways is the conflict depicted in "Gregory" similar (albeit involving a different ethnic group) to that reported by Slavenka Drakulić in "The Balkan Express"? What common features do they share?

✦ Extending Viewpoints Through Writing

1. In your opinion, is Gregory a good person or just a fool who is stupid enough to get killed when he does not have to die?

2. If you were in the narrator's shoes, what would you have done? Do you think you would have had to make yourself hate Gregory, as the narrator did, in order to be able to kill him?

3. In an essay, explore the effects of British colonialism in Cyprus, Antigua (see Jamaica Kincaid's "A Small Place," Chapter 5), and Kenya (see Ngũgĩ wa Thiong'o's "Decolonising the Mind," Chapter 6).

Connecting Cultures

◆

Golda Meir, We Have Our State

What contrasting perspectives on Israel and Palestine and on the value of a homeland do you get from the accounts by Golda Meir and Edward Said (see "Reflections on Exile," Chapter 7)?

Albert Camus, The Guest

To what extent do the protagonists in the stories by Albert Camus and Gloria Anzaldúa (see "Cervicide," Chapter 7) find themselves in no-win situations?

Slavenka Drakulić, The Balkan Express

How is the impact of the accounts by Slavenka Drakulić and Luis Alberto Urrea (see "Border Story," Chapter 7) heightened as a result of the everyday settings in which dreadful things occur?

Ngũgĩ wa Thiong'o, Decolonising the Mind

How do both Rigoberta Menchú's "Birth Ceremonies" (see Chapter 1) and Ngũgĩ wa Thiong'o's account enhance your understanding of what life is like for a native people living under the domination of a different culture (the *ladino* in Guatemala and the colonial British bureaucracy in Kenya)?

Jon Swain, The Eyes of Vietnam

How does Edward Said's analysis of exile (see "Reflections on Exile," Chapter 7) provide additional insight into the predicament of the refugees described by Jon Swain?

Nien Cheng, The Red Guards

To what extent does the concept of the destruction or devaluation of authentic cultural artifacts play a role in the accounts by Nien Cheng and R. K. Narayan (see "Misguided 'Guide'," Chapter 4)?

Feng Jicai, *The Tall Woman and Her Short Husband*

Compare the picture of marriage you get in terms of monogamy and polygamy in the stories by Feng Jicai and Sembene Ousmane (see "Her Three Days," Chapter 3).

Panos Ioannides, *Gregory*

In what sense are the protagonists in the stories by Panos Ioannides and Gloria Anzaldúa (see "Cervicide," Chapter 7) coerced into killing someone or something they care about because of the political circumstances in which they find themselves?

7

Strangers in a
Strange Land

◆————————

In some ways, our age—the age of the refugee, of the displaced person, and of mass immigration—is defined by the condition of exile. Being brought up in one world and then emigrating to a different culture inevitably produces feelings of alienation. Moving to another country involves living among people who dress differently, eat different foods, have different customs, and speak a different language. Understandably, forming relationships with people whose cultural frame of reference is often radically different from one's own invariably leads to "culture shock," to a greater or lesser degree. Without insight into the norms that govern behavior in a new environment, it is often difficult for immigrants to interpret the actions of others: to know what particular facial expressions and gestures might mean, what assumptions govern physical contact, how people express and resolve conflicts, or what topics of conversation are deemed appropriate.

The jarring, intense, and often painful emotional experience of having to redefine oneself in a strange land, of trying to reconcile conflicting cultural values, forces immigrants to surrender all ideas of safety, the comfort of familiar surroundings, and a common language. Ironically, the condition of *not* belonging, of being caught between two cultures, at home in neither, gives the exile the chance to develop a tolerance for conflicting messages and the ability to see things from outside the controlling frame of reference of a single culture.

The works in this chapter explore the need of those who have left home, whether as refugees, immigrants, or travelers, to make sense of their lives in a new place. These selections offer many perspectives on the experience of learning a new language and the void created by the failure to communicate, the intolerance of the dominant culture toward minorities, and the chance to create a new life for oneself. Edward Said, in "Reflections on Exile," explores how the psychological characteristics of exile—isolation, loneliness, persecution, and the re-creation of a lost homeland—play a central role in the works of twentieth-century writers. William M. Kephart, in "The Gypsies," describes the lifestyle of a group that exists permanently on the margins of societies around the world. In "Miami: The Cuban Presence," Joan Didion reports on the dramatic success story of the Cuban immigrants in Dade County, Florida, and the resistance they encounter from the Anglo community. After emigrating to America from Vietnam, Le Ly Hayslip relates the challenges and rewards of adapting to her new American husband, family, and culture, in "Yearning to Breathe Free." The survival of the human spirit in the harrowing conditions in Tijuana, on the United States–Mexican border, is graphically portrayed by Luis Alberto Urrea in "Border Story." Poranee Natadecha-Sponsel, in "Individualism as an American Cultural Value," describes the often perplexing cultural differences that she experienced after moving to the United States from Thailand. The Chicana writer Gloria Anzaldúa, in "Cervicide," tells a poignant story of a Mexican-American family living on the Texas border.

Edward Said

Reflections on Exile

◆

*Edward Said (born in 1935) is a Palestinian who was educated in Pales-
tine and Egypt when those countries were under British jurisdiction. Said
is the Parr Professor of English and Comparative Literature at Columbia
University. Said is best known for his critical works, including* Oriental-
ism *(1978), a lively analysis of how the West has created certain cultural
stereotypes about the East;* The World, Text, and the Critic *(1983); (with
Christopher Hitchens)* Blaming the Victims: Spurious Scholarship
and the Palestinian Question *(1987); and* Culture and Imperialism
(1993). "Reflections on Exile," which first appeared in Granta *(Autumn
1984), offers a penetrating analysis of the plight of the exiled and the role
this condition has played in literature of the twentieth century.*

1   Exile is strangely compelling to think about but terrible to experience. It is the unhealable rift forced between a human being and a native place, between the self and its true home: its essential sadness can
never be surmounted. And while it is true that literature and history
contain heroic, romantic, glorious, even triumphant episodes in an exile's life, these are no more than efforts meant to overcome the crippling
sorrow of estrangement. The achievements of exile are permanently
undermined by the loss of something left behind for ever.

2   Exiles look at non-exiles with resentment. *They* belong in their surroundings, you feel, whereas an exile is always out of place. What is it
like to be born in a place, to stay and live there, to know that you are of
it, more or less for ever?

3   Although it is true that anyone prevented from returning home is
an exile, some distinctions can be made between exiles, refugees, expatriates and émigrés. Exile originated in the age-old practice of banishment. Once banished, the exile lives an anomalous and miserable life,
with the stigma of being an outsider. Refugees, on the other hand, are a
creation of the twentieth-century state. The word 'refugee' has become
a political one, suggesting large herds of innocent and bewildered
people requiring urgent international assistance, whereas 'exile' carries
with it, I think, a touch of solitude and spirituality.

4   Expatriates voluntarily live in an alien country, usually for personal or social reasons. Hemingway and Fitzgerald were not forced to
live in France. Expatriates may share in the solitude and estrangement

430

of exile, but they do not suffer under its rigid proscriptions. Émigrés enjoy an ambiguous status. Technically, an émigré is anyone who emigrates to a new country. Choice in the matter is certainly a possibility. Colonial officials, missionaries, technical experts, mercenaries and military advisers on loan may in a sense live in exile, but they have not been banished. White settlers in Africa, parts of Asia and Australia may once have been exiles, but as pioneers and nation-builders the label 'exile' dropped away from them.

Much of the exile's life is taken up with compensating for disorienting loss by creating a new world to rule. It is not surprising that so many exiles seem to be novelists, chess players, political activists, and intellectuals. Each of these occupations requires a minimal investment in objects and places a great premium on mobility and skill. The exile's new world, logically enough, is unnatural and its unreality resembles fiction. Georg Lukács, in *Theory of the Novel,* argued with compelling force that the novel, a literary form created out of the unreality of ambition and fantasy, is *the* form of 'transcendental homelessness'. Classical epics, Lukács wrote, emanate from settled cultures in which values are clear, identities stable, life unchanging. The European novel is grounded in precisely the opposite experience, that of a changing society in which an itinerant and disinherited middle-class hero or heroine seeks to construct a new world that somewhat resembles an old one left behind for ever. In the epic there is no *other* world, only the finality of *this* one. Odysseus returns to Ithaca after years of wandering; Achilles will die because he cannot escape his fate. The novel, however, exists because other worlds *may* exist, alternatives for bourgeois speculators, wanderers, exiles.   5

No matter how well they may do, exiles are always eccentrics who *feel* their difference (even as they frequently exploit it) as a kind of orphanhood. Anyone who is really homeless regards the habit of seeing estrangement in everything modern as an affectation, a display of modish attitudes. Clutching difference like a weapon to be used with stiffened will, the exile jealousy insists on his or her right to refuse to belong.   6

This usually translates into an intransigence that is not easily ignored. Wilfulness, exaggeration, overstatement: these are characteristic styles of being an exile, methods for compelling the world to accept your vision—which you make more unacceptable because you are in fact unwilling to have it accepted. It is yours, after all. Composure and serenity are the last things associated with the work of exiles. Artists in exile are decidedly unpleasant, and their stubbornness insinuates itself into even their exalted works. Dante's vision in *The Divine Comedy* is tremendously powerful in its universality and detail, but even the beatific peace achieved in the *Paradiso* bears traces of the vindictiveness and severity of judgement embodied in the *Inferno.* Who but an exile like Dante, banished from Florence, would use eternity as a place for settling old scores?   7

8   James Joyce *chose* to be in exile: to give force to his artistic vocation. In an uncannily effective way—as Richard Ellmann has shown in his biography—Joyce picked a quarrel with Ireland and kept it alive so as to sustain the strictest opposition to what was familiar. Ellmann says that 'whenever his relations with his native land were in danger of improving, [Joyce] was to find a new incident to solidify his intransigence and to reaffirm the rightness of his voluntary absence.' Joyce's fiction concerns what in a letter he once described as the state of being 'alone and friendless.' And although it is rare to pick banishment as a way of life, Joyce perfectly understood its trials.

9   But Joyce's success as an exile stresses the question lodged at its very heart: is exile so extreme and private that any instrumental use of it is ultimately a trivialization? How is it that the literature of exile has taken its place as a *topos* of human experience alongside the literature of adventure, education or discovery? Is this the *same* exile that quite literally kills Yanko Goorall and has bred the expensive, often dehumanizing relationship between twentieth-century exile and nationalism? Or is it some more benign variety?

10   Much of the contemporary interest in exile can be traced to the somewhat pallid notion that non-exiles can share in the benefits of exile as a redemptive motif. There is, admittedly, a certain plausibility and truth to this idea. Like medieval itinerant scholars or learned Greek slaves in the Roman Empire, exiles—the exceptional ones among them—do leaven their environments. And naturally 'we' concentrate on that enlightening aspect of 'their' presence among us, not on their misery or their demands. But looked at from the bleak political perspective of modern mass dislocations, individual exiles force us to recognize the tragic fate of homelessness in a necessarily heartless world.

11   A generation ago, Simone Weil posed the dilemma of exile as concisely as it has ever been expressed. 'To be rooted,' she said, 'is perhaps the most important and least recognized need of the human soul.' Yet Weil also saw that most remedies for uprootedness in this era of world wars, deportations and mass exterminations are almost as dangerous as what they purportedly remedy. Of these, the state—or, more accurately, statism—is one of the most insidious, since worship of the state tends to supplant all other human bonds.

12   Weil exposes us anew to that whole complex of pressures and constraints that lie at the centre of the exile's predicament, which, as I have suggested, is as close as we come in the modern era to tragedy. There is the sheer fact of isolation and displacement, which produces the kind of narcissistic masochism that resists all efforts at amelioration, acculturation and community. At this extreme the exile can make a fetish of exile, a practice that distances him or her from all connections and commitments. To live as if everything around you were temporary and per-

haps trivial is to fall prey to petulant cynicism as well as to querulous lovelessness. More common is the pressure on the exile to join—parties, national movements, the state. The exile is offered a new set of affiliations and develops new loyalties. But there is also a loss—of critical perspective, of intellectual reserve, of moral courage.

It must also be recognized that the defensive nationalism of exiles often fosters self-awareness as much as it does the less attractive forms of self-assertion. Such reconstitutive projects as assembling a nation out of exile (and this is true in this century for Jews and Palestinians) involve constructing a national history, reviving an ancient language, founding national institutions like libraries and universities. And these, while they sometimes promote strident ethnocentrism, also give rise to investigations of self that inevitably go far beyond such simple and positive facts as 'ethnicity.' For example, there is the self-consciousness of an individual trying to understand why the histories of the Palestinians and the Jews have certain patterns to them, why in spite of oppression and the threat of extinction a particular ethos remains alive in exile.

Necessarily, then, I speak of exile not as a privilege, but as an *alternative* to the mass institutions that dominate modern life. Exile is not, after all, a matter of choice: you are born into it, or it happens to you. But, provided that the exile refuses to sit on the sidelines nursing a wound, there are things to be learned: he or she must cultivate a scrupulous (not indulgent or sulky) subjectivity.

Perhaps the most rigorous example of such subjectivity is to be found in the writing of Theodor Adorno, the German-Jewish philosopher and critic. Adorno's masterwork, *Minima Moralia,* is an autobiography written while in exile; it is subtitled *Reflexionen aus dem beschädigten Leben (Reflections from a Mutilated Life).* Ruthlessly opposed to what he called the 'administered' world, Adorno saw all life as pressed into ready-made forms, prefabricated 'homes.' He argued that everything that one says or thinks, as well as every object one possesses, is ultimately a mere commodity. Language is jargon, objects are for sale. To refuse this state of affairs is the exile's intellectual mission.

Adorno's reflections are informed by the belief that the only home truly available now, though fragile and vulnerable, is in writing. Elsewhere, 'the house is past. The bombings of European cities, as well as the labour and concentration camps, merely precede as executors, with what the immanent development of technology had long decided was to be the fate of houses. These are now good only to be thrown away like old food cans.' In short, Adorno says with a grave irony, 'it is part of morality not to be at home in one's home.'

To follow Adorno is to stand away from 'home' in order to look at it with the exile's detachment. For there is considerable merit in the practice of noting the discrepancies between various concepts and

13

14

15

16

17

ideas and what they actually produce. We take home and language for granted; they become nature, and their underlying assumptions recede into dogma and orthodoxy.

18   The exile knows that in a secular and contingent world, homes are always provisional. Borders and barriers, which enclose us within the safety of familiar territory, can also become prisons, and are often defended beyond reason or necessity. Exiles cross borders, break barriers of thought and experience.

19   Hugo of St Victor, a twelfth-century monk from Saxony, wrote these hauntingly beautiful lines:

> It is, therefore, a source of great virtue for the practised mind to learn, bit by bit, first to change about invisible and transitory things, so that afterwards it may be able to leave them behind altogether. The man who finds his homeland sweet is still a tender beginner; he to whom every soil is as his native one is already strong; but he is perfect to whom the entire world is as a foreign land. The tender soul has fixed his love on one spot in the world; the strong man has extended his love to all places; the perfect man has extinguished his.

Erich Auerbach, the great twentieth-century literary scholar who spent the war years as an exile in Turkey, has cited this passage as a model for anyone wishing to transcend national or provincial limits. Only by embracing this attitude can a historian begin to grasp human experience and its written records in their diversity and particularity; otherwise he or she will remain committed more to the exclusions and reactions of prejudice than to the freedom that accompanies knowledge. But note that Hugo twice makes it dear that the 'strong' or 'perfect' man achieves independence and detachment by *working through* attachments, not by rejecting them. Exile is predicated on the existence of, love for, and bond with, one's native place; what is true of all exile is not that home and love of home are lost, but that loss is inherent in the very existence of both.

20   Regard experiences as if they were about to disappear. What is it that anchors them in reality? What would you save of them? What would you give up? Only someone who has achieved independence and detachment, someone whose homeland is 'sweet' but whose circumstances makes it impossible to recapture that sweetness, can answer those questions. (Such a person would also find it impossible to derive satisfaction from substitutes furnished by illusion or dogma.)

21   This may seem like a prescription for an unrelieved grimness of outlook and, with it, a permanently sullen disapproval of all enthusiasm or buoyancy of spirit. Not necessarily. While it perhaps seems peculiar to speak of the pleasures of exile, there are some positive things to be said for a few of its conditions. Seeing 'the entire world as a foreign land' makes possible originality of vision. Most people are princi-

pally aware of one culture, one setting, one home; exiles are aware of at least two, and this plurality of vision gives rise to an awareness of simultaneous dimensions, an awareness that—to borrow a phrase from music—*is contrapuntal.*

For an exile, habits of life, expression or activity in the new environment inevitably occur against the memory of these things in another environment. Thus both the new and the old environments are vivid, actual, occurring together contrapuntally. There is a unique pleasure in this sort of apprehension, especially if the exile is conscious of other contrapuntal juxtapositions that diminish orthodox judgement and elevate appreciative sympathy. There is also a particular sense of achievement in acting as if one were at home wherever one happens to be.   22

This remains risky, however: the habit of dissimulation is both wearying and nerve-racking. Exile is never the state of being satisfied, placid, or secure. Exile, in the words of Wallace Stevens, is 'a mind of winter' in which the pathos of summer and autumn as much as the potential of spring are nearby but unobtainable. Perhaps this is another way of saying that a life of exile moves according to a different calendar, and is less seasonal and settled than life at home. Exile is life led outside habitual order. It is nomadic, decentred, contrapuntal; but no sooner does one get accustomed to it than its unsettling force erupts anew.   23

✦ *Evaluating the Text*

1. How does someone born in a place knowing he or she will be there forever experience that place differently from someone who has recently arrived? How is the experience of exile connected with not being able to put down roots? Why would it be difficult for an exile to settle into a new place if she or he always had to be ready to return to the homeland?

2. What is the distinction Said draws between an exile (i.e., anyone prevented from returning home) and the circumstances of being a refugee, an expatriate, or an émigré? How is being an exile an isolating psychological condition, whereas being a refugee a communal experience that connects one with all other refugees?

3. Why are so many exiles chess players, novelists, and intellectuals? How is much of the exile's life "taken up with compensating for disorienting loss by creating a new world to rule"?

4. In Said's view, how does the idea on which the modern European novel is based differ from classic literary epics? How is one an imaginative compensation for lost reality while the other is an exploration and return to a known world? In what way are the great fictional works of Dante and Joyce a projection into an imaginative form of the

psychological characteristics of exile—isolation, loneliness, persecution, and imaginative compensation for a lost reality?

5. How does the exile's simultaneous awareness of the culture left behind and the culture presently inhabited give rise to a dual perspective that could be beneficial? Why would it be valuable to be able to see the customs of the country you are living in from an outside perspective? How might this give you freedom to choose or reject these customs as you wished?

✦ Exploring Different Perspectives

1. Explore the differences between the condition of exile described in Said and the situation of the Cubans in Miami in Joan Didion's "Miami: The Cuban Presence" account. To what extent has the Cuban community adjusted to being in exile? What role does the premise of someday returning to Cuba play?

2. How does Le Ly Hayslip's account "Yearning to Breathe Free" reveal some of the positive aspects of exile in terms of Hayslip's ability to see her new country with "originality of vision," in Said's terms?

✦ Extending Viewpoints Through Writing

1. What personal experience have you had living in or visiting places other than where you grew up? What insights into different cultural perspectives did you gain from your experiences?

2. Have you or any members of your family experienced any of the psychological problems associated with a forced or voluntary dislocation? To what extent do your experiences confirm Said's observations of both the negative and positive results associated with exile? Do you think it is really possible to develop detachment and flexibility, and to avoid identifying with property and material goods in the way Said describes? Keep in mind that exile can be both a literal experience and a psychological experience resulting from a feeling of being out of place anywhere.

3. What recent world development has highlighted the problem of refugees, displaced persons, or immigrants?

William M. Kephart

The Gypsies

◆

"The Gypsies" is drawn from William M. Kephart's book Extraordinary
Groups *(1987). The author is a professor emeritus at the University of
Pennsylvania.*

The Gypsies are most incredible. For several years now, I have 1
studied them, interviewed them, and—on occasion—mingled with
them, but I still find it difficult to grasp their culture patterns. Other
writers have experienced similar difficulties, for the Gypsies have a
life-style that comes close to defying comprehension. On the dust
jacket of Peter Maas' controversial and widely read *King of the Gypsies*,
for example, the following blurb appears:

> There are perhaps a million or more Gypsies in the United States—no-
> body knows exactly how many, not even the government. They no
> longer live in horse-drawn caravans on dusty roads; they live in cities,
> drive cars, have telephones and credit cards. Yet they do not go to
> school, neither read nor write, don't pay taxes, and keep themselves
> going by means of time-honored ruses and arrangements. Gypsies
> themselves recognize the contrast they make, and they are proud of it.[1]

Given the nature of modern journalism, can this statement be true? 2
The answer is not a simple one, and each of the above points requires
some explanation.

It is true that no one knows how many Gypsies there are in the 3
United States, although the million figure commonly reported in the
press may be too high. More reliable estimates place the figure closer to
500,000.[2] If the latter figure is correct, it would mean that only two
other countries in the world have larger Gypsy populations: Yugoslavia (750,000), and Romania (680,000).[3]

Although 500,000 seems a reasonable estimate, it is unlikely that 4
the real figure will ever be known. The fact of the matter is that Gypsies
move about so much, have so many different names and aliases, and
are generally so secretive that it is often difficult to pinpoint the numbers for a given city let alone for the nation at large.

Gypsies live in cities and drive cars? Indeed they do. They are not 5
likely to be found on farms or in the suburbs. They will not be found on
the water. They are urban dwellers—towns and cities—and they reside

in nearly all of the fifty states. At the same time, Gypsies are, and always have been, great travelers. They may be the greatest travelers the world has ever known. (In England, the terms "Gypsy" and "Traveler" are often used interchangeably.) As we shall see, traveling serves as an integral part of Gypsy life-style.

6   As for the cars, Gypsies not only drive them but sometimes make their living repairing them. The days of the horse-drawn wagons and caravans have long since gone, but Gypsies—as is their wont—have adapted remarkably well to motorized transportation. Indeed, despite the fact that they are a low-income group, Gypsies often drive Cadillacs.

7   Gypsies do not go to school? Not very often—and not for very long. They feel that formal education is not germane to their way of life and that the American school system would tend to "de-Gypsyize" their youngsters. Both claims are at least partially true, and the subject will be discussed later.

8   Gypsies neither read nor write? True. A large proportion of them are functionally illiterate. They cannot even read or write their own language, Romany, for it is a spoken rather than a written tongue. The literacy situation is improving, but so far progress has been slow. In spite of their self-imposed linguistic handicap, however, Gypsies have made a remarkable adaptation to their environment.

9   Gypsies do not pay taxes? Some observers would reply: "Not if they can help it." And it is true that many Gypsies do not pay property taxes because they have no taxable property. They often prefer to rent rather than to buy a dwelling-place. Also, many Gypsies work irregularly and have low-paying jobs, so that their income taxes would be negligible. A fair number are on welfare. On the other hand, at least some Gypsies are moving into white-collar occupations, and their tax payments are probably commensurate with those of other white-collar workers.

10   Gypsies keep themselves going by means of time-honored ruses and arrangements? A complicated question, surely, but then the Gypsies are a complicated people. As it true of all ethnic groups, there are honest Gypsies and there are dishonest Gypsies. Unfortunately, however, many Gypsies continue to believe that all *gadje** (non-Gypsies) are fair game. And more than occasionally this belief does culminate in ruses and petty swindles.

11   At the same time, Gypsy attitudes toward the *gadje* have been shaped in part by the *gadje* themselves. As will be shown, Gypsies have not been met with open arms by the various host countries. On the contrary, they have experienced near-universal prejudice and discrimina-

---

*Interestingly enough, the Gypsy language has not been standardized. As a result, most of their terms have a variety of spellings. In the present account, spelling has been adapted to fit the pronunciation.

tion. Social distance studies in several countries, including the United States, simply confirm the obvious; namely, that Gypsies rank at the absolute bottom of the status scale.[4]

Through it all, the Gypsies have survived. Gypsies always survive. If they haven't exactly flourished, they have in many ways given a very good account of themselves. It is not easy to be a Gypsy. As one writer put it: "Only the fit need apply."[5] It is hoped that in the following pages the full implications of this statement will become clear.

Who Are the Gypsies?

Like so many other aspects of their life, Gypsy origins are draped in mystery. The word "Gypsy" derives from "Egyptian," for the Gypsies were mistakenly thought to have originated in Egypt. This was a belief that they themselves did little to discourage. In fact, some Gypsies still believe in their Egyptian roots, although it has now been rather well established that their original homeland was India. (Romany, the Gypsy language, has its roots in Sanskrit.)

Exactly when the Gypsies left India—or what their status was—is still being debated. They have been variously described as being descended from the Criminal and Wandering Tribes, as being deported prisoners of war, and as being "a loose federation of nomadic tribes, possibly outside the Indian caste system entirely."[6] Rishi contends that "the majority of Gypsies, before migrating from India, formed a vital part of the upper strata of the Indian population, such as the Rajputs, Kshatriyas, and Jats."[7]

Whatever their class or caste origins, it seems likely that the proto-Gypsies left India at different times—and from different areas—perhaps during the first few centuries A.D.[8] By the fifth century, they seem to have settled in and around Persia and Syria. And although their early migration patterns are anything but clear, Gypsies were reported in Southeastern Europe (Greece, Hungary, Romania, Serbia) by the 1300s, and in Western Europe (France, Germany, Italy, Holland, Switzerland, Spain) by the 1400s.[9] Today there are Gypsies in practically every European country. They are also well established in North Africa, the Near East, South America, the United States, and Canada.

The term "Gypsy," incidentally, is not a Romany term. Gypsies refer to themselves as "Rom." (In the present account, the two terms will be used interchangeably.) And while there is much physical variation, the Rom tend to have dark hair, dark eyes, and medium to dark complexions. On the whole, they are of average or a little below average height. Several writers have noticed that Gypsies tend to become obese as they age.

(Some groups who are often thought of as Gypsies are not in fact true Gypsies, or Rom. These would include the Tinkers of Ireland and

Scotland, and the Taters of Norway.[10] The Irish Tinkers, for example, are of Celtic origin, and they speak Shelte, a Celtic dialect.[11] In the present account, we are concerned only with the Rom.)

18   As they spread throughout Europe, Gypsies came to be—above all else—travelers. "A Gypsy who does not keep on the move," wrote Block just prior to World War II, "is not a Gypsy."[12] Actually, there have always been a fair number of sedentary Gypsies, or *Sinte*. Lockwood reports that in Yugoslavia there is currently a community of some 40,000 Gypsies.[13]

19   Nevertheless, *Sinte* or no *Sinte*, it was the horse-drawn wagons and gaily decorated caravans that seemed to strike a responsive chord in people of all ages. Jan Yoors, author of one of the most widely read books on Gypsy life, ran away as a young boy and lived for many years with a Gypsy group.[14] Webb, another writer, states that

> for as long as I can remember, Gypsies have fascinated me. These dark-skinned strangers, indifferent to the rest of the world, mysterious in their comings and goings, traveling the roads with parades of highly colored raggedness, fired my imagination. I was curious about them and wanted to know more. But, nobody, it seemed, could tell me more.[15]

20   The Rom themselves seemed captivated by the caravan style of life. Indeed, some still talk about the good old (premotorized) days. Whether, in fact, caravan life was all that good can be debated. Yoors himself writes as follows:

> One year, for the first time, I stayed with the Rom throughout the winter. Lying half awake in the cold stillness of the long nights in Pulika's huge wagon, I heard the snapping noise of the nails in the boards as they creaked under the effect of the severe frost. The windows had been covered up with boards, old overcoats and army blankets, straw or pieces of tar paper, but the wind blasted through cracks too many to fill.
>
> The dogs whimpered all night. The drinking water froze in the buckets, and washing in the morning became an ordeal. Hands chapped, lips cracked and bled. The men ceased to shave. The small children cried bitterly when they were put outside and chased away from the wagons near which they had wanted to relieve themselves. Clothes could not be washed. The air inside the wagons was thick and unbreathable, mixed with the coal fumes from the red-hot stove, from which small children had to be kept away.
>
> During the winter months, not enough dead wood could be gathered outside to keep the fires going all day and part of the night, so the Rom were forced to buy, beg, or steal coal.[16]

21   No combination of elements, however, could dampen the Gypsy spirit—or their fondness for bright colors, especially greens, yellows,

and reds. As one effervescent Gypsy put it, "I wear bright beads and bright colors because we're a bright race. We don't like anything drab."[17]

The Gypsy Paradox

With their unusual life-style, there is no doubt that Gypsies have   22
held a real fascination for the *gadje,* almost irrespective of the country involved. Novels, plays, operettas, movies, and songs have portrayed—and sometimes glorified—the romantic wanderings of the Gypsy vagabond. Popular pieces like "Gypsy Love Song" and "Play Gypsy, Dance Gypsy" have become part of the worldwide musical repertoire.

Yet side by side with the attraction and fascination has come ha-   23
rassment and persecution. This is the Gypsy paradox: attraction on the one hand, persecution on the other. The climax of persecution came during World War II, when the Nazis murdered between 250,000 and 500,000 Rom. Moreover, the extermination took place without the Gypsies even being given a reason!

Despite worldwide persecution, however, the Gypsies have man-   24
aged to survive. Gypsies always survive. As Gropper puts it:

> For 500 years Gypsies have succeeded in being themselves against all odds, fiercely maintaining their identity in spite of persecution, prejudice, hatred, and cultural forces compelling them to change. We may have something to learn from them on how to survive in a drastically changing world.[18]

The Modern Period

Following World War II, urbanization and industrialization—   25
together with population expansion—literally cramped the Gypsies' life-style. There was less and less room on the modern highway for horse-drawn caravans. Camping sites became harder to find, and the open countryside seemed to shrink. But—as always—the Gypsies adapted. Travel continued, albeit on a reduced scale. Caravans and wagons were replaced by automobiles, trucks, campers, and trailers. Somehow, by one method or another, the Rom managed to get by. And they did so without sacrificing their group identity or their freedom.

Their identity was not maintained without a price, however, for   26
prejudice and harassment continued. Gypsy nomads were often hounded from one locale to another. The *Sinte* or sedentary Rom—whose proportion tended to increase—were also met by hostility and discrimination. "No Gypsies Allowed" signs came more and more to be posted in public places.

The issue was hardly one-sided. From the view of local authorities,   27
Gypsies were using community services without paying their share of

the taxes. Indeed, they were often not paying any taxes at all! Addition-ally, the Rom were dirty, they would not use indoor toilets, they lied, they cheated, and they stole. Sometimes the charges were true; often they were unfounded. (Interestingly, the Rom have rarely been accused of crimes of violence.)

28   Fortunately, the Gypsies also had friends and supporters, and in a number of countries efforts were made to set up camping sites, estab-lish housing facilities, provide legal assistance, and otherwise improve the lot of the Rom. By the 1970s, a number of national and international committees and councils had been organized—with Gypsy representa-tion. The purpose of these groups has been not only to protect the inter-ests of the Rom but to dispel stereotypes, combat false portrayals in the media, and act as a clearinghouse for information about Gypsies.

29   When all is said and done, however, there is not doubt that the Rom continue to have problems. According to Dodds, the idea of their having a carefree, romantic life is a myth. In reality, "the Gypsy's life is one of perpetual insecurity."[19]

30   And yet . . . contrast the foregoing statement with the following, by Clebert: "Gypsies themselves are Lords of the Earth. . . . All real Gyp-sies are united in their love of freedom, and in their eternal flight from the bonds of civilization, in their desire to be their own masters, and in their contempt for what we pompously call the 'consequences.'"[20]

31   Which of the two views is correct? Perhaps both are. In some ways, the Rom do indeed have a difficult life. Their relationship with the *gadje* often takes on the appearance of an interminable contest. At the same time, Gypsies show little inclination to assimilate. They are demonstra-bly proud that they are Gypsies, an attitude that is unlikely to change.

32   How many Gypsies are there in the world today? Estimates vary from five to ten million, with the latter figure probably being closer to the truth. (More than half are in Eastern Europe.) There is general—though not unanimous—agreement that the Rom are divided into four tribes or nations (*natsiyi*): the Lowara, Machwaya, Kalderasha, and Churara. While there are linguistic and cultural differences among the four *natsiyi*, surprisingly little has been written on this score. . . .

Difficulties in Studying the Rom

> *If you ask a dozen Gypsies the same question, you will probably get a dozen different answers. If you ask one Gypsy the same question a dozen times, you will still probably get a dozen different answers.*
>
> —Anon

33   Although there are many versions, this adage contains more than a little truth. Gypsies live—and always have lived—in alien cultures. The boundaries between Rom and *gadje* are sharp, and the Rom have every intention of maintaining the sharpness. Deception, avoidance, misrep-

resentation, and lying are part of the Gypsies' arsenal, and they have had hundreds of years to perfect and embellish their defenses. In many ways, investigating the Rom is like trying to penetrate a secret society. As Evans-Pritchard observes:

> I am sure that it is much easier to enter into a primitive Melanesian or African community than that of the Gypsies. The Melanesian or African has not had to build his barricades as the Gypsies have had to do. . . . Gypsies have been for centuries living in societies in which they have not belonged.[21]

Perhaps the most formidable obstacle the researcher has to face is   34
the avoidance syndrome. The Rom ordinarily do not mingle with the *gadje*; in fact, except for a possible visit to a fortune-teller, most Americans never come into contact with a Gypsy. Almost certainly they never see the inside of a Romany dwelling. Researchers face much the same problem. The fact that they are accredited university personnel means little to the Rom. Generally speaking, Gypsies have no intention of divulging their life-style and customs to social scientists or to anybody else.

Marimé

Central to any understanding of the Rom is their concept of *ma-*   35
rimé. It is *marimé* that is the key to their avoidance of the *gadje*, and it is *marimé* that serves as a powerful instrument of social control.

Marimé means defilement or pollution, and as used by the Gypsies   36
it is both an object and a concept. And since there is really no comparable term used by non-Gypsies, it is sometimes difficult for the latter to comprehend the meaning. "*Marimé*," writes Miller, "extends to all areas of Rom life, under-writing a hygienic attitude toward the world. . . . Lines are drawn between Gypsy and non-Gypsy, the clean and the unclean, health and disease, the good and the bad, all of which are made obvious and visible through the offices of ritual avoidance."[22]

The most striking aspects of *marimé* have to do with the demarca-   37
tion of the human body. The upper parts, particularly the head and the mouth, are looked upon as pure and clean. The lower portions, especially the genital and anal regions, are considered *marimé*. As the Rom see it, the upper and lower halves of the body must not "mix" in any way, and objects that come into contact with one half must not come into contact with the other.

There are countless examples of this hygienic-ritualistic separation.   38
Ronald Lee, who is himself a Gypsy, writes that

> you can't wash clothes, dishes, and babies in the same pan, and every Gypsy has his own eating utensils, towels, and soap. Other dishes and

utensils are set aside for guests, and still others for pregnant women. Certain towels are for the face, and others for the nether regions—and there are different colored soaps in the sink, each with an allotted function.[23]

39   *Marimé* apparently originated in the early-caravan period, when—for hygienic purposes—it was imperative that certain areas of the camp be set aside for cooking, cleaning, washing, taking care of body functions, and the like. Also, within the close confines of the wagons and tents, it was important that rules pertaining to sex be carefully spelled out and enforced. As is so often the case, however, over the years the various hygienic and sexual taboos proliferated. Miller notes, for example, that at the present time:

> Items that come into contact with the upper portions of the body are separately maintained and washed in running water or special basins. These items would include soap, towels, razors and combs, clothes, pillows, furniture like the backs of chairs and the tops of tables, tablecloths, aprons, sinks, utensils, and, of course, food itself, which is prepared, served, and eaten with the greatest consideration for ritual quality. . . .
>
> Any contact between the lower half of the body, particularly the genitals, which are conceptually the ultimate source of *marimé,* and the upper body is forbidden. The inward character of the genitals, especially the female genitalia—which are associated with the mysteries of blood and birth—make them consummately impure. Items that have contact with this area are carefully segregated because they contain a dangerous threat to the status of pure items and surfaces. The most dreadful contact, of course, would be between the genitals and the oral cavity.[24]

40   Gropper states that "a woman is *marimé* during and after childbirth, and during her monthly period. . . . A *marimé* woman may not cook or serve food to men. She may not step over anything belonging to a man or allow her skirts to touch his things. Women's clothing must be washed separately from men's."[25]

41   Even such a natural phenomenon as urination may cause difficulties for the Rom. "One old lady called off a visit to a friend because she was indisposed and felt it would be too embarrassing to urinate frequently. Men often go outside to urinate rather than do so in their own homes, especially if guests are present."[26]

42   Interestingly and—given their conception of *marimé*—quite logically, Gypsy women attach shame to the legs rather than the breasts. Sutherland points out that it is shameful for a woman to have too much leg exposed, and that women who wear short skirts are expected to cover them with a sweater when they sit. On the other hand:

Women use their brassieres as their pocketbooks, and it is quite common for a man, whether he be the husband, son, father, or unrelated, to reach into her brassiere to get cigarettes or money. When women greet each other after a certain absence, they squeeze each other's breasts. They will also squeeze the breasts to show appreciation of a witty story or joke.[27]

Quasi-Legal and Illegal Activities

Although most of the economic activities of the Rom are legal in nature, some are quasi-legal while others are clearly illegal. Blacktopping and sealing of driveways, for instance, are perfectly legal operations. But when the asphalt is laid at only one-third of the required thickness, and when the sealer has been surreptitiously diluted, the legality becomes questionable. Similarly, auto-body repair is legal, but if instead of actually removing the dents a thick coating of "paint and putty" is used, the practice is obviously unethical.

43

Fortune-Telling

Fortune-telling is a special case, for if there is one field that has been monopolized by the Rom it is certainly fortune-telling. Indeed, the terms "Gypsy" and "fortune-teller" seem to go hand in hand—and with good reason, as the following account by Andersen indicates:

44

> The little girl is expected to be a fortune-teller or reader and advisor, as early as thirteen or fourteen, and as a child she is trained for this profession. Fortune-telling as a means of livelihood is a tradition among Gypsy women, and many little girls observe their mothers, aunts, and other female relatives performing within this tradition every day.
> They are taught that they have a natural gift for the practice, that they received this gift from God, and that as fortune-tellers they will be performing a type of psychological counseling service for non-Gypsies.[28]

Fortune-telling is not a difficult occupation to learn, overhead expenses are negligible, and—depending on the location—business may be good. Clark cites the old Gypsy saying: "A fortune cannot be true unless silver changes hands."[29] And there have always been enough *gadje* who believe in this aphorism to make crystal gazing, palmistry, and card reading profitable ventures. Fees typically range from $2 to $5 per session, with a surprising number of repeat customers. Most of the latter are reportedly drawn from the lower socio-economic ranks. As Bercovici puts it: "The Gypsy fortune-teller is the psychoanalyst of the poor."[30]

45

Do Gypsies themselves believe in fortune-telling? The answer is yes and no. Despite what they may nominally teach their youngsters,

46

all Rom realize that readings performed for the *gadje* are entirely fallacious. Paradoxically, however, some Gypsy women are believed to possess occult powers of prediction, at least when applied to other
Gypsies. Older Gypsy women, therefore—who are felt to be experts in
dream interpretation and card reading—are sometimes consulted.[31]

47   The specifics of Gypsy fortune-telling vary somewhat, though not
a great deal. In a few areas, Romni still travel in pairs, telling fortunes
on a catch-as-catch-can basis. The most common practice, however, is
to set up a fortune-telling parlor, or *ofisa,* with living quarters in the
rear. The actual location of an *ofisa* depends in good part on the avail-
ability of large numbers of shoppers or passersby, which is why resort
and vacation areas are considered choice places to set up shop.

48   I know one Gypsy fortune-teller who has been a fixture on the Atlantic City boardwalk for more than thirty years, although this is a
rather exceptional case. In many instances, the life-span of an *ofisa* is
relatively short-lived, some lasting for only a summer or winter holiday season. Another common practice is for the *ofisa* to remain at the
same location, with the same decorations but with a series of different
proprietors.

49   Although crystal gazing and palmistry are still seen, many Gypsy
fortune-tellers prefer tarot cards. Trigg writes that "a tarot pack consists
of 78 gaily decorated cards marked with a number of archaic
symbols. . . . Each card has its own astrological, alchemical, numerolog-
ical, and philosophical meaning. . . . There are, of course, many different methods which are used for interpreting the tarot cards."[32]

50   What do Gypsy fortune-tellers think of their customers? The following statement speaks for itself:

> Gypsies cannot understand why the *gadje* take bogus readings so seri-
> ously; they assume that it is because non-Gypsies are stupid. What the
> Rom fail to take into account is that it is mostly the less intelligent or
> maladjusted who come to them for readings. Occasionally, the Gypsies
> are approached by younger people or a courting couple who want
> their palms read merely for a lark. . . .
>   In the large cities, fortune-telling stores are often seen in under-
> privileged neighborhoods; few are seen in affluent sections.[33]

Prejudice and Discrimination

51   Prejudice and discrimination are realities that virtually all Gypsies
must learn to face—and live with. The sad fact is that the Rom have
been persecuted in practically every county they have ever inhabited.
As was mentioned, the Nazis murdered hundreds of thousands during
World War II. Entire *vitsi* were wiped out. Furthermore, Kenrick and
Puxon note that during the many months of the Nuremberg war crimes

trial, not a single Gypsy was ever called as a witness![34] Nor was any monetary restitution ever made to the surviving Romany groups.

Although the wholesale slaughter ceased with the downfall of Hitler, Gypsy problems continued in both Western and Eastern Europe. About three-quarters of the European Gypsy population currently reside in Communist countries. Seeger writes about them:

> In dozens of Budapest restaurants, Gypsy orchestras perform for foreign tourists and local citizens in Eastern Europe's most pleasurable city. These musicians, however, are the fortunate handful among tens of thousands of Gypsies who are an unassimilated, poverty-stricken, despised minority scattered across Central and Western Europe. . . .
>
> Thirty years after the end of World War II, when thousands of Gypsies were exterminated by the Nazis along with the Jews, the Gypsy population is large enough to present Communist governments with major social problems.
>
> At a recent session of the U.N. subcommission on the Prevention of Discrimination, Grattan Puxon, general secretary of the World Romany Congress, said that the five million Gypsies living in Eastern Europe were "at the bottom of the social pile despite 30 years of socialism."
>
> The U.N. body responded to the plea by asking that "those countries that have Gypsies within their borders give them the full rights to which they are entitled."[35]

American Gypsies, too, continue to face prejudice and discrimination. Some large cities—like New York and Chicago—have special police assigned to the Rom. In the smaller towns, sheriffs will often escort Gypsies to the county line, glad to be rid of them. A recent issue of *The Police Chief* contains an article advising the police on how to keep their districts free of Gypsies.[36] Hancock reports that:

> various states have also directed laws against Gypsies. As recently as 1976, a family was expelled from the state of Maryland, where the law requires Gypsies to pay a licensing fee of $1,000 before establishing homes or engaging in business, and there is a bounty of $10 on the head of any Gypsy arrested who has not paid this fee.
>
> In New Hampshire in 1977, two families were legally evicted from the state without being charged with any crime, solely for reasons of their ethnic identity.[37]

Why does the persecution continue? Some observers contend that it is a matter of ethnic prejudice, similar to that experienced by blacks, Chicanos, and certain immigrant groups. Others, however, simply feel that the Rom are perceived as non-productive trouble-makers. As one police official put it, "they're nothing but economic parasites." The truth of the matter can be debated, but that is beside the point. If people

52

53

54

perceive of Gypsies as non-productive dissidents, then unfortunately for all concerned, prejudice and discrimination might be looked upon as justifiable retaliation.

Adaptability: The Gypsy Trademark

55   It is doubtful whether the Rom spend much time thinking about the causes of discrimination. Being realists, they expect it. And being Gypsies, they learn to live with it. In fact, being Gypsies, they learn to live with a great many things they do not like or agree with. This, indeed, is the Gypsies' trademark: adaptability.

56   In addition to coping with discrimination, Gypsies have also had to adapt to a vast panorama of social change. Times change, customs change, governments change—sometimes it seems that nothing is permanent—but whatever the transformation, the Rom seem to make the necessary adjustments. *They adapt without losing their cultural identity.*

57   Examples of their adaptation are numerous. Gypsies have never had their own religion. In all their wanderings and migrations, they have simply adapted to the religion—or religions—of the host country. The same is largely true of clothing styles, although as Polster observes, Gypsy women often do wear colorful outfits.[38] And aside from a seeming fondness for spicy dishes, the Rom adapt to the foods and cuisine of the country or area they are living in.

58   During the days of the caravan, Gypsy nomads camped outside the towns and cities—off the beaten track. When changing conditions forced them from the road, they took to the cities, where they have adapted rather well. Today, most of the American Rom are to be found in urban areas.

59   When horses were replaced by mechanized transportation, the Rom adapted. Instead of being horse traders, they learned auto-body repair and motor maintenance. When metal working—long a Gypsy specialty—was superseded by factory-type technology, the Rom turned to roofing and blacktopping. When fortune-telling became illegal in various places, Gypsies became "readers" and "advisors." And when these latter efforts were challenged, the Rom resorted to bribery and police "cooperation."

60   Gypsies make no claim to being quality workers, or even to being industrious. But both in America and elsewhere they are versatile. *They adapt.* As one Gypsy remarked to Adams and her colleagues, "Put me down anywhere in the world, and I'll make a living."[39]

FOOTNOTES

1. Peter Maas, *King of the Gypsies* (New York: Viking, 1975).
2. See Ian Hancock, "Gypsies," in Stephan Thernstrom, ed., *Harvard Encyclopedia of American Ethnic Groups* (Cambridge, Mass.: Harvard University Press, 1980), p. 441.

3. See William Lockwood, "Balkan Gypsies: An Introduction," in Joanne Grumet, ed., *Papers from the Fourth and Fifth Annual Meetings, Gypsy Lore Society, North American Chapter* (New York: Gypsy Lore Society, Publication No. 2, 1985), pp. 91–99.

4. Cited in Matt Salo and Sheila Salo, *The Kalderasha in Eastern Canada* (Ottawa: National Museums of Canada, 1977), p. 17.

5. Rena C. Gropper, *Gypsies in the City* (Princeton, N.J.: Darwin, 1975), p. 189.

6. Donald Kenrick and Grattan Puxon, *The Destiny of Europe's Gypsies* (New York: Basic Books, 1972), pp. 13–14.

7. P. W. R. Rishi, "Roma Preserves Hindu Mythology," *Roma* (January 1977): 13.

8. See the discussion in T. A. Acton, "The Social Construction of the Ethnic Identity of Commercial Nomadic Groups," in Grumet, *Papers,* pp. 5–23.

9. See Gropper, *Gypsies in the City,* pp. 1–16.

10. Frederick Barth, "The Social Organization of a Parish Group in Norway," in Farnham Rehfisch, ed., *Gypsies, Tinkers, and Other Travelers* (New York: Academic Press, 1975), pp. 285–99.

11. For an interesting discussion, see George Gmelch, *The Irish Tinkers* (Prospect Heights, Ill.: Waveland Press, 1985).

12. Martin Block, *Gypsies: Their Life and Their Customs* (New York: Appleton-Century, 1939), p. 1.

13. William Lockwood, "Balkan Gypsies: An Introduction," in Grumet, *Papers,* p. 92.

14. Jan Yoors, *The Gypsies* (New York: Simon and Schuster, 1967).

15. G. E. C. Webb, *Gypsies: The Secret People* (London: Herbert Jenkins, 1960), p. 9.

16. Yoors, *Gypsies,* p. 86.

17. Jeremy Sandford, *Gypsies* (London: Secker & Warburg, 1973), p. 13.

18. Gropper, *Gypsies in the City,* p. 1.

19. Norman Dodds, *Gypsies, Didikois, and Other Travelers* (London: Johnson, 1976), p. 16.

20. Jean-Paul Clebert, *The Gypsies* (London: Vista, 1963), pp. xvii–xix.

21. E. E. Evans-Pritchard, quoted in Elwood Trigg, *Gypsy Demons and Divinities* (Secaucus, N.J.: Citadel, 1973), p. x.

22. Carol Miller, "American Rom and the Ideology of Defilement," in Rehfisch, *Gypsies,* p. 41.

23. Ronald Lee, *Goddam Gypsy: An Autobiographical Novel* (Montreal: Tundra, 1971), pp. 29–30.

24. Miller, "American Rom," p. 42. See also Trigg, *Gypsy Demons,* p. 64.

25. Gropper, *Gypsies in the City,* pp. 92–93.

26. Anne Sutherland, *Gypsies: The Hidden Americans* (New York: Free Press, 1975), p. 21.

27. Ibid., p. 264.

28. Andersen, "Symbolism," in Salo, *American Kalderasha, p. 14.*

29. Clark, "Vanishing Vagabonds," p. 205.

30. Konrad Bercovici, *Gypsies: Their Life, Lore, and Legends* (New York: Greenwich House, 1983), p. 236.

31. See Silverman, "Everyday Drama," p. 394; Gropper, *Gypsies in the City,* p. 44; Yoors, *Gypsies,* p. 7.

32. Trigg, *Gypsy Demons,* p. 48.

33. Gropper, *Gypsies in the City,* p. 43.

34. Kenrick and Puxon, *Destiny of Europe's Gypsies,* p. 189.

35. Murray Seeger, "The Gypsies," *Philadelphia Inquirer,* October 9, 1977.

36. Hancock, "Gypsies," p. 44.

37. Ibid.

38. Polster, "Gypsies of Bunniton," p. 139.

39. Adams et al, *Gypsies and Government Policy,* p. 132.

SELECTED READINGS

Clebert, Jean-Paul. *The Gypsies.* London: Vista, 1963.

Dodds, Norman. *Gypsies, Didikois, and Other Travelers.* London: Johnson, 1976.

Gmelch, George. *The Irish Tinkers.* Prospect Heights, Ill.: Waveland Press, 1985.

Gropper, Rena C. *Gypsies in the City.* Princeton, N.J.: Darwin, 1975.

Hancock, Ian. "Gypsies." In the *Harvard Encyclopedia of American Ethnic Groups,* ed. by Stephan Thernstrom, pp. 440–45. Cambridge, Mass.: Harvard University Press, 1980.

Lee, Ronald. *Goddam Gypsy: An Autobiographical Novel.* Montreal: Tundra, 1971.

Lockwood, William G. "Balkan Gypsies: An Introduction." In *Papers From the Fourth and Fifth Annual Meetings, Gypsy Lore Society, North American Chapter,* ed. by Joanne Grumet, pp. 91–99. New York: Gypsy Lore Society, 1985.

Maas, Peter. *King of the Gypsies.* New York: Viking, 1975.

Rehfisch, Farnham, ed. *Gypsies, Tinkers, and Other Travelers.* New York: Academic Press, 1975.

Salo, Matt, and Salo, Sheila. *The Kalderasha in Eastern Canada.* Ottawa: National Museums of Canada, 1977.

Salo, Matt T., ed., *The American Kalderasha: Gypsies in the New World.* Hackettstown, N.J.: Gypsy Lore Society, 1981.

Silverman, Carol. "Everyday Drama: Impression Management of Urban Gypsies." In Matt Salo, ed., *Urban Anthropology, Special Issue,* 11, Number 3–4 (Fall-Winter, 1982): 377–398.

Sutherland, Anne. *Gypsies: The Hidden Americans.* New York: Free Press, 1975.

Yoors, Jan. *The Gypsies.* New York: Simon and Schuster, 1967.

———. *The Gypsies of Spain.* New York: Macmillan, 1974.

✦ *Evaluating the Text*

1. What aspects of the unusual lifestyle of the Gypsies help explain their marginal status in so many cultures around the world? How does their attitude toward non-Gypsies (*gadje*) help explain their avoidance of any involvement or commitment in the societies in which they find themselves?

2. What, in your view, explains the fascination that Gypsies have held for so many generations across cultures?

3. In your own words, explain the concept of *marimé* and the important role that it plays in many facets of Gypsy life and in the Gypsies' relationship to the outside world.

✦ *Exploring Different Perspectives*

1. What characteristics of exiled groups described by Edward Said in "Reflections on Exile" are shared by the Gypsies, according to William M. Kephart's analysis?

2. Compare and contrast the Cubans depicted by Joan Didion in "Miami: The Cuban Presence" with the Gypsies, as described in Kephart's ac-

count, to discover different strategies that different marginalized groups use to survive.

✦ *Extending Viewpoints Through Writing*

1. In a short essay, discuss the stereotypes about Gypsies that Kephart attempts to refute with regard to how they make a living and other aspects of their lives. You may draw upon your own experiences, if any, you have had with Gypsies.

Joan Didion

Miami: The Cuban Presence

———————◆———————

*Joan Didion was born in 1934 in Sacramento, a sixth-generation Califor-
nian. After graduating from the University of California at Berkeley, she
worked as a features editor at* Vogue *magazine. Her published work includes novels such as* Play It as It Lays *(1971);* A Book of Common
Prayer *(1977), and* Democracy *(1984); three collections of essays,* Slouch-
ing Towards Bethlehem *(1968),* The White Album *(1979), and* After
Henry *(1993); and a book-length account of her experiences as a reporter,
entitled* Salvador *(1983). "Miami: The Cuban Presence" originally appeared in the* New York Review of Books *for May 28, 1987, and evolved
into her book* Miami *(1987). This enlightening essay challenges views of
longtime Dade County residents with facts and statistics that reveal the
vital part that Cuban immigrants have played in the rebirth of Miami.*

1   On the 150th anniversary of the founding of Dade County, in February of 1986, the Miami *Herald* asked four prominent amateurs of local
history to name "the ten people and the ten events that had the most
impact on the county's history." Each of the four submitted his or her
own list of "The Most Influential People in Dade's History," and
among the names mentioned were Julia Tuttle ("pioneer business-
woman"), Henry Flagler ("brought the Florida East Coast Railway to
Miami"), Alexander Orr, Jr. ("started the research that saved Miami's
drinking water from salt"), Everest George Sewell ("publicized the city
and fostered its deepwater seaport"). . . . There was Dr. James M. Jackson, an early Miami physician. There was Napoleon Bonaparte Bro-
ward, the governor of Florida who initiated the draining of the
Everglades. There appeared on three of the four lists the name of the
developer of Coral Gables, George Merrick. There appeared on one of
the four lists the name of the coach of the Miami Dolphins, Don Shula.

2   On none of these lists of "The Most Influential People in Dade's
History" did the name Fidel Castro appear, nor for that matter did the
name of any Cuban, although the presence of Cubans in Dade County
did not go entirely unnoted by the *Herald* panel. When it came to naming the Ten Most Important "Events," as opposed to "People," all four
panelists mentioned the arrival of the Cubans, but at slightly off angles
("Mariel Boatlift of 1980" was the way one panelist saw it), and as if the
arrival had been just another of those isolated disasters or innovations
which deflect the course of any growing community, on an approxi-

mate par with the other events mentioned, for example the Freeze of 1895, the Hurricane of 1926, the opening of the Dixie Highway, the establishment of Miami International Airport, and the adoption, in 1957, of the metropolitan form of government, "enabling the Dade County Commission to provide urban services to the increasingly populous unincorporated area."

This set of mind, in which the local Cuban community was seen as   3
a civic challenge determinedly met, was not uncommon among Anglos to whom I talked in Miami, many of whom persisted in the related illusions that the city was small, manageable, prosperous in a predictable broadbased way, southern in a progressive Sunbelt way, American, and belonged to them. In fact 43 percent of the population of Dade County was by that time "Hispanic," which meant mostly Cuban. Fifty-six percent of the population of Miami itself was Hispanic. The most visible new buildings on the Miami skyline, the Arquitectonica buildings along Brickell Avenue, were by a firm with a Cuban founder. There were Cubans in the board rooms of the major banks, Cubans in clubs that did not admit Jews or blacks, and four Cubans in the most recent mayoralty campaign, two of whom, Raul Masvidal and Xavier Suarez, .
had beaten out the incumbent and all other candidates to meet in a runoff, and one of whom, Xavier Suarez, a thirty-six-year-old lawyer who had been brought from Cuba to the United States as a child, was by then mayor of Miami.

The entire tone of the city, the way people looked and talked and   4
met one another, was Cuban. The very image the city had begun presenting of itself, what was then its newfound glamour, its "hotness" (hot colors, hot vice, shady dealings under the palm trees), was that of prerevolutionary Havana, as perceived by Americans. There was even in the way women dressed in Miami a definable Havana look, a more distinct emphasis on the hips and décolletage, more black, more veiling, a generalized flirtatiousness of style not then current in American cities. In the shoe departments at Burdine's and Jordan Marsh there were more platform soles than there might have been in another American city, and fewer displays of the running shoe ethic. I recall being struck, during an afternoon spent at La Liga Contra el Cancer, a prominent exile charity which raises money to help cancer patients, by the appearance of the volunteers who had met that day to stuff envelopes for a benefit. Their hair was sleek, of a slightly other period, immaculate pageboys and French twists. They wore Bruno Magli pumps, and silk and linen dresses of considerable expense. There seemed to be a preference for strictest gray or black, but the effect remained lush, tropical, like a room full of perfectly groomed mangoes.

This was not, in other words, an invisible 56 percent of the popula-   5
tion. Even the social notes in *Diario Las Americas* and in *El Herald*, the

daily Spanish edition of the *Herald* written and edited for *el exilio,* suggested a dominant culture, one with money to spend and a notable willingness to spend it in public. La Liga Contra el Cancer alone sponsored, in a single year, two benefit dinner dances, one benefit ball, a benefit children's fashion show, a benefit telethon, a benefit exhibition of jewelry, a benefit presentation of Miss Universe contestants, and a benefit showing, with Saks Fifth Avenue and chicken *vol-au-vent,* of the Adolfo (as it happened, a Cuban) fall collection.

6   One morning *El Herald* would bring news of the gala at the Pavillon of the Amigos Latinamericanos del Museo de Ciencia y Planetarium; another morning, of an upcoming event at the Big Five Club, a Miami club founded by former members of five fashionable clubs in prerevolutionary Havana: a *coctel,* or cocktail party, at which tables would be assigned for yet another gala, the annual "Baile Imperial de las Rosas" of the American Cancer Society, Hispanic Ladies Auxiliary. Some members of the community were honoring Miss America Latina with dinner dancing at the Doral. Some were being honored themselves, at the Spirit of Excellence Awards Dinner at the Omni. Some were said to be enjoying the skiing at Vail; others to prefer Bariloche, in Argentina. Some were reported unable to attend (but sending checks for) the gala at the Pavillon of the Amigos Latinamericanos del Museo de Ciencia y Planetarium because of a scheduling conflict, with *el coctel de* Paula Hawkins.

7   Fete followed fete, all high visibility. Almost any day it was possible to drive past the limestone arches and fountains which marked the boundaries of Coral Gables and see little girls being photographed in the tiaras and ruffled hoop skirts and maribou-trimmed illusion capes they would wear at their *quinces,* the elaborate fifteenth-birthday parties at which the community's female children come of official age. The favored facial expression for a *quince* photograph was a classic smolder. The favored backdrop was one suggesting Castilian grandeur, which was how the Coral Gables arches happened to figure. Since the idealization of the virgin implicit in the *quince* could exist only in the presence of its natural foil, *machismo,* there was often a brother around, or a boyfriend. There was also a mother, in dark glasses, not only to protect the symbolic virgin but to point out the better angle, the more aristocratic location. The *quinceanera* would pick up her hoop skirts and move as directed, often revealing the scuffed Jellies she had worn that day to school. A few weeks later there she would be, transformed in *Diario Las Americas,* one of the morning battalion of smoldering fifteen-year-olds, each with her arch, her fountain, her borrowed scenery, the gift if not exactly the intention of the late George Merrick, who built the arches when he developed Coral Gables.

8   Neither the photographs of the Cuban *quinceaneras* nor the notes about the *coctel* at the Big Five were apt to appear in the newspapers

read by Miami Anglos, nor, for that matter, was much information at all about the daily life of the Cuban majority. When, in the fall of 1986, Florida International University offered an evening course called "Cuban Miami: A Guide for Non-Cubans," the *Herald* sent a staff writer, who covered the classes as if from a distant beat. "Already I have begun to make some sense out of a culture, that, while it totally surrounds us, has remained inaccessible and alien to me," the *Herald* writer was reporting by the end of the first meeting, and, by the end of the fourth:

> What I see day to day in Miami, moving through mostly Anglo corridors of the community, are just small bits and pieces of that other world, the tip of something much larger than I'd imagined.... We may frequent the restaurants here, or wander into the occasional festival. But mostly we try to ignore Cuban Miami, even as we rub up against this teeming, incomprehensible presence.

Only thirteen people, including the *Herald* writer, turned up for the first meeting of "Cuban Miami: A Guide for Non-Cubans" (two more appeared at the second meeting, along with a security guard, because of telephone threats prompted by what the *Herald* writer called "somebody's twisted sense of national pride"), an enrollment which suggested a certain willingness among non-Cubans to let Cuban Miami remain just that, Cuban, the "incomprehensible presence." In fact there had come to exist in South Florida two parallel cultures, separate but not exactly equal, a key distinction being that only one of the two, the Cuban, exhibited even a remote interest in the activities of the other. "The American community is not really aware of what is happening in the Cuban community," an exiled banker named Luis Botifoll said in a 1983 *Herald* Sunday magazine piece about ten prominent local Cubans. "We are clannish, but at least we know who is whom in the American establishment. They do not." About another of the ten Cubans featured in this piece, Jorge Mas Canosa, the *Herald* had this to say:

> He is an advisor to US Senators, a confidant of federal bureaucrats, a lobbyist for anti-Castro US policies, a near unknown in Miami. When his political group sponsored a luncheon speech in Miami by Secretary of Defense Caspar Weinberger, almost none of the American business leaders attending had ever heard of their Cuban host.

The general direction of this piece, which appeared under the cover line "THE CUBANS: *They're ten of the most powerful men in Miami. Half the population doesn't know it,*" was, as the *Herald* put it,

> to challenge the widespread presumption that Miami's Cubans are not really Americans, that they are a foreign presence here, an exile

9

10

community that is trying to turn South Florida into North Cuba. . . . The top ten are not separatists; they have achieved success in the most traditional ways. They are the solid, bedrock citizens, hard-working humanitarians who are role models for a community that seems determined to assimilate itself into American society.

11   This was interesting. It was written by one of the few Cubans then on the *Herald* staff, and yet it described, however unwittingly, the precise angle at which Miami Anglos and Miami Cubans were failing to connect: Miami Anglos were in fact interested in Cubans only to the extent that they could cast them as aspiring immigrants, "determined to assimilate," a "hard-working" minority not different in kind from other groups of resident aliens. (But had I met any Haitians, a number of Anglos asked when I said that I had been talking to Cubans.) Anglos (who were, significantly, referred to within the Cuban community as "Americans") spoke of cross-culturalization, and of what they believed to be a meaningful second-generation preference for hamburgers, and rock-and-roll. They spoke of "diversity," and of Miami's "Hispanic flavor," an approach in which 56 percent of the population was seen as decorative, like the Coral Gables arches.

12   Fixed as they were on this image of the melting pot, of immigrants fleeing a disruptive revolution to find a place in the American sun, Anglos did not on the whole understand that assimilation would be considered by most Cubans a doubtful goal at best. Nor did many Anglos understand that living in Florida was still at the deepest level construed by Cubans as a temporary condition, an accepted political option shaped by the continuing dream, if no longer the immediate expectation, of a vindicatory return. *El exilio* was for Cubans a ritual, a respected tradition. *La revolución* was also a ritual, a trope fixed in Cuban political rhetoric at least since José Martí, a concept broadly interpreted to mean reform, or progress, or even just change. Ramón Grau San Martín, the president of Cuba during the autumn of 1933 and from 1944 until 1948, had presented himself as a revolutionary, as had his 1948 successor, Carlos Prío. Even Fulgencio Batista had entered Havana life calling for *la revolución*, and had later been accused of betraying it, even as Fidel Castro was now.

13   This was a process Cuban Miami understood, but Anglo Miami did not, remaining as it did arrestingly innocent of even the most general information about Cuba and Cubans. Miami Anglos for example still had trouble with Cuban names, and Cuban food. When the Cuban novelist Guillermo Cabrera Infante came from London to lecture at Miami-Dade Community College, he was referred to by several Anglo faculty members to whom I spoke as "Infante." Cuban food was widely seen not as a minute variation on that eaten throughout both the Caribbean and the Mediterranean but as "exotic," and full of garlic. A typical

Thursday food section of the *Herald* included recipes for Broiled Lemon-Curry Cornish Game Hens, Chicken Tetrazzini, King Cake, Pimiento Cheese, Raisin Sauce for Ham, Sauteed Spiced Peaches, Shrimp Scampi, Easy Beefy Stir-Fry, and four ways to used dried beans ("Those cheap, humble beans that have long sustained the world's poor have become the trendy set's new pet"), none of them Cuban.

This was all consistent, and proceeded from the original construction, that of the exile as an immigration. There was no reason to be curious about Cuban food, because Cuban teenagers preferred hamburgers. There was no reason to get Cuban names right, because they were complicated, and would be simplified by the second generation, or even by the first, "Jorge L. Mas" was the way Jorge Mas Canosa's business card read. "Raul Masvidal" was the way Raul Masvidal y Jury ran for mayor of Miami. There was no reason to know about Cuban history, because history was what immigrants were fleeing.

Even the revolution, the reason for the immigration, could be covered in a few broad strokes: "Batista," "Castro," "26 Julio," this last being the particular broad stroke that inspired the Miami Springs Holiday Inn, on July 26, 1985, the thirty-second anniversary of the day Fidel Castro attacked the Moncada Barracks and so launched his six-year struggle for power in Cuba, to run a bar special on Cuba Libres, thinking to attract local Cubans by commemorating their holiday. "It was a mistake," the manager said, besieged by outraged exiles. "The gentleman who did it is from Minnesota."

There was in fact no reason, in Miami as well as in Minnesota, to know anything at all about Cubans, since Miami Cubans were now, if not Americans, at least aspiring Americans, and worthy of Anglo attention to the exact extent that they were proving themselves, in the *Herald*'s words, "role models for a community that seems determined to assimilate itself into American society"; or, as George Bush put it in a 1986 Miami address to the Cuban American National Foundation, "the most eloquent testimony I know to the basic strength and success of America, as well as to the basic weakness and failure of Communism and Fidel Castro."

The use of this special lens, through which the exiles were seen as a tribute to the American system, a point scored in the battle of the ideologies, tended to be encouraged by those outside observers who dropped down from the northeast corridor for a look and a column or two. George Will, in *Newsweek,* saw Miami as "a new installment in the saga of America's absorptive capacity," and Southwest Eighth Street as the place where "these exemplary Americans," the seven Cubans who had been gotten together to brief him, "initiated a columnist to fried bananas and black-bean soup and other Cuban contributions to the tanginess of American life." George Gilder, in *The Wilson Quarterly,* drew pretty much the same lesson from Southwest Eighth Street, finding it "more effervescently thriving than its crushed prototype," by which he seemed to mean Havana. In fact Eighth Street was for George Gilder a street that seemed to "percolate with the forbidden commerce of the dying island to the south . . . the Refrescos Cawy, the Competidora and El Cuño cigarettes, the *guayaberas*, the Latin music pulsing from the storefronts, the pyramids of mangoes and tubers, gourds and plantains, the iced coconuts served with a straw, the new theaters showing the latest anti-Castro comedies."

18   There was nothing on this list, with the possible exception of the "anti-Castro comedies," that could not most days be found on Southwest Eighth Street, but the list was also a fantasy, and a particularly *gringo* fantasy, one in which Miami Cubans, who came from a culture which had represented western civilization in this hemisphere since before there was a United States of America, appeared exclusively as vendors of plantains, their native music "pulsing" behind them. There was in any such view of Miami Cubans an extraordinary element of condescension, and it was the very condescension shared by Miami Anglos, who were inclined to reduce the particular liveliness and sophistication of local Cuban life to a matter of shrines on the lawn and love potions in the *botanicas*, the primitive exotica of the tourist's Caribbean.

19   Cubans were perceived as most satisfactory when they appeared most fully to share the aspirations and manners of middle-class Americans, at the same time adding "color" to the city on appropriate occasions, for example at their *quinces* (the *quinces* were one aspect of Cuban life almost invariably mentioned by Anglos, who tended to present them as evidence of Cuban extravagance, i.e., Cuban irresponsibility, or childishness), or on the day of the annual Calle Ocho Festival, when they could, according to the *Herald*, "samba" in the streets and stir up a paella for two thousand (ten cooks, two thousand mussels, two hundred and twenty pounds of lobster, and four hundred and forty pounds of rice), using rowboat oars as spoons. Cubans were perceived as least satisfactory when they "acted clannish," "kept to themselves," "had their own ways," and, two frequent flash points, "spoke Spanish when they didn't need to" and "got political"; complaints, each of them, which suggested an Anglo view of what Cubans should be at significant odds with what Cubans were.

20   This question of language was curious. The sound of spoken Spanish was common in Miami, but it was also common in Los Angeles, and Houston, and even in the cities of the Northeast. What was unusual about Spanish in Miami was not that it was so often spoken, but that it was so often heard: In, say, Los Angeles, Spanish remained a language only barely registered by the Anglo population, part of the ambient noise, the language spoken by the people who worked in the car wash and came to trim the trees and cleared the tables in restaurants. In Mi-

ami Spanish was spoken by the people who ate in the restaurants, the people who owned the cars and the trees, which made, on the socio-auditory scale, a considerable difference. Exiles who felt isolated or de-classed by language in New York or Los Angeles thrived in Miami. An entrepreneur who spoke no English could still, in Miami, buy, sell, ne-gotiate, leverage assets, float bonds, and, if he were so inclined, attend galas twice a week, in black tie. "I have been after the *Herald* ten times to do a story about millionaires in Miami who do not speak more than two words in English," one prominent exile told me. "'Yes' and 'no.' Those are the two words. They come here with five dollars in their pockets and without speaking another word of English they are millionaires."

The truculence a millionaire who spoke only two words of English   21
might provoke among the less resourceful native citizens of a nomi-nally American city was predictable, and manifested itself rather di-rectly. In 1980, the year of Mariel, Dade County voters had approved a referendum requiring that county business be conducted exclusively in English. Notwithstanding the fact that this legislation was necessarily amended to exclude emergency medical and certain other services, and notwithstanding even the fact that many local meetings continued to be conducted in that unbroken alternation of Spanish and English which had become the local patois ("I will be in Boston on Sunday and *desafortunadamente yo tengo un compromiso en* Boston *qu no puedo romper y yo no podre estar con Vds.,*" read the minutes of a 1984 Miami City Commission meeting I had occasion to look up. "*En espiritu, estaré, pero* the other members of the commission I am sure are invited . . .").[1] the very existence of this referendum, was seen by many as ground re-gained, a point made. By 1985 a St. Petersburg optometrist named Rob-ert Melby was launching his third attempt in four years to have English declared the official language of the state of Florida, as it would be in 1986 of California. "I don't know why our legislators here are so, how should I put it?—spineless," Robert Melby complained about those South Florida politicians who knew how to count. "No one down here seems to want to run with the issue."

Even among those Anglos who distanced themselves from such ef-   22
forts, Anglos who did not perceive themselves as economically or so-cially threatened by Cubans, there remained considerable uneasiness on the matter of language, perhaps because the inability or the disincli-nation to speak English tended to undermine their conviction that as-similation was an ideal universally shared by those who were to be assimilated. This uneasiness had for example shown up repeatedly

---

[1]"I will be in Boston on Sunday and unfortunately I have an appointment in Boston that I can't break and I won't be able to be with you. In spirit, I will be, but the other members of the commission I am sure are invited. . . ."

during the 1985 mayoralty campaign, surfacing at odd but apparently irrepressible angles. The winner of that contest, Xavier Suarez, who was born in Cuba but educated in the United States, a graduate of Harvard Law, was reported in a wire service story to speak, an apparently unexpected accomplishment, "flawless English."

23   A less prominent Cuban candidate for mayor that year had unsettled reporters at a televised "meet the candidates" forum by answering in Spanish the questions they asked in English. "For all I or my dumbstruck colleagues knew," the *Herald* political editor complained in print after the event, "he was reciting his high school's alma mater or the ten Commandments over and over again. The only thing I understood was the occasional *Cubanos vota Cubano* he tossed in." It was noted by another *Herald* columnist that of the leading candidates, only one, Raul Masvidal, had a listed telephone number, but: ". . . if you call Masvidal's 661-0259 number on Kiaora Street in Coconut Grove—during the day, anyway—you'd better speak Spanish. I spoke to two women there, and neither spoke enough English to answer the question of whether it was the candidate's number."

24   On the morning this last item came to my attention in the *Herald* I studied it for some time. Raul Masvidal was at that time the chairman of the board of the Miami Savings Bank and the Miami Savings Corporation. He was a former chairman of the Biscayne Bank, and a minority stockholder in the M Bank, of which he had been a founder. He was a member of the Board of Regents for the state university system of Florida. He had paid $600,000 for the house on Kiaora Street in Coconut Grove, buying it specifically because he needed to be a Miami resident (Coconut Grove is part of the city of Miami) in order to run for mayor, and he had sold his previous house, in the incorporated city of Coral Gables, for $1,100,000.

25   The Spanish words required to find out whether the number listed for the house on Kiaora Street was in fact the candidate's number would have been roughly these: "*¿Es la casa de Raul Masvidal?*" The answer might have been "*Si*," or the answer might have been "*No.*" It seemed to me that there must be very few people working on daily newspapers along the southern borders of the United States who would consider this exchange entirely out of reach, and fewer still who would not accept it as a commonplace of American domestic life that daytime telephone calls to middle-class urban households will frequently be answered by women who speak Spanish.

26   Something else was at work in this item, a real resistance, a balkiness, a coded version of the same message Dade County voters had sent when they decreed that their business be done only in English: WILL THE LAST AMERICAN TO LEAVE MIAMI PLEASE BRING THE FLAG, the famous bumper stickers had read the year of Mariel. "It was the last American stronghold in Dade County," the owner of the Gator Kicks Longneck Saloon,

out where Southwest Eighth Street runs into the Everglades, had said after he closed the place for good the night of Super Bowl Sunday, 1986. "Fortunately or unfortunately, I'm not alone in my inability," a *Herald* columnist named Charles Whited had written a week or so later, in a column about not speaking Spanish. "A good many Americans have left Miami because they want to live someplace where everybody speaks one language: theirs." In this context the call to the house on Kiaora Street in Coconut Grove which did or did not belong to Raul Masvidal appeared not as a statement of literal fact but as shorthand, a glove thrown down, a stand, a cry from the heart of a beleaguered raj.

✦ Evaluating the Text

1. How does Didion use striking examples and news items to establish the impact of the 56 percent of Miami's population that is Cuban and the extent to which Cubans are an integral part of the political and social structure of the city?

2. What evidence does Didion provide to show that the Cuban majority is more powerful politically and economically and more independent than most Anglos would care to admit?

3. Why is it significant that *The Miami Herald* did not have a Cuban on the staff reporting on cultural events in the Cuban community when they constitute 56 percent of Dade County's population? What other evidence does Didion offer to show that Anglos living side by side with Cubans in Miami are unaware of activities taking place in their community?

4. What are *quinces,* and how are they perceived very differently by Anglos and by the Cuban community? How does the difference in perception of *quinces* underscore Didion's thesis?

5. Why is it significant that Dade County business is conducted in both English and Spanish? How is the history of resistance to using Spanish for county business a reflection of the political struggle of Cubans in Dade County?

✦ Exploring Different Perspectives

1. What factors explain the difference between Cuban success in Dade County and the marginal existence of Mexicans along the border described by Luis Alberto Urrea in "Border Story"?

2. In what significant ways do Cubans differ from Edward Said's characterization of exiles? What factors are responsible for these differences?

✦ *Extending Viewpoints Through Writing*

1. What series of historical events resulted in the Cuban exodus after the rise to power of Fidel Castro? What would you infer about their situation in Cuba at the time Castro took over? How do the Cubans who came to Miami differ from most groups of immigrants that come to America?

2. Write a brief essay describing the role played by a particular ethnic group in a town or city with which you are familiar. Highlight the contributions of this group in real and specific ways to the spirit and culture of the city.

3. How is the issue of language connected to refugees and immigrants moving to an area in the United States? Discuss this idea in relationship to proposals that English should be the official state language in Florida, California, and in other states that have large immigrant populations? What is your view on whether English should be declared the official language in your state?

4. Didion said of the book that evolved from this essay, "*Miami* [1987], its title not withstanding, is mainly about what I think is wrong in Washington" (quoted by James Chase in *The New York Times Book Review*, October 25, 1987). How does Didion's characterization of politicians in Washington point out a reluctance to come to terms with the enormously influential role Hispanics play and will continue to play in American culture?

Le Ly Hayslip

Yearning to Breathe Free

———————◆———————

Le Ly Hayslip, the youngest of six children in a close-knit Buddhist family, was twelve years old when U.S. helicopters landed in Ky La, in central Vietnam. Before she was sixteen, Le Ly experienced near starvation, imprisonment, torture, rape, and the deaths of family members. After a courageous escape to America, she settled in Los Angeles with her three sons, where she started the East Meets West Foundation, a charitable relief organization. Her eloquent memoir, When Heaven and Earth Changed Places *(with Jay Wurts, 1989) details her return to Vietnam after thirty years. A 1993 movie,* Heaven and Earth *(directed by Oliver Stone), was based on her experiences. The following account, from* Child of War, Woman of Peace *(with James Hayslip, 1993), describes the challenge she faced in emigrating to the United States. Hayslip's narrative offers insight into the lives of great numbers of Vietnamese who fled the country during and after the war.*

Honolulu's warm breeze caressed me like a mother's hands. A pretty hula girl put a flowered lei—a victor's garland—around my neck. For the first time in my life, I gulped the heady air of a world at peace.

May 27, 1970, the day I stepped onto the ramp at Honolulu International Airport after fleeing the war in Vietnam, marked the beginning of my new life as an apprentice American. It may have been my imagination, but the attendants on the big American jetliner from Saigon seemed exceptionally kind to me and my two boys—three-year-old Jimmy (whose father, a wealthy Saigon industrialist, he never knew) and Tommy, the three-month-old son of my new American husband, Ed Munro, whom we were on our way to join. Liberty and good-will, like corruption and cruelty, seem to hold each other's hand.

Still, Hawaii was too much like Vietnam to really count as the United States. For one, it was a tropical island—covered with palms and sand—and Honolulu, despite its modern hotels and shops and restaurants, was too much like Saigon: filled with Asians and GIs, tawdry bars and taxis, and people in transit, *khong hieu qua khu*—without a past or future, like me. The thrill of great America would have to wait for our next landing.

As it turned out, San Diego was another Honolulu, if written on a larger page. Our plane arrived after midnight, not a good time for

463

sightseeing, especially by timid immigrants. In Vietnam, the Viet Cong feared the light, so "friendly" areas—cities, towns, air bases, and outposts—were lit up like American Christmas trees. Perhaps to show it was safe for GIs coming back from the war, San Diego, too, left its lights burning all night.

5   Ed met us at the arrival gate, just as he'd promised. He had been staying with his mother, Erma, in the suburb of El Cajon. Although he looked tanned and healthy and was a welcome familiar face after thousands of miles of strangers, my heart sagged when I saw him. Born in 1915 (seven years after my mother's birth) in Mount Vernon, Washington, he was old enough to be my father—no twenty-year-old's dream husband. Yet, with two brothers and three sisters, he was no stranger to small towns and big families—one reason, in addition to his own maturity, that he understood me so well. His mother had been a waitress at something called a "drive-in" and his father, like mine, had died. Both had been honest, family-loving men who tackled life barehanded. My father had been a farmer who seldom went farther than a day's walk from our home village of Ky La. Ed's dad had been a carpenter and hunter who ventured to Alaska: a wondrous place where, Ed said, ice fell stinging from the sky. In all, Ed's relatives were solid working-class people. Like my peasant family, they loved one another, loved their country, and lived their values every day.

6   Ed had been married twice before. He knew, as I did, how it felt to lose the game of love. His first wife gave him two sons, Ron and Ed Jr. (navy boys whom we visited in Vietnam), then divorced him and moved to Nevada. His second wife was unfaithful and when Ed found out about it, he did not beat her as a Vietnamese husband would, but sent her a dozen roses and wished her good luck with her new man. In a way, that was what Ed was all about. He put the wishes of those he loved above his own right to be happy. This constant sacrifice, I think, whittled him down and eventually cost him what he treasured most. In this, I would discover, he was not alone among Americans.

7   The long drive from San Diego's Lindbergh Field to El Cajon was not much different from a drive to Saigon's suburbs, except for more cars and fewer motorbikes on the highway's six broad lanes. Off the freeway, we drove through blocks of tidy homes, all dark except for streetlamps standing like GI basketball hoops in the gloom. We parked in the driveway of a pale yellow house—"ranch style," Ed said, although I couldn't smell any animals—and we went up the narrow walk to a front door bright with light. Before Ed could reach the bell, a shadow hobbled up behind the curtain. The door opened onto a large American woman in curlers, backlit in a nightgown as big as a sheet.

8   Startled, I bowed low—to be polite and to put the big creature out of sight while I collected my sleep-starved wits.

"Ohhh!" Erma, Ed's sister, screamed, slapping her cheeks, and 9
pulling me to her with beefy arms. "She's so cute—like a little china
doll! I want to hug her to pieces!"

She very nearly did—a big, sloppy American bearhug, a show of 10
emotion no proper Vietnamese would dare display on first meeting. It
amazed me how quick Americans were to show affection to strangers,
even those their menfolk had gone so far from home to destroy.

"And the children—?" Erma peeked around my helmet of ratted 11
hair. Ed had shown her pictures of my two sons.

"In the car!" He poked a dad's boastful thumb over his shoulder. 12

"Ooo—I can't wait to see them!" Erma scuttled down the walk. 13
"I'll just eat them up!"

Eat them up—my god! Of course, it was just another American fig- 14
ure of speech. I was beginning to discover that English was as full of
booby traps as the jungle outside Ky La.

Anyway, Ed's new family impressed her, for better *and* for worse. 15
Jimmy was cranky from crossing time zones, and since he spoke mostly
Vietnamese, he cried when this giant brown-haired bear-lady tried to
crush him with her paws. Tommy, however, who had slept fourteen
hours on the plane and was ready for fun, screeched with delight. Erma
knew right away which boy had the bright, upstanding, red-white-and-
blue American father and which child was the pitiful third-world refugee. First impressions are lasting. I think that midnight meeting forever
biased her in Tommy's favor, although I never dreamed of saying it.

We unloaded the luggage and put the boys to bed, where I stayed 16
with them until they fell asleep. From the depths of this strange-smelling,
thick-walled American house, I listened to Ed and Erma chat in too fast
English over coffee. I still didn't know what to make of my new environment: American kitchens smelled like sickly hospitals, reeking of
disinfectant, not *Ong Tao*, "Mr. Stove's," healthy food. The darkness
outside the house was as terrifying as a midnight cadre meeting. I
wanted to join them and gossip and laugh like real family, but I understood only a fraction of what they said and part of that was whispered,
which to me meant danger, not good manners. Fortunately, the deep,
even breathing of the kids won me over and I fell asleep, reminding
myself to pay special attention to any spirits who might visit me in my
first American dream.

My first full day as an American housewife didn't go so well. I 17
slept poorly in Erma's tight-sealed house and my body still awoke and
made water and got hungry on Saigon time. Nobody explained jet lag
to me and I thought my strange waves of sleepiness in the middle of
the day and spunkiness at four in the morning were just signs of how
out of place Orientals were in round-eyed America. I hoped it would

pass, like the flu, without my having to consult the neighborhood psychic or witch doctor.

18   My alarm dock on that first day was a playful slap on the rump.

19   "Get up, sleepyhead!" Ed yelled with a grin as wide as the band of sunlight streaming in through the window. He looked so happy to have his wife and family with him again that I thought he was going to burst. Like a slug in my mother's garden, I slithered around the sunburst to the shower where I took another ten minutes to wake up.

20   I dressed and made up with great care, partly because of my new surroundings (unlike Vietnamese peasant houses, American homes have their owner's fingerprints all over them: no two housewives ever put wastebaskets and tissues in the same place!) and partly because I could take no chances with my appearance. Daylight and in-laws are terrible critics.

21   "Hurry up and dress the kids," Ed commanded. "After breakfast, I want you to meet my mother!"

22   In Vietnam, meeting in-laws is always a tricky business. This is true especially when the marriage has not been arranged through matchmakers and the couple are of vastly different ages, let alone races—*quen nha ma, la nha chong,* I am at home in my mother's house, but a stranger to my in-laws! I would sooner have met an American battle tank on Erma's lawn than to walk next door unescorted and introduce myself to Ed's mother—which, for some unknown reason, was my husband's harebrained plan.

23   When Jimmy was dressed and fed (Tommy was still asleep and nobody had the courage to wake him) Ed booted us out and pointed to the shingled green house next door.

24   "Oh, go on!" he laughed. "You girls get acquainted. Mom won't bite your head off!"

25   Well, I certainly hoped not, but Ed hadn't met a real Vietnamese mother-in-law. Back in Danang, my mother had never accepted our marriage, and so never treated Ed like a new family-member-in-training, with all the horror the position inspires. I dragged my son across the sunny lawn like a goat on the way to the slaughterhouse.

26   I squeezed Jimmy's spit-slick fingers and knocked on the door. Dog-barks from hell—we jumped back! The shadow of a big, Erma-like figure waddled toward us behind lacy curtains. A grandmother's high-pitched voice scolded the yappy dogs.

27   Had this been a Vietnamese house, I would have known instantly what to do. I would have bowed low, recited the ritual greeting of an unworthy daughter-in-law to the witch-queen who would transform me over the next few years into a deserving wife for her son, then gone into the kitchen and made us both some tea, humbly serving it with two hands, the old-fashioned way. Then I would have sat silently and waited to be instructed.

But this was an American house: a great sand-castle trap for a Viet-   28
namese fish out of water. In Vietnam, a matchmaker would have prepared the way—sold my mother-in-law on my maidenly virtues, few as
those might be. Now I would have to do my own selling, encumbered
with my fatherless child, remembering how I had lost my virginity not
once, but *three* times: bodily to the Viet Cong who raped me after my
kangaroo court-martial; spiritually to Anh, Jimmy's father, with whom
I fell into girlish love; and morally to the sad little GI in Danang who
kept my family off the street by paying me four hundred U.S. dollars
green money for a last happy memory of my country. By any measure, I
was unworthy to stand on this fine woman's stoop, let alone pretend to
the honors and duties of a daughter-in-law. It was only because of my
continuing bad karma that the earth did not swallow me up.

Despite my fears, the door opened onto the most angelic old face I   29
had ever seen.

Leatha (whom I would always call "Mom Munro" and *never* impo-   30
litely by her first name) was seventy-five and had silver-blond hair that
circled her cherub face the way white smoke twists around a storybook
cottage. In Vietnam, such women aged like plucked berries: from the
blush of virgin freshness to old age it was quick and downhill. Although
a woman's post-birth *buon de* ritual, like our daily regimen of outdoor
labor, kept our bodies lean and hard, we had no time or money for
beauty treatments. Indeed, in a culture where reaching old age was a
real accomplishment, we revered our elderly for being one step closer to
the ancestors we worshiped. Old women and old men were sometimes
mistaken for one another, and that was no cause for shame. In a way,
this blending of sexes with its release from the trials of youth—concern
for appearance and catching a mate—was one of aging's big rewards.

But not for Leatha.   31

Although Ed and Erma later assured me that she was "just an aver-   32
age grandma," I thought her angelic hair, well-fed happy face, plump
saggy arms, solid girth, and movie star makeup made her even more
spectacular than the painted Buddhas in the shrine beneath Marble
Mountain near my village. Her appearance was even more astonishing,
since in Vietnam I had seen no American women over fifty. (Most outsiders were men—soldiers or civilian contractors like Ed—or young female nurses.) Although her big hug made me feel better, I continued to
stare at her. I tried to imagine my mother's face beneath the silver
wreath and felt strangely envious and sad. Until I later found out how
most Americans treat their elderly parents, the thought of growing old,
fat, and pretty in America seemed to be another dividend of peace.

Of course, Leatha knew who I was at once and invited us inside.   33
We talked only a minute before our polite smiles hurt and our rootless
conversation slowed to head nods and empty laughter. I volunteered to
make tea but she insisted that was the hostess's duty. Unfortunately,

such was my mood that even this unexpected kindness seemed like a slap in the face—a reminder of my foreignness and incapacity. How bad must a daughter-in-law be, I thought, not even to merit a stern lecture on family rules?

34   Eventually, Ed and Erma came over with Tommy and I felt more at ease. To be strictly proper, I should have sung the "new bride" song in the presence of both my husband and his mother—a kind of ceremonial acceptance of the collar of obedience:

> A risen moon is supposed to shine
> Except through clouds, when it is dim and weak,
> I come young and innocent to be your wife
> Please speak of me kindly in your mother's ear.
> People plant trees to grow big and strong,
> People have children to prosper and protect them.
> I cross my arms and bow my head
> To please my husband and his mother.
> If I do something wrong, please teach me right.
> Don't beat me or scold me in public
> For some will laugh and others will say
> The fist is my husband,
> The tongue is she from whence he came.

35   Instead, Ed put his arm around his mother and told her all about Vietnam, leaving out everything of importance in my black and bloody past—most of which he didn't know himself. Instead, he bragged about his mother's blue-ribbon pies at the Skagit Valley Fair, and I nodded enthusiastically even though I hadn't the slightest idea what pies, blue ribbons, or county fairs really were. After Ed's father died, I learned, Leatha had moved south to California where she took up residence next door to Erma, who shared a house with her husband, Larry, and adult son, Larry Jr., who was seldom around.

36   I saw much more of her pixie-faced daughter, Kathy, a young woman about my age, who lived with her husband in the neighboring town of Santee. Why Leatha didn't move in with her daughter, who had more than enough room and could share housekeeping and cooking chores Vietnamese style, was beyond my understanding. I guessed that Americans loved their possessions so much that even a lonely old woman valued her own TV set, kitchen, bathroom, spare bedrooms, and garage for a car she couldn't drive more than living with a daughter in her sunset years.

37   Anyway, the longing in Leatha's eyes told me that she probably would have traded all her possessions for a little room among her family. Her "children" these days were six little dogs that jumped around like kids and yapped at the TV and pestered you for snacks and atten-

tion whenever you sat down. She even bought canned food for them at the store, which I thought was the height of decadence.

In Vietnam, a dog was a guardian first, then a pet, and sometimes 38
dinner. It fed itself by foraging, not at the family's expense. I chalked up Leatha's behavior to American ignorance, and it helped me feel less like a bumpkin in their magnificent homes. After all, if they knew that the soul of the dog was really a transient spirit (usually a greedy person who had to earn a new human body by suffering a dog's life—most of it spent guarding someone else's wealth), they wouldn't be so quick to put them up on pedestals and deny them penance. I shuddered to think how Leatha's six "children" must have laughed among themselves in dogbark about their naive American mistress.

Ed and Leatha gossiped away the morning until Erma's son, Larry, 39
joined us. I soon felt like a decorative china doll Erma had dubbed me when I arrived—just unwrapped and put on a shelf, worthy of an occasional glance but no conversation. Jet lag (as Ed now explained it) soon caught up with me again and, depressed and exhausted, I bowed and apologized in Vietnamese, which I knew would sound more sincere, and went for a nap, leaving Ed to contend with the kids. I fell asleep wondering how quickly Ed's womenfolk would begin to complain about the "lazy new wife" he had brought to California.

When I awoke, most of our things had been moved from Erma's 40
house to Leatha's. Ed preferred the company of his aged mom to imposing on his sister, and I agreed enthusiastically. Whereas Leatha seemed to look down on me as one of her puppies, Erma just seemed to look down. I was not prepared for this reversal of roles, for the sister-in-law was supposed to be the young bride's ally—someone who would comfort her when the rigors of wife-training got too bad. In America, it seems, who you are is more important than the role society gives you. Even as Ed's wife, though, I did not seem to be worth too much.

That evening, Erma and Larry came over and I tried to help the 41
women fix dinner. Unfortunately, between my ignorance of American kitchens and a strong desire to avoid looking dumber than I had already, I didn't contribute much.

The first thing that astounded me was the refrigerators—a two- 42
door monster that dwarfed our knee-high Vietnamese models—every nook and cranny of which was packed with food! It occurred to me that this was why Americans got so big: the bigger the refrigerators, the bigger the people. I thanked fate or luck or god that Jimmy would now grow up to be twice the size of Anh, his wealthy Vietnamese father. For a second I held a fantasy reunion: me, more rich and beautiful than Lien (Anh's wife who had thrown me out of their mansion when I got pregnant); my mother—plump and queenly as Leatha; and Jimmy—called Phung Quoc Hung in Vietnamese—tall and powerful as an

American Green Beret, stooping to shake his father's little hand. It was a scene that could never come true, although, as everybody said, all things are possible in America.

43   Erma took out a frosty box with the picture of a glowering green giant (no doubt a character from American fables who devoured children who didn't eat their vegetables), then a slab of meat, frozen solid in a little Styrofoam boat covered with plastic.

44   "How we eat this?" I asked as the clumpy peas, hard as marbles, rattled into a pan. I was not ready to live in a country where vegetables and meat were sucked like ice cubes.

45   "Oh, the peas will cook in no time," Erma said, adding water and flipping on her stove's magic, matchless flame. "The round steak we'll have tomorrow. I'll just defrost it in the fridge."

46   Why not just go to the market and get what you want before you eat it? Maybe that was why Americans had to invent frozen food, so they would have something to put in their expensive freezers. Little by little, I was beginning to understand capitalism.

47   We sat down for my first American dinner and I shyly waited to see what everyone else did first. I knew some Americans said prayers for their food, perhaps to honor the dead animal they were about to eat, but this seemed like a silly custom. There was a time for praying and a time for eating. Did those same people say prayers when they did other ordinary things—when they made love or went shopping or relieved themselves? I just didn't understand their reasoning, particularly since Americans didn't seem like a particularly spiritual people. Their houses lacked shrines for their ancestors where prayers were said. Anyway, I was happy to see the Munros reach for the food all at once—"digging in," as Leatha called it—like an Oriental family, as soon as we sat down.

48   My next hurdle was faking the use of their cumbersome eating utensils. In Vietnam, all food was taken with chopsticks or slurped from a bowl. Here, Americans employed as many utensils as the cook had used to prepare the meal. I was sure I'd never master them all, particularly the fork, which everyone held like a pencil, then juggled like acrobats between hands to cut their meat. Why didn't the cook just slice the food into bite-sized strips the way we did in the Orient? I went along with the game as far as I could, grasping my fork like a club and politely smacking my lips very loudly so that Erma and Leatha would know I enjoyed the meal—despite the rich sauces that filled me up after two bites. Fortunately, after a few seconds of this, nobody looked at me anymore and Jimmy and I finished our meal winking and poking each other at the kids' end of the table.

49   After dinner, I wanted to show my new mother-in-law that I could be a good housewife, so I volunteered to do dishes. At first, I was shocked by all the uneaten food. In Vietnam, we believed that the more

food you waste in this life, the hungrier you'll be in the next. Then I remembered the full refrigerator and guessed that if people rationed their food as we did in Vietnam, all the freezers and freezer makers would be out of business and go hungry; so, in America, waste was really thrift. I began scraping the plates into the garbage can and, predictably, Ed came up behind me and laughed his amused-daddy laugh.

"No, no," he said. "Dump the garbage into the sink."   50

"What?" I knew he must be kidding. "You want to clog drain?" I   51
might be new to America, but I wasn't born yesterday.

"It won't get stopped up. Go ahead. Just dump it down the drain.   52
I'll show you some magic."

I peevishly did as he instructed. *Okay, Mister Smart Man, if you want*   53
to play plumber after your supper, that's okay with me!

When a heap of leavings blocked the drain, I turned on the tap and   54
stood back. Sure enough, the water started to rise. Without blinking an
eye, Ed threw a switch over the stove and the pile of sludge became a
shaking, squirting volcano, and miraculously, the pile collapsed and
disappeared. The grinding earthquake became a hum and Ed turned
off the switch. Tap water ran merrily down the drain.

Pale and humiliated—again—I could only look at the floor. Tears   55
came to my eyes.

"Here now," Ed put his arm around me. "I didn't mean to scare   56
you. That's just a garbage disposal. A motor under the sink grinds everything up."

I took the wrapper the peas came in and started to shove it down   57
the monster's rubbery throat.

"No, no," Ed corrected me again.   58

I stopped and blew a wisp of hair from my face.   59

"No paper," Ed warned, "or bones or plastic or anything like that."   60

"But you say put trash in sink!" This American miracle now   61
seemed a little fickle to be real magic.

"No trash. Just soft food."   62

Again, I did as I was told, feeling Erma's critical eyes on my back.   63
With the sink now empty, I could at last get on with washing the dishes—
something even an ignorant Vietnamese farm girl knew quite well how
to do.

"No, no," Ed said when he saw me stacking the dishes in the sink.   64
"Just load them in the dishwasher." He had the same irritating little
smile and I had absolutely no idea if he was making fun of me or trying
to be helpful.

"What you talk about?" I slammed the silverware into the sink. I was   65
getting tired again and my tone was not properly humble and subservient. I looked over my shoulder into the dining room. Erma and Leatha
politely pretended to be absorbed in their coffee and conversation.

66   "Here—" Ed flipped down the big metal door beside the sink. Inside was a queer wire basket. "Just put the dishes here." He demonstrated with a plate.

67   "Okay, but how we wash them when they inside?" It seemed a logical question, but it only made Ed laugh. Under his close supervision, I loaded all the dishes in the stupid machine, wondering how even these mechanically inclined Americans got greasy plates and the tines of their silly, useless forks clean without rags and fingers. When I was finished, he poured some powder into a little box on the door and shut it tight. He punched a few buttons and turned a big dial and the growling noise began again. I thought for a minute that the dishes would be ground up, but the whirring was friendlier this time and I could hear the water splashing.

68   "See?" Ed smiled proudly. "Nothing to it!"

69   "Okay," I replied, "so how long we wait to dry them?" I fished for a dishtowel.

70   Ed laughed again. "You don't have to wait. You wipe the counter and go watch TV!"

71   *Okay—I can do that!* My first long day in America was coming to an end and I was ready to accept anything he said at face value. I decided I wouldn't even ask about the machine that put the dishes away.

✦ *Evaluating the Text*

1. What differences and similarities does Hayslip make the reader aware of that separates her and connects her to her American husband, his family, and her new home?

2. How would you characterize Hayslip's first meeting with her new mother-in-law? How did it differ from what would have taken place in Vietnam?

3. What differences in cultural attitudes emerge from Hayslip's account about how aging is viewed in Vietnamese and in American cultures?

✦ *Exploring Different Perspectives*

1. Discuss Hayslip's trying to adapt to her new home in America in terms of the psychological assumptions elaborated in Edward Said's "Reflections on Exile."

2. How do the accounts by Le Ly Hayslip and Poranee Natadecha-Sponsel ("Individualism as an American Cultural Value") dramatize the difficulties that language causes in cross-cultural communication?

✦ *Extending Viewpoints Through Writing*

1. Describe your own experiences, feelings, and impressions upon meeting your boyfriend or girlfriend's family for the first time. How did you react to each other?

2. Describe a common household appliance or utility as if you were seeing it for the first time: for example, a microwave oven, VCR, television set, popcorn maker, or vacuum cleaner.

3. Have you ever been romantically involved with someone from a completely different ethnic, racial, religious, or political background? Describe your experiences and discuss the kinds of pressures from family and friends to which you were subjected. What was the outcome of this relationship?

4. Describe your experiences moving from one place to another. To what extent did your difficulties in adjusting to a new environment resemble those experienced by Le Ly Hayslip?

Luis Alberto Urrea

Border Story

---◆---

Luis Alberto Urrea was born in Tijuana to an American mother and a Mexican father. He was raised in San Diego and graduated from the University of California in 1977. After working as a film extra, he worked as a volunteer from 1978 to 1982 with Spectrum Ministries, a Protestant organization with headquarters in San Diego that provided food, clothing, and medicine to the poor on the Mexican side of the border. In 1982, he went to Massachusetts, where he taught expository writing at Harvard. He currently lives in Boulder, Colorado. His latest work is a novel entitled In Search of Snow *(1994).* Across the Wire: Life and Hard Times on the Mexican Border *(1993), from which "Border Story" is taken, offers a compassionate and unprecedented account of what life is like for those refugees living on the Mexican side of the border.*

Mexico was inhabited as far back as 20,000 B.C. *Before the arrival of the Spanish in the early sixteenth century, great Indian civilizations, such as the Aztecs and Mayas, flourished. A wave of Spanish explorers, including Hernán Cortés, arrived in the 1500s, overthrew the Aztec empire, and turned Mexico into a colony of Spain, until Mexico achieved its independence in 1821. Although recently Mexico's economy has been on the rebound, previous cycles of economic instability and the earthquake that devastated Mexico City (one of the largest cities in the world with a population of nearly 17 million) in 1985, have led many to cross the border into the United States in hope of finding work.*

In 1988, Carlos Salinas de Gortari was elected president, promising to bring democratic reforms. Legislative elections in 1991 endorsed Gortari's efforts. Mexico, along with Canada and the United States, negotiated the North American Free Trade Agreement (NAFTA), which is intended to reduce tariffs and increase trade between these countries. A new government was formed in 1994 under the leadership of Ernesto Zedillo of the Institutional Revolutionary Party (PRI). Following the devaluation of the peso in December 1994, an emergency economic plan was introduced to reduce inflation and stimulate investment, and it appears to have been successful.

1   When I was younger, I went to war. The Mexican border was the battlefield. There are many Mexicos; there are also many Mexican borders, any one of which could fill its own book. I, and the people with me, fought on a specific front. We sustained injuries and witnessed

deaths. There were machine guns pointed at us, knives, pistols, clubs, even skyrockets. I caught a street-gang member trying to stuff a lit cherry bomb into our gas tank. On the same night, a drunk mariachi opened fire on the missionaries through the wall of his house.

We drove five beat-up vans. We were armed with water, medicine, shampoo, food, clothes, milk, and doughnuts. At the end of a day, like returning veterans from other battles, we carried secrets in our hearts that kept some of us awake at night, gave others dreams and fits of crying. Our faith sustained us—if not in God or "good," then in our work.

Others of us had no room for or interest in such drama, and came away unscathed—and unmoved. Some of us sank into the mindless joy of fundamentalism, some of us drank, some of us married impoverished Mexicans. Most of us took it personally. Poverty *is* personal: it smells and it shocks and it invades your space. You come home dirty when you get too close to the poor. Sometimes you bring back vermin: they hide in your hair, in your underpants, in your intestines. These unpleasant possibilities are a given. They are the price you occasionally have to pay.

In Tijuana and environs, we met the many ambassadors of poverty: lice, scabies, tapeworm, pinworm, ringworm, fleas, crab lice. We met diphtheria, meningitis, typhoid, polio, *turista* (diarrhea), tuberculosis, hepatitis, VD, impetigo, measles, chronic hernia, malaria, whooping cough. We met madness and "demon possession."

These were the products of dirt and disregard—bad things afflicting good people. Their world was far from our world. Still, it would take you only about twenty minutes to get there from the center of San Diego.

For me, the worst part was the lack of a specific enemy. We were fighting a nebulous, all-pervasive *It*. Call it hunger. Call it despair. Call it the Devil, the System, Capitalism, the Cycle of Poverty, the Fruits of the Mexican Malaise. It was a seemingly endless circle of disasters. Long after I'd left, the wheel kept on grinding.

At night, the Border Patrol helicopters swoop and churn in the air all along the line. You can sit in the Mexican hills and watch them herd humans on the dusty slopes across the valley. They look like science fiction crafts, their hard-focused lights raking the ground as they fly.

Borderlands locals are so jaded by the sight of nightly people-hunting that it doesn't even register in their minds. But take a stranger to the border, and she will *see* the spectacle: monstrous Dodge trucks speeding into and out of the landscape; uniformed men patrolling with flashlights, guns, and dogs; spotlights; running figures; lines of people hurried onto buses by armed guards; and the endless clatter of the helicopters with their harsh white beams. A Dutch woman once told me it seemed altogether "un-American."

9   But the Mexicans keep on coming—and the Guatemalans, the Salvadorans, the Panamanians, the Colombians. The seven-mile stretch of Interstate 5 nearest the Mexican border is, at times, so congested with Latin American pedestrians that it resembles a town square.

10   They stick to the center island. Running down the length of the island is a cement wall. If the "illegals" (currently, "undocumented workers"; formerly, "wetbacks") are walking north and a Border Patrol vehicle happens along, they simply hop over the wall and trot south. The officer will have to drive up to the 805 interchange, or Dairy Mart Road, swing over the overpasses, then drive south. Depending on where this pursuit begins, his detour could entail five to ten miles of driving. When the officer finally reaches the group, they hop over the wall and trot north. Furthermore, because freeway arrests would endanger traffic, the Border Patrol has effectively thrown up its hands in surrender.

11   It seems jolly on the page. But imagine poverty, violence, natural disasters, or political fear driving you away from everything you know. Imagine how bad things get to make you leave behind your family, your friends, your lovers; your home, as humble as it might be; your church, say. Let's take it further—you've said good-bye to the graveyard, the dog, the goat, the mountains where you first hunted, your grade school, your state, your favorite spot on the river where you fished and took time to think.

12   Then you come hundred—or thousands—of miles across territory utterly unknown to you. (Chances are, you have never traveled farther than a hundred miles in your life.) You have walked, run, hidden in the backs of trucks, spent part of your precious money on bus fare. There is no AAA or Travelers Aid Society available to you. Various features of your journey north might include police corruption; violence in the forms of beatings, rape, murder, torture, road accidents; theft; incarceration. Additionally, you might experience loneliness, fear, exhaustion, sorrow, cold, heat, diarrhea, thirst, hunger. There is no medical attention available to you. There isn't even Kotex.

13   Weeks or months later, you arrive in Tijuana. Along with other immigrants, you gravitate to the bad parts of town because there is nowhere for you to go in the glittery sections where the *gringos* flock. You stay in a run-down little hotel in the red-light district, or behind the bus terminal. Or you find you way to the garbage dumps, where you throw together a small cardboard nest and claim a few feet of dirt for yourself. The garbage-pickers working this dump might allow you to squat, or they might come and rob you or burn you out for breaking some local rule you cannot possibly know beforehand. Sometimes the dump is controlled by a syndicate, and goon squads might come to you within a day. They want money, and if you can't pay, you must leave or suffer the consequences.

In town, you face endless victimization if you aren't streetwise. The   14
police come after you, street thugs come after you, petty criminals
come after you; strangers try your door at night as you sleep. Many
shady men offer to guide you across the border, and each one wants all
your money now, and promises to meet you at a prearranged spot.
Some of your fellow travelers end their journeys right here—relieved
of their savings and left to wait on a dark corner until they realize they
are going nowhere.

If you are not Mexican, and can't pass as *tijuanense,* a local, the tough   15
guys find you out. Salvadorans and Guatemalans are routinely beaten
up and robbed. Sometimes they are disfigured. Indian—Chinantecas,
Mixtecas, Guasaves, Zapotecas, Mayas—are insulted and pushed
around; often they are lucky—they are merely ignored. They use this to
their advantage. Often they don't dream of crossing into the United
States: a Mexican tribal person would never be able to blend in, and
they know it. To them, the garbage dumps and street vending and begging in Tijuana are a vast improvement over their former lives. As
Doña Paula, a Chinanteca friend of mine who lives at the Tijuana garbage dump, told me, "This is the garbage dump. Take all you need.
There's plenty here for *everyone!*"

If you are a woman, the men come after you. You lock yourself in   16
your room, and when you must leave it to use the pestilential public
bathroom at the end of your floor, you hurry, and you check every
corner. Sometimes the lights are out in the toilet room. Sometimes men
listen at the door. They call you "good-looking" and "bitch" and
"*mamacita,*" and they make kissing sounds at you when you pass.

You're in the worst part of town, but you can comfort yourself—at   17
least there are no death squads here. There are no torturers here, or
bandit land barons riding into your house. This is the last barrier, you
think, between you and the United States—*los Yunaites Estaites.*

You still face police corruption, violence, jail. You now also have a   18
wide variety of new options available to you: drugs, prostitution, white
slavery, crime. Tijuana is not easy on newcomers. It is a city that has always thrived on taking advantage of a sucker. And the innocent are the
ultimate suckers in the Borderlands.

If you have saved up enough money, you go to one of the *coyotes*   19
(people-smugglers), who guide travelers through the violent canyons
immediately north of the border. Lately, these men are also called *polleros,* or "chicken-wranglers. " Some of them are straight, some are land
pirates. Negotiations are tense and strange: *polleros* speak a Spanish
you don't quite understand—like the word *polleros.* Linguists call the
new border-speak "Spanglish," but in Tijuana, Spanglish is mixed with
slang and *pochismos* (the polyglot hip talk of Mexicans infected with
gringoismo; the *cholos* in Mexico, or Chicanos on the American side).

20   Suddenly, the word for "yes," *sí*, can be *simón* or *siról*. "No" is *chale*. "Bike" (*bicicleta*) is *baica*. "Wife" (*esposa*) is *wafia*. "The police" (*la policía*) are *la chota*. "Women" are *rucas* or *morras*. You don't know what they're talking about.

21   You pay them all your money—sometimes it's your family's life-long savings. Five hundred dollars should do it. "*Orale*," the dude tells you, which means "right on." You must wait in Colonia Libertad, the most notorious *barrio* in town, ironically named "Liberty."

22   The scene here is baffling. Music blares from radios. Jolly women at smoky taco stands cook food for the journeys, sell jugs of water. You can see the Border Patrol agents cruising the other side of the fence; they trade insults with the locals.

23   When the appointed hour comes, you join a group of *pollos* (chickens) who scuttle along behind the *coyote*. You crawl under the wires, or, if you go a mile east, you might be amazed to find that the famous American Border Fence simply stops. To enter the United States, you merely step around the end of it. And you follow your guide into the canyons. You might be startled to find groups of individuals crossing the line without *coyotes* leading them at all. You might wonder how they have mastered the canyons, and you might begin to regret the loss of your money.

24   If you have your daughters or mothers or wives with you—or if you are a woman—you become watchful and tense, because rape and gang rape are so common in this darkness as to be utterly unremarkable. If you have any valuables left after your various negotiations, you try to find a sly place to hide them in case you meet *pandilleros* (gang members) or *rateros* (thieves—ratmen). But, really, where can you put anything? Thousands have come before you, and the hiding places are pathetically obvious to robbers: in shoulder bags or clothing rolls, pinned inside clothes, hidden in underwear, inserted in body orifices.

25   If the *coyote* does not turn on you suddenly with a gun and take everything from you himself, you might still be attacked by the *rateros*. If the *rateros* don't get you, there are roving zombies that you can smell from fifty yards downwind—these are the junkies who hunt in shambling packs. If the junkies somehow miss you, there are the *pandilleros*—gang-bangers from either side of the border who are looking for some bloody fun. They adore "taking off" illegals because it's the perfect crime: there is no way they can ever be caught. They are Tijuana *cholos*, or Chicano *vatos*, or Anglo head-bangers.

26   Their sense of fun relies heavily on violence. Gang beatings are their preferred sport, though rape in all its forms in common, as always. Often the *coyote* will turn tail and run at the first sight of *pandilleros*. What's another load of desperate chickens to him? He's just making a living, taking care of business.

If he doesn't run, there is a good chance he will be the first to be as- 27
saulted. The most basic punishment these young toughs mete out is a
good beating, but they might kill him in front of the *pollos* if they feel
the immigrants need a lesson in obedience. For good measure, these
boys—they are mostly *boys,* aged twelve to nineteen, bored with Super
Nintendo and MTV—beat people and slash people and thrash the
women they have just finished raping.

Their most memorable tactic is to hamstring the *coyote* or anyone 28
who dares speak out against them. This entails slicing the muscles in
the victim's legs and leaving him to flop around in the dirt, crippled. If
you are in a group of *pollos* that happens to be visited by these furies,
you are learning border etiquette.

Now, say you are lucky enough to evade all these dangers on your 29
journey. Hazards still await you and your family. You might meet
white racists, complimenting themselves with the tag "Aryans"; they
"patrol" the scrub in combat gear, carrying radios, high-powered flashlights, rifles, and bats. Rattlesnakes hide in bushes—you didn't count
on that complication. Scorpions, tarantulas, black widows. And, of
course, there is the Border Patrol (*la migra*).

They come over the hills on motorcycles, on horses, in huge Dodge 30
Ramcharger four-wheel drives. They yell, wear frightening goggles,
have guns. Sometimes they are surprisingly decent; sometimes they are
too tired or too bored to put much effort into dealing with you. They
collect you in a large group of fellow *pollos,* and a guard (a Mexican
Border Patrol agent!) jokes with your group in Spanish. Some cry, some
sulk, most laugh. Mexicans hate to be rude. You don't know what to
think—some of your fellow travelers take their arrest with aplomb.
Sometimes the officers know their names. But you have been told repeatedly that the Border Patrol sometimes beats or kills people. Everyone talks about the Mexican girl molested inside its building.

The Border Patrol puts you into trucks that take you to buses that 31
take you to compounds that load you onto other buses that transport
you back to Tijuana and put you out. Your *coyote* isn't bothered in the
least. Some of the regulars who were with you go across and get
brought back a couple of times a night. But for you, things are different.
You have been brought back with no place to sleep. You have already
spent all your money. You might have been robbed, so you have only
your clothes—maybe not all of them. The robbers may have taken your
shoes. You might be bloodied from a beating by *pandilleros,* or an "accident" in the Immigration and Naturalization Service compound. You
can't get proper medical attention. You can't eat, or afford to feed your
family. Some of your compatriots have been separated from their wives
or their children. Now their loved ones are in the hands of strangers, in

the vast and unknown United States. The Salvadorans are put on planes and flown back to the waiting arms of the military. As you walk through the cyclone fence, back into Tijuana, the locals taunt you and laugh at your misfortune.

32　　　If you were killed, you have nothing to worry about.

33　　　Now what?

34　　　Perhaps you'll join one of the other groups that break through the Tortilla Curtain every night. The road-runners. They amass at dusk along the cement canal that separates the United States from Mexico. This wide alley is supposedly the Tijuana River, but it's usually dry, or running with sewage that Tijuana pumps toward the U.S. with great gusto.

35　　　As soon as everybody feels like it—there are no *coyotes* needed here—you join the groups passing through the gaping holes in the fence. Houses and alleys and cantinas back up against it, and in some spots, people have driven stolen cars into the poles to provide a wider passage. You rush across the canal and up the opposite slope, timing your dash between passing *migra* trucks and the overflights of helicopters. Following the others, you begin your jog toward the freeway. Here, there are mostly just Border Patrol officers to outrun—not that hard if you're in good shape. There are still some white-supremacist types bobbling around, but the cops will get them if they do anything serious. No, here the problem is the many lanes of I-5.

36　　　You stand at the edge of the road and wonder how you're going to cut across five lanes of traffic going sixty miles an hour. Then, there is the problem of the next five lanes. The freeway itself is constructed to run parallel to the border, then swing north. Its underpasses and storm-drain pipes offer another subterranean world, but you don't know about them. All you know is you have to get across at some point, and get far from the hunters who would take you back.

37　　　If you hang around the shoulder of I-5 long enough, you will find that many of your companions don't make it. So many have been killed and injured that the *gringos* have put up warning signs to motorists to watch for running people. The orange signs show a man, a woman, and a child charging across. Some *gringos* are so crazy with hate for you that they speed up, or aim for you as you run.

38　　　The vague blood of over a hundred slain runners shadows the concrete.

39　　　On either side of the border, clustered near the gates, there are dapper-looking men, dressed in nice cowboy clothes, and they speak without looking anyone in the eye. They are saying, "Los Angeles, San Bernardino, San Francisco."

They have a going concern: business is good. 40

Once you've gotten across the line, there will always be the question of *Where do I go now?* "Illegal aliens" have to eat, sleep, find work. Once across, you must begin another journey. 41

Not everyone has the energy to go on. Even faith—in Jesus, the Virgin Mary, or the Streets of Gold—breaks down sooner or later. Many of these immigrants founder at the border. There is a sad swirl of humanity in Tijuana. Outsiders eddy there who have simply run out of strength. If North America does not want them, Tijuana wants them even less. They become the outcasts of an outcast region. We could all see them if we looked hard enough: they sell chewing gum. Their children sing in traffic. In bars downtown, the women will show us a breast for a quarter. They wash our windshields at every stoplight. But mostly, they are invisible. To see them, we have to climb up the little canyons all around the city, where the cardboard shacks and mud and smoke look like a lost triptych by Hieronymus Bosch. We have to wade into the garbage dumps and the orphanages, sit in the little churches and the hospitals, or go out into the back country, where they raise their goats and bake red bricks and try to live decent lives. 42

They are not welcome in Tijuana. And, for the most part, Tijuana itself is not welcome in the Motherland. Tijuana is Mexico's cast-off child. She brings in money and *gringos,* but nobody would dare claim her. As a Mexican diplomat once confided to me, "We both know Tijuana is not Mexico. The border is nowhere. It's a no-man's-land." 43

I was born there. 44

My Story

I was born in Tijuana, to a Mexican father and an American mother. I was registered with the U.S. government as an American Citizen, Born Abroad. Raised in San Diego, I crossed the border all through my boyhood with abandon, utterly bilingual and bicultural. In 1977, my father died on the border, violently. (The story is told in detail in a chapter entitled "Father's Day.") 45

In the Borderlands, anything can happen. And if you're in Tijuana long enough, anything *will* happen. Whole neighborhoods appear and disappear seemingly overnight. For example, when I was a boy, you got into Tijuana by driving through the Tijuana River itself. It was a muddy floodplain bustling with animals and belching old cars. A slum that spread across the riverbed was known as "Cartolandia." In borderspeak, this meant "Land of Cardboard." 46

Suddenly, it was time for Tijuana to spruce up its image to attract more American dollars, and Cartolandia was swept away by a flash 47 flood of tractors. The big machines swept down the length of the river, crushing shacks and toppling fences. It was like magic. One week, there were choked multitudes of sheds; the next, a clear, flat space awaiting the blank concrete of a flood channel. Town—no town.

48   The inhabitants of Cartolandia fled to the outskirts, where they were better suited to Tijuana's new image as Shopping Mecca. They had effectively vanished. Many of them homesteaded the Tijuana municipal garbage dump. The city's varied orphanages consumed many of their children.

49   Tijuana's characteristic buzz can be traced directly to a mixture of dread and expectation: there's always something coming.

50   I never intended to be a missionary. I didn't go to church, and I had no reason to believe I'd be involved with a bunch of Baptists. But in 1978, I had occasion to meet a remarkable preacher known as Pastor Von (Erhardt George von Trutzschler III, no less): as well as being a minister, he was a veteran of the Korean War, a graphic artist, a puppeteer, a German baron, an adventurer, and a practical joker. Von got me involved in the hardships and discipline he calls "Christian Boot Camp."

51   After working as a youth pastor in San Diego for many years, he had discovered Mexico in the late sixties. His work there began with the typical church do-good activities that everyone has experienced at least once: a bag of blankets for the orphans, a few Christmas toys, alms for the poor. As Protestantism spread in Mexico, however, interest in Von's preaching grew. Small churches and Protestant orphanages and Protestant *barrios*, lacking ministers of their own, began asking Von to teach. Preaching and pastoring led to more work; work led to more needs; more needs pulled in more workers. On it went until Von had put in thirty or so years slogging through the Borderlands mud, and his little team of die-hard renegades and border rats had grown to a nonprofit corporation (Spectrum Ministries, Inc.), where you'll find him today.

52   Von's religious ethic is similar in scope to Teresa of Calcutta's. Von favors actual works over heavy evangelism. Spectrum is based on a belief Christians call "living the gospel." This doctrine is increasingly rare in America, since it involves little lip service, hard work, and no glory.

53   Von often reminds his workers that they are "ambassadors of Christ" and should comport themselves accordingly. Visitors are indelicately stripped of their misconceptions and prejudices when they discover that the crust on Von and his crew is a mile thick: the sight of teenybopper Bible School girls enduring Von's lurid pretrip briefing is priceless. Insouciantly, he offers up his litany: lice, worms, pus, blood; diarrhea, rattletrap outhouses, no toilet paper; dangerous water and food; diseased animals that will leave you with scabies; rats, maggots, flies; *odor*. Then he confuses them by demanding love and respect for

the poor. He caps his talk with: "Remember—you are not going to the zoo. These are people. Don't run around snapping pictures of them like they're animals. Don't rush into their shacks saying, 'Ooh, gross!' They live there. Those are their homes."

Because border guards often "confiscate" chocolate milk, the car- 54 tons must be smuggled into Mexico under bags of clothes. Because the floors of the vans get so hot, the milk will curdle, so the crew must first freeze it. The endless variations of challenge in the Borderlands keep Von constantly alert—problems come three at a time and must be solved on the run.

Like the time a shipment of tennis shoes was donated to Spectrum. 55 They were new, white, handsome shoes. The only problem was that no two shoes in the entire shipment matched. Von knew there was no way the Mexican kids could use *one* shoe, and they—like teens everywhere— were fashion-conscious and wouldn't be caught dead in unmatching sneakers.

Von's solution was practical and witty. He donned unmatched 56 shoes and made his crew members wear unmatched shoes. Then he an- nounced that it was the latest California surfer rage; kids in California weren't considered hip unless they wore unmatched shoes. The ship- ment was distributed, and shoeless boys were shod in the *faux* fashion craze begun by Chez Von.

Von has suffered for his beliefs. In the ever more conservative at- 57 mosphere of American Christianity (read: Protestantism), the efforts of Spectrum have come under fire on several occasions. He was once de- nounced because he refused to use the King James Bible in his sermons— clearly the sign of a heretic.

Von's terse reply to criticism: "It's hard to 'save' people when 58 they're dead."

Von has a Monday night ministerial run into Tijuana, and in his 59 heyday, he was hitting three or four orphanages a night. I was curious, unaware of the severity of the poverty in Tijuana. I knew it was there, but it didn't really mean anything to me. One night, in late October 1978, my curiosity got the better of me. I didn't believe Von could show me anything about my hometown that I didn't know. I was wrong. I quickly began to learn just how little I really knew.

He managed to get me involved on the first night. Actually, it was 60 Von and a little girl named América. América lived in one of the or- phanages barely five miles from my grandmother's house in the hills above Tijuana.

She had light hair and blue eyes like mine—she could have been 61 my cousin. When she realized I spoke Spanish, she clutched my fingers and chattered for an hour without a break. She hung on harder when Von announced it was time to go. She begged me not to leave. América resorted to a tactic many orphanage children master to keep visitors from leaving—she wrapped her legs around my calf and sat on my foot. As I peeled her off, I promised to return on Von's next trip.

62   He was waiting for me in the alley behind the orphanage.

63   "What did you say to that girl?" he asked.

64   "I told her I'd come back next week."

65   He glared at me. "Don't *ever* tell one of my kids you're coming back," he snapped. "Don't you know she'll wait all week for you? Then she'll wait for months. Don't say it if you don't mean it."

66   "I mean it!" I said.

67   I went back the next time to see her. Then again. And, of course, there were other places to go before we got to América's orphanage, and there were other people to talk to after we left. Each location had people waiting with messages and questions to translate. It didn't take long for Von to approach me with a proposition. It seemed he had managed the impressive feat of spending a lifetime in Mexico without picking up any Spanish at all. Within two months, I was Von's personal translator.

68   It is important to note that translation is often more delicate an art than people assume. For example, Mexicans are regularly amused to read *TV Guide* listings for Spanish-language TV stations. If one were to leave the tilde (~) off the word años, or "years," the word becomes the plural for "anus." Many cheap laughs are had when "The Lost Years" becomes "The Lost Butt Holes."

69   It was clear that Von needed reliable translating. Once, when he had arranged a summer camping trip for *barrio* children, he'd written a list of items the children needed to take. A well-meaning woman on the team translated the list for Von, and they Xeroxed fifty or sixty copies.

70   The word for "comb" in Spanish is *peine,* but leave out a letter, and the word takes on a whole new meaning. Von's note, distributed to every child and all their families, read:

> You must bring CLEAN CLOTHES
> TOOTH PASTE
> SOAP
> TOOTHBRUSH
> SLEEPING BAG
> and BOYS—You Must Remember
> to BRING YOUR PENIS!

71   Von estimates that in a ten-year period his crew drove several *million* miles in Mexico without serious incident. Over five-hundred people came and went as crew members. They transported more than sixty thousand visitors across the border.

72   In my time with him, I saw floods and three hundred-mile-wide prairie fires, car wrecks and gang fights, monkeys and blood and shit. I

saw human intestines and burned flesh. I saw human fat through deep red cuts. I saw people copulating. I saw animals tortured. I saw birthday parties in the saddest sagging shacks. I looked down throats and up wombs with flashlights. I saw lice, rats, dying dogs, rivers black with pollywogs, and a mound of maggots three feet wide and two feet high. One little boy in the back country cooked himself with an overturned pot of boiling *frijoles;* when I asked him if it hurt, he sneered like Pancho Villa and said, "Nah." A maddened Pentecostal tried to heal our broken-down van by laying hands on the engine block. One girl who lived in a brickyard accidentally soaked her dress in diesel fuel and lit herself on fire. When I went in the shed, she was standing there, naked, her entire front burned dark brown and red. The only part of her not burned was her vulva; it was a startling cleft, a triangular island of white in a sea of burns.

I saw miracles, too. A boy named Chispi, deep in a coma induced 73 by spinal meningitis, suffered a complete shutdown of one lobe of his brain. The doctors in the intensive care unit, looking down at his naked little body hard-wired to banks of machinery and pumps, just shook their heads. He was doomed to be a vegetable, at best. His mother, fished out of the cantinas in Tijuana's red-light district, spent several nights sitting in the hospital cafeteria sipping vending-machine coffee and telling me she hoped there were miracles left for people like her.

Chispi woke up. The machines were blipping and pinging, and he 74 sat up and asked for Von. His brain had regenerated itself. They unhitched him, pulled out the catheters, and pulled the steel shunt out of his skull. He went home. There was no way anybody could explain it. Sometimes there were happy endings, and you spent as much time wondering about them as grieving over the tragedies.

God help me—it was fun. It was exciting and nasty. I strode, fear- 75 less, through the Tijuana garbage dumps and the Barrio of Shallow Graves. I was doing good deeds, and the goodness thrilled me. But the squalor, too, thrilled me. Each stinking gray *barrio* gave me a wicked charge. I was arrested one night by Tijuana cops; I was so terrified that my knees wobbled like Jell-O. After they let me go, I was happy for a week. Mexican soldiers pointed machine guns at my testicles. I thought I was going to die. Later, I was so relieved, I laughed about it for days. Over the years, I was cut, punctured, sliced: I love my scars. I had girlfriends in every village, in every orphanage, at each garbage dump. For a time, I was a hero. And at night, when we returned, caked in dried mud, smelly, exhausted, and the good Baptists of Von's church looked askance at us, we felt dangerous. The housewives, grandmothers, fundamentalists, rock singers, bikers, former drug dealers, schoolgirls, leftists, republicans, jarheads, and I were all transformed into *The Wild Bunch.*

It added a certain flair to my dating life as well. It was not uncom- 76 mon for a Mexican crisis to track me down in the most unlikely places.

I am reminded of the night I was sitting down to a fancy supper at a woman's apartment when the phone rang. A busload of kids from one of our orphanages had flipped over, killing the American daughter of the youth minister in charge of the trip. All the *gringos* had been arrested. The next hour was spent calling Tijuana cops, Mexican lawyers, cousins in Tijuana, and Von. I had to leave early to get across the border.

77   Incredibly, in the wake of this tragedy, the orphanage kids were taken to the beach by yet another *gringo* church group, and one of the boys was hit by a car and killed.

78   My date was fascinated by all this, no doubt.

79   Slowly, it became obvious that nobody outside the experience understood it. Only among ourselves was hunting for lice in each other's hair considered a nice thing. Nobody but us found humor in the appalling things we saw. No one else wanted to discuss the particulars of our bowel movements. By firsthand experience, we had become diagnosticians in the area of gastrointestinal affliction. Color and content spoke volumes to us: pale, mucus-heavy ropes of diarrhea suggested amoebas. Etc.

80   One of Von's pep talks revolved around the unconscionable wealth in the United States. "Well," he'd say to some unsuspecting *gringo,* "you're probably not rich. You probably don't even have a television. Oh, you *do?* You have three televisions? One in each room? Wow. But surely you don't have furniture? You do? Living room furniture and beds in the bedrooms? Imagine that!

81   "But you don't have a floor, do you? Do you have carpets? Four walls? A roof! What do you use for light—candles? *Lamps!* No way. Lamps.

82   "How about your kitchen—do you have a stove?"

83   He'd pick his way through the kitchen: the food, the plates and pots and pans, the refrigerator, the ice. Ice cream. Soda. Booze. The closets, the clothes in the closets. Then to the bathroom and the miracle of indoor plumbing. Whoever lived in that house suddenly felt obscenely rich.

84   I was never able to reach Von's level of commitment. The time he caught scabies, he allowed it to flourish in order to grasp the suffering of those from whom it originated. He slept on the floor because the majority of the world's population could not afford a bed.

✦ *Evaluating the Text*

1. What impression do you get of the narrator's personal involvement in the conditions he describes? Why was he there, and what did he hope to accomplish?

2. How does Urrea's description of what it feels like to be in the situation of those he describes make it possible to empathize with them? What details did you find especially effective in communicating this experience?

3. What are some of the dangers one faces that might be encountered when crossing the border? What future awaits those who turn back?

✦ Exploring Different Perspectives

1. How are the circumstances different for the would-be immigrants in Urrea's account from those of Le Ly Hayslip (see "Yearning to Breathe Free")?

2. Compare and contrast the accounts by Luis Alberto Urrea and William M. Kephart in terms of the marginal existence of the respective ethnic groups they describe.

✦ Extending Viewpoints Through Writing

1. Have you or a member of your family ever had to relocate from one country to another? Was the situation physically or psychologically similar to the one Urrea describes?

2. Putting yourself in the same situation, after reading Urrea's description of the dangers that might befall one trying to cross the border, would you take the chance if you already knew what might await you? Why or why not?

Poranee Natadecha-Sponsel

Individualism as an American Cultural Value

◆

Poranee Natadecha-Sponsel was born and raised in a multiethnic Thai and Malay region in the southern part of Thailand. She received her B.A. with honors in English and philosophy from Chulalongkorn University in Bangkok, Thailand, in 1969. She has lived in the United States for over fifteen years, earning her M.A. in philosophy at Ohio University, in Athens, in 1973 and her Ed.D. in 1991 from the University of Hawaii at Manoa. She currently teaches interdisciplinary courses in women's studies and coordinates the mentoring program for new women faculty at the University of Hawaii at Manoa.

1   "Hi, how are you?" "Fine, thank you, and you?" These are greetings that everybody in America hears and says every day—salutations that come ready-made and packaged just like a hamburger and fries. There is no real expectation for any special information in response to these greetings. Do not, under any circumstances, take up anyone's time by responding in depth to the programmed query. What or how you may feel at the moment is of little, if any, importance. Thai people would immediately perceive that our concerned American friends are truly interested in our welfare, and this concern would require polite reciprocation by spelling out the details of our current condition. We become very disappointed when we have had enough experience in the United States to learn that we have bored, amused, or even frightened many of our American acquaintances by taking the greeting "How are you?" so literally. We were reacting like Thai, but in the American context where salutations have a different meaning, our detailed reactions were inappropriate. In Thai society, a greeting among acquaintances usually requests specific information about the other person's condition, such as "Where are you going?" or "Have you eaten?"

2   One of the American contexts in which this greeting is most confusing and ambiguous is at the hospital or clinic. In these sterile and ritualistic settings, I have always been uncertain exactly how to answer when the doctor or nurse asks "How are you?" If I deliver a packaged answer of "Fine," I wonder if I am telling a lie. After all, I am there in

(For additional information about Thailand, see p. 252.)

the first place precisely because I am not so fine. Finally, after debating for some time, I asked one nurse how she expected a patient to answer the query "How are you?" But after asking this question, I then wondered if it was rude to do so. However, she looked relieved after I explained to her that people from different cultures have different ways to greet other people and that for me to be asked how I am in the hospital results in awkwardness. Do I simply answer, "Fine, thank you," or do I reveal in accurate detail how I really feel at the moment? My suspicion was verified when the nurse declared that "How are you?" was really no more than a polite greeting and that she didn't expect any answer more elaborate than simply "Fine." However, she told me that some patients do answer her by describing every last ache and pain from which they are suffering.

A significant question that comes to mind is whether the verbal pattern of greetings reflects any social relationship in American culture. The apparently warm and sincere greeting may initially suggest interest in the person, yet the intention and expectations are, to me, quite superficial. For example, most often the person greets you quickly and then walks by to attend to other business without even waiting for your response! This type of greeting is just like a package of American fast food! The person eats the food quickly without enjoying the taste. The convenience is like many other American accoutrements of living such as cars, household appliances, efficient telephones, or simple, systematic, and predictable arrangements of groceries in the supermarket. However, usually when this greeting is delivered, it seems to lack a personal touch and genuine feeling. It is little more than ritualized behavior.

I have noticed that most Americans keep to themselves even at social gatherings. Conversation may revolve around many topics, but little, if anything, is revealed about oneself. Without talking much about oneself and not knowing much about others, social relations seem to remain at an abbreviated superficial level. How could one know a person without knowing something about him or her? How much does one need to know about a person to really know that person?

After living in this culture for more than a decade, I have learned that there are many topics that should not be mentioned in conversations with American acquaintances or even close friends. One's personal life and one's income are considered to be very private and even taboo topics. Unlike my Thai culture, Americans do not show interest or curiosity by asking such personal questions, especially when one just meets the individual for the first time. Many times I have been embarrassed by my Thai acquaintances who recently arrived at the University of Hawaii and the East-West Center. For instance, one day I was walking on campus with an American friend when we met another Thai woman to whom I had been introduced a few days earlier. The

Thai woman came to write her doctoral dissertation at the East-West Center where the American woman worked, so I introduced them to each other. The American woman greeted my Thai companion in Thai language, which so impressed her that she felt immediately at ease. At once, she asked the American woman numerous personal questions such as, How long did you live in Thailand? Why were you there? How long were you married to the Thai man? Why did you divorce him? How long have you been divorced? Are you going to marry a Thai again or an American? How long have you been working here? How much do you earn? The American was stunned. However, she was very patient and more or less answered all those questions as succinctly as she could. I was so uncomfortable that I had to interrupt whenever I could to get her out of the awkward situation in which she had been forced into talking about things she considered personal. For people in Thai society, such questions would be appropriate and not considered too personal let alone taboo.

6   The way Americans value their individual privacy continues to impress me. Americans seem to be open and yet there is a contradiction because they are also aloof and secretive. This is reflected in many of their behavior patterns. By Thai standards, the relationship between friends in American society seems to be somewhat superficial. Many Thai students, as well as other Asians, have felt that they could not find genuine friendship with Americans. For example, I met many American classmates who were very helpful and friendly while we were in the same class. We went out, exchanged phone calls, and did the same things as would good friends in Thailand. But those activities stopped suddenly when the semester ended.

7   Privacy as a component of the American cultural value of individualism is nurtured in the home as children grow up. From birth they are given their own individual, private space, a bedroom separate from that of their parents. American children are taught to become progressively independent, both emotionally and economically, from their family. They learn to help themselves at an early age. In comparison, in Thailand, when parents bring a new baby home from the hospital, it shares the parents' bedroom for two to three years and then shares another bedroom with older siblings of the same sex. Most Thai children do not have their own private room until they finish high school, and some do not have their own room until another sibling moves out, usually when the sibling gets married. In Thailand, there are strong bonds within the extended family. Older siblings regularly help their parents to care for younger ones. In this and other ways, the Thai family emphasizes the interdependence of its members.

8   I was accustomed to helping Thai babies who fell down to stand up again. Thus, in America when I saw babies fall, it was natural for me to try to help them back on their feet. Once at a summer camp for East-West Center participants, one of the supervisors brought his wife and

their ten-month-old son with him. The baby was so cute that many students were playing with him. At one point he was trying to walk and fell, so all the Asian students, males and females, rushed to help him up. Although the father and mother were nearby, they paid no attention to their fallen and crying baby. However, as the students were trying to help and comfort him, the parents told them to leave him alone; he would be all right on his own. The baby did get up and stopped crying without any assistance. Independence is yet another component of the American value of individualism.

Individualism is even reflected in the way Americans prepare, serve, and consume food. In a typical American meal, each person has a separate plate and is not supposed to share or taste food from other people's plates. My Thai friends and I are used to eating Thai style, in which you share food from a big serving dish in the middle of the table. Each person dishes a small amount from the serving dish onto his or her plate and finishes this portion before going on with the next portion of the same or a different serving dish. With the Thai pattern of eating, you regularly reach out to the serving dishes throughout the meal. But this way of eating is not considered appropriate in comparison to the common American practice where each person eats separately from his or her individual plate.

One time my American host, a divorcée who lived alone, invited a Thai girlfriend and myself to an American dinner at her home. When we were reaching out and eating a small portion of one thing at a time in Thai style, we were told to dish everything we wanted onto our plates at one time and that it was not considered polite to reach across the table. The proper American way was to have each kind of food piled up on your plate at once. If we were to eat in the same manner in Thailand, eyebrows would have been raised at the way we piled up food on our plates, and we would have been considered to be eating like pigs, greedy and inconsiderate of others who shared the meal at the table.

Individualism as a pivotal value in American culture is reflected in many other ways. Material wealth is not only a prime status marker in American society but also a guarantee and celebration of individualism—wealth allows the freedom to do almost anything, although usually within the limits of law. The pursuit of material wealth through individual achievement is instilled in Americans from the youngest age. For example, I was surprised to see an affluent American couple, who own a large ranch house and two BMW cars, send their nine-year-old son to deliver newspapers. He has to get up very early each morning to deliver the papers, even on Sunday! During summer vacation, the boy earns additional money by helping in his parents' gift shop from 10 A.M. to 5 P.M. His thirteen-year-old sister often earns money by babysitting, even at night.

In Thailand, only children from poorer families work to earn money to help the household. Middle- and high-income parents do not encourage their children to work until after they have finished their education. They provide economic support in order to free their children to concentrate on and excel in their studies. Beyond the regular schooling, families who can afford it pay for special tutoring as well as training in music, dance, or sports. However, children in low- and middle-income families help their parents with household chores and the care of younger children.

13   Many American children have been encouraged to get paid for their help around the house. They rarely get any gifts free of obligations. They even have to be good to get Santa's gifts at Christmas! As they grow up, they are conditioned to earn things they want; they learn that "there is no such thing as a free lunch." From an early age, children are taught to become progressively independent economically from their parents. Also, most young people are encouraged to leave home at college age to be on their own. From my viewpoint as a Thai, it seems that American family ties and closeness are not as strong as in Asian families whose children depend on family financial support until joining the work force after college age. Thereafter, it is the children's turn to help support their parents financially.

14   Modern American society and economy emphasize individualism in other ways. The nuclear family is more common than the extended family, and newlyweds usually establish their own independent household rather than initially living with either the husband's or the wife's parents. Parents and children appear to be close only when the children are very young. Most American parents seem to "lose" their children by the teenage years. They don't seem to belong to each other as closely as do Thai families. Even though I have seen more explicit affectionate expression among American family members than among Asian ones, the close interpersonal spirit seems to be lacking. Grandparents have relatively little to do with the grandchildren on any regular basis, in contrast to the extended family, which is more common in Thailand. The family and society seem to be graded by age to the point that grandparents, parents, and children are separated by generational subcultures that are evidently alienated from one another. Each group "does its own thing." Help and support are usually limited to whatever does not interfere with one's own life. In America, the locus of responsibility is more on the individual than on the family.

15   In one case I know of, a financially affluent grandmother with Alzheimer's disease is taken care of twenty-four hours a day by hired help in her own home. Her daughter visits and relieves the helper occasionally. The mature granddaughter, who has her own family, rarely visits. Yet they all live in the same neighborhood. However, each lives in a different house, and each is very independent. Although the mother worries about the grandmother, she cannot do much. Her husband also needs her, and she divides her time between him, her daugh-

ters and their children, and the grandmother. When the mother needs to go on a trip with her husband, a second hired attendant is required to care for the grandmother temporarily. When I asked why the granddaughter doesn't temporarily care for the grandmother, the reply was that she has her own life, and it would not be fair for the granddaughter to take care of the grandmother, even for a short period of time. Yet I wonder if it is fair for the grandmother to be left out. It seems to me that the value of individualism and its associated independence account for these apparent gaps in family ties and support.

In contrast to American society, in Thailand older parents with a long-term illness are asked to move in with their children and grandchildren if they are not already living with them. The children and grandchildren take turns attending to the grandparent, sometimes with help from live-in maids. Living together in the same house reinforces moral support among the generations within an extended family. The older generation is respected because of the previous economic, social, and moral support for their children and grandchildren. Family relations provide one of the most important contexts for being a "morally good person," which is traditionally the principal concern in the Buddhist society of Thailand.   16

In America, being young, rich, and/or famous allows one greater freedom and independence and thus promotes the American value of individualism. This is reflected in the mass appeal of major annual television events like the Super Bowl and the Academy Awards. The goal of superachievement is also seen in more mundane ways. For example, many parents encourage their children to take special courses and to work hard to excel in sports as a shortcut to becoming rich and famous. I know one mother who has taken her two sons to tennis classes and tournaments since the boys were six years old, hoping that at least one of them will be a future tennis star like Ivan Lendl. Other parents focus their children on acting, dancing, or musical talent. The children have to devote much time and hard work as well as sacrifice the ordinary activities of youth in order to develop and perform their natural talents and skills in prestigious programs. But those who excel in the sports and entertainment industries can become rich and famous, even at an early age, as for example Madonna, Tom Cruise, and Michael Jackson. Television and other media publicize these celebrities and thereby reinforce the American value of individualism, including personal achievement and financial success.   17

Although the American cultural values of individualism and the aspiration to become rich and famous have had some influence in Thailand, there is also cultural and religious resistance to these values. Strong social bonds, particularly within the extended family, and the hierarchical structure of the kingdom run counter to individualism. Also, youth gain social recognition through their academic achievement.   18

From the perspective of Theravada Buddhism, which strongly influences Thai culture, aspiring to be rich and famous would be an illustration of greed, and those who have achieved wealth and fame do not celebrate it publicly as much as in American society. Being a good, moral person is paramount, and ideally Buddhists emphasize restraint and moderation.

19   Beyond talent and skill in the sports and entertainment industries, there are many other ways that young Americans can pursue wealth. Investment is one route. One American friend who is only a sophomore in college has already invested heavily in the stock market to start accumulating wealth. She is just one example of the 1980s trend for youth to be more concerned with their individual finances than with social, political, and environmental issues. With less attention paid to public issues, the expression of individualism seems to be magnified through emphasis on lucrative careers, financial investment, and material consumption—the "Yuppie" phenomenon. This includes new trends in dress, eating, housing (condominiums), and cars (expensive European imports). Likewise, there appears to be less of a long-term commitment to marriage. More young couples are living together without either marriage or plans for future marriage. When such couples decide to get married, prenuptial agreements are made to protect their assets. Traditional values of marriage, family, and sharing appear to be on the decline.

20   Individualism as one of the dominant values in American culture is expressed in many ways. This value probably stems from the history of the society as a frontier colony of immigrants in search of a better life with independence, freedom, and the opportunity for advancement through personal achievement. However, in the beliefs and customs of any culture there are some disadvantages as well as advantages. Although Thais may admire the achievements and material wealth of American society, there are costs, especially in the value of individualism and associated social phenomena.

✦ Evaluating the Text

1. For the Thais, what are the kinds of private topics about which it would be rude to inquire? How do these differ from the topics that are taboo among Americans?

2. How do concepts of friendship and privacy differ in Natadecha-Sponsel's experience with the Thai and American cultures?

3. How do the examples involving the child who has fallen, the way food is served and eaten, and the newspaper route provide the author with significant insights into American cultural values? Do you agree with her interpretations?

✦ Exploring Different Perspectives

1. How do the accounts by Le Ly Hayslip ("Yearning to Breathe Free") and Poranee Natadecha-Sponsel dramatize the kinds of language problems immigrants face in everyday conversation?

2. To what extent does Buddhism fail to provide guidance for immigrants in American culture in the accounts by Poranee Natadecha-Sponsel and Le Ly Hayslip ("Yearning to Breathe Free")?

✦ Extending Viewpoints Through Writing

1. How do concepts of the care of the elderly and Buddhist philosophy provide strikingly different models for behavior in Thailand and in the United States? What incidents in your own experience illustrate the value placed on individualism in American culture, a value that those from other cultures might find strange?

Gloria Anzaldúa

Cervicide

◆

Gloria Anzaldúa is a Chicana poet and fiction writer who grew up in south Texas. She has edited several highly praised anthologies. This Bridge Called My Back: Writings by Radical Women of Color *won the 1986 Before Columbus Foundation American Book Award.* Borderlands—La Frontera, the New Mestiza *was selected as one of the best books of 1987 by* Library Journal. *Her recent work includes* Making Face, Making Soul *(1990),* La Prieta *(1991), and a children's book,* Friends from the Other Side *(1993). She has been a contributing editor for* Sinister Wisdom *since 1984 and has taught Chicano studies, feminist studies, and creative writing at the University of Texas at Austin, San Francisco State University, and the University of California, Santa Cruz. "Cervicide" first appeared in* Labyris *(vol. 4, no. 11, Winter 1983). In it, Anzaldúa tells the poignant story of a Mexican-American family living on the Texas border who are forced to kill a pet deer whose detection by the game warden would result in an unaffordable fine or the father's imprisonment.*

1   *La venadita.* The small fawn. They had to kill their pet, the fawn. The game warden was on the way with his hounds. The penalty for being caught in possession of a deer was $250 or jail. The game warden would put *su papí en la cárcel.*

2   How could they get rid of the fawn? Hide it? No, *la guardia's* hounds would sniff Venadita out. Let Venadita loose in the *monte?* They had tried that before. The fawn would leap away and seconds later return. Should they kill Venadita? The mother and Prieta looked toward *las carabinas* propped against the wall behind the kitchen door—the shiny barrel of the .22, the heavy metal steel of the 40-40. No, if *they* could hear his pickup a mile and a half down the road, he would hear the shot.

3   Quick, they had to do something. Cut Venadita's throat? Club her to death? The mother couldn't do it. She, Prieta, would have to be the one. The game warden and his *perros* were a mile down the road. Prieta loved her *papí.*

Cervicide—the killing of a deer. In archetypal symbology the Self appears as a deer for women.
su papí en la cárcel—her father in jail.
monte—the woods.
Prieta—literally one who is dark-skinned, a nickname.

496

In the shed behind the corral, where they'd hidden the fawn, Prieta   4
found the hammer. She had to grasp it with both hands. She swung it
up. The weight folded her body backwards. A thud reverberated on
Venadita's skull, a wave undulated down her back. Again, a blow behind the ear. Though Venadita's long lashes quivered, her eyes never
left Prieta's face. Another thud, another tremor. *La guardia* and his
hounds were driving up the front yard. The *venadita* looked up at her,
the hammer rose and fell. Neither made a sound. The tawny, spotted
fur was the most beautiful thing Prieta had ever seen. She remembered
when they had found the fawn. She had been a few hours old. A hunter
had shot her mother. The fawn had been shaking so hard, her long thin
legs were on the edge of buckling. Prieta and her sister and brothers
had bottle-fed Venadita, with a damp cloth had wiped her skin, had
watched her tiny, perfectly formed hooves harden and grow.

Prieta dug a hole in the shed, a makeshift hole. She could hear the   5
warden talking to her mother. Her mother's English had suddenly gotten bad—she was trying to stall *la guardia*. Prieta rolled the fawn into
the hole, threw in the empty bottle. With her fingers raked in the dirt.
Dust caked on her arms and face where tears had fallen. She patted the
ground flat with her hands and swept it with a dead branch. The game
warden was strutting toward her. His hounds sniffing, sniffing, sniffing the ground in the shed. The hounds pawing pawing the ground.
The game warden, straining on the leashes *les dio un tirón, sacó los perros.* He inspected the corrals, the edge of the woods, then drove away in
his pickup.

✦ Evaluating the Text

1. To what pressures is the family subject because they are illegal
   immigrants?

2. Discuss the consequences for the narrator of having to make such a
   choice and perform such an action. In your opinion, how will she be
   different from now on? In what sense might the deer symbolize the
   self that can no longer exist?

✦ Exploring Different Perspectives

1. How does Luis Alberto Urrea's description in "Border Story" of what
   life is like at the United States–Mexican border help explain why the
   protagonist in "Cervicide" is faced with such a terrible choice?

les dio un tirón, sacó los perros—jerked the dogs out.

2. Compare and contrast the coping mechanisms of Mexican-Americans with those of Gypsies (see William M. Kephart's "The Gypsies") in terms of the ability to survive in American culture.

✦ Extending Viewpoints Through Writing

1. Would you ever consider killing your pet for food if you were in a circumstance where you and your children were starving?

2. How does being forced to choose between a deer she loves and her loyalty to her father whom she loves illustrate the kind of predicament in which those without power find themselves?

3. What actions did a pet of yours take that led you to believe it showed evidence of consciousness, motivation, and intelligence?

4. Describe your search for a name for your pet. What character traits important to you or your family does this name reveal?

5. What could your pet say about you that no human being knows?

Connecting Cultures

◆

Edward Said, Reflections on Exile

To what extent does the narrative of Napoleon A. Chagnon (see "Doing Fieldwork Among the Yąnomamö," Chapter 8) dramatize the "culture shock" of trying to adjust to a completely new environment? What evidence can you find within this work that supports Said's observations?

William M. Kephart, The Gypsies

How does Constance Classen's theory of the "other" (see "The Odour of the Other," Chapter 5) help explain the concept of *marimé,* or what is perceived to be clean or unclean in Gypsy culture?

Joan Didion, Miami: The Cuban Presence

In what respects can the *quinces* depicted in Joan Didion's article be seen as an initiation ceremony much like those described by Tepilit Ole Saitoti (see "The Initiation of a Maasai Warrior," Chapter 2)? How do the differences between the two reflect differences in cultural values between Cubans in Miami and the Maasai in Kenya?

Le Ly Hayslip, Yearning to Breathe Free

We usually think of "culture shock" as Napoleon A. Chagnon (see "Doing Fieldwork Among the Yąnomamö," Chapter 8) uses the term, that is, to characterize the unexpected conditions explorers and anthropologists encounter. In what sense can one speak of the "culture shock" experienced by Vietnamese immigrants to the United States?

Luis Alberto Urrea, Border Story

What similarities can you discover in the treatment of those trying to escape from one country to another in the accounts by Luis Alberto Urrea and Jon Swain (see "The Eyes of Vietnam," Chapter 6)?

Poranee Natadecha-Sponsel, Individualism as an American Cultural Value

What specifically Buddhist values inform the accounts by Poranee Natadecha-Sponsel and Aung San Suu Kyi (see "My Country and People," Chapter 9)?

Gloria Anzaldúa, Cervicide

How do the stories by Gloria Anzaldúa and Mahdokht Kashkuli (see "The Button," Chapter 5) dramatize the predicament of families faced with dehumanizing choices?

8

The Role Customs Play in Different Cultures

◆

In the customs that guide behavior within a particular society, we can see most clearly the hidden cultural logic and unconscious assumptions people in that society rely on to interpret everything that goes on in their world. Customs and rituals that may seem bizarre or strange to an outsider appear entirely normal and natural to those within the culture. Unfortunately, the potential for conflict exists as soon as people from different cultures whose "natural" ways do not coincide make contact with each other.

As communications, immigration, and travel make the world smaller, the potential for cross-cultural misunderstanding accelerates. Correspondingly, the need to become aware of the extent to which our own and other people's conclusions about the world are guided by different cultural presuppositions grows. Analysis of the customs of cultures other than our own allows us to temporarily put aside our taken-for-granted ways of seeing the world, even if we are normally unaware of the extent to which we rely on these implicit premises—to understand that the meanings we give to events, actions, and statements are not their only possible meanings.

The range and diversity of the selections in this chapter will allow you to temporarily replace your own way of perceiving the world and become aware, perhaps for the first time, of your own cultural assumptions that govern your interpretation of the world.

Nick Fiddes offers an intriguing analysis of "The Power of Meat" in societies where meat eating is connected with aggression and violence. In Napoleon A. Chagnon's account, "Doing Fieldwork Among the Yąnomamö," we can experience the meaning of "culture shock" as we read about Chagnon's growing awareness of the vast difference in values and attitudes that separated him culturally from the people in this Brazilian tribe among whom he lived for forty-one months. In Gretel Ehrlich's "To Live in Two Worlds," we benefit from the opportunity she was granted to observe the Kiowa Sun Dance, the most sacred ceremony of this Plains Tribe. Raymonde Carroll, in "Home," provides a penetrating analysis of the different culturally based interpretations of privacy among the French and Americans. In "The Language of Clothes," Alison Lurie investigates the cultural symbolism of various kinds of clothing and body decorations. David R. Counts, in "Too Many Bananas," reveals the many lessons he learned while doing fieldwork in New Guinea. Octavio Paz, in "The Day of the Dead," explores the important role fiestas play in Mexican culture and their relationship to the Mexican national character. The Egyptian writer Nabil Gorgy, in "Cairo Is a Small City," tells how a ruthless engineer is held accountable to the traditional Bedouin concept of justice in modern-day Egypt.

Nick Fiddes

The Power of Meat

◆

Nick Fiddes teaches social anthropology at the University of Edinburgh in Scotland. "The Power of Meat" is drawn from his 1991 book Meat: a Natural Symbol, *a work that grew out of his doctoral thesis. Mr. Fiddes has operated a catering business and is a self-proclaimed meat eater with many friends who are vegetarians.*

Belief in human dominion does not merely legitimate meat eating— the reverse is also true: meat reinforces that presumption. Killing, cooking, and eating other animals' flesh provides perhaps the ultimate authentication of human superiority over the rest of nature, with the spilling of their blood a vibrant motif. Thus, for individuals and societies to whom environmental control is an important value meat consumption is typically a key symbol. Meat has long stood for Man's proverbial 'muscle' over the natural world.

Sixteenth- and seventeenth-century moral theology, for example, seems almost directly to equate civilisation with the conquest of other creatures. Keith Thomas illustrates, for example, the sadistic vocabulary then attached to the important task of carving meat:

> Break that deer; . . . rear that goose; lift that swan; sauce that chicken; unbrace that mallard; unlace that cony; dismember that heron; display that crain; disfigure that peacock; unjoint that bittern; . . . mince that plover; . . . splay that bream; . . . tame that crab . . .
>
> —(Thomas 1983: 25–27)

Even today, the slaughter of sentient creatures is not just a (perhaps regrettable) necessity in producing a valuable foodstuff. Bloodshed is central to meat's value. Indeed, the visible domination of other creatures is so important that cruelty is widely reputed to be *necessary* to producing high quality meat—veal production is one example. An advertisement protesting at South Korean treatment of 'pets,' similarly, alleges that 'Kittens, cats and dogs will suffer appalling cruelty as they are slowly hanged . . . strangled . . . clubbed . . . or tossed alive into boiling water. Terror stricken animals, it's claimed, taste better' (IFAW 1988: 3). In eighteenth century Britian too, Jennifer Stead notes that:

> Living fish were slashed to make the flesh contract. This was called 'crimping.' Eels were skinned alive, lobsters roasted alive, crammed

poultry were sewn up in the guts, turkeys were suspended by the feet and bled to death by the mouth, bulls were baited before slaughter to make the meat more tender, pigs and calves were lashed for the same reason. One of William Kitchiner's recipes begins 'Take a red cock that is not too old and beat him to death.'

—(Stead 1985: 26)

4   Such practices, viewed as cruel from our perspective, were not simply wanton. Glorification of human dominance was then in its heyday so the harsh treatment of other animals is unsurprising. Meat was, and remains, a venerable symbol of potency, and indeed of civilisation itself. 'I do not believe', wrote a Swedish visitor, for example, 'that any Englishman who is his own master has ever eaten a dinner without meat' (Kalm 1748; quoted in Thomas 1983: 26). Even today meat is often linked with similar values: 'After nearly 12 years of negotiations, the tastiest symbols of American cultural imperialism are coming to Moscow in the form of McDonald's hamburgers' (*Guardian* 1987b: 6).

5   The humble hamburger is an appropriate, if somewhat clichéd, metaphor for North American culture since it embodies so many of the multi-faceted ideals on which the society is reputedly founded—of power and freedom, efficiency, and ease. When the ubiquitous McDonald's eventually began business in the Soviet Union, the hamburger's symbolic relevance did not go unremarked: '"It's like the coming of civilisation to Moscow," enthused Mr. Yuri Tereshchenko, licking his fingers as he finished off a Big Mac' (Reuter 1990: 20).

6   The global 'hamburger joint' is the apotheosis of standardised production-line catering—its product a fitting food for industrial society, pre-cooked and camouflaged by the bread roll that relieves the stark savagery of raw red meat. The cherished image of sterile order seeks to reassure the patron that its '100% pure' beef product is above suspicion. And so successful has this strategy been that rising red meat sales in this market have offset otherwise falling consumption. Like so much industrial production, the mass-produced hamburger effectively divorces consumption from its ecological context. Fast-flesh emporia entice the consumer with sanitised gratification; here everybody smiles, whilst health, welfare, and environmental implications are banished to another less seductive world. In this role the hamburger has become the routine exemplar of 'junk' food, and the regular target for protesters' complaints. But the core symbol remains the ground beef by which the 'quarterpounder' or 'halfpounder' is measured, and the vital, virile, potency which that apparently endows . . . ideas by which even Gandhi was once influenced:

It began to grow on me that meat-eating was good, that it would make me strong and daring, and that, if the whole country took to meateating, the English could be overcome. . . . We went in search of a lonely spot by the river, and there I saw, for the first time in my life—meat. There was baker's bread also. I relished neither. The goat's meat was as tough as leather. I simply could not eat it. I was sick and had to leave off eating. I had a very bad night afterwards. A horrible nightmare haunted me. Every time I dropped off to sleep it would seem as though a wild goat were bleating inside me, and I would jump up full of remorse . . . If my mother and father came to know of my having become a meat-eater, they would be deeply shocked. This knowledge was gnawing at my heart.

—(Gandhi 1949: 3–4)

Gandhi sought the power of technology which he saw ruthlessly harnessed to subdue his people, just as it is otherwise brought to bear on the natural world. He thought that he might gain the desired force by physically consuming meat, mistaking the *medium* of expression of a more domineering tradition than his own with the *source* of its power. 7

Like Gandhi, and like many peoples who think that by consuming a physical substance one can somehow partake of its essence (see Chapter 12), we in the modern western world also seem to believe that meat alone can endow us with its unique vitality. We most favour the animal's muscle flesh since, metaphorically, we consume its strength. Unlike nutrition or crude economic logic, this helps explain our valuation of 'better' cuts of meat, for as Sahlins points out: 8

> The social value of steak or roast, as compared with tripe or tongue, would be difficult to defend. Moreover, steak remains the most expensive meat even though its absolute supply is much greater than that of tongue; there is much more steak to the cow than there is tongue.
>
> —(Sahlins 1976: 176)

It is steak that constitutes the astronaut's ritual pre-flight meal (Twigg 1983: 23), affirming our technological control of the planet—technology on which the pilots' tenuous link is soon to be so dependent. Meat satisfies our bodies but it also feeds our minds. We eat not only the animal's flesh; with it we drain their lifeblood and so seize their strength. And it is not only that animal which we so utterly subjugate; consuming its flesh is a statement that we are the unquestioned masters of the world. 9

The motif of blood is central to the meat system. Indeed, it appears, by association with the colour red, blood is fundamental to much human thought. Berlin and Kay's cross-cultural enquiry into 'basic color terms' discovered that all languages have terms at least for black and for white (or dark and light), but that if a language contains three terms then the third will be for red. Red is the first true colour term to emerge as complex language develops (Berlin and Kay 1969). 10

11   Around the world red serves to suggest ideas of danger, violence, or revolution. Red is the colour of aggression, of power, of anger, of warning. It stands out and attracts our attention—hence its ubiquitous use in advertising and on fire alarms. As Edmund Leach notes of the oppositions we draw between red and other colours:

> When we make paired oppositions of this kind, red is consistently given the same value, it is treated as a danger sign: hot taps, live electric wires, debit entries on account books, stop signs on roads and railways. This is a pattern which turns up in many other cultures besides our own and in these other cases there is often a quite explicit recognition that the 'danger' of red derives from its 'natural' association with blood.
>
> —(Leach 1974: 22)

12   Blood's mortal significance is indeed widespread. Blood is the stream of life itself—perhaps since life ends when too much is spilled. We faint at the sight of it. To have blood on our hands implies guilt—Lady Macbeth found a spot of it impossible to remove as she was driven mad. It signifies kinship: as in blood brotherhood, noble blood, or blood feud. It is used as the arbiter of inheritance as when we talk of blood lineage or say that some attribute is in the blood. The British upper classes are termed blue-blooded, as if so civilised as to be beyond mortality, no longer characterised by that most natural sign of red blood. Red meat might be suitable food for such beings, but it is apparently an inappropriate conception of their own physiology.

13   At Christian communion we drink the blood of Christ to form a mystical bond in which we partake of the Holy Spirit. In our horror stories characters such as Dracula drink the blood of living people to drain them of their life force. Blood is also the source of our passion—to be hot blooded is to be wild, spirited, lusty, impulsive; to be cold blooded is to be cruel, calculating, inhuman. The concept of lifeblood is evident throughout our culture, either directly or through association with the colour red. It is the so-called red meats, in which the blood is most vividly evident, which have traditionally been held in highest esteem in western society. It is red meats which today are most regularly reviled as unhealthy. It is also red meats which have been most zealously rejected by vegetarians.

14   Significantly, the image of red-coloured fruit and vegetables such as tomatoes or red apples seems to be largely unaffected by this association, possibly since by being categorically opposed to meat in the food system the link between their pigment and that of blood carries little meaning. Liquid red wine can, however, have something of the same reputation, upon which some 'full-bodied' brands such as Bull's Blood deliberately play, and as is made explicit in Christian commun-

ion. It is through red meat, however, that this gory image is most tellingly expressed:

> The concept of blood as the river of life continues to exert a hold even today. It is a force that no vegetarian should underestimate. It surely underlies the general disinclination of the average housewife to provide her family with soya protein instead of chunks of stewing: no amount of arguing about the nutritional sufficiency of soya products, it seems, can overcome this residual unconscious belief in blood ... Vegetarians, therefore, are people who have somehow conquered this mythopoeic belief in the regenerative power of blood ... Blood is the very stuff of life and meat partakes of its qualities and of its mythical and psychological associations. Sometimes no amount of factual evidence or moral exhortations can conquer this primordial logic.
>
> —(Cox and Crockett 1979: 18–19)

Meat remains a graphic vehicle through which notions of natural human power are widely conveyed, and the image of blood is central to its efficacy. Cross-references between meat eating and such attributes as civilisation, instinct, ease and convenience, prestige, affluence, mental and physical well-being, potency, and skill, are routine, indeed endemic, in our belief, thought, and action, a common thread being the principle of environmental control and the benefits with which that civilised status reputedly endows us.   15

Cooking and Processing

We do not generally eat animal flesh in its crude state. With the exception of periodic vogues for raw foods such as the Japanese sushi, or for certain culinary specialities such as *steak tartare,* flesh almost invariably undergoes a transformation before we allow it to enter our mouths: we cook it. The next chapter considers in more detail the range of foods we classify as edible raw, and those which must be cooked, but meat is predominantly of the latter type. This apparently mundane observation is of singular significance since every known society cooks at least some of its food, and we are the only species which does so. Routine and ritual cooking of food is one trait by which all human groups can be categorically distinguished from all other animals. Or, more accurately, in this way we *distinguish ourselves* from other animals. The dichotomy between us and them is our mental creation.   16

Time and again, around the world, myths deal with the origins of fire, and fire and cooking play a key role in ritual, signifying its elementary importance to humanity. Prometheus stole fire from the Gods. The South American Gê people stole fire and the skill of cooking from the Jaguar (Lévi-Strauss 1970: 66). The Chukchi of Siberia have strict rules   17 about the generation and transfer of 'genuine fire', their fireboards are revered as family heirlooms, and both play an important part in the sacrifice of reindeer. Amongst their neighbours, the Koryak, fire 'signifies the source whence [domestic] reindeer originated' (Jochelson 1908: 87; Ingold 1986: 267–269). In Northern Canada it is reported that 'the Chipewyan distinguish themselves from animals and eskimo' by avoidance of raw food (Sharp 1981: 231). And Audrey Richards notes that the 'savage' is quite erroneously supposed 'under the guidance of some superior natural instinct denied to his civilised fellows' to eat his vegetables raw (1939: 1). Clearly the notional savage, whom we invented to stand in contrast to our own supposed civilisation, will be characterised by general contradiction of cultivated behaviour; if we distinguish ourselves from barbarity by the cooking of meat it is hardly surprising that savages should be presumed to consume not cooked meat but raw vegetables.

18   The importance of cooking has been noted by many writers. Guy-Gillet (1981) argues psychoanalytically that humans, through cookery, unconsciously act as intermediaries between three orders: cosmological, zoological, and cultural. Carleton Coon (1955: 63) suggests that cooking was the 'decisive factor in leading man from a primarily animal existence into one that was more fully human', as did Boswell before him (Hill 1964: iii.245, v.33n). Dando too, investigating the history of famine, states that control 'of fire was a great step in emancipating humans from constraints found in the physical environment. Humans are distinguished from other animals by their general preference for cooked food' (1980:13).

19   But it was Lévi-Strauss who underscored the notion of cooking as the fundamental articulation of the distinction between nature and culture. He noted that every known society processes at least some of its food 'by cooking, which, it has never been sufficiently emphasised, is with language a truly universal form of activity' (1966: 937). The transformation (by fire) which 'universally brings about the cultural transformation of the raw' (1970: 142) is, for Lévi-Strauss, the most profound and privileged expression of the transformation from nature to culture—or in other words of the way in which human beings conceive themselves as different from the rest of the natural world.

20   Of course vegetables may be cooked as well as meat, but vegetables are also eaten raw—for example in salads. Meat, however, is almost invariably transformed from its natural state, if not by cooking then through processing such as drying, marinating, or pickling. The processing of bacon by salting or smoking may indeed contribute to its image as a lesser meat, since its subsequent cooking will mean that it has been doubly transformed by the time it is consumed. It is not sold dripping blood as is 'real' meat. Bacon would rarely form the centrepiece of an important meat dinner. It can, however, be served as part of the Great British Breakfast, at a meal when meat is otherwise absent

in Britain (although even this custom is in decline). And, unlike most meats, it can be served to support other flesh or animal products, in a game casserole, with chicken, or in an omelette, for example. Bacon is a subsidiary meat, of which even some 'vegetarians' remain fond.

Sausages, cooked pies, chopped ham, corned beef, or pâtés, like-   21
wise, rarely enjoy the same prestige as a piece of proper meat. Except in cases of hardship, they are better suited to the day's secondary meal, or perhaps as an appetiser at the main event. These lower-status meats may be seen as more appropriate to children than to Real Men who need real meat. They can be sold by any grocers, rather than only by proper butchers. Such items provide us with animal flesh in accessible form, but much of meat's peculiar mystique is dissipated in the process.

Cooking and other techniques metamorphose meat from a corpo-   22
real substance to an artifact of our culinary culture. When still in its raw state, in the kitchen or on the butcher's slab, meat is not yet the stuff of mouthwatering delight. But as the vivid redness of blood becomes a less hostile shade of brown, so the flesh turns from distasteful to tasty:

> *Betty:* 'It's funny though. I can look at a lump of meat, like a chicken, and do all the bits with it, and all the necessary stuff, and take out its entrails and what have you . . .'
>
> *Steve:* 'I bet you couldn't pluck it though!'
>
> *Betty:* 'Oh, I think I could because when I'm looking at it like that I'm looking at it, like . . . differently . . .'
>
> *Steve:* 'Something to eat . . .'
>
> *Betty:* 'No, that's the thing! I'm not looking at it like something to eat; I'm looking at it as this . . . thing here that I've got to do this with, in the same way that in biology you'd dissect . . . animals and rats and . . . you'd just do it. It's not something to eat until you've actually got it in the pan and you're cooking it and adding to it . . . and once it's beginning to cook. Then it becomes something to eat, but while it's just . . . a bit of animal lying on your chopping board it's just something that you've got to do.'

> 'I was visiting my cousin in London, and she can't have been completely vegetarian yet then but she certainly didn't normally eat much meat. But she knew that I did eat meat, so for some reason when I came to stay she thought she should cook it for me . . . So she bought this mince for us but then she was too squeamish to actually deal with it herself until it had gone brown! I had to fry it and stir it until all the red colour had gone—and then she took over and did the rest.'

Raw meat, dripping blood, is what is eaten by wild, carnivorous an-   23
imals, not by civilised humans. We position ourselves above animals in

general by eating meat, and above other carnivores by cooking it. Raw meat is bestial and cooking sets us apart. Appropriately, the genre of horror fiction involving degenerate individuals is an area where we often encounter the image of humans eating raw flesh. For example, an infamous 'video nasty', outlawed by the British censors in the early 1980s, was a film entitled *Cannibal Holocaust*, the cover for which featured savage-looking women tearing with their teeth at raw, supposedly human, flesh—cleverly combining transgression of the cannibalism taboo with the added shock of seeing (female) humans consuming raw meat.

24   Many people today are reluctant to handle raw meat at all, reporting that whilst they do not mind eating it once cooked they find it difficult to deal with a substance in which the blood is still evident. Likewise, the smell of blood from raw meat is enough to dissuade many meat eaters from entering traditional butchers' shops, since superstores offer an attractively sanitised alternative. It is perhaps not surprising that the odour emanating from raw meat should find relative disfavour, although the smell is unpleasant in no absolute sense any more than the scent of a sizzling steak is automatically appetising. Either can be attractive or repellent according to our disposition. But smell can be highly evocative, capable of conjuring distant memories literally out of thin air. It is the associations which we find distasteful—the scent of bloody raw meat cueing us to consider the animal's death.

25   There are, however, occasions when the vulgar ubiquity of cooked meat is insufficient to communicate the desired message—when the potency of the symbol 'in the raw' perfectly conveys the severity of spirit implied. The stark barbarity represented by uncooked flesh has a rare capacity to disconcert us when its imagery is invoked in particular contexts. Raw meat, oozing blood, most strikingly represents the brute power of nature, undiminished by acculturation. In modern fields of combat, therefore, the idea of raw meat as the very essence of brutal nature, red in tooth and claw, can be an effective statement of extreme ruthlessness:

> Lloyd Honeyghan, looking every inch the magazine-cover picture of a world champion, returned to London yesterday . . . to announce the next defence of his WBC and IBF welterweight [boxing] titles . . .
>
> Honeyghan, resplendent in a £1,500 leather suit complete with studs, buckles, chains and horsehair epaulets—'they're the scalps of my last two opponents'—will fight the WBC's No 1 contender . . .
>
> It will also be Honeyghan's second title defence in two months, but he declared: 'I want to fight as often as possible. I'm still so hungry for success I've been living on raw steak.'
>
> —(Massarik 1987: 28)

'Oh yes, I know it's something that some businessmen do quite deliberately. You take the guy you're negotiating with to a fancy restaurant for a business lunch and then order steak tartare. It totally unnerves the other guy seeing you eating this raw meat with blood dripping out of it, and actually does make a difference—it can just give you that edge.'

Processing such as cooking transforms meat from a natural sub- 26 stance to a cultural artifact. Thus, the more skilfully its manipulation is effected, the better it expresses the supremacy of human civilisation. Cooked meat places us above the mere animal, and its appreciation affirms to us our privileged status, to which can be attributed at least part of its added value. Skill is for this reason expected of farmers, butchers, and chefs. The greater is the skill required in the processing the higher is the value of the end-product, and those we entrust with meat's provision must discharge their responsibility with diligence. In restaurants the chef's skill is paramount, since this is the arena of the specialist. Beef steak—cow's muscle—remains the most popular choice of entrée in British restaurants, and its preparation is a matter of grave concern, curious though this may seem to a vegetarian:

'I don't know if I'm just being really biased but I went out for a meal yesterday with my dad and my brother and his girlfriend and they all had meat and I had an omelette because they didn't have any veggie stuff on the menu and none of them liked their food! I keep noticing that whenever I go out with people and they eat meat and I don't and they don't like their food and I do. I've decided that either people don't know how to cook meat or people who eat meat are really fussy! It's either too tough or it's not cooked enough . . . and meanwhile I'm always quite happily munching into my pasta with tomato sauce or whatever I'm having and there's never anything wrong with that. People just never seem to be satisfied with it. Maybe they expect too much: like they order a big juicy steak, and it's not big and it's not juicy. It's just so important to people that it should be just as they want it and it never is.'

The entire process of procuring and preparing meat bears evidence 27 of a relationship between powerful, predatory, 'civilised', humans and our 'legitimate resource' of non-civilised animals. The proper texture for meat presented at table, for example, is a matter of fine discrimination. If cooking, which tends to make meat more tender to the tooth, represents to us the qualities of humanity, it is perhaps not surprising that tenderness should be a quality highly valued in cooked meat:

'And I did sirloin steaks in wine. Then again, that was in the casserole, because I find steaks can be a bit . . . no matter how good your steaks are, grilling them can be a bit tricky, you know. They can be tough, which, you know, can be a bit upsetting if you produce a tough steak to a guest.'

28   On the other hand, meat should certainly have some 'bite' to it: something to get one's teeth into, that puts up a bit of resistance—a quality with which the value of challenge in hunting curiously reverberates. Of all foods, only meat is held to have this proper texture that gives full eating satisfaction which is why, for many, meatless meals are incomplete.

29   If, as an anthropology textbook claims, central 'to every culture is its way of obtaining food' then strictly speaking we are no longer gatherers, nor hunters, nor even farmers, but we live in an age of industrial food provision. We 'go to the supermarket to choose among thousands of products marketed mostly by large corporations. Increasingly, these corporations control every step of the process of food production and preparation from the farmer's field to the fast-food restaurant' (McElroy and Townsend 1985: 175). And in this world, we are repeatedly told, meat is the ideal convenience food.

30   But convenience is more than a rational objective. Convenience is a by-word for the civilised society in which we have elevated ourselves above the daily grind of days gone by. In the words of the television advertisement: *'Menu Masters* help you make time to live your life'. We are masters. No longer do we merely save time—we make it, God-like. Convenience is leisure; convenience is the power to have the work done by other means; convenience is to be on top of the heap—and meat signals convenience. Why? Surely not for its functional attributes, since a slice of bread or a tin of baked beans would be equally convenient, nutritional, and filling. Meat is called a convenience food because it already stands as an expression of those same core values of modern western society: of power, of superiority . . . of civilisation.

✦ Evaluating the Text

1. How, in Fiddes's view, does meat eating express a theme of control over the environment? What is the significance of past recipes that incorporated what would seem to us today to be cruelty to animals?

2. How has the traditional symbolism of meat in various cultures been associated with blood and violence?

3. What symbolic importance of cooking meat has Fiddes discovered in his research?

✦ Exploring Different Perspectives

1. How are the idea of violence and the value of meat connected in accounts by Nick Fiddes and Napoleon A. Chagnon ("Doing Fieldwork Among the Yąnomamö")?

2. Compare the analysis by Nick Fiddes with that of David R. Counts in "Too Many Bananas" in terms of societies where meat occupies no role and reciprocity rather than aggression is the dominant social value.

✦ Extending Viewpoints Through Writing

1. Would you ever consider becoming a vegetarian? Why or why not?

2. Have you ever known anyone who became a vegetarian? Have you discussed it with them? What led them to this decision?

Napoleon A. Chagnon

Doing Fieldwork
Among the Yąnomamö

◆

*Napoleon A. Chagnon is a renowned anthropologist whose research into
the social aspects of tribal warfare among the Indians of South America
are best represented by* Yąnomamö: The Fierce People *(1968) and*
Studying the Yąnomamö *(1974). In addition, he has written and produced more than twenty documentary films about the Yąnomamö, a tribe
of roughly 10,000, living mostly in southern Venezuela and Brazil, for
which he was awarded the Grand Prize of the Brussels' Film Festival in
1970.*

    *The largest South American country, Brazil occupies almost half of
the continent and is the only country in South America whose culture,
history, and language were shaped by Portugal, whose first permanent
settlement in what is present-day São Paulo occurred in 1532. Since the
Europeans landed in 1500, the population of native tribes has been reduced from an estimated 6 million to 200,000 today. Brazil's population is
an amalgam of Indian, black, and European strains. Native Indians of
several tribes (including the Yąnomamö studied by Chagnon) live along
the Amazon River, which flows across northern Brazil to the Atlantic
Ocean. The Yąnomamö have been subject to the steady encroachment of
civilization as the Brazilian government, despite international pressure,
has permitted wholesale destruction of the rain forest in the Amazon
River basin. Despite being the world's largest coffee producer, in 1989
Brazil experienced the devastating combination of 600 percent inflation
rates and the largest foreign debt of any developing nation. In 1990,
President Collor instituted a program of price freezes, privatization of
industry, higher utility rates, and devaluation of the currency (cruzado
novo) designed to revive the economy. These measures only crippled the
economy further and along with suspicions of Collor's corruption led to
his resignation in December 1992. Itamar Franco assumed the presidency
in a transitional capacity until the next elections scheduled for 1994. In
the elections of October 1994, Fernando Henrique Cardoso was elected
president.*

The Yąnomamö[1] indians live in southern Venezuela and the adjacent   1
portions of northern Brazil. Some 125 widely scattered villages have
populations ranging from 40 to 250 inhabitants, with 75 to 80 people the
most usual number. In total numbers their population approaches
10,000 people, but this is merely a guess. Many of the villages have not
yet been contacted by outsiders, and nobody knows for sure exactly
how many uncontacted villages there are, or how many people live in
them. By comparison to African or Melanesian tribes, the Yąnomamö
population is small. Still, they are one of the largest unacculturated
tribes left in all of South America.

But they have a significance apart from tribal size and cultural pu-   2
rity: the Yąnomamö are still actively conducting warfare. It is in nature
of man to fight, according to one of their myths, because the blood of
"Moon" spilled on this layer of the cosmos, causing men to become
fierce. I describe the Yąnomamö as "the fierce people" because that is
the most accurate single phrase that describes them. That is how they
conceive themselves to be, and that is how they would like others to
think of them.

I spent nineteen months with the Yąnomamö,[2] during which time I   3
acquired some proficiency in their language and, up to a point, sub-
merged myself in their culture and way of life. The thing that impressed me most was the importance of aggression in their culture. I
had the opportunity to witness a good many incidents that expressed
individual vindictiveness on the one hand and collective bellicosity on
the other. These ranged in seriousness from the ordinary incidents of
wife beating and chest pounding to dueling and organized raiding by
parties that set out with the intention of ambushing and killing men
from enemy villages. One of the villages discussed in the chapters that
follow was raided approximately twenty-five times while I conducted
the fieldwork, six times by the group I lived among.

[1]The word Yąnomamö is nasalized through its entire length, indicated by the diacritical
mark [ą]. When this mark appears on a word, the entire word is nasalized. The terminal
vowel [-ö] represents a sound that does not occur in the English language. It corresponds
to the phone [ɨ] of linguistic orthography. In normal conversation, Yąnomamö is pronounced like "Yah-no-mama," except that it is nasalized. Finally, the words having the [-ä]
vowel are pronounced as that vowel with the "uh" sound of "duck." Thus the name
Kąobawä would be pronounced "cow-ba-wuh," again nasalized.

[2]I spent a total of twenty-three months in South America of which nineteen were spent
among the Yąnomamö on three separate field trips. The first trip, November 1964
through February 1966, was to Venezuela. During this time I spent thirteen months in direct contact with the Yąnomamö, using my periodic trips back to Caracas to visit my family and to collate the genealogical data I had collected up to that point. On my second
trip, January through March 1967, I spent two months among Brazilian Yąnomamö and
one more month with the Venezuelan Yąnomamö. Finally, I returned to Venezuela for
three more months among the Yąnomamö, January through April 1968.

4   The fact that the Yąnomamö live in a state of chronic warfare is reflected in their mythology, values, settlement pattern, political behavior, and marriage practices. Accordingly, I have organized this case study in such a way that students can appreciate the effects of warfare on Yąnomamö culture in general and on their social organization and politics in particular.

5   I collected the data under somewhat trying circumstances, some of which I will describe in order to give the student a rough idea of what is generally meant when anthropologists speak of "culture shock" and "fieldwork." It should be borne in mind, however, that each field situation is in many respects unique, so that the problems I encountered do not necessarily exhaust the range of possible problems other anthropologists have confronted in other areas. There are a few problems, however, that seem to be nearly universal among anthropological fieldworkers, particularly those having to do with eating, bathing, sleeping, lack of privacy and loneliness, or discovering that primitive man is not always as noble as you originally thought.

6   This is not to state that primitive man everywhere is unpleasant. By way of contrast, I have also done limited fieldwork among the Yąnomamö's northern neighbors, the Carib-speaking Makiritare Indians. This group was very pleasant and charming, all of them anxious to help me and honor bound to show any visitor the numerous courtesies of their system of etiquette. In short, they approached the image of primitive man that I had conjured up, and it was sheer pleasure to work with them. The recent work by Colin Turnbull (1966) brings out dramatically the contrast in personal characteristics of two African peoples he has studied.

7   Hence, what I say about some of my experiences is probably equally true of the experiences of many other fieldworkers. I write about my own experiences because there is a conspicuous lack of fieldwork descriptions available to potential fieldworkers. I think I could have profited by reading about the private misfortunes of my own teachers; at least I might have been able to avoid some of the more stupid errors I made. In this regard there are a number of recent contributions by fieldworkers describing some of the discomforts and misfortunes they themselves sustained.[3] Students planning to conduct fieldwork are urged to consult them.

8   My first day in the field illustrated to me what my teachers meant when they spoke of "culture shock." I had traveled in a small, alumi-

---

[3]Maybury-Lewis 1967, "Introduction," and 1965*b*; Turnbull, 1966; L. Bohannan, 1964. Perhaps the most intimate account of the tribulations of a fieldworker is found in the posthumous diary of Bronislaw Malinowski (1967). Since the diary was not written for publication, it contains many intimate, very personal details about the writer's anxieties and hardships.

num rowboat propelled by a large outboard motor for two and a half days. This took me from the Territorial capital, a small town on the Orinoco River, deep into Yąnomamö country. On the morning of the third day we reached a small mission settlement, the field "headquarters" of a group of Americans who were working in two Yąnomamö villages. The missionaries had come out of these villages to hold their annual conference on the progress of their mission work, and were conducting their meetings when I arrived. We picked up a passenger at the mission station, James P. Barker, the first non-Yąnomamö to make a sustained, permanent contact with the tribe (in 1950). He had just returned from a year's furlough in the United States, where I had earlier visited him before leaving for Venezuela. He agreed to accompany me to the village I had selected for my base of operations to introduce me to the Indians. This village was also his own home base, but he had not been there for over a year and did not plan to join me for another three months. Mr. Barker had been living with this particular group about five years.

We arrived at the village, Bisaasi-teri, about 2:00 PM and docked the   9
boat along the muddy bank at the terminus of the path used by the Indians to fetch their drinking water. It was hot and muggy, and my clothing was soaked with perspiration. It clung uncomfortably to my body, as it did thereafter for the remainder of the work. The small, biting gnats were out in astronomical numbers, for it was the beginning of the dry season. My face and hands were swollen from the venom of their numerous stings. In just a few moments I was to meet my first Yąnomamö, my first primitive man. What would it be like? I had visions of entering the village and seeing 125 social facts running about calling each other kinship terms and sharing food, each waiting and anxious to have me collect his genealogy. I would wear them out in turn. Would they like me? This was important to me; I wanted them to be so fond of me that they would adopt me into their kinship system and way of life, because I had heard that successful anthropologists always get adopted by their people. I had learned during my seven years of anthropological training at the University of Michigan that kinship was equivalent to society in primitive tribes and that it was a moral way of life, "moral" being something "good" and "desirable." I was determined to work my way into their moral system of kinship and become a member of their society.

My heart began to pound as we approached the village and heard   10
the buzz of activity within the circular compound. Mr. Barker commented that he was anxious to see if any changes had taken place while he was away and wondered how many of them had died during his absence. I felt into my back pocket to make sure that my notebook was still there and felt personally more secure when I touched it. Otherwise, I would not have known what to do with my hands.

11   The entrance to the village was covered over with brush and dry palm leaves. We pushed them aside to expose the low opening to the village. The excitement of meeting my first Indians was almost unbearable as I duck-waddled through the low passage into the village clearing.

12   I looked up and gasped when I saw a dozen burly, naked, filthy, hideous men staring at us down the shafts of their drawn arrows! Immense wads of green tobacco were stuck between their lower teeth and lips making them look even more hideous, and strands of dark-green slime dripped or hung from their noses. We arrived at the village while the men were blowing a hallucinogenic drug up their noses. One of the side effects of the drug is a runny nose. The mucus is always saturated with the green powder and the Indians usually let it run freely from their nostrils. My next discovery was that there were a dozen or so vicious, underfed dogs snapping at my legs, circling me as if I were going to be their next meal. I just stood there holding my notebook, helpless and pathetic. Then the stench of the decaying vegetation and filth struck me and I almost got sick. I was horrified. What sort of a welcome was this for the person who came here to live with you and learn your way of life, to become friends with you? They put their weapons down when they recognized Barker and returned to their chanting, keeping a nervous eye on the village entrances.

13   We had arrived just after a serious fight. Seven women had been abducted the day before by a neighboring group, and the local men and their guests had just that morning recovered five of them in a brutal club fight that nearly ended in a shooting war. The abductors, angry because they lost five of the seven captives, vowed to raid the Bisaasiteri. When we arrived and entered the village unexpectedly, the Indians feared that we were the raiders. On several occasions during the next two hours the men in the village jumped to their feet, armed themselves, and waited nervously for the noise outside the village to be identified. My enthusiasm for collecting ethnographic curiosities diminished in proportion to the number of times such an alarm was raised. In fact, I was relieved when Mr. Barker suggested that we sleep across the river for the evening. It would be safer over there.

14   As we walked down the path to the boat, I pondered the wisdom of having decided to spend a year and a half with this tribe before I had even seen what they were like. I am not ashamed to admit, either, that had there been a diplomatic way out, I would have ended my fieldwork then and there. I did not look forward to the next day when I would be left alone with the Indians; I did not speak a word of their language, and they were decidedly different from what I had imagined them to be. The whole situation was depressing, and I wondered why I ever decided to switch from civil engineering to anthropology in the first place. I had not eaten all day, I was soaking wet from perspiration,

the gnats were biting me, and I was covered with red pigment, the result of a dozen or so complete examinations I had been given by as many burly Indians. These examinations capped an otherwise grim day. The Indians would blow their noses into their hands, flick as much of the mucus off that would separate in a snap of the wrist, wipe the residue into their hair, and then carefully examine my face, arms, legs, hair, and the contents of my pockets. I asked Mr. Barker how to say "Your hands are dirty"; my comments were met by the Indians in the following way: They would "clean" their hands by spitting a quantity of slimy tobacco juice into them, rub them together, and then proceed with the examination.

Mr. Barker and I crossed the river and slung our hammocks. When   15
he pulled his hammock out of a rubber bag, a heavy, disagreeable odor of mildewed cotton came with it. "Even the missionaries are filthy," I thought to myself. Within two weeks, everything I owned smelled the same way, and I lived with that odor for the remainder of the fieldwork. My own habits of personal cleanliness reached such levels that I didn't even mind being examined by the Indians, as I was not much cleaner than they were after I had adjusted to the circumstances.

So much for my discovery that primitive man is not the picture of   16
nobility and sanitation I had conceived him to be. I soon discovered that it was an enormously time-consuming task to maintain my own body in the manner to which it had grown accustomed in the relatively antiseptic environment of the northern United States. Either I could be relatively well fed and relatively comfortable in a fresh change of clothes and do very little fieldwork, or, I could do considerably more fieldwork and be less well fed and less comfortable.

It is appalling how complicated it can be to make oatmeal in the   17
jungle. First, I had to make two trips to the river to haul the water. Next, I had to prime my kerosene stove with alcohol and get it burning, a tricky procedure when you are trying to mix powdered milk and fill a coffee pot at the same time: the alcohol prime always burned out before I could turn the kerosene on, and I would have to start all over. Or, I would turn the kerosene on, hoping that the element was still hot enough to vaporize the fuel, and start a small fire in my palm-thatched hut as the liquid kerosene squirted all over the table and walls and ignited. It was safer to start over with the alcohol. Then I had to boil the oatmeal and pick the bugs out of it. All my supplies, of course, were carefully stored in Indian-proof, rat-proof, moisture-proof, and insect-proof containers, not one of which ever served its purpose adequately. Just taking things out of the multiplicity of containers and repacking them afterward was a minor project in itself. By the time I had hauled the water to cook with, unpacked my food, prepared the oatmeal, milk, and coffee, heated water for dishes, washed and dried the dishes, repacked the food in the containers, stored the containers in locked

trunks and cleaned up my mess, the ceremony of preparing breakfast had brought me almost up to lunch time!

18   Eating three meals a day was out of the question. I solved the problem by eating a single meal that could be prepared in a single container, or, at most, in two containers, washed my dishes only when there were no clean ones left, using cold river water, and wore each change of clothing at least a week to cut down on my laundry problem, a courageous undertaking in the tropics. I was also less concerned about sharing my provisions with the rats, insects, Indians, and the elements, thereby eliminating the need for my complicated storage process. I was able to last most of the day on *café con leche,* heavily sugared espresso coffee diluted about five to one with hot milk. I would prepare this in the evening and store it in a thermos. Frequently, my single meal was no more complicated than a can of sardines and a package of crackers. But at least two or three times a week I would do something sophisticated, like make oatmeal or boil rice and add a can of tuna fish or tomato paste to it. I even saved time by devising a water system that obviated the trips to the river. I had a few sheets of zinc roofing brought in and made a rain-water trap; I caught the water on the zinc surface, funneled it into an empty gasoline drum, and then ran a plastic hose from the drum to my hut. When the drum was exhausted in the dry season, I hired the Indians to fill it with water from the river.

19   I ate much less when I traveled with the Indians to visit other villages. Most of the time my travel diet consisted of roasted or boiled green plantains . . . that I obtained from the Indians, but I always carried a few cans of sardines with me in case I got lost or stayed away longer than I had planned. I found peanut butter and crackers a very nourishing food, and a simple one to prepare on trips. It was nutritious and portable, and only one tool was required to prepare the meal, a hunting knife that could be cleaned by wiping the blade on a leaf. More importantly, it was one of the few foods the Indians would let me eat in relative peace. It looked too much like animal feces to them to excite their appetites.

20   I once referred to the peanut butter as the dung of cattle. They found this quite repugnant. They did not know what "cattle" were, but were generally aware that I ate several canned products of such an animal. I perpetrated this myth, if for no other reason than to have some peace of mind while I ate. Fieldworkers develop strange defense mechanisms, and this was one of my own forms of adaptation. On another occasion I was eating a can of frankfurters and growing very weary of the demands of one of my guests for a share in my meal. When he asked me what I was eating, I replied: "Beef." He then asked, "What part of the animal are you eating?" to which I replied, "Guess!" He stopped asking for a share.

21   Meals were a problem in another way. Food sharing is important to the Yąnomamö in the context of displaying friendship. "I am hungry," is

almost a form of greeting with them. I could not possibly have brought enough food with me to feed the entire village, yet they seemed not to understand this. All they could see was that I did not share my food with them at each and every meal. Nor could I enter into their system of reciprocities with respect to food; every time one of them gave me something "freely," he would dog me for months to pay him back, not with food, but with steel tools. Thus, if I accepted a plantain from some-one in a different village while I was on a visit, he would most likely visit me in the future and demand a machete as payment for the time that he "fed" me. I usually reacted to these kinds of demands by giving a banana, the customary reciprocity in their culture—food for food— but this would be a disappointment for the individual who had visions of that single plantain growing into a machete over time.

Despite the fact that most of them knew I would not share my food   22
with them at their request, some of them always showed up at my hut during mealtime. I gradually became accustomed to this and learned to ignore their persistent demands while I ate. Some of them would get angry because I failed to give in, but most of them accepted it as just a peculiarity of the subhuman foreigner. When I did give in, my hut quickly filled with Indians, each demanding a sample of the food that I had given one of them. If I did not give all a share, I was that much more despicable in their eyes.

A few of them went out of their way to make my meals unpleasant,   23
to spite me for not sharing; for example, one man arrived and watched me eat a cracker with honey on it. He immediately recognized the honey, a particularly esteemed Yąnomamö food. He knew that I would not share my tiny bottle and that it would be futile to ask. Instead, he glared at me and queried icily, "Shaki![4] What kind of animal semen are you eating on that cracker?" His question had the desired effect, and my meal ended.

Finally, there was the problem of being lonely and separated from   24
your own kind, especially your family. I tried to overcome this by seek-ing personal friendships among the Indians. This only complicated the matter because all my friends simply used my confidence to gain priv-ileged access to my cache of steel tools and trade goods, and looted me. I would be bitterly disappointed that my "friend" thought no more of me than to finesse our relationship exclusively with the intention of getting at my locked up possessions, and my depression would hit new lows every time I discovered this. The loss of the possession bothered

---

[4]"Shaki," or, rather, "Shakiwä," is the name they gave me because they could not pro-nounce "Chagnon." They like to name people for some distinctive feature when possible. *Shaki* is the name of a species of noisome bee; they accumulate in large numbers around ripening bananas and make pests of themselves by eating into the fruit, showering the people below with the debris. They probably adopted this name for me because I was also a nuisance, continuously prying into their business, taking pictures of them, and, in general, being where they did not want me.

me much less than the shock that I was, as far as most of them were concerned, nothing more than a source of desirable items; no holds were barred in relieving me of these, since I was considered something subhuman, a non-Yąnomamö.

25   The thing that bothered me most was the incessant, passioned, and aggressive demands the Indians made. It would become so unbearable that I would have to lock myself in my mud hut every once in a while just to escape from it: Privacy is one of Western culture's greatest achievements. But I did not want privacy for its own sake; rather, I simply had to get away from the begging. Day and night for the entire time I lived with the Yąnomamö I was plagued by such demands as: "Give me a knife, I am poor!"; "If you don't take me with you on your next trip to Widokaiya-teri I'll chop a hole in your canoe!"; "Don't point your camera at me or I'll hit you!"; "Share your food with me!"; "Take me across the river in your canoe and be quick about it!"; "Give me a cooking pot!"; "Loan me your flashlight so I can go hunting tonight!"; "Give me medicine . . . I itch all over!"; "Take us on a week-long hunting trip with your shot-gun!"; and "Give me an axe or I'll break into your hut when you are away visiting and steal one!" And so I was bombarded by such demands day after day, months on end, until I could not bear to see an Indian.

26   It was not as difficult to become calloused to the incessant begging as it was to ignore the sense of urgency, the impassioned tone of voice, or the intimidation and aggression with which the demands were made. It was likewise difficult to adjust to the fact that the Yąnomamö refused to accept "no" for an answer until or unless it seethed with passion and intimidation—which it did after six months. Giving in to a demand always established a new threshold; the next demand would be for a bigger item or favor, and the anger of the Indians even greater if the demand was not met. I soon learned that I had to become very much like the Yąnomamö to be able to get along with them on their terms: sly, aggressive, and intimidating.

27   Had I failed to adjust in this fashion I would have lost six months of supplies to them in a single day or would have spent most of my time ferrying them around in my canoe or hunting for them. As it was, I did spend a considerable amount of time doing these things and did succumb to their outrageous demands for axes and machetes, at least at first. More importantly, had I failed to demonstrate that I could not be pushed around beyond a certain point, I would have been the subject of far more ridicule, theft, and practical jokes than was the actual case. In short, I had to acquire a certain proficiency in their kind of interpersonal politics and to learn how to imply subtly that certain potentially undesirable consequences might follow if they did such and such to me. They do this to each other in order to establish precisely the point at which they cannot goad an individual any further without pre-

cipitating retaliation. As soon as I caught on to this and realized that much of their aggression was stimulated by their desire to discover my flash point, I got along much better with them and regained some lost ground. It was sort of like a political game that everyone played, but one in which each individual sooner or later had to display some sign that his bluffs and implied threats could be backed up. I suspect that the frequency of wife beating is a component of this syndrome, since men can display their ferocity and show others that they are capable of violence. Beating a wife with a club is considered to be an acceptable way of displaying ferocity and one that does not expose the male to much danger. The important thing is that the man has displayed his potential for violence and the implication is that other men better treat him with respect and caution.

After six months, the level of demand was tolerable in the village I 28 used for my headquarters. The Indians and I adjusted to each other and knew what to expect with regard to demands on their part for goods, favors, and services. Had I confined my fieldwork to just that village alone, the field experience would have been far more enjoyable. But, as I was interested in the demographic pattern and social organization of a much larger area, I made regular trips to some dozen different villages in order to collect genealogies or to recheck those I already had. Hence, the intensity of begging and intimidation was fairly constant for the duration of the fieldwork. I had to establish my position in some sort of pecking order of ferocity at each and every village.

For the most part, my own "fierceness" took the form of shouting 29 back at the Yąnomamö as loudly and as passionately as they shouted at me, especially at first, when I did not know much of their language. As I became more proficient in their language and learned more about their political tactics, I became more sophisticated in the art of bluffing. For example, I paid one young man a machete to cut palm trees and make boards from the wood. I used these to fashion a platform in the bottom of my dugout canoe to keep my possessions dry when I traveled by river. That afternoon I was doing informant work in the village; the long-awaited mission supply boat arrived, and most of the Indians ran out of the village to beg goods from the crew. I continued to work in the village for another hour or so and went down to the river to say "hello" to the men on the supply boat. I was angry when I discovered that the Indians had chopped up all my palm boards and used them to paddle their own canoes[5] across the river. I knew that if I overlooked this incident I would have invited them to take even greater liberties with my goods in the future. I crossed the river, docked amidst their dugouts, and shouted for the Indians to come out and see me. A few of

[5]The canoes were obtained from missionaries, who, in turn, got them from a different tribe.

the culprits appeared, mischievous grins on their faces. I gave a spirited lecture about how hard I had worked to put those boards in my canoe, how I had paid a machete for the wood, and how angry I was that they destroyed my work in their haste to cross the river. I then pulled out my hunting knife and, while their grins disappeared, cut each of their canoes loose, set it into the current, and let it float away. I left without further ado and without looking back.

30   They managed to borrow another canoe and, after some effort, recovered their dugouts. The headman of the village later told me with an approving chuckle that I had done the correct thing. Everyone in the village, except, of course, the culprits, supported and defended my action. This raised my status.

31   Whenever I took such action and defended my rights, I got along much better with the Yąnomamö. A good deal of their behavior toward me was directed with the forethought of establishing the point at which I would react defensively. Many of them later reminisced about the early days of my work when I was "timid" and a little afraid of them, and they could bully me into giving goods away.

32   Theft was the most persistent situation that required me to take some sort of defensive action. I simply could not keep everything I owned locked in trunks, and the Indians came into my hut and left at will. I developed a very effective means for recovering almost all the stolen items. I would simply ask a child who took the item and then take that person's hammock when he was not around, giving a spirited lecture to the others as I marched away in a faked rage with the thief's hammock. Nobody ever attempted to stop me from doing this, and almost all of them told me that my technique for recovering my possessions was admirable. By nightfall the thief would either appear with the stolen object or send it along with someone else to make an exchange. The others would heckle him for getting caught and being forced to return the item.

33   With respect to collecting the data I sought, there was a very frustrating problem. Primitive social organization is kinship organization, and to understand the Yąnomamö way of life I had to collect extensive genealogies. I could not have deliberately picked a more difficult group to work with in this regard: They have very stringent name taboos. They attempt to name people in such a way that when the person dies and they can no longer use his name, the loss of the word in the language is not inconvenient. Hence, they name people for specific and minute parts of things, such as "toenail of some rodent," thereby being able to retain the words "toenail" and "(specific) rodent," but not being able to refer directly to the toenail of that rodent. The taboo is maintained even for the living: One mark of prestige is the courtesy others show you by not using your name. The sanctions behind the taboo seem to be an unusual combination of fear and respect.

I tried to use kinship terms to collect genealogies at first, but the   34
kinship terms were so ambiguous that I ultimately had to resort to
names. They were quick to grasp that I was bound to learn everybody's
name and reacted, without my knowing it, by inventing false names
for everybody in the village. After having spent several months collecting names and learning them, this came as a disappointment to me: I
could not cross-check genealogies with other informants from distant
villages.

They enjoyed watching me learn these names. I assumed, wrongly,   35
that I would get the truth to each question and that I would get the best
information by working in public. This set the stage for converting a serious project into a farce. Each informant tried to outdo his peers by inventing a name even more ridiculous than what I had been given
earlier, or by asserting that the individual about whom I inquired was
married to his mother or daughter, and the like. I would have the informant whisper the name of the individual in my ear, noting that he was
the father of such and such a child. Everybody would then insist that I
repeat the name aloud, roaring in hysterics as I clumsily pronounced
the name. I assumed that the laughter was in response to the violation
of the name taboo or to my pronunciation. This was a reasonable interpretation, since the individual whose name I said aloud invariably became angry. After I learned what some of the names meant, I began to
understand what the laughter was all about. A few of the more colorful
examples are: "hairy vagina," "long penis," "feces of the harpy eagle,"
and "dirty rectum." No wonder the victims were angry.

I was forced to do my genealogy work in private because of the   36
horseplay and nonsense. Once I did so, my informants began to agree
with each other and I managed to learn a few new names, real names. I
could then test any new informant by collecting a genealogy from him
that I knew to be accurate. I was able to weed out the more mischievous
informants this way. Little by little I extended the genealogies and
learned the real names. Still, I was unable to get the names of the dead
and extend the genealogies back in time, and even my best informants
continued to deceive me about their own close relatives. Most of them
gave me the name of a living man as the father of some individual in
order to avoid mentioning that the actual father was dead.

The quality of a genealogy depends in part on the number of gener-   37
ations it embraces, and the name taboo prevented me from getting any
substantial information about deceased ancestors. Without this information, I could not detect marriage patterns through time. I had to rely
on older informants for this information, but these were the most reluctant of all. As I became more proficient in the language and more skilled
at detecting lies, my informants became better at lying. One of them in
particular was so cunning and persuasive that I was shocked to discover that he had been inventing his information. He specialized in

making a ceremony out of telling me false names. He would look around to make sure nobody was listening outside my hut, enjoin me to never mention the name again, act very nervous and spooky, and then grab me by the head to whisper the name very softly into my ear. I was always elated after an informant session with him, because I had several generations of dead ancestors for the living people. The others refused to give me this information. To show my gratitude, I paid him quadruple the rate I had given the others. When word got around that I had increased the pay, volunteers began pouring in to give me genealogies.

38   I discovered that the old man was lying quite by accident. A club fight broke out in the village one day, the result of a dispute over the possession of a woman. She had been promised to Rerebawä, a particularly aggressive young man who had married into the village. Rerebawä had already been given her older sister and was enraged when the younger girl began having an affair with another man in the village, making no attempt to conceal it from him. He challenged the young man to a club fight, but was so abusive in his challenge that the opponent's father took offense and entered the village circle with his son, wielding a long club. Rerebawä swaggered out to the duel and hurled insults at both of them, trying to goad them into striking him on the head with their clubs. This would have given him the opportunity to strike them on the head. His opponents refused to hit him, and the fight ended. Rerebawä had won a moral victory because his opponents were afraid to hit him. Thereafter, he swaggered around and insulted the two men behind their backs. He was genuinely angry with them, to the point of calling the older man by the name of his dead father. I quickly seized on this as an opportunity to collect an accurate genealogy and pumped him about his adversary's ancestors. Rerebawä had been particularly nasty to me up to this point, but we became staunch allies: We were both outsiders in the local village. I then asked about other dead ancestors and got immediate replies. He was angry with the whole group and not afraid to tell me the names of the dead. When I compared his version of the genealogies to that of the old man, it was obvious that one of them was lying. I challenged his information, and he explained that everybody knew that the old man was deceiving me and bragging about it in the village. The names the old man had given me were the dead ancestors of the members of a village so far away that he thought I would never have occasion to inquire about them. As it turned out, Rerebawä knew most of the people in that village and recognized the names.

39   I then went over the complete genealogical records with Rerebawä, genealogies I had presumed to be in final form. I had to revise them all because of the numerous lies and falsifications they contained. Thus, after five months of almost constant work on the genealogies of just one group, I had to begin almost from scratch!

Discouraging as it was to start over, it was still the first real turning   40
point in my fieldwork. Thereafter, I began taking advantage of local arguments and animosities in selecting my informants, and used more
extensively individuals who had married into the group. I began traveling to other villages to check the genealogies, picking villages that
were on strained terms with the people about whom I wanted information. I would then return to my base camp and check with local informants the accuracy of the new information. If the informants became
angry when I mentioned the new names I acquired from the unfriendly
group, I was almost certain that the information was accurate. For this
kind of checking I had to use informants whose genealogies I knew
rather well: they had to be distantly enough related to the dead person
that they would not go into a rage when I mentioned the name, but not
so remotely related that they would be uncertain of the accuracy of the
information. Thus, I had to make a list of names that I dared not use in
the presence of each and every informant. Despite the precautions, I occasionally hit a name that put the informant into a rage, such as that of
a dead brother or sister that other informants had not reported. This always terminated the day's work with that informant, for he would be
too touchy to continue any further, and I would be reluctant to take a
chance on accidentally discovering another dead kinsman so soon after
the first.

These were always unpleasant experiences, and occasionally dan-   41
gerous ones, depending on the temperament of the informant. On one
occasion I was planning to visit a village that had been raided about a
week earlier. A woman whose name I had on my list had been killed by
the raiders. I planned to check each individual on the list one by one to
estimate ages, and I wanted to remove her name so that I would not say
it aloud in the village. I knew that I would be in considerable difficulty
if I said this name aloud so soon after her death. I called on my original
informant and asked him to tell me the name of the woman who had
been killed. He refused, explaining that she was a close relative of his. I
then asked him if he would become angry if I read off all the names on
the list. This way he did not have to say her name and could merely
nod when I mentioned the right one. He was a fairly good friend of
mine, and I thought I could predict his reaction. He assured me that
this would be a good way of doing it. We were alone in my hut so that
nobody could overhear us. I read the names softly, continuing to the
next when he gave a negative reply. When I finally spoke the name of
the dead woman he flew out of his chair, raised his arm to strike me,
and shouted: "You son-of-a-bitch! If you ever say that name again, I'll
kill you!" He was shaking with rage, but left my hut quickly. I shudder
to think what might have happened if I had said the name unknowingly in the woman's village. I had other, similar experiences in different villages, but luckily the dead person had been dead for some time

and was not closely related to the individual into whose ear I whispered the name. I was merely cautioned to desist from saying any more names, lest I get people angry with me. . . .

✦ Evaluating the Text

1. What was Chagnon's purpose in going to study the Yąnomamö Indians of Brazil, the largest known culturally intact native tribe in the Americas?

2. What incidents reveal the major part that aggression plays in Yąnomamö culture? Does the way aggression is expressed toward Chagnon seem to differ from the way they express it toward each other?

3. What is the phenomenon known as *culture shock,* and what details does Chagnon give that most effectively illustrate it? Specifically, what contrasts can you discover between Chagnon's expectations and the experience of his first encounter with the Yąnomamö?

4. How do the Yąnomamö try to use reciprocal gift-giving to extract Chagnon's prized possessions?

5. Discuss how the taboo involving revealing tribal names, of the living as well as the dead, presented an obstacle to Chagnon's research on the Yąnomamö's genealogy.

6. From Chagnon's account, what do you infer about the role of women in Yąnomamö society?

✦ Exploring Different Perspectives

1. How does Napoleon A. Chagnon bring an expectation of privacy to Brazil in ways that remind you of Raymonde Carroll's analysis in "Home"? Is privacy merely a Western concept?

2. Compare the degree of "culture shock" Chagnon experiences with that described by David R. Counts in "Too Many Bananas."

✦ Extending Viewpoints Through Writing

1. Have you ever experienced what might be called *culture shock?* Describe the circumstances and discuss what about the experience was so unsettling and challenged your expectations. What about this experience enables you to better understand Chagnon's reaction to the Yąnomamö?

2. To what extent does the psychology underlying reciprocal gift giving operate in contemporary American society among your family and friends? What are some of the similarities and differences from the way it operates in Yąnomamö culture?

3. Have you ever tried to construct a family tree? Describe your experiences. To what extent did you hit on the same methods of cross confirmation that Chagnon used?

Gretel Ehrlich

To Live in Two Worlds

◆

Gretel Ehrlich was born and raised in California, educated at Bennington College, UCLA Film School, and the New School for Social Research, and first went to Wyoming as a documentary film maker. Her work has appeared in The New York Times, The Atlantic, *and* Harper's. *She has worked on ranches, branding cattle and herding sheep, and currently lives with her husband on a ranch in Shell, Wyoming. "To Live in Two Worlds" is her fascinating first hand account of the Kiowa Indian Sun Dance, from her book* The Solace of Open Spaces *(1986).*

1   July. Last night from one in the morning until four, I sat in the bed of my pickup with a friend and watched meteor showers hot dance over our heads in sprays of little suns that looked like white orchids. With so many stars falling around us I wondered if daylight would come. We forget that our sun is only a star destined to someday burn out. The time scale of its transience so far exceeds our human one that our unconditional dependence on its life-giving properties feels oddly like an indiscretion about which we'd rather forget.

2   The recent news that astronomers have discovered a new solar system in-the-making around another sun-star has startled us out of a collective narcissism based on the assumption that we dominate the cosmic scene. Now we must make room for the possibility of new life— not without resentment and anticipation—the way young couples make room in their lives for a baby. By chance, this discovery came the same day a Kiowa friend invited me to attend a Sun Dance.

3   I have Indian neighbors all around me—Crow and Cheyenne to the north, Shoshone and Arapaho to the south—and though we often ranch, drink, and rodeo side by side, and dress in the same cowboy uniforms— Wrangler jeans, tall boots, wide-brimmed, high-crowned hats—there is nothing in our psyches, styles, or temperaments that is alike.

4   Because Christians shaped our New World culture we've had to swallow an artificial division between what's sacred and what's profane. Many westerners, like Native Americans, have made a life for themselves out in the raw wind, riding the ceremony of seasons with a fine-tuned eye and ear for where the elk herd is hidden or when in fall

*(For information on the Kiowas, see p. 127.)

to bring the cattle down. They'll knock a sage hen in the head with a rock for dinner and keep their bearings in a ferocious storm as ably as any Sioux warrior, but they won't become visionaries, diviners, or healers in the process.

On a Thursday I set off at two in the morning and drove to the reservation. It was dark when I arrived and quiet. On a broad plain bordered in the west by mountains, the families of the hundred men who were pledging the dance had set up camps: each had a white canvas tipi, a wall tent, and a rectangular brush arbor in a circle around the Lodge, where for the next four days the ceremony would take place. At 5 A.M. I could still see stars, the Big Dipper suspended in the northwest as if magnified, and to the east, a wide band of what looked like blood. I sat on the ground in the dark. Awake and stirring now, some of the "dancers" filed out of the Lodge, their star quilts pulled tightly over their heads. When they lined up solemnly behind two portable johns, I thought I was seeing part of the dance. Then I had to laugh at myself but at the same time understood how the sacredness of this ceremony was located not just in the Lodge but everywhere.

Sun Dance is the holiest religious ceremony of the Plains tribes, having spread from the Cheyenne to the Sioux, Blackfoot, Gros Ventre, Assiniboine, Arapaho, Bannock, and Shoshone sometime after the year 1750. It's not "sun worship" but an inoculation of regenerative power that restores health, vitality, and harmony to the land and all tribes.

For the hundred dancers who have volunteered to dance this year (the vow obligates them to dance four times during their lives) Sun Dance is a serious and painful undertaking; called "thirsty standing," they eat no food and drink no water for four days. This year, with the hundred-degree heat we've been having, their suffering will be extreme. The ceremonies begin before dawn and often last until two or three in the morning. They must stay in the Lodge for the duration. Speaking to or making eye contact with anyone not dancing is forbidden, and it's considered a great disgrace to drop out of the dance before it is over.

Sun Dance was suppressed by the government in the 1880s, and its full revival has only been recent. Some tribes practiced the ceremony secretly, others stopped. George Horse Capture, a Gros Ventre who lives near me and has completed one Sun Dance, has had to read the same sources I have—Dorsey, Kroeber, and Peter Powell—to reeducate himself in his tradition.

"Did you sleep here last night?" an old man, one of the elders of the tribe, asked. Shrunken and hawk-nosed, he wore a blue farmer's cap and walked with a crudely carved pine cane. "No, I drove from Shell," I answered, sounding self-conscious because I seemed to be the only white person around. "Oh . . . you have a very good spirit to get up so early and come all this way. That's good . . . I'm glad you are here," he said. His round eyes narrowed and he walked away. On the other side of the shed where the big drum was kept he approached three teenage girls. "You sober?" he asked. "Yes," they replied in unison. "Good," he said. "Don't make war on anyone. If you're not drunk, there's peace." He hobbled past me again out into the parched field between the circle of tents and the Lodge. Coleman lanterns were being lighted and the tipis behind him glowed. He put both hands on top of the cane and, in a hoarse voice that carried far across the encampment, sang an Arapaho morning song: "Get up, Everybody get up . . . ," it began, followed by encouragements to face the day.

10   The sky had lightened; it was a shield of pink. The new moon, white when I had arrived, now looked blue. Another voice—sharp, gravelly, and less patient, boomed from the north, his song overlapping that of the first Crier's. I looked: he was a younger man but bent at the shoulders like a tree. He paced the hard ground as he sang, and the tweed jacket he wore, which gave him a Dickensian look, hung from him and swayed in the breeze. Now I could hear two other Criers to the south and west. The four songs overlapped, died out, and started again. The men, silhouetted, looked ghostlike against the horizon, almost disembodied, as though their age and authority were entirely in the vocal cords.

11   First light. In the Lodge the dancers were dressing. Over gym shorts (the modern substitute for breechclouts), they pulled on long, white, sheath skirts, to which they fastened, with wide beaded belts, their dance aprons: two long panels, front and back, decorated with beads, ribbons, and various personal insignias. Every man wore beaded moccasins, leaving legs and torsos bare. Their faces, chests, arms, and the palms of their hands were painted yellow. Black lines skittered across chests, around ankles and wrists, and encircled each face. Four bundles of sage, which represents healing and breath, were tucked straight up in the apron fronts; thin braided wreaths of it were slipped onto the dancer's wrists and ankles, and a crown of sage ending in two loose sprays looked like antennae.

12   Light begets activity—the Lodge began filling up. It's a log arbor, forty yards across, covered with a thatchwork of brush. Its sixteen sides radiate from a great center pole of cottonwood—the whole trunk of a hundred-year-old tree whose forked top looked like antlers. A white cloth was tied with rope around the bark, and overhead, on four of the pine stringers, tribal members had hung bandanas, silk cowboy scarves, and shawls that all together form a loose, trembling hieroglyph spelling out personal requests for health and repair.

13   Alongside the dancers, who stood in a circle facing east, a group of older men filed in. These were the "grandfathers" (ceremonially related, not by blood) who would help the younger dancers through their four-day ordeal.

The little shed against which I had leaned in the premorning light   14
opened and became an announcer's stand. From it the drum was rolled
out and set up at the entrance to the Lodge.

Light begets activity begets light. The sky looked dry, white, and in-   15
flammable. Eleven drummers who, like "the grandfathers," were probably ranchers sat on metal folding chairs encircling the drum. A stream
of announcements in both Arapaho and English flooded the air. Friends
and relatives of the dancers lined up in front of the Lodge. I found myself in a group of Indian women. The drumming, singing, and dancing
began all at once. It's not really a dance with steps but a dance of con-
tainment, a dance in place. Facing east and blowing whistles made of
eagle wing bones in shrill unison, the men bounced up and down on
their heels in time to the drumbeat. Series after series of songs, composed especially for Sun Dance, were chanted in high, intense voices.
The ropey, repeating pulse was so strong it seemed to pull the sun up.

There were two important men at the back of the Lodge I hadn't   16
noticed. That their faces were painted red, not yellow, signified the status of Instructor, Pledger, or Priest. The taller of the two held a hoop
(the sun) with eagle feathers (the bird of day) fastened around it. The
"grandfather" standing in back of him raised the hoop-holding hand
and, from behind, pushed the arm up and down in a wide, swinging
arc until it took flight on its own.

I felt warmth on my shoulder. As the sun topped the horizon, the   17
dancers stretched their arms straight out, lifting them with the progress
of the sun's rising. Songs pushed from the backs of the drummers'
throats. The skin on the dancer's chests bounced as though from some
interior tremor. When the light hit their faces, they looked as if they
were made of sun.

The sunrise ceremony ended at eight. They had danced for nearly two   18
hours and already the heat of the day was coming on. Pickups rambled
through camps, children played quietly everywhere. Walking to a
friend's camp, I began to understand how the wide ampleness of the Indian body stands for a spirit of accommodation. In the ceremony I had
just witnessed, no one—dancer, observer, child, priest, or drummer—
had called attention to himself. There was no applause, no frivolous-
ness. Families ambled back to their camps as though returning from a
baseball game. When I entered my friend's brush arbor (already a relief
from the sun) and slid behind the picnic table bench she handed me the
cup of coffee I'd been hoping for. "They're dancing for all of us," she
said. Then we drained our cups in silence.

Though I came and went from the Sun Dance grounds (it was too   19
hot to stand around in the direct sun) the ceremonies continued all day
and most of each night. At nine the "runners" drove to the swamp to
cut reeds from which they fashioned beds for the dancers. The moisture
in the long, bladelike leaves helped cool the men off. At ten, special

food eaten by the dancers' families was blessed in the Lodge, and this was surely to become one of the dancers' daily agonies: the smell of meat, stew, and fry bread filling the space, then being taken away. The sunrise drummers were spelled by new ones, and as the songs began again those dancers who could stood in their places and danced. Each man was required to dance a certain number of hours a day. When he was too weak or sick or reeling from hallucination, he was allowed to rest on his rush mat.

20 "What happens if it rains during Sun Dance?" I asked my Kiowa friend. "It doesn't," she answered curtly. By eleven, it was ninety-nine degrees. We drove west away from the grounds to the land she owned and went skinny-dipping in the river. Her brown body bobbed up and down next to my white one. Behind us a wall of colored rock rose out of the water, part of a leathery bluff that curved for miles. "That's where the color for the Sun Dance paints comes from," my friend's husband said, pointing to a cave. He'd just floated into view from around an upstream bend. With his big belly glinting, he had the complacent look of a man who lords over a houseful of women: a wife, two daughters, a young tutor for his girls. The night before, they'd thrown an anniversary party at this spot. There were tables full of Mexican food, a five-piece Mexican band whose members looked like reformed Hell's Angels, a charro with four skinny horses and a trick-riding act, two guests who arrived from the oil fields by helicopter, and a mutual friend who's Jewish and a Harvard professor who popped bikini-clad out of a giant plywood cake.

21 The men in the Rabbit Lodge danced as late as the party-goers. The next morning when I arrived at four-thirty the old man with the cane walked directly to me. "Where's your coat? Aren't you cold?" he asked gruffly, though I knew he was welcoming me. The dancers spit bile and shuffled back and forth between the johns and the Lodge. A friend had asked one of them how he prepared for Sun Dance. He replied, "I don't. There's no way to prepare for pain." As the dancers began to look more frail, the singing became raucous. The astounding volume, quick rises in pitch, and forays into falsetto had an enlivening effect on all of us. Now it was the drummers who made the dancers make the sun rise.

22 Noon. In the hottest midday sun the dancers were brought out in front of the Lodge to be washed and freshly painted. The grandfathers dipped soft little brooms of sage in water and swabbed the men down; they weren't allowed to drink. Their families gathered around and watched while the dancers held their gaze to the ground. I couldn't bring myself to stand close. It seemed a violation of privacy. It wasn't nudity that rendered the scene so intimate (they still had their gym shorts on), but the thirst. Behind me, someone joked about dancing for rain instead of sun.

I was wrong about the bathing scene. Now the desolation of it   23
struck me as beautiful. All afternoon the men danced in the heat—two,
eight, or twenty of them at a time. In air so dry and with their juices
squeezed out, the bouncing looked weightless, their bodies thin and
brittle as shells. It wasn't the pain of the sacrifice they were making that
counted but the emptiness to which they were surrendering themselves. It was an old ritual: separation, initiation, return. They'd left
their jobs and families to dance. They were facing physical pain and
psychological transformation. Surely, the sun seared away preoccupation and pettiness. They would return changed. Here, I was in the presence of a collective hero. I searched their faces and found no martyrs,
no dramatists, no antiheroes either. They seemed to pool their pain and
offer it back to us, dancing not for our sins but to ignite our hearts.

Evening. There were many more spectators tonight. Young Indian   24
women cradling babies moved to the front of the Lodge. They rocked
them in time with the drums and all evening not one child cried. Cur-
rents of heat rose from the ground; in fact, everything seemed to be rising: bone whistles, arms, stars, penises, the yeast in the fry bread, the
smell of sage. My breasts felt full. The running joke in camp was about
"Sun Dance Babies." Surely the expansive mood in the air settled over
the tipis at night, but there was more to it than that. Among some tribes
a "Sacred Woman" is involved in the ceremony. The sun is a "man
power" symbol. When she offers herself to the priest, their union represents the rebirth of the land, water, and people. If by chance a child is
conceived, he or she is treated with special reverence for a lifetime.

Dawn. This morning I fainted. The skinny young man dancing in   25
front of me appeared to be cringing in pain. Another dancer's face had
been painted green. I'm not saying they made me faint—maybe I
fainted for them. With little ado, the women behind me picked me up.
Revived and feeling foolish, I stood through to the end. "They say
white people don't have the constitution to go without water for so
many days," a white friend commented later. It sounded like a racist
remark to me. She'd once been offered a chance to fast with a medicine
man and refused. "I think it has more to do with one's concepts of hope
and fear," I mumbled as she walked through the field to her car.

Afternoon. At five, only two dancers were standing. Because of the   26
heat, the smell of urine had mixed with the sage.

Later in the evening I stood next to two teenage boys from Okla-   27
homa. Not realizing I was old enough to be their mother, they flirted
with me, then undercut the dares with cruelty. "My grandmother hates
white tourists," the one who had been eyeing my chest said to me.
"You're missing the point of this ceremony," I said to him. "And racism
isn't a good thing anywhere." They walked away, but later, when I
bumped into them, they smiled apologetically.

28   When I had coffee in a friend's brush arbor during a break in the dancing, the dancer's wife looked worried. "He looks like death warmed over," she said. A young man with black braids that reached his belt buckle was dangling a baby on each knee; I've never seen men so gentle and at ease with children. A fresh breeze fanned us. The round-the-clock rhythm of drumbeats and dancing made day and night seem the same. Sleeping became interchangeable with waiting, until, finally, there was no difference between the two.

29   Sunday. Two American flags were raised over the Lodge today—both had been owned by war veterans. The dance apron of a man near me had U.S. Navy insignias sewn into the corners. Here was a war hero, but he'd earned his medal far from home. Now the ritual of separation, initiation, and return performed in Vietnam, outside the context of community, changes into separation, benumbment, and exile.

30   Throughout the afternoon's dancing there was a Give-Away, an Indian tradition to honor friends, relatives, and admirers with a formal exchange of gifts. In front of the announcer's stand there was a table chock-full of food and another stacked high with Pendleton blankets, shawls, and beadwork. The loudspeaker overwhelmed the drumming until all the gifts were dispersed. Pickups streamed through the camps and a layer of dust muted the hard brightness of the day. After his first Sun Dance one old man told me he had given nearly everything he owned away: horse, wagons, clothes, winter blankets. "But it all comes back," he said, as if the day and night rhythm of this ceremony stood for a bigger tidal cadence as well.

31   Evening. They've taken the brush away from the far side of the Lodge. Now the dancers face west. All hundred men, freshly painted with a wild dappling of dots, stripes, and crooked lines, bounced up and down vigorously and in short strokes waved eagle fans in front of their bodies as if to clear away any tiredness there.

32   When I asked why the Sun Dance ended at night, my friend said, "So the sun will remember to make a complete circle, and so we'll always have night and day." The sun drained from the dancers' faces and sank into a rack of thunderclouds over the mountains. Every movement coming from the Lodge converged into a single trajectory, a big "V" like a flock of birds migrating toward me. This is how ritual speaks with no words. The dancing and whistling surged; each time a crescendo felt near, it ebbed. In the southwest, the first evening star appeared, and the drumming and singing, which had begun to feel like a hard dome over my head, stopped.

33   Amid cries of relief and some clapping I heard hoarse expulsions of air coming from dancers, like whales breaching after being under water too long. They rushed forward to the front of the Lodge, throwing off the sage bracelets and crowns, knelt down in turn by wooden bowls of chokecherry juice, and drank their first liquid in four days.

The family standing next to me approached the Lodge cautiously. 34
"There he is," I heard the mother say. They walked toward the dancer,
a big, lumbering man in his thirties whose waist, where rolls of fat had
been, now looked concave. The man's wife and father slid their arms
around his back, while his mother stood in front and took a good look
at him. He gave her the first drink of sweet water from his bowl. "I
tried to be there as much as possible today. Did you see me?" his wife
asked. He nodded and smiled. Some of the young children had rushed
into the Lodge and were swinging the flattened reeds that had been the
dancers' beds around and around in the air. One of the drummers, an
energetic man with an eccentric, husky voice, walked up to a group of
us and started shaking our hands. He didn't know us but it didn't matter. "I'm awfully glad you're here," he kept saying, then walked away
laughing ecstatically. The dancer I had been watching was having
trouble staying on his feet. He stumbled badly. A friend said he worked
for Amoco and tomorrow he'd be back in the oil fields. Still supporting
him with their arms, his family helped him toward their brush arbor,
now lit with oil lamps, where he would vomit, then feast.

✦ Evaluating the Text

1. What is the Sun Dance designed to accomplish?

2. Ehrlich's account appears in the form of a journal entry for July. What
   is the thematic relationship between the entries based on her observation of meteor showers and the underlying imagery of the Sun Dance?

3. Describe the preparation of the dancers for taking part in the Sun
   Dance. What is the significance of the different elements of the costume and the kinds of colors worn as it relates to the purpose of the
   dance?

4. How are different stages of the dance designed to mimic events in the
   natural world? For example, how is the sun "pulled up"?

5. What provisions are made for the dancers to rest between "shifts"?

6. What can you infer about Ehrlich's relationship with her Kiowa
   friend? What encounters does Ehrlich have with different people in
   the camp? At which moments does she feel more like an insider and
   less like an outsider?

7. How is the ritual conducted so as to progress through phases of separation, initiation, and return?

8. Why is it important that the dancers not make eye contact with each
   other or the crowd?

9. What kind of events occur on the third day that seem, to Ehrlich, to re-veal the regenerative effects of the Sun Dance?

10. Ehrlich's account takes the form of a first-person narrative, of the kind that might be found in a journal or diary. Yet her account has been re-fined from initial notes and observations. At what points do you think Ehrlich is attempting to make her original account "more literary"? What specific words and phrases can you cite that support this?

11. How would you characterize Ehrlich's attitude toward the events she describes? How does she seem to have been changed by the experi-ence of witnessing the Sun Dance of the Kiowas?

✦ Exploring Different Perspectives

1. How does the idea of reciprocity play as important a role in Kiowa cul-ture as it does in New Guinea, according to David R. Counts's analysis in "Too Many Bananas"?

2. In what way are rituals in the Sun Dance of the Kiowa and fiestas in Mexico described by Octavio Paz in "The Day of the Dead" based on the principle that if you give away or divest yourself of worldly pos-sessions or use all the money you have for religious festivals, the orig-inal amounts and more will be returned to you? Discuss the psychology of sacrifice that underlies this belief.

✦ Extending Viewpoints for Writing

1. Were you ever invited by someone from another culture to witness or take part in a ceremony or ritual that was important to them? Describe your experiences, and tell how the actual event was different from what you had expected.

2. What is the longest period of time you have ever gone without food and water? Have you ever fasted for religious or spiritual reasons? Write a narrative explaining how you felt before, during, and after your fast.

3. Have you ever participated in a religious ceremony that entailed dep-rivation, fasting, or other voluntary suffering? Describe the meaning and purpose of the ritual.

4. How is the Sun Dance similar to and different from what we usually call dancing? Discuss as many significant similarities and differences as you can discover (e.g., how are differences in eye contact or lack of it between the dancers and the crowd, apparel, makeup, musical ac-

companiment, movement of the dancers, eating and drinking while dancing, all related to different purposes of the Sun Dance versus regular dancing?)

5. Ehrlich observes that although she and her Indian neighbors "often ranch, drink, and rodeo side by side, and dress in the same cowboy uniforms . . . there is nothing in our psyches, styles, or temperaments, that is alike." Unlike secular culture, American Indian culture does not segregate the sacred from everyday life. Discuss how the details in the performance of the Sun Dance reveal this lack of separation.

Raymonde Carroll

Home

◆

Raymonde Carroll was born in Tunisia and educated in France and the United States. She was trained as an anthropologist and studied the culture of Micronesia while she lived for three years on a Pacific atoll. She presently teaches in the Department of Romance Languages at Oberlin College. "Home" is a chapter from her book Cultural Misunderstandings: The French-American Experience *(translated by Carol Volk, 1988). This investigation of the misperceptions that can arise between the French and Americans reveals how important implicit cultural assumptions are in shaping conceptions of space, territory, and privacy in the home.*

1   Several years ago, an American anthropologist returning from France, where he had spent the summer on his way back from Africa, told me that what had really struck him was the distrustfulness of the French, who always kept their shutters closed. Just the idea of shutters . . . They made the streets particularly gloomy, as if the villages were uninhabited, or as if people were spying on you from behind them (This anthropologist did not do research in France.)

2   When my mother came to visit me in the United States, she liked the style of American houses, the way they stood separate from each other, the big lawns, the architectural diversity, the space. One day, we were quietly seated in the living room when she suddenly became aware of the large bay window and, visibly shocked, said to me, "My goodness, you live in the street!" And I understood exactly what she was feeling. It took me years to get used to "living in the street." And when I stroll around my neighborhood in the evening, I am still somewhat surprised at being able to see right into each home. People read, watch television, throw parties, eat dinner, do the dishes, or whatever without closing their drapes, and they are apparently not the least bit bothered by the possibility of a stranger's eyes peering into their lives. And even today, I'm the one who always closes the drapes in our home, much to the amusement of my American husband.

3   The lawns surrounding American houses display this same refusal to separate the street and the house. In certain American cities the side-

*(For information on France, see p. 286.)

walk itself disappears, the lawn ends where the street begins, and the owner of the house is responsible for its upkeep (as he or she would be for the upkeep of the sidewalk). Space substitutes for walls, railings, or fences, which are sometimes replaced by bushes or trees. But the cutoff point is not clearly defined. Thus, in spring and summer, it is common to see passing strollers sit awhile on your lawn to rest, without, however, going beyond an implicit limit. Backyards and gardens blend into each other in certain small American cities, but more often they are separated by low hedges, across which neighbors exchange produce from their gardens or simply chat. According to an old American tradition, when a family moves into a neighborhood the neighbors immediately come to welcome them, bringing hot coffee and cakes. I benefited from this type of welcome in two different cities, each with over one hundred thousand inhabitants. (I'm speaking here about moving into houses, not apartments.)

We can therefore understand an American's surprise when faced   4
with the walls, gates, shutters, and drawn curtains that "protect" French houses, as well as the uneasiness of a French person before these "open" American houses. But these differences do not really cause any problems. It is inside the house that blunders or misunderstandings have a greater chance of arising.

Dick and Jill are invited to dinner at Pierre and Jeanne's. The con-   5
versation becomes lively during cocktails. Pierre speaks enthusiastically about a book he thinks would interest Dick a great deal. He has it in fact, and goes to look for it in his study. He is taken aback, as he heads toward the room, when he realizes that Dick is following him. Jeanne goes to the kitchen to check if something is burning. She is just as taken aback when she sees Jill walk in right behind her. Jill offers to help. "No, no thank you, everything is ready . . ." Or at the end of the meal, Jill gets up to clear the table and carries the dishes into the kitchen, or else Dick offers to do the dishes. Pierre and Jeanne protest; if they are unfamiliar with American habits, they might very well consider Jill and Dick to be "intrusive" or "inconsiderate," or they might be "ashamed" that Dick or Jill has seen the rooms "in a terrible mess." ("But what could I do? I wasn't expecting him to follow me all over the house, I didn't know how to stop him.") In fact, it would have sufficed to say "I'll be back in a minute" for Dick not to have gotten up, for him not to have felt obliged to accompany Pierre because Pierre was going out of his way for him.

French people are often surprised when, the first time they enter an   6
American home, their hosts show them around the house, and they interpret this as "showing off." Without excluding this possibility, it is important to understand that an American considers this an attempt to

make you "feel at home" by immediately giving you an opportunity to orient yourself, so to speak. Thus, instead of taking your coat when you arrive at a party, the host will show you in which bedroom and on what floor "the coats go." This, among other things, allows you to check your hair, or whatever you like, in the bathroom mirror next door. And if the party is a success, it will spill over into every room on the ground floor, with a definite preference for the kitchen. Guests serve themselves at the bar set up for the occasion (unless the party is more "formal"), help themselves to beer from the refrigerator—in short, they try hard to do as much as they can by themselves so as not to "bother" their host, who also has a right to have fun. This means that the cupboards and drawers are likely to be opened and closed freely, which would give French people the sense that they were being "intruded upon" or that their guests had "been all over the place."

7   These few examples, and there are many others, already show how different the relationship to the home is in these two cultures.

8   A French informant told me that he had never entered the kitchen at his grandmother's house, where he ate lunch once a week, until she became very old and less mobile and resigned herself to sending him to get things from the kitchen during meals. While the division between public and private is clearly marked outside the house by its division from the street, thanks to the walls, gates, and drawn curtains mentioned earlier, it is not so clearly marked inside the French home. But the dividing line, though implicit, exists just the same.

9   One can, in fact, determine the degree of intimacy between two people if one knows to which rooms one person has access in the other's house. The unknown person, the stranger, stays at the door. The next step consists in access to the foyer, then to the living room, then to the dining room (and, if need be, to the toilet). Many visitors will never go any further. A child's friends may have access to the room of that child, as well as to the kitchen for something to drink or for a snack, if they are regular guests in the house. The bathroom, which is separate from the toilet, is off-limits and is reserved for those who could be invited to spend the night. The refrigerator, the closets and the drawers are rarely accessible, except to those considered to be true "intimates" of the house. The room that remains sacred is the parents' bedroom. Of course we are talking about a house that has all these rooms, but space is not the significant factor in this context. Rather, it is the way in which this space is opened, or not opened, to all those who are not part of the "immediate" family (comprised of the parents and children). Thus, if my father-in-law or mother-in-law, or even my father or mother, lives under my roof, that does not automatically give him or her access to my bedroom. On the contrary. "Well brought up" French people know all this. But one can easily imagine the misunderstandings that can

arise when Americans are invited to French homes or when they live (as students) with French families for a period of time.

Similarly, there are misunderstandings in the reverse direction, which may seem surprising given the "relaxed" attitude with which Americans receive guests. A French writer, whose name I will not mention, wrote a book explaining Americans to the French. He enthusiastically tells us that when the lady of the house receives you wearing curlers, it is precisely to make you relax and "feel at home." No problem up to that point. The writer, grateful and admiring, describes the comfort of the room reserved for him, mentions the small touches like letter paper and stamps on the desk. Then the maid (rather a rare character, except in certain social spheres) asks him if he is going to dine with his hosts, and what he would like for dinner. The first evening, he tells us, he goes down to eat with his hosts. Then the second evening, because of the "relaxed" attitude and "kindness" of his hosts, and because he has a great deal of work to do, he decides to eat dinner in his room and "orders a steak and french fries from the maid."

If the writer in question actually did this, his hosts undoubtedly respected his wishes. But it is also more than likely that they attributed his request to "the well-known arrogance" of the French, or at least that they were deeply shocked by the "vulgarity" of this French person, whom, nevertheless, they would never think of enlightening as to his "monstrous" blunder. (The two questions he was asked probably mean "Are you planning to go out for dinner?" and "We'll do our best to please you," or something of that nature.) An unfortunate misunderstanding crowns the best of intentions in this case: the writer-character comes off as a boor, whereas it is his enthusiasm for American hospitality (as he understands it) that makes him unknowingly behave in an impolite fashion.

The misunderstanding is easy to comprehend. Indeed, when you are a house guest in an American home, your hosts immediately show you your room, the "bathroom" (which includes the toilet), the place where towels are kept (or where you can get new ones, if there are already some in your room), the kitchen, including everything you need to make a cup of coffee or tea if you wake up in the middle of the night, and, finally, the refrigerator. At the same time, they invite you to "make yourself at home" and to "help yourself to anything you want." It is therefore possible that one's enthusiasm for "so much openness" might leave one with the impression of having all the advantages of a hotel at home, and that this would result in one's taking the invitation not to stand on ceremony literally. It is, in fact, almost impossible, without cultural analysis, to know where the line is drawn, a line which remains completely implicit. All the Americans to whom I told this story were shocked by the blunder, surprised that such a mistake was possible.

One need only, however, carry the logic beyond the invisible line to make such an error.

13   An American student who spent a year living with a French family told me that an uncomfortable situation had developed toward the end of her stay, that there had been a kind of estrangement, for reasons which she did not understand. After she answered all kinds of questions from me, we reconstructed the misunderstanding as follows. At the beginning of her stay, as she did not yet know the family, she spent a good deal of time chatting with the mother and children on returning from school, before going to work in her room. Since she didn't feel quite comfortable yet, she kept the door to her room open. Much later, when she thought that she had become "a member of the family" and really felt at home, she (unconsciously) began acting exactly as she did at home. That is, on returning from school, she simply said hello and went directly to her room to work, automatically closing one door. It was at this point that the family, who must have felt she was rejecting them without understanding why, began to treat her with greater distance, "like a foreigner." Only after our discussion did she realize that what was for her a kind of compliment to the family (they made her feel at home) was on the contrary an insult (undeserved, and therefore all the more baffling) to the family, who had treated her as one of them.

14   Another student, this time one who lived in a small hotel which had been transformed into a residence for foreign students, told me of an unpleasant experience which she didn't understand. This story, once again, involves a door. One Saturday morning, as neither she nor her roommate had classes, they told the cleaning woman that they would make their beds themselves because they wanted to sleep late. The cleaning woman, according to them, left looking very angry. The following Saturday, in order to assure that they would not be awakened, they put a "do not disturb" sign on the outer doorknob. This in no way stopped the cleaning woman, who knocked and entered. The two young women didn't stop her, because the "only other solution, which is very difficult for Americans, would have been to tell her to leave." What shocked them most of all was that the cleaning woman knocked and entered almost simultaneously, without giving them a chance to answer. What they considered to be an inviolable space, a room with a closed door, was simply invaded, as if by right. The student who told me of this experience summarized the source of the misunderstanding in this way: "In France, people knock on the door to announce that they are entering, whereas in the United States, it is to ask for permission to enter (for which one must wait) or to make certain the room is empty." I myself remember that, after having spent several years in the United States, I was shocked when a new colleague, who had just arrived from France, knocked and "barged into" my office. Everyone else waited for

a "come in," including French people who had been living in the
United States for a longer period of time.

A young American, who was boarding with a family in the six- 15
teenth arrondissement in Paris, began, he says, to "behave like a member of the family" until the day when, to his great disappointment, the
mother told him that she had rented him the room for purely economic
reasons and not to establish a quasi-familial relationship with him. He
could not understand how one could have someone in one's home and
at one's table and at the same time treat that person "like a stranger." In
an equivalent case in the United States, a family who rents a room to a
student gives him access to the kitchen ("kitchen privileges") but not to
the dining table without a special invitation. A permanent invitation to
share the family meal calls for "member of the family" behavior, which
undoubtedly explains why the "pension" system does not exist nowadays in most places.

A French student in the United States explained to another French 16
woman, in my presence, that she had moved into a room she liked very
much and which an American professor, known for his fine cooking,
rented to her. When the woman asked if she ate with the professor's
family, the student protested, with both an amused and indignant air,
"Oh, no! He made it clear that meals were not part of the deal, and that I
shouldn't feel tempted, no matter what kinds of smells emanated from
the kitchen. . . . He promised to invite me to dinner. . . . I can't wait." The
dividing line had been clearly indicated in this particular case—a rare
occurrence. But this clarification did not seem to have prevented the
French student from feeling somewhat ruffled, so difficult it is to get
used to the assumptions of others. It is all the more difficult for a French
person to understand this attitude, since "everyone knows" that Americans invite "people they meet on the street" to dinner, "warmly" open
their homes to people they hardly know, easily lend their houses to
friends so that friends of their friends, whom they don't know, can use it
in their absence. The nonexistence of the boarding system can be explained by the fact that an American will easily put his possessions and
himself at your disposal if you are his guest but will not agree to "sell"
you his services right inside his home, to give you the rights of a "paying
customer" over him and over his freedom. In the French family, everyone usually eats dinner together. The meal must therefore be prepared in
any case, and one more person at the table doesn't make much difference. In the American family, on the other hand, it is possible for each
family member to eat dinner separately on certain evenings, when it is
most convenient for her or him, because schedules are often difficult to
coordinate. Having a boarder and owing him or her a meal every day
would demand more of the "parents" than the children do themselves.

17   It is now clear that French and American houses differ not only in the exterior. Their differences are in fact reproduced, but less visibly, inside the house. The distinct separation between the inside and the outside in French culture anticipates the barriers to be crossed once inside. Access to different rooms denotes the path toward intimacy, so to speak, and corresponds to the visible/invisible division. What I mean is that the rooms which are "off limits" are closed and hidden from the eyes of those who have not been specifically admitted. By the same token, someone who stands close to a window, perfectly visible from the street, should adopt an "outside" form of behavior, even though he is separated from the outside by the window.

18   On the other hand, the American house is as open to strangers as it is visible from the street. In the evening, lit up on a dark street, it even attracts attention. If this does not seem to bother an American, it is because such openness in no way encroaches on his privacy, which he defines by setting up the barriers of his choice—by closing the door to his room, by surrounding himself by huge lawns or thick trees, by refusing all boarders, or simply by stopping you on your way to a room by saying "I'd rather you didn't see the mess," or "I'll be right back." Fences, walls, and high hedges give him the impression of being closed in and seem to deprive him of the spectacle of the street, the forest, or the beach bordering his house. And he will consider as an invasion of his privacy any intrusion made without his knowledge or against his wishes (electronic surveillance, of course, but also a door opened without waiting for permission, and the like). An American colleague does not enter your office without being invited: he or she remains on the threshold, even if the door is wide open. If your window is near the street, passersby will make it their business "not to see you," and if by chance your gazes meet through the window, they will smile or make a friendly gesture as if to say that they were looking into your house "by accident."

19   If I take the logic of the preceding analysis to its limit, I obtain two literally inverse situations. In French culture, the person who enters my house is responsible for knowing the rules, for remaining within the spatial limits that our relationship authorizes. (Thus I must be wary of a stranger who would invite me to skip some steps, to penetrate the depths of his house immediately.) I therefore have no defense against guests who feel "at ease" in my home, like Americans who follow me into the kitchen. In American culture, on the other hand, I am the one who is responsible for indicating the limits beyond which a person entering my house must not venture. What is troubling for French people is that these limits can change according to my mood. Here is an example: Tom (American) is putting up the parents of his wife (French), who

are vacationing in the United States. On certain evenings, Tom is "charming" and sociable, whereas on others he comes home from work, barely says hello, takes a beer from the refrigerator ("without even offering them one"), sinks into his chair, and reads the paper. In this case, Tom, for personal reasons which, according to American culture, he need not explain, is indicating that he does not want his "space," his privacy, to be invaded. It is very probable that Tom would behave in exactly the same way in the absence of his in-laws, that his desire for solitude has nothing to do with them. But the in-laws, not knowing how to interpret this message, are hurt and do not understand why Tom "has them at his home, only to treat them this way."

As we can see, hardly have we crossed the threshold when the intercultural misunderstandings begin. We can easily imagine that these won't be the last.

✦ Evaluating the Text

1. In Carroll's view, how are American cultural expectations in regard to privacy reflected in the architecture of American homes in ways that are diametrically opposite to those of the French in terms of the placement of walls, gates, railings, fences, trees, and other natural and artificial barriers?

2. How does the example of Dick and Jill being invited to dinner at Pierre and Jeanne's illustrate Carroll's insights into the differences in cultural expectations between the French and Americans regarding privacy, space, and territory?

3. How do the experiences of students renting a room with a French family illustrate the unspoken cultural assumptions that distinguish French from American culture? How might these different assumptions lead to cross-cultural misunderstandings? How does knocking on the door give rise to different expectations in each culture?

✦ Exploring Different Perspectives

1. What distinctive attitude toward possessions and privacy do you find in the analyses by Raymonde Carroll and Napoleon A. Chagnon (see "Doing Fieldwork Among the Yąnomamö")?

2. How do the accounts by Raymonde Carroll and Gretel Ehrlich (see "To Live in Two Worlds") develop the theme of boundaries, that is, what you are permitted to do and see?

✦ Extending Viewpoints Through Writing

1. Discuss what the term *privacy* means to you, and relate any experiences you have had that suggested a dramatically different understanding of this concept between you and family members or friends.

2. Discuss a situation (for example, one that involved showing affection in public, interactions between parents and children, conceptions of privacy, telephone manners) through which it was obvious to you that people from different cultures relied on different assumptions to interpret the same action or situation.

Alison Lurie

The Language of Clothes

———◆———

*Alison Lurie, born in 1926 in Chicago, is professor of American literature
at Cornell University. Lurie is the author of several novels, including*
Love and Friendship *(1962),* Imaginary Friends *(1967),* The War Between the Tates *(1974), later made into a movie, and* Foreign Affairs,
*which won a Pulitzer Prize for fiction in 1985. Her fiction is character-
ized by a sense of the fragility of social relationships and by compassionate
insight into fragmented lives. The following essay, "The Language of
Clothes," appeared in* Human Ecology *in 1991. Lurie explains how
clothes can serve as a language with its own grammar and vocabulary
that conveys thoughts, feelings, and social position in the context of cultural conventions.*

For thousands of years human beings have communicated with
one another first in the language of dress. Long before I am near
enough to talk to you on the street, in a meeting, or at a party, you announce your sex, age and class to me through what you are wearing—
and very possibly give me important information (or misinformation)
as to your occupation, origin, personality, opinions, tastes, sexual desires and current mood. I may not be able to put what I observe into
words, but I register the information unconsciously; and you simultaneously do the same for me. By the time we meet and converse we have
already spoken to each other in an older and more universal language.

The statement that clothing is a language, though made occasionally with the air of a man finding a flying saucer in his backyard, is not
new. Balzac, in *Daughter of Eve* (1830), observed that dress is a "contin-
ual manifestation of intimate thoughts, a language, a symbol." Today,
as semiotics becomes fashionable, sociologists tell us that fashion too is
a language of signs, a nonverbal system of communication.

None of these theorists, however, has gone on to remark what
seems obvious: that if clothing is a language, it must have a vocabulary
and a grammar like other languages. Of course, as with human speech,
there is not a single language of dress, but many: some (like Dutch and
German) closely related and others (like Basque) almost unique. And
within every language of clothes there are many different dialects and
accents, some almost unintelligible to members of the mainstream culture. Moreover, as with speech, each individual has his own stock of
words and employs personal variations of tone and meaning.

1

2

3

4   The vocabulary of dress includes not only items of clothing, but also hair styles, accessories, jewelry, make-up and body decoration. Theoretically at least this vocabulary is as large as or larger than that of any spoken tongue, since it includes every garment, hair style, and type of body decoration ever invented. In practice, of course, the sartorial resources of an individual may be very restricted. Those of a sharecropper, for instance, may be limited to five or ten "words" from which it is possible to create only a few "sentences" almost bare of decoration and expressing only the most basic concepts. A so-called fashion leader, on the other hand, may have several hundred "words" at his or her disposal, and thus be able to form thousands of different "sentences" that will express a wide range of meanings. Just as the average English-speaking person knows many more words than he or she will ever use in conversation, so all of us are able to understand the meaning of styles we will never wear.

Magical Clothing

5   Archaeologists digging up past civilizations and anthropologists studying primitive tribes have come to the conclusion that, as Rachel Kemper [*Costume*] puts it, "Paint, ornament, and rudimentary clothing were first employed to attract good animistic powers and to ward off evil." When Charles Darwin visited Tierra del Fuego, a cold, wet, disagreeable land plagued by constant winds, he found the natives naked except for feathers in their hair and symbolic designs painted on their bodies. Modern Australian bushmen, who may spend hours decorating themselves and their relatives with patterns in colored clay, often wear nothing else but an amulet or two.

6   However skimpy it may be, primitive dress almost everywhere, like primitive speech, is full of magic. A necklace of shark's teeth or a girdle of cowrie shells or feathers serves the same purpose as a prayer or spell, and may magically replace—or more often supplement—a spoken charm. In the first instance a form of *contagious* magic is at work: the shark's teeth are believed to endow their wearer with the qualities of a fierce and successful fisherman. The cowrie shells, on the other hand, work through *sympathetic* magic: since they resemble the female sexual parts, they are thought to increase or preserve fertility.

7   In civilized society today belief in the supernatural powers of clothing—like belief in prayers, spells and charms—remains widespread, though we denigrate it with the name "superstition." Advertisements announce that improbable and romantic events will follow the application of a particular sort of grease to our faces, hair or bodies; they claim that members of the opposite (or our own) sex will be drawn to us by the smell of a particular soap. Nobody believes those ads, you may say. Maybe not, but we behave as though we did: look in your bathroom cabinet.

The supernatural garments of European folk tales—the seven-league boots, the cloaks of invisibility and the magic rings—are not forgotten, merely transformed, so that today we have the track star who can only win a race in a particular hat or shoes, the plainclothes cop who feels no one can see him in his raincoat and the wife who takes off her wedding ring before going to a motel with her lover. 8

Sympathetic or symbolic magic is also often employed, as when we hang crosses, stars or one of the current symbols of female power and solidarity around our necks, thus silently involving the protection of Jesus, Jehovah or Astarte. Such amulets, of course, may be worn to announce our allegiance to some faith or cause rather than as a charm. Or they may serve both purposes simultaneously—or sequentially. The crucifix concealed below the parochial-school uniform speaks only to God until some devilish force persuades its wearer to remove his or her clothes: then it acts—or fails to act—as a warning against sin as well as a protective talisman. 9

Articles of clothing, too, may be treated as if they had mana, the impersonal supernatural force that tends to concentrate itself in objects. When I was in college it was common to wear a particular "lucky" sweater, shirt or hat to final examinations, and this practice continues today. Here it is usually contagious magic that is at work: the chosen garment has become lucky by being worn on the occasion of some earlier success, or has been given to its owner by some favored person. The wearing of such magical garments is especially common in sports, where they are often publicly credited with bringing their owners luck. Their loss or abandonment is thought to cause injury as well as defeat. Actors also believe ardently in the magic of clothes, possibly because they are so familiar with the near-magical transforming power of theatrical costume. 10

Fashion and Status

Clothing designed to show the social position of its wearer has a long history. Just as the oldest languages are full of elaborate titles and forms of address, so for thousands of years certain modes have indicated high or royal rank. Many societies passed decrees known as *sumptuary laws* to prescribe or forbid the wearing of specific styles by specific classes of persons. In ancient Egypt only those in high position could wear sandals; the Greeks and Romans controlled the type, color and number of garments worn and the sorts of embroidery with which they could be trimmed. During the Middle Ages almost every aspect of dress was regulated at some place or time—though not always with much success. The common features of all sumptuary laws—like that of edicts against the use of certain words—seem to be that they are difficult to enforce for very long. 11

Laws about what could be worn by whom continued to be passed in Europe until about 1700. But as class barriers weakened and wealth 12 could be more easily and rapidly converted into gentility, the system by which color and shape indicated social status began to break down. What came to designate high rank instead was the evident cost of a costume: rich materials, superfluous trimmings and difficult-to-care-for styles, or as Thorstein Veblen later put it [in *The Theory of the Leisure Class*], Conspicuous Waste and Conspicuous Leisure. As a result, it was assumed that the people you met would be dressed as lavishly as their income permitted. In Fielding's *Tom Jones,* for instance, everyone judges strangers by their clothing and treats them accordingly; this is presented as natural. It is a world in which rank is very exactly indicated by costume, from the rags of Molly the gamekeeper's daughter to Sophia Western's riding habit "which was so very richly laced" that "Partridge and the postboy instantly started from their chairs, and my landlady fell to her curtsies, and her ladyships, with great eagerness." The elaborate wigs characteristic of this period conferred status partly because they were both expensive to buy and expensive to maintain.

13   By the early eighteenth century the social advantages of conspicuous dress were such that even those who could not afford it often spent their money on finery. This development was naturally deplored by supporters of the status quo. In Colonial America the Massachusetts General Court declared its "utter detestation and dislike, that men or women of mean condition, should take upon them the garb of Gentlemen, by wearing Gold or Silver lace, or Buttons, or Points at their knees, or to walk in great Boots; or Women of the same rank to wear Silk or Tiffiny hoods, or Scarfes. . . ." What "men or women of mean condition"—farmers or artisans—were supposed to wear were coarse linen or wool, leather aprons, deerskin jackets, flannel petticoats and the like.

14   To dress above one's station was considered not only foolishly extravagant, but deliberately deceptive. In 1878 an American etiquette book complained,

> It is . . . unfortunately the fact that, in the United States, but too much attention is paid to dress by those who have neither the excuse of ample means nor of social claims. . . . We Americans are lavish, generous, and ostentatious. The wives of our wealthy men are glorious in garb as are princesses and queens. They have a right so to be. But when those who can ill afford to wear alpaca persist in arraying themselves in silk . . . the matter is a sad one.

Color and Pattern

15   Certain sorts of information about other people can be communicated in spite of a language barrier. We may not be able to understand

Welsh or the thick Southern dialect of the Mississippi delta, but when we hear a conversation in these tongues we can tell at once whether the speakers are excited or bored, cheerful or miserable, confident or frightened. In the same way, some aspects of the language of clothes can be read by almost anyone.

The first and most important of these signs, and the one that makes the greatest and most immediate impact, is color. Merely looking at different colors, psychologists have discovered, alters our blood pressure, heartbeat and rate of respiration, just as hearing a harsh noise or a harmonious musical chord does. When somebody approaches from a distance the first thing we see is the hue of his clothes; the closer he comes, the more space this hue occupies in our visual field and the the greater its effect on our nervous system. Loud, clashing colors, like loud noises or loud voices, may actually hurt our eyes or give us a headache; soft, harmonious hues, like music and soft voices, thrill or soothe us. Color in dress is also like tone of voice in speech in that it can completely alter the meaning of what is "said" by other aspects of the costume: style, fabric and trimmings. Just as the words "Do you want to dance with me?" can be whispered shyly or flung as a challenge, so the effect of a white evening dress is very different from that of a scarlet one of identical fabric and pattern. In certain circumstances some hues, like some tones of voice, are beyond the bounds of polite discourse. A bride in a black wedding dress, or a stockbroker greeting his clients in a shocking-pink three-piece suit, would be like people screaming aloud. 16

Although color often indicates mood, it is not by any means an infallible guide. For one thing, convention may prescribe certain hues. The urban businessman must wear a navy blue, dark gray or (in certain regions) brown or tan suit, and can express his feelings only through his choice of shirt and tie, or tie alone; and even here the respectable possibilities may be very limited. Convention also alters the meaning of colors according to the place and time at which they are worn. Vermilion in the office is not the same as vermilion at a disco; and hot weather permits the wearing of pale hues that would make one look far more formal and fragile in midwinter. 17

There are other problems. Some people may avoid colors they like because of the belief or illusion that they are unbecoming, while others may wear colors they normally dislike for symbolic reason: because they are members or fans of a certain football team, for instance. In addition, some fashionable types may select certain hues merely because they are "in" that year. 18

Finally, it should be noted that the effect of any color in dress is modified by the colors that accompany it. In general, therefore, the following remarks should be taken as applying mainly to costumes composed entirely or almost entirely of a single hue. 19

20   The mood of a crowd, as well as that of an individual, can often be read in the colors of clothing. In the office of a large corporation, or at a professional convention, there is usually a predominance of conventional gray, navy, beige, tan and white—suggesting a general attitude of seriousness, hard work, neutrality, propriety and status. The same group of people at a picnic are a mass of lively, relaxed blue, red and brown, with touches of yellow and green. In the evening, at a disco, they shimmer under the rotating lights in dramatic combinations of purple, crimson, orange, turquoise, gold, silver and black.

21   Apart from the chameleon, man is the only animal who can change his skin to suit his background. Indeed, if he is to function successfully he must do so. The individual whose clothes do not fall within the recognized range of colors for a given situation attracts attention, usually (though not always) unfavorable attention. When a child puts its pet chameleon down on the earth and it does not turn brown, we know the creature is seriously ill. In the same way, men or women who begin to come to work in a conservative office wearing disco hues and a disco mood are regarded with anxiety and suspicion. If they do not blush a respectable beige, navy or gray within a reasonable length of time, their colleagues know that they will not be around for long.

✦ Evaluating the Text

1. At each point in drawing an analogy between clothes and language, Lurie touches on similarities or draws equivalences between elements of vocabulary, syntax, and grammar and different items of dress or appearance. Which of the examples cited by Lurie to support her extended analogy between language and clothes seem especially convincing?

2. How can clothes serve a magical function? Do you have an article of clothing that you feel brings you good luck? Describe the item and how it came to have this meaning.

3. How have cultural conventions operated to define the kinds of clothing that could be worn in different societies by different classes?

✦ Exploring Different Perspectives

1. How does Alison Lurie's analysis provide a frame of reference within which to understand Gretel Ehrlich's description of body decorations and costumes worn by the Kiowa during the Sun Dance? (See "To Live in Two Worlds.")

2. In what sense does clothing function as a disguise according to Octavio Paz (in "The Day of the Dead") in ways that evoke Alison Lurie's analysis?

✦ Extending Viewpoints Through Writing

1. Go through your own wardrobe and classify items of clothing you wear according to the "statement" you want to make in different contexts. What is your very favorite outfit? What do you think it says about you? Alternatively, analyze any ad for clothing (for example, Jordache or Nike) with regard to the range of possible meanings (as well as thoughts, feelings, social conventions, status of the model) that advertisers invoke for their audiences.

David R. Counts

Too Many Bananas

◆

David R. Counts teaches in the anthropology department at McMaster University in Ontario, Canada. Together with his wife, Dorothy A. Counts, he has edited a number of works, including Coping with the Final Tragedy: Dying and Grieving in Cross-Cultural Perspective *(1991) and* Aging and Its Transformations: Moving Toward Death in Pacific Societies *(1992). This selection is drawn from his book* The Humbled Anthropologist: Tales from the Pacific *(1990).*

New Guinea, the world's second-largest island after Greenland, is located in the Southwestern Pacific Ocean north of Australia. The western half of the island, known as Irian Jaya, is administered by Indonesia. Papua, which occupies the eastern half of New Guinea, was formerly a territory of Australia. It became the independent nation of Papua New Guinea in 1975. As one might gather from David R. Counts's article, the chief food crops are bananas, taro roots, and yams. The economy of New Guinea is one of the least developed of any area in the world. Most of the people farm land and grow their own food.

No Watermelon at All

1   The woman came all the way through the village, walking between the two rows of houses facing each other between the beach and the bush, to the very last house standing on a little spit of land at the mouth of the Kaini River. She was carrying a watermelon on her head, and the house she came to was the government "rest house," maintained by the villagers for the occasional use of visiting officials. Though my wife and I were graduate students, not officials, and had asked for permission to stay in the village for the coming year, we were living in the rest house while the debate went on about where a house would be built for us. When the woman offered to sell us the watermelon for two shillings, we happily agreed, and the kids were delighted at the prospect of watermelon after yet another meal of rice and bully beef. The money changed hands and the seller left to return to her village, a couple of miles along the coast to the east.

2   It seemed only seconds later that the woman was back, reluctantly accompanying Kolia, the man who had already made it clear to us that he was the leader of the village. Kolia had no English, and at that time, three or four days into our first stay in Kandoka Village on the island of

New Britain in Papua New Guinea, we had very little Tok Pisin. Language difficulties notwithstanding, Kolia managed to make his message clear: The woman had been outrageously wrong to sell us the watermelon for two shillings and we were to return it to her and reclaim our money immediately. When we tried to explain that we thought the price to be fair and were happy with the bargain, Kolia explained again and finally made it clear that we had missed the point. The problem wasn't that we had paid too much; it was that we had paid at all. Here he was, a leader, responsible for us while we were living in his village, and we had shamed him. How would it look if he let guests in his village *buy* food? If we wanted watermelons, or bananas, or anything else, all that was necessary was to let him know. He told us that it would be all right for us to give little gifts to people who brought food to us (and they surely would), but *no one* was to sell food to us. If anyone were to try—like this woman from Lauvore—then we should refuse. There would be plenty of watermelons without us buying them.

The woman left with her watermelon, disgruntled, and we were   3
left with our two shillings. But we had learned the first lesson of many about living in Kandoka. We didn't pay money for food again that whole year, and we did get lots of food brought to us . . . but we never got another watermelon. That one was the last of the season.

LESSON 1: *In a society where food is shared or gifted as part of social life, you may not buy it with money.*

Too Many Bananas

In the couple of months that followed the watermelon incident, we   4
managed to become at least marginally competent in Tok Pisin, to negotiate the construction of a house on what we hoped was neutral ground, and to settle into the routine of our fieldwork. As our village leader had predicted, plenty of food was brought to us. Indeed, seldom did a day pass without something coming in—some sweet potatoes, a few taro, a papaya, the occasional pineapple, or some bananas—lots of bananas.

We had learned our lesson about the money, though, so we never   5
even offered to buy the things that were brought, but instead made gifts, usually of tobacco to the adults or chewing gum to the children. Nor were we so gauche as to haggle with a giver over how much of a return gift was appropriate, though the two of us sometimes conferred as to whether what had been brought was a "two-stick" or a "three-stick" stalk, bundle, or whatever. A "stick" of tobacco was a single large leaf, soaked in rum and then twisted into a ropelike form. This, wrapped in half a sheet of newsprint (torn for use as cigarette paper), sold in the local trade stores for a shilling. Nearly all of the adults in the

village smoked a great deal, and they seldom had much cash, so our stocks of twist tobacco and stacks of the Sydney *Morning Herald* (all, unfortunately, the same day's issue) were seen as a real boon to those who preferred "stick" to the locally grown product.

6   We had established a pattern with respect to the gifts of food. When a donor appeared at our veranda we would offer our thanks and talk with them for a few minutes (usually about our children, who seemed to hold a real fascination for the villagers and for whom most of the gifts were intended) and then we would inquire whether they could use some tobacco. It was almost never refused, though occasionally a small bottle of kerosene, a box of matches, some laundry soap, a cup of rice, or a tin of meat would be requested instead of (or even in addition to) the tobacco. Everyone, even Kolia, seemed to think this arrangement had worked out well.

7   Now, what must be kept in mind is that while we were following their rules—or seemed to be—we were *really still buying food*. In fact we kept a running account of what came in and what we "paid" for it. Tobacco as currency got a little complicated, but since the exchange rate was one stick to one shilling, it was not too much trouble as long as everyone was happy, and meanwhile we could account for the expenditure of "informant fees" and "household expenses." Another thing to keep in mind is that not only did we continue to think in terms of our buying the food that was brought, we thought of them as *selling it*. While it was true they never quoted us a price, they also never asked us if we needed or wanted whatever they had brought. It seemed clear to us that when an adult needed a stick of tobacco, or a child wanted some chewing gum (we had enormous quantities of small packets of Wrigley's for just such eventualities) they would find something surplus to their own needs and bring it along to our "store" and get what they wanted.

8   By late November 1966, just before the rainy reason set in, the bananas were coming into flush, and whereas earlier we had received banana gifts by the "hand" (six or eight bananas in a cluster cut from the stalk), donors now began to bring bananas, "for the children," by the *stalk!* The Kaliai among whom we were living are not exactly specialists in banana cultivation—they only recognize about thirty varieties, while some of their neighbors have more than twice that many—but the kinds they produce differ considerably from each other in size, shape, and taste, so we were not dismayed when we had more than one stalk hanging on our veranda. The stalks ripen a bit at the time, and having some variety was nice. Still, by the time our accumulation had reached *four* complete stalks, the delights of variety had begun to pale a bit. The fruits were ripening progressively and it was clear that even if we and the kids ate nothing but bananas for the next week, some would still fall from the stalk onto the floor in a state of gross

overripeness. This was the situation as, late one afternoon, a woman came bringing yet another stalk of bananas up the steps of the house.

Several factors determined our reaction to her approach: one was that there was literally no way we could possibly use the bananas. We hadn't quite reached the point of being crowded off our veranda by the stalks of fruit, but it was close. Another factor was that we were tired of playing the gift game. We had acquiesced in playing it—no one was permitted to sell us anything, and in turn we only gave things away, refusing under any circumstances to sell tobacco (or anything else) for money. But there had to be a limit. From our perspective what was at issue was that the woman wanted something and she had come to trade for it. Further, what she had brought to trade was something we neither wanted nor could use, and it should have been obvious to her. So we decided to bite the bullet.

The woman, Rogi, climbed the stairs to the veranda, took the stalk from where it was balanced on top of her head, and laid it on the floor with the word, "Here are some bananas for the children." Dorothy and I sat near her on the floor and thanked her for her thought but explained, "You know, we really have too many bananas—we can't use these; maybe you ought to give them to someone else. . . ." The woman looked mystified, then brightened and explained that she didn't want anything for them, she wasn't short of tobacco or anything. They were just a gift for the kids. Then she just sat there, and we sat there, and the bananas sat there, and we tried again. "Look," I said, pointing up to them and counting, "we've got four stalks already hanging here on the veranda—there are too many for us to eat now. Some are rotting already. Even if we eat only bananas, we can't keep up with what's here!"

Rogi's only response was to insist that these were a gift, and that she didn't want anything for them, so we tried yet another tack: "Don't *your* children like bananas?" When she admitted that they did, and that she had none at her house, we suggested that she should take them there. Finally, still puzzled, but convinced we weren't going to keep the bananas, she replaced them on her head, went down the stairs, and made her way back through the village toward her house.

As before, it seemed only moments before Kolia was making his way up the stairs, but this time he hadn't brought the woman in tow. "What was wrong with those bananas? Were they no good?" he demanded. We explained that there was nothing wrong with the bananas at all, but that we simply couldn't use them and it seemed foolish to take them when we had so many and Rogi's own children had none. We obviously didn't make ourselves clear because Kolia then took up the same refrain that Rogi had—he insisted that we shouldn't be worried about taking the bananas, because they were a gift for the children and Rogi hadn't wanted anything for them. There was no reason, he added, to send her away with them—she would be ashamed. I'm afraid we must have seemed as if we were hard of hearing or thought he was, for our only response was to repeat our reasons. We went through it again—there they hung, one, two, three, *four* stalks of bananas, rapidly ripening and already far beyond our capacity to eat— we just weren't ready to accept any more and let them rot (and, we added to ourselves, pay for them with tobacco, to boot).

13   Kolia finally realized that we were neither hard of hearing nor intentionally offensive, but merely ignorant. He stared at us for a few minutes, thinking, and then asked: "Don't you frequently have visitors during the day and evening?" We nodded. Then he asked, "Don't you usually offer them cigarettes and coffee or milo?" Again, we nodded. "Did it ever occur to you to suppose," he said, "that your visitors might be hungry?" It was at this point in the conversation, as we recall, that we began to see the depth of the pit we had dug for ourselves. We nodded, hesitantly. His last words to us before he went down the stairs and stalked away were just what we were by that time afraid they might be. "When your guests are hungry, *feed them bananas!*"

Lesson 2: *Never refuse a gift, and never fail to return a gift. If you cannot use it, you can always give it away to someone else—there is no such thing as too much—there are never too many bananas.*

Not Enough Pineapples

14   During the fifteen years between that first visit in 1966 and our residence there in 1981 we had returned to live in Kandoka village twice during the 1970s, and though there were a great many changes in the village, and indeed for all of Papua New Guinea during that time, we continued to live according to the lessons of reciprocity learned during those first months in the field. We bought no food for money and refused no gifts, but shared our surplus. As our family grew, we continued to be accompanied by our younger children. Our place in the village came to be something like that of educated Kaliai who worked far away in New Guinea. Our friends expected us to come "home" when we had leave, but knew that our work kept us away for long periods of time. They also credited us with knowing much more about the rules of their way of life than was our due. And we sometimes shared the delusion that we understood life in the village, but even fifteen years was not long enough to relieve the need for lessons in learning to live within the rules of gift exchange.

15   In the last paragraph I used the word *friends* to describe the villagers intentionally, but of course they were not all our friends. Over the years some really had become friends, others were acquaintances, others remained consultants or informants to whom we turned when we needed information. Still others, unfortunately, we did not like at all.

We tried never to make an issue of these distinctions, of course, and to be evenhanded and generous to all, as they were to us. Although we almost never actually refused requests that were made of us, over the long term our reciprocity in the village was balanced. More was given to those who helped us the most, while we gave assistance or donations of small items even to those who were not close or helpful.

One elderly woman in particular was a trial for us. Sara was the eldest of a group of siblings and her younger brother and sister were both generous, informative, and delightful persons. Her younger sister, Makila, was a particularly close friend and consultant, and in deference to that friendship we felt awkward in dealing with the elder sister.   16

Sara was neither a friend nor an informant, but she had been, since she returned to live in the village at the time of our second trip in 1971, a constant (if minor) drain on our resources. She never asked for much at a time. A bar of soap, a box of matches, a bottle of kerosene, a cup of rice, some onions, a stick or two of tobacco, or some other small item was usually all that was at issue, but whenever she came around it was always to ask for something—or to let us know that when we left, we should give her some of the furnishings from the house. Too, unlike almost everyone else in the village, when she came, she was always empty-handed. We ate no taro from her gardens, and the kids chewed none of her sugarcane. In short, she was, as far as we could tell, a really grasping, selfish old woman—and we were not the only victims of her greed.   17

Having long before learned the lesson of the bananas, one day we had a stalk that was ripening so fast we couldn't keep up with it, so I pulled a few for our own use (we only had one stalk at the time) and walked down through the village to Ben's house, where his five children were playing. I sat down on his steps to talk, telling him that I intended to give the fruit to his kids. They never got them. Sara saw us from across the open plaza of the village and came rushing over, shouting, "My bananas!" Then she grabbed the stalk and went off gorging herself with them. Ben and I just looked at each other.   18

Finally it got to the point where it seemed to us that we had to do something. Ten years of being used was long enough. So there came the afternoon when Sara showed up to get some tobacco—again. But this time, when we gave her the two sticks she had demanded, we confronted her.   19

First, we noted the many times she had come to get things. We didn't mind sharing things, we explained. After all, we had plenty of tobacco and soap and rice and such, and most of it was there so that we could help our friends as they helped us, with folktales, information, or even gifts of food. The problem was that she kept coming to get things, but never came to talk, or to tell stories, or to bring some little something that the kids might like. Sara didn't argue—she agreed. "Look," we suggested, "it doesn't have to be much, and we don't mind giving   20 you things—but you can help us. The kids like pineapples, and we don't have any—the next time you need something, bring something—like maybe a pineapple." Obviously somewhat embarrassed, she took her tobacco and left, saying that she would bring something soon. We were really pleased with ourselves. It had been a very difficult thing to do, but it was done, and we were convinced that either she would start bringing things or not come. It was as if a burden had lifted from our shoulders.

21   It worked. Only a couple of days passed before Sara was back, bringing her bottle to get it filled with kerosene. But this time, she came carrying the biggest, most beautiful pineapple we had seen the entire time we had been there. We had a friendly talk, filled her kerosene container, and hung the pineapple up on the veranda to ripen just a little further. A few days later we cut and ate it, and whether the satisfaction it gave came from the fruit or from its source would be hard to say, but it was delicious. That, we assumed, was the end of that irritant.

22   We were wrong, of course. The next afternoon, Mary, one of our best friends for years (and no relation to Sara), dropped by for a visit. As we talked, her eyes scanned the veranda. Finally she asked whether we hadn't had a pineapple there yesterday. We said we had, but that we had already eaten it. She commented that it had been a really nice-looking one, and we told her that it had been the best we had eaten in months. Then, after a pause, she asked, "Who brought it to you?" We smiled as we said, "Sara!" because Mary would appreciate our coup—she had commented many times in the past on the fact that Sara only *got* from us and never gave. She was silent for a moment, and then she said, "Well, I'm glad you enjoyed it—my father was waiting until it was fully ripe to harvest it for you, but when it went missing I thought maybe it was the one you had here. I'm glad to see you got it. I thought maybe a thief had eaten it in the bush."

LESSON 3: *Where reciprocity is the rule and gifts are the idiom, you cannot demand a gift, just as you cannot refuse a request.*

23   It says a great deal about the kindness and patience of the Kaliai people that they have been willing to be our hosts for all these years despite our blunders and lack of good manners. They have taught us a lot, and these three lessons are certainly not the least important things we learned.

✦ Evaluating the Text

1. How does Counts's initial experience of offering money for watermelon lead him to learn his first important lesson about the culture of New Guinea?

2. How does the idea of "too many bananas" sum up the important principle of reciprocity that Counts learns? In your own words, describe the principle involved.

3. How does the experience Counts has with Sara lead to his ironic realization of the third lesson about the culture of New Guinea?

✦ Exploring Different Perspectives

1. How is the society of the Yąnomamö described by Napoleon A. Chagnon (see "Doing Fieldwork Among the Yąnomamö") set up on an entirely different basis from that described by Counts?

2. In what ways does the theme of reciprocity underlie both Bedouin culture as dramatized by Nabil Gorgy in his story "Cairo Is a Small City" and the culture of New Guinea as described by Counts?

✦ Extending Viewpoints Through Writing

1. What experiences have you had that involved a principle of reciprocity in your relationship with another? Discuss one incident and the lesson you learned.

Octavio Paz

The Day of the Dead

◆

Octavio Paz, born on the outskirts of Mexico City in 1914, is a poet, essay-
ist, and unequalled observer of Mexican society. He served as a Mexican
diplomat in France and Japan and as Ambassador to India before resign-
ing from the diplomatic service to protest the Tlatelolco Massacre (govern-
ment massacre of 300 students in Mexico City) in 1968. His many
volumes of poetry include Sun Stone *(1958), a new reading of the Aztec*
myths; Marcel Duchamp *(1968);* The Children of the Mire *(1974);*
and The Monkey Grammarian *(1981). In 1990, Paz was awarded the*
Nobel Prize for Literature. As an essayist whose works have helped rede-
fine the concept of Latin American culture, Paz wrote The Other Mexico
(1972) and The Labyrinth of Solitude, *translated by Lysander Kemp*
(1961), from which "The Day of the Dead" is taken. In the following essay,
Paz offers insight, conveyed with his typical stylistic grace and erudition,
into the deep psychological needs met by fiestas in Mexican culture.

1   The solitary Mexican loves fiestas and public gatherings. Any occasion for getting together will serve, any pretext to stop the flow of time
and commemorate men and events with festivals and ceremonies. We
are a ritual people, and this characteristic enriches both our imaginations and our sensibilities, which are equally sharp and alert. The art of
the fiesta has been debased almost everywhere else, but not in Mexico.
There are few places in the world where it is possible to take part in a
spectacle like our great religious fiestas with their violent primary colors, their bizarre costumes and dances, their fireworks and ceremonies
and their inexhaustible welter of surprises: the fruit, candy, toys and
other objects sold on these days in the plazas and open-air markets.

2   Our calendar is crowded with fiestas. There are certain days when
the whole country, from the most remote villages to the largest cities,
prays, shouts, feasts, gets drunk and kills, in honor of the Virgin of
Guadalupe or Benito Juaréz. Each year on the fifteenth of September, at
eleven o'clock at night, we celebrate the fiesta of the *Grito*[1] in all the plazas of the Republic, and the excited crowds actually shout for a whole
hour . . . the better, perhaps, to remain silent for the rest of the year.
During the days before and after the twelfth of December,[2] time comes

[1]Padre Hildalgo's call-to-arms against Spain, 1810.—*Tr.*
[2]Fiesta of the Virgin of Guadalupe.—*Tr.*

to a full stop, and instead of pushing us toward a deceptive tomorrow that is always beyond our reach, offers us a complete and perfect today of dancing and revelry, of communion with the most ancient and secret Mexico. Time is no longer succession, and becomes what it originally was and is: the present, in which past and future are reconciled.

But the fiestas which the Church and State provide for the country as a whole are not enough. The life of every city and village is ruled by a patron saint whose blessing is celebrated with devout regularity. Neighborhoods and trades also have their annual fiestas, their ceremonies and fairs. And each one of us—atheist, Catholic, or merely indifferent—has his own saint's day, which he observes every year. It is impossible to calculate how many fiestas we have and how much time and money we spend on them. I remember asking the mayor of a village near Mitla, several years ago, "What is the income of the village government?" "About 3,000 pesos a year. We are very poor. But the Governor and the Federal Government always help us to meet our expenses." "And how are the 3,000 pesos spent?" "Mostly on fiestas, señor. We are a small village, but we have two patron saints." 3

This reply is not surprising. Our poverty can be measured by the frequency and luxuriousness of our holidays. Wealthy countries have very few: there is neither the time nor the desire for them, and they are not necessary. The people have other things to do, and when they amuse themselves they do so in small groups. The modern masses are agglomerations of solitary individuals. On great occasions in Paris or New York, when the populace gathers in the squares or stadiums, the absence of people, in the sense of a people, is remarkable: there are couples and small groups, but they never form a living community in which the individual is at once dissolved and redeemed. But how could a poor Mexican live without the two or three annual fiestas that make up for his poverty and misery? Fiestas are our only luxury. They replace, and are perhaps better than, the theater and vacations, Anglo-Saxon weekends and cocktail parties, the bourgeois reception, the Mediterranean café. 4

In all of these ceremonies—national or local, trade or family—the Mexican opens out. They all give him a chance to reveal himself and to converse with God, country, friends or relations. During these days the silent Mexican whistles, shouts, sings, shoots off fireworks, discharges his pistol into the air. He discharges his soul. And his shout, like the rockets we love so much, ascends to the heavens, explodes into green, red, blue, and white lights, and falls dizzily to earth with a trail of golden sparks. This is the night when friends who have not exchanged more than the prescribed courtesies for months get drunk together, trade confidences, weep over the same troubles, discover that they are brothers, and sometimes, to prove it, kill each other. The night is full of songs and loud cries. The lover wakes up his sweetheart with an orchestra. There are jokes and conversations from balcony to balcony, 5 sidewalk to sidewalk. Nobody talks quietly. Hats fly in the air. Laughter and curses ring like silver pesos. Guitars are brought out. Now and then, it is true, the happiness ends badly, in quarrels, insults, pistol shots, stabbings. But these too are part of the fiesta, for the Mexican does not seek amusement: he seeks to escape from himself, to leap over the wall of solitude that confines him during the rest of the year. All are possessed by violence and frenzy. Their souls explode like the colors and voices and emotions. Do they forget themselves and show their true faces? Nobody knows. The important thing is to go out, open a way, get drunk on noise, people, colors. Mexico is celebrating a fiesta. And this fiesta, shot through with lightning and delirium, is the brilliant reverse to our silence and apathy, our reticence and gloom.

6   According to the interpretation of French sociologists, the fiesta is an excess, an expense. By means of this squandering the community protects itself against the envy of the gods or of men. Sacrifices and offerings placate or buy off the gods and the patron saints. Wasting money and expending energy affirms the community's wealth in both. This luxury is a proof of health, a show of abundance and power. Or a magic trap. For squandering is an effort to attract abundance by contagion. Money calls to money. When life is thrown away it increases; the orgy, which is sexual expenditure, is also a ceremony of regeneration; waste gives strength. New Year celebrations, in every culture, signify something beyond the mere observance of a date on the calendar. The day is a pause: time is stopped, is actually annihilated. The rites that celebrate its death are intended to provoke its rebirth, because they mark not only the end of an old year but also the beginning of a new. Everything attracts its opposite. The fiesta's function, then, is more utilitarian than we think: waste attracts or promotes wealth, and is an investment like any other, except that the returns on it cannot be measured or counted. What is sought is potency, life, health. In this sense the fiesta, like the gift and the offering, is one of the most ancient of economic forms.

7   This interpretation has always seemed to me to be incomplete. The fiesta is by nature sacred, literally or figuratively, and above all it is the advent of the unusual. It is governed by its own special rules, that set it apart from other days, and it has a logic, an ethic and even an economy that are often in conflict with everyday norms. It all occurs in an enchanted world: time is transformed to a mythical past or a total present; space, the scene of the fiesta, is turned into a gaily decorated world of its own; and the persons taking part cast off all human or social rank and become, for the moment, living images. And everything takes place as if it were not so, as if it were a dream. But whatever happens, our actions have a greater lightness, a different gravity. They take on other meanings and with them we contract new obligations. We throw down our burdens of time and reason.

In certain fiestas the very notion of order disappears. Chaos comes   8
back and license rules. Anything is permitted: the customary hierarchies vanish, along with all social, sex, caste, and trade distinctions.
Men disguise themselves as women, gentlemen as slaves, the poor as
the rich. The army, the clergy, and the law are ridiculed. Obligatory sacrilege, ritual profanation is committed. Love becomes promiscuity.
Sometimes the fiesta becomes a Black Mass. Regulations, habits and
customs are violated. Respectable people put away the dignified expressions and conservative clothes that isolate them, dress up in gaudy
colors, hide behind a mask, and escape from themselves.

Therefore the fiesta is not only an excess, a ritual squandering of   9
the goods painfully accumulated during the rest of the year; it is also a
revolt, a sudden immersion in the formless, in pure being. By means of
the fiesta society frees itself from the norms it has established. It ridi-
cules its gods, its principles, and its laws: it denies its own self.

The fiesta is a revolution in the most literal sense of the word. In the   10
confusion that it generates, society is dissolved, is drowned, insofar as it
is an organism ruled according to certain laws and principles. But it
drowns in itself, in its own original chaos or liberty. Everything is united:
good and evil, day and night, the sacred and the profane. Everything
merges, loses shape and individuality and returns to the primordial
mass. The fiesta is a cosmic experiment, an experiment in disorder, re-
uniting contradictory elements and principles in order to bring about a
renascence of life. Ritual death promotes a rebirth; vomiting increases
the appetite; the orgy, sterile in itself, renews the fertility of the mother
or of the earth. The fiesta is a return to a remote and undifferentiated
state, prenatal or presocial. It is a return that is also a beginning, in accordance with the dialectic that is inherent in social processes.

The group emerges purified and strengthened from this plunge   11
into chaos. It has immersed itself in its own origins, in the womb from
which it came. To express it in another way, the fiesta denies society as
an organic system of differentiated forms and principles, but affirms it
as a source of creative energy. It is a true "re-creation," the opposite of
the "recreation" characterizing modern vacations, which do not entail
any rites or ceremonies whatever and are as individualistic and sterile
as the world that invented them.

Society communes with itself during the fiesta. Its members return   12
to original chaos and freedom. Social structures break down and new
relationships, unexpected rules, capricious hierarchies are created. In
the general disorder everybody forgets himself and enters into otherwise forbidden situations and places. The bounds between audience
and actors, officials and servants, are erased. Everybody takes part in
the fiesta, everybody is caught up in its whirlwind. Whatever its
mood, its character, its meaning, the fiesta is participation, and this trait

distinguishes it from all other ceremonies and social phenomena. Lay or religious, orgy or saturnalia, the fiesta is a social act based on the full participation of all its celebrants.

13   Thanks to the fiesta the Mexican opens out, participates, communes with his fellows and with the values that give meaning to his religious or political existence. And it is significant that a country as sorrowful as ours should have so many and such joyous fiestas. Their frequency, their brilliance and excitement, the enthusiasm with which we take part, all suggest that without them we would explode. They free us, if only momentarily, from the thwarted impulses, the inflammable desires that we carry within us. But the Mexican fiesta is not merely a return to an original state of formless and normless liberty: the Mexican is not seeking to return, but to escape from himself, to exceed himself. Our fiestas are explosions. Life and death, joy and sorrow, music and mere noise are united, not to re-create or recognize themselves, but to swallow each other up. There is nothing so joyous as a Mexican fiesta, but there is also nothing so sorrowful. Fiesta night is also a night of mourning.

14   If we hide within ourselves in our daily lives, we discharge ourselves in the whirlwind of the fiesta. It is more than an opening out: we rend ourselves open. Everything—music, love, friendship—ends in tumult and violence. The frenzy of our festivals shows the extent to which our solitude closes us off from communication with the world. We are familiar with delirium, with songs and shouts, with the monologue . . . but not with the dialogue. Our fiestas, like our confidences, our loves, our attempts to reorder our society, are violent breaks with the old or the established. Each time we try to express ourselves we have to break with ourselves. And the fiesta is only one example, perhaps the most typical, of this violent break. It is not difficult to name others, equally revealing: our games, which are always a going to extremes, often mortal; our profligate spending, the reverse of our timid investments and business enterprises; our confessions. The somber Mexican, closed up in himself, suddenly explodes, tears open his breast and reveals himself, though not without a certain complacency, and not without a stopping place in the shameful or terrible mazes of his intimacy. We are not frank, but our sincerity can reach extremes that horrify a European. The explosive, dramatic, sometimes even suicidal manner in which we strip ourselves, surrender ourselves, is evidence that something inhibits and suffocates us. Something impedes us from being. And since we cannot or dare not confront our own selves, we resort to the fiesta. It fires us into the void; it is a drunken rapture that burns itself out, a pistol shot in the air, a skyrocket.

Translated by Lysander Kemp

✦ Evaluating the Text

1. What factors contribute to the popularity of fiestas in Mexico, especially in relationship to the Mexican national character, as described by Paz?

2. In what way are people's experience of time during the fiesta period qualitatively different from their experience of time during the rest of the year?

3. How would you characterize Paz's understanding of the underlying psychological and cultural motivations for Mexican fiestas? For example, how is the love of fiestas related to what Paz calls the "solitude" of Mexicans?

4. How does Paz's use of economic information as to the cost and frequency of fiestas help explain the extraordinary importance they play in Mexican life?

5. In what sense does a fiesta provide an opportunity for the solitary individual to be "at once resolved and redeemed"? What do you think Paz means by this?

6. Evaluate the explanation for fiestas offered by French sociologists. In your opinion, what would be an "American" version of such conspicuous, ill-afforded squandering of money? Would the interpretations be the same? If not, in what ways might they differ?

7. How do Paz's comparisons between Mexican attitudes toward celebrations, life, and death with those of Europeans and North Americans make it easier for his readers to understand his analysis?

✦ Exploring Different Perspectives

1. In what ways does the fiesta create its own world, set off from time, demarcated in space, and encourage forms of behavior normally not permitted in everyday life? To what extent are fiestas (involving as they do costumes, dances, ceremonies, and expenditure of material possessions and energy) similar to and different from the Kiowa Indian Sun Dance (see Gretel Ehrlich's "To Live in Two Worlds")? In what sense are the goals of both of these ritual celebrations the same?

2. How do the accounts by Octavio Paz and Napoleon A. Chagnon (see "Doing Fieldwork Among the Yąnomamö") make you aware of the important role played by ritualized expressions of violence among the Yąnomamö and Mexicans?

✦ Extending Viewpoints Through Writing

1. Have you ever been at a party that came close in spirit to the Mexican fiesta where people use the occasion to renew friendships, get drunk together, and discover kinships? If so, describe your experiences and discuss the similarities and differences in terms of emotional transformation such celebrations encourage.

2. If you are familiar with the Mardi Gras in Brazil or in New Orleans, the Ash Wednesday Celebration in Trinidad, or any comparable event, describe how it serves many of the same purposes as the Mexican fiesta.

3. To what extent do celebrations such as weddings, baptisms, bar mitzvahs, and vacations serve much the same function in the United States as fiestas do in Mexico? Discuss the similarities and differences.

Nabil Gorgy

Cairo Is a Small City

━━━━━◆━━━━━

Nabil Gorgy was born in Cairo in 1944 and studied civil engineering at Cairo University. After working as an engineer in New York City, he returned to Cairo, where he now runs his own art gallery and writes. His interests in mysticism, Egyptology, and Sufi traditions are reflected in his novel The Door *(1981). His most recent collection of short stories is* The Slave's Dream and Other Stories *(1991). In "Cairo Is a Small City," translated by Denys Johnson-Davies (1983), an upper-class Egyptian engineer falls victim to an age-old Bedouin tradition.*

On the balcony of his luxury flat Engineer Adil Salim stood watching some workmen putting up a new building across the wide street along the centre of which was a spacious garden. The building was at the foundations stage, only the concrete foundations and some of the first-floor columns having been completed. A young ironworker with long hair was engaged in bending iron rods of various dimensions. Adil noticed that the young man had carefully leant his Jawa motorcycle against a giant crane that crouched at rest awaiting its future tasks. "How the scene has changed!" Adil could still remember the picture of old-time master craftsmen, and of the workers who used to carry large bowls of mixed cement on their calloused shoulders.   1

The sun was about to set and the concrete columns of a number of new constructions showed up as dark frameworks against the light in this quiet district at the end of Heliopolis.   2

As on every day at this time there came down into the garden dividing the street a flock of sheep and goats that grazed on its grass, and behind them two bedouin women, one of whom rode a donkey, while the younger one walked beside her. As was his habit each day, Adil fixed his gaze on the woman walking in her black gown that not so much hid as emphasized the attractions of her body, her waist being tied round with a red band. It could be seen that she wore green plastic slippers on her feet. He wished that she would catch sight of him on the balcony of his luxurious flat; even if she did so, Adil was thinking, those bedouin had a special code of behaviour that differed greatly from what he was used to and rendered it difficult to make contact with them. What, then, was the reason, the motive, for wanting to think   3

*(For information on Egypt, see p. 107.)

up some way of talking to her? It was thus that he was thinking, following her with his gaze as she occasionally chased after a lamb that was going to be run over by a car or a goat left far behind the flock.

4   Adil, who was experienced in attracting society women, was aware of his spirit being enthralled: days would pass with him on the balcony, sunset after sunset, as he watched her without her even knowing of his existence.

5   Had it not been for that day on which he had been buying some fruit and vegetables from one of the shopkeepers on Metro Street, and had not the shopkeeper seen another bedouin woman walking behind another flock, and had he not called out to her by name, and had she not come, and had he not thrown her a huge bundle of waste from the shop, after having flirted with her and fondled her body—had it not been for that day, Adil's mind would not have given birth to the plan he was determined, whatever the cost, to put through, because of that woman who had bewitched his heart.

6   As every man, according to Adil's philosophy of life, had within him a devil, it was sometimes better to follow this devil in order to placate him and avoid his tyranny. Therefore Engineer Adil Salim finally decided to embark upon the terrible, the unthinkable. He remembered from his personal history during the past forty years that such a temporary alliance with this devil of his had gained him a courage that had set him apart from the rest of his colleagues, and through it he had succeeded in attaining this social position that had enabled him to become the owner of this flat whose value had reached a figure which he avoided mentioning even in front of his family lest they might be upset or feel envy.

7   Thus, from his balcony on the second floor in Tirmidhi Street, Engineer Adil Salim called out in a loud voice "Hey, girl!" as he summoned the one who was walking at the rear of the convoy. When the flock continued on its way without paying any attention, he shouted again: "Hey, girl—you who sell sheep," and before the girl moved far away he repeated the word "sheep." Adil paid no attention to the astonishment of the doorman, who had risen from the place where he had been sitting at the entrance, thinking that he was being called. In fact he quietly told him to run after the two bedouin women and to let them know that he had some bread left over which he wanted to give them for their sheep.

8   From the balcony Adil listened to the doorman calling to the two women in his authoritative Upper Egyptian accent, at which they came to a stop and the one who was riding the donkey looked back at him. Very quickly Adil was able to make out her face as she looked towards him, seeking to discover what the matter was. As for the young girl, she continued on behind the flock. The woman was no longer young and had a corpulent body and a commanding look which she did not seek to hide from him. Turning her donkey round, she crossed the street separating the garden from his building and waited in front of the gate for

some new development. Adil collected up all the bread in the house and hurried down with it on a brass tray. Having descended to the street, he went straight up to the woman and looked at her. When she opened a saddlebag close by her leg, he emptied all the bread into it.

"Thanks," said the woman as she made off without turning to- 9 wards him. He, though, raising his voice so that she would hear, called out, "And tomorrow too."

During a period that extended to a month Adil began to buy bread 10 which he did not eat. Even on those days when he had to travel away or to spend the whole day far from the house, he would leave a large paper parcel with the doorman for him to give to the bedouin woman who rode the donkey and behind whom walked she for whom the engineer's heart craved.

Because Adil had a special sense of the expected and the probable, 11 and after the passing of one lunar month, and in his place in front of the building, with the bread on the brass tray, there occurred that which he had been wishing would happen, for the woman riding the donkey had continued on her way and he saw the other, looking around her carefully before crossing the road, ahead of him, walking towards him. She was the most beautiful thing he had set eyes on. The speed of his pulse almost brought his heart to a stop. How was it that such beauty was to be found without it feeling embarrassed at ugliness, for after it any and every thing must needs be so described? When she was directly in front of him, and her kohl-painted eyes were scrutinizing him, he sensed a danger which he attributed to her age, which was no more than twenty. How was it that she was so tall, her waist so slim, her breasts so full, and how was it that her buttocks swayed so enticingly as she turned away and went off with the bread, having thanked him? His imagination became frozen even though she was still close to him: her pretty face with the high cheekbones, the fine nose and delicate lips, the silver, crescent-shaped earrings, and the necklace that graced her bosom? Because such beauty was "beyond the permissible," Adil went on thinking about Salma—for he had got to know her name, her mother having called her by it in order to hurry her back lest the meeting between the lovers be prolonged.

Adil no longer troubled about the whistles of the workers who had 12 now risen floor by floor in the building opposite him, being in a state of infatuation, his heart captured by this moonlike creature. After the affair, in relation to himself, having been one of boldness, to end in seeing or greeting her, it now became a matter of necessity that she turn up before sunset at the house so that he might not be deprived of the chance of seeing her. So it was that Engineer Adil Salim fell in love with the beautiful bedouin girl Salma. And just as history is written by historians, so it was that Adil and his engineering work determined the history of this passion in the form of a building each of whose columns represented a day and each of whose floors was a month. He noted that, at the completion of twenty-eight days and exactly at full moon, Salma would come to him in place of her mother to take the bread. And so, being a structural engineer, he began to observe the moon, his yearning increasing when it was in eclipse and his spirits sparkling as its fullness drew near till, at full moon, the happiness of the lover was completed by seeing the beloved's face.

13   During seven months he saw her seven times, each time seeing in her the same look she had given him the first time: his heart would melt, all resolution would be squeezed out of him and that fear for which he knew no reason would be awakened. She alone was now capable of granting him his antidote. After the seventh month Salma, without any preamble, had talked to him at length, informing him that she lived with her parents around a spring at a distance of an hour's walk to the north of the airport, and that it consisted of a brackish spring alongside which was a sweet one, so that she would bathe in the first and rinse herself clean in the other, and that there were date palms around the two springs, also grass and pasturage. Her father, the owner of the springs and the land around them, had decided to invite him and so tomorrow "he'll pass by you and invite you to our place, for tomorrow we attend to the shearing of the sheep."

14   Adil gave the lie to what he was hearing, for it was more than any stretch of the imagination could conceive might happen.

15   The following day Adil arrived at a number of beautifully made tents, where a vast area of sand was spread out below date palms that stretched to the edge of a spring. Around the spring was gathered a large herd of camels, sheep and goats that spoke of the great wealth of the father. It was difficult to believe that such a place existed so close to the city of Cairo. If Adil's astonishment was great when Salma's father passed by him driving a new Peugeot, he was yet further amazed at the beauty of the area surrounding this spring. "It's the land of the future," thought Adil to himself. If he were able to buy a few *feddans* now he'd become a millionaire in a flash, for this was the Cairo of the future. "This is the deal of a lifetime," he told himself.

16   On the way the father asked a lot of questions about Adil's work and where he had previously lived and about his knowledge of the desert and its people. Though Adil noticed in the father's tone something more than curiosity, he attributed this to the nature of the Bedouin and their traditions.

17   As the car approached the tents Adil noticed that a number of men were gathered under a tent whose sides were open, and as the father and his guest got out of the car the men turned round, seated in the form of a horse-shoe. With the father sitting down and seating Engineer Adil Salim alongside him, one of the sides of the horse-shoe was

completed. In front of them sat three men on whose faces could be seen the marks of time in the form of interlaced wrinkles.

The situation so held Adil's attention that he was unaware of   18
Salma except when she passed from one tent to another in the direction he was looking and he caught sight of her gazing towards him.

The man who was sitting in a squatting position among the three   19
others spoke. Adil heard him talking about the desert, water and sheep, about the roads that went between the oases and the *wadi*, the towns and the springs of water, about the bedouin tribes and blood ties; he heard him talking about the importance of protecting these roads and springs, and the palm trees and the dates, the goats and the milk upon which the suckling child would be fed; he also heard him talk about how small the *wadi* was in comparison to this desert that stretched out endlessly.

In the same way as Adil had previously built the seven-storey   20
building that represented the seven months, each month containing twenty-eight days, till he would see Salma's face whenever it was full moon, he likewise sensed that this was the tribunal which had been set up to make an enquiry with him into the killing of the man whom he had one day come across on the tracks between the oases of Kharga and Farshout. It had been shortly after sunset when he and a friend, having visited the iron ore mines in the oases of Kharga had, instead of taking the asphalt road to Assiout, proceeded along a rough track that took them down towards Farshout near to Kena, as his friend had to make a report about the possibility of repairing the road and of extending the railway line to the oases. Going down from the high land towards the *wadi*, the land at a distance showing up green, two armed men had appeared before them. Adil remembered how, in a spasm of fear and astonishment, of belief and disbelief, and with a speed that at the time he thought was imposed upon him, a shot had been fired as he pressed his finger on the trigger of the revolver which he was using for the first time. A man had fallen to the ground in front of him and, as happens in films, the other had fled. As for him and his friend, they had rushed off to their car in order to put an end to the memory of the incident by reaching the *wadi*. It was perhaps because Adil had once killed a man that he had found the courage to accept Salma's father's invitation.

"That day," Adil heard the man address him, "with a friend in a   21
car, you killed Mubarak bin Rabia when he went out to you, Ziyad al-Mihrab being with him."

This was the manner in which Engineer Adil Salim was executed   22
in the desert north-west of the city of Cairo: one of the men held back his head across a marble-like piece of stone, then another man plunged the point of a tapered dagger into the spot that lies at the bottom of the neck between the two bones of the clavicle.

✦ *Evaluating the Text*

1. How is the engineer, Adil Salim, characterized? What incidents reveal these character traits most clearly? How does he see himself? To what does he attribute his success and affluence?

2. Under what circumstances does the engineer first meet the Bedouin girl? What is his attitude toward her?

3. How do Gorgy's descriptions of modern urban Cairo and the Bedouin encampment underscore the conflicting set of values this story explores?

4. After reading the story, discuss the significance of the title, especially as it sheds light on the surprising consequences for the engineer. To what extent does the title suggest that the Cairo of the Bedouins and the Cairo of the engineer, although seemingly very different, are basically the same?

✦ *Exploring Different Perspectives*

1. What function is played by the ritualized resolution of conflict among the Bedouin in Nabil Gorgy's story and among the Yąnomamö in Napoleon A. Chagnon's account "Doing Fieldwork Among the Yąnomamö"?

2. How does reciprocity organize societies in Nabil Gorgy's story and in David R. Counts's narrative, "Too Many Bananas"?

✦ *Extending Viewpoints Through Writing*

1. In a short essay, discuss Gorgy's attitude toward ancient cultural traditions as they emerge in the story.

2. Adil's actions and reactions indicate that he is in love. What actions and reactions of your own or someone you know serve as sure-fire signs of being in love?

Connecting Cultures

◆────────────◆

Nick Fiddes, The Power of Meat

What insight do the analyses by Nick Fiddes and Tepilit Ole Saitoti's account (see "The Initiation of a Maasai Warrior," Chapter 2) provide into the symbolic value associated with eating beef and ritual slaughter?

Napoleon A. Chagnon, Doing Fieldwork Among the Yąnomamö

How does the research of Napoleon A. Chagnon and Colin Turnbull (see "The Mbuti Pygmies," Chapter 1) reveal how cultures may be founded on principles of cooperation or on competition and aggression?

Gretel Ehrlich, To Live in Two Worlds

In what way are Gretel Ehrlich's account and Bessie Head's story (see "Looking for a Rain God," Chapter 9) based on the premise that religious rituals influence the world of nature?

Raymonde Carroll, Home

Which aspects of life in America does Le Ly Hayslip (see "Yearning to Breathe Free," Chapter 7) misinterpret or fail to understand because of the kinds of cultural differences in interpretation discussed by Raymonde Carroll?

Alison Lurie, The Language of Clothes

Discuss Alison Lurie's theory of the meanings communicated by the clothes we wear in relation to the wedding costumes described by Nicholas Bornoff (see "The Marriage Go-Round," Chapter 1).

David R. Counts, Too Many Bananas

How does the concept of reciprocity underlie David R. Counts's essay and Bessie Head's story (see "Looking for a Rain God," Chapter 9)?

Octavio Paz, *The Day of the Dead*

Discuss the psychology of sacrificing what normally would be conserved to placate the gods and attract abundance, as revealed in Octavio Paz's essay and Bessie Head's story "Looking for a Rain God" (Chapter 9).

Nabil Gorgy, *Cairo Is a Small City*

Compare the cultural factors and expectations that come into play in arranging marriages, as described by Nabil Gorgy in this story and by Serena Nanda in "Arranging a Marriage in India" (Chapter 1).

9

The Unseen World

———————◆———————

At one time or another in their lives, most people reflect on their relationship to a higher order of existence, whether one perceives it as an eternal force, the universe around us, a defined spiritual entity, or a concept that answers to a basic human need for a sense of order underlying the turbulence of everyday life.

In all societies religions attempt to deal with the most fundamentally mysterious questions of human existence. Religions in various forms offer answers to the ultimate questions of life and death, the existence of evil, and the attainment of good through cosmologies that explain how things have come to be the way they are.

In some cultures, shamans or priests are designated from birth or by experience and training as the religious practitioners. In other cultures, professional religious clergy, such as priests, ministers, and rabbis, are formally appointed and assume responsibility for leading that community in the performance of its religious rituals. Cultures have also existed where each person in the community performs these rituals directly without intermediaries.

Whatever form they take in terms of ceremonies, gestures, words, objects, actions, and mythology, religious rituals are performed in all cultures with a view toward influencing supernatural entities or forces on behalf of the petitioners. For example, in traditional agricultural societies, religious ceremonies were designed to ensure the health and fertility of human beings, animals, and crops through the offering of sacrifices, food, and libations to deities or ancestral spirits.

The methods and rituals used to influence supernatural powers or to communicate with spirits have traditionally taken the form of prayers, petitioning the deity, gifts, sacrifices and offerings, and spirit possession, in which a supernatural being takes over control of a medium and allows others to talk directly with someone from the spirit world.

The capacity to believe in the existence of a spiritual order is an act of faith that is the most fundamental aspect of all religions. At the same time, few people have ever unquestioningly trusted in the existence of a spiritual order without having to wrestle with uncertainty and doubt. Some works in this chapter examine the idea that faith must be tested by depicting protagonists who must overcome the skepticism of others and their own uncertainty.

Some people are content to continue within the religious traditions in which they were raised whereas others are drawn to systems of belief that they find match their needs and perceptions of the spiritual dimension. The readings in this chapter illustrate a multiplicity of different responses to the universal or cosmic. The chapter presents works that reflect how people in many different cultures and societies throughout the world look at themselves in relationship to the absolute, the eternal, the supernatural, or the concept of an ultimate truth.

We gain insight into how rituals ensure a cohesive system of social control in Gino Del Guercio's "The Secrets of Haiti's Living Dead" by discovering that the practice of voodoo, in contrast to its stereotyped image in the popular media, is an integral force in Haitian society. Leslie Marmon Silko, in "Language and Literature from a Pueblo Indian Perspective," discusses the attitude of Native-Americans toward the interconnection between the natural and spiritual worlds. Bessie Head relates a fact-based story, "Looking for a Rain God," that tells how a family in drought-plagued Botswana was driven beyond the limits of physical and psychological endurance and resorted to an outlawed tribal ritual of sacrificing their children in exchange for rain. Aung San Suu Kyi, in "My Country and People," explores the pervasive influence of Buddhism on all aspects of Burmese culture. Abioseh Nicol, from Sierra Leone, tells a bittersweet ghost story, "Life Is Sweet at Kumansenu," in which a son's reappearance before his mother after his death repays her lifelong devotion to him. The Egyptian writer Naguib Mahfouz creates an intriguing parable that compresses the experience of a lifetime into "Half a Day." Carol Spindel describes how important "Blessings" are in everyday village life in Côte d'Ivoire. The great Indian writer Premchand, in "Deliverance," dramatizes the fateful encounter between a village tanner and a Brahman priest.

Gino Del Guercio

The Secrets
of Haiti's Living Dead

◆

Gino Del Guercio is a national science writer for United Press Interna-
tional and was a MACY fellow at Boston's television station WGBH.
"The Secrets of Haiti's Living Dead" was first published in Harvard
Magazine *(January/February 1986). In 1982, Wade Davis, a Harvard-*
trained ethnobotanist, whose exploits formed the basis for this article, trav-
eled into the Haitian countryside to investigate accounts of Zombies—the
infamous living dead of Haitian folklore. Davis's research led him to ob-
tain the poison associated with the process. His findings were first pre-
sented in The Serpent and the Rainbow *(1988), a work that served as*
the basis for the movie of the same name, directed by Wes Craven, and
later in Passage of Darkness *(1988). Davis is currently research associ-*
ate in ethnobotany at the New York Botanical Garden.

The republic of Haiti in the West Indies occupies the western third of
the island of Hispaniola, which it shares with the Dominican Republic.
French rule of Haiti lasted from 1697, until Toussaint l'Ouverture, a
former slave, led Haiti to become the second independent nation in the
Americas, in 1804. For the most part, Haiti's history has been fraught
with intrigue and violence. In 1957, François "Papa Doc" Duvalier es-
tablished a dictatorship and was succeeded by his son Jean Claude ("Baby
Doc"), who fled the country in 1986. In December 1990, the Reverend
Jean Bertrand Aristide, a champion of the poor, was elected head of the
government in Haiti's first democratic elections. Aristide was subse-
quently forced into exile, and the government was placed under military
control. After the expulsion of the United Nations and the Organization
of American States (OAS) missions by a military junta in July 1994, fif-
teen thousand American troops moved into Haiti in September. President
Aristide briefly returned to office in October of 1994. Guercio's report re-
veals the extent to which Haitian life is controlled by voodoo, a religious
belief, West African in origin, that is characterized by induced trances
and magical rituals. Until this century, Voodoo was the state religion and
continues to flourish despite opposition from Roman Catholicism, the
other major religion in Haiti.

Five years ago, a man walked into l'Estére, a village in central Haiti,   1
approached a peasant woman named Angelina Narcisse, and identified

himself as her brother Clairvius. If he had not introduced himself using a boyhood nickname and mentioned facts only intimate family members knew, she would not have believed him. Because, eighteen years earlier, Angelina had stood in a small cemetery north of her village and watched as her brother Clairvius was buried.

2   The man told Angelina he remembered that night well. He knew when he was lowered into his grave, because he was fully conscious, although he could not speak or move. As the earth was thrown over his coffin, he felt as if he were floating over the grave. The scar on his right cheek, he said, was caused by a nail driven through his casket.

3   The night he was buried, he told Angelina, a voodoo priest raised him from the grave. He was beaten with a sisal whip and carried off to a sugar plantation in northern Haiti where, with other zombies, he was forced to work as a slave. Only with the death of the zombie master were they able to escape, and Narcisse eventually returned home.

4   Legend has it that zombies are the living dead, raised from their graves and animated by malevolent voodoo sorcerers, usually for some evil purpose. Most Haitians believe in zombies, and Narcisse's claim is not unique. At about the time he reappeared, in 1980, two women turned up in other villages saying they were zombies. In the same year, in northern Haiti, the local peasants claimed to have found a group of zombies wandering aimlessly in the fields.

5   But Narcisse's case was different in one crucial respect; it was documented. His death had been recorded by doctors at the American-directed Schweitzer Hospital in Deschapelles. On April 30, 1962, hospital records show, Narcisse walked into the hospital's emergency room spitting up blood. He was feverish and full of aches. His doctors could not diagnose his illness, and his symptoms grew steadily worse. Three days after he entered the hospital, according to the records, he died. The attending physicians, an American among them, signed his death certificate. His body was placed in cold storage for twenty hours, and then he was buried. He said he remembered hearing his doctors pronounce him dead while his sister wept at his bedside.

6   At the Centre de Psychiatrie et Neurologie in Port-au-Prince, Dr. Lamarque Douyon, a Haitian-born, Canadian-trained psychiatrist, has been systematically investigating all reports of zombies since 1961. Though convinced zombies were real, he had been unable to find a scientific explanation for the phenomenon. He did not believe zombies were people raised from the dead, but that did not make them any less interesting. He speculated that victims were only made to *look* dead, probably by means of a drug that dramatically slowed metabolism. The victim was buried, dug up within a few hours, and somehow reawakened.

7   The Narcisse case provided Douyon with evidence strong enough to warrant a request for assistance from colleagues in New York. Douyon

wanted to find an ethnobotanist, a traditional-medicines expert, who could track down the zombie potion he was sure existed. Aware of the medical potential of a drug that could dramatically lower metabolism, a group organized by the late Dr. Nathan Kline—a New York psychiatrist and pioneer in the field of psychopharmacology—raised the funds necessary to send someone to investigate.

The search for that someone led to the Harvard Botanical Museum, one of the world's foremost institutes of ethnobiology. Its director, Richard Evans Schultes, Jeffrey professor of biology, had spent thirteen years in the tropics studying native medicines. Some of his best-known work is the investigation of curare, the substance used by the nomadic people of the Amazon to poison their darts. Refined into a powerful muscle relaxant called D-tubocurarine, it is now an essential component of the anesthesia used during almost all surgery.   8

Schultes would have been a natural for the Haitian investigation, but he was too busy. He recommended another Harvard ethnobotanist for the assignment, Wade Davis, a 28-year-old Canadian pursuing a doctorate in biology.   9

Davis grew up in the tall pine forests of British Columbia and entered Harvard in 1971, influenced by a *Life* magazine story on the student strike of 1969. Before Harvard, the only Americans he had known were draft dodgers, who seemed very exotic. "I used to fight forest fires with them," Davis says. "Like everybody else, I thought America was where it was at. And I wanted to go to Harvard because of that *Life* article. When I got there, I realized it wasn't quite what I had in mind."   10

Davis took a course from Schultes, and when he decided to go to South America to study plants, he approached his professor for guidance. "He was an extraordinary figure," Davis remembers. "He was a man who had done it all. He had lived alone for years in the Amazon." Schultes sent Davis to the rain forest with two letters of introduction and two pieces of advice: wear a pith helmet and try ayahuasca, a powerful hallucinogenic vine. During that expedition and others, Davis proved himself an "outstanding field man," says his mentor. Now, in early 1982, Schultes called him into his office and asked if he had plans for spring break.   11

"I always took to Schultes's assignments like a plant takes to water," says Davis, tall and blond, with inquisitive blue eyes. "Whatever Schultes told me to do, I did. His letters of introduction opened up a whole world." This time the world was Haiti.   12

Davis knew nothing about the Caribbean island—and nothing about African traditions, which serve as Haiti's cultural basis. He certainly did not believe in zombies. "I thought it was a lark," he says now.   13

Davis landed in Haiti a week after his conversation with Schultes, armed with a hypothesis about how the zombie drug—if it existed— might be made. Setting out to explore, he discovered a country materi-   14 ally impoverished, but rich in culture and mystery. He was impressed by the cohesion of Haitian society; he found none of the crime, social disorder, and rampant drug and alcohol abuse so common in many of the other Caribbean islands. The cultural wealth and cohesion, he believes, spring from the country's turbulent history.

15   During the French occupation of the late eighteenth century, 370,000 African-born slaves were imported to Haiti between 1780 and 1790. In 1791, the black population launched one of the few successful slave revolts in history, forming secret societies and overcoming first the French plantation owners and then a detachment of troops from Napoleon's army, sent to quell the revolt. For the next hundred years Haiti was the only independent black republic in the Caribbean, populated by people who did not forget their African heritage. "You can almost argue that Haiti is more African than Africa," Davis says. "When the west coast of Africa was being disrupted by colonialism and the slave trade, Haiti was essentially left alone. The amalgam of beliefs in Haiti is unique, but it's very, very African."

16   Davis discovered that the vast majority of Haitian peasants practice voodoo, a sophisticated religion with African roots. Says Davis, "It was immediately obvious that the stereotypes of voodoo weren't true. Going around the countryside, I found clues to a whole complex social world." Vodounists believe they communicate directly with, indeed are often possessed by, the many spirits who populate the everyday world. Vodoun society is a system of education, law, and medicine; it embodies a code of ethics that regulates social behavior. In rural areas, secret vodoun societies, much like those found on the west coast of Africa, are as much or more in control of everyday life as the Haitian government.

17   Although most outsiders dismissed the zombie phenomenon as folklore, some early investigators, convinced of its reality, tried to find a scientific explanation. The few who sought a zombie drug failed. Nathan Kline, who helped finance Davis's expedition, had searched unsuccessfully, as had Lamarque Douyon, the Haitian psychiatrist. Zora Neale Hurston, an American black woman, may have come closest. An anthropological pioneer, she went to Haiti in the Thirties, studied vodoun society, and wrote a book on the subject, *Tell My Horse*, first published in 1938. She knew about the secret societies and was convinced zombies were real, but if a powder existed, she too failed to obtain it.

18   Davis obtained a sample in a few weeks.

19   He arrived in Haiti with the names of several contacts. A BBC reporter familiar with the Narcisse case had suggested he talk with Marcel Pierre. Pierre owned the Eagle Bar, a bordello in the city of Saint Marc. He was also a voodoo sorcerer and had supplied the BBC with a physiologically active powder of unknown ingredients. Davis found him willing to negotiate. He told Pierre he was a representative of

"powerful but anonymous interests in New York," willing to pay generously for the priest's services, provided no questions were asked. Pierre agreed to be helpful for what Davis will only say was a "sizable sum." Davis spent a day watching Pierre gather the ingredients—including human bones—and grind them together with mortar and pestle. However, from his knowledge of poison, Davis knew immediately that nothing in the formula could produce the powerful effects of zombification.

Three weeks later, Davis went back to the Eagle Bar, where he found Pierre sitting with three associates. Davis challenged him. He called him a charlatan. Enraged, the priest gave him a second vial, claiming that this was the real poison. Davis pretended to pour the powder into his palm and rub it into his skin. "You're a dead man," Pierre told him, and he might have been, because this powder proved to be genuine. But, as the substance had not actually touched him, Davis was able to maintain his bravado, and Pierre was impressed. He agreed to make the poison and show Davis how it was done. 20

The powder, which Davis keeps in a small vial, looks like dry black dirt. It contains parts of toads, sea worms, lizards, tarantulas, and human bones. (To obtain the last ingredient, he and Pierre unearthed a child's grave on a nocturnal trip to the cemetery.) The poison is rubbed into the victim's skin. Within hours he begins to feel nauseated and has difficulty breathing. A pins-and-needles sensation afflicts his arms and legs, then progresses to the whole body. The subject becomes paralyzed; his lips turn blue for lack of oxygen. Quickly—sometimes within six hours—his metabolism is lowered to a level almost indistinguishable from death. 21

As Davis discovered, making the poison is an inexact science. Ingredients varied in the five samples he eventually acquired, although the active agents were always the same. And the poison came with no guarantee. Davis speculates that sometimes instead of merely paralyzing the victim, the compound kills him. Sometimes the victim suffocates in the coffin before he can be resurrected. But clearly the potion works well enough often enough to make zombies more than a figment of Haitian imagination. 22

Analysis of the powder produced another surprise. "When I went down to Haiti originally," says Davis, "my hypothesis was that the formula would contain *concombre zombi,* the 'zombie's cucumber,' which is a *Datura* plant. I thought somehow *Datura* was used in putting people down." *Datura* is a powerful psychoactive plant, found in West Africa as well as other tropical areas and used there in ritual as well as criminal activities. Davis had found *Datura* growing in Haiti. Its popular name suggested the plant was used in creating zombies. 23

But, says Davis, "there were a lot of problems with the *Datura* hypothesis. Partly it was a question of how the drug was administered. *Datura* would create a stupor in huge doses, but it just wouldn't produce 24 the kind of immobility that was key. These people had to appear dead, and there aren't many drugs that will do that."

25   One of the ingredients Pierre included in the second formula was a dried fish, a species of puffer or blowfish, common to most parts of the world. It gets its name from its ability to fill itself with water and swell to several times its normal size when threatened by predators. Many of these fish contain a powerful poison known as tetrodotoxin. One of the most powerful nonprotein poisons known to man, tetradotoxin turned up in every sample of zombie powder that Davis acquired.

26   Numerous well-documented accounts of puffer fish poisoning exist, but the most famous accounts come from the Orient, where *fugu* fish, a species of puffer, is considered a delicacy. In Japan, special chefs are licensed to prepare *fugu*. The chef removes enough poison to make the fish nonlethal, yet enough remains to create exhilarating physiological effects—tingles up and down the spine, mild prickling of the tongue and lips, euphoria. Several dozen Japanese die each year, having bitten off more than they should have.

27   "When I got hold of the formula and saw it was the *fugu* fish, that suddenly threw open the whole Japanese literature," says Davis. Case histories of *fugu* poisoning read like accounts of zombification. Victims remain conscious but unable to speak or move. A man who had "died" after eating *fugu* recovered seven days later in the morgue. Several summers ago, another Japanese poisoned by *fugu* revived after he was nailed into his coffin. "Almost all of Narcisse's symptoms correlated. Even strange things such as the fact that he said he was conscious and could hear himself pronounced dead. Stuff that I thought had to be magic, that seemed crazy. But, in fact, that is what people who get *fugu*-fish poisoning experience."

28   Davis was certain he had solved the mystery. But far from being the end of his investigation, identifying the poison was, in fact, its starting point. "The drug alone didn't make zombies," he explains. "Japanese victims of puffer-fish poisoning don't become zombies, they become poison victims. All the drug could do was set someone up for a whole series of psychological pressures that would be rooted in the culture. I wanted to know why zombification was going on," he says.

29   He sought a cultural answer, an explanation rooted in the structure and beliefs of Haitian society. Was zombification simply a random criminal activity? He thought not. He had discovered that Clairvius Narcisse and "Ti Femme," a second victim he interviewed, were village pariahs. Ti Femme was regarded as a thief. Narcisse had abandoned his children and deprived his brother of land that was rightfully his. Equally suggestive, Narcisse claimed that his aggrieved brother had sold him to a *bokor,* a voodoo priest who dealt in black magic; he made cryptic reference to having been tried and found guilty by the "masters of the land."

Gathering poisons from various parts of the country, Davis had   30
come into direct contact with the vodoun secret societies. Returning to
the anthropological literature on Haiti and pursuing his contacts with
informants, Davis came to understand the social matrix within which
zombies were created.

Davis's investigations uncovered the importance of the secret soci-   31
eties. These groups trace their origins to the bands of escaped slaves
that organized the revolt against the French in the late eighteenth century. Open to both men and women, the societies control specific territories of the country. Their meetings take place at night, and in many
rural parts of Haiti the drums and wild celebrations that characterize
the gatherings can be heard for miles.

Davis believes the secret societies are responsible for policing their   32
communities, and the threat of zombification is one way they maintain
order. Says Davis, "Zombification has a material basis, but it also has a
societal logic." To the uninitiated, the practice may appear a random
criminal activity, but in rural vodoun society, it is exactly the opposite—a
sanction imposed by recognized authorities, a form of capital punishment. For rural Haitians, zombification is an even more severe punishment than death, because it deprives the subject of his most valued
possessions: his free will and independence.

The vodounists believe that when a person dies, his spirit splits   33
into several different parts. If a priest is powerful enough, the spiritual
aspect that controls a person's character and individuality, known as *ti
bon ange*, the "good little angel," can be captured and the corporeal aspect, deprived of its will, held as a slave.

From studying the medical literature on tetrodotoxin poisoning,   34
Davis discovered that if a victim survives the first few hours of the poisoning, he is likely to recover fully from the ordeal. The subject simply
revives spontaneously. But zombies remain without will, in a trance-
like state, a condition vodounists attribute to the power of the priest.
Davis thinks it possible that the psychological trauma of zombification
may be augmented by *Datura* or some other drug; he thinks zombies
may be fed a *Datura* paste that accentuates their disorientation. Still, he
puts the material basis of zombification in perspective: "Tetrodotoxin
and *Datura* are only templates on which cultural forces and beliefs may
be amplified a thousand times."

Davis has not been able to discover how prevalent zombification is   35
in Haiti. "How many zombies there are is not the question," he says. He
compares it to capital punishment in the United States: "It doesn't really
matter how many people are electrocuted, as long as it's a possibility."
As a sanction in Haiti, the fear is not of zombies, it's of becoming one.

Davis attributes his success in solving the zombie mystery to his   36
approach. He went to Haiti with an open mind and immersed himself
in the culture. "My intuition unhindered by biases served me well," he

says. "I didn't make any judgments." He combined this attitude with what he had learned earlier from his experiences in the Amazon. "Schultes's lesson is to go and live with the Indians as an Indian." Davis was able to participate in the vodoun society to a surprising degree, eventually even penetrating one of the Bizango societies and dancing in their nocturnal rituals. His appreciation of Haitian culture is apparent. "Everybody asks me how did a white person get this information? To ask the question means you don't understand Haitians—they don't judge you by the color of your skin."

37   As a result of the exotic nature of his discoveries, Davis has gained a certain notoriety. He plans to complete his dissertation soon, but he has already finished writing a popular account of his adventures. To be published in January by Simon and Schuster, it is called *The Serpent and the Rainbow,* after the serpent that vodounists believe created the earth and the rainbow spirit it married. Film rights have already been optioned; in October Davis went back to Haiti with a screenwriter. But Davis takes the notoriety in stride. "All this attention is funny," he says. "For years, not just me, but all Schultes's students have had extraordinary adventures in the line of work. The adventure is not the end point, it's just along the way of getting the data. At the Botanical Museum, Schultes created a world unto itself. We didn't think we were doing anything above the ordinary. I still don't think we do. And you know," he adds, "the Haiti episode does not begin to compare to what others have accomplished—particularly Schultes himself."

✦ Evaluating the Text

1. To what extent does Guercio's account gain credibility because he begins with the mysterious case of Clairvius Narcisse? How is Narcisse's identification by his sister intended to put the case beyond all doubt and leave the process of zombification as the only possible explanation for his otherwise inexplicable "death"?

2. Why is it important to Guercio's account that he mentions physicians from the United States as well as Haitian doctors who certified the "death" of Clairvius Narcisse? What is Guercio's attitude toward this phenomenon? How is this attitude revealed in the way he constructs his report?

3. What is the relationship between the vodoun religion and African tribal customs? Why is it important that Haiti was the only independent black republic in the Caribbean, populated by a people who launched one of the few successful slave revolts in history?

4. How does the threat of zombification serve as a preventative measure that ensures social control in deterring crimes against the community?

How did it operate in the cases of Clairvius Narcisse and "Ti Femme"? In what ways is the reality of the social mechanism of zombification quite different from how it has been presented in movies and popular culture?

5. What kinds of independent confirmation of the effects of tetrodotoxin, a potent neurotoxin that drastically reduces metabolism and produces paralysis, did Davis discover in his research on the effects of Japanese victims of *fugu* fish poisoning?

✦ Exploring Different Perspectives

1. How do the social processes and different religious beliefs concerning control of the person's soul described by Davis differ from those explored in Abioseh Nicol's "Life Is Sweet at Kumansenu"?

2. How does the concept of death and resurrection enter into the account by Gino Del Guercio and Bessie Head's story "Looking for a Rain God"?

✦ Extending Viewpoints Through Writing

1. If you are familiar with or interested in the processes by which various religious cults enlist and program their members, you might compare their methods to those of the vodoun priests in terms of positive and negative reinforcement of psychological, sociological, and physiological conditioning.

2. If you have had the opportunity to see the movie *The Serpent and the Rainbow* (1988), directed by Wes Craven, you might wish to compare its representation of the events described in this article or Wade Davis's book *The Serpent and the Rainbow* (1985). For further research on this subject, you might consult Wade Davis, *Passage of Darkness: The Ethnobiology of the Haitian Zombie* (1988), an in-depth study of the political, social, and botanical mechanisms of zombification.

3. For a research project, you might pursue the fascinating interconnections between François Duvalier's rise to political power (president from 1957 until his succession by his son, Jean-Claude Duvalier) in Haiti and his prior life as a physician, vodoun priest, and well-regarded anthropologist.

Leslie Marmon Silko

Language and Literature from a Pueblo Indian Perspective

◆

Leslie Marmon Silko was born in 1948 in Albuquerque, New Mexico. Silko's writing draws on her heritage as a Native American of mixed ancestry (Laguna, Mexican, and white). She grew up on the Laguna Pueblo reservation in New Mexico and attended the University of New Mexico, graduating in 1969 with a B.A. in English. She then briefly attended law school, but decided to be a writer and teacher instead. Her first short story, "The Man to Send Rain Clouds," was published in New Mexico Quarterly *in 1969. She taught for two years at the Navajo Community College at Many Farms, Arizona, following which she spent two years in Ketchikan, Alaska. Her first novel,* Ceremony *(1977), about an Indian veteran of World War II and his search for sanity, is shaped by her innovative use of Pueblo oral storytelling techniques as are her later works* Laguna Woman *(1974),* Storyteller *(1981), a collection of poems and stories, her second novel,* Almanac of the Dead *(1991) and her most recent work,* Sacred Water *(1993). Her work has been widely praised. In 1981 she was the recipient of a MacArthur Foundation grant. In her 1991 essay, "Language and Literature from a Pueblo Indian Perspective," Silko discusses and illustrates the relationship between Laguna Pueblo religious beliefs and the tradition of storytelling in Laguna society.*

According to Laguna tradition, the Laguna tribe migrated into the area close to Albuquerque, New Mexico, on the south bank of the San Jose River, after having been forced south by drought. The settlement at Laguna dates from the early 1700s and currently comprises a population of several thousand scattered among several small farming villages. The Laguna people together with their close cultural relatives, the Acoma, share a language that derives from the Keresan family. The name Laguna, *Spanish for "lake," was inspired by a large pond located west of the pueblo or settlement. Traditional features of Pueblo society required all young men to be initiated into the Katcina (pronounced "kachina") cult and to take part in masked dances in which they impersonated the rain gods to bring rain. Also, numerous secret medicine societies perform ceremonies and dances to cure the sick, bring good crops, control the weather, and ensure the health and well-being of the Pueblo. Traditional culture and language remain important despite contact with the outside world that began with the building of railroad lines and the introduction of Protestantism. To this day, when a Laguna Indian dies, he or she may be painted with many colors, buried along with bowls of food and water, with the head pointing to the east. In a ceremony conducted by a shaman, using feathered prayer sticks, the spirit of the deceased is sent on the third day to the land of the dead.*

Where I come from, the words most highly valued are those spoken from the heart, unpremeditated and unrehearsed. Among the Pueblo people, a written speech or statement is highly suspect because the true feelings of the speaker remain hidden as she reads words that are detached from the occasion and the audience. I have intentionally not written a formal paper because I want you to *hear* and to experience English in a structure that follows patterns from the oral tradition. For those of you accustomed to being taken from point A to point B to point C, this presentation may be somewhat difficult to follow. Pueblo expression resembles something like a spider's web—with many little threads radiating from the center, crisscrossing each other. As with the web, the structure emerges as it is made and you must simply listen and trust, as the Pueblo people do, that meaning will be made. 1

My task is a formidable one: I ask you to set aside a number of basic approaches that you have been using, and probably will continue to use, and instead, to approach language from the Pueblo perspective, one that embraces the whole of creation and the whole of history and time. 2

What changes would Pueblo writers make to English as a language for literature? I have some examples of stories in English that I will use to address this question. At the same time, I would like to explain the importance of storytelling and how it relates to a Pueblo theory of language. 3

So, I will begin, appropriately enough, with the Pueblo Creation story, an all-inclusive story of how life began. In this story, Tséitsínako, Thought Woman, by thinking of her sisters, and together with her sisters, thought of everything that is. In this way, the world was created. Everything in this world was a part of the original creation; the people at home understood that far away there were other human beings, also a part of this world. The Creation story even includes a prophecy, which describes the origin of European and African peoples and also refers to Asians. 4

This story, I think, suggests something about why the Pueblo people are more concerned with story and communication and less concerned with a particular language. There are at least six, possibly seven, distinct languages among the twenty pueblos of the southwestern United States, for example, Zuñi and Hopi. And from mesa to mesa there are subtle differences in language. But the particular language being spoken isn't as important as what a speaker is trying to say, and this emphasis on the story itself stems, I believe, from a view of narrative particular to the Pueblo and other Native American peoples—that is, that language *is* story. 5

6   I will try to clarify this statement. At Laguna Pueblo, for example, many individual words have their own stories. So when one is telling a story, and one is using words to tell the story, each word that one is speaking has a story of its own, too. Often the speakers or tellers will go into these word-stories, creating an elaborate structure of stories-within-stories. This structure, which becomes very apparent in the actual telling of a story, informs contemporary Pueblo writing and storytelling as well as the traditional narratives. This perspective on narrative—of story within story, the idea that one story is only the beginning of many stories, and the sense that stories never truly end—represents an important contribution of Native American cultures to the English language.

7   Many people think of storytelling as something that is done at bedtime, that it is something done for small children. But when I use the term *storytelling*, I'm talking about something much bigger than that. I'm talking about something that comes out of an experience and an understanding of that original view of creation—that we are all part of a whole; we do not differentiate or fragment stories and experiences. In the beginning, Tséitsínako, Thought Woman, thought of all things, and all of these things are held together as one holds many things together in a single thought.

8   So in the telling (and you will hear a few of the dimensions of this telling) first of all, as mentioned earlier, the storytelling always includes the audience, the listeners. In fact, a great deal of the story is believed to be inside the listener; the storyteller's role is to draw the story out of the listeners. The storytelling continues from generation to generation.

9   Basically, the origin story constructs our identity—within this story, we know who we are. We are the Lagunas. This is where we come from. We came this way. We came by this place. And so from the time we are very young, we hear these stories, so that when we go out into the world, when one asks who we are, or where we are from, we immediately know: we are the people who came from the north. We are the people of these stories.

10   In the Creation story, Antelope says that he will help knock a hole in the earth so that the people can come up, out into the next world. Antelope tries and tries; he uses his hooves, but is unable to break through. It is then that Badger says, "Let me help you." And Badger very patiently uses his claws and digs a way through, bringing the people into the world. When the Badger clan people think of themselves, or when the Antelope people think of themselves, it is as people who are of *this* story, and this is *our* place, and we fit into the very beginning when the people first came, before we began our journey south.

11   Within the clans there are stories that identify the clan. One moves, then, from the idea of one's identity as a tribal person into clan identity, then to one's identity as a member of an extended family. And it is the notion of "extended family" that has produced a kind of story that

some distinguish from other Pueblo stories, though Pueblo people do not. Anthropologists and ethnologists have, for a long time, differentiated the types of stories the Pueblos tell. They tended to elevate the old, sacred, and traditional stories and to brush aside family stories, the family's account of itself. But in Pueblo culture, these family stories are given equal recognition. There is no definite, preset pattern for the way one will hear the stories of one's own family, but it is a very critical part of one's childhood, and the storytelling continues throughout one's life. One will hear stories of importance to the family—sometimes wonderful stories—stories about the time a maternal uncle got the biggest deer that was ever seen and brought it back from the mountains. And so an individual's identity will extend from the identity constructed around the family—"I am from the family of my uncle who brought in this wonderful deer and it was a wonderful hunt."

Family accounts include negative stories, too; perhaps an uncle did   12
something unacceptable. It is very important that one keep track of all these stories—both positive and not so positive—about one's own family and other families. Because even when there is no way around it— old Uncle Pete *did* do a terrible thing—by knowing the stories that originate in other families, one is able to deal with terrible sorts of things that might happen within one's own family. If a member of the family does something that cannot be excused, one always knows stories about similarly inexcusable things done by a member of another family. But this knowledge is not communicated for malicious reasons. It is very important to understand this. Keeping track of all the stories within the community gives us all a certain distance, a useful perspective, that brings incidents down to a level we can deal with. If others have done it before, it cannot be so terrible. If others have endured, so can we.

The stories are always bringing us together, keeping this whole to-   13
gether, keeping this family together, keeping this clan together. "Don't go away, don't isolate yourself, but come here, because we have all had these kinds of experiences." And so there is this constant pulling together to resist the tendency to run or hide or separate oneself during a traumatic emotional experience. This separation not only endangers the group but the individual as well—one does not recover by oneself.

Because storytelling lies at the heart of Pueblo culture, it is absurd   14
to attempt to fix the stories in time. "When did they tell the stories?" or "What time of day does the storytelling take place?"—these questions are nonsensical from a Pueblo perspective, because our storytelling goes on constantly: as some old grandmother puts on the shoes of a child and tells her the story of a little girl who didn't wear her shoes, for instance, or someone comes into the house for coffee to talk with a teenage boy who has just been in a lot of trouble, to reassure him that someone else's son has been in that kind of trouble, too. Storytelling is an ongoing process, working on many different levels.

15   Here's one story that is often told at a time of individual crisis (and I want to remind you that we make no distinctions between types of story—historical, sacred, plain gossip—because these distinctions are not useful when discussing the Pueblo *experience* of language). There was a young man who, when he came back from the war in Vietnam, had saved up his army pay and bought a beautiful red Volkswagen. He was very proud of it. One night he drove up to a place called the King's Bar right across the reservation line. The bar is notorious for many reasons, particularly for the deep *arroyo* located behind it. The young man ran in to pick up a cold six-pack, but he forgot to put on his emergency brake. And his little red Volkswagen rolled back into the *arroyo* and was all smashed up. He felt very bad about it, but within a few days everybody had come to him with stories about other people who had lost cars and family members to that *arroyo*, for instance, George Day's station wagon, with his mother-in-law and kids inside. So everybody was saying, "Well, at least your mother-in-law and kids weren't in the car when it rolled in," and one can't argue with that kind of story. The story of the young man and his smashed-up Volkswagen was now joined with all the other stories of cars that fell into that *arroyo*.

16   Now I want to tell you a very beautiful little story. It is a very old story that is sometimes told to people who suffer great family or personal loss. This story was told by my Aunt Susie. She is one of the first generation of people at Laguna who began experimenting with English—who began working to make English speak for us—that is, to speak from the heart. (I come from a family intent on getting the stories told.) As you read the story, I think you will hear that. And here and there, I think, you will also hear the influence of the Indian school at Carlisle, Pennsylvania, where my Aunt Susie was sent (like being sent to prison) for six years.

17   This scene is set partly in Acoma, partly in Laguna. Waithea was a little girl living in Acoma and one day she said, "Mother, I would like to have some *yashtoah* to eat." *Yashtoah* is the hardened crust of corn mush that curls up. *Yashtoah* literally means "curled up." She said, "I would like to have some *yashtoah*," and her mother said, "My dear little girl, I can't make you any *yashtoah* because we haven't any wood, but if you will go down off the mesa, down below, and pick up some pieces of wood and bring them home, I will make you some *yashtoah*." So Waithea was glad and ran down the precipitous cliff of Acoma mesa. Down below, just as her mother had told her, there were pieces of wood, some curled, some crooked in shape, that she was to pick up and take home. She found just such wood as these.

18   She brought them home in a little wicker basket. First she called to her mother as she got home, *"Nayah, deeni!* Mother, upstairs!" The Pueblo people always called "upstairs" because long ago their homes were two, three stories, and they entered from the top. She said, *"Deeni!*

UPSTAIRS!" and her mother came. The little girl said, "I have brought the wood you wanted me to bring." And she opened her little wicker basket to lay out the pieces of wood but here they were snakes. They were snakes instead of the crooked sticks of wood. And her mother said, "Oh my dear child, you have brought snakes instead!" She said, "Go take them back and put them back just where you got them." And the little girl ran down the mesa again, down below to the flats. And she put those snakes back just where she got them. They were snakes instead and she was very hurt about this and so she said, "I'm not going home. I'm going to *Kawaik,* the beautiful lake place, *Kawaik,* and drown myself in that lake, *byn'yah'nah* [the "west lake"]. I will go there and drown myself."

So she started off, and as she passed by the Enchanted Mesa near   19
Acoma she met an old man, very aged, and he saw her running, and he said, "My dear child, where are you going?" "I'm going to *Kawaik* and jump into the lake there." "Why?" "Well, because," she said, "my mother didn't want to make any *yashtoah* for me." The old man said, "Oh, no! You must not go my child. Come with me and I will take you home." He tried to catch her, but she was very light and skipped along. And every time he would try to grab her she would skip faster away from him.

The old man was coming home with some wood strapped to his   20
back and tied with yucca. He just let that strap go and let the wood drop. He went as fast as he could up the cliff to the little girl's home. When he got to the place where she lived, he called to her mother. *"Deeni!"* "Come on up!" And he said, "I can't. I just came to bring you a message. Your little daughter is running away. She is going to *Kawaik* to drown herself in the lake there." "Oh my dear little girl!" the mother said. So she busied herself with making the *yashtoah* her little girl liked so much. Corn mush curled at the top. (She must have found enough wood to boil the corn meal and make the *yashtoah.*)

While the mush was cooling off, she got the little girl's clothing, her   21
manta dress and buckskin moccasins and all her other garments, and put them in a bundle—probably a yucca bag. And she started down as fast as she could on the east side of Acoma. (There used to be a trail there, you know. It's gone now, but it was accessible in those days.) She saw her daughter way at a distance and she kept calling: "Stsamaku! My daughter! Come back! I've got your *yashtoah* for you." But the little girl would not turn. She kept on ahead and she cried: "My mother, my mother, she didn't want me to have any *yashtoah.* So now I'm going to *Kawaik* and drown myself." Her mother heard her cry and said, "My little daughter, come back here!" "No," and she kept a distance away from her. And they came nearer and nearer to the lake. And she could see her daughter now, very plain. "Come back, my daughter! I have your *yashtoah.*" But no, she kept on, and finally she reached the lake and she stood on the edge.

22 She had tied a little feather in her hair, which is traditional (in death they tie this feather on the head). She carried a feather, the little girl did, and she tied it in her hair with a piece of string, right on top of her head she put the feather. Just as her mother was about to reach her, she jumped into the lake. The little feather was whirling around and around in the depths below. Of course the mother was very sad. She went, grieved, back to Acoma and climbed her mesa home. She stood on the edge of the mesa and scattered her daughter's clothing, the little moccasins, the *yashtoah*. She scattered them to the east, to the west, to the north, to the south. And the pieces of clothing and the moccasins and *yashtoah*, all turned into butterflies. And today they say that Acoma has more beautiful butterflies: red ones, white ones, blue ones, yellow ones. They came from this little girl's clothing.[1]

23 Now this is a story anthropologists would consider very old. The version I have given you is just as Aunt Susie tells it. You can occasionally hear some English she picked up at Carlisle—words like "precipitous." You will also notice that there is a great deal of repetition, and a little reminder about *yashtoah,* and how it is made. There is a remark about the cliff trail at Acoma—that it was once there, but is there no longer. This story may be told at a time of sadness or loss, but within this story many other elements are brought together. Things are not separated out and categorized; all things are brought together, so that the reminder about the *yashtoah* is valuable information that is repeated— a recipe, if you will. The information about the old trail at Acoma reveals that stories are, in a sense, maps, since even to this day there is little information or material about trails that is passed around with writing. In the structure of this story the repetitions are, of course, designed to help you remember. It is repeated again and again, and then it moves on.

24 The next story I would like to tell is by Simon Ortiz, from Acoma Pueblo. He is a wonderful poet who also works in narrative. One of the things I find very interesting in this short story is that if you listen very closely, you begin to hear what I was talking about in terms of a story never beginning at the beginning, and certainly never ending. As the Hopis sometimes say, "Well, it has gone this far for a while." There is always that implication of a continuing. The other thing I want you to listen for is the many stories within one story. Listen to the kinds of stories contained within the main story—stories that give one a family identity and an individual identity, for example. This story is called "Home Country":

25 "Well, it's been a while. I think in 1947 was when I left. My husband had been killed in Okinawa some years before. And so I had

[1]See Leslie Marmon Silko, *Storyteller* (1981).

no more husband. And I had to make a living. O I guess I could have looked for another man but I didn't want to. It looked like the war had made some of them into a bad way anyway. I saw some of them come home like that. They either got drunk or just stayed around a while or couldn't seem to be satisfied anymore with what was there. I guess now that I think about it, that happened to me too although I wasn't in the war not in the Army or even much off the reservation just that several years at the Indian School. Well there was that feeling things were changing not only the men the boys, but things were changing.

"One day the home nurse the nurse that came from the Indian   26
health service was at my mother's home my mother was getting near the end real sick and she said that she had been meaning to ask me a question. I said what is the question. And the home nurse said well your mother is getting real sick and after she is no longer around for you to take care of, what will you be doing you and her are the only ones here. And I said I don't know. But I was thinking about it what she said made me think about it. And then the next time she came she said to me Eloise the government is hiring Indians now in the Indian schools to take care of the boys and girls I heard one of the supervisors saying that Indians are hard workers but you have to supervise them a lot and I thought of you well because you've been taking care of your mother real good and you follow all my instructions. She said I thought of you because you're a good Indian girl and you would be the kind of person for that job. I didn't say anything I had not ever really thought about a job but I kept thinking about it.

"Well my mother she died and we buried her up at the old   27
place the cemetery there it's real nice on the east side of the hill where the sun shines warm and the wind doesn't blow too much sand around right there. Well I was sad we were all sad for a while but you know how things are. One of my aunties came over and she advised me and warned me about being too sorry about it and all that she wished me that I would not worry too much about it because old folks they go along pretty soon life is that way and then she said that maybe I ought to take in one of my aunties kids or two because there was a lot of them kids and I was all by myself now. But I was so young and I thought that I might do that you know take care of someone but I had been thinking too of what the home nurse said to me about working. Hardly anybody at our home was working at something like that no woman anyway. And I would have to move away.

"Well I did just that. I remember that day very well. I told my   28
aunties and they were all crying and we all went up to the old highway where the bus to town passed by everyday. I was wearing

an old kind of bluish sweater that was kind of big that one of my cousins who was older had got from a white person a tourist one summer in trade for something she had made a real pretty basket. She gave me that and I used to have a picture of me with it on it's kind of real ugly. Yeah that was the day I left wearing a baggy sweater and carrying a suitcase that someone gave me too I think or maybe it was the home nurse there wasn't much in it anyway either. I was scared and everybody seemed to be sad I was so young and skinny then. My aunties said one of them who was real fat you make sure you eat now make your own tortillas drink the milk and stuff like candies is no good she learned that from the nurse. Make sure you got your letter my auntie said. I had it folded into my purse. Yes I had one too a brown one that my husband when he was still alive one time on furlough he brought it on my birthday it was a nice purse and still looked new because I never used it.

29 "The letter said that I had a job at Keams Canyon the boarding school there but I would have to go to the Agency first for some papers to be filled and that's where I was going first. The Agency. And then they would send me out to Keams Canyon. I didn't even know where it was except that someone of our relatives said that it was near Hopi. My uncles teased me about watching out for the Hopi men and boys don't let them get too close they said well you know how they are and they were pretty strict too about those things and then they were joking and then they were not too and so I said aw they won't get near to me I'm too ugly and I promised I would be careful anyway.

30 "So we all gathered for a while at my last auntie's house and then the old man my grandfather brought his wagon and horses to the door and we all got in and sat there for a while until my auntie told her father okay father let's go and shook his elbow because the poor old man was old by then and kind of going to sleep all the time you had to talk to him real loud. I had about ten dollars I think that was a lot of money more than it is now you know and when we got to the highway where the Indian road which is just a dirt road goes off the pave road my grandfather reached into his blue jeans and pulled out a silver dollar and put it into my hand. I was so shocked. We were all so shocked. We all looked around at each other we didn't know where the old man had gotten it because we were real poor two of my uncles had to borrow on their accounts at the trading store for the money I had in my purse but there it was a silver dollar so big and shining in my grandfather's hand and then in my hand.

31 "Well I was so shocked and everybody was so shocked that we all started crying right there at the junction of that Indian road and the pave highway I wanted to be a little girl again running after the

old man when he hurried with his long legs to the cornfields or went for water down to the river. He was old then and his eye was turned gray and he didn't do much anymore except drive the wagon and chop a little bit of wood but I just held him and I just held him so tightly.

"Later on I don't know what happened to the silver dollar it had a date of 1907 on it but I kept it for a long time because I guess I wanted to have it to remember when I left my home country. What I did in between then and now is another story but that's the time I moved away," is what she said.[2]   32

There are a great many parallels between Pueblo experiences and those of African and Caribbean peoples—one is that we have all had the conqueror's language imposed on us. But our experience with English has been somewhat different in that the Bureau of Indian Affairs schools were not interested in teaching us the canon of Western classics. For instance, we never heard of Shakespeare. We were given Dick and Jane, and I can remember reading that the robins were heading south for the winter. It took me a long time to figure out what was going on. I worried for quite a while about our robins in Laguna because they didn't leave in the winter, until I finally realized that all the big textbook companies are up in Boston and *their* robins do go south in the winter. But in a way, this dreadful formal education freed us by encouraging us to maintain our narratives. Whatever literature we were exposed to at school (which was damn little), at home the story-telling, the special regard for telling and bringing together through the telling, was going on constantly.   33

And as the old people say, "If you can remember the stories, you will be all right. Just remember the stories." When I returned to Laguna Pueblo after attending college, I wondered how the storytelling was continuing (anthropologists say that Laguna Pueblo is one of the more acculturated pueblos), so I visited an English class at Laguna-Acoma High School. I knew the students had cassette tape recorders in their lockers and stereos at home, and that they listened to Kiss and Led Zeppelin and were well informed about popular culture in general. I had with me an anthology of short stories by Native American writers, *The Man to Send Rain Clouds.* One story in the book is about the killing of a state policeman in New Mexico by three Acoma Pueblo men in the early 1950s.[3] I asked the students how many had heard this story and steeled myself for the possibility that the anthropologists were right, that the old traditions were indeed dying out and the students would   34

[2]Simon J. Ortiz, *Howbah Indians* (Tucson: Blue Moon Press, 1978).

[3]See Simon J. Ortiz, "The Killing of a State Cop," in *The Man to Send Rain Clouds,* ed. Kenneth Rosen (New York: Viking Press, 1974), pp. 101–108.

be ignorant of the story. But instead, all but one or two raised their hands—they had heard the story, just as I had heard it when I was young, some in English, some in Laguna.

35   One of the other advantages that we Pueblos have enjoyed is that we have always been able to stay with the land. Our stories cannot be separated from their geographical locations, from actual physical places on the land. We were not relocated like so many Native American groups who were torn away from their ancestral land. And our stories are so much a part of these places that it is almost impossible for future generations to lose them—there is a story connected with every place, every object in the landscape.

36   Dennis Brutus has talked about the "yet unborn" as well as "those from the past," and how we are still *all* in *this* place, and language—the storytelling—is our way of passing through or being with them, or being together again. When Aunt Susie told her stories, she would tell a younger child to go open the door so that our esteemed predecessors might bring in their gifts to us. "They are out there," Aunt Susie would say. "Let them come in. They're here, they're here with us *within* the stories."

37   A few years ago, when Aunt Susie was 106, I paid her a visit, and while I was there she said, "Well, I'll be leaving here soon. I think I'll be leaving here next week, and I will be going over to the Cliff House." She said, "It's going to be real good to get back over there." I was listening, and I was thinking that she must be talking about her house at Paguate Village, just north of Laguna. And she went on, "Well, my mother's sister (and she gave her Indian name) will be there. She has been living there. She will be there and we will be over there, and I will get a chance to write down these stories I've been telling you." Now you must understand, of course, that Aunt Susie's mother's sister, a great storyteller herself, has long since passed over into the land of the dead. But then I realized, too, that Aunt Susie wasn't talking about death the way most of us do. She was talking about "going over" as a journey, a journey that perhaps we can only begin to understand through an appreciation for the boundless capacity of language that, through storytelling, brings us together, despite great distances between cultures, despite great distances in time.

✦ Evaluating the Text

1. What peripheral stories can you discern radiating from the central story "Home Country" by Simon Ortiz? How does this story express the concept that no story is ever really self-contained?

2. How do "origin stories" function as myths in Laguna society? What questions do they answer? How do they provide a sense of identity and continuity?

3. Why is it significant that the Pueblo tradition of storytelling makes no distinction between types of stories, such as historical, sacred, or just plain gossip?

4. How is the function of storytelling illustrated in this essay by the story told by Aunt Susie? What moral values and ethical principles does the story express?

✦ Exploring Different Perspectives

1. How is the interweaving or lack of separation between everyday life and the spiritual a feature of Native-American culture, as seen in Silko's article, or in Buddhist culture, as described by Aung San Suu Kyi in "My Country and People."

2. How do the accounts by Leslie Marmon Silko and Gino Del Guercio ("The Secrets of Haiti's Living Dead") describe cultures that interweave the secular and spiritual in everyday life?

✦ Extending Viewpoints Through Writing

1. In a short essay, discuss the distinctive qualities that define the way stories are told in Native-American cultures. How do these differ from what you consider to be a traditional story?

2. What legends or stories have come down from the past and have been told and retold in your family or community?

Bessie Head

Looking for a Rain God

◆

Bessie Head (1937–1986) was born in Pietermaritzburg, South Africa, the daughter of a black father and a white mother. She suffered the childhood trauma of being "reclassified"; she was taken from her mother at birth and brought up by foster parents as a Coloured. Her mother was treated as insane because of her relationship with a black man. Head was raised by her foster parents until she was thirteen, when she was placed in a mission orphanage. The emotional scars of her childhood are powerfully recorded in the widely acclaimed A Question of Power *(1973), a fictional study of madness produced by the violence of the apartheid system. After completing her education, she taught grammar school and wrote fiction for a local newspaper. In 1963, Head moved to a farm commune in Serowe, Botswana, with her son. She lived there, working as a teacher and a gardener in a local village until her death.*

Head's writing grows directly out of her experience of village life. Her first novel, When Rain Clouds Gather *(1968), presents the epic struggle of a village trying to survive a devastating drought. Her next two novels,* Maru *(1971) and* A Question of Power *(1973), depict women struggling to overcome oppression in their societies and earned her the distinction of being one of Africa's major female writers. As a chronicler of village life, Head wrote two histories,* Serowe: Village of the Rain Wind *(1981) and* A Bewitched Crossroad *(1985). "Looking for a Rain God," from* The Collector of Treasures and Other Botswana Tales *(1977), is based on a shocking local incident revealing how an ancient tribal ritual resurfaced after years of drought in modern-day Botswana.*

Located in South-Central Africa, Botswana became independent from British rule in 1966. Because of its land-locked location, Botswana continues to be economically dependent on South Africa and Zimbabwe, which controls railroad routes through Botswana. Religious practices are divided equally between Christianity and traditional tribal beliefs. The conditions of drought so graphically described by Bessie Head in her 1977 story were again confronted by the country during six successive years of drought between 1981 and 1987.

1   It is lonely at the lands where the people go to plough. These lands are vast clearings in the bush, and the wild bush is lonely too. Nearly all the lands are within walking distance from the village. In some parts of the bush where the underground water is very near the surface,

people made little rest camps for themselves and dug shallow wells to quench their thirst while on their journey to their own lands. They experienced all kinds of things once they left the village. They could rest at shady watering places full of lush, tangled trees with delicate pale-gold and purple wildflowers springing up between soft green moss and the children could hunt around for wild figs and any berries that might be in season. But from 1958, a seven-year drought fell upon the land and even the watering places began to look as dismal as the dry open thornbush country; the leaves of the trees curled up and withered; the moss became dry and hard and, under the shade of the tangled trees, the ground turned a powdery black and white, because there was no rain. People said rather humorously that if you tried to catch the rain in a cup it would only fill a teaspoon. Toward the beginning of the seventh year of drought, the summer had become an anguish to live through. The air was so dry and moisture-free that it burned the skin. No one knew what to do to escape the heat and tragedy was in the air. At the beginning of that summer, a number of men just went out of their homes and hung themselves to death from trees. The majority of the people had lived off crops, but for two years past they had all returned from the lands with only their rolled-up skin blankets and cooking utensils. Only the charlatans, incanters, and witch doctors made a pile of money during this time because people were always turning to them in desperation for little talismans and herbs to rub on the plough for the crops to grow and the rain to fall.

The rains were late that year. They came in early November, with a   2
promise of good rain. It wasn't the full, steady downpour of the years of good rain but thin, scanty, misty rain. It softened the earth and a rich growth of green things sprang up everywhere for the animals to eat. People were called to the center of the village to hear the proclamation of the beginning of the ploughing season; they stirred themselves and whole families began to move off to the lands to plough.

The family of the old man, Mokgobja, were among those who left   3
early for the lands. They had a donkey cart and piled everything onto it, Mokgobja—who was over seventy years old; two girls, Neo and Boseyong; their mother Tiro and an unmarried sister, Nesta; and the father and supporter of the family, Ramadi, who drove the donkey cart. In the rush of the first hope of rain, the man, Ramadi, and the two women, cleared the land of thornbush and then hedged their vast ploughing area with this same thornbush to protect the future crop from the goats they had brought along for milk. They cleared out and deepened the old well with its pool of muddy water and still in this light, misty rain, Ramadi inspanned two oxen and turned the earth over with a hand plough.

The land was ready and ploughed, waiting for the crops. At night,   4
the earth was alive with insects singing and rustling about in search of

food. But suddenly, by mid-November, the rain flew away; the rain clouds fled away and left the sky bare. The sun danced dizzily in the sky, with a strange cruelty. Each day the land was covered in a haze of mist as the sun sucked up the last drop of moisture out of the earth. The family sat down in despair, waiting and waiting. Their hopes had run so high; the goats had started producing milk, which they had eagerly poured on their porridge, now they ate plain porridge with no milk. It was impossible to plant the corn, maize, pumpkin, and watermelon seeds in the dry earth. They sat the whole day in the shadow of the huts and even stopped thinking, for the rain had fled away. Only the children, Neo and Boseyong, were quite happy in their little-girl world. They carried on with their game of making house like their mother and chattered to each other in light, soft tones. They made children from sticks around which they tied rags, and scolded them severely in an exact imitation of their own mother. Their voices could be heard scolding the day long: "You stupid thing, when I send you to draw water, why do you spill half of it out of the bucket!" "You stupid thing! Can't you mind the porridge pot without letting the porridge burn!" And then they would beat the rag dolls on their bottoms with severe expressions.

5   The adults paid no attention to this; they did not even hear the funny chatter; they sat waiting for rain; their nerves were stretched to breaking-point willing the rain to fall out of the sky. Nothing was important, beyond that. All their animals had been sold during the bad years to purchase food, and of all their herd only two goats were left. It was the women of the family who finally broke down under the strain of waiting for rain. It was really the two women who caused the death of the little girls. Each night they started a weird, high-pitched wailing that began on a low, mournful note and whipped up to a frenzy. Then they would stamp their feet and shout as though they had lost their heads. The men sat quiet and self-controlled; it was important for men to maintain their self control at all times but their nerve was breaking too. They knew the women were haunted by the starvation of the coming year.

6   Finally, an ancient memory stirred in the old man, Mokgobja. When he was very young and the customs of the ancestors still ruled the land, he had been witness to a rain-making ceremony. And he came alive a little, struggling to recall the details which had been buried by years and years of prayer in a Christian church. As soon as the mists cleared a little, he began consulting in whispers with his youngest son, Ramadi. There was, he said, a certain rain god who accepted only the sacrifice of the bodies of children. Then the rain would fall; then the crops would grow, he said. He explained the ritual and as he talked, his memory became a conviction and he began to talk with unshakable authority. Ramadi's nerves were smashed by the nightly wailing of the women and soon the two men began whispering with the two women.

The children continued their game: "You stupid thing! How could you have lost the money on the way to the shop! You must have been playing again!"

After it was all over and the bodies of the two little girls had been spread across the land, the rain did not fall. Instead, there was a deathly silence at night and the devouring heat of the sun by day. A terror, extreme and deep, overwhelmed the whole family. They packed, rolling up their skin blankets and pots, and fled back to the village.

People in the village soon noted the absence of the two little girls. They had died at the lands and were buried there, the family said. But people noted their ashen, terror-stricken faces and a murmur arose. What had killed the children, they wanted to know? And the family replied that they had just died. And people said amongst themselves that it was strange that the two deaths had occurred at the same time. And there was a feeling of great unease at the unnatural looks of the family. Soon the police came around. The family told them the same story of death and burial at the lands. They did not know what the children had died of. So the police asked to see the graves. At this, the mother of the children broke down and told everything.

Throughout that terrible summer the story of the children hung like a dark cloud of sorrow over the village, and the sorrow was not assuaged when the old man and Ramadi were sentenced to death for ritual murder. All they had on the statute books was that ritual murder was against the law and must be stamped out with the death penalty. The subtle story of strain and starvation and breakdown was inadmissible evidence at court; but all the people who lived off crops knew in their hearts that only a hair's breadth had saved them from sharing a fate similar to that of the Mokgobja family. They could have killed something to make the rain fall.

✦ Evaluating the Text

1. Why does Head not withhold knowledge of the ending in telling this story? How does knowing what happened shift the focus of the story into an attempt to try to understand how it happened?

2. How does the author lay the psychological groundwork for what otherwise would come as a shock—the choice of the two young girls in the family as sacrificial victims? Look carefully at how the girls must appear to everyone else in the family, especially in a culture where everyone, to survive, must contribute to the welfare of all. Looked at in this way, how do details such as their sloppiness (spilling food or water) and disobedience contribute to the family's decision to kill them in exchange for rain? How do the games Neo and Boseyong play provide further insight into how they are already being treated by the adults?

3. How does overwhelming stress reactivate a belief in rituals that lie just below the surface of collective tribal memory? From the details concerning the slaughter and dismemberment of the girls, how, in your opinion, was this ritual supposed to have worked?

4. Even though the police respond, as representatives of Neo and Boseyong and the social order, and execute Mokgobja and Ramadi for killing their children, why is it significant that Head ends the story with the statement that the other villagers "could have killed something to make the rain fall"? What does this tell you about Head's attitude toward the events in the story?

✦ Exploring Different Perspectives

1. How, in both this story set in Botswana and in Gino Del Guercio's "The Secrets of Haiti's Living Dead" account of voodoo in Haiti, are officially unsanctioned rituals resorted to in times of extreme political, environmental, and psychological stress—in situations where faith in the powers that be fails?

2. What differences can you discover between the religious beliefs in Bessie Head's story and Buddhism as described by Aung San Suu Kyi in "My Country and People"?

✦ Extending Viewpoints Through Writing

1. To what extent does "Looking for a Rain God" give you insight into situations so extreme (such as a soccer team stranded in a snow-filled mountain pass becoming cannibals to survive) that the normal conceptions of what is right or wrong give way to the question of survival?

2. To what extent does this story give you insight into the lives of people who live in colonized nations where Western Christian values are superimposed on tribal customs and beliefs? As a follow-up research project you might wish to investigate the practice of Santéria, a religion originating in Africa, brought to the United States by Cuban émigrées. See Joseph M. Murphy's *Santéria: An African Religion in America* (1988), Judith Gleason's *Santéria, Bronx* (1975), Migene Gonzalez-Wippler's *The Santéria Experience* (1982), and *Rituals and Spells of Santéria* (1984).

3. Did your family have a secret that they kept either from someone in the family or from the outside world? If it can now be revealed, tell what it was. Does the secret seem as significant as it did at the time?

Aung San Suu Kyi

My Country and People

◆————————————

*Born in 1945, Aung San Suu Kyi is the daughter of Burma's national
hero, Aung San, who was assassinated when she was two years old, just
before Burma gained the independence to which he had dedicated his life.
Educated in Rangoon, Delhi, and at Oxford University, she worked at the
United Nations in New York and in Bhutan and raised her family in England before returning to Burma in 1988 to care for her dying mother. Her
return coincided with the outbreak of a revolt against twenty-six years of
political repression. Aung San Suu Kyi emerged as a most effective human rights activist and leader of Burma's national league for democracy.
Despite being detained and put under house arrest in 1989 by the ruling
military junta, the party she founded went on to win an electoral victory
in May 1990. The military junta that now rules Burma has since released
her. In 1990 Aung San Suu Kyi was awarded the Sakharov Prize for Freedom of Thought by the European Parliament and in 1991 her indomitable
efforts were recognized when she received the Nobel Peace Prize. A collection of her writings entitled* Freedom from Fear *(1991) was edited by
her husband, Michael Aris, a professor of Tibetan studies at Harvard, who
was permitted to visit his wife only a few times after her house arrest. The
selection from this book that follows provides an overview of the influence
that Buddhism has had on the cultural heritage of Burma.*

*Officially known in English as the Union of Myanmar, this country
is bordered by Bangladesh, India, and the Bay of Bengal to the west, China
to the north and northeast, Laos and Thailand to the east, and the Anda-
man Sea to the south. A Burmese–Tibetan people, the Pyus or Burmese,
settled in what is now Burma in the first century. Hinayana Buddhism
was introduced to the region by King Anawrahta in the eleventh century
and has remained the dominant religion of a majority of the Burmese. The
Burmese kingdom of Pagan founded in the ninth century stood until its
destruction in 1287 by the Mongol hoardes under Kubla Khan. Subsequently, Burma flourished under dynastic rule until it was overthrown by
the British in 1885. Occupied by Japan during World War II, Burma
achieved complete independence in 1948, in part because of the efforts of
Aung San Suu Kyi's father in organizing a Nationalist party. Decades of
insurgent activity and rebellions among the Karen and Kachin peoples
have led to a series of military coups and the imposition of martial law. Although international pressures forced the government to release Aung*

San Suu Kyi, it began a campaign against her supporters in September, 1996, imprisoning many of them.

The Burmese

1   The one single factor which has had the most influence on Burmese culture and civilization is Theravada Buddhism. In all parts of the country where the Burmese people live there are pagodas and Buddhist monasteries. The graceful tapering shape of a pagoda, painted white or gilded to a shining gold, is a basic part of any Burmese landscape. Burma is often called the 'Land of Pagodas.'

2   Buddhism teaches that suffering is an unavoidable part of existence. At the root of all suffering are such feelings as desire, greed and attachment. Therefore to be free from suffering it is necessary to be free from those undesirable feelings. This freedom can be obtained by following the Noble Eightfold Path:

> Right Understanding
> Right Thought
> Right Speech
> Right Action
> Right Livelihood
> Right Effort
> Right Mindfulness
> Right Concentration

This path is also known as the Middle Way, because it avoids two extremes: one extreme is the search for happiness through the pursuit of pleasure, the other extreme is the search for happiness through inflicting pain on oneself. The final goal of a Buddhist is to be liberated from the cycle of existence and rebirth, called *samsara*. Once this final liberation is achieved, one may be said to have attained *nirvana;* this word means 'extinction' and might be explained as Ultimate Reality for all Buddhists.

3   The teachings of the Buddha are known as the Dharma, and these teachings are generally passed on to ordinary people by the Buddhist monks, collectively known as the Sangha. Therefore, the Buddha, the Dharma and the Sangha are called the 'Triple Gem.' Because the Lord Buddha was a great teacher, the Burmese have a great reverence for all teachers. Parents are also regarded with 'awe, love and respect.' Consequently, the Triple Gem, teachers and parents make up the 'five that must be revered' by Burmese Buddhists.

4   All good Buddhists undertake to abide by the Five Precepts: not to take life, not to steal, not to commit adultery, not to tell lies, not to take intoxicating drinks. Although the taking of life is considered such an

evil that many Burmese will go out of their way to avoid stepping on an insect, there are few who avoid eating meat. This is considered inconsistent by some people. The Burmese would probably argue that the Lord Buddha himself ate meat. The Burmese people are a practical people. They have also been described as happy-go-lucky.

As might be expected, many Burmese festivals are based on Buddhist events. Festival days are determined by the Burmese calendar, which is calculated according to the phases of the moon. The full moon days of the month of *Kason* (April/May), *Waso* (June/July), and *Thidingyut* (October/November) are special days for the Buddhists. The full moon day of *Kason* celebrates the birth, enlightenment and death of the Buddha. The Buddha achieved enlightenment—that is, he finally shed all false beliefs and saw through to the ultimate truth—underneath a *bodhi* tree. On the full moon of *Kason,* therefore, people pour offerings of water on *bodhi* trees.

The full moon day of *Waso* also celebrates important events in the life of the Buddha, in particular the first sermon he preached on the truth he had learnt. In addition, this day marks the beginning of the 'Buddhist Lent,' which lasts for three months. During this time the monks are not allowed to travel. Many Buddhists observe what are known as the Eight Precepts on all the holy days during Lent. The Buddhist holy days are the day of the dark moon, the eighth day of the new moon, the day of the full moon and the eighth day after the full moon. The Eight Precepts are four of the basic Five Precepts (not to kill, steal, lie or take intoxicating drinks) with the addition of four others: not to commit any immoral acts, not to take any food after twelve noon, not to indulge in music, dancing and the use of perfume, not to sleep in high places. (The last is taken to mean that one should not sleep in a luxurious bed.) Some devout Buddhists keep these eight precepts throughout the three months of Lent. Because it is a time when people should be thinking of their spiritual development, Buddhists should not get married during this period. Marriage brings family life and therefore greater ties and attachments. Thus it is likely to make the achieving of *nirvana* more difficult.

The end of Lent coincides with the end of the monsoon rains in October. It is a time for happiness and rejoicing. Tradition has it that the Lord Buddha spent one Lent in the *Tavatimsa* heaven to preach to his mother. (His mother had died in giving birth to him and had been reborn in *Tavatimsa,* one of the many Buddhist heavens.) At the end of Lent, he came back to earth and the people of the world welcomed him with lights. In celebration of this, during the three days of the *Thidingyut* festival, pagodas, monasteries and homes are decorated with lights and lanterns. Cities like Rangoon and Mandalay are ablaze with coloured lights, and there are competitions to see which part of the town is the most beautifully decorated. *Thidingyut* is a time for expressing reverence towards older people. Many Burmese visit older friends and relatives to bow down before them and to offer gifts.

8   There are other Buddhist festivals apart from the ones described above. In addition, many pagodas have their own festival day. One of the most important pagoda festivals is that of the great Shwedagon in Rangoon, which takes place in March. Soaring to a height of almost 100 metres (over 300 feet), covered with layers of solid gold leaf and topped with a hollow gold orb encrusted with many precious gems, the Shwedagon is the most famous landmark in the country. Foreigners come to look at it with curiosity and wonder. For the Burmese it is not just an interesting and beautiful monument, but a very central part of their religious life—and not just on festival days. Every day, an endless stream of people climb up to the Shwedagon from one of its four great stairways (an electric lift has also been installed near one stairway). They buy flowers, incense sticks, gold leaves and candles to offer at the pagoda from the stalls that line the stairs. (These stalls sell a variety of other things apart from religious objects.)

9   The atmosphere of the Shwedagon is steeped in the religious faith of the people who have worshipped there for generations. Everywhere are the sounds of prayers and the clear ring of prayer gongs. On the platform which surrounds the pagoda are many smaller pagodas, shrines and pavilions. Each person goes to his or her favourite place of worship to pray there and to make offerings. Apart from the main prayer pavilions, the eight planetary posts which mark the days of the week are popular places of worship. (Each day of the week, together with Rahu—Wednesday night—has its own planet.) People go to the post marking the day of their birth to pray, fight candles and incense sticks and to make offerings of flowers and water. In a hot country like Burma, the coolness of water is symbolic of peace.

10   All Burmese know the day of the week on which they were born. The name given on a person's birth horoscope is decided according to the day of birth. For example, those born on a Monday should have names beginning with the letters *ka, hka, ga, nga,* those born on a Tuesday are given names beginning with *sa, hsa, za, nya,* and so on. Not just horoscope names but also those given by parents are usually chosen according to these rules. The horoscope shows the position of the planets at the time of a person's birth. Astrologers use it to make predictions about the future. This practice is not really in line with the teachings of the Buddha, according to which one's future is decided by one's own actions rather than by the stars.

11   Another side of Burmese life which is not strictly in accordance with Buddhist teachings is spirit-worship. Like the other peoples of Burma, the Burmese were spirit-worshippers before the arrival of Buddhism. The Burmese use the word *nat* to mean supernatural beings, the good ones who dwell in the various heavens as well as the frightening

ones who interfere in the affairs of the human world. Little *nat* shrines can often be seen in Burma, especially under big trees which are believed to harbour spirits. The most powerful of all the *nats* are the *Thonzekhuna Min,* or 'Thirty-Seven Lords'. There are people who take *nat* worship very seriously in spite of their belief in Buddhism. Even those who avoid having anything to do with spirit-worship will not do anything which is known to be offensive to *nats.*

The most important place for *nat* worship in Burma is Mount Popa,   12 an extinct volcano. Mount Popa is considered to be the home of two of the thirty-seven powerful *nats.* A great festival takes place there every year which attracts people from all over the country, *nat* worshippers as well as curious observers.

It is often asked why even educated Burmese can sometimes be   13 found taking part in *nat* worship. Perhaps the answer lies in two aspects of Burmese life. One is the strong hold which old beliefs from the days before Buddhism still have on the minds of the people. The other is the extreme self-reliance which Buddhism demands from the individual. In Buddhism there are no gods to whom one can pray for favours or help. One's destiny is decided entirely by one's own actions. While accepting the truth of this, most people find it difficult to resist the need to rely on supernatural powers, especially when times are hard.

The Burmese may put great importance on their religious life, but   14 that does not stop them from being a fun-loving people. This is particularly obvious during the celebrations for the Burmese New Year, which takes place in April. *Thingyan* is also known as the Water Festival because the last three days of the old year are a time for people to throw water at one another all over the country. This is very refreshing at a time of year when the hot weather is at its worst. The water-throwing can sometimes get too rough, but nobody is supposed to get angry.

Thingyan is also a time when many Burmese boys celebrate one of   15 the most important landmarks of their life. This is the *shinbyu,* when a Buddhist boy enters the monastery for a short time as a novice monk. All Burmese parents see it as their duty to make sure that their sons are admitted to the religious life in this way. The *shinbyu* ceremony can be performed once the boy is old enough to say certain Buddhist prayers correctly, manage the robes of a monk and 'drive away crows from his begging bowl.' This period of novicehood during which boys live the life of monks (although they do not keep all the rules which adult monks must observe) is a good introduction to the religious life. Burmese men like to enter monastic life at least three times during their lifetime: once as a boy, once as a young man and once as an adult.

The *shinbyu* ceremony is a joyful occasion. The candidate for nov-   16 icehood *(shinlaung)* is usually dressed in princely costume. This recalls the fact that the Buddha was a prince before he gave up his royal position to follow the religious life. The *shinlaung* is paraded through the

streets with great ceremony before his head is shaved and he is given
the robes of a novice. How simple or elaborate a *shinbyu* ceremony is
depends on the inclinations and resources of the family. Often a number of boys take part in a single ceremony. Apart from the *Thingyan* period, the Buddhist Lent is a popular time for *shinbyu* ceremonies.

17   When brothers are having their *shinbyu*, it is usual for the sisters to
have their ears pierced. This gives the girls a chance to dress up as prin-
cesses and have their share of fuss and attention. Many see this as an
expression of the Burmese belief in the equality of men and women. Although, theoretically, men are considered nobler because only a man
can become a Buddha, Burmese women have never really had an inferior status. They have always had equal rights of inheritance and led
active, independent lives. Secure in the knowledge of her own worth,
the Burmese woman does not mind giving men the kind of respectful
treatment that makes them so happy!

18   A big *shinbyu* ceremony may be accompanied by a *pwe*. *Pwe* is a particularly Burmese word which can mean a festival, feast, celebration,
ceremony, gathering or public performance. One common use of the
word is to describe a popular entertainment which is a marvellous mixture of dance, drama, music and clowning.

19   The origins of Burmese dance are considered to go back at least to
the Pagan period, judging from old wall paintings and references in
stone inscriptions. However, many of the dances performed today owe
a considerable amount to Thai influences introduced in the eighteenth
century when a son of Alaungpaya brought back many artists from his
invasions of Thailand. The movements of both male and female dancers are very graceful, involving beautiful hand gestures and extremely
skilled footwork.

20   Burmese drama, which is a little like western opera with music,
singing and much dramatic action, also owes a considerable amount to
the tradition of court plays brought back from Thailand in the eighteenth century. Popular dramas such as the *Yamazat,* based on the famous *Ramayana* epic of India, are performed again and again. The
nineteenth century produced many fine Burmese dramatists whose
works also remain popular to this day.

21   Dance drama is always accompanied by orchestral music. Burmese
musical instruments fall into five categories: bronze instruments,
stringed instruments, leather instruments, hollow wind instruments
and non-metallic percussion instruments used for keeping time. Burmese orchestral music has a great range, from soft, gentle tunes to the
loud, stirring clashes which so often announce the presence of a *pwe*.
The leading instrument of the orchestra is the *hsaingwaing,* a circle of
twenty-one small leather-faced drums which are played with amazing
virtuosity by the performer, who sits in the centre. Another instrument
considered particularly Burmese is the gently curving harp, which is
held in the lap of the performer as he plays.

There are many different types of classical Burmese song. To men-   22
tion a few, there are the *kyo* (meaning string), which is always preceded
by little phrases of music on the *hsaingwaing;* and the *bawle,* invented by
a princess of the last royal dynasty at Mandalay.

Although classical music is always performed at the much loved   23
pwes, modern music showing a strong western influence is increasingly
gaining popularity, especially among young people. However, Burmese music and dance have not only strong traditions but also the support and encouragement of the government. There is, therefore, little
danger that they will fall into decline, in spite of modern developments.

One form of entertainment which has lost some of its popular ap-   24
peal is the puppet show. This was first introduced in the late eighteenth
or early nineteenth century for the amusement of the royal court. A traditional puppet show has twenty-eight characters, including *nats,* a
king, queen, courtiers and various animals and birds. Different kinds of
wood must be used to make different characters. There are many other
rules, such as the order in which the characters come on stage and the
direction from which they emerge. Puppeteering is, therefore, a very
specialized art. It is a great pity that the public no longer seem very interested in this fascinating form of entertainment.

Today, the cinema has much appeal for the Burmese. The Burmese   25
film industry began before the Second World War. As in other countries,
actors and actresses have many fans. But although successful film stars
can make a good living, they do not become as rich as the big stars in the
western countries. Traditionally, actors and dancers were considered an
inferior class, but these old prejudices are fast disappearing. Television,
which was introduced several years ago, is quickly gaining in popularity.

The Burmese are an agricultural people, depending on the land for   26
their living. Even today, in spite of some industries and the many professions open to people in the towns, agriculture is the backbone of the
country. The number of those engaged in such professions as medicine,
engineering and teaching is increasing all the time. The Burmese have
always had a high proportion of people who could read and write. This
is due to the custom of sending children to the local monastery for their
schooling. Traditionally the monasteries limited themselves to religious teachings, but gradually more and more of them added modern
subjects to their teaching programme. Nowadays, with the growth of
state education, there are few monasteries serving as schools. However,
there are still many Burmese who owe their early education to Buddhist monks.

It has already been mentioned that Burmese writing first began to   27
develop in the Pagan period. Much of the traditional literature was concerned with religious themes. But there is also a considerable body of
classical works, mainly verse, which deals with nonreligious matters.
Before the nineteenth century, the Burmese seem to have preferred poetry to prose. However, since the first novel in Burmese was published

at the beginning of the twentieth century, prose writing, especially fiction, has developed greatly. Today, Burmese is a vigorous, continuously developing language.

28   The Burmese have a great respect for education. There is a popular old saying that riches can vanish as if by magic, but knowledge is a truly precious treasure which nobody can take away. Traditionally, education was seen not just as the acquisition of knowledge but as the development of Buddhist values. The needs of the present age have led to more emphasis on formal qualifications, but parents still place importance on bringing children up as good Buddhists.

29   The family is very important in Burma. Children are brought up to honour and respect their elders. It is believed that the love and care given by parents are beyond repayment. Burmese are taught that even though the Lord Buddha showed his mother the way to *nirvana,* he did not manage to repay more than a minute portion of what he owed her.

30   In spite of the strong feelings of family, the Burmese do not have a system of family names. Each individual has his or her own personal name, which is often quite different from those of everybody else in the family. Moreover, women do not change their names on marriage. For example, the father may be called U Thein, the mother Daw Saw Tin, the son Maung Tun Aye and the daughter Ma Khin Khin. *U, Daw, Maung* and *Ma* are prefixes like 'Mr' or 'Mrs.' In Burma, age is an important factor in deciding which prefix to use. *U* literally means 'uncle' and *Daw* means 'aunt,' so these cannot be used for young children. *Maung,* meaning 'younger brother,' is suitable for a boy, but when he is older the prefix *Ko* ('older brother') will be used. However, *Ma* ('sister') is the only prefix used for girls. Sometimes it is the person's position that decides which prefix should be used. A young man who has achieved a very important position will be addressed as *U,* while an older man, if his status is low, may still be addressed as *Ko* or *Maung.*

31   A person's position may decide how much respect is shown to him, but Burmese society has no rigid class system. It is not possible to tell from a person's name or accent whether his father is a manual labourer or a wealthy businessman. Even his appearance is not always an indication of his background, as there is not a great deal of difference in the kinds of clothes people wear. Many of those who are in high positions come from humble homes. A person is judged by his own achievements rather than by his family.

32   An important part of Burmese life is food. Both Burmese men and women take a lively interest in cooking. The basic item of a Burmese meal is usually rice, taken with what westerners would describe as a 'curry.' However, Burmese 'curries' are not quite the same as the better-known Indian ones. The Burmese use less spices but more garlic and ginger. Fish products are an important part of Burmese cooking. Fish sauce and dried shrimps are used for flavouring. *Ngapi,* a paste of pre-

served fish with a very strong smell, is taken as a relish at almost every meal. Meat is not eaten in large quantities. A great variety of vegetables are available all the year round and Burmese cooking makes full use of them. It has been said that no tender leaf or shoot is safe from the Burmese.

The number of Indians and Chinese in Burma have added further variety to the food of the country. In the towns there are many restaurants and food stalls. It is quite usual for people to stop by the roadside to have a snack or a meal. Two of the most popular dishes are *mohinga* and *khaukswe*. *Mohinga* is a dish of slightly fermented rice noodles eaten with a thick fish soup. *Khaukswe* simply means noodles, and these can be prepared in many different ways. But the *khaukswe* dish considered most typically Burmese is the one eaten with a kind of chicken stew cooked in coconut milk. 33

In general, the Burmese do not eat many sweets. Hot, spicy snacks are more to their taste. Fruits often take the place of puddings. As in many other South Asian countries, the mango is very popular. There are many varieties and the Burmese eat them in a number of ways. Small green mangoes are taken with *ngapi* as part of the main meal, or eaten as a snack dipped in salt and chili powder. Larger, slightly underripe mangoes can be made into a curry. But of course there is nothing to compare with a ripe, sweet mango eaten on its own. 34

Green tea is one of the most usual drinks in Burma. Tea with milk and sugar is also taken, but this is usually brewed in such a way that foreigners do not always recognize it as tea. As Buddhists, the Burmese frown upon alcoholic drinks, but there are strong country liquors made from the juice of the toddy palm. Bottled beer of the western variety is also produced nowadays. 35

Food is a popular subject of conversation. It is quite usual for friends and acquaintances to ask each other on meeting: 'And what did you have for lunch today?' This constant interest makes Burmese cooking one of the most imaginative and varied in the world. 36

Both Burmese men and women wear the *longyi,* a long tube of cloth which they wrap around themselves and tuck in at the waist. Men wear western-style shirts with their *longyis* and women wear short, fitted tops. Young girls have now taken to wearing western-style blouses and T-shirts. For formal occasions, men wear collarless shirts with short jackets and a *gaungbaung* (a kind of turban) on their heads. Chains of sweet-smelling white jasmines coiled around a knot of glossy black hair are one of the most attractive sights. Traditionally, both Burmese men and women kept their hair very long. Men started to cut their hair soon after British rule was established in the country. However, men with large top-knots can still be seen in the villages. Women have continued to keep their hair long, but in recent years it has become fashionable for girls to adopt short, westernized hairstyles. 37

38   Burmese women are noted for their fine complexions. It is thought that they owe this in some degree to the use of *thanakha*. This is a paste made by grinding the bark of the *thanakha* tree. It gives the skin protection from the sun and is also thought to have medicinal properties. *Thanakha* is a yellow-beige paste and when applied thickly can make the face look as though it has been smeared with mud. In spite of this, it remains the most important item of a Burmese woman's beauty treatment. Even the arrival of modern cosmetics has not diminished the popularity of *thanakha*.

39   In Burma, as in many Asian countries, western goods are much sought after. Western ideas and attitudes have also crept in through books, films and foreign visitors. Under the policy of the present government, tourists are only allowed into the country for one week at a time. This goes some way towards keeping out foreign influences and, compared with most Southeast Asian countries, Burma has done a much better job of preserving its own culture and traditions. The country is to some extent isolated from the rest of the world through restrictions on Burmese wishing to travel abroad as well as on foreigners wishing to come to Burma. This enforced isolation has resulted in giving things foreign the appeal of 'forbidden fruit' for some Burmese. It also means that in many areas of scientific and technological education, Burma has fallen behind modern developments.

40   Whatever attraction western goods and culture may hold for some of the Burmese people, Buddhism is still the greatest influence on their daily lives. Young people who dress in T-shirts and listen eagerly to western-style pop music still visit the pagodas frequently. The religious life of the Burmese is not separated from their social life. Most Burmese gatherings are centred around a religious event. The most common social occasion is perhaps the *hsoongway*, offering of food to monks. Friends will come to help, listen to the sermons and join in the chanting of prayers. It is usual to repeat the Five Precepts and undertake to keep them. On holy days people undertake to keep the Eight Precepts. After the monks have left, friends and family will eat together. It will have been an enjoyable as well as a spiritually rewarding occasion.

41   By international standards, Burma is not a wealthy country and life is hard for many of its people. But there is still a quality of calmness and serenity which is very precious. For this the Burmese are greatly indebted to their religion.

✦ Evaluating the Text

1. How do the goals and methods of Buddhism shape Burmese life and culture? In what facets of Burmese life can you see this influence most clearly?

2. What impression do you get as to the coexistence of Buddhism with other beliefs with which it might seem to be incompatible? What factors explain the persistence of these beliefs?

3. What place do music and other forms of entertainment occupy in Burmese culture? What characteristics define the forms they take?

✦ Exploring Different Perspectives

1. Compare the influence of Buddhism in shaping Burmese culture with that of voodoo in Haiti as described by Gino Del Guercio in "The Secrets of Haiti's Living Dead."

2. To what extent is Islam as described by Carol Spindel in "Blessings" a feature of everyday life in ways that remind you of the influence of Buddhism as described by Aung San Suu Kyi?

✦ Extending Viewpoints Through Writing

1. Describe a feast day in which you participated. Explain the significance of its customs.

2. Have you ever gone on a pilgrimage either as part of a religion or as part of an obligation that was personal to you? Describe where you went, the purpose, and your experiences.

3. Has any major religious text, such as the Koran, the Old Testament, the New Testament, the Mahabarata, or the Buddhist Saddharma-Pundarika (The Lotus of the True Law), had a profound impact in shaping your ideas and attitudes? Discuss your experiences.

Abioseh Nicol

Life Is Sweet at Kumansenu

◆

Abioseh Nicol (whose given name was Davidson Sylvester Hector Wil-loughby Nicol) was born in 1924 in Sierra Leone. As a child he was edu-cated in both his native Sierra Leone and in Nigeria. He received a medical degree from Cambridge University and has worked as a physician in both England and Africa and as a school administrator in Sierra Leone. He has also held a wide range of posts with the United Nations. Although he has written many articles on medical subjects, education, and politics, it was only through the efforts of the late African-American writer Langston Hughes that his poetry and short stories were published. Collections of his works include The Truly Married Woman and Other Stories *(1965)* and Two African Tales *(1972). "Life Is Sweet at Kumansenu" is typical of Nicol's work in its mixture of the old and the new in Africa, showing authentic and traditional animistic beliefs coexisting with urban culture.*

Sierra Leone, located on the coast of West Africa, is bordered by the Atlantic Ocean to the west, Guinea to the north and east, and Liberia to the south. Although there are Christian and Moslem minorities, the great majority of the people are of the Mende and the Temne tribes, who follow traditional religious beliefs. Those who convert to a formal religion, usu-ally Christianity or Islam, usually retain traditional animist beliefs as well and often belong to secret societies where animism is practiced. From the twelfth to the sixteenth centuries, Sierra Leone was dominated by the Sudanic kingdoms of West and Northwest Africa. In 1462 Portuguese ex-plorers along the coast named the territory Lion Range *(Serra Lyoa) be-cause of the thunderous roars heard coming from the steep mountain range. After the American Revolution the attempt to resettle freed slaves led to the establishment of Freetown as the capital in 1792. Britain took over Freetown in 1808 and during the next fifty years about 50,000 liber-ated slaves were settled there. Sierra Leone became independent in 1961, and after a series of military coups, the All People's Congress under the leadership of Siaka Stevens gained control and the country was ruled as a one-party state until he retired in 1985. His successor Joseph Momoh was forced from power in 1992 following a coup. Valentine Strasser, leader of that coup took power as president and first scheduled and later canceled free elections.*

1   The sea and the wet sand to one side of it; green tropical forest on the other; above it the slow tumbling clouds. The clean round blinding

disc of sun and the blue sky covered and surrounded the small African village, Kameni.

A few square mud houses with roofs like helmets, here thatched 2 and there covered with corrugated zinc where the prosperity of cocoa and trading had touched the head of the family.

The widow Bola stirred her palm-oil stew and thought of nothing 3 in particular. She chewed a kola nut[1] rhythmically with her strong toothless jaws and soon unconsciously she was chewing in rhythm with the skipping of Asi, her granddaughter. She looked idly at Asi as the seven-year-old brought the twisted palm-leaf rope smartly over her head and jumped over it, counting in English each time the rope struck the ground and churned up a little red dust. Bola herself did not understand English well, but she could count easily up to twenty in English for market purposes. Asi shouted six and then said nine, ten. Bola called out that after six came seven. And I should know, she sighed. Although now she was old, there was a time when she bore children regularly every two years. Six times she had borne a boy child and six times they had died. Some had swollen up and with weak plaintive cries had faded away. Others had shuddered in sudden convulsions, with burning skins, and had rolled up their eyes and died. They had all died. Or rather he had died, Bola thought, because she knew it was one child all the time whose spirit had crept up restlessly into her womb to be born and to mock her.[2] The sixth time Musa, the village magician whom time had transformed into a respectable Muslim, had advised her and her husband to break the bones of the quiet little corpse and mangle it so that it couldn't come back to torment them alive again. But she held on to the child, and refused to let them handle it. Secretly she had marked it with a sharp pointed stick at the left buttock before it was wrapped in a mat and they had taken it away. When, the seventh time she had borne a son, and the purification ceremonies had taken place, she had turned it slyly to see whether the mark was there. It was. She showed it to the old woman who was the midwife and asked her what that was, and she had forced herself to believe the other who said it was an accidental scratch made whilst the child was being scrubbed. But this child had stayed. Meji, he had been called. And he was now thirty years of age and a second-class clerk in government offices in a town ninety miles away. Asi, his daughter, had been left with her to do the things an old woman wanted a small child for, to run and take messages to the neighbors, to fetch a cup of water from the earthenware pot in the kitchen, to sleep with her and be fondled.

---

[1]*kola nut*, the bitter seed of an African evergreen tree, used in making medicines and soft drinks.

[2]*One child . . . to mock her*, a reference to a West African belief in a spirit-child who does not live to maturity but returns in a series of rebirths.

4   She threw the washed and squeezed cassava[3] leaves into the red boiling stew, putting in a finger's pinch of salt, and then went indoors, carefully stepping over the threshold to look for the dried red pepper. She found it, and then dropped it, leaning against the wall with a little cry. He turned round from the window and looked at her with a twisted half smile of love and sadness. In his short-sleeved, open-necked white shirt and gray gabardine trousers, a gold wristwatch and brown suede shoes, he looked like the pictures in African magazines of a handsome clerk who would get to the top because he ate the correct food, or regularly took the correct laxative, which was being advertised. His skin was grayish brown and he had a large handkerchief tied round his neck.

5   "Meji, God be praised," Bola cried. "You gave me quite a turn. My heart is weak and I can no longer take surprises. When did you come? How did you come? By lorry,[4] by fishing boat? And how did you come into the house? The front door was locked. There are so many thieves nowadays. I'm so glad to see you, so glad," she mumbled and wept, leaning against his breast.

6   Meji's voice was hoarse, and he said: "I am glad to see you too, Mother," beating her back affectionately.

7   Asi ran in and cried, "Papa, Papa," and was rewarded with a lift and a hug.

8   "Never mind how I came, Mother," Meji said, laughing. "I'm here, and that's all that matters."

9   "We must make a feast, we must have a big feast. I must tell the neighbors at once. Asi, run this very minute to Mr. Addai, the catechist, and tell him your papa is home. Then to Mami Gbera to ask her for extra provisions, and to Pa Babole for drummers and musicians . . ."

10   "Stop," said Meji raising his hand. "This is all quite unnecessary. I don't want to see *anyone,* no one at all; I wish to rest quietly and completely. No one is to know I'm here."

11   Bola looked very crestfallen. She was proud of Meji, and wanted to show him off. The village would never forgive her for concealing such an important visitor. Meji must have sensed this because he held her shoulder comfortingly and said: "They will know soon enough. Let us enjoy each other, all three of us, this time. Life is too short."

12   Bola turned to Asi, picked up the packet of pepper, and told her to go and drop a little into the boiling pot outside, taking care not to go too near the fire or play with it. After the child had gone, Bola said to her son, "Are you in trouble? Is it the police?"

13   He shook his head. "No," he said, "it's just that I like returning to you. There will always be this bond of love and affection between us,

---

[3]*cassava* (kä sä′vä), a tropical plant with starchy roots.
[4]*lorry,* truck. [British]

and I don't wish to share it. It is our private affair and that is why I've
left my daughter with you," he ended up irrelevantly; "girls somehow
seem to stay with relations longer."

"And don't I know it," said Bola. "But you look pale," she contin-   14
ued, "and you keep scraping your throat. Are you ill?" She laid her
hand on his brow. "And you're cold, too."

"It's the cold wet wind," he said, a little harshly. "I'll go and rest   15
now if you can open and dust my room for me. I'm feeling very tired.
Very tired indeed. I've traveled very far today and it has not been an
easy journey."

"Of course, my son, of course," Bola replied, bustling away hur-   16
riedly but happily.

Meji slept all afternoon till evening, and his mother brought his   17
food to his room, later took the empty basins away. Then he slept again
till morning.

The next day, Saturday, was a busy one, and after further promis-   18
ing Meji that she would tell no one he was about, Bola went off to market. Meji took Asi for a long walk through a deserted path and up into
the hills. She was delighted. They climbed high until they could see the
village below in front of them, and the sea in the distance, and the boats
with their wide white sails. Soon the sun had passed its zenith and was
halfway towards the west. Asi had eaten all the food, the dried fish and
the flat tapioca pancakes and the oranges. Her father said he wasn't
hungry, and this had made the day perfect for Asi, who had chattered,
eaten, and then played with her father's fountain pen and other things
from his pocket. They soon left for home because he had promised they
would be back before dark; he had carried her down some steep boulders and she had held on to his shoulders because he had said his neck
hurt so and she must not touch it. She had said: "Papa, I can see behind
you and you haven't got a shadow. Why?"

He had then turned her round to face the sun. Since she was get-   19
ting drowsy, she had started asking questions, and her father had joked
with her and humored her. "Papa, why has your watch stopped at
twelve o'clock?" "Because the world ends at noon." Asi had chuckled
at that. "Papa, why do you wear a scarf always round your neck?" "Because my head would fall off if I didn't." She had laughed out loud at
that. But soon she had fallen asleep as he bore her homewards.

Just before nightfall, with his mother dressed in her best, they had   20
all three, at her urgent request, gone to his father's grave, taking a secret route and avoiding the main village. It was a small cemetery, not
more than twenty years or so old, started when the Rural Health Department had insisted that no more burials take place in the backyards
of households. Bola took a bottle of wine and a glass and four split
halves of kola, each a half sphere, two red and two white. They reached
the graveside and she poured some wine into the glass. Then she spoke

to the dead man softly and caressingly. She had brought his son to see him, she said. This son whom God had given success, to the confusion and discomfiture of their enemies. Here he was, a man with a pension-able clerk's job and not a farmer, fisherman, or a mechanic. All the years of their married life people had said she was a witch because her children had died young. But this boy of theirs had shown that she was a good woman. Let her husband answer her now, to show that he was listening. She threw the four kola nuts up into the air and they fell on the grave. Three fell with the flat face upwards and one with its flat face downwards. She picked them up again and conversed with him once more and threw the kola nuts up again. But still there was an odd one or sometimes two.

21   They did not fall with all four faces up, or with all four faces down, to show that he was listening and was pleased. She spoke endearingly, she cajoled, she spoke sternly. But all to no avail. Then she asked Meji to perform. He crouched by the graveside and whispered. Then he threw the kola nuts and they rolled a little, Bola following them eagerly with her sharp old eyes. They all ended up face downwards. Meji emp-tied the glass of wine on the grave and then said that he felt nearer his father at that moment than he had ever done before in his life.

22   It was sundown, and they all three went back silently home in the short twilight. That night, going outside the house near her son's room window, she found, to her sick disappointment, that he had been throw-ing away all the cooked food out there. She did not mention this when she went to say goodnight, but she did sniff and say that there was a smell of decay in the room. Meji said he thought there was a dead rat up in the rafters, and he would clear it away after she had gone to bed.

23   That night it rained heavily, and sheet lightning turned the dark-ness into brief silver daylight for one or two seconds at a time. Then the darkness again and the rain. Bola woke soon after midnight and thought she could hear knocking. She went to Meji's room to ask him to open the door, but he wasn't there. She thought he might have gone out for a while and been locked out by mistake. She opened the door quickly, holding an oil lamp upwards. He stood on the veranda, curi-ously unwet, and refused to come in.

24   "I have to go away," he said hoarsely, coughing.

25   "Do come in," she said.

26   "No," he said, "I have to go, but I wanted to thank you for giving me a chance."

27   "What nonsense is this?" she said. "Come in out of the rain."

28   "I did not think I should leave without thanking you."

29   The rain fell hard, the door creaked, and the wind whistled.

30   "Life is sweet, Mother dear, good-by, and thank you."

31   He turned round and started running.

There was a sudden diffuse flash of lightning and she saw that the   32
yard was empty. She went back heavily, and fell into a restless sleep.
Before she slept she said to herself that she must see Mr. Addai next
morning, Sunday, or, better still, Monday, and tell him about this in
case Meji was in trouble. She hoped Meji would not be annoyed. He
was such a good son.

But it was Mr. Addai who came instead, on Sunday afternoon,   33
quiet and grave, and saw Bola sitting on an old stool in the veranda,
dressing Asi's hair in tight thin plaits.

Mr. Addai sat down and, looking away, he said: "The Lord giveth   34
and the Lord taketh away." And soon half the village were sitting
round the veranda and in the yard.

"But I tell you, he was here on Friday and left Sunday morning,"   35
Bola said. "He couldn't have died on Friday."

Bola had just recovered from a fainting fit after being told of her   36
son's death in town. His wife, Asi's mother, had come with the news,
bringing some of his property. She said Meji had died instantly at noon
on Friday and had been buried on Saturday at sundown. They would
have brought him to Kameni for the burial. He had always wished that.
But they could not do so in time as bodies did not last much after a day.

"He was here, he was here," Bola said, rubbing her forehead and   37
weeping.

Asi sat by quietly. Mr. Addai said comfortingly, "Hush, hush, he   38
couldn't have been, because no one in the village saw him."

"He said we were to tell no one," Bola said.   39

The crowd smiled above Bola's head, and shook their heads. "Poor   40
woman," someone said, "she is beside herself with grief."

"He died on Friday," Mrs. Meji repeated, crying. "He was in the of-   41
fice and he pulled up to the window to look out and call the messenger.
Then the sash broke. The window fell, broke his neck, and the sharp
edge almost cut his head off; they say he died at once."

"My papa had a scarf around his neck," Asi shouted suddenly.   42

"Hush," said the crowd.   43

Mrs. Meji dipped her hand into her bosom and produced a small   44
gold locket and put it round Asi's neck, to quieten her. "Your papa had
this made last week for your Christmas present. You may as well have
it now."

Asi played with it and pulled it this way and that.   45

"Be careful, child," Mr. Addai said, "it was your father's last gift."   46

"I was trying to remember how he showed me yesterday to open   47
it." Asi said.

"You have never seen it before," Mrs. Meji said sharply, trembling   48
with fear mingled with anger.

She took the locket and tried to open it.

50   "Let me have it," said the village goldsmith, and he tried whispering magic words of incantation. Then he said, defeated, "It must be poor-quality gold; it has rusted. I need tools to open it."

51   "I remember now," Asi said in the flat complacent voice of childhood.

52   The crowd gathered round quietly and the setting sun glinted on the soft red African gold of the dangling trinket. The goldsmith handed the locket over to Asi and asked in a loud whisper: "How did he open it?"

53   "Like so," Asi said and pressed a secret catch. It flew open and she spelled out gravely the word inside: "ASI."

54   The silence continued.

55   "His neck, poor boy," Bola said a little wildly, "that is why he could not eat the lovely meals I cooked for him."

56   Mr. Addai announced a service of intercession after vespers that evening. The crowd began to leave quietly.

57   Musa, the magician, was one of the last to leave. He was now very old and bent. In times of grave calamity, it was known that even Mr. Addai did not raise objection to Musa being consulted.

58   He bent over further and whispered in Bola's ear: "You should have had his bones broken and mangled thirty-one years ago when he went for the sixth time and then he would not have come back to mock you all these years by pretending to be alive. I told you so. But you women are naughty and stubborn."

59   Bola stood up, her black face held high, her eyes terrible with maternal rage and pride.

60   "I am glad I did not," she said, "and that is why he came back specially to thank me before he went for good."

61   She clutched Asi to her. "I am glad I gave him the opportunity to come back, for life is sweet. I do not expect you to understand why I did so. After all, you are only a man."

◆ *Evaluating the Text*

1. Why did Bola refuse to perform the ritual Musa recommended after her first six sons had died in infancy?

2. How might each of the following details serve as a clue to Meji's true state: his hoarse voice, his pallor and temperature, the fact that he casts no shadow, his joke to his daughter when she asks him about the handkerchief tied around his neck, the fact that he does not eat anything his mother offers him, the flash of lightning that marks his departure? What other clues can you cite?

3. What role does the locket play in convincing the skeptical villagers that Meji had really returned? How does the emphasis placed on this object signal its symbolic status?

4. How is Meji's visit an expression of gratitude to Bola for the chance to have lived?

✦ Exploring Different Perspectives

1. Discuss the persistence of tribal beliefs in this story and in Bessie Head's "Looking for a Rain God." How do the protagonists return to older belief systems?

2. How does the theme of fearing the dead operate both in this story and in Gino Del Guercio's discussion in "The Secrets of Haiti's Living Dead"?

✦ Extending Viewpoints Through Writing

1. Did you ever have a lucky charm, talisman, or amulet? How did you acquire it and how has it brought you good luck?

2. Have you ever had the feeling you were being contacted by a spirit or the ghost of someone who died? What form did the communication take? Describe your experience.

3. You have made a pact with the devil. Discuss in detail what you want in return for your soul.

Naguib Mahfouz

Half a Day

◆

Naguib Mahfouz was born in 1911 in Ganaliyya—an old quarter of Cairo that served as a setting for several of his novels—to a family that earned its living from trade. In 1930 he entered the Secular University in Cairo where he studied philosophy. Like his predecessor, Tewfik al-Hakim, Mahfouz developed a narrative technique through which he could criticize the government without running the risk of antagonizing the authorities. In this way, Mahfouz veiled his criticism of the ruling powers through the framework of historical novels set in ancient Egypt, most notably in The Mockery of Fate *(1939),* Radobais *(1943), and* The Struggle of Thebes *(1944). In the late 1940s and 1950s he turned to a more realistic style, setting his stories in modern Egypt. Between 1956 and 1957 he produced his famous Cairo Trilogy, a sequence of novels that chronicles the changes in three generations of a middle-class Cairo family.*

Widely regarded as Egypt's leading literary figure, Naguib Mahfouz is the first Arabic-language author awarded the Nobel Prize in literature (1988) and only the second from the African continent (Wole Soyinka, a Nigerian, had won two years earlier). Generations of Arabs have read his works and sixteen of his novels have been adapted for films in Egypt. He brought enormous changes to Arab prose by synthesizing traditional literary style and modern speech to create a language understood by Arabs everywhere.

Mahfouz's prose works have been compared in spirit and tone to the social realism of Balzac and Dickens because of both the extent to which they reflect Egypt's volatile political history, and their accurate depiction of the distressing conditions under which the poor live. He has held a variety of government posts and has served as director of the Foundation for Support of the Cinema. In 1989, when Mahfouz spoke out against the Ayatollah Khomeini's death sentence on Salman Rushdie (for his novel The Satanic Verses*), Mahfouz was himself subject to death threats by Muslim fundamentalists. In English, his most recently translated works include* Midag Alley *(1981),* Miramar *(1983), and* The Time and The Place and Other Stories *(1991), in which "Half a Day," translated by Davies Denys-Johnson, first appeared. This story is typical of Mahfouz's later works in its extensive use of allegory, symbolism, and experimental narrative techniques to explore spiritual themes.*

*(For information on Egypt, see p. 107.)

I proceeded alongside my father, clutching his right hand, running   1
to keep up with the long strides he was taking. All my clothes were
new: the black shoes, the green school uniform, and the red tarboosh.
My delight in my new clothes, however, was not altogether unmarred,
for this was no feast day but the day on which I was to be cast into
school for the first time.

My mother stood at the window watching our progress, and I   2
would turn toward her from time to time, as though appealing for help.
We walked along a street lined with gardens; on both sides were extensive fields planted with crops, prickly pears, henna trees, and a few
date palms.

"Why school?" I challenged my father openly. "I shall never do   3
anything to annoy you."

"I'm not punishing you," he said, laughing. "School's not a punish-   4
ment. It's the factory that makes useful men out of boys. Don't you
want to be like your father and brothers?"

I was not convinced. I did not believe there was really any good to   5
be had in tearing me away from the intimacy of my home and throwing me into this building that stood at the end of the road like some
huge, high-walled fortress, exceedingly stern and grim.

When we arrived at the gate we could see the courtyard, vast and   6
crammed full of boys and girls. "Go in by yourself," said my father,
"and join them. Put a smile on your face and be a good example to
others."

I hesitated and clung to his hand, but he gently pushed me from   7
him. "Be a man," he said. "Today you truly begin life. You will find me
waiting for you when it's time to leave."

I took a few steps, then stopped and looked but saw nothing. Then   8
the faces of boys and girls came into view. I did not know a single one
of them, and none of them knew me. I felt I was a stranger who had lost
his way. But glances of curiosity were directed toward me, and one boy
approached and asked, "Who brought you?"

"My father," I whispered.   9

"My father's dead," he said quite simply.   10

I did not know what to say. The gate was closed, letting out a piti-   11
able screech. Some of the children burst into tears. The bell rang. A lady
came along, followed by a group of men. The men began sorting us
into ranks. We were formed into an intricate pattern in the great courtyard surrounded on three sides by high buildings of several floors;
from each floor we were overlooked by a long balcony roofed in wood.

"This is your new home," said the woman. "Here too there are   12
mothers and fathers. Here there is everything that is enjoyable and beneficial to knowledge and religion. Dry your tears and face life joyfully."

We submitted to the facts, and this submission brought a sort of   13
contentment. Living beings were drawn to other living beings, and

from the first moments my heart made friends with such boys as were to be my friends and fell in love with such girls as I was to be in love with, so that it seemed my misgivings had had no basis. I had never imagined school would have this rich variety. We played all sorts of different games: swings, the vaulting horse, ball games. In the music room we chanted our first songs. We also had our first introduction to language. We saw a globe of the Earth, which revolved and showed the various continents and countries. We started learning the numbers. The story of the Creator of the universe was read to us, we were told of His present world and of His Hereafter, and we heard examples of what He said. We ate delicious food, took a little nap, and woke up to go on with friendship and love, play and learning.

14 As our path revealed itself to us, however, we did not find it as totally sweet and unclouded as we had presumed. Dust-laden winds and unexpected accidents came about suddenly, so we had to be watchful, at the ready, and very patient. It was not all a matter of playing and fooling around. Rivalries could bring about pain and hatred or give rise to fighting. And while the lady would sometimes smile, she would often scowl and scold. Even more frequently she would resort to physical punishment.

15 In addition, the time for changing one's mind was over and gone and there was no question of ever returning to the paradise of home. Nothing lay ahead of us but exertion, struggle, and perseverance. Those who were able took advantage of the opportunities for success and happiness that presented themselves amid the worries.

16 The bell rang announcing the passing of the day and the end of work. The throngs of children rushed toward the gate, which was opened again. I bade farewell to friends and sweethearts and passed through the gate. I peered around but found no trace of my father, who had promised to be there. I stepped aside to wait. When I had waited for a long time without avail, I decided to return home on my own. After I had taken a few steps, a middle-aged man passed by, and I realized at once that I knew him. He came toward me, smiling, and shook me by the hand, saying, "It's a long time since we last met—how are you?"

17 With a nod of my head, I agreed with him and in turn asked, "And you, how are you?"

18 "As you can see, not all that good, the Almighty be praised!"

19 Again he shook me by the hand and went off. I proceeded a few steps, then came to a startled halt. Good Lord! Where was the street lined with gardens? Where had it disappeared to? When did all these vehicles invade it? And when did all these hordes of humanity come to rest upon its surface? How did these hills of refuse come to cover its sides? And where were the fields that bordered it? High buildings had taken over, the street surged with children, and disturbing noises

shook the air. At various points stood conjurers showing off their tricks and making snakes appear from baskets. Then there was a band announcing the opening of a circus, with clowns and weight lifters walking in front. A line of trucks carrying central security troops crawled majestically by. The siren of a fire engine shrieked, and it was not clear how the vehicle would cleave its way to reach the blazing fire. A battle raged between a taxi driver and his passenger, while the passenger's wife called out for help and no one answered. Good God! I was in a daze. My head spun. I almost went crazy. How could all this have happened in half a day, between early morning and sunset? I would find the answer at home with my father. But where was my home? I could see only tall buildings and hordes of people. I hastened on to the crossroads between the gardens and Abu Khoda. I had to cross Abu Khoda to reach my house, but the stream of cars would not let up. The fire engine's siren was shrieking at full pitch as it moved at a snail's pace, and I said to myself, "Let the fire take its pleasure in what it consumes." Extremely irritated, I wondered when I would be able to cross. I stood there a long time, until the young lad employed at the ironing shop on the corner came up to me. He stretched out his arm and said gallantly, "Grandpa, let me take you across."

✦ Evaluating the Text

1. What can you infer about the boy's relationship with his father from their conversation on the way to school?

2. When did you suspect that the events in the story covered more than the narrator's first day at school?

3. How does the boy's encounter with the middle-aged man, and what the boy discovers when he returns to the street where he expects to find his home, suggest something out of the ordinary has happened?

4. How does the image of fire at the end of the story symbolize the effect of time on people, places, and things?

5. In what way is the story an expression of the journey archetype? How does the structure of the story personalize this universal theme?

✦ Exploring Different Perspectives

1. Compare Naguib Mahfouz's "Half a Day" with storytelling as it is described in Leslie Marmon Silko's "Language and Literature from a Pueblo Indian Perspective" in terms of differences in style and values expressed.

2. What evidence in Naguib Mahfouz's story suggests an implicit Islamic perspective in ways that remind you of Carol Spindel's account in "Blessings"?

✦ *Extending Viewpoints Through Writing*

1. Have you ever had experiences that made you aware that time is more subjective than simply counting the minutes that pass on the clock?

2. What images or pictures come to mind in connection with the term *infinity?* What literal description can you offer that would represent infinity for you?

Carol Spindel

Blessings

◆────────────◆

*Carol Spindel was born in Memphis, Tennessee, and received a B.F.A.
from the University of Iowa in 1977 and an M.A. in art history from the
University of Illinois in 1988. In 1981, she lived in a village in northern
Côte d'Ivoire and described the experiences she had there in* The Shadow
of the Sacred Grove *(1989), from which "Blessings" is taken. Spindel is
currently teaching creative nonfiction at the University of Illinois.*

*Côte d'Ivoire is a republic in western Africa on the Gulf of Guinea,
bordered by Ghana to the east, Burkina Faso and Mali to the north, and
Guinea and Liberia to the west. French control of the area began after
World War II and lasted until 1960, when Côte d'Ivoire (or the Ivory
Coast) declared itself independent. It is one of the most prosperous and politically stable nations in Africa. In the elections of October 1990, Felix
Houphouet-Boigny was elected president for a seventh five-year term by
an overwhelming 81 percent majority of the voters but died unexpectedly
in 1993 before he could serve out his term.*

Before Adama became our interpreter, the constant exchange of
blessings made me a little uneasy. After all, the one I received most frequently was, "May Allah give you children." In Berkeley, having a
child was a weighty personal decision, something one pondered for
years and went to therapy to resolve, not something one wished lightly
on others like, "Have a good day." When the blessing was given in Senufo, the deity was Kolotyolo, and so I could translate it, "May Ancient
Mother give you children." I preferred the Senufo version because I
thought that Ancient Mother was more likely to understand my feelings on the matter: children were desirable, but there were better and
worse times to receive them. As far as Allah was concerned, I imagined
him to be the Grand Old Patriarch with a white beard who had never
actually carried a baby on his back or wiped a runny nose, and I figured that his main concern in the matter was the production of more
little Moslems. If this were true, an infidel like me was probably safe
from his schemes for the grand design of things. Nevertheless, the constant collective desire of sixteen hundred people to see me become
pregnant as expressed through frequent fervent blessings gave me
pause for thought.

Whenever I gained a few pounds or was sick to my stomach, I
could see their eyes light up hopefully. Against this strong a collective

631

desire, I worried that my diaphragm would prove too weak. After all, it was designed to repel mere matter. Could it really stand up against something as powerful as the collective faith of an entire village who daily invoked two different deities to aid them in their desire to see me bear a child? Did a man-made scrap of rubber, an upstart human invention, have a chance against a desire that strong and that ancient? This is what I asked myself uneasily as I muttered *"amina"* to their blessings.

3   Whenever Adama translated the blessings, he always used the French word *Dieu* for God, and this also made me feel uneasy. I wasn't sure I believed in one. Certainly I believed in vague "forces" or "powers" in the universe, but I felt more comfortable if I left my forces in an unnamed state of spiritual ambiguity. Like many people I knew, I claimed to believe in Something. I just didn't want that Something defined too clearly.

4   But the forces I felt in the universe were not something I invoked as personally and specifically as the people of Kalikaha invoked theirs. When Sita prayed at dawn, she seemed to open her heart to Allah in a way I had never considered doing. And when my neighbors gave me blessings, they were always concrete and specific. They asked God to give me a good afternoon or a peaceful night or to help with my work that day, to give me a child, a harmonious marriage, a safe trip back from Korhogo, and a long life. At first, I tapped my forehead to help the blessing sink in and muttered *"amina"* as a matter of course. I was pleased that I was able to catch the first word, *Allah,* and that I could respond appropriately by saying "amen."

5   Being around Adama changed me. When we went into the village to do interviews, Adama gave out blessings to everyone. This was something Yardjuma had never done. If someone told Adama of a death or an illness, he immediately responded with a heartfelt blessing. *"Allah ka nagoya kay.* May God make it better. *Allah ka hinara.* May this person go to heaven." The blessings soothed the roughness of the moment. This did not mean that Adama did not try to help. He did. But first, he always invoked God's aid.

6   "May God give your children life," Adama said fervently to every mother. And they all, no matter how young and hopeful or how old and wizened, whispered intently, *"amina"* and their eyes thanked Adama for expressing the concern that they lived with daily in their hearts.

7   This giving out of blessings was more than polite utterance. It was a way of sharing hope, for people in Kalikaha needed hope to survive. No abstract relationship with deities who lived far above, this was a gritty daily contact with two deities who seemed, through people's words, to be always present in the village with us. Nor were the deities themselves estranged in enmity. Sometimes Adama spoke in Senufo of Ancient Mother, sometimes in Dyula of Allah; to us he spoke in French

of *Dieu*. When I questioned him about distinctions, he said it didn't matter, that God was always the same.

Tom and I, at the end of interviews and conversations, found our-   8
selves making up our own blessings and asking Adama to translate and deliver them for us. I didn't do this unconsciously, the way I some-times picked up new words. Rather, I found myself wanting to hand out blessings and feeling sincerely touched and, in the most appropri-ate word, *blessed*, when I received them.

I started a page in my Dyula notebook for blessings and began to   9
learn the hundreds of different ones that applied to particular situa-tions. "I need a blessing to help the potters with their work," I would say to Adama. "One that says 'May the firing turn out well.'"

"*Allah an jayma*," replied Adama instantly. "May Allah help us in   10
our work."

Adama regarded my new relationship to blessings with obvious   11
approval, and the page of blessings in my dog-eared Dyula notebook was quickly filled. There was a blessing for the young Dyula girls who wandered through the village selling bits of soap or bouillon cubes. "God help the alleyways to please you." When someone bought a new piece of cloth in the market, you said, "May it wear out before you do," a pragmatic blessing if ever there was one. At about three-thirty, I could bring smiles to the stony faces of even the most proper Dyula elders by saying as I passed them on their way to the mosque, "May the after-noon prayers be good."

When I gave out my favorite blessing, I could never keep a totally   12
straight face—a certain irrepressible delight in the phrase itself always came out with it. It was so idiomatic, so absolutely, essentially Dyula in character, that villagers crowed with delight at the absurdity of hearing it from me. I could astonish Dyula guests in the village by casually say-ing as I told them good night, "*Allah yan kelen kelen wuli*." Literally, it means "May everyone here wake up one at a time."

"Do you know the value of waking up one at a time?" the Dyula   13
man who taught me this blessing asked me. I had to admit that I had no idea.

"If there is some disaster in the night," he replied, "like a fire or a   14
death or a war, someone will call out, and we will all wake up at once. But if the night passes in peace, each of us will wake up in the morning at our own moment, one at a time."

When someone gave a gift, everyone present showered the giver   15
with blessings. The most frequent was "*Allah i baraji*." "May God give you something even greater than what you have given me." This bless-ing represents most clearly the sense in traditional African thought of the communal good. For it will probably not be me who will repay you. Life is not that neat, and Africans do not pretend that it is. To assume

the responsibility for equity yourself is a form of arrogance in Kalikaha. You receive from those more fortunate than you—older, wiser, or wealthier. You give to those less fortunate. The age class system is based on these precepts. Somehow, the gift will be returned. It will not come back in the same form. Nor will it come back from the same hand. Years may pass.

16   It was not only knowing the blessing which was important but also saying it at the proper time, with (of utmost importance) the proper pauses. If I blurted out a blessing at the wrong moment, no one understood. They didn't say *"amina,"* even though I was sure I had gotten the words right.

17   Not only did I need to know the right words. I needed to know the appropriate situations in which blessings were given and the appropriate moments at which to give them. Once Tom and I had mastered that, we progressed to multiple blessings. Blessings flowed nicely when they came in three's. "May God heal you. May God grant you happiness. May God give you a long life." We learned to pronounce them one after another with just the right pause between. Then we were rewarded with a long chorus of head-tapping and the soft sound of *"amina, amina, amina here be."* The best reward of all was seeing the soft look of appreciation, that moment of blessedness that came over people when they received a string of heartfelt blessings.

18   The sound of the three blessings reminded me of services when I was a girl and how, at the end, the rabbi always raised his arms. We were supposed to bow our heads, but I always looked up to see his black bell-shaped sleeves stretched out like wings as he gave three singsong blessings in Hebrew and English, with a long pause between each one—the same long pause they used in Kalikaha. But in Kalikaha, I didn't need to be a rabbi and I didn't need a long black robe.

19   I do not feel nearly so powerful nor so rational as I did before I went to Kalikaha. There, I saw my good intentions go awry too many times. In Kalikaha, I tried to save a child, a month-old baby. I failed. The baby died. And when Adama said, "It is God's will. May the child go to heaven," I felt a little bit comforted. Not everything is within our will or understanding. Not everything can be harnessed by our rational powers. In Kalikaha, I felt a spirituality that was threaded through every small encounter. I no longer hesitate to call on the help of other powers and to wish that help on my friends. When I speak to myself, I call these blessings what they truly are: prayers.

✦ *Evaluating the Text*

1. What function do "blessings" have in the culture of the Ivory Coast village in which Spindel is staying? What cultural values are expressed in these "blessings"?

2. How do these "blessings" attest to the importance of a belief in Allah that is integral to this society? Why is it significant that many of these "blessings" shift the focus from what one would want for oneself to what would be objectively desired for the good of the many?

3. What examples best illustrate the extent to which the idea of a communal good is an essential feature of this Moslem culture?

✦ Exploring Different Perspectives

1. In what ways do Carol Spindel's account and Bessie Head's story "Looking for a Rain God" dramatize different attitudes toward children in two different African countries?

2. How does Carol Spindel's analysis relate to equivalent features in Leslie Marmon Silko's account ("Language and Literature from a Pueblo Indian Perspective") of the influence of unseen powers in everyday life that can be invoked through specific sayings?

✦ Extending Viewpoints Through Writing

1. What blessings are you familiar with in your culture? Describe one of these and discuss its religious and philosophical implications. Alternatively, you might wish to compose a "blessing" of your own that expresses some deeply felt communal value.

Premchand

Deliverance

—————◆—————

*Premchand (a pseudonym for Dhanpat Rai) (1880–1936), who is argu-
ably the greatest writer in Hindi, was born near Benares (present-day
Varanasi), India. Although not from a wealthy family, he received a good
education in Persian and Urdu. His earliest fiction was influenced by
Dickens, Tolstoy, and Gandhi and from the outset was directed toward social reform. He produced an astonishing amount of work of the highest
caliber, including fourteen novels, three hundred short stories, and several
hundred essays in addition to numerous plays, screenplays, and transla-
tions. His short story "Deliverance" was made into a film by the great Indian film director Satyajit Ray.*

1   Dukhi the tanner was sweeping in front of his door while Jhuriya,
his wife, plastered the floor with cow-dung. When they both found a
moment to rest from their work Jhuriya said, 'Aren't you going to the
Brahman to ask him to come? If you don't he's likely to go off somewhere.'

2   'Yes, I'm going,' Dukhi said, 'But we have to think about what he's
going to sit on.'

3   'Can't we find a cot somewhere? You could borrow one from the
village headman's wife.'

4   'Sometimes the things you say are really aggravating! The people
in the headman's house give me a cot? They won't even let a coal out of
their house to light your fire with, so are they going to give me a cot?
Even when they're where I can go and talk to them if I ask for a pot of
water I won't get it, so who'll give me a cot? A cot isn't like the things
we've got—cow-dung fuel or chaff or wood that anybody who wants
can pick up and carry off. You'd better wash our own cot and set it
out—in this hot weather it ought to be dry by the time he comes.'

5   'He won't sit on our cot,' Jhuriya said. 'You know what a stickler he
is about religion and doing things according to the rule.'

6   A little worried, Dukhi said, 'Yes, that's true. I'll break off some *mohwa* leaves and make a mat for him, that will be the thing. Great gentlemen eat off *mohwa* leaves, they're holy. Hand me my stick and I'll break
some off.'

*(For information on India, see p. 58.)

'I'll make the mat, you go to him. But we'll have to offer him some 7
food he can take home and cook, won't we? I'll put it in my dish—'

'Don't commit any such sacrilege!' Dukhi said. 'If you do, the offer- 8
ing will be wasted and the dish broken. *Baba* will just pick up the dish
and dump it. He flies off the handle very fast, and when he's in a rage
he doesn't even spare his wife, and he beat his son so badly that even
now the boy goes around with a broken hand. So we'll put the offering
on a leaf too. Just don't touch it. Take Jhuri the *Gond*'s daughter to the
village merchant and bring back all the things we need. Let it be a complete offering—a full two pounds of flour, a half of rice, a quarter of
gram, an eighth of *ghee*, salt, turmeric, and four *annas* at the edge of the
leaf. If you don't find the *Gond* girl then get the woman who runs the
parching oven, beg her to go if you have to. Just don't touch anything
because that will be a great wrong.'

After these instructions Dukhi picked up his stick, took a big bundle 9
of grass and went to make his request to the Pandit. He couldn't go
empty-handed to ask a favour of the Pandit; he had nothing except the
grass for a present. If Panditji ever saw him coming without an offering, he'd shout abuse at him from far away.

* * *

Pandit Ghasiram was completely devoted to God. As soon as he 10
awoke he would busy himself with his rituals. After washing his hands
and feet at eight o'clock, he would begin the real ceremony of worship,
the first part of which consisted of the preparation of *bhang*. After that
he would grind sandalwood paste for half-an-hour, then with a straw
he would apply it to his forehead before the mirror. Between two lines
of sandalwood paste he would draw a red dot. Then on his chest and
arms he would draw designs of perfect circles. After this he would take
out the image of the Lord, bathe it, apply the sandalwood to it, deck it
with flowers, perform the ceremony of lighting the lamp before it and
ringing a little bell. At ten o'clock he'd rise from his devotions and after
a drink of the *bhang* go outside where a few clients would have gathered: such was the reward for his piety; this was his crop to harvest.

Today when he came from the shrine in his house he saw Dukhi 11
the Untouchable tanner sitting there with a bundle of grass. As soon as
he caught sight of him Dukhi stood up, prostrated himself on the
ground, stood up again and folded his hands. Seeing the Pandit's glorious figure his heart was filled with reverence. How godly a sight!—a
rather short, roly-poly fellow with a bald, shiny skull, chubby cheeks
and eyes aglow with brahmanical energy. The sandalwood markings
bestowed on him the aspect of the gods. At the sight of Dukhi he in-
toned, 'What brings you here today, little Dukhi?'

12   Bowing his head, Dukhi said, 'I'm arranging Bitiya's betrothal. Will your worship help us to fix an auspicious date? When can you find the time?'

13   'I have no time today,' Panditji said. 'But still, I'll manage to come toward evening.'

14   'No, maharaj, please come soon. I've arranged everything for you. Where shall I set this grass down?'

15   'Put it down in front of the cow and if you'll just pick up that broom sweep it clean in front of the door,' Panditji said. 'Then the floor of the sitting room hasn't been plastered for several days so plaster it with cowdung. While you're doing that I'll be having my lunch, then I'll rest a bit and after that I'll come. Oh yes, you can split that wood too, and in the storeroom there's a little pile of hay—just take it out and put it into the fodder bin.'

16   Dukhi began at once to carry out the orders. He swept the doorstep, he plastered the floor. This took until noon. Panditji went off to have his lunch. Dukhi, who had eaten nothing since morning, was terribly hungry. But there was no way he could eat here. His house was a mile away—if he went to eat there Panditji would be angry. The poor fellow suppressed his hunger and began to split the wood. It was a fairly thick tree trunk on which a great many devotees had previously tried their strength and it was ready to match iron with iron in any fight. Dukhi, who was used to cutting grass and bringing it to the market, had no experience with cutting wood. The grass would bow its head before his sickle but now even when he bought the axe down with all his strength it didn't make a mark on the trunk. The axe just glanced off. He was drenched in sweat, panting, he sat down exhausted and got up again. He could scarcely lift his hands, his legs were unsteady, he couldn't straighten out his back. Then his vision blurred, he saw spots, he felt dizzy, but still he went on trying. He thought that if he could get a pipeful of tobacco to smoke then perhaps he might feel refreshed. This was a Brahman village, and Brahmans didn't smoke tobacco at all like the low castes and Untouchables. Suddenly he remembered that there was a *Gond* living in the village too, surely he would have a pipeful. He set off at a run for the man's house at once, and he was in luck. The *Gond* gave him both pipe and tobacco, but he had no fire to light it with. Dukhi said, 'Don't worry about the fire, brother, I'll go to Panditji's house and ask him for a light, they're still cooking there.'

17   With this he took the pipe and came back and stood on the verandah of the Brahman's house, and he said, 'Master, if I could get just a little bit of light I'll smoke this pipeful.'

18   Panditji was eating and his wife said, 'Who's that man asking for a light?'

19   'It's only that damned little Dukhi the tanner. I told him to cut some wood. The fire's lit, so go give him his light.'

Frowning, the Panditayin said, 'You've become so wrapped up in   20
your books and astrological charts that you've forgotten all about caste
rules. If there's a tanner or a washerman or a birdcatcher why he can
just come walking right into the house as though he owned it. You'd
think it was an inn and not a decent Hindu's house. Tell that good-for-
nothing to get out or I'll scorch his face with a firebrand.'

Trying to calm her down, Panditji said, 'He's come inside—so   21
what? Nothing that belongs to you has been stolen. The floor is clean, it
hasn't been desecrated. Why not just let him have his light—he's doing
our work, isn't he? You'd have to pay at least four *annas* if you hired
some labourer to split it.'

Losing her temper, the Panditayin said, 'What does he mean com-   22
ing into this house!'

'It was the son of a bitch's bad luck, what else?' the Pandit said.   23

'It's all right,' she said, 'This time I'll give him his fire but if he ever   24
comes into the house again like that I'll give him the coals in his face.'

Fragments of this conversation reached Dukhi's ears. He repented: 25
it was a mistake to come. She was speaking the truth—how could a tanner ever come into a Brahman's house? These people were clean and
holy, that was why the whole world worshipped and respected them.
A mere tanner was absolutely nothing. He had lived all his life in the
village without understanding this before.

Therefore when the Pandit's wife came out bringing coals it was   26
like a miracle from heaven. Folding his hands and touching his forehead to the ground he said, 'Panditayin, Mother, it was very wrong of
me to come inside your house. Tanners don't have much sense—if we
weren't such fools why would we get kicked so much?'

The Panditayin had brought the coals in a pair of tongs. From a few   27
feet away, with her veil drawn over her face, she flung the coals toward
Dukhi. Big sparks fell on his head and drawing back hastily he shook
them out of his hair. To himself he said, 'This is what comes of dirtying
a clean Brahman's house. How quickly God pays you back for it! That's
why everybody's afraid of Pandits. Everybody else gives up his money
and never gets it back but who ever got any money out of a Brahman?
Anybody who tried would have his whole family destroyed and his
legs would turn leprous.'

He went outside and smoked his pipe, then took up the axe and   28
started to work again.

Because the sparks had fallen on him the Pandit's wife felt some   29
pity for him. When the Pandit got up from his meal she said to him,
'Give this tanner something to eat, the poor fellow's been working for a
long time, he must be hungry.'

Panditji considered this proposal entirely outside of the behavior   30
expected of him. He asked, 'Is there any bread?'

'There are a couple of pieces left over.'   31

32   'What's the good of two or three pieces for a tanner? Those people need at least a good two pounds.'

33   His wife put her hands over her ears. 'My, my, a good two pounds! Then let's forget about it.'

34   Majestically Panditji said, 'If there's some bran and husks mix them in flour and make a couple of pancakes. That'll fill the bastard's belly up. You can never fill up these low-caste people with good bread. Plain millet is what they need.'

35   'Let's forget the whole thing,' the Panditayin said, 'I'm not going to kill myself cooking in weather like this.'

*   *   *

36   When he took up the axe again after smoking his pipe, Dukhi found that with his rest the strength had to some extent come back into his arms. He swung the axe for about half-an-hour, then out of breath he sat down right there with his head in his hands.

37   In the meantime the *Gond* came. He said, 'Why are you wearing yourself out, old friend? You can whack it all you like but you won't split this trunk. You're killing yourself for nothing.'

38   Wiping the sweat from his forehead Dukhi said, 'I've still got to cart off a whole wagon-load of hay, brother.'

39   'Have you had anything to eat? Or are they just making you work without feeding you? Why don't you ask them for something?'

40   'How can you expect me to digest a Brahman's food, Chikhuri?'

41   'Digesting it is no problem, you have to get it first. He sits in there and eats like a king and then has a nice little nap after he tells you you have to split his wood. The government officials may force you to work for them but they pay you something for it, no matter how little. This fellow's gone one better, calling himself a holy man.'

42   'Speak softly, brother, if they hear you we'll be in trouble.'

43   With that Dukhi went back to work and began to swing the axe. Chikhuri felt so sorry for him that he came and took the axe out of Dukhi's hands and worked with it for a good half hour. But there was not even a crack in the wood. Then he threw the axe down and said, 'Whack it all you like but you won't split it, you're just killing yourself,' and he went away.

44   Dukhi began to think, 'Where did the *Baba* get hold of this trunk that can't be split? There's not even a crack in it so far. How long can I keep smashing into it? I've got a hundred things to do at home by now. In a house like mine there's no end to the work, something's always left over. But he doesn't worry about that. I'll just bring him his hay and tell him, '*Baba*, the wood didn't split. I'll come and finish it tomorrow.'

45   He lifted up the basket and began to bring the hay. From the store-room to the fodder bin was no less than a quarter of a mile. If he'd

really filled up the basket the work would have been quickly finished, but then who could have hoisted up the basket on his head? He couldn't raise a fully loaded basket, so he took just a little each time. It was four o'clock by the time he'd finished with the hay. At this time Pandit Ghasiram woke up, washed his hands and face, took some *paan* and came outside. He saw Dukhi asleep with the basket still on his head. He shouted, '*Arrey*, Dukhiya, sleeping? The wood's lying there just the way it was. What's taken you so long? You've used up the whole day just to bring in a little fistful of hay and then gone and fallen asleep! Pick up the axe and split that wood. You haven't even made a dent in it. So if you don't find an auspicious day for your daughter's marriage, don't blame me. This is why they say that as soon as an Untouchable gets a little food in his house he can't be bothered with you any more.'

Dukhi picked up the axe again. He completely forgot what he'd been thinking about before. His stomach was pasted against his backbone—he hadn't so much as eaten breakfast that morning, there wasn't any time. Just to stand up seemed an impossible task. His spirit flagged, but only for a moment. This was the Pandit, if he didn't fix an auspicious day the marriage would be a total failure. And that was why everybody respected the Pandits—everything depended on getting the right day set. He could ruin anybody he wanted to. Panditji came close to the log and standing there began to goad him. 'That's right, give it a real hard stroke, a real hard one. Come on now, really hit it! Don't you have any strength in your arm? Smash it, what's the point of standing there thinking about it? That's it, it's going to split, there's a crack in it.' 46

Dukhi was in a delirium some kind of hidden power seemed to have come into his hands. It was as though fatigue, hunger, weakness, all had left him. He was astonished at his own strength. The axe-strokes descended one after another like lightning. He went on driving the axe in this state of intoxication until finally the log split down the middle. And Dukhi's hands let the axe drop. At the same moment, overcome with dizziness, he fell, the hungry, thirsty, exhausted body gave up. 47

Panditji called, 'Get up, just two or three more strokes. I want it in small bits.' Dukhi did not get up. It didn't seem proper to Pandit Ghasiram to insist now. He went inside, drank some *bhang*, emptied his bowels, bathed and came forth attired in full Pandit regalia. Dukhi was still lying on the ground. Panditji shouted, 'Well, Dukhi, are you going to just stay lying here? Let's go, I'm on my way to your house! Everything's set, isn't it?' But still Dukhi did not get up. 48

A little alarmed, Panditji drew closer and saw that Dukhi was absolutely stiff. Startled half out of his wits he ran into the house and said to his wife, 'Little Dukhi looks as though he's dead.' 49

Thrown into confusion Panditayin said, 'But hasn't he just been chopping wood?' 50

51   'He died right while he was splitting it. What's going to happen?'

52   Calmer, the Panditayin said, 'What do you mean what's going to happen? Send word to the tanners settlement so they can come and take the corpse away.'

53   In a moment the whole village knew about it. It happened that except for the *Gond* house everyone who lived there was Brahman. People stayed off the road that went there. The only path to the well passed that way—how were they to get water? Who would come to draw water with a tanner's corpse nearby? One old woman said to Panditji, 'Why don't you have this body thrown away? Is anybody in the village going to be able to drink water or not?'

54   The *Gond* went from the village to the tanners' settlement and told everyone the story. 'Careful now!' he said. 'Don't go to get the body. There'll be a police investigation yet. It's no joke that somebody killed this poor fellow. The somebody may be a pandit, but just in his own house. If you move the body you'll get arrested too.'

55   Right after this Panditji arrived. But there was nobody in the settlement ready to carry the corpse away. To be sure, Dukhi's wife and daughter both went moaning to Panditji's door and tore their hair and wept. About a dozen other women went with them, and they wept too and they consoled them, but there was no man with them to bear up the body. Panditji threatened the tanners, he tried to wheedle them, but they were very mindful of the police and not one of them stirred. Finally Panditji went home disappointed.

*   *   *

56   At midnight the weeping and lamentation were still going on. It was hard for the Brahmans to fall asleep. But no tanner came to get the corpse, and how could a Brahman lift up an Untouchable's body? It was expressly forbidden in the scriptures and no one could deny it.

57   Angrily the Panditayin said, 'Those witches are driving me out of my mind. And they're not even hoarse yet!'

58   'Let the hags cry as long as they want. When he was alive nobody cared a straw about him. Now that he's dead everybody in the village is making a fuss about him.'

59   'The wailing of tanners is bad luck,' the Panditayin said.

60   'Yes, very bad luck.'

61   'And it's beginning to stink already.'

62   'Wasn't that bastard a tanner? Those people eat anything, clean or not, without worrying about it.'

63   'No sort of food disgusts them!'

64   'They're all polluted!'

65   Somehow or other they got through the night. But even in the morning no tanner came. They could still hear the wailing of the women. The stench was beginning to spread quite a bit.

Panditji got out a rope. He made a noose and managed to get it 66 over the dead man's feet and drew it tight. Morning mist still clouded the air. Panditji grabbed the rope and began to drag it, and he dragged it until it was out of the village. When he got back home he bathed immediately, read out prayers to Durga for purification, and sprinkled Ganges water around the house.

Out there in the field the jackals and kites, dogs and crows were 67 picking at Dukhi's body. This was the reward of a whole life of devotion, service and faith.

✦ Evaluating the Text

1. What position is Dukhi the tanner in relative to the Brahman whose advice he seeks regarding an auspicious date for his daughter's wedding? What insight does their relationship give you into the role caste distinctions play in India and into the value of the Brahman in scheduling important events?

2. How does Premchand's description of the Brahman's daily activities when contrasted to Dukhi's labors offer an ironic perspective? How is this story a portrait of religious hypocrisy?

3. In view of what happens to Dukhi and the nature of the society in which he lives and dies, what might the title be taken to mean?

✦ Exploring Different Perspectives

1. How does the belief in religious tradition enter into Premchand's story and Bessie Head's story "Looking for a Rain God"?

2. How do the stories by Premchand and Abioseh Nicol offer unflattering portraits of religious authority figures?

✦ Extending Viewpoints Through Writing

1. In your view, does this story argue for social reform and, if so, what kind do you think Premchand might have had in mind?

Connecting Cultures

◆

Gino Del Guercio, The Secrets of Haiti's Living Dead

Discuss the similarities between the Haitian belief that a voodoo priest can gain power over the essential part of the self and the naming taboo that governs the circumstances under which a Yąnomamö can be called by his or her given name (see Napoleon A. Chagnon's "Doing Fieldwork Among the Yąnomamö," Chapter 8).

Leslie Marmon Silko, Language and Literature from a Pueblo Indian Perspective

How do the accounts by Leslie Marmon Silko and N. Scott Momaday (see "The Names," Chapter 2) depend on the concept that the stories associated with particular landmarks and landscapes provide a history that is continuous?

Bessie Head, Looking for a Rain God

How do Bessie Head's story and Ngũgĩ wa Thiong'o's account (see "Decolonising the Mind," Chapter 6) reveal the dual nature of tribal society in Botswana and Kenya? What attitude do both works reveal toward the recently imposed layer of colonial "civilization"?

Aung San Suu Kyi, My Country and People

What impression do you get of the way objects produced by artists are perceived as having a secular aesthetic function as well as a religious or sacred meaning in the cultures of Burma and Guinea (see Camara Laye's "The Village Goldsmith," Chapter 4)?

Abioseh Nicol, Life Is Sweet at Kumansenu

How does the story by Abioseh Nicol and the account by Christy Brown (see "The Letter 'A'," Chapter 2) depict mothers who fight prevailing cultural views to defend their children?

Naguib Mahfouz, Half a Day

How does the work the reader has to perform in the stories of Naguib Mahfouz and Dino Buzzati (see "The Falling Girl," Chapter 2) depend on making sense out of the displacement of the real by the surreal?

Carol Spindel, Blessings

What similarities can you discover in the culturally based lessons learned by Carol Spindel in Côte d'Ivoire and David R. Counts (see "Too Many Bananas," Chapter 8) in New Guinea?

Premchand, Deliverance

To what extent are Premchand and Mahdokht Kashkuli (see "The Button," Chapter 5) sympathetic as storytellers to characters who belong to a lower stratum of society?

Rhetorical Index

◆

IRONY, HUMOR, AND SATIRE

AUTOBIOGRAPHY

JOURNALS AND DIARIES

SPEECHES

FICTION

Albert Camus   "The Guest"
Feng Jicai   "The Tall Woman and Her Short Husband"
Panos Ioannides   "Gregory"
Gloria Anzaldúa   "Cervicide"
Nabil Gorgy   "Cairo Is a Small City"
Bessie Head   "Looking for a Rain God"
Abioseh Nicol   "Life Is Sweet at Kumansenu"
Naguib Mahfouz   "Half a Day"
Premchand   "Deliverance"

Geographical Index

———————◆———————

AFRICA

ASIA

AUSTRALIA

EUROPE

LATIN AMERICA

THE MIDDLE EAST

NORTH AMERICA

Acknowledgments

◆────────

Gloria Anzaldúa, "Cervicide," from *Borderlands/La Frontera: The New Mestiza.* Copyright © 1987 by Gloria E. Anzaldúa. Reprinted with the permission of Aunt Lute Books.

Aung San Suu Kyi, "My Country and People," from *Freedom from Fear and Other Writings*, translated by Michael Aris (New York: Penguin, 1991). Reprinted with the permission of Viking Penguin, a division of Penguin Books USA Inc.

Roland Barthes, "Ornamental Cookery," translated by Annette Lavers, from *Mythologies.* Translation copyright © 1972 by Jonathan Cape, Ltd. Reprinted with the permission of Hill and Wang, a division of Farrar, Straus & Giroux, Inc., and Jonathan Cape, Ltd.

Nicholas Bornoff, "The Marriage Go-Round," from *Pink Samurai.* Copyright © 1991 by Nicholas Bornoff. Reprinted with the permission of Pocket Books, a division of Simon & Schuster, Inc.

Christy Brown, "The Letter 'A'," from *My Left Foot.* Copyright © 1955 by Christy Brown. Reprinted with the permission of Martin Secker & Warburg, Ltd.

Dino Buzzati, "The Falling Girl," from *Restless Nights*, translated by Lawrence Venuti. Translation copyright © 1983 by Lawrence Venuti. Reprinted with the permission of the translator and Arnoldo Mondadori.

Albert Camus, "The Guest," from *Exile and the Kingdom*, translated by Justin O'Brien. Copyright © 1957, 1958 by Alfred A. Knopf, Inc Reprinted with the permission of the publisher.

Raymonde Carroll, "Home," from *Cultural Misunderstandings: The French-American Experience.* Copyright © 1988 by The University of Chicago. Reprinted with the permission of the author and The University of Chicago Press.

Napoleon A. Chagnon, "Doing Fieldwork Among the Yąnomamö," from *Yąnomamö: The Fierce People, Second Edition.* Copyright © 1977 by Holt, Rinehart & Winston, Inc. Reprinted with the permission of the publisher.

John Cheever, "Reunion," from *The Stories of John Cheever.* Copyright © 1962 by John Cheever. Reprinted with the permission of Alfred A. Knopf, Inc.

Nien Cheng, "The Red Guards," from *Life and Death in Shanghai.* Copyright © 1986 by Nien Cheng. Reprinted with the permission of Grove/Atlantic, Inc. and HarperCollins Publishers, Ltd.

Kim Chernin, "The Flesh and the Devil," from *The Obsession: Reflections on the Tyranny of Slenderness*, Copyright © 1981 by Kim Chernin. Reprinted with the permission of HarperCollins Publishers, Inc.

Edward T. Hall, "Hidden Culture," from *Beyond Culture* by Edward T. Hall. Copyright © 1976, 1981 by Edward T. Hall. Reprinted with the permission of Doubleday, a division of Bantam Doubleday Dell Publishing Group, Inc.

Le Ly Hayslip, "Yearning to Breathe Free," from *Child of War, Woman of Peace.* Copyright © 1993 by Le Ly Hayslip and Charles Jay Warts. Reprinted with the permission of Doubleday, a division of Bantam Doubleday Dell Publishing Group, Inc.

Lesley Hazleton, "Confessions of a Fast Woman," from *Confessions of a Fast Woman.* Copyright © 1992 by Lesley Hazleton. Reprinted with the permission of Addison-Wesley Publishing Company.

Bessie Head, "Looking for a Rain God," from *The Collector of Treasures and Other Botswana Village Tales.* Copyright © 1977 by the Estate of Bessie Head. Reprinted with the permission of John Johnson, Authors' Agent, Ltd., and Heinemann Publishers Oxford.

Panos Ioannides, "Gregory," translated by Marion Byron and Catherine Raizis, from *The Charioteer: A Review of Modern Greek Literature.* Copyright © 1989 by Panos Ioannides. English translation copyright © 1989 by Marion Byron and Catherine Raizis. Reprinted with the permission of Pella Publishing Company, Inc.

Mahdokht Kashkuli, "The Button," from *Stories by Iranian Women Since the Revolution,* translated by Sorayua Sullivan (Austin: Center for Middle Eastern Studies, University of Texas at Austin, 1991). Reprinted with the permission of Center for Middle Eastern Studies, The University of Texas at Austin.

William M. Kephart, "The Gypsies,"from *Extraordinary Groups, Third Edition.* Copyright © 1987 by St. Martin's Press, Inc. Reprinted with the permission of the publishers.

Jamaica Kincaid, "A Small Place," from *A Small Place.* Copyright © 1988 by Jamaica Kincaid. Reprinted with the permission of Farrar, Straus & Giroux, Inc.

Kon Krailet, "In the Mirror," from Trevor Carolan, ed., *The Colors of Heaven: Short Stories from the Pacific Rim* (New York: Random House, 1991). Reprinted by permission.

Camara Laye, "The Village Goldsmith," Chapter Two of *The Dark Child*, translated by James Kirkup and Ernest Jones. Copyright 1954 and renewed © 1982 by Camara Laye. Reprinted with the permission of Farrar, Straus & Giroux, Inc.

Rosa Liksom, excerpt from *One Night Stands,* translated by Anselm Hollo. Copyright © 1993. Reprinted with the permission of Serpent's Tail.

Catherine Lim, "Paper," from *Little Ironies: Stories of Singapore.* Copyright © 1986. Reprinted with the permission of Heinemann Asia/Reed International (Singapore) Pte Ltd.

Alison Lurie, "The Language of Clothes," from *Human Ecology,* Spring 1991. Copyright © 1991 by Alison Lurie. Reprinted with the permission of the Melanie Jackson Agency.

Pronunciation Key to Names and Places

$\blacklozenge$

The pronunciation of each of the following names is shown in parentheses according to the following pronunciation key.

1. A heavy accent ′ is placed after a syllable with the primary accent.
2. A lighter accent ´ is placed after a syllable with the secondary accent.
3. The letters and symbols used to represent given sounds are pronounced as in the examples below.

a	bat, nap	o	box, hot
ā	way, cape	ō	boat, go
â	dare, air	ô	ought, order
ä	art, far	oi	voice, joy
		oo	ooze, rule
b	cabin, back	ou	loud, out
ch	beach, child		
d	do, red	p	pot, paper
		r	read, run
e	bet, merry	s	see, miss
ē	equal, beet	sh	show, push
ė	learn, fern		
		t	tell, ten
f	fit, puff	th	thin, path
g	give, go	th	that, smooth
h	how, him		
		u	up, butter
i	pin, big	u̇	put, burn
ī	deny, ice	ü	rule, ooze
j	jam, fudge		
k	keep, kind	v	river, save
		w	west, will
l	love, all	y	yes, yet
m	my, am	z	zeal, lazy
n	in, now	zh	vision, measure
ng	sing, long		

ə occurs only in unaccented syllables and indicates the sound of

a	in alone
e	in taken
i	in pencil
o	in gallop
u	in circus

FOREIGN SOUNDS

a	as in French *ami*
Y	as in French *do;* or as in German *über*
œ	as in French *feu;* or as in German *schön*
N	as in French *bon*
H	as in German *ach;* or as in Scottish *loch*
R	as in Spanish *pero;* or as in German *mare*

Hanan al-Shaykh (hä′ nän′ al shāk′)
Napoleon A. Chagnon (nə pō′lē ən shan′ yən′)
Slavenka Drakulić (slə ven′ kə dra kül′ ik)
Nawal El Saadawi (na′ wäl′ əl sä dou′ wē)
Le Ly Hayslip (lā lē hā′ slip′)
Mahdokht Kashkuli (mə dōkt′ käsh′ kü′ lē)
Kon Krailet (kon krā′ let)
Camara Laye (kä′ mə rä lā)
Abioseh Nicol (äbē ōsə̄ nik ol′)
Sembene Ousmane (sem be′ nā o͞oz män′)
Shirley Saad (shŭr′lē säd)
Tepilit Ole Saitoti (te′ pə lit′ ō′lē sī tō′tē)
Aung San Suu Kyi (ong sän sü kē)
Ngũgĩ wa Thiong'o (nə go͞o′ gē wä tē ong′ō)
Luis Alberto Urrea (loo ēs′ al bâr′tō oo Rē-ə)

Index of Authors and Titles

◆

(U.S.)

Canada

United States

Atlantic Ocean

Cuba

Puerto Rico

Mexico

Haiti

Antigua

Guatemala

Colombia

Pacific Ocean

Brazil

Only countries mentioned in
selections are labeled on this map.